RHS
GARDEN
FINDER
2001-2002

EDITOR
CHARLES QUEST-RITSON

A Dorling Kindersley Book

Dorling Kindersley

LONDON, NEW YORK, SYDNEY, DELHI, PARIS, MUNICH AND JOHANNESBURG

First published in Great Britain in 2001 by
Dorling Kindersley Limited
9 Henrietta Street, London WC2E 8PS

A Pearson Company

1 3 5 7 9 8 6 4 2

Note: whilst every care has been taken to ensure that the information
contained in this directory is both accurate and up-to-date, neither the
author, the Royal Horticultural Society nor the publisher accept any
liability to any party for loss or damage occurred by reliance placed
on the information contained in this book or through omission
or errors, howsoever caused.

A CIP catalogue record for this book is available from the British Library.

ISBN 0751313122

The opinions expressed in this work are the opinions of the author and
not of the publishers or the Royal Horticultural Society.

Data management and typesetting by
HWA Text and Data Management, Tunbridge Wells

Printed and bound in Italy by Legoprint

See our complete catalogue at
www.dk.com

THE ROYAL
HORTICULTURAL
SOCIETY

Step into a world of inspirational gardens

Join the Royal Horticultural Society and enjoy free access to over 60 inspirational gardens in the UK.

Let the RHS help you make the most from your garden and enjoy all the benefits that Membership brings. Throughout the year, Members can receive advice, ideas and inspiration through the acclaimed RHS Gardens Wisley, Rosemoor and Hyde Hall as well as from the excellent monthly magazine *The Garden*, privileged access to the world's most famous Flower Shows including Chelsea, Hampton Court Palace and Tatton Park and discounted tickets to RHS talks, events and garden tours across Britain.

RHS Membership Special Offer - Save £5

RHS Membership is normally £36 (£29 plus a one-off joining fee of £7) but you can save £5 and pay just £31 or save an additional £2 when you join by direct debit and pay just £29, which can be set up by calling the Membership Hotline.

To join, simply complete the application form overleaf or call the Membership Hotline on

020 7821 3401

and quote code 1716

Registered charity no. 222879

Subscription rate valid until 31 October 2001.   www.rhs.org.uk

THE ROYAL HORTICULTURAL SOCIETY

Membership Application Form

Please return to:

Membership Department,
The Royal Horticultural Society,
PO Box 313, London SW1P 2PE

In becoming a Member of the RHS I agree that information relating to my Membership will be passed to carefully selected third parties for processing purposes only. I also agree to receive information from the RHS relating to RHS events and products.

Please tick

☐ **Individual Membership at £31.**

Your details

Title	Initial(s)
Surname	
Address	
Postcode	
Daytime Tel. No.	

Payment Details

Payment by credit or debit card

Please tick

☐ RHS Mastercard   ☐ Mastercard   ☐ Visa

☐ Delta   ☐ Amex   ☐ Diners

Card details

☐☐☐☐ ☐☐☐☐ ☐☐☐☐ ☐☐☐☐

Expiry Date [/   ]

Cardholder's name

Signature

Date [   ]

Payment by Cheque (UK bank/building society accounts only

I enclose a cheque made payable to

The Royal Horticultural Society for £ [   ]

☐ Please tick the box if you wish to receive information about other products and services offered by our carefully selected partners.

If you would like to purchase Premier Gift Membership for gardening friends or relations, please call our Membership Hotline on
020 7821 3401.

CONTENTS

Introduction 6

GARDENS TO VISIT
England 14

Scotland 338

Wales 376

Northern Ireland 390

Republic of Ireland 396

RHS Gardens Overseas 410

PLANT-LOVER'S GUIDES
NCCPG National Collections 418

Where to See Particular Plants 425

Maps 431

Useful Addresses 454

Index 474

INTRODUCTION

Garden visiting

Welcome to the first edition of *The RHS Garden Finder 2001–2002*. This new publication has grown out of the *RHS Gardener's Yearbook*, the indispensable guide which has been published annually since 1994 and is now substantially represented by information on the Royal Horticultural Society's website (www.rhs.org.uk). The thinking behind *The RHS Garden Finder 2001–2002* is simple: none of the existing guides to visiting gardens in Britain and Ireland concentrates on plants. The *RHS Plant Finder* tells you where to find the right nurseries for plants: *The RHS Garden Finder 2001–2002* will tell you where to see the same plants growing in gardens which are open to the public. This is all the more important now that membership of the Royal Horticultural Society brings free access for its members to nearly eighty gardens up and down the United Kingdom and abroad.

The aim of this book is to supply sufficient detail to enable readers to decide if and when to plan a visit. The list is not exhaustive. It offers a selection of the different types of garden which are open to the public: ancient and modern, large and small, public and private. The editor welcomes suggestions for additions, deletions or alterations to entries. All major gardens which are open regularly are listed as a matter of course. These include many gardens of the National Trust and the National Trust for Scotland as well as botanic and public gardens and those attached to stately homes. But many gardens do not open to visitors regularly: the National Gardens Scheme lists over three 3,500. We have found space for a selection of these gardens which open only once a year or by appointment. Some guides would omit them on the grounds that it is not worthwhile to give publicity to gardens which so few people can visit. We take the view that, if a good garden is seldom open, it is all the more important to know when the opportunity to see it will arise. We also concentrate upon gardens with plants: we have written little about some of the great historic gardens of the eighteenth century because their landscapes are rather short on horticultural content. On the other hand, some of the best gardens for plants are those which have large 'living collections' for teaching purposes – botanic gardens and those attached to horticultural colleges. It is important to stress that almost all such gardens nowadays are extremely conscious of the need to offer ornamental and horticultural features to please visitors. Public amenity is usually the principal justification now for maintaining the historic plant collections which were systematically amassed in the nineteenth and early twentieth centuries.

Nurseries

Because this book is plant-led, we have also included about 200 leading nurseries. Almost all have a demonstration garden attached to them, just as most gardens have a nursery or plant stall. This is a recent development – it started about twenty years ago – but is now quite normal: visitors to a nursery like to see plants growing in a garden before making their purchases, and visitors to a garden like the opportunity to buy some of the plants they have seen there. It would not be right to exclude a garden like Bridgemere Garden World or Barnsdale just because it is attached to a commercial enterprise that sells plants.

How to use this book

Gardens are listed by county or region (for Scotland), and then alphabetically by name. The order is England, Scotland, Wales, Northern Ireland, Republic of Ireland and RHS Gardens Overseas. In general, we have stuck to the familiar 1974 counties of England and Wales and to the Scottish regional divisions. There are three exceptions: the counties of Avon, Cleveland and Humberside have been redistributed to Gloucestershire and Somerset, North Yorkshire and Lincolnshire. We have also divided Hereford & Worcester into its two component parts again. We have been careful to ensure, so far as possible, that gardens are listed in the counties or region in which they actually lie – which is not always the county or region their postal addresses suggest, or where their owners believe themselves to live. Thus the Savill Garden lies in Surrey, even though most of Windsor Great Park is in Berkshire. And the gardens at Burford House near Tenbury Wells are neither in Herefordshire nor in Worcestershire, but across the border in Shropshire. To find information about a specific garden turn to the index at the back: it should take you straight to the page you need.

Practical details

Our source for practical information about directions, opening times, admission charges, parking, lavatories, disabled facilities and refreshments has been the owners or their staff, backed up by our own enquiries where appropriate. The accuracy of these details is not guaranteed, but is believed to be correct at the time of going to press. We rely to a great extent on information which has been submitted to us by third parties. Not everyone who was approached has replied – or replied in time – and this explains some gaps. A paperless version of the book is on-line as part of the Royal Horticultural Society's website (www.rhs.org.uk) and updates will be made as and when they are available. Inclusion or exclusion either in this book or on the society's website should not be construed as a recommendation or condemnation. And, though this book carries the Royal Horticultural Society's endorsement, its comments and opinions are the editor's, and his alone.

Contacting gardens

In order to assist readers with special needs, or who are hoping to arrange a group visit by special appointment, we list the telephone and fax numbers to which enquiries should be directed. In many cases this is the private telephone line of the owners: readers are urged to respect their privacy. If telephone and fax numbers have been omitted, this is because the owners prefer to receive such requests by letter.

Websites

There has been a great increase in the number of gardens and nurseries with dedicated internet sites. Many are beautifully designed and extremely informative. These help to attract visitors, especially groups from gardening clubs and tour operators. Please remember that website addresses change frequently and inexplicably. We have checked all the hundreds in this book during the autumn of 2000 and have only included the ones which are up and running and seem to us to offer useful information. Many websites are of excellent quality: some of the nursery sites permit on-line ordering. Others exist only as registered names: we have omitted them. And far too many people seem to think that, once they have launched their website, there is nothing more that they need to do. One very important plantsman's nursery was still inviting web customers last December to download a catalogue which they specifically described as valid only until 1 September.

Visiting times

Many gardens are attached to other attractions – most typically, a house which is also open to the public. The visiting times we have given relate only to the garden. Please remember that most gardens have a last admission time. Typically it will be thirty or forty-five minutes before they close, but it can be much longer. The last admission to Stowe is one hour before it closes, while Stratfield Saye actually closes its gates at 3 pm, two hours before visitors are required to leave. Remember, too, that a pre-booked group can often make a visit at a time or season when the garden is not open to individual visitors.

Prices

As with times, so with prices. The admission prices we have given relate only to the garden. If the house or some other attraction is open at the same time, a supplement may be payable. Some owners insist on you buying a full ticket: it costs £10 to see Alan Bloom's garden at Bressingham, because the price includes entrance to Foggy Bottom garden (not always open) and the Bressingham Steam Experience (which may not interest you) plus a £5 voucher redeemable against Blooms Heritage Collection plants (which you may not want). Fortunately, most visitor attraction managers are more reasonable. It is true that some gardens may seem rather expensive but, generally speaking, the market rules of supply and demand apply and you get what you pay for. And it should be said that for every garden which is over-priced there are ten wonderful plantsman's gardens, run by their owners on a strictly non-commercial basis, where you can be certain of wonderful flowers, good design and a genuine welcome.

Many gardens offer special rates to groups and, if details are not given, it may be worth asking whether a reduction is available and what minimum number is acceptable. Please remember, however, that not all gardens permit parties: popular gardens which already suffer from wear and tear may not welcome increased visitor numbers. Special rates for families are sometimes available, especially at larger gardens attached to stately homes, where the garden is only one of many entertainments offered to the visitor. There are endless permutations on the numbers of adults and/or children which constitute a 'family' and the age at which a child becomes an adult and has to pay the full entry price. Season tickets are sometimes available, and good value for people who live near a large garden or stately home.

Entrance fees vary, and a few owners have told us that they may increase fees in the middle of the season. Some have a high season for a month or so – like Exbury in spring. Others have a special day of the week or open days for charity when the entrance fee is higher. A few owners had not yet fixed their 2001 times or admission charges by the time we went to press and we have therefore indicated that the times or prices quoted are for 2000. All entrance fees are, in any event, liable to be changed: visitors would do well to take more money than they think they will need. Some gardens have honesty boxes, and it is also important to take lots of change, so that you are not forced to choose between paying too much or too little.

It is always worth remembering that National Trust members are usually admitted free to Trust properties. Readers are strongly recommended to join the National Trust in any event: its portfolio of blue chip gardens is so comprehensive that no garden tour is complete without a visit to one or more of its properties.

Facilities

This guide uses a variety of symbols to show whether a garden has such facilities as public conveniences or plants for sale. We have indicated whether parking is available: this may be at the garden itself or on a public road very close to it. Parking may be at some distance from the house. At Saltram it is 500 yards away, and this is by no means exceptional. You can however expect better parking facilities at a popular property which offers a wide range of entertainments than at a small plantsman's garden in a country lane.

It is often a condition of admission that no photograph taken within a garden there may be sold or used for public reproduction without the consent of the property owner. Visitors should also remember that almost all gardens accept dogs only if they are kept on leads. Some restrict dogs to particular areas of a property, like the car park, or the woods and parkland rather than the garden proper. Private owners are generally better disposed towards dogs than corporate owners like the National Trust or English Heritage. A few owners go out of their way to say that dogs are actually welcome, but not all have shaded areas for parking.

Disabled visitors

We have generally indicated which gardens are suitable for disabled people, though it is important to stress that access may only be partial. Often an area around the house or entrance is accessible for people in wheelchairs, but the more remote parts of the garden are quite unsuitable. It is best to ring before your visit to check. The same is true of other disabled facilities. We have not specified the nature of those facilities, but in most cases it includes lavatories and ramps which are suitable for the wheelchair-bound. It is best to enquire in advance of a visit if particular items of special equipment are required. The National Trust is especially good at adapting its properties to accommodate the needs of disabled visitors and publishes an excellent free booklet called *Information for Visitors with Disabilities*, which details the many special facilities available at those of its properties which are suitable for disabled visitors. It is available from the National Trust's head office in London.

Refreshments

Many gardens now offer refreshments to visitors. The signs which indicate whether there are facilities for light refreshments or a more substantial meal refer only to what is offered within the garden itself, and not to what may be available in restaurants, tea-rooms and public houses nearby.

Size of gardens

We have asked owners to let us publish a note of the size of their garden and the number of people who work in it. Taken together, these two statistics help to suggest how intensively a garden is worked and how long you need to allow for your visit. The number or gardeners must be interpreted flexibly. Some owners have told us how many paid gardeners they employ: others have included their own contributions and based their figure on how much time they and their family give to the garden. The size of gardens is expressed in acres, even though some owners prefer to use hectares. We have been more accommodating where other measurements are concerned – for example, the heights of trees and lengths of borders. Here we have used both imperial and metric measurements with no apparent consistency, in order to follow, so far as possible, the system which the owners and other sources of information have used. We have found that professionals tend to talk metric, while owners think imperial.

The NCCPG

Two common abbreviations are used freely throughout the text: RHS for the Royal Horticultural Society and NCCPG for the National Council for the Conservation of Plants and Gardens. We have noted the NCCPG National Collections which are held at the gardens and nurseries we list and supplied a separate index of them towards the end of the book. Not all genera are the subject of a National Collection: there are still some horticulturally important groups of plants which have not yet been seriously collected and studied under the auspices of the NCCPG. Other genera have been split into a number of different collections. This is particularly necessary in the case of such a large genus as *Rhododendron* or those, like *Euphorbia*, which require a great variety of growing conditions. Moreover, the NCCPG has wisely introduced a system of duplicate collections to insure against the risks which face every collection of rare plants so that plants are grown in two or more gardens. The need to maintain duplicate collections and split large genera explains why certain names occur several times in the list of National Collections towards the end of the book. That list is taken from information supplied to us by the NCCPG in November last year. The 2001 edition of the National Plant Collections Directory will shortly be published and lists some 650 National Plant Collections: copies are available from bookshops or directly from the NCCPG, The Stable Courtyard, Wisley Garden, Woking, Surrey GU23 6QB (£4.95 plus £1.25 p&p).

Champion trees

For most gardens, we give a brief list of Plant Highlights. These include general information like 'good collection of trees'

and more specific facts like 'tallest *Quercus cerris* in the UK'. Occasionally we have added some highlights which are not strictly plants, but do add enormously to the character of a garden and the reasons for making a visit. Information about outsize trees is taken from the records kept by the Tree Register of the British Isles and from a fascinating publication *Champion Trees in the British Isles* by Alan F Mitchell, Victoria E Schilling and John E J White (4th Edition 1994, HMSO £5). There are two ways of measuring trees: height and girth. Sometimes the tallest specimen will also have the thickest trunk – but not always. Both the tallest and the biggest can claim to be the champion tree, and we have sometimes made this distinction when noting record breakers in gardens. Tree measurements can never be fully up to date: some records have not been verified since the great gales of 1987 and 1990.

The 2000 season

Most of the owners we spoke to in the course of compiling this book told us that their gardens had fewer visitors in 2000 than in 1999. They tended to attribute this downturn in numbers to the exceptionally wet weather – though 1999 was also a wet year. Some also believe that the petrol strike in September prevented them from recovering at the end of the season. On the other hand, it was widely acknowledged that, though visitor numbers were down, visitor 'spend' was actually up, thus confirming the impression that more people have higher disposable incomes nowadays. The net result was that most garden-owners were not too disappointed by their final figures.

It remains to be seen whether visitor numbers perk up again in 2001 and 2002. Many gardens – especially the larger ones – consider that they are in competition for visitors with other tourist attractions, other entertainments and other activities like shopping. Their reaction has been to put more emphasis upon special events in gardens. These vary from those like plant sales, study days and garden walks which are designed to attract keen gardeners, to broad-based entertainments like concerts, craft fairs and car rallies. Many are listed in the Event Finder on the Royal Horticultural Society's website (www.rhs.org.uk). What no-one can yet gauge is the effect which all these activities may have upon the numbers of people visiting smaller gardens. Nor it is yet clear whether we are seeing the beginning of a decline in garden visiting, as some people have suggested, or a temporary variation in visitor numbers caused by exceptionally unfriendly weather.

Acknowledgements

The editor is very grateful to the many people who have helped in the compilation of this work. First and foremost he thanks all the garden owners, nurseries, horticulturists, colleges, societies and every one else who has responded to his requests for information. He is greatly indebted to them, and regrets that it is not always possible to give each the personal attention which is their due. Particular thanks go the staff of the Alpine Garden Society; the National Trust; the National Trust for Scotland; Rodger Bain at the NCCPG; Tony Lord of the *RHS Plant Finder*; Bill Simpson of the Alpine Garden Society; Peter Moore from the Cyclamen Society; Sally Furness at the Henry Doubleday Research Association (HDRA); Anne Snell of the Heather Society; Shirley Bassett of the Delphinium Society; Deni Brown of the Herb Society; Clive Lane of the Cottage Garden Society; and Josephine Warren and Miranda Gunn of the RHS Rhododendron, Camellia & Magnolia Group. Special thanks are also due to Wendy Crammond, Susanne Mitchell and others at the Royal Horticultural Society and especially to Karen Wilson in the publications department. The editor also acknowledges the considerable input of others who have worked with us on this project: John Hodgson, Barbara Levy, David Lamb and our colleagues at Dorling Kindersley. Finally thanks are due for their patience and endeavours to Madeline Quest-Ritson, Christopher and Katharine Blair, Camilla Roberts; and above all to Brigid Quest-Ritson whose labours are represented throughout these pages.

KEY TO SYMBOLS

(P) Parking available

(🐕) Dogs permitted

(WC) Toilet facilities

(♿) Access for the disabled

(🌱) Plants for sale

(🎁) Gift shop

(🍴) Restaurant

(☕) Light refreshments/afternoon teas

GARDENS
TO
VISIT

ENGLAND

The purpose of this short introduction is to highlight some of the considerations which apply to gardens in England, but not to those in other parts of the UK or abroad. The first point to make is that gardens and gardening are essentially an English phenomenon. England has always taken the lead within the British Isles, and gardening is still – to some extent – one of our most important cultural, artistic and scientific exports. Within England there are differences of garden emphasis and style between regions. Alpine gardening has many followers in the north of England; Cornish gardens tend to be rhododendron woodland gardens; the smart designers tend to practice in and around London. Gardening is probably at its strongest as a national pursuit in the south-east of the country, where more than half the Royal Horticultural Society's members live. But there are good gardens of every kind open to the public in every part of the country. In fact they are also fairly evenly distributed throughout England, except perhaps for the east Midlands, which has fewer good gardens than its rich agriculture might suggest. Gardens and garden-making depend as much upon social and economic influences as soil and climate.

A word about the grading of historic gardens is needed. During the 1980s, English Heritage's predecessors compiled a register of gardens and parks of special historic interest. The aim was to draw attention to the nation's heritage, so that designed landscapes were not overlooked, for example in plans for new development. There are three gradings, each of which assesses the historic layout, features and architectural ornaments. Grade I parks and gardens are 'of exceptional interest'; Grade II* parks and gardens are 'of great quality'. Grade II – parks and gardens are 'of special interest'. These gradings reflect the importance of a particular garden or park and compare it with others in England as a whole. The register is in 46 parts, one for each of the 1974 English counties, and copies are available from English Heritage. The information they contain about the individual gardens is very comprehensive. It covers the site; area; dates and designers of key surviving elements; surviving features of the garden or park; and other interesting aspects such as historic associations.

The best source of reference for plants and nurseries is *The RHS Plant Finder*, whose 2001–2002 edition will be published shortly. It shows where the main concentrations of nurseries are – in Surrey, for example – and where there are few, like northern Cornwall. It lists only a handful of garden centres, which is a pity because most people buy their plants at local garden centres rather than specialist nurseries. There is no publication which tells you where to find a good garden centre, though the Garden Centre Association does have a very helpful searchable website on (www.gca.org.uk). The advantage of buying from garden which belongs to the Garden Centre Association is that members offer a high level of service and a good range of plants and associated products, together with professional advice and information. They are subject to annual inspections by an independent auditor and must satisfy stringent standards to remain members.

The starting point for garden visiting English gardens must be the 'Yellow Book' which the National Gardens Scheme publishes annually in February under the full title *Gardens of England & Wales Open to the Public.* The Yellow Book is a best seller. Its sales immediately after publication exceed 5,000 copies per week, three times the success rate of its nearest rival among best-selling paperback reference books. It is wonderfully comprehensive and totally undiscriminating. The owners write their own garden entries, with the result that a really good garden may come across as self-deprecatingly boring, while an exciting description can often lead to disappointment. Beware of self-publicists: you can usually spot the hype. The Yellow Book lists over 3,600 gardens and is the single most important guide to visiting gardens in England and Wales, and the least expensive. Copies of *Gardens of England & Wales Open to the Public in 2001* will be available as from the end of February from bookshops or directly from the National Gardens Scheme, Hatchlands Park, East Clandon, Guildford, Surrey GU4 7RT. (£4.50 plus p&p).

The leading guide to the whole of the British Isles is *The Good Gardens Guide 2001* by Peter King. Others that we can recommend are *The Gardener's Guide to Britain* by Patrick Taylor (Dorling Kindersley, £12.99) and *The Garden Lover's Guide to Britain* by Kathryn Bradley-Hole (BBC Publications, £12.99). The Royal National Rose Society has published a very useful *Guide to Rose Gardens to Visit,* which lists all the best gardens for seeing roses and many of the leading rose nurseries too. The Alpine Garden Society publishes a *Garden Open Directory* for members of the AGS who are willing to show other members round their garden.

Members of the RHS enjoy free entry to many gardens throughout England. Some are free throughout the year: others for only a month or so. In some cases the privilege applies only to member of the RHS not to any guests who accompany them. Nevertheless, it is an impressive list, and worth spelling out in full. In addition to the three RHS Gardens at Hyde Hall, Rosemoor and Wisley, members have free access to the following gardens in England: Abbotsbury Sub-Tropical Gardens, Bedgebury National Pinetum, Bluebell Arboretum, Borde Hill, Broadview Gardens, Brogdale, Burnby Hall, Cabbages & Kings, Catforth Gardens, Cholmondeley Castle, Cottesbrooke Hall, Dalemain, Dunge Valley, East Ruston Old Vicarage, Fairhaven Woodland & Water Garden, Felley Priory, Forde Abbey, Harlow Carr, Hidcote Manor, Knoll Gardens, Longframlington Gardens, Loseley Park, Millgate House, Newby Hall, Normanby Hall, Nymans, Pound Hill House, Probus Gardens, Ryton Organic Gardens, Sheffield Park, Stillingfleet Lodge, Tatton Park, The Abbey House at Malmesbury, the Picton Garden at Old Court Nurseries, The Quinta, the Hillier Arboretum, Trebah, Trewithen, Waddesdon Manor, Waterperry, Westonbirt, Wollerton Old Hall and Yalding Organic Gardens in Kent. We should add that this list has grown considerably in recent years, and that the Royal Horticultural Society hopes to expand it yet further.

In addition to its Free Access gardens, the Royal Horticultural Society has a system of running lectures at a number of partner nurseries in England, most of which are listed in this book, with a note of how to find out further details. The Society's own *Members' Handbook 2001* gives full details of these and of the many lectures, demonstrations, workshops, garden walks and other events held at RHS Partner Colleges.

BEDFORDSHIRE

Both the Grade I gardens in Bedfordshire – Woburn Abbey and Wrest Park
– are open to the public. Few of its other important gardens remain open to
visitors, though every garden-visitor should seek out the gloriously eccentric
Swiss Garden (Grade II*). The headquarters of the Royal Society for the
Protection of Birds, The Lodge at Sandy, is also rated as a Grade II garden.
It is regrettable that Luton Hoo has been closed to the public for some years
now, and that there is no immediate prospect of this changing. Bedfordshire
is horticulturally underdeveloped. It is not over-endowed with arboreta,
though Woburn has a fine collection of trees. Surprisingly few private gardens
open for the National Gardens Scheme and the county has only one
National Collection. There are few nurseries too: best known is Blom's Bulbs
at Melchbourne, close to the border with Northamptonshire, but it is not
open to visitors. One para-horticultural curiosity worth seeing is the
'Tree Cathedral' near Chessington Zoo.

The Manor House

CHURCH ROAD, STEVINGTON,
BEDFORD MK43 7QB

Tel 01234 822064   **Fax** 01234 825531
Location 5 miles north-west of Bedford, off A428
Opening hours 2 pm – 6 pm; 22 April & 24 June. Plus
2 July in evening. And groups at other times by
appointment.
Admission fee Adults £2.50; Children free

This is a very interesting newish garden –
the owners moved here in 1991 and have
designed and planted it with a sense of style
that is contemporary rather than nostalgic.
Kathy Brown is a garden-writer and
cookery-writer, and these interests have
overlapped in such titles as *The Edible
Flower Garden* (1999). But she has also
written books about container gardening,
bulbs and cottage gardening – all of which
have to some extent been worked out in the
garden here. She is very good on structure:
the French garden is an essay in formal
design. It starts right outside the house, with
a terrace that has a *gâteau* of tiles and stone
at its centre: box cones and gravelled
parterres lead down to a circular fountain.
Planting is another of her skills: the
containers are exuberantly filled with all
kinds of unconventional material – lupins
for example – and this is one of the few
garden where groundcover roses have been
made to grow well as loosely pendulous
container-plants. Elsewhere are masses of
bulbs, some in grass and other in beds which
may later be filled with herbs and roses.
Gazebos, pergolas, a parterre filled with
grasses, a cottage garden and a wisteria walk
are among the many other features.

Definitely a garden to see now and return to watch it develop in future.

Owned by Simon & Kathy Brown
Number of gardeners owners only
Size 3 acres

Seal Point

7 WENDOVER WAY, LUTON LU2 7LS

Tel 01582 611567
Location North-east Luton: turn north off Stockingstone Road (A505) into Felstead Way, then second left
Opening hours 2 pm – 6 pm; first Tuesday of month; May to September. And 2 May for Red Cross, and by appointment
Admission fee Adults £2.50

This small town garden on a difficult site has been much praised. It manages to combine a large number of different features with an overall oriental theme, including a bonsai garden arranged on a slate moraine. Plants are important too: the trees are well-chosen for their ornamental effect, and the owners use foliage plants and grasses to intensify the dramatic impact of the plantings. Mrs Johnston was BBC Gardener of 1999 for the south-east region.

Owned by David & Danae Johnston
Number of gardeners owners only
Size 1 acre

Swiss Garden

OLD WARDEN, BIGGLESWADE

Tel 01767 626255   **Fax** 01767 627443
Website swissgarden@deed.bedfordshire.gov.uk
Location 1½ miles west of Biggleswade
Opening hours 1 pm – 6 pm (but 10 am – 6 pm on Sundays & Bank Holidays); daily; March to September.
11 am – 3 pm; Sundays & New Year's Day; January, February & October
Admission fee Adults £3; Concessions £2

This rustic, gothic landscape garden was largely developed by the Shuttleworth family in the nineteenth century. It is a remarkable relic: a pleasure ground of winding paths and sinuous waterways, little cast-iron bridges and picturesque huts, quaint kiosks and soaring ironwork arches, gullies and ferneries, vast conifers and cheerful rhododendrons, and an early grotto- glasshouse (note the small panes of glass) planted as a fernery.

Owned by Bedfordshire County Council
English Heritage grade II*

Toddington Manor

TODDINGTON LU5 6HJ

Tel 01525 872576   **Fax** 01525 874555
Location Signed from village
Opening hours 12 noon – 5 pm; Monday – Saturday; May to August
Admission fee Adults £3.50; OAPs £2.50; Children £1.50

This garden is now in its prime, and has all been made by the owners since 1979 around some magnificent old trees. It has some excellent features, notably a lime avenue which leads into a cherry walk, and a wonderfully high standard of maintenance. The walled garden has long beds of delphiniums and peonies and a fine garden of herbs, while the double herbaceous border has recently been extended and is now 100 metres long and 6 metres wide. There is also good modern rose garden of white and yellow floribundas interplanted with philadelphus. Further away from the house are a wild garden and three small ponds: visiting children may borrow nets to go dipping.

Plant Highlights Woodland walks; roses (mainly old-fashioned); herbs; mature conifers; good herbaceous borders; largest *Tilia tomentosa* 'Petiolaris' in the British Isles.

Owned by Sir Neville & Lady Bowman-Shaw

Woburn Abbey

WOBURN MK17 9WA

Tel 01525 290666   **Fax** 01525 290271
Location 1½ miles from Woburn on A4012
Opening hours 11 am – 4 pm; daily; 26 March to
30 September. 11 am – 4 pm; Saturdays & Sundays;
1 January to 25 March, and 1 to 28 October. Private
gardens open for National Gardens Scheme:
11 am – 5 pm; 8 April & 2 July
Admission fee Park: £5 per car: National Gardens
Scheme extra

Woburn may not have the reputation of a gardeners' garden, but Humphry Repton, who designed the park, considered it one of his finest achievements. The deer park is home to ten different types of deer: one is the Muntjac deer from China, some of which escaped during World War II and have spread through much of England. Nearer the house are a pinetum and a quercetum (a collection of oaks), cedars, redwoods, huge swamp cypresses and such rarities as mature specimens of the hardy 'rubber tree' *Eucommia ulmoides* and *Acer triflorum*. Elsewhere are lily ponds, fritillaries, wild orchids and masses of naturalised *Narcissus* – more than 100 daffodil cultivars. The private gardens are simple and formal, mainly nineteenth- century and Italianate, but they include a circular hornbeam maze with a Chinese pavilion in the centre, herbaceous borders, a rose garden, a camellia house, and lots of good statues.

 Plant Highlights Mature conifers; fine collection of trees; deer park; tallest *Zelkova sinica* (17m) in the British Isles.

Owned by The Marquess of Tavistock
Size 42 acres
English Heritage grade I

Wrest Park

SILSOE MK45 4HS

Tel 01525 860152 (weekends)
Location ¾ mile east of Silsoe
Opening hours 10 am – 6 pm; Saturdays, Sundays &
Bank Holiday Mondays; April to September. Plus
10 am – 5 pm; Saturdays & Sundays; October
Admission fee Adults £3.40; Concessions £2.60; Children
£1.70

The 'English Versailles' is dominated by a graceful long canal which runs down to the classical domed pavilion built by Thomas Archer in 1710. Capability Brown came here later, but worked around the earlier design. Many historic garden buildings have survived, some from as far back as the 1730s and others from the nineteenth century, including the orangery, the Mithraic altar, the bowling green house and the Chinese temple and bridge. In the walled garden and around the house are a rose garden, bedding displays and glasshouses. In the park are handsome specimen trees, including a fine example of the purple-leaved birch (*Betula pendula*) 'Purpurea'.

 Plant Highlights Grand parterres; long vistas; largest pink chestnut (*Aesculus × carnea*) in the British Isles.

Owned by English Heritage
Size 90 acres
English Heritage grade I

BERKSHIRE

Even in its attenuated post-1974 shape, Berkshire is well provided with good gardens. Few of its great historic gardens and landscapes are open to the public, though Berkshire's only Grade I landscape, Windsor Great Park, is of course open all the time, while Inkpen House (Grade II*) and Donnington Grove (Grade II) both open for the National Gardens Scheme. Lutyens's great masterpiece Folly Farm (Grade II*) changed hands recently, and is at present no longer visitable. There are good specimen trees in Windsor Great Park and the grounds of Eton College. Nurseries are less common than garden centres: Henry Street Garden Centre at Arborfield is one of the more individual ones, with a special line in roses. Berkshire has comparatively few National Collections, though the Crown Estates have no less than eight of them at the Savill Gardens and Valley Gardens, just over the border into Surrey.

Blencathra

OFF THE RIDGES, FINCHAMPSTEAD, WOKINGHAM RG40 3SS

Tel 0118 973 4563
Location Down a private drive at the north-west end of the Finchampstead ridges
Opening hours For National Gardens Scheme and other charities. And by appointment
Admission fee Adults £2.50; Children free

Dr & Mrs Gifford bought this 11-acre plot in 1964, built their house on it and set about making a garden without little or no hired help. Now they enjoy a woodland garden where the natural flowers (bluebells, dog mercury, primroses) are supplemented by ornamental shrubs – especially rhododendrons, azaleas, conifers and heathers. Three small lakes and a bog garden have increased the opportunities. The result is a model for our times – maximum returns for minimum effort.

Owned by Dr & Mrs F W Gifford
Number of gardeners owners only
Size 11 acres

Englefield House

ENGLEFIELD, THEALE, READING RG7 5EN

Tel 0118 930 2221   **Fax** 0118 930 2226
Website www.englefield-est.demon.co.uk
Location On A340, 1 mile from M4 Jct12
Opening hours 10 am – dusk; Mondays (plus Tuesdays – Thursdays from 1 April to 1 October); all year
Admission fee Adults £3; Children free

Englefield is a substantial estate, with a deer park and landscaped park around the imposing house. The lake alone extends to forty-five acres. Along the south front of the house is a balustraded terrace and a series of formal beds built in the 1850s. Lanning Roper reworked them in 1976. Above the house is a splendid woodland garden, laid out by Wallace & Barr in 1936: mature native trees like oak and beech are mixed with Victorian conifers and underplanted with maples, azaleas, viburnums, magnolias and many good shrubs.

Owned by Sir William & Lady Benyon
English Heritage grade II

Foxgrove

SKINNERS GREEN, ENBORNE,
NEWBURY RG14 6RE

Tel 01635 40554
Location On edge of village
Opening hours For National Gardens Scheme. Groups welcome by appointment
Admission fee Adults £2; Children free (2000 rates)

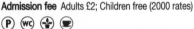

Foxgrove is a plantsman's garden, linked to Louise Vockins's nursery next door: Audrey Vockins is her aunt. Bulbs, alpines and herbaceous plants are Audrey's great interest. The hellebores, crocus and snowdrops give a great display in early spring. There are good shrubs, roses and handsome small trees too. Louise's nursery is open from 10 am – 5 pm from Wednesday to Sunday but closed in August. It carries an interesting range of hardy and cottage garden plants, including several new *Saxifraga* cultivars from the Czech Republic. Its speciality is snowdrops, which are sold by mail order 'in the green'. Other specialities – worth visiting the nursery to see – are hellebores, grasses and penstemons. Louise Vockins's planted-up troughs have been a great feature of RHS spring flower shows recently.

Owned by Miss Audrey Vockins

Frogmore Gardens

THE HOME PARK, WINDSOR CASTLE,
WINDSOR SL4 2JG

Tel 01753 869898   **Fax** 01753 832290
Location Access varies: please contact 01753 869898 ext. 2347
Opening hours 10 am – 5.30 pm; 15, 16 & 17 May. 10 am – 7 pm; 25, 26 & 27 August
Admission fee Adults £3; Children free in May. Adults £5.20; Children £3.20 in August

Frogmore is a royal residence: most of the house dates from the reign of George III. The grounds were first laid out in 1793, when the lake was excavated and the spoil used to create a series of mounds and banks. The many garden buildings include a gothic temple, an Indian kiosk, a tea house and the royal mausoleum where many members of the royal family have been buried since the middle of the nineteenth century. During the 1920s and 1930s, the gardens were extensively developed by the planting of ornamental trees and shrubs, underplanted by bulbs. The May openings are more expensive than the August ones, because the price for the latter includes a visit to the house. The house may also be visited in May, but there is a separate charge for it then. The mausoleum will also be open on 23 May (the closest Wednesday to Queen Victoria's birthday).

Owned by The Royal Family
Number of gardeners 6
Size 35 acres
English Heritage grade II*

The Harris Garden

PLANT SCIENCES LABORATORY, UNIVERSITY OF READING,
WHITEKNIGHTS, READING RG6 2AS

Tel 0118 931 8071   **Fax** 0118 975 0630
Location On A327, 1 mile south-east of Reading
Opening hours 2 pm – 6 pm; 13 May, 24 June, 22 July
& 23 September
Admission fee Adults £1.50; Children free

The Harris Garden was begun as recently as 1988, though it occupies what was once part of a famous landscape garden created by the 4th Duke of Marlborough between 1798 and 1817. The idea was to develop a garden as an adjunct to the teaching of horticulture, landscape and botany by the School of Plant Sciences at the University. It is very much a gardener's garden, full of horticultural interest. Annuals, for example, are grown both in traditional drifts of individual plants, and in experimental mixtures. There is a foliage border of tender plants grown solely for their spectacular sub-tropical effects. The winter garden concentrates upon plants whose flowers, bark or form gives particular pleasure in the dark months of the year. The orchard is not a fruit garden, but a collection of ornamental crab apples underplanted with wild flowers and bulbs which flower from January to the time when apple blossom fills the air. There is a large heather garden, where plants are in turn interplanted with dwarf pines: it is designed to lead naturally to a wild flower meadow. The walled garden has been developed as a traditional kitchen garden, with fruit trained on the walls, vegetables, herbs and flowers. The formal gardens include an area where Gertrude Jekyll's famous flower borders at Munstead Wood have been reproduced to illustrate her ideas on colour planting – Richard Bisgrove is the great expert on Jekyll's planting style and one of the team behind the Harris Garden. But there is much more to see, including the woodland garden, a golden garden, a nut garden, a cherry bowl (flowering cherries around a circular clearing with bulbs which flower at the same time), a primula dell, a pond garden, an autumn foliage bed and a splendid mixed border nearly 150 yards long. The garden is well supported by a friends organisation – details are available from the Hon. Secretary at the School of Plant Sciences.

Owned by University of Reading
Number of gardeners 4
Size 12 acres
NCCPG National Collections *Iris* (species)

The Living Rainforest

HAMPSTEAD NORREYS, THATCHAM, NEWBURY RG18 0TN

Tel 01635 202444 **Fax** 01635 202440
Website www.livingrainforest.org
Location Signed from Jct13 on M4
Opening hours 10 am – 5.15 pm; daily; all year. Closed 25 & 26 December
Admission fee Adults £4.50; Concessions £3; Children £2.50

The Living Rainforest consists of two large landscaped glasshouses, computer-set to create two different rainforest climates. Each has a thickly planted collection of exotic plants of every kind, many of them endangered or vulnerable to extinction. There is a particularly fine and near-comprehensive collection of tropical aroids, including the epiphytic *Anthurium warocqueanum* from Colombia and the terrestial *A. watermaliense* from Costa Rica. The flowering plants are wonderful in winter when the tropical orchids flower, and in spring when the jade vine (*Strongylodon macrobotrys*) flowers for several months – it has even set seed here. Later, in the summer, *Victoria amazonica* becomes one of the great attractions when it fills one of the pools. But the Living Rainforest is fascinating whatever the season or the weather outside, and there are tropical monkeys too.

Owned by The Living Rainforest
Size 20,000 sq ft of glass

Old Rectory Cottage

TIDMARSH, PANGBOURNE RG8 8ER

Tel 0118 984 3241
Location Small lane off A340 on right 200 yards north of Tidmarsh village
Opening hours By appointment
Admission fee £2

This is the marvellous garden of a great plantsman who has collected in all four corners of the world – the introducer of such staples as *Geranium palustre* and *Symphytum caucasicum*. The garden is a treasure house of unusual species, forms and home-made hybrids. Snowdrops, crocus, cyclamen, hellebores and winter stem colours justify a visit in February. Lilies are a special interest in early July – Bill Baker breeds them in thousands.

Plant Highlights A great plantsman's collection of plants; woodland garden; roses; herbs; good herbaceous plants; fine collection of trees; cyclamen; colchicums; hardy geraniums; snowdrops; plants collected in the wild; small lake; collection of birds; wonderful lilies.

Owned by Mr & Mrs A W A Baker

Old Rectory

BURGHFIELD RG3 3TH

Tel 0118 983 3200
Location Right at Hatch Gate Inn & first entrance on right
Opening hours 11 am – 4 pm; last Wednesday in month;
February to October
Admission fee Adults £2; Children free

This highly acclaimed garden was designed and planted by Esther Merton, a first-rate plantswoman who knew exactly what she wanted to achieve in her garden. She had a very good eye for plants, and collected them herself all over the world, as well as exchanging gifts with her gardening friends throughout Britain. Her legacy includes wonderful roses, lush summer bedding, quantities of spring bulbs (some of them rare), tiny alpines and unusual hellebores – all of them extremely well grown. The *tour de force* is a double herbaceous border where plants build up their impact through repetition, backed by yew hedges which get taller towards the end, to cheat the perspective. It leads to a pool framed by dense plantings of strong foliage – ferns, hostas, maples.

Owned by A R Merton
Number of gardeners 2
Size 4½ acres

Opening hours By appointment: parties welcome
Admission fee Adults £3

The garden at Scotlands has been made by the owners over many years. The house is an early (1930s) barn conversion and the lawns in front of it run down to a small lake with a fine swamp cypress (*Taxodium distichum*) on one side and a pinewood summerhouse after the style of Repton on the other. Further down still are more ponds and waterside plantings in a woodland garden where azaleas, camellias and pieris are underplanted with naturalised bluebells and primroses. The kitchen garden, partially walled, has rather more flowers than vegetables: a formal herb garden and a rose garden are each more prominent than edible crops. It is formally laid out in such a way that you appreciate the dynamism of the design but linger among the plants. There is one other very handsome lay-out – a lawn with an oval swimming pool in the centre, backed by yew hedges which are stepped and staggered like a stage-set. Swimming pools are difficult to fit into a garden: this is one of the best integrated we know.

Owned by Mr Michael & The Hon Mrs Payne
Number of gardeners 1
Size 4 acres

Scotlands

COCKPOLE GREEN, WARGRAVE, READING RG10 8QP

Tel 01628 822648
Location At Holly Cross, in the triangle between the A4130, the A321 & the A4

BUCKINGHAMSHIRE

Buckinghamshire is wonderfully stocked with large estates and grand, historic gardens. All three Grade I landscapes – Cliveden, Stowe and West Wycombe Park – are regularly open to the public, as are the two Rothschild gardens at Ascott and Waddesdon. These estates also have many fine trees. The National Gardens Scheme is active in the county, and lists over fifty gardens to visit, often in village clusters. Dorneywood Gardens at Burnham are particularly worth seeing on their all-too-rare openings for the National Gardens Scheme. There are comparatively few National Collections in the county, though the *Pleione* species and hybrids at Butterfields Nursery in Bourne End, visitable only by appointment (01628 525455), have long been a feature of RHS shows. There is a good selection of garden centres in the county: Buckingham Nurseries & Garden Centre is one of the best known and there is a large Blooms of Bressingham Garden Centre in the old walled garden at Dorney Court.

Ascott

WING, LEIGHTON BUZZARD LU7 0PS

Tel 01296 688242 **Fax** 01296 681904
Website www.nationaltrust.org.uk
Location ½ mile east of Wing
Opening hours Garden only: 2 pm – 6 pm; Tuesday – Sunday; 1 – 30 April and 7 August to 14 September. Plus Wednesdays & last Sundays in month; 1 May to 1 August
Admission fee Garden only: £4 Adults; £2 Children

Ascott is an opulent late-Victorian extravaganza. It was largely planned by Leopold de Rothschild and planted with trees and shrubs supplied by Sir Harry Veitch. The Dutch garden, the Venus garden and the topiary sundial date from this period – roughly 1880–1920. The topiary sundial is famous: its Roman numerals are planted in box and the gnomon at the centre is made of golden yew grafted onto a green Irish yew. The motto – in Latin – reads 'Light and shade by turn, but love always'. Much in these old gardens has been restored, re-made and re-planted in recent years. The bedding in the Dutch garden relies heavily upon the sumptuous leaves of coleus (*Solenostemon* cvs.), cannas and the ornamental cabbage 'Tokio': all were popular one hundred years ago. Other parts of the garden have been re-designed in a more modern idiom. The 'long walk' now has a serpentine shape. The old fern garden has been replanted as a box parterre and is now known as the sunken garden. And there is a new 'planet topiary garden', built to resemble the astrological symbols of the twelve planets and showing their position in the sky at the very moment Sir Evelyn and Lady de Rothschild were each born. But there are fine old trees, and new plantings too, including a young collection of modern magnolias and groups of *Davidia*

involucrata, Aesculus indica and *Juglans nigra.*

 Plant Highlights Woodland garden; topiary; mature conifers; good herbaceous borders; spring bulbs; Dutch garden; tallest *Cedrus atlantica* 'Aurea' in the British Isles.

Owned by The National Trust
English Heritage grade II*

Blossoms

COBBLERS HILL, GREAT MISSENDEN
HP16 9PW

Tel & Fax 01494 863140
Location In Cobblers Hill Lane, on road between Wendover Dean & Hampden Bottom
Opening hours By appointment only
Admission fee £1.50 for National Gardens Scheme

Ⓟ ♿ ☕

The bones of this fascinating plantsman's garden go back to 1925 when a previous owner started to plant up a four-acre field and an acre of beech wood filled with bluebells. Dr and Mrs Hytten have lived here since 1975 and have benefited from the substantial windbreaks planted in the 1920s and 1930s. Having once been open – there is still a fine view of the Lisbourne Valley – Blossoms is essentially a woodland garden now, with an established apple orchard and some lusty specimen trees including a liquidamber and a fern-leaved *Fagus sylvatica* 'Asplenifolia'. The Hyttens have thickened up the woodland themselves and made good collections of maples, eucalyptus and willows, together with some more unusual trees, such as *Tetradium danielli*, *Davidia* and *Metasequoia*. Add in a herbaceous border, a scree garden, a rock garden, a rare collection of herbaceous plants, a cutting garden, a number of very

large climbing roses, a small lake, smaller ponds, patios and statues (mostly wood-carvings) – and the scale and variety of the owners' achievement will be apparent. The owners say that spring and autumn are the best seasons, but like all good plantsmen's gardens there is lots of interest throughout the year.

Owned by Dr & Mrs Frank Hytten
Number of gardeners owners only
Size 5 acres

Buckingham Nurseries & Garden Centre

10 TINGEWICK ROAD, BUCKINGHAM
MK18 4AE

Tel 01280 813556
Website www.buckingham-nurseries.co.uk
Location 1½ miles west of Buckingham, on A421
Opening hours Summer: 8.30 am – 6 pm; Monday – Friday. 9.30 am – 6 pm; Sundays. Winter: 8.30 am – 5.30 pm; Monday – Friday. 9.30 am – 5.30 pm; Sundays. Open late on Thursdays: 8 pm in summer & 7 pm in winter

Ⓟ

Buckingham Nurseries is a well-established nursery attached to a flourishing garden centre where you can find all the extras which are so much a part of visiting a garden centre today – pots, furniture, retailing areas, a restaurant and an aquatics centre. But the nursery's speciality is hedging – it produces a very wide range of bare-root hedging plants and tree plants for ornamental and forestry use. In the display garden are lots of sample strips of hedging, some mature and others more recently planted: these give customers an opportunity to see how a hedge will develop over the years. The website is helpful, too.

Butterfields Nursery

HARVEST HILL, BOURNE END SL8 5JJ

Tel 01628 525455
Location Off B476
Opening hours 9 am – 5 pm (usually)

Butterfields Nursery has two very different specialities: pleiones and dahlias. Ian Butterfield is far and away the most important breeder and seller of pleiones, having bred and selected forms and hybrids for many years – and created quite a sensation when he exhibits at shows like the Chelsea Flower Show. Two-thirds of all the species, hybrids, forms and grexes of pleiones sold in England are unique to Butterfields Nursery. The dahlias are primarily for exhibition (though all are good garden plants too) and range right across the classes from the largest decoratives to the smallest pompons. The dahlias do not dominate the market in quite the same way but, that said, Butterfields lists an impressive number which are unique to it in the same way that the pleiones are – the pale lilac pompon 'Rhonda Suzanne', for example, and the orange-flowered miniature semi-cactus 'Andries Orange'.

Campden Cottage

51 CLIFTON ROAD, CHESHAM BOIS, AMERSHAM HP6 5PN

Tel 01494 726818
Location Signed from A416 between Amersham on the Hill & Chesham
Opening hours 2 pm – 6 pm; 4 March, 8 April, 13 May, 10 June, 15 July, 5 August, 2 September, 7 October
Admission fee Adults £1.50; Children free

This plantsman's garden crams a vast number of rare and interesting plants into its half acre and, like all good gardens, has lots to enjoy at every time of the year. The owners have given the garden a good structure and placed plants together to show the contrasts and harmonies of their colours and shapes. They say they are busiest at their March opening when people come to see the hellebores.

Owned by Mr & Mrs P Liechti
Number of gardeners 1
Size ½ acre

Chenies Manor

CHENIES, RICKMANSWORTH WD3 6ER

Tel & Fax 01494 762888
Location Centre of Chenies village
Opening hours 2 pm – 5 pm; Wednesdays, Thursdays & Bank Holidays; April to October
Admission fee Garden only, £3; House & garden, £5

The richly planted gardens at Chenies Manor are full of variety but designed to complement the Elizabethan house. Their most spectacular period is spring – April and early May – when 300 different cultivars of tulip come into flower in and around the sunken garden, modelled on Hampton Court. All come from Bloms and all are clearly labelled: each is grown in groups of ten to fifty bulbs and offers a wonderful opportunity to learn about tulips. Later comes the summer bedding, interspersed with herbaceous plantings – red dahlias with white forms of *Campanula latiloba*, for example. And there are colour borders everywhere: one very easy but effective one mixes *Alchemilla mollis* with catmint and *Sisyrinchium striatum*. Add in a Physic garden for herbs, a grass labyrinth, and some beautiful old lawns and yew hedges, and you have a garden of great harmony.

 Plant Highlights Bulbs; topiary; herbs; fruit; physic garden; award-winning maze.

Owned by Mrs A MacLeod Matthews
Number of gardeners 2½
Size 4½ acres
English Heritage grade II*

Cliveden

TAPLOW, MAIDENHEAD SL6 0JA

Tel 01628 605069   **Fax** 01628 669461
Website www.nationaltrust.org.uk
Location 2 miles north of Taplow, M4 Jct7
Opening hours 11 am – 6 pm (4 pm in November & December); daily; 14 March to 31 December. Closed 10 July
Admission fee Adults (Grounds) £5; Children £2.50

Cliveden is a vast landscape garden, filled with whatever money could buy: balustrading from the Villa Borghese in Rome, the dramatic 'Fountain of Love' and a huge parterre below the house. The best parts are the Arcadian ilex wood, quite magical, and newly restored rose garden, originally made by Geoffrey Jellicoe in 1932.

 Plant Highlights Woodland garden; snowdrops; roses (mainly modern); fruit; good herbaceous borders; bluebells; good autumn colour; tallest *Juglans cinerea* (24m) in the British Isles.

Owned by The National Trust
NCCPG National Collections *Catalpa*
English Heritage grade I

Great Barfield

BRADENHAM, HIGH WYCOMBE HP14 4HP

Tel 01494 563741
Location Turn into village from A4010 at Red Lion & first right – ½ mile
Opening hours For National Gardens Scheme, and by appointment
Admission fee Adults £1.50; Children (under 16) free (2000 prices)

One of the best modern plantsman's gardens in southern England, not least because it is beautifully designed, labelled and maintained. Whatever the season, Great Barfield amazes the visitor by the number and variety of plants in flower and their thoughtful placing.

 Plant Highlights Woodland garden; snowdrops; roses (mainly old-fashioned); plantsman's collection of plants; good herbaceous borders; wonderful hellebores in February; lilies (notably martagons) naturalising; colchicums; good autumn colour & fruits.

Owned by Richard Nutt
NCCPG National Collections *Iris unguicularis*; *Leucojum*

Hughenden Manor

HIGH WYCOMBE HP14 4LA

Tel 01494 755573   **Fax** 01494 755564
Website www.nationaltrust.org.uk
Location 1½ miles north of High Wycombe
Opening hours noon – 5 pm; Saturdays & Sundays in March; then Wednesday – Sunday plus Bank Holiday Mondays from 1 April to 31 October
Admission fee Garden only £1.50. Park & woodland free

Hughenden is not a great garden, but interesting for its association with Disraeli. The garden was made by his wife in the 1860s and is a classic formal design of its period. Recently restored, using photographs taken in 1881, the parterre is once again planted with Victorian bedding.

 Plant Highlights Good herbaceous borders; 61 old apple varieties; rolling parkland; formal Victorian parterres with bright bedding out as in Disraeli's day.

Owned by The National Trust
English Heritage grade II

Lower Icknield Farm

LOWER ICKNIELD WAY, GREAT KIMBLE, AYLESBURY HP17 9TX

Tel & Fax 01844 343436
Location On B4009 between Great Kimble & Longwick
Opening hours 9 am – 5.30 pm; daily; all year. Closed from Christmas to New Year
Admission fee None

The owners say that the display garden attached to Lower Icknield Farm Nurseries is best from July to September when their National Collection of *Argyranthemum* is in flower. They now have over 110 cultivars of these shrubby daisies from Madeira and the Canaries: this is at least four times as many as any other nursery offers. But they also have a good collection of tender salvias, mainly the Mexican species like *S. greggii* and the *S. × jamensis* hybrids, and a fair list of hardy grasses. All the plants they sell are raised on the nursery – none are bought in – and they sell no sundries apart from their own brand of growing compost. Plants are what they raise, and there is a succession of half-hardy patio and house-plants for sale throughout the year, as well as hardy bedding.

Owned by Mr & Mrs J Baldwin
Number of gardeners 1
Size 2 acres
NCCPG National Collections *Argyranthemum*

The Manor House

BLEDLOW, PRINCES RISBOROUGH HP27 9PB

Tel 020 7584 4243   **Fax** 020 7823 1476
Location Off B4009
Opening hours 2 pm – 6 pm; 6 May & 17 June for National Gardens Scheme. And by appointment
Admission fee £4.50

This is one of the greatest gardens of our times: beautifully planted and well maintained, it has all been made on thin chalk soil since 1969. There are four parts: first, the garden 'proper' round the house, enclosed by hedges of beech, hornbeam or yew. Best is the armillary garden, an exercise in topiary with the sphere at its centre, surrounded by four cubes of yew, smaller hedges and labels of box. Next comes the walled garden with a gazebo in the centre whose eight trellised posts are planted with clematis and rambling roses. The central grass walk is lined with apple trees trained as spheres around a wire globe: they rise from parterre boxes of teucrium, each planted with a different herb – sage, chives, Greek oregano and so on. The third part of the garden is quite different – two and a half acres of sculpture garden started in 1991 and already remarkably mature. The land has been contoured to maximise the movement of the surface, and give contrast of height and depth. Its fluid modern design is a great foil to the formal gardens around the house. The presiding spirit is a life-size gorilla by Michael Cooper. The fourth part of the garden is different again – four acres of water garden, started in 1979 on the site of three old watercress beds. The thirteen springs which issue from its sides are the headwaters of the River Lyde, a tributary of the Thames. The steep valley sides are thickly planted with shrubs and herbaceous plants. A wooden walkway, Japanese in style, takes you round the edge of the lakes at the bottom. The muddy banks are planted with candelabra primroses, gunneras, hostas and astilbes. Unlike the rest of the garden, this part is open daily (and free) from dawn to dusk.

Owned by Lord & Lady Carrington

Stowe Landscape Gardens

STOWE, BUCKINGHAM MK18 5EH

Tel 01280 822850   **Fax** 01280 822437
Website www.nationaltrust.org.uk
Location 3 miles north-west of Buckingham
Opening hours 10 am – 5.30 pm or dusk (last admissions 4 pm); Wednesday – Sunday plus Bank Holiday Mondays; 3 March to 28 October. Plus 10 am – 4 pm; Wednesday – Sunday; 1 to 23 December
Admission fee Adults £4.60

This mega-landscape, considered by some the most important in the history of gardens. The National Trust acquired control from the boys' public school in 1989 and the restoration will take many years. Go if you have not been already, and go again if you have. Stowe is not obvious: stomp round slowly, and contemplate the history and symbolism of each feature. Read the National Trust's excellent guide and then go round again, this year, next year, every year, and commune with the *genius loci*.

Plant Highlights Tallest *Fraxinus angustifolia* 'Lentiscifolia' (24m) and largest × *Crataemespilus grandiflora* (9m) in the British Isles.

Owned by The National Trust
English Heritage grade I

Turn End

TOWNSIDE, HADDENHAM, AYLESBURY HP17 8BG

Tel 01844 291383
Location Turn at Rising Sun in Haddenham, then 300 yards on left. Park in street
Opening hours 10 am – 4 pm; 6, 13, 20 & 27 June. 2 pm – 6 pm, 1 April, 7 May & 23 September for National Gardens Scheme. Groups by appointment
Admission fee Adults £2; Children 50p

Peter Aldington was once a young architect, much influenced by Le Corbusier and James Stirling. In 1963 he and his wife bought this plot and built their house – a modern architectural classic, much photographed, cited, visited and copied. Aldington believed that his job as an architect was to make connections and create forms which enclosed spaces for people to use and enjoy. He then set out to apply the same principles to his garden, drawing upon his love of textures and materials to design and plant it. The garden, like the house, became one of the most acclaimed to be made in the latter half of the twentieth century. Over the years he was able to increase its size by small additions. It still covers less than one acre, but never was space so used to create an illusion of size. A brilliant series of enclosed gardens, sunken or raised, sunny or shady, each different and yet harmonious, contrasts with lawns, borders and glades. The story is told in *A Garden & Three Houses* by Jane Brown (Garden Art Press, 1999). Visitors are requested to park well away from the house, please.

Owned by Mr & Mrs Peter Aldington

Waddesdon Manor

AYLESBURY HP18 0JH

Tel 01296 653212   **Fax** 01296 653211
Website www.waddesdon.org.uk
Location A41 Bicester & Aylesbury; 20 miles from Oxford
Opening hours 10 am – 5 pm; Wednesday – Sunday
& Bank Holiday Mondays; 28 February to 23 December
Admission fee Grounds only: Adults £3; Children £1.50.
RHS members free in March & October

The garden at Waddesdon was laid out in
the 1870s and 1880s for Baron Ferdinand de
Rothschild by the French landscape designer
Elie Lainé: it is one of the finest Victorian
gardens in Britain. A grand Victorian park,
splendid formal gardens, a rococo aviary
and extravagant bedding are the first fruits
of restoring the grounds of this amazing
Rothschild palace. New features for 2001
include a rose garden and a children's
garden – and carpet bedding designed by
Oscar de la Renta.

Owned by The National Trust
English Heritage grade II*

West Wycombe Park

WEST WYCOMBE HP14 3AJ

Tel 01494 513569
Website www.nationaltrust.org.uk
Location West end of West Wycombe on A40
Opening hours 2 pm – 6 pm; Sunday – Thursday; June to
August. Plus, gardens only, Sundays, Wednesdays & Bank
Holidays in April & May
Admission fee Adults £2.60

This early landscape park, with a lake in the
shape of a swan, has been well restored and
embellished by modern additions, including
three modern eye-catchers designed by
Quinlan Terry.

Owned by The National Trust
English Heritage grade I

CAMBRIDGESHIRE

Cambridgeshire has a good number of historic gardens. Though Wimpole Hall is the only one rated as Grade I, there is a great cluster of Grade II* and Grade II landscapes in Cambridge itself: these include the Botanic gardens and the following colleges – Christ's, Emmanuel, King's, Queen's, St John's and Trinity (including Trinity Hall). The Backs are also rated Grade I – and one of the few places in the country where the strange but beautiful parasitic *Lathraea clandestina* has naturalised (Wisley is another). The Cambridge University Botanic Garden has by far the most exciting and comprehensive collection of plants in the county and is remarkable for those trees which grow particularly well in the dry climate: many are the tallest of their kind in the British Isles. The National Gardens Scheme is well-supported in Cambridgeshire, and has quite a number of villages where several smaller gardens open together. In Cambridge itself, several colleges open for the National Gardens Scheme, including Clare, Emmanuel, King's, Newnham, Selwyn and Trinity. The county is thinly supplied with nurseries and garden centres, but Monksilver Nursery is a magnet for keen plantsman and of international importance as a source of rare plants. Cambridgeshire has its fair share of National Collections – here too the lead is set by the University Botanic Garden with no less than nine National Collections from *Alchemilla* to *Tulipa*. The College of West Anglia at Milton, near Cambridge, is a RHS Partner College.

Abbots Ripton Hall

ABBOTS RIPTON PE17 2PQ

Tel 01487 773555   **Fax** 01487 773545
Location Off B1090
Opening hours 2 pm – 5 pm; 20 May, 24 June, 8 July, 22 July & 5 August, for various local charities
Admission fee Adults £3; Children (under 16) £1.50

Humphrey Waterfield, Lanning Roper and Jim Russell all worked here, and few garden owners have had as many gardening friends as the late Lord & Lady De Ramsey, who made and remade this garden over more than 50 years. The result is a garden of stylish individuality – as witness the gothic trellis work and the bobbles of yellow philadelphus – but also of great unity. The present Lady De Ramsey has retained the unity of style while replanting many of the borders. In early summer it can fairly claim to be the most beautiful garden in England.

Plant Highlights Irises; grey border; Chinese bridge; trellis work; splendid herbaceous borders; tallest *Pyrus pyraster* (12m) in the British Isles; new arboretum of rare oaks.

Owned by Lord De Ramsey
Number of gardeners 1, plus 3 part-time
Size 8 acres
English Heritage grade II

Anglesey Abbey

LODE CB5 9EJ

Tel 01223 811243
Website www.nationaltrust.org.uk/angleseyabbey
Location Off B1102
Opening hours 10.30 am – 5.30 pm (or dusk if sooner, last entry 4.30 pm); Wednesday – Sunday, plus Bank Holiday Mondays; 28 March to 21 October. Plus Mondays & Tuesdays from 2 July to 9 September. Winter Walk open Thursday – Sunday from 6 January to 24 March and from 24 October to 23 December
Admission fee Gardens: Adults £3.80, but £3.30 in winter

Seventy years old, no more, but the grounds at Anglesey already deserve to be famous, for they are the grandest made in England during the twentieth century. Majestic avenues and 35 acres of grass are the stuff of it: visit Anglesey when the horse chestnuts are out and tulips glow in the meadows. Large formal gardens, carved out of the flat site by yew hedges, house the first Lord Fairhaven's collection of classical and renaissance sculpture. Then there are smaller gardens, said to be more intimate, where thousands of dahlias and hyacinths hit the eye: glorious or vainglorious, Anglesey has no match.

 Plant Highlights Snowdrops; good herbaceous borders; landscaping on the grandest scale; long avenues of trees; dahlias; cyclamen; good autumn colour; new winter walk (1999).

Owned by The National Trust
English Heritage grade II*

Clare College Fellows' Garden

CLARE COLLEGE, CAMBRIDGE
CB2 1TL

Tel 01223 333222 **Fax** 01223 333219
Website www.clare.cam.ac.uk
Location Enter from Clare Old Court, Trinity Lane or Queens Road
Opening hours Not known as we went to press. In 2000 the garden was open 10.30 am – 4.30 pm; daily; April to September
Admission fee £2 (in 2000)

Two acres of views and vistas, walks and Hidcote-style enclosures filled with exquisite spring bulbs, spectacular hot-colour borders dating from the 1950s and brilliant bedding which is changed twice a year.

Owned by The Master & Fellows

Crossing House Garden

MELDRETH ROAD, SHEPRETH,
ROYSTON SG8 6PS

Tel 01763 261071
Location 8 miles south of Cambridge off A10
Opening hours Dawn – dusk; daily; all year
Admission fee Donation to National Gardens Scheme

One of the wonders of modern gardening, the Crossing House celebrates the achievements of its makers since 1969, on an unpropitious site right beside the main railway line to Cambridge. Box-edged beds separated by granite paths contain thousands and thousands of different plants, densely planted in the cottage style. Shrubs, herbaceous plants, alpines and bulbs are planted in the same beds, to maximise the effect at all seasons. Peat beds, screes, arches,

Cambridge University Botanic Garden

CORY LODGE, BATEMAN STREET, CAMBRIDGE CB2 1JF

Tel 01223 336265 **Fax** 01223 336278
Location Entrance on Bateman Street, 1 mile to the south
of the City Centre
Opening hours 10 am – 4 pm in winter, (5 pm in spring
& autumn, 6 pm in summer); daily, except Christmas Day
& Boxing Day
Admission fee Adults £2; OAPs & Children £1.50

This exceptionally attractive botanic garden is essential visiting for any garden lover who does not already know it. It has so many good and interesting features that you could spend all day here and not be bored. Cambridge's is also one of the most beautiful and best maintained botanic gardens in the country. The limestone rock garden is one of its major attractions, where the plantings are arranged geographically. It overlooks the small lake whose surface is covered in water lilies. Late spring is the time to see the nearby woodland garden. Here are fine tree specimens, including *Dipteronia sinensis*, *Tetracentron sinense* and the hardy paw-paw *Asimina triloba*, and a dawn redwood (*Metasequoia glyptostroboides*) grown from the original introduction of seed into the UK in 1948. Along the sides of the little stream which runs through the wood are candelabra primulas, astilbes, irises and a bed of the giant horse tail *Equisetum telmateia*. Late spring is also the time to see the horse chestnuts in flower, the Persian lilacs and the National Collections of shrubby *Lonicera* and *Ribes*. The garden has a very good collection of peony species, which are in some places interplanted with its hardy geraniums: perhaps one reason why the garden is so attractive is that its National Collections are of supreme horticultural value. The garden also maintains two acres of (mainly herbaceous) systematic beds, a feature which dates back 150 years. A more modern addition is the genetic garden, whose scientific purpose is to demonstrate the natural effects of genes on plant morphology. Everywhere, too, are wonderful trees: was there ever a tree more beautiful than the type specimen of *Quercus* 'Warburgii'? The superb series of linked glasshouses are a blessed sanctuary to horticulturally smart undergraduates during the cold months of an East Anglian winter, but every aspect of the garden's existence is educationally aware and it goes out of its way to attract and interest school-children too.

Plant Highlights Plants under glass; good herbaceous borders; fine collection of trees; important rock garden; species roses; new 'dry' garden (1998); new 'genetic' bed (1999); tallest *Broussonetia papyrifera* (15m) in the British Isles (and 22 other record trees).

Owned by University of Cambridge
NCCPG National Collections *Alchemilla*; *Bergenia* (species & primary hybrids); *Fritillaria* (European species); *Geranium* (species & primary hybrids); *Lonicera* (species & primary hybrids); *Ribes* (species & primary hybrids); *Ruscus*; *Saxifraga* (European species); *Tulipa* (species & primary hybrids)
English Heritage grade II*

topiary, pools and raised beds are some of the features which add variety to the most intensely and intensively planted small garden in England. And every few minutes a London express whizzes past.

Owned by Mr & Mrs D G Fuller and Mr J Marlar
Number of gardeners owners only
Size ¼ acre

Docwra's Manor

SHEPRETH, ROYSTON SG8 6PS

Tel 01763 260235/261557
Location Off A10 to Shepreth
Opening hours Not known as we went to press. In 2000 the garden was open 10 am – 4 pm; Wednesdays and Fridays; all year; 2 pm – 4 pm, first Sunday of April to October. And by appointment
Admission fee £2, but £3 for special openings (2000 prices)

This is very much a plantsman's garden, whose lush profusion defies the dry, cold site. Docwra's Manor is a series of small gardens – walled, wild, paved and so on – each brimming with interesting plants and good combinations. There is a sense of abundance, whatever the season. Do read John Raven's charming and erudite *The Botanist's Garden*, now in print again.

Owned by Mrs John Raven

Elsworth Herbs

AVENUE FARM COTTAGE, 31 SMITH STREET, ELSWORTH, CAMBRIDGE CB3 8HY

Tel & Fax 01954 267414
Location Smith Street is the road through the middle of Elsworth; the nursery is towards the western end
Opening hours By appointment

This is an excellent example of a nursery attached to a National Collection – in this case two of them, *Artemisia* and *Nerium oleander*. Its range is wide – over 50 oleanders, for example, which is twice as many as anyone else – but the owners do not carry large stocks, so they are happy to propagate to order. The list of *Artemisia* species is quite unique – a triumph of plantsmanship.

Owned by Dr J Twibell
NCCPG National Collections *Artemisia; Nerium oleander*

Elton Hall

PETERBOROUGH PE8 6SH

Tel 01832 280468   **Fax** 01832 280584
Location A605, 8 miles west of Peterborough
Opening hours Not known as we went to press. In 2000 the garden was open 2 pm – 5 pm; Wednesdays; June to August. Also Thursdays & Sundays in July & August
Admission fee Garden only: Adults £2.50; Children free (2000 prices)

The house is a castellated extravaganza, but the Victorian gardens have been energetically restored in recent years and make Elton highly visitable. The knot garden and the collection of old roses are the high spots, best in June.

Owned by Mr & Mrs William Proby
English Heritage grade II*

Hardwicke House

HIGH DITCH ROAD, FEN DITTON,
CAMBRIDGE CB5 8TF

Tel & Fax 01223 292246
Location ½ mile east of village
Opening hours 2 pm – 5 pm on 27 May. And by
appointment
Admission fee Adults £3; Children 50p

This is an excellent plantsman's garden with
an emphasis on herbaceous plants, roses and
bulbs. The owner has a particular interest in
Asia Minor, as witness an area devoted to
Turkish bulbs.

Owned by John Drake
NCCPG National Collections *Aquilegia*

Monksilver Nursery

OAKINGTON ROAD, COTTENHAM
CB4 4TW

Tel 01954 251555   **Fax** 01223 502887
Website www.monksilver.com
Location North of Cambridge: between Oakington &
Cottenham
Opening hours 10 am – 4 pm; Friday – Saturday; March
to June, and October

This remarkable nursery is deservedly
fashionable. Monksilver specialises in
finding and rescuing really rare plants. They
say that their areas of speciality include
Anthemis, Arum, Astrantia, Aster, bulbs,
Euphorbia, ferns, *Galanthus*, grasses and
sedges, *Hemerocallis* species, herbaceous
perennials, *Lamium, Lathyrus, Monarda*,
Pink Sheet plants ('pink sheets' are NCCPG
search lists), *Pulmonaria, Ranunculus ficaria,
Sedum, Solidago, Vinca*, rare shrubs and
trees, variegated and wild collected plants.

But the truth is that they list hundreds of
other plants which are equally interesting.
Many nurseries claim to have 'rare and
unusual' plants: in the case of Monksilver,
the boast is consistently true. A fifth of the
catalogue changes each year.

NCCPG National Collections *Vinca*

Netherhall Manor

TANNERS LANE, SOHAM, ELY
CB7 5AB

Tel 01353 720269
Location In middle of village: turn right off the main road
into Tanners Lane
Opening hours 2 pm – 5 pm; 1 April, 6 May,
5 & 12 August
Admission fee Adults £2

This is an unusual garden, worth seeing for
its individual collections of genera and plant
groups which offer something of interest at
every season. The hellebores are good in
spring: a thirty-year old bed is devoted to
the true *Helleborus* 'Potter's Wheel' and
another to white seedlings from Helen
Ballard. Elsewhere are the seldom-seen
Helleborus 'Günther Jürgl' (the first of the
upright-facing cultivars), *H.* 'Circe' (long
thought to be extinct) and *H.* 'Taurus'.
Other goodies include *Primula auricula*
'Duke of Edinburgh' (also thought to be
extinct) and a complete collection of
Fritillaria imperialis cultivars. Better still is
the collection of nineteenth-century
Pelargonium cultivars, including 'Turtle's
Surprise', and 'Sophie Dumaresque': all are
grown from cuttings every year. Calceolarias,
heliotropes, turban ranunculus and
hyacinths are other specialities. The one-
acre garden is immaculately maintained
– its lawns are completely weedless – and
includes a neat kitchen garden area.

Owned by Timothy Clark
Number of gardeners 1 part-time
Size 1 acre

Padlock Croft

WEST WRATTING CB1 5LS

Tel 01223 290383
Location 2½ miles off B1307 (was A604) between Linton & Horseath
Opening hours 2 pm – 6 pm; 26 & 28 May, 16 & 23 June, and 14 July. And by appointment on weekdays
Admission fee £1

Less than an acre of plantsmanship, Padlock Croft is 'interesting' rather than 'exquisite' say the owners. But they do themselves an injustice, because this is a fascinating garden. There are four National Collections of *Campanulaceae* and the *Campanula* collection itself includes every section of the genus. Visit the garden from mid-June onwards, when the campanulas are a knock-out.

Owned by Peter & Susan Lewis
Number of gardeners owners
Size ¾ acre
NCCPG National Collections *Adenophora*; *Campanula*; *Platycodon*; *Symphyandra*

Peckover House

NORTH BRINK, WISBECH PE13 1JR

Tel & Fax 01945 583463
Website www.nationaltrust.org.uk
Location Signed from Wisbech
Opening hours Garden only: 12.30 pm – 5.30 pm; Saturday – Thursday; 31 March to 4 November
Admission fee £2.50

Peckover is a charming example of a not-too-grand Victorian garden, complete with monkey puzzle, fernery and spotted laurel shrubberies. One of the orange trees in the conservatory is 200 years old.

Plant Highlights Fernery; Malmaison carnations; tallest *Acer negundo* (18m) in the British Isles.

Owned by The National Trust
English Heritage grade II

Wimpole Hall

ARRINGTON, ROYSTON SG8 0BW

Tel 01223 207257 **Fax** 01223 207838
Website www.wimpole.org
Location On A603, south-west of Cambridge
Opening hours 10.30 am – 5 pm; daily except Monday & Friday (but open Good Friday & Bank Holiday Mondays); 17 March to 4 November. Open on Fridays in August
Admission fee Garden: £2.50. Park: free

Wimpole is an important classical eighteenth-century landscape where Bridgeman, Brown and Repton have all left their mark. The grand Victorian parterres have 72 flower-beds arranged as eight Union Jack patterns and bright with 24,000 bedding plants.

Owned by The National Trust
NCCPG National Collections *Juglans*
English Heritage grade I

CHESHIRE

Cheshire has a fair number of important historic landscapes, including Adlington
Hall, Arley Hall, Eaton Hall, Lyme Park and Tatton Park, but none is important
enough to be accorded Grade I status by English Heritage. Nevertheless, Cheshire
has a good reputation for gardens and gardening: it is a prosperous county, with
rich soils and plenty of rainfall. This makes it a good area for nurseries and garden
centres. Probably the best known are Bridgemere Nurseries and Stapeley Water
Gardens, both at Bridgemere where the International Water Lily Society also has its
base. Collinwood Nurseries at Mottram St Andrew is one of the leading growers of
chrysanthemums, with an exceptionally comprehensive list of cultivars. Other
specialist nurseries are Caddick's Clematis Nursery at Thelwall and the two rose
nurseries C & K Jones at Tarvin and Fryer's Roses at Knutsford. The National
Gardens Scheme lists a fair number of middle-sized gardens: azaleas and
rhododendrons are particularly popular. Reaseheath College near Nantwich
is a RHS Partner College. The RHS Flower Show at Tatton Park will take place
from 18 to 22 July (ticket hotline 0870 906 3810).

Adlington Hall

MACCLESFIELD SK10 4LF

Tel 01625 829206   **Fax** 01625 828756
Website www.adlingtonhall.com
Location 5 miles north of Macclesfield off A523
Opening hours 2 pm – 5 pm; Mondays & Wednesdays;
June & July. And by prior appointment at any time for
groups of 20 or more: telephone the guide on 01625
820875
Admission fee £4.50 per person; £4 for groups of
26 or more

It is good to see this important historic
garden regularly open to the public again,
and to know that the owners are adding
their own improvements in another part of
the estate. These include a young maze and a
rose garden. Many of the historical features
have been restored in recent years: some are
still awaiting their turn, but the owners'
intention is to repair and rebuild them as
soon as possible. One of the oldest is an
avenue of yews planted in 1660. An ancient
avenue of lime trees, planted in 1688 to
celebrate the accession of William and Mary,
leads to a woodland wilderness with follies.
These include a Shell Cottage (1750s), a
Temple to Diana, a Chinese bridge and a
Hermitage.

Owned by Mrs C J C Legh
English Heritage grade II*

Arley Hall

GREAT BUDWORTH, NORTHWICH
CW9 6NA

Tel 01565 777353   **Fax** 01565 777465
Website www.arleyestate.zuunet.co.uk
Location 5 miles west of Knutsford
Opening hours 11 am – 5 pm; Tuesday – Sunday; 14 April
to 30 September
Admission fee Adults £4.40; OAPs £3.80; Children £2.20

Arley has pleached limes, red *Primula
florindae*, clipped ilex cylinders (30 feet
high) and pretty old roses. But its claim to
fame is the double herbaceous border, backed
and buttressed by yew hedges, one of the
oldest and still one of the best in England.

Plant Highlights Woodland garden;
topiary; roses (mainly old-fashioned);
good herbaceous borders; newly restored
kitchen garden (1999); HHA/Christie's
Garden of the Year in 1987.

Owned by Viscount Ashbrook
Number of gardeners 4
English Heritage grade II*

Bridgemere Garden World

BRIDGEMERE, NANTWICH CW5 7QB

Tel 01270 521100   **Fax** 01270 520215
Location M6 Jct15 & 16: follow signs
Opening hours 8 am – 8 pm (5 pm in winter); daily; all
year except 25 & 26 December
Admission fee Garden World: free. Honesty box
(donations to Cancer Research) for Victorian garden

More than twenty immaculate show gardens
in different styles and the television set of

Gardeners' Diary are just some of
Bridgemere's many attractions. All have
recently been re-made, together with a
complete replica of the garden which won
top prize at the RHS Tatton Park Flower
Show in 1999. Definitely worth a visit,
whatever the season.

Owned by J Ravenscroft
Size 6 acres
NCCPG National Collections *Cimicifuga*; *Clematis
orientalis*; *Thalictrum*

Capesthorne Hall

SIDDINGTON, MACCLESFIELD
SK11 9JY

Tel 01625 861221   **Fax** 01625 861619
Location A34, 3 miles south of Alderley Edge
Opening hours 12 noon – 6 pm; Wednesdays,
Sundays & Bank Holidays; April to October
Admission fee Adults £4; OAPs £3; Children £2

There are lots of interesting things to see at
Capesthorne Hall, provided you are
prepared to explore the grounds and find
them. Fine trees are certainly a feature: the
Victorian arboretum contains some very
vigorous wellingtonias and chestnuts,
supplemented by recent plantings over the
last fifty years. Vernon Russell-Smith
designed the formal lakeside gardens in the
1960s: mixed borders of shrub roses and
herbaceous plants. Along the rhododendron
walk is a splendid mixture of hardy hybrids
interspersed with *Rhododendron ponticum*
and the sweet scented *Rhododendron luteum*.
They flourish under a canopy of tall English
oaks and wild cherries. Here too are two
cork trees, *Quercus suber*. By the time
you have discovered the rose arbour, the
avenue of American hawthorns, the ice
house and the golden glade (planted to
commemorate the golden wedding of Sir

Walter and Lady Bromley-Davenport in 1983), you will have some measure of just how much the garden has to offer.

Owned by W A Bromley-Davenport
Number of gardeners 2

Cholmondeley Castle Gardens

MALPAS SY14 8AH

Tel & Fax 01829 720383
Location Off A49 Tarporley-Whitchurch road
Opening hours 11.30 am – 5 pm; Wednesdays, Thursdays, Sundays & Bank Holiday Mondays. 2 April to 30 September. Closed 21 April
Admission fee Adults £3; OAPs £2.50; Children £1.50. RHS members free in June

The gardens below this handsome early nineteenth-century castle set in rolling parkland have been redeveloped since the 1960s with horticultural advice from Jim Russell. The new plantings have been well integrated into the classical landscape and have added an entirely new horticultural dimension to the landscape. The exquisite temple garden, curling the whole way around a small lake, is breathtakingly beautiful. Highly recommended.

Owned by The Marchioness of Cholmondeley
English Heritage grade II

Dorfold Hall

NANTWICH CW5 8LD

Tel 01270 625245   **Fax** 01270 628723
Location 1 mile west of Nantwich on A534
Opening hours 2 pm – 5 pm; Tuesdays & Bank Holiday Mondays; April to October. Also 2 pm – 5.30 pm on 20 May for National Gardens Scheme

Admission fee House & gardens: Adults £4.50; Children £3. National Gardens Scheme day: Adults £2; Children 75p

William Nesfield designed the formal approach but the main reason for visiting the gardens at Dorfold Hall is the new woodland garden of rhododendrons and other shrubs, leading down to a stream where *Primula pulverulenta* has naturalised in its thousands. Do not miss the incredible hulk of an ancient Spanish chestnut in the stable yard.

Owned by R C Roundell
English Heritage grade II

Dunge Valley Gardens

KETTLESHULME, HIGH PEAK SK23 7RF

Tel & Fax 01663 733787
Location 1 mile south of Kettleshulme: turn down a minor road in the village
Opening hours 10.30 am – 5.30 pm; daily; April to August
Admission fee Adults £3; OAPs £2.50; Children 50p. RHS members free on weekdays in April & May

These hidden gardens 1,000m up in the Pennines are a surprise and a delight: few are so high, and fewer still so full of colour. It is not only the number of plants which gives such pleasure, but the surprise of finding so many that one might suppose too tender – embothriums, desfontainias and mahonias, for example. But there are also fine rhododendrons, old-fashioned roses and flowering borders in an almost Himalayan setting.

Owned by David Kettley

Granada Arboretum

JODRELL BANK, MACCLESSFIELD
SK11 9DL

Tel 01477 571339 **Fax** 01477 571695
Location On A535 between Holmes Chapel and Chelford
Opening hours 10.30 am – 5.30 pm; daily; March to
October. 11 am – 4.30 pm; Tuesday – Sunday; November
to February
Admission fee Grounds, Science Centre & Planetarium:
Adults £4.90; Concessions £3.50; Children £2.50

Originally known as the Jodrell Bank
Arboretum and founded by Sir Bernard
Lovell in 1971, this wonderful arboretum
specialises in alders, birches, crab apples,
pine and *Sorbus*. Long straight drives lead
spaciously into the distance, by way of large
collections of heaths (*Erica*) and heathers
(*Calluna*). The plantings are young and
vigorous, the groupings imaginative. A huge
radio telescope dominates the site: an
awesome presence.

Owned by Manchester University
NCCPG National Collections *Malus*; *Sorbus*

Grosvenor Garden Centre

WREXHAM ROAD, BELGRAVE,
CHESTER CH4 9EB

Tel 01244 682856
Location South of Chester, on B5445
Opening hours 9 am – 6 pm (5 pm in winter); Monday –
Saturday. 11 am – 5 pm; Sundays

This is a large garden centre with a full range
of plants and products, and a series of
garden-related events throughout the year.

Hare Hill Garden

GARDEN LODGE, OVER ALDERLEY,
MACCLESSFIELD SK10 4QB

Tel 01625 828981
Website www.nationaltrust.org.uk
Location Between Alderley Edge & Prestbury
Opening hours 10 am – 5.30 pm; Wednesdays,
Thursdays, Saturday, Sundays & Bank Holiday Mondays
(but daily from 10 to 30 May for rhododendrons & azaleas);
1 April to 30 October
Admission fee Adults £2.50; Children £1.25

Hare Hill is a woodland garden, thickly
planted with trees and underplanted with
rhododendrons, azaleas and shrubs by Jim
Russell in the 1960s. In the middle is a
walled garden which has been developed as a
flower garden with a pergola, arbour and
tender plants against the walls. Planting
continues: much *Rhododendron ponticum*
has been cleared recently and replaced by
new cultivars. Perhaps best in May, there are
still some rhododendrons to flower with the
roses in July.

Owned by The National Trust

Little Moreton Hall

CONGLETON CW12 4SD

Tel 01260 272018
Website www.nationaltrust.org.uk
Location 4 miles south of Congleton on A34
Opening hours 11 am – 5 pm (or dusk, if earlier);
Wednesday – Sunday & Bank Holiday Mondays; 31 March
to 4 November. 11.30 am – 4 pm; Saturdays & Sundays;
10 November to 22 December
Admission fee Adults £4.40; Children £2.20

Little Moreton Hall is the handsomest
timber-framed house in England. When the

National Trust asked Graham Thomas to design and plant a suitable period garden, he specified box-edged parterres with yew topiary and gravel infilling – and very fine they are too. In the kitchen garden, a speciality has been made of old varieties of fruit and vegetables. Peaceful, charming and orderly.

Owned by The National Trust
English Heritage grade I

Lodge Lane Nursery & Bluebell Cottage Gardens

BLUEBELL COTTAGE, LODGE LANE, DUTTON, WARRINGTON WA4 4HP

Tel & Fax 01928 713718
Location Turn off A533 midway between Runcorn & Northwich
Opening hours Nursery open 10 am – 5 pm; Wednesday – Sunday & Bank Holidays; mid March to mid September. Garden open 10 am – 5 pm; Friday – Sunday & Bank Holidays; May to August
Admission fee Adults £2. RHS members free from June to August. Nursery free at all times

Lodge Lane Nursery is a RHS Partner Nursery selling more than 1,500 different herbaceous plants: it is particularly strong on penstemons, but also good for aquilegias, asters, campanulas, diascias, nepeta and salvias, among others. Bluebell Cottage Gardens are the nursery's show garden, well worth a visit in their own right. Both were started as recently as 1993. The garden has been developed as a series of smaller gardens-within-the-garden. Each has a different theme: among them are the herb garden, the yellow garden, the ornamental grass garden and the scree bed. Several

island beds are used to display herbaceous plants: the owners believe that there is nothing to beat them for colour (and sheer garden value) from early to late summer. The wildflower meadow was started in 1994 – three acres of native flowers (mainly perennial) among the grasses, including ox-eye daisies, yarrows, clovers and meadow cranesbill. Right at the far side is a stretch of native woodland, carpeted with bluebells in May. Four RHS special events will take place during 2001: details from 020 7821 3408.

Owned by Mr & Mrs R Casey
Number of gardeners owners, plus a little part-time help
Size 1½ acres, plus meadow & woodland

Lyme Park

DISLEY SK12 2NX

Tel 01663 762023   **Fax** 01663 765035
Website www.nationaltrust.org.uk
Location 6½ miles south-east of Stockport on A6, just west of Disley
Opening hours 11 am – 5 pm (but 1 pm – 5 pm on Wednesdays & Thursdays); daily; March to 30 October. 12 noon – 3 pm; Saturdays & Sundays; 1 November to 18 December
Admission fee Garden only: Adults £2.50; Children £1.20. Plus £3.50 for car (National Trust members free)

There is much of horticultural interest at Lyme, as well as the razzmatazz of a country park: traditional bedding out, two enormous camellias in the conservatory, and a Jekyll-type herbaceous border by Graham Thomas whose colours run from orange to deepest purple. Best of all is the sunken Dutch garden whose looping box and ivy parterres contain the most extravagant bedding displays. The National Trust has now assumed full control of the garden and begun to restore the structure. Lyme Park

featured as Pemberley in the BBC's
Pride & Prejudice.

 Plant Highlights Roses (mainly old-fashioned); good herbaceous borders; spring bulbs; bedding out; orangery by Wyatt; 'Dutch' garden.

Owned by The National Trust
NCCPG National Collections Vicary Gibbs plants
English Heritage grade II*

Mellors Garden

HAIGH HOLE HOUSE, RAINOW,
MACCLESFIELD SK10 5UW

Tel 01625 573251　**Fax** 01625 572389
Location In Sugar Lane
Opening hours 2 pm – 5 pm; 28 May & 29 August. And by appointment
Admission fee £1.50

Ⓟ ⒲ⓒ 🍴

This remarkable small garden was laid out in the nineteenth century as an allegory of Christian's journey in Pilgrim's Progress and planted only with plants that are mentioned in the Bible. Features represent such places as the Way of Salvation, the Cave of the Holy Sepulchre, Vanity Fayre, the Dark River, the Delectable Mountains, Doubting Castle and the Celestial City. A spiritual and historical experience more than a horticultural one.

Owned by Mr & Mrs A Rigby

Norton Priory Museum & Gardens

TUDOR ROAD, RUNCORN WA7 1SX

Tel 01928 569895
Location Well signed locally

Opening hours 12 noon – 5 pm (but 4 pm in March, and 6 pm at weekends & Bank Holidays from April on); daily; March – October
Admission fee Adults £3.75; OAPs £2.50

 Ⓟ ⒲ⓒ ♿ 🌱 🏛 🍴

The old walled garden at Norton Priory has a new layout modelled on eighteenth-century precedents and intended to instruct and please visitors. A cottage garden border, a medicinal herb garden and orchard rub shoulders with colour borders, children's gardens and a scented garden. Beyond are sixteen acres of woodland garden with Georgian summerhouses and glades by the stream.

 Plant Highlights Roses (ancient & modern); rock garden; herbs; fruit; good herbaceous borders.

Owned by Norton Priory Museum Trust (Cheshire County Council)
Number of gardeners 3
Size 38 acres
NCCPG National Collections Cydonia oblonga

Peover Hall

OVER PEOVER, KNUTSFORD
WA16 6SW

Tel 01565 722656
Location 3 miles south of Knutsford
Opening hours 2 pm – 5 pm; Mondays & Thursdays; April to October
Admission fee Adults £2; Children £1

Ⓟ ⒲ⓒ ♿

First a classic eighteenth-century parkland, then an Edwardian overlay of formal gardens – yew hedges and brick paths. Now Peover has modern plantings too – borders in colour combinations, a herb garden, and a rhododendron dell in the woods.

Ness Botanic Gardens

NESTON CH64 4AY

Tel 0151 353 0123 **Fax** 0151 353 1004
Website www.merseyworld.com/nessgardens/
Location Signed off A540, Chester to Hoylake
Opening hours 9.30 am – 4 pm (5 pm from March to October); 4 January to 24 December
Admission fee Adults £4.70; Concessions £4.30. £3.70 in January & February

Ness was the creation of a rich Liverpool cotton merchant, Arthur Bulley, who laid out the garden in 1898 and started to plant it with new species from abroad. He was particularly interested in Himalayan and Chinese plants: he believed that many could become established in cultivation in Britain and he therefore sponsored such plant collectors as George Forrest and Frank Kingdon Ward. It is to Bulley that we owe such plants as *Gentiana sino-ornata* and *Pieris formosa* var. *forrestii*, and it was at Ness that many Chinese plants were first grown in Europe – notably the candelabra primulas. Ness was presented to the University of Liverpool by Bulley's daughter in 1948 and has continued to develop as a public amenity, a tourist attraction and a teaching garden, while still retaining the 'feel' of a private garden. It is beautifully laid out in a sequence of incidents: both its design and plantings have continued to improve year by year. The main features are as follows: a 'sorbus lawn', where the type plant of *Sorbus forrestii* grows; a laburnum arch; a herb garden; a rhododendron border (long and deep) underplanted with many lilies; an excellent heather garden; sandstone terraces where tender plants like *Ribes speciosum* and two wild-collected forms of *Lobelia tupa* flourish; a rock garden with an enormous range of different environments, south-facing and north-facing, limestone and sandstone, sunny, shaded and damp; a water garden; a camellia collection; an arboretum; a willow collection recognised by the NCCPG as a National Collection; a rose garden which illustrates the history of the rose; herbaceous borders; and a series of glasshouses with temperate, arid and tropical sections for such plants respectively as *Lonicera hildebrandiana*, the crown of thorns (*Euphorbia milii*) and important economic plants like cotton, sugar cane, kapok and papyrus. As with all botanic gardens, there is no end of things to see whatever the season, and your visit can be as short or as long as it suits. In practice, however, Ness is one of those gardens where you tend to spend much longer than you intended. The website is very comprehensive.

Plant Highlights Roses (mainly old-fashioned); rock garden; plants under glass; mature conifers; fine collection of trees; 30-metre laburnum arch; new Camellia Walk (2000); tallest *Alnus cremastogyne* (3.3m) in the British Isles.

Owned by University of Liverpool
English Heritage grade II

Owned by R Brooks Ltd
English Heritage grade II

The Quinta

SWETTENHAM VILLAGE, CONGLETON
CW12 2LD

Tel 01270 610180 **Fax** 01270 610430
Location Access through the garden of Swettenham Arms
Opening hours Dawn – dusk; daily; all year
Admission fee Adults £2; Children £1. free to RHS
members from April to October

The Quinta Arboretum was created by Sir
Bernard Lovell, originator of the Jodrell
Bank Radio Telescope, and is now owned by
the Cheshire Wildlife Trust. The garden
features more than 5,000 trees and shrubs,
with beautiful views over the River Dane
meanders. Grand avenues lead to the
ancient woodland nature reserve with
flower-rich meadows grazed by rare-breed
sheep. A wonderful site to visit in all seasons.

Owned by Cheshire Wildlife Trust
Size 40 acres
NCCPG National Collections *Fraxinus*; *Pinus*

Reaseheath College

NANTWICH CW5 6DF

Tel 01270 625131 **Fax** 01270 625665
Location 1 mile north of Nantwich on A51
Opening hours 2 pm – 4 pm; Wednesdays; 23 & 30 May,
and 6 June. College Open Day 11 am – 5 pm on 20 May
Admission fee Donation

Reaseheath's 30 acres have been thoroughly
replanted recently: there is an enormous
amount to enjoy and learn here. Highlights
include a woodland garden, rose garden,
heather garden, rock garden, good bedding
on the formal terraces and splendid mixed
borders.

Owned by Reaseheath College

Rode Hall

CHURCH LANE, SCHOLAR GREEN,
STOKE ON TRENT ST7 3QP

Tel 01270 882961 **Fax** 01270 882962
Location 5 miles south-west of Congleton between
A34 & A50
Opening hours 2 pm – 5 pm; Tuesday – Thursday & Bank
Holidays; 4 April to 28 September. Plus 1.30 pm – 5.30 pm
on 13 May for National Gardens Scheme and 12 noon
– 4 pm from 4 to 18 February for snowdrops
Admission fee Garden only: Adults £2.50; OAPs £1.50

Stand on the terraces at Rode Hall and take
in the prospect: Nesfield's 1860s rose garden
and Repton's landscape beyond. The 'pool'
is nearly a mile long and 150 yards wide. But
horticulture is also here in abundance: take
the boathouse walk past the old stew pond
(pretty marginals and a waterfall) to the wild
flower garden (terraced rock garden – early
nineteenth-century – *very* early for this sort
of garden) where snowdrops, sarcococcas,
hellebores (lots), ferns, primroses and
soldanellas flourish in the lee of
rhododendrons. Note the splendid Loderi
crosses, which smell of sugared almonds and
extend the flowering season into early June.
Admire Professor Pratt's scented azaleas
(would that more people knew and grew
them) and note how the plantings of
rhododendron species are being extended
into the adjacent Old Wood. Then visit the
walled kitchen garden (about two acres) and
see the rows of decorative vegetables set
between cornflowers, poppies, marigolds
and flowers for drying. Espaliered fruit trees
cover the walls between 12ft abutilons:

Cheshire has a mild climate. Look inside the greenhouses and see the many geraniums with scented leaves. And ponder the industry of the head gardener, Kelvin Archer, who grows over forty cultivars of gooseberry here and holds the world record for the largest gooseberry fruit.

Owned by Sir Richard Baker Wilbraham
Number of gardeners 2
Size 6 acres
English Heritage grade II

Stapeley Water Gardens

LONDON ROAD, STAPELEY, NANTWICH CW5 7LH

Tel 01270 623868 **Fax** 01270 624919
Website www.stapeleywatergardens.com
Location A51, 1 mile south of Nantwich
Opening hours 10 am – 5.30 pm (5 pm in winter); daily; all year except 25 December. Nursery opens at 9 am Monday – Friday & 10 am on Saturdays & Sundays; closes at 6 pm (but 4 pm on Sundays, 7 pm on winter Wednesdays & 8 pm on summer Wednesdays)
Admission fee Palms Tropical Oasis: Adults £3.85; OAPs £3.25; Children £2

Part entertainment, part nursery and part display garden, the Palms Tropical Oasis is worth a visit in its own right. A long rectangular pool in the Moorish style is flanked by tall palms, strelitzias and other showy tropical flowers. Visit in winter. But the display gardens are fascinating all through the year, especially the water gardens where all the waterlilies grow.

Owned by Stapeley Water Garden Ltd
NCCPG National Collections *Nymphaea*

Tatton Park

KNUTSFORD WA16 6QN

Tel 01625 534400
Website www.nationaltrust.org.uk
Location Off M6 Jct19 & M56 Jct7 – well signed
Opening hours 10.30 am – 6 pm (but 11 am – 4 pm from October to March); Tuesday – Sunday, plus Bank Holiday Mondays; all year
Admission fee Adults £3; Children £2. RHS members free

Humphry Repton laid out the parkland at Tatton. Joseph Paxton designed both the formal Italian garden and the exquisite fernery, claimed as the finest in the UK. Later came a Japanese garden and Shinto temple (1910), such follies as the African hut, and the mass plantings of rhododendrons and azaleas. Tatton Park is wonderfully well organised for visitors, and gets better every year. Be prepared for a long and absorbing visit. The highly successful RHS Flower Show at Tatton Park will take place from 18 to 22 July: tickets from 0870 906 3810. Two further RHS special events will take place during 2001: details from 020 7821 3408.

Plant Highlights Good herbaceous borders; fine collection of trees; rhododendrons & azaleas in May; biggest *Quercus × schochiana* in the British Isles.

Owned by The National Trust (managed by Cheshire County Council)
NCCPG National Collections *Adiantum*
English Heritage grade II*

Tirley Garth Trust

UTKINTON, TARPORLEY CW6 0LZ

Tel 01829 732301   **Fax** 01829 732265
Website www.tirleygarth.org
Location 2½ miles north of Tarporley, just north of
Utkinton on road to Kelsall
Opening hours 2 pm – 6 pm; 10 & 11 April; 13, 20,
27 & 28 May, 10 July, 11 & 14 October
Admission fee Adults £3; Children 50p

Tirley Garth (originally Tirley Court) is a
famous example of Thomas Mawson's work:
wonderful terraces, paths, retaining walks
and garden buildings. It is this structure
which underpins the planting, including
the rhododendrons and azaleas in the
woodland below. Restoration, replanting
and improvement have continued in
recent years.

Owned by The Tirley Garth Trust
Number of gardeners 2, plus one trainee
Size 39 acres
English Heritage grade II

CORNWALL

Many of the great historic gardens of Cornwall are also the most interesting horticulturally. Mount Edgcumbe and Tresco are both rated Grade I gardens of national importance, while Caerhays Castle, Lanhydrock, Tregrehan and Trewithen are Grade II* and Antony, Carclew, Chyverton, Cotehele, Glendurgan, Heligan, Lamellen, Pencarrow, Penjerrick, St Michael's Mount, Trebah, Trelissick and Trengwainton are all Grade II. It is a proud list, unmatched by any other county, and evidence of how the big estates have always dominated the gardening scene in Cornwall. The county still has its own horticultural organisation the Cornwall Garden Society: its spring show is dominated by camellias and rhododendrons. About 80 gardens open every year for the Cornwall Festival of Spring Gardens which runs from mid-March to the end of May: details from the Cornwall Tourist Board on 01872 322900. Almost all the gardens have fine collections of trees too: those at Trebah, Tregrehan and Trewithin are particularly noted for the age and size of their specimens, while the woodlands of Caerhays contain an exceptional number of well-grown rarities. A new type of Cornish garden has however been emerging over the last 25 years, where the owners have taken advantage of the climate to grow a very wide range of newer plants: Pine Lodge, Lamorran and Bosvigo are good examples and will doubtless be followed by others. The county's National Collections reflect the opportunities which the Cornish weather makes possible: among them are *Escallonia* at Duchy College (a RHS Partner College), *Crocosmia* at Lanhydrock, *Azara* at Trelissick, *Grevillea* at Pine Lodge and *Acacia* at Tresco. Finest of all is the National Collection of *Dahlia* at Varfell Farm at Long Rock, just off the A30, where some 2,000 species and cultivars can be seen by the public from 10 am to 5 pm on 1 & 2 September 2001 and by prior appointment (further details from 01736 710744). Cornish nurseries cater well for the local market: the Duchy of Cornwall Nursery at Lostwithiel has the largest stock of all, while tender exotica are the speciality of Trevena Cross Garden Centre near Helston and Lower Kenneggy Nurseries near Penzance. Best known is Burncoose & South Down Nurseries, a regular winner of Gold Medals for its spectacular displays of flowering trees and shrubs at RHS shows throughout the year.

Antony House

TORPOINT PL11 2QA

Tel & Fax 01752 812364
Website www.nationaltrust.org.uk
Location 5 miles west of Plymouth, 2 miles north-west of Torpoint
Opening hours 1.30 pm – 5.30 pm; Tuesday – Thursday & Bank Holidays; 4 April to 1 November; also 1.30 pm – 5.30 pm on Sundays from June to August. Last admissions 4.45 pm
Admission fee Adults £2; Children £1

Antony has been an historic and important garden for centuries – and every generation seems to have left its mark. Its classic late-eighteenth-century landscape is still superb, though there is considerable debate as to whether Humphry Repton designed it or the Pole-Carews (as they were then called) listened to Repton's advice but did what they wanted to do for themselves. The yew walk with its lead statues of a shepherd and his shepherdess and the huge Chinese temple bell, flanked by stone lanterns, date from the nineteenth century. The position is superb – an elevated promontory above the Tamar estuary, technically in Cornwall, but just across Plymouth Sound from Devon. Most of the horticultural interest was created by Sir John Carew Pole in the middle of the twentieth century – 300 camellias, millions of bulbs, the lime-tree avenue on either side of the drive, over 500 early *Hemerocallis* hybrids from USA, a 30-ft loquat tree (*Eriobotrya japonica*) against the house, the vast cork oak (*Quercus suber*) on the main lawn and the beautiful March-flowering *Magnolia campbellii* 'Charles Raffill' (another record-breaker) out on the edge of the woodland. Sir Richard & Lady Carew Pole, who now live at Antony, have continued to intensify and extend the horticultural interest: more spring-flowering trees and shrubs have been planted, alongside the creation of gardens for summer and autumn interest. The Summer Garden is particularly effective: hybrid musk roses are underplanted with lavender, irises, dianthus and peonies and its walls covered in clematis, climbing roses, lemon-scented verbena and *Cytisus battandieri*. But there is much to see at every season – the magnolia walk in spring, the lilac walk in May (the 'lilacs' are ceanothus – known as California lilac), the knot garden in high summer and free-standing fig-trees *Ficus carica* 'White Marseilles' in autumn. And it is a large garden, so you need to allow lots of time to do it justice.

Plant Highlights Mature conifers; good herbaceous borders; magnolias; yew hedges; tallest Japanese loquat *Eriobotrya japonica* (8m) in the British Isles (and two other tree records).

Owned by The National Trust
NCCPG National Collections *Hemerocallis*
English Heritage grade II

Antony Woodland Garden

ANTONY HOUSE, TORPOINT
PL11 2QA

Tel & Fax 01752 812364
Location 5 miles west of Plymouth, 2 miles north-west of Torpoint
Opening hours 11 am – 5.30 pm; daily except Mondays & Fridays (but open on Bank Holidays); March to October
Admission fee Adults £3; Accompanied children free

This is the 'Cornish' part of the grounds at Antony, still controlled by the Carew Pole family rather than the National Trust. They have planted it with the best modern forms of rhododendrons, azaleas, magnolias, camellias and other trees.

Owned by The Carew Pole Garden Trust
NCCPG National Collections Camellia japonica

The Barbara Hepworth Museum & Sculpture Garden

2 BARNOON HILL, ST IVES
TR26 1TG

Tel 01736 796226   Fax 01736 794480
Location In town centre
Opening hours 10.30 am – 5.30 pm; Tuesday – Sunday; all year. Plus Mondays in July & August
Admission fee Adults £3.75; Concessions £2

Dame Barbara Hepworth's studio and garden have been run by the Tate Gallery since 1980. She designed the garden as a permanent setting to exhibit her works. Visiting it gives you a remarkable insight into one of the twentieth century's most important sculptors.

Owned by Tate Gallery & Hepworth Estate
Number of gardeners 2
Size ½ acre

Bosvigo

BOSVIGO LANE, TRURO TR1 3NH

Tel & Fax 01872 275774
Location Turn off A390 at Highertown near Sainsbury's roundabout, then 500 yards down Dobbs Lane
Opening hours 11 am – 6 pm; Thursday – Saturday; 1 March to 29 September
Admission fee Adults £3; Children £1

Not a typical Cornish garden, the emphasis at Bosvigo is upon herbaceous plants, chosen for their individual qualities and planted in fine colour combinations. The woodland garden is more traditional, and underplanted with snowdrops, hellebores, wood anemones, erythroniums and epimediums, but the rest of the garden is at its best in summer and keeps well into the autumn. Over the last twenty years or so, Wendy & Michael Perry have created a series of small walled or hedged garden 'rooms' around the mainly Georgian house. Each has its own colour theme: the walled garden heaves with polite blues, mauves and pinks while another is mainly of gold and white. Reds and oranges co-exist in a 'hot' garden which, according to the Perrys, 'blows your socks off'. Many of the plants are rare, and some are sold in the small specialist nursery. The nursery is also open for the sale of hellebores from 10 am to 4 pm on Fridays & Saturdays in February.

Owned by Wendy & Michael Perry
Number of gardeners owners only
Size 2 acres

Burncoose Nurseries & Gardens

GWENNAP, REDRUTH TR16 6BJ

Tel 01209 860316   **Fax** 01209 860011
Website www.burncoose.co.uk
Location On A393 between Lanner & Ponsanooth
Opening hours 8.30 am – 5 pm (open 11 am on Sundays); daily except 25 December; all year
Admission fee Adults £2; Children free

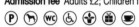

Burncoose Nurseries specialise in rare and unusual plants: they list over 2,500 different ones – mainly ornamental trees and shrubs – which makes them one of the best for sheer choice in all Europe. Their real specialities are camellias, rhododendrons, magnolias and conservatory plants. Burncoose has won gold medals at all but one of the last twelve Chelsea Flower Shows and, over two years, have won more awards and gold medals at UK flower shows than any other exhibitor. The garden is a woodland garden, carpeted with bluebells, primroses, snowdrops and wild violets in spring. Two monkey puzzles *Araucaria araucana* are over 100ft high and a *Eucryphia* × *nymansensis* reaches 40ft. Most of the ornamental plants have been planted since 1900 and the older ones have been matched in recent years by substantial additions.

Owned by F J Williams CBE
Number of gardeners 1
Size 30 acres

Carclew Gardens

PERRAN-AR-WORTHAL, TRURO TR3 7PB

Tel 01872 864070
Location A39 east at Perran-ar-Worthal, 1 mile to garden
Opening hours 2 pm – 5.30 pm. 22 & 29 April, 6, 13, 20 & 27 May. And at any time by appointment
Admission fee Adults £2.50; Children 50p

Carclew's garden first opened to the public in 1927 and has continued to do so for charity every year since then. It was once the greatest rhododendron garden in the south-west: some of the oldest rhododendrons were grown from Sir Joseph Hooker's Himalayan collections nearly one 150 years ago. The many fine trees include a large ginkgo and a form of *Quercus* × *hispanica* which is *not* 'Lucombeana'. Mrs Chope has been busy replanting and restoring the garden: the waterfall is now repaired again.

Plant Highlights Woodland garden; roses (mainly modern); rhododendrons; tallest *Pseudolarix amabilis* (23m) in the British Isles.

Owned by Mrs Robert Chope
English Heritage grade II

Carwinion

MAWNAN SMITH, FALMOUTH TR11 5JA

Tel 01326 250258
Location From Mawnan Smith, turn left at Red Lion, 500 yards up hill on right
Opening hours 10 am – 5.30 pm; daily or by appointment; all year
Admission fee Adults £2.50; Children free

Caerhays Castle Gardens

GORRAN, ST AUSTELL PL26 6LY

Tel 01872 501310   **Fax** 01872 501870
Website www.caerhays.co.uk
Location Between Mevagissey & Portloe
Opening hours 10 am – 4 pm; Monday – Friday; 12 March to 18 May. Charity openings: 25 March, 15 April & 7 May
Admission fee Adults £3.50; Children £1.50

Caerhays has belonged to the Williams family since 1853, but it was not until the young J C Williams took over the estate in the 1890s that they began to develop the gardens. It seems that the original inspiration came from an RHS daffodil conference: it sparked JCW's lifelong interest in hybridising. By 1903 he was sponsoring E H Wilson's collections in China and this was followed by a partnership with George Forrest. Of the many plants that these expeditions introduced, Caerhays is best known for its magnolias, but JCW is also remembered as a great hybridiser of rhododendrons and camellias. *Camellia × williamsii* was named for him: some of the originals still flourish at Caerhays, including 'J.C. Williams', 'Mary Christian' and 'St. Ewe'. The present owner and his son Charles Williams have been no less involved in conserving and improving the remarkable plant collections at Caerhays. They make a point of trying to accommodate rare and unusual plants, whose cultural requirements take precedence over the niceties of garden design. And the Williams are still involved in wide scale plantings – especially since the garden suffered serious damage in the 1990 great gale. Magnolias remain a major interest and almost all the new forms and cultivars coming out of Australia, USA and New Zealand have been added to the garden

and have grown away well. One of the joys of Caerhays is to stumble upon magnificent old specimens deep in its 100 acres of woodland. Among the many rare trees are fine specimens of *Laurus azorica, Lithocarpus cleistocarpa, Lithocarpus henryi*; magnolias like *M. delavayi, M. nitida, M. robusta* and *M. salicifolia*; and such oaks as *Quercus acuta, Q. crassifolia, Q. glauca, Q. ilicifolia, Q. lamellosa, Q. lanata, Q. Lodicosa, Q. oxyodon* and *Q. phillyreoides*. Almost all these species are known to few of us: this litany of names is a measure of the importance of Caerhays. There is much to discover, so you should allow plenty of time. And see the website – very informative.

Plant Highlights Woodland garden; plantsman's collection of plants; mature conifers; fine collection of trees; camellias; magnolias; rhododendrons; tallest specimen of *Emmenopterys henryi* (17m) in the British Isles, and 37 further record-breaking trees (including eight *Acer* species).

Owned by F J Williams CBE
Number of gardeners 4
Size 60 acres
English Heritage grade II*

Ten acres of Cornish jungle, exotically thick with rhododendrons, camellias, drimys and the largest collection of bamboos in the south-west.

Owned by Anthony Rogers

Chyverton

ZELAH, TRURO TR4 9HD

Tel 01872 540324
Location 1 mile south-west of Zelah on A30
Opening hours By appointment at any time
Admission fee Adults £4; Children (under 16) free; Groups (20+) £3.50

Chyverton started out as a Georgian landscape garden. Then the owners planted a pinetum in the 1860s. The horticultural plantings have however been very much extended since the 1920s, initially with some advice from Sir Harold Hillier, but latterly by the owners themselves. Nigel Holman is a distinguished plantsman: Hugh Johnson calls his garden 'a magic jungle'. Magnolias are a particular interest: several Chyverton seedlings now bear cultivar names. Many other established plants have also been grown from seed: rhododendron hybrids from Brodick, for instance. But there is much more to interest the plantsman. A large *Berberidopsis corallina* and a lanky red-stemmed hedge of *Luma apiculata* below the house are both outstanding. And the planting continues.

Plant Highlights Woodland garden; plantsman's collection of plants; mature conifers; magnolias, including four record-breakers; nothofagus; new herbaceous plantings (2000); tallest *Rhododendron* 'Cornish Red' (14m) in the British isles.

Owned by Nigel Holman
Size 120 acres
English Heritage grade II

Cotehele

ST DOMINICK, SALTASH PL12 6TA

Tel 01579 351346 **Fax** 01579 351222
Website www.nationaltrust.org.uk
Location 14 miles from Plymouth via Saltash
Opening hours 10.30 am – dusk; daily; all year
Admission fee £3.40

Broad Victorian terraces below the house support many tender climbers such as *Jasminum mesnyi*, while the beds beneath have wallflowers and roses. Down the wooded valley are camellias, rhododendrons and shade-loving plants which thrive in an ancient woodland, kept damp by a small stream. The National Trust has undertaken much gentle restoration and renewal in recent years.

Plant Highlights Woodland garden; topiary; roses (mainly modern); daffodils; fine collection of trees; palms; ferns; pretty dovecote; largest *Davidia involucrata* in the British Isles.

Owned by The National Trust
English Heritage grade II

Duchy of Cornwall Nursery

COTT ROAD, LOSTWITHIEL PL22 0BW

Tel 01208 872668 **Fax** 01208 872835
Location 1½ miles off A390 at Lostwithiel

Opening hours 9 am – 5 pm; Monday – Saturday. 10 am – 5 pm; Sundays. Closed Bank Holidays

The Duchy nursery stocks an extensive general range of all types of plants, and will interest even the most discriminating plantsman. Its policy does not compromise on quality: it offers the cultivars which it considers the best. These range from reliable old favourites to rare and recent cultivars. The nursery is especially good on hardy fuchsias, and hopes that its collection will one day be recognised by the NCCPG. It is also one of the few nurseries which still supply bare-rooted stock in winter.

The Eden Project

WATERING LANE NURSERY, PENTEWAN, ST AUSTELL PL26 6BE

Tel 01726 811911   **Fax** 01726 811912
Website www.edenproject.com
Location Signed from A30, A390 & A391
Opening hours Times & dates not yet known, but expected to open in April 2001
Admission fee Adults £9.50; OAPs £7.50; Children £4

This imaginative project is expected to be completed in spring 2001. The promoters hope to provide visitors with an understanding of the world of plants, and their importance to human welfare. The area under glass is described as being the size of thirty football pitches. One of the gigantic conservatories – all made in a disused clay-pit near St Austell – is landscaped as a rainforest, while others are Mediterranean, South African and Californian. Staples like cocoa, coffee, bananas and rubber will be grown alongside plants used in paper, wine, scent and brewing.

Owned by The Eden Trust
Size 37 acres

Glendurgan Gardens

HELFORD RIVER, MAWNAN SMITH, FALMOUTH TR11 5TR

Tel 01326 250906   **Fax** 01326 865808
Website www.nationaltrust.org.uk
Location 1 mile west of Mawnan Smith, west to Trebah
Opening hours 10.30 am – 5.30 pm (last admissions 4.30 pm); Tuesday – Saturday, plus Bank Holiday Mondays; 17 February to 3 November. Closed Good Friday
Admission fee Adults £3.60; Children £1.80

Glendurgan is a steep, sub-tropical valley garden on the Helford River with a good collection of old rhododendrons and camellias. It also boasts an extraordinary 1830s maze of clipped cherry laurel, recently restored and best seen from the new viewing platform above. Indeed, the whole garden is almost best when viewed from the top – but the temptation to wander down and into it is irresistible.

Plant Highlights Woodland garden; sub-tropical plants; mature conifers; laurel maze; wild flowers; huge tulip tree; tallest *Eucryphia lucida* (13m) in the British Isles; new Bhutanese valley planting (1996).

Owned by The National Trust
English Heritage grade II

Headland

POLRUAN-BY-FOWEY PL23 1PW

Tel 01726 870243
Location Find Polruan: go to the bottom of Fore Street, along West Street, left up Battery Lane to end

Opening hours 2 pm – 6 pm; Thursdays; 3 May to 13 September
Admission fee Adults £2; Children £1

A cliff garden with the sea on three sides and its own sandy beach, Headland is a lesson in what will tolerate salt-laden winds: eucalyptus, acacias, foxgloves, columbines and junipers, but especially cacti and succulents – agaves, aloes, echeverias, sedums and crassulas. The design and the variety of the planting make it seem much larger than its 1¼ acres.

Owned by Jean & John Hill
Size 1¼ acres

Heligan Gardens

PENTEWAN, ST AUSTELL PL26 6EN

Tel 01726 845100   **Fax** 01726 845101
Location St Austell to Mevagissey Road, following brown tourist signs
Opening hours 10 am – 6 pm; daily; all year except 24 & 25 December
Admission fee Adults £5.50; OAPs £5; Children £2.50

Heligan calls itself 'The Lost Gardens of Heligan' and its 22 acres have been spectacularly rescued since 1990 from a jungle of neglect. Its kitchen garden is of particular interest: look for pineapple pits, and melon, citrus, peach and vine houses. Newly recovered features emerge with incredible speed: recent restorations include the Northern Summerhouse garden and several rides within the 30-acre 'Lost Valley.' The enthusiasm of the restorers is infectious and their achievements are already substantial. The owners are brilliant at getting financial support and publicity – with the result that the garden can get very crowded.

Owned by Heligan Gardens Ltd
English Heritage grade II

Ken Caro

BICTON, LISKEARD PL14 5RF

Tel 01579 362446
Location Signed from A390, midway between Callington & Liskeard
Opening hours 2 pm – 6 pm; Sunday – Thursday; 15 April to 30 August
Admission fee Adults £2.50; Children £1

Ken Caro was started in 1970 as two acres of intensely planted formal gardens in different styles, and extended in 1993 by taking in a further two acres. It is very much a plantsman's garden with good herbaceous plants and shrubs, not at all a traditional Cornish garden. The owners are flower arrangers: look for architectural plants and original combinations.

Plant Highlights Plantsman's collection of plants; mature conifers; good herbaceous borders; new garden extension (2000); new water-lily pond (1998).

Owned by Mr & Mrs K R Willcock
Size 4½ acres

Lamorran House

UPPER CASTLE ROAD, ST MAWES TR2 5BZ

Tel 01326 270800   **Fax** 01326 270801
Location ½ mile from village centre
Opening hours 10.30 am – 5 pm; Wednesdays, Fridays & the first Saturday of the month; April to September

Admission fee Adults £3.50; Groups £3; Children free

The garden at Lamorran has been almost entirely made since 1980, on a steep site above Falmouth Bay. It is tightly designed in the Italian style, but also full of unusual plants – an English Mediterranean garden in Cornwall, say the owners, or a mainland Tresco, though it is closest to the great English garden at La Mortola on the Italian Riviera. One of their latest ventures has been a bank planted with cacti and succulents: another has seen an increase in the number of cycads in the garden. But tender rhododendrons from Asia are yet another interest, and plants from Australia too. The collection of unusual plants is simply amazing: very adventurous. The planting is guided by a desire to experiment with hardiness and tempered by the aesthetic demands of the whole garden. So the garden is not a *botanic* collection, but an extremely good *horticultural* one, and the plants are chosen and placed for their decorative merit and their contribution to the whole.

Owned by Mr & Mrs Robert Dudley-Cooke
Number of gardeners 2
Size 4½ acres

Lanhydrock

BODMIN PL30 5AD

Tel 01208 73320   **Fax** 01298 74084
Website www.nationaltrust.org.uk
Location 2½ miles south-east of Bodmin
Opening hours 10 am – 6 pm (dusk, if sooner); daily; all year. Closes at 5 pm from 17 February to 31 March, and throughout October.
Admission fee Garden only £3.70

Lanhydrock is a grand mansion, mainly nineteenth-century, with one of the best formal gardens in Cornwall – clipped yews, box parterres and bedding out, as well as large herbaceous borders which contain the National Collection of *Crocosmia*. The woodlands behind are impressive for their size and colourful rhododendrons in spring. But it is the magnolias which impress the visitor most: 140 different species and cultivars.

Owned by The National Trust
NCCPG National Collections *Crocosmia*
English Heritage grade II*

Mount Edgcumbe Gardens

CREMYLL, TORPOINT PL10 1HZ

Tel 01752 822236   **Fax** 01752 822199
Location At the end of the B3247 in south-east Cornwall, or by ferry from Plymouth
Opening hours Formal gardens & park: dawn to dusk; all year. House & Earl's Garden: 11 am – 4.30 pm; daily; April to September
Admission fee House & Earl's Garden: Adults £4.50; OAPs £3.50; Children £2.25. Formal gardens & park: free

A long, stately grass drive runs down from the house to Plymouth Sound, through oak woods interplanted with large ornamental trees. Here is the National Collection of *Camellia*, meticulously labelled, which will eventually include all 32,000 known cultivars. The formal gardens are right down on the waterside, protected by a clipped ilex hedge 30ft high. There are no less than ten acres of gardens here, including an Italian garden (made in about 1790), a French garden (Regency), a modern American garden, a New Zealand garden complete with geyser, the eighteenth-century Milton's Temple, an orangery with newly acquired orange trees, and the fern dell recently replanted with ivies and tree ferns. Allow plenty of time to do justice to these majestic pleasure gardens.

 Plant Highlights Sub-tropical plants; plants under glass; daffodils; good herbaceous borders; fine collection of trees; summer bedding; deer park; formal gardens; fern dell; genuine Victorian rose garden; tallest cork oak *Quercus suber* (26m) in the British Isles.

Owned by Cornwall County Council & Plymouth City Council
Number of gardeners 3
Size 10 acres, plus huge park
NCCPG National Collections *Camellia*
English Heritage grade I

Pencarrow

WASHAWAY, BODMIN PL30 3AG

Tel 01208 841369 **Fax** 01208 841722
Website www.pencarrow.co.uk
Location 4 miles north-west of Bodmin – signed off the A389 at Washaway
Opening hours Dawn – dusk; 1 April to 28 October
Admission fee Adults £2.50; Children free

The mile-long drive at Pencarrow leads to an avenue of rhododendrons and rare conifers before you eventually come to the pretty Anglo-Palladian house. On one side are the outlines of an Italian garden, complete with fountain, laid out in the 1830s, and next to it a great granite rock garden where vast boulders from Bodmin Moor lie strewn among the trees and shrubs. Pencarrow is famous for its conifers: an ancestor planted one of every known variety in the mid-nineteenth century and the survivors are so venerable that the great Alan Mitchell wrote a guide to them. Since about 1970 the owners have steadily

retrieved the garden from the state of dereliction in which it was left at the end of World War II and added a further 200 or so conifers. Recent plantings have involved the addition of over 700 of the best modern rhododendrons, 70 camellias and many other broad-leaved trees and shrubs. It is good to see the fortunes of such a distinguished garden revived.

Owned by The Trustees of the Molesworth-St Aubyn Family
English Heritage grade II

Penjerrick

BUDOCK WATER, FALMOUTH TR11 5ED

Tel 01872 870105
Location 3 miles south-west of Falmouth, entrance at junction of lanes opposite Penmorvah Manor Hotel
Opening hours 1.30 pm – 4.30 pm; Wednesdays, Fridays & Sundays; March to September
Admission fee Adults £2; Children £1

The garden at Penjerrick was begun by the Fox family in the mid-nineteenth century. It is a great plantsman's garden, famous in particular for its Barclayi and Penjerrick hybrid rhododendrons. Some of the original plants still survive in the woodland garden thick with exotics: tender plants thrive in the lush, sheltered valley. The garden is recovering well from a period of neglect: it sums up all that was best about Cornish gardens 100 years ago

 Plant Highlights Woodland garden; rhododendrons; camellias; tree ferns; waterfall improved (1998).

Owned by Mrs Rachel Morin
Number of gardeners ½
Size 10 acres
English Heritage grade II

Probus Gardens

PROBUS, TRURO TR2 4HQ

Tel 01726 882597   **Fax** 01726 883868
Website www.probusgardens.org.uk
Location Off the A390 just east of the village
Opening hours 10 am – 4 pm (5 pm from March to
November); daily; all year. Closed from 21 December to
8 January and at weekends in January & February
Admission fee Adults £3; OAPs £2.50; Children free. RHS
members free from May to October

Probus likes to call itself the 'Gardener's
Garden' or the 'Really Useful Garden'.
Both nicknames are correct: Probus is quite
simply the best place in Cornwall to learn
about gardening. Everything is clearly
labelled: everyone will gain more from a visit
than they ever imagined possible. Within it
are innumerable garden rooms which
illustrate and demonstrate the attraction of
gardening with plants: among them are the
ornamental grass garden, the seaside garden,
the plantsman's garden, the exotic garden,
the Japanese garden and the scented garden.
The winter garden has a fine array of
hellebores, primulas, narcissi and heathers,
planted amongst pieris and cornus. There
are collections of bamboos, camellias,
clematis, conifers, dye-plants, eucalyptus,
hebes, herbs, hollies, hydrangeas and many
others. Nor is the garden just about plants: it
has innumerable demonstration plots for
lawns, methods of cultivation, composting
and shelter. There are nine greenhouses
dedicated to demonstrating techniques of
propagation and water-saving: the garden
has its own rainwater collection system and
is completely independent of the mains.
Fruit and vegetables are also grown under
glass, together with a range of unusual
tender shrubs and perennials – Probus is not
in the balmiest part of Cornwall. The low
allergen garden shows which plants will help
asthma-sufferers. The fruit and vegetable
gardens grow modern cultivars of particular
use to amateurs, and serve as part of the
Gardening Which? trials. The latest addition
is a large millennium herbaceous garden, set
within low stone walls and planted as a
Celtic colour wheel. One highly original
feature is a geological map of Cornwall,
made from rock specimens from all over the
county. Here too are many of the *Salvia*
collection (130 cultivars) which the garden
hopes may one day be recognised as a
National Collection by the NCCPG.

Owned by The Friends of Probus Garden
Number of gardeners 1, plus 20 part-time volunteers
Size 5 acres

Pine Lodge

CUDDRA, ST AUSTELL PL25 3RQ

Tel & Fax 01726 73500
Website www.pine-lodge.co.uk
Location East of St Austell between Holmbush
& Tregrehan
Opening hours 10 am – 5 pm; Wednesday – Sunday, plus
Bank Holidays; April to September. And by appointment for
groups at any time of year
Admission fee Adults £3.50; Children £2

This modern 30-acre garden is rather
different from the typical Cornish garden. It
has several different styles and contains over
6,000 different plants, all of which are
labelled. In addition to the rhododendrons,
magnolias and camellias so familiar in
Cornish gardens there are Mediterranean
and southern-hemisphere plants grown for
year-round interest, herbaceous borders, a
fernery, a formal garden, a Japanese garden,
a woodland walk and shrubberies. The water
features include a large wildlife pond, an
ornamental pond, a lake with an island and
marsh gardens. Trees are a particular
interest: Pine Lodge has an acer glade, a
young four-acre pinetum, and an
arboretum. And a new wild flower meadow
has just been planted with over 7,000 bulbs
and flowers. The pace of the garden's
development is very exciting and the
owners' appetite for new plants grows even
stronger every year.

Owned by Mr & Mrs Raymond Clemo
Number of gardeners 4
Size 30 acres
NCCPG National Collections Grevillea

St Michael's Mount

MARAZION TR17 0HT

Tel 01736 710507   **Fax** 01736 711544
Website www.stmichaelsmount.co.uk
Location 1 mile south of Marazion
Opening hours 10.30 am – 5.30 pm; Monday – Friday;
2 April to 2 November. Plus some weekends in summer
Admission fee £2.25

A triumph of man's ingenuity in the face of
Atlantic gales, salt spray and bare rock with
sand for garden soil. Careful experiment
over the generations has enabled the owners
to plant a remarkable garden of plants which
resist the elements: *Luma apiculata*, Rugosa
roses, correas, nerines, Hottentot figs and
naturalised agapanthus. On the north side, a
sparse wood of sycamores and pines gives
protection to camellias, azaleas and
hydrangeas. Nigel Nicolson calls it 'the
largest and loveliest rock-garden in
England'. There is nothing rare about the
plants: the wonder is that they grow at all.

Owned by Lord St Levan & The National Trust
English Heritage grade II

Trebah Garden Trust

MAWNAN SMITH, FALMOUTH
TR11 5JZ

Tel 01326 250448   **Fax** 01326 250781
Website www.trebah-garden.co.uk
Location 4 miles south-west of Falmouth, signed from
Hillhead roundabout on A39 approach to Falmouth
Opening hours 10.30 am – 5 pm (last admission); daily;
all year
Admission fee Adults £3.75; OAPs £3.50; Children
(5 – 15) & disabled visitors £2; Children (under 5) free.

RHS members free at all times. National Trust members free November to February

Trebah has been vigorously restored and improved since the Hibberts bought it in 1980. The view from the top is magical – a beautiful, secret, wooded valley which runs right down to the Helford estuary. A stream cascades over waterfalls, through two acres of blue and white hydrangeas, and spills out over the beach. Vast trees, natural and exotic, line the steep sides, while the central point is held by a group of elegant tall palms. Glades of huge sub-tropical tree ferns mingle with giant gunneras, furcraeas and echiums, while along the sides and overhead is the rolling canopy of 100-year-old rhododendrons. A paradise for plantsmen, but Trebah is also popular with children, whose curiosity is aroused by trails, quizzes and educational games. It is a garden for all people and for all seasons – open *every day of the year*.

 Plant Highlights Woodland garden; sub-tropical plants; plantsman's collection of plants; fine collection of trees; massed hydrangeas; lilies and candelabra primulas; extensive new plantings of palms & succulents at the top of the water garden; tallest hardy palm *Trachycarpus fortunei* (15m) in the British Isles and three other tree records.

Owned by The Trebah Garden Trust
English Heritage grade II

Tregrehan

PAR PL24 2SJ

Tel 01726 812438   **Fax** 01726 814389
Location 1 mile west of St Blazey on A390
Opening hours 10.30 am – 5 pm; Wednesday – Sunday (except Easter Sunday); mid-March to mid-June

Admission fee Adults £3; Children free

An old Cornish garden whose 20 acres include a fine range of Victorian conservatories, tall conifers and lanky rhododendrons. Tregrehan is best known for the camellias bred there by the late Gillian Carlyon, especially 'Jennifer Carlyon' which won her the Cory Cup from the RHS. But Tom Hudson's collections in Yunnan have also made a big impact on the garden.

Owned by T C Hudson
English Heritage grade II*

Trehane

PROBUS, TRURO TR2 4JG

Location Signed from A39 by Tresillian Bridge

The Trehane family have recently (December 2000) sold this beautiful and historic woodland garden. The new owners will need a year or so to decide whether they feel able to welcome visitors, so for the time being Trehane remains closed.

Owned by Mr & Mrs John Connell

Trelissick Garden

FEOCK, TRURO TR3 6QL

Tel 01872 862090   **Fax** 01872 865808
Website www.nationaltrust.org.uk
Location Take B3289 off main Truro – Falmouth Road
Opening hours 10.30 am (12 noon on Sundays) – 5.30 pm; daily; 17 February to 4 November. Closes at 5 pm in February, March & October
Admission fee Adults £4.40; Children £2.20

Once famous for its fig garden, still maintained by the National Trust, Trelissick

is particularly colourful in August and September when the hydrangeas are in full flower. There are over 100 cultivars, some in a special walk. But venerable conifers and tender plants are also features: *Rosa bracteata* and *Yucca whipplei* are among the many good things to admire in summer, not to mention daffodils, rhododendrons and camellias in spring.

 Plant Highlights Woodland garden; plantsman's collection of plants; mature conifers; aromatic plant garden; fig garden; hydrangeas; tallest tree fern *Dicksonia antarctica* (6m) in the British Isles.

Owned by The National Trust
NCCPG National Collections *Azara; Photinia*
English Heritage grade II

Trengwainton Gardens

MADRON, PENZANCE TR20 8RZ

Tel 01736 363148   **Fax** 01736 368142
Location 2 miles north-west of Penzance, ½ mile west of Heamoor
Opening hours 10 am – 5.30 pm (5 pm in February, March & October); Sunday – Thursday & Good Friday; 18 February to 4 November
Admission fee Adults £3.50; Children £1.75

Trengwainton has the best collection of tender plants on the Cornish mainland, all thanks to the Bolitho family who started planting seriously only in 1925. Much came from original seed from such collectors as Kingdon Ward: some rhododendrons flowered here for the first time in the British Isles, among them *R. macabeanum*, *R. elliottii* and *R. taggianum*. The plants in many Cornish gardens are past their best. Not so at Trengwainton, where so many are in their prime. It is a garden to wander

through slowly, giving yourself as much time as you need to enjoy its riches.

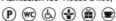 **Plant Highlights** Woodland garden; sub-tropical plants; roses (mainly old-fashioned); lilies; acacias; *Myosotidium hortensia*; tree ferns; tallest *Xanthoceras sorbifolium* (7m) in the British Isles (and two record trees).

Owned by Lt Col E T Bolitho & The National Trust
English Heritage grade II

Trerice

NEWQUAY TR8 4PG

Tel 01637 875404   **Fax** 01637 879300
Website www.nationaltrust.org.uk
Location 3 miles south-east of Newquay – turn right off A3058 at Kestle Mill
Opening hours 11 am – 5.30 pm (5 pm in October); daily except Tuesdays & Saturdays (but open every day from 17 July to 11 September); 1 April to 4 November
Admission fee House £4.30; Garden free

Ⓟ ⓦⓒ ⑤ ⊕ ⌖ ⊕

A perfect West Country manor house with pretty Dutch gables, Trerice is unusual among Cornish gardens. It is small and comparatively formal: the design and herbaceous plantings are its best points. It is not surrounded by swirling rhododendron woodland. There is a perfect harmony between the Jacobean architecture and the gardens. Somewhat anomalously, it boasts the largest collection of mid-Victorian to current-day lawn mowers in the country. They are both interesting and fun to visit.

Owned by The National Trust

Tresco Abbey

ISLES OF SCILLY TR24 0QQ

Tel 01720 424105   **Fax** 01720 422868
Website www.tresco.co.uk
Location Direct helicopter flight from Penzance
Opening hours 10 am – 4 pm; daily; all year
Admission fee Adults £6.50; Children free

The sub-tropical gardens on Tresco are unique in the British Isles. They were first designed and planted by Augustus Smith in 1834: his successors have been equally passionate in their search for tender plants that will grow outside on Tresco's south-facing terraces as nowhere else in Britain. The collection is especially strong in plants from South Africa, Australia and New Zealand but, even though any account of Tresco reads like a list of plants, it is still very much an ornamental garden which strives for horticultural effect. The oldest specimens include Canary Island palms, a large number of aeoniums from both the Canary Islands and Madeira, agaves from America and puyas from Chile. After the great gale of 1990, the gardens have been extensively replanted in recent years, with hundreds of exotic plants from Kew, all protected by extensive new shelterbelts. No matter what time of the year, there is always a lot of colour and much of interest: proteas and acacias in winter; the shrubby foxglove (*Isoplexis sceptrum*); mesembryanthemums and agapanthus in summer. There is also a shady area where tree ferns and *Musschia wollastonii* flourish. Many people come here year after year to admire the displays of plants which cannot be seen elsewhere in Britain. The standards of maintenance are exemplary. There is only one disadvantage: the helicopter service may make access from the mainland easier and quicker than ever,

but the noise from its arrivals and departures does distract you while actually visiting the garden.

Plant Highlights Sub-tropical plants; plantsman's collection of plants; mature conifers; cacti; succulents; South African, Australian and New Zealand plants; tallest *Luma apiculata* (20m), *Metrosideros excelsa* (20m) and *Cordyline australis* (15m) in the British Isles.

Owned by Robert Dorrien Smith
Number of gardeners 5, plus 2 students
Size 17 acres
NCCPG National Collections *Acacia*
English Heritage grade I

Trewithen

GRAMPOUND ROAD, TRURO
TR2 4DD

Tel 01726 883647   **Fax** 01726 882301
Location A390 between Probus & Grampound
Opening hours 10 am – 4.30 pm; Monday – Saturday
(& Sundays in April & May); March to September
Admission fee Adults £3.75; Children £2

Trewithen's setting is magnificent. Instead of the steep terraces of most Cornish gardens, there is a spacious flat lawn that stretches for 200 yards into the distance, with gentle banks of rhododendrons, magnolias and rare shrubs on all sides. It sets the tone for the garden's grandeur, which was entirely the work of George Johnstone in the first half of the twentieth century. Johnstone was a great plantsman. He subscribed to plant hunting expeditions, such as those of Frank Kingdon Ward. Note how he used laurel hedges to divide up the woodland and give structure to the garden. He also had an eye for placing plants to advantage. As a breeder, he gave us *Rhododendron* 'Alison Johnstone', *Ceanothus* 'Trewithen Blue' and *Camellia saluensis* 'Trewithen White'. There is an excellent guidebook written by Nigel Holman. The Michelin Guide gives Trewithen its top award of three stars – *vaut le voyage*!

Plant Highlights Woodland garden; rhododendrons & azaleas; plantsman's collection of plants; camellias; good herbaceous borders; fine collection of trees; magnolias; quarry garden; cyclamen; new fountain (1999); tallest *Magnolia campbellii* subsp. *mollicomata* (19m) in the British Isles and 16 more record-breaking tree species.

Owned by A M J Galsworthy
Number of gardeners 4
Size 30 acres
English Heritage grade II*

CUMBRIA

Cumbria came into being in 1974, an amalgam of the old counties of Cumberland, Westmorland and the northern part of Lancashire. Gardening in Cumbria is dominated by the Lake District: both Wordsworth's garden Rydal Mount and Ruskin's at Brantwood are open to visitors. There are good historic gardens of the grander sort, too. Though few in number, almost all the most important ones are open to the public: Levens is rated Grade I, while Dalemain, Holker, Muncaster and Sizergh are all Grade II*. Cumbria's acid soils and the highest rainfall in England are very favourable to the growth of conifers: many of the older gardens have fine specimens of *Abies*, *Picea* and *Pinus*, while Muncaster also offers an extensive collection of *Nothofagus* species. The National Gardens Scheme is active in the county, and particularly successful in persuading garden-owners in and around the Lake District to open for charity. Cumbria has comparatively few nurseries, but the ones we list below are exceptionally good. The county has its fair share of National Collections, with clusters of genera at three of the larger gardens: *Halesia*, *Pterostyrax*, *Styrax*, *Sinojackia* and other *Styracaceae* at Holker; *Astilbe*, *Hydrangea* and *Polystichum* at Holehird; and *Asplenium scolopendrium*, *Cystopteris*, *Dryopteris*, and *Osmunda* at Sizergh. Newton Rigg near Penrith is a RHS Partner College, with lectures, demonstrations and garden walks throughout the year.

Acorn Bank Garden

ACORN BANK, TEMPLE SOWERBY, PENRITH CA10 1SP

Tel 01768 361893   **Fax** 01768 361467
Website www.nationaltrust.org.uk
Location North of Temple Sowerby, 6 miles east of Penrith on A66
Opening hours 10 am – 5 pm; daily; 31 March to 4 November
Admission fee Adults £2.50; Children £1.25

Acorn Bank claims to have the largest collection (250 varieties) of culinary and medicinal plants in the north, but it is almost better visited in spring when thousands and thousands of daffodils fill the woodland slopes, and the fruit trees flower in the old walled garden. Best of all is the huge quince tree, a wondrous sight in flower or fruit.

Owned by The National Trust

Brantwood

CONISTON LA21 8AD

Tel 01539 441396
Website www.brantwood.org.uk
Location East side of Coniston Water, 2½ miles from Coniston, 4 miles from Hawkshead
Opening hours 11 am – 5.30 pm; daily; 13 March to 13 November. 11 am – 4.30 pm; Wednesday – Sunday; rest of year
Admission fee Adults £2; Children £1

These 20 acres of woodland garden were laid out by John Ruskin from 1871 onwards but somewhat altered and neglected after his death in 1900. Working with the natural materials of the site, Ruskin developed a series of experimental gardens within the ancient woodland and on the high moor behind. When the Brantwood Trust began the task of reclamation, it decided to restore the garden partly as it was in Ruskin's lifetime, and partly as a modern re-interpretation of his ideas. Below Ruskin's 'living laboratory', exotic ornamental plantings frame wonderful views across Coniston Water.

Owned by The Brantwood Trust

Charney Well

HAMPSFELL ROAD,
GRANGE-OVER-SANDS LA11 6BE

Tel 01539 534526 **Fax** 01539 535765
Website www.charneywell.com
Location Up behind Main Street: park in town centre
Opening hours 11 am – 4.30 pm; 21 & 22 July. And groups by appointment
Admission fee Adults £2

The Mediterranean effects of this tiered and terraced modern classic have been achieved by planting lots of phormiums, together with cordylines, palms, yuccas, pittosporums and cypress trees. Bold foliage and a flamboyant personality is what the owners seek in their plants, so they are chosen for such seasonal highlights as striking bark or foliage. It follows that Charney Well is full of evergreen foliage – eucalyptus, acacia, bamboos, *Viburnum tinus* and *Mahonia* 'Charity', for example. The underplantings too are rich and every patch is thickly covered: do not expect to see anything so conventional as a lawn. The site is steep, dry and rocky – not a promising place for traditional English gardening, but perfect for the exotic plants the owners choose to grow. And the garden is forever changing, especially after trips to see real Mediterranean gardens.

Owned by Messrs C Holliday & R Roberts
Number of gardeners 1
Size ½ acre
NCCPG National Collections *Phormium*

Dalemain

PENRITH CA11 0HB

Tel 01768 486450 **Fax** 01768 486223
Location M6 (Jct40), A66, A592
Opening hours 10.30 am – 5 pm; Sunday – Thursday; 25 March to 7 October
Admission fee Gardens only: £3. RHS members free from 3 June to 13 July

Dalemain has been belonged to the Hasell family since 1679. The history of the garden starts, however, with a sixteenth-century terrace, of which very few remain anywhere in the British Isles. Then comes a kitchen garden with fruit trees planted 250 years ago, though the overall 'feel' of Dalemain is

Edwardian. Most of the plantings are modern, including the formal knot garden and the long and richly planted herbaceous border which overlooks the park and the Lakeland Fells. The mixed borders and roses are dreamily English, particularly the Rose Walk, which boasts more than 100 old-fashioned roses. Nearby is the wild garden with drifts of meconopsis and martagon lilies in late spring, though it is fair to say that this is a garden which looks good at all seasons. Plants are well labelled and well grown.

 Plant Highlights Woodland garden; roses (mainly old-fashioned); herbs; meconopsis; old flower and fruit varieties; good herbaceous and mixed borders; biggest *Abies cephalonica* in the British Isles.

Owned by Robert Hasell-McCosh
English Heritage grade II*

Graythwaite Hall

ULVERSTON, HAWKSHEAD LA12 8BA

Tel 01539 531248   **Fax** 01539 530060
Location Between Newby Bridge & Hawkshead
Opening hours 10 am – 6 pm; daily; April to June
Admission fee Adults £2; Children free

Graythwaite shows Thomas Mawson on home ground and at his best. Formal gardens in the Arts & Crafts style by the house drop down to sweeping lawns; beyond the stream is a woodland of rhododendrons and azaleas. The yew topiary is good – some castellated and some with a mixture of green and gold cultivars.

Owned by Graythwaite Estate Trustees
Number of gardeners 1
Size 6 acres

Hartside Nursery Garden

ALSTON CA9 3BL

Tel & Fax 01434 381372
Location ¼ mile south-west of Alston on the A686 to Penrith
Opening hours 9.30 am – 4.30 pm; Monday – Friday. 12.30 pm – 4 pm; Saturdays & Sundays. March to October. Other months by appointment

This high-level (1000+ ft) nursery specialises in alpines, particularly in primulas (lots of interesting forms of *Primula gracillipes*, for example), dwarf shrubs, conifers and hardy ferns: all are home-grown in the cold North Pennines. The display gardens are worth a visit and maintained in a relaxed style: there is lots to admire.

Holehird

LAKELAND HORTICULTURAL SOCIETY, PATTERDALE ROAD, WINDERMERE LA23 1NP

Tel 01539 446008
Location 1 mile north of Windermere town, off A592
Opening hours Dawn – dusk; daily; all year
Admission fee Donation (min. £2)

Holehird is a demonstration and trial garden, maintained entirely by some seventy volunteers, all members of the Lakeland Horticultural Society. The society's aim is to 'promote and develop the science, practice and art of horticulture, particularly with regard to the conditions prevailing in the Lake District'. The gardens occupy an old walled garden and rockery and have recently been extended to about ten acres. The interesting thing for visitors is to see what flourishes in a cool damp climate: alpines, azaleas, heathers, bulbs, ferns and much, much more.

Owned by Lakeland Horticultural Society
Number of gardeners about 70 volunteers
Size 10 acres
NCCPG National Collections Astilbe; Hydrangea; Polystichum

Holker Hall

CARK-IN-CARTMEL,
GRANGE-OVER-SANDS LA11 7PL

Tel 01539 558328 **Fax** 01539 558776
Location Jct36 off M6, follow brown & white tourist signs
Opening hours 10 am – 6 pm (last admission 4.30 pm); Sunday – Friday; April to October
Admission fee Adults £3.50; Children £2 (2000 prices, subject to review)

The nineteenth-century formal gardens below the house are scrumptiously planted as herbaceous borders, the first of many imaginative modern designs and plantings throughout this extensive garden. The woodland has foxgloves, rhododendrons and splendid trees: Joseph Paxton supplied a monkey puzzle and Lord George Cavendish the cedars grown from seeds he brought back from the Holy Land.

Plant Highlights Woodland garden; roses (ancient & modern); rhododendrons; formal gardens; fine limestone cascade & fountain; HHA/Christie's Garden of the Year in 1991; tallest *Ilex latifolia* (15m) in the British Isles (and two other tree records).

Owned by Lord Cavendish of Furness
Number of gardeners 6
Size 26 acres
NCCPG National Collections Styracaceae (incl. *Halesia, Pterostyrax, Styrax, Sinojackia*)
English Heritage grade II*

Hutton-in-the-Forest

SKELTON, PENRITH CA11 9TH

Tel 01768 484449 **Fax** 01768 484571
Location 3 miles from Exit 41 of M6 on B5305
Opening hours Gardens: 11 am – 5 pm; all year except Saturdays
Admission fee Gardens only: Adults £2.50; Children free

The house at Hutton-in-the-Forest is old, handsomely sited and built onto a mediaeval pele tower. Salvin refashioned it in the nineteenth century and Gilpin restored the terraces at about the same time: the fine topiary is a little later. Beyond the terraces is a woodland garden where large conifers are underplanted by billowing rhododendrons. In the walled garden, a double herbaceous border runs from end to end, screened from the growing vegetables by thick yew hedges. This is a very traditional garden of great serenity.

Owned by Lord Inglewood
Number of gardeners 1
Size 11 acres
English Heritage grade II

Levens Hall

KENDAL LA8 0PD

Tel 01539 560321 **Fax** 01539 560669
Website www.levenshall.co.uk
Location 5 miles south of Kendal on A6

Opening hours 10 am – 5 pm; Sunday – Thursday;
1 April to 11 October
Admission fee Adults £4.50; Children £2.20

Levens means topiary: huge overgrown chunks of box and yew. Some is left over from a simple formal parterre laid out in 1694 and supplemented by golden yews in the nineteenth century. Some is more recent – successive generations have been good about replacing plants and restoring the garden when necessary. The arbours and high yew hedges, some of them crenellated, are spangled with *Tropaeolum speciosum* and the parterres planted annually with 15,000 plants, which makes Levens one of the best places to study the expensive art of bedding out. Well maintained.

Owned by C H Bagot
English Heritage grade I

Muncaster Castle

RAVENGLASS CA18 1RQ

Tel 01229 717614   **Fax** 01229 717010
Website www.muncastercastle.co.uk
Location A595 1 mile east of Ravenglass on west coast of Cumbria
Opening hours 10.30 am – 6 pm; daily; all year
Admission fee Adults £5; Children £3

Visit Muncaster in May, when the rhododendrons are at their peak. Many are grown from the original seed introduced by such plant hunters as Forrest and Kingdon Ward in the 1920s and 1930s. The owners have made an excellent job of identifying them and labelling them: some have turned out to be the tallest of their kind in England. Alongside this vigorous work of restoration, Muncaster also has a developing collection of hardy hybrid rhododendrons and a

nursery which sells 500+ cultivars. The castle was revamped by Salvin in the 1860s: stand on its wonderful long curved terrace (*very* long – half a mile) above the steep slopes and soak up the intensely romantic landscape of the Lakeland hills around. Ruskin called it 'the gateway to Paradise'. The new MeadowVole (*sic*) Maze will appeal to younger visitors.

 Plant Highlights Woodland garden; mature conifers; rhododendrons; camellias; maples; masses of new plantings; bluebells; tallest *Nothofagus obliqua* (31m) in the British Isles; lots of new plantings.

Owned by Mrs P R Gordon-Duff-Pennington
Number of gardeners 4, plus some part-time help
Size 77 acres
English Heritage grade II*

Rydal Mount

AMBLESIDE LA22 9LU

Tel 01539 433002   **Fax** 01539 431738
Location 1½ miles north of Ambleside on A591, turn up Rydal Hill
Opening hours 9.30 am – 5 pm, March to October; 10 am – 4 pm, November to February
Admission fee Adults £1.75

Kept very much as it was in the poet's day, the garden at Rydal Mount is a memorial to William Wordsworth. He believed that a garden should be informal in its design, harmonise with the country and keep its views open.

Plant Highlights Daffodils; bluebells; trees; rhododendrons; Dora Wordsworth's terrace undergoing restoration (1997).

Owned by Rydal Mount Trust (Wordsworth Family)
Number of gardeners 1
English Heritage grade II

Sizergh Castle

KENDAL LA8 8AE

Tel 015396 60070
Website www.nationaltrust.org.uk
Location 3½ miles south of Kendal
Opening hours 12.30 pm – 5.30 pm; Sunday – Thursday;
April to October
Admission fee Garden only: Adult £2.40

One of the best National Trust gardens,
Sizergh has lots of interest from wild
daffodils and alpines in April to hydrangeas
and a hot half-hardy border in September –
Beschorneria yuccoides and *Buddleja colvilei*.
Best of all is the 1920s rock garden, made of
local limestone, and home to an important
(and beautiful) collection of ferns.

Owned by The National Trust
NCCPG National Collections *Asplenium scolopendrium*;
Cystopteris; *Dryopteris*; *Osmunda*
English Heritage grade II*

DERBYSHIRE

Derbyshire has no less than five historic gardens which are listed as Grade I: Chatsworth, Haddon, Hardwick, Kedleston and Melbourne. All are regularly open to the public. The National Gardens Scheme is very active in the county, with a good number of medium-sized and small gardens listed in the Yellow Book.

Nevertheless it is the larger gardens on old estates which offer the most horticultural interest. Much of Derbyshire is high and cold in winter, yet it also has some excellent nurseries and garden centres. Bluebell Nursery & Arboretum, right in the south of the county, has one of the most exciting new collections of trees and shrubs in the British Isles, while Abbey Brook Cactus Nursery in Matlock has for long been the UK's leading specialist nursery for cacti and succulents. Its National Collections of *Conophytum, Haworthia* and *Lithops* are unmatched by any other collection holder. Begonias and gladiolus are popular in Derbyshire, and fine displays are often seen at local flower shows. Broomfield College at Morley is a RHS Partner College with a wide range of workshops and lectures throughout the year: details from 01332 836600.

Abbey Brook Cactus Nursery

BAKEWELL ROAD, MATLOCK DE4 2QJ

Tel 01629 580306 **Fax** 01629 55852
Website www.abbeybrookcacti.com
Location On A6, 2 miles north of Matlock
Opening hours 1 pm – 4 pm; daily, except Tuesday. Opens 12.15 pm on Sundays. Closed 1 January, 25 & 26 December
Admission fee free

Abbey Brook is the UK's leading cactus nursery, now 90% wholesale and with 1,000,000 plants in stock. The retail list is remarkable – it lists over 2,000 cultivars, and has at least the same number again among its stock plants. The nursery is worth a visit at any time of the year – so is the website, which offers a full-colour catalogue and on-line ordering. Cactus buffs need no introduction to Abbey Brook, but the nursery is also extremely interesting for those whose gardening interests are quite different. It displays the wonder and beauty of these plants in such a way that you cannot help responding to them – and their extraordinary diversity.

NCCPG National Collections *Conophytum*; *Echinopsis* hybrids; *Gymnocalycium*; *Haworthia*; *Lithops*

Bluebell Nursery & Arboretum

ANNWELL LANE, SMISBY,
ASHBY-DE-LA-ZOUCH LE65 2TA

Tel 01530 413700   **Fax** 01530 417600
Website www.bluebellnursery.com
Location 200 yards south of Smisby Church. Follow
brown tourist signs to arboretum
Opening hours 9 am – 5 pm (4 pm from November
to February); Monday – Saturday; all year.
10.30 am – 4.30 pm; Sundays; March to October
Admission fee Adults £1.50; Children free

Bluebell Nursery has been a stalwart
supporter of RHS shows for some years now
and has won many medals for its displays of
rare trees and shrubs. The six-acre
arboretum has expanded every year since it
was first planted in 1992, but the owners are
keen to emphasise that 'you should not
expect to find a Westonbirt, Wisley or
Wakehurst' yet. Nevertheless, it is already a
most interesting place to visit, not least to
see what will grow in the cold Midlands.
Most visitors are intrigued by the many
cultivars of dogwoods (*Cornus*), maples
(*Acer*) and beech (*Fagus sylvestris*). Other
highlights include an avenue of witch-hazel
cultivars (*Hamamelis*), the largest collection
of deciduous hollies *Ilex verticillata* in
Europe and a seven-year old Vallonea oak
which they call *Quercus macrolepis*
'Hemelrijk Silver' and which already carries
'acorns the size of door knockers'. The
website allows on-line ordering: the nursery
sells many more plants than those in its
excellent catalogue.

Owned by Mr & Mrs Robert Vernon
Size 5 acres

Calke Abbey

TICKNALL DE7 1LE

Tel 01332 863822   **Fax** 01332 865272
Website www.nationaltrust.org.uk
Location 10 miles south of Derby in village of Ticknall
Opening hours 11 am – 5.30 pm; Saturday – Wednesda
31 March to 4 November
Admission fee £2.50

The 'sleeping beauty' house is not really
matched by its garden, but when funds are
available it will be replanted in the early
nineteenth-century style, with period
ornamental and fruit varieties, a physic
garden and an orangery. The drive runs
along a magnificent avenue of ancient lime
In the walled garden is the only surviving
Auricula Theatre, originally built to display
the perfection of these beautiful 'florist's'
plants.

Plant Highlights Vegetables; fruit;
good herbaceous borders; dahlias;
good Victorian-style bedding; deer park;
horse-chestnut trees; local varieties of
apples & soft fruit.

Owned by The National Trust
English Heritage grade II*

Dam Farm House

EDNASTON, ASHBOURNE DE6 3BA

Tel 01335 360291
Location Turn off A52 to Bradley, opposite Ednaston La
end
Opening hours 11 am – 4 pm on 29 April (plant sale).
2 pm – 4.30 pm on 20 May, & 12 August. Parties by
arrangement from April to October
Admission fee Adults £2.50; Children free

Chatsworth

AKEWELL DE45 1PP

01246 582204   **Fax** 01246 583536
bsite www.chatsworth-house.co.uk
:ation 8 miles north of Matlock off B6012
ening hours 11 am (10.30 am from June to
ust) – 6 pm (last admissions 5 pm); daily; 21 March to
October
mission fee Adults £4; OAPs £3; Children £1.75; Family
:et £9.50

hatsworth sits near the bottom of a high
valley on the edge of the Peak District
rrounded by over 100 acres of beautiful
dscaped park – the work of Capability
own. Into this naturalistic setting
ccessive Dukes of Devonshire have
serted formal designs, flower gardens and
agnificent garden buildings. Despite their
ecemeal history, the gardens at
atsworth all come together as a single
nament for the house. They have been
en to the public for nearly 200 years. The
ory days of Chatsworth's garden were the
30s when Sir Joseph Paxton and the
achelor Duke' built the Emperor fountain,
e rock garden (huge boulders surrounded
conifers), the arboretum, the pinetum
d the 'conservative wall', which was
tended to keep the heat and ripen fruit
es (and protects an enormous *Camellia
ticulata* 'Captain Rawes' with trunks 80cm
ick). The present Duchess has been
sponsible for some stylish additions such
the serpentine hedges which lead from the
ctorian ring pond to a bust of the sixth
ike. Perhaps the best known features at
atsworth today are the Great Cascade,
ilt in about 1700 and unique in England
d the Canal, dug at the same time as a
rmal sheet of water to set off the southern
ade of the house. But there is much of

horticultural interest too: a tulip tree avenue,
the bamboo walk, Victorian yews of
different hues, the rose garden, the cottage
garden, the kitchen garden, the
blue-and-white and the orange borders and
record trees like *Pinus peuce*. Chatsworth has
also long been famous for its camellias and
glasshouse grapes, both of which have won
many prizes at RHS shows. But perhaps the
greatest joy of Chatsworth is the sense,
which still pervades the entire estate, that it
is a private garden in which every visitor
feels that he is a welcome guest.

Plant Highlights Woodland garden;
topiary; roses (mainly modern); rock
garden; rhododendrons & azaleas; fine
collection of trees; pinetum; maze; tulip tree
avenue; millennium planting of 100 oaks in
50 different varieties; tallest *Pinus strobus*
(42m) in the British Isles.

Owned by Chatsworth House Trust
Number of gardeners 21
Size 105 acres
English Heritage grade I

Mrs Player (born a Loder) has made this outstanding garden on a greenfield site since 1980. The design is firm, and the planting exuberant. Clipped hedges enclose a series of separate gardens which flow into each other, but in contrast to the firm design, the planting belongs to the cottage garden tradition. There is a formal garden by the house which ends in a delicate white wire gazebo. The borders are richly planted with the best of modern plants – *Cercis canadensis* 'Forest Pansy' for example and *Viburnum sargentii* 'Onondaga'. Clematis are a favourite and there is a surprisingly large number of plants which one might suppose too tender for Derbyshire – cistus, ceanothus and penstemons. This garden is now in its prime: the trees are semi-mature and the plants have lost none of their youthful vigour. Rare plants abound, but it is their treatment which makes the garden such an exciting place to visit and learn from: their planting, training and cultivation are a model for our times.

Owned by Mrs Jean Player
Number of gardeners part-time only
Size 3 acres

Elvaston Castle

BORROWASH ROAD, ELVASTON DE72 3EP

Tel 01332 571342   **Fax** 01332 758751
Location 5 miles south-east of Derby. Signed from A6 & A52
Opening hours Dawn – dusk (Old English Garden, 9 am – 5 pm, but 4 pm in winter); daily; all year
Admission fee Gardens free. Car park 70p midweek, £1.30 weekends

This is an historic garden, once famous for its topiary: it was saved from oblivion by Derby County Council 25 years ago. The

parterres have been replaced and the walled garden replanted with roses and herbaceous plants, and renamed the Old English Garden. However, there is a possibility that it might be sold later this year.

Owned by Derbyshire County Council
Number of gardeners 6
English Heritage grade II*

Haddon Hall

BAKEWELL DE45 1LA

Tel 01629 812855   **Fax** 01629 814379
Website www.haddonhall.co.uk
Location 1½ miles south of Bakewell on A6
Opening hours 10.30 am – 5 pm; daily; April to September. Plus Monday – Thursday in October (closes at 4.30 pm). Closed 15 July
Admission fee House & garden: Adults £5.90; OAPs £5; Children £3

Haddon Hall is a substantial house which dates mainly from about 1600. The gardens, however, are less than 100 years old, having been laid out by the ninth Duchess of Rutland in the 1910s and 1920s along the much older terraces. The Duchess planted formal features like yew trees to add to the structure, but her great passion was for roses, and it is for these most beautiful of flowers that the garden is now known. The collection is a good one and, though it lacks any real rarities, it is kept up to date by the addition of all the best repeat-flowering cultivars, which means that there is a good selection of modern roses among the older ramblers and noisettes. The hybrid teas include the bright crimson 'Royal William' and pink 'Paul Shirville' and among the floribundas are yellow 'Arthur Bell' and the dark red 'The Times' rose. But shrub roses and wild rose species are also well represented. There are 60 different cultivars of delphinium in the herbaceous borders, which are supplemented by tender perennials and annuals, hardy and half-hardy. In June and July there is no more beautiful and romantic garden in England.

 Plant Highlights Topiary; good herbaceous borders; roses of every kind; clematis; delphiniums; Christie's/HHA Garden of the Year in 1994.

Owned by Lord Edward Manners
Number of gardeners 2
English Heritage grade I

Hardwick Hall

DOE LEA, CHESTERFIELD S44 5QJ

Tel 01246 850430   **Fax** 01246 854200
Website www.nationaltrust.org.uk
Location Signed from M1 Jct29
Opening hours Gardens: 12 noon – 5.30 pm; daily; 31 March to 28 October
Admission fee Garden only: Adults £3.30; Children £1.60

The formal gardens are extensive: avenues of hornbeam and yew and a newly restored 'Elizabethan' (actually 1970s) herb garden (lavender and eglantine) in the kitchen garden. Hardwick has wonderful old fruit trees, nutteries, a mulberry avenue, old roses and modern borders in the Jekyll style. In the park are fine cedars and Hungarian oaks. This is one of the best National Trust gardens, and getting still better.

Owned by The National Trust
NCCPG National Collections Scabiosa caucasica
English Heritage grade I

Kedleston Hall

DERBY DE22 5JH

Tel 01332 842191   **Fax** 01332 841972
Website www.nationaltrust.org.uk
Location 5 miles north-west of Derby
Opening hours 11 am – 6 pm; Saturday – Wednesday; 31 March to 4 November
Admission fee Park & garden only £2.30

Kedleston is an important historic garden. The eighteenth-century landscaped park runs down to a long lake. The house is matched by a Robert Adam summerhouse in the circular garden: impressive and important. Lord Curzon moved it to its present position at the side of the lawns. The park has some splendid trees, most notably a fern-leaved beech (*Fagus sylvatica* 'Asplenifolia').

Owned by The National Trust
English Heritage grade I

Lea Gardens

LEA, MATLOCK DE4 5GH

Tel 01629 534380   **Fax** 01629 534260
Location 3 miles south-east of Matlock
Opening hours 10 am – 5.30 pm; daily; 20 March to 30 June
Admission fee Adults £3; Children 50p; Season ticket £5; wheelchair-bound free

These rhododendron gardens were started in 1935 by John Marsden-Smedley who was so inspired by his visits to Bodnant and Exbury that he decided to plant his own rhododendron collection. He was then aged 68: by the time he died aged 92 in 1959, the garden contained some 350 cultivars of rhododendron and azaleas. Since that time, it has belonged to the Tye family, who have continued to maintain and develop it. The standard of maintenance is extremely high and it is one of the most beautiful gardens to visit in season. Much is on a steep slope and some of the paths are narrow, but the principal areas are fairly open and there are large numbers of modern, low-growing rhododendron and azalea hybrids underplanted with naturalised bluebells. Little attempt has been made to segregate the colours but the plants are graded for height, so you stand on a path and look at a mass of rhododendrons of every imaginable hue rising from knee level right back to huge giants far behind. There have been some interesting interplantings with other plants in recent years – ornamental trees, especially conifers, and herbaceous plants like gunneras, celmisias, *Dactylorhiza foliosa* and *Meconopsis betonicifolia*. It should also be said that the garden is extremely well organised for visitors to enjoy themselves.

Owned by Mr & Mrs J Tye
Number of gardeners 3
Size 4½ acres

Melbourne Hall

MELBOURNE DY3 1EN

Tel 01332 862502   **Fax** 01322 862263
Location 8 miles south of Derby
Opening hours 1.30 pm – 5.30 pm; Wednesdays, Saturdays, Sundays & Bank Holiday Mondays; April to September
Admission fee Adults £3; OAPs £2

Melbourne is a near-perfect example of an early eighteenth-century garden, influenced by Le Nôtre. Much has been simplified over the centuries and the original plantings (some by the royal gardener Henry Wise) are rather overgrown now. But there are terraces, circular *bassins*, palisades of limes, intersecting *allées*, lumpy old hedges and the famous yew tunnel to fire the visitor's imagination. The lead statues (from Jan van Nost's foundry in Piccadilly in about 1710) are unique: so is the large urn known as the Four Seasons, which was originally cast for Queen Anne.

Owned by Lord Ralph Kerr
Number of gardeners 2
English Heritage grade I

Renishaw Hall

RENISHAW, SHEFFIELD S31 9WB

Tel 01246 432042   **Fax** 01246 430760
Website www.sitwell.co.uk
Location 2½ miles from M1 Jct30
Opening hours 10.30 am – 4.30 pm; Friday – Sunday, plus Bank Holiday Mondays; 6 April to 30 September. Plus Thursdays in July & August
Admission fee Adults £3; Concessions £2.50

The gardens at Renishaw were laid out in around 1900 by Sir George Sitwell, grandfather of the present owner. Sir George was an expert on Italian gardens and his book *On the Making of Gardens* (1909) is a gardening classic. He applied the principles of Italian renaissance gardens to the garden he made at Renishaw: symmetry, proportion, scale and shadow. What we see today are yew hedges, pools, fountains, grass and statues – a garden which would not be out of place in Tuscany or the Veneto. Gertrude Jekyll advised Sir George on the planting, but he did not follow her advice. The modern plantings are mainly herbaceous, and kept within pastel shades to emphasise the line of the formal garden: scarlet geraniums, for example, would bring those lines too far forward. The soft colours of old-fashioned roses are perfect: Renishaw has three separate rose gardens with over 1,000 roses. In the woodland garden and against the walls of the kitchen garden, tender plants thrive that seldom survive in Derbyshire – acacias, *Cytisus battandieri* and dendromecons. Renishaw is also worth visiting in the spring, when daffodils fill the lime avenue: they were first planted in 1680 on the advice of no lesser authority than John Evelyn. In the recently restored orangery, the National Collection of yuccas is displayed against an Arizona landscape.

Owned by Sir Reresby Sitwell
Number of gardeners 4
Size 7 acres formal, plus woodlands
NCCPG National Collections *Yucca*
English Heritage grade II*

DEVON

No county has such an abundance of good gardens and nurseries as Devon: Devonians maintain that it is the best place in the world for gardening with plants. Rich soils ('Devon acres') and high rainfall make for excellent growth, but the county's microclimates are immensely variable, from the cold, windswept uplands of Dartmoor to valleys along the southern coast which are virtually frost-free. The Royal Horticultural Society's West Country flagship at Rosemoor shows what can be done to develop a major horticultural garden in little more than ten years. And there is no private garden in England to match the lifetime achievements of Dr Smart at Marwood Hill. Devon has some fine general nurseries and garden centres like Hill House near Ashburton, but surely no county ever had such an abundance of specialist nurseries. These specialists include hostas (Roger and Ann Bowden near Okehampton), rare perennials (Carol Klein's Glebe Cottage Plants – a favourite at RHS shows), violets (Devon Violet Nursery at Rattery), clematis (Peveril Clematis Nursery near Exeter), rare trees (Thornhayes Nursery near Cullompton) and penstemon (Shirley Reynolds at Seaton). Devon has more National Collection holders than any other county, including many tender genera like *Azara* and *Agapanthus*. There are comparatively few top-class historic gardens and – such as they are – they tend to date from the nineteenth century like Bicton. Nevertheless the history of Devon gardens is extremely well documented and the Devon Gardens Trust has a large and vigorous membership. Bicton, Killerton and Endsleigh have splendid collections of old trees: in Edwardian times the avenue of monkey puzzles (*Araucaria araucana*) at Bicton was one of the wonders of English horticulture. The National Gardens Scheme also does exceptionally well in Devon, with more gardens open for their charity than anywhere else in the south-west. Devon is indeed a county of horticultural superlatives.

Arlington Court

ARLINGTON, BARNSTAPLE EX31 4LP

Tel 01271 850296   **Fax** 01271 850625
Website www.nationaltrust.org.uk
Location 8 miles north of Barnstaple on A39
Opening hours 10.30 am – 5.30 pm; Wednesday
– Monday – Friday; 31 March to 4 November
Admission fee Gardens only: Adults £3.40

Arlington offers mature parkland on a dead
flat site in front of a fine Georgian house. Its
has a pretty Victorian formal garden and
conservatory. But watch the restoration of
the walled garden: nineteenth-century fruit
and vegetables grow alongside local
cultivars.

Owned by The National Trust
English Heritage grade II

Bicton Park Gardens

EAST BUDLEIGH, BUDLEIGH SALTERTON EX9 7DP

Tel & Fax 01395 568465
Location On A376 north of Budleigh Salterton
Opening hours 10 am – 6 pm (5 pm in winter); daily
except Christmas Day
Admission fee Adults £4.75; OAPs £3.75; Children £2.75

Sixty acres of fascinating features, including:
an Italian garden; important trees; the
oriental garden; three walled gardens;
historic parkland; formal gardens; an
American garden; a collection of dwarf
conifers; more than 2,000 heathers; an
avenue of monkey puzzles; a hermitage; and
the finest pre-Paxton palm house built
1815–20 from thousands of tiny panes of
glass. The Bicton College of Agriculture has
National Collections of *Agapanthus* and
Pittosporum and is a RHS Partner College.

 Plant Highlights Woodland garden;
roses (ancient & modern); plantsman's
collection of plants; plants under glass;
mature conifers; good herbaceous borders;
fine collection of trees; tallest monkey puzzle
Araucaria araucana (30m) in the British
Isles (and nine further record-breaking
trees).

Owned by Simon Lister
English Heritage grade I

Ann & Roger Bowden

HOSTAS, STICKLEPATH, OKEHAMPTON EX20 2NN

Tel 01837 840481   **Fax** 01837 840482
Location Near Okehampton, in centre of Sticklepath, near
turning signed 'Skaigh'
Opening hours By appointment only

Ann and Roger Bowden know everything
there is to know about hostas: they are the
UK's leading ambassadors for these useful
and easy-to-grow beauties. They sell them
from a handsome catalogue with excellent
photographs. Prices are fair and range from
£2.50 for basic species to £15 for the latest
imported hybrids. But the choice is
magnificent: some 320 different hostas, of
which a large number are new or
re-introduced. Their garden at Cleave
House in Sticklepath (NB there are two
Sticklepaths in Devon – this is the
Okehampton one) has been developed over
the last 30 years with mixed plantings for
year-round interest. But the display beds for
their National Collection of hostas are here
too – an incredible 800 cultivars.

Buckland Abbey

YELVERTON PL20 6EY

Tel 01822 853607   **Fax** 01822 855448
Website www.nationaltrust.org.uk
Location Signed from A386 at Yelverton
Opening hours 10.30 am – 5.30 pm; Friday – Wednesday;
23 March to 4 November. 2 pm – 5 pm; Saturdays &
Sundays; November & December. Closed 24 December
2001 & 15 February 2001
Admission fee Adults £2.40

(P) (WC) (✿) (☕)

Originally a Cistercian Abbey, then the
house of Sir Francis Drake, the main interest
for garden lovers is the charming herb
garden along the side of the Great Barn.

 Plant Highlights Herbs; new
Elizabethan herb garden begun (1999).

Owned by The National Trust

Burrow Farm Gardens

DALWOOD, AXMINSTER EX13 7ET

Tel 01404 831285   **Fax** 01404 831844
Location Turn north off A35 at Taunton Cross: follow
brown tourist signs for ½ mile
Opening hours 10 am – 7 pm; daily; April to September
Admission fee Adults £3; Children 50p

(P) (🐕) (WC) (✿)

There are seven acres of plantsmanship at
Burrow Hill, and long views over the
sweeping hills. A formal pergola walk is
lined with old-fashioned shrubs and
climbing roses, while the woodland garden
is underplanted with rhododendrons,
azaleas and interesting herbaceous plants.
The candelabra primulas have naturalised all
through the bog garden. And the garden is
still growing – both in its size and in the
intensity of its planting.

Owned by Mr & Mrs J Benger
Number of gardeners 2
Size 7 acres

Castle Drogo

DREWSTEIGNTON EX6 6PB

Tel 01647 433306   **Fax** 01647 433186
Website www.nationaltrust.org.uk
Location Drewsteignton village: signs from A30 & A382
Opening hours 10.30 am – dusk; daily; all year
Admission fee Adults £2.80 (gardens only)

(P) (WC) (♿) (✿) (🎁) (☕)

This is a major 1920s garden, 900 feet up on
the edge of Dartmoor and made to match
the last castle built in Britain – a granite folly
which was one of Lutyens's most remarkable
works. The gardens too are grand and
grandiose. They are mainly within a large
enclosed area, tightly hedged against the
wind with thick, clipped yew. The design is
formal and terraced with granite steps and
walls. The vast and vivid herbaceous borders
contrast with the austere castle on its windy
bluff. Weather-beaten, lichen-heavy *Prunus*
and acers survive in the woodland spring
garden on the slopes below.

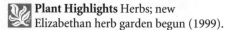 **Plant Highlights** Woodland garden;
roses (ancient & modern); rock
garden; good herbaceous borders; tallest
Acer capillipes (16m) in the British Isles.

Owned by The National Trust
English Heritage grade II*

Coleton Fishacre Garden

COLETON, KINGSWEAR, DARTMOUTH
TQ6 0EQ

Tel 01803 752466   **Fax** 01803 753017
Website www.nationaltrust.org.uk
Location 3 miles from Kingswear off Lower-Ferry Road
Opening hours 11 am – 5 pm; Sundays in March.
10.30 am – 5.30 pm (or dusk, if earlier); Wednesday
– Sundays & Bank Holidays; April to October
Admission fee Adults £3.80

The Lutyens-style house at Coleton Fishacre
was built by Oswald Milne for Sir Rupert
and Lady Dorothy D'Oyly Carte in 1925.
Rare bulbs flourish in the warm terraces
which surround it. The woodland garden,
thickly planted with rhododendrons and
camellias, crashes down a secret valley to the
sea. A stream runs down the valley, dammed
to make small pools along the way, where
damp-loving perennials luxuriate. Almost
frost-free, the range and size of Southern
Hemisphere trees and shrubs is astounding.

Plant Highlights Woodland garden;
sub-tropical plants; plantsman's
collection of plants; good herbaceous
borders; rhododendrons; rare trees; tallest
Catalpa bungei in the British Isles (and two
other record trees); interesting new
plantings in the 'Holiwell' area.

Owned by The National Trust
English Heritage grade II

Dartington Hall

DARTINGTON, TOTNES TQ9 6EL

Tel & Fax 01803 862367
Website www.dartington.u-net.com

Location 2 miles north-west of Totnes
Opening hours Dawn – dusk; daily; all year. Groups by
prior appointment only
Admission fee Donation (£2 suggested)

Dartington is one of the best examples of
grand mid-twentieth century gardening in
England: it was made with American money
at a time when few Englishmen could afford
to spend on such a scale. Some famous
designers are associated with it: Beatrix
Farrand designed the courtyard and
influenced the woodland plantings; Percy
Cane built the long staircase and opened up
some of the long vistas; Henry Moore
deposited a reclining woman. The scale is
magnificent, and wholly appropriate to the
house and landscape. The gardens are very
well maintained and full of horticultural
interest, but the detail is never allowed to
obscure the greater scheme of it. Dartington
also has fine mature trees and some
interesting modern additions like the
Japanese garden.

Owned by Dartington Hall Trust
Number of gardeners 4
Size 28 acres
English Heritage grade II*

Docton Mill

LYMEBRIDGE, HARTLAND, BIDEFORD
EX39 6EA

Tel & Fax 01237 441369
Website www.doctonmill.co.uk
Location Take road from Hartland to Stoke & follow signs
towards Elmscott
Opening hours 10 am – 6 pm; daily; March to October
Admission fee Adults £3.25; OAPs £3;
Children (under 14) £1

The main attraction at Docton is a working water mill, but the garden is developing quickly and the new owners have already made further improvements. Last year they planted up a small field with magnolias and flowering shrubs. This year they are planting up a large new glasshouse. Much of the garden is natural bluebell woodland, into which shrubs like rhododendrons have been planted over the last 20 years. But there is also a fine bog garden (candelabra primulas in late spring) and a collection of old roses underplanted with herbaceous and ground-cover plants.

Owned by Mr & Mrs J Borrett
Number of gardeners 2
Size 8½ acres

Escot

OTTERY ST MARY, EXETER EX11 1LU

Tel 01404 822188   **Fax** 01404 822903
Website www.escot-devon.co.uk
Location Signed from A30 at Fairmile
Opening hours 10 am – 6 pm; daily; Easter to October
Admission fee Adults £3.50; OAPs & Children £3; under fours free

Escot is an up-and-coming low-budget old/new garden, responding well to vigorous replanting. It surrounds an aquatic centre and incorporates a wildlife centre. The house is an elegant Regency sugarlump, with distant views to East Hill (Capability Brown advised on the prospect), but the woodlands around the house are full of good Victorian rhododendrons and the walled garden sports a basic collection of old and English roses.

Owned by John-Michael Kennaway

Exeter University Gardens

EXETER EX4 4PX

Tel 01392 263059   **Fax** 01392 264547
Website www.ex.ac.uk
Location 3 miles north of City Centre, all around University
Opening hours Dawn – dusk; daily; all year
Admission fee free

From the horticultural point of view, Exeter has the most interesting university campus in England: the gardens are educational, attractive and important. At the centre are the gardens around Reed Hall, laid out by Veitch in the 1860s at the then phenomenal cost of £70,000. This explains the framework of splendid mature trees and shrubs which give such character to the whole site – especially conifers, rhododendrons, magnolias and hardy palm trees. Modern plantings have kept pace: there is a particularly fine collection of Australasian plants including acacias, callistemons and eucalyptus. Other tender plants that grow outside include *Albizia julibrissin*, cacti like *Opuntia humifusa* and the beautiful parrot-bill plant (*Clianthus puniceus*) from New Zealand. In the glasshouses, a collection of good ornamental tropical plants is maintained. The gardeners also practice with great artistry the Victorian art of bedding out.

Owned by The University of Exeter
Number of gardeners 25
Size 250 acres
NCCPG National Collections *Azara*

Gidleigh Park Hotel

CHAGFORD TQ13 8HH

Tel 01647 432367 **Fax** 01647 432574
Website www.gidleigh.com
Location 20 miles west of Exeter. Approach from
Chagford: do NOT go to Gidleigh
Opening hours Guests of the hotel & restaurant only
Admission fee free to hotel & restaurant clients

Gidleigh has 45 acres of woodland (much of
it recently replanted) on the edge of
Dartmoor. Most of the rhododendrons and
conifers were planted in the nineteenth
century and are wonderfully mature.
Around the Tudorised house – now a top
hotel – is a 1920s garden. Below is a fine
1930s water garden. The garden contains
nothing very rare or special, but the position
is stupendous and the sense of space, even
grandeur, is enhanced by immaculate
maintenance. The hotel and restaurant have
received innumerable awards over many
years. Finding it needs careful map-reading:
in Chagford Square turn right at Lloyds
Bank and, after 150 yards, take the first fork
to the right and follow the lane for two miles
to its end.

Owned by Paul Henderson
Number of gardeners 4
Size 45 acres

Glebe Cottage Plants

PIXIE LANE, WARKLEIGH,
UMBERLEIGH EX37 9DH

Tel 01769 540554
Location 4 miles south-west of South Molton
Opening hours 10 am – 1 pm & 2 pm – 5 pm; Wednesday
– Friday. The garden is open from 2 pm – 5 pm in aid of the

National Gardens Scheme on 18 & 25 March, 15 April,
3 June, 29 July, 26 August & 9 September

Carol Klein has a sharp eye for worthwhile
new introductions, yet does not forget the
reliable old classics: her talents have brought
her television popularity and five Gold
Medals at Chelsea 1992–96 (and again in
2000). Her nursery has an exceptional list of
perennials, including lots of newly
discovered species and promising cultivars.

Gnome Reserve
& Wild Flower Garden

WEST PUTFORD, BRADWORTHY
EX22 7XE

Tel 01409 241435
Website www.ndia.ndirect.co.uk/gnomes
Location Between Bideford & Holsworthy, signed from
A39, A386 & A388
Opening hours 10 am – 6 pm; daily; 21 March to
31 October
Admission fee Adults £2.45; OAPs £2.20; Children £1.90

There are four reasons to visit this
remarkable conservation centre which has
been featured on television more than 50
times: first, the two-acre gnome reserve in a
beech wood with a stream; second the
two-acre pixies' wildflower meadow, with
250 labelled species; third, the kiln where
pottery gnomes and pixies are born; fourth,
the museum of rare early gnomes. A large
slice of gardening history is displayed in
this garden and its museum, while the
wildflower meadow is one of the best in
the country.

Owned by The Atkin Family

Higher Knowle

LUSTLEIGH, NEWTON ABBOT
TQ13 9SP

Tel 01647 277275   **Fax** 0870 131 5914
Location 3 miles north-west of Bovey Tracey, just south of Wrayland
Opening hours 2 pm – 6 pm; Sundays & Bank Holiday Mondays; 18 March to 3 June
Admission fee Adults £2.50; Children free

Higher Knowle was built by a pupil of Lutyens on a wooded slope on the south-eastern edge of Dartmoor: a stream flows down towards the Bovey valley. The first plantings date from the late 1950s – mature azaleas and magnolias around and above the house. The present owners bought the house in 1966 and have since planted up the lower woodland area with camellias, modern magnolias and rhododendrons. Bluebells, primroses and huge boulders of natural granite add to its charm, especially in spring.

Owned by Mr & Mrs David Quicke
Number of gardeners owners only
Size 3 acres

Hill House Nursery & Garden

LANDSCOVE, ASHBURTON, NEWTON ABBOT TQ13 7LY

Tel & Fax 01803 762273
Location Off A384, follow signs for Landscove
Opening hours 11 am – 5 pm; daily; all year (including bank holidays)
Admission fee free

This Victorian Old Vicarage was made famous by Edward Hyams' *An Englishman's Garden* but for many years now it is has

been the centre of an excellent plantsman's nursery. Family-owned and family-run, the three-acre nursery has an excellent range of unusual or 'hard-to-find' plants – a list of over 3,000 in all, most of them available at any one time. In the glasshouses are handsome large specimens, particularly of fuchsias and passion flowers. Most of the stock is raised in the nursery. Raymond Hubbard also breeds plants: this is where *Nemesia* 'Bluebird' originated and he expects to benefit this year from sales of over two million. He is also the breeder of *Dianthus* 'Old Mother Hubbard' (an RHS Award of Garden Merit plant) and *Plectranthus argentatus* 'Hill House'.

Owned by Raymond, Valerie & Matthew Hubbard

Killerton

BROADCLYST, EXETER EX5 3LE

Tel 01392 881345   **Fax** 01392 883112
Website www.nationaltrust.org.uk
Location West side of B3181, Exeter to Cullompton Road
Opening hours 10.30 am – dusk; daily; all year
Admission fee Adults £3.70 (but reduced rate in winter)

Killerton is an historic giant among gardens. Its long connections with Veitch's Nursery have bequeathed it a great tree collection. These include innumerable record-breaking specimens, many from collectors' seed, but one's sense of awe may be a little spoilt by droning traffic on the M5 below.

Plant Highlights Snowdrops; rock garden; rhododendrons & azaleas; daffodils; fine collection of trees; bluebells; tallest *Ostrya carpinifolia* (22m) in the British Isles (and eight further record trees); magnolia; drifts of *Crocus tommasinianus*.

Owned by The National Trust
English Heritage grade II*

The Garden House

BUCKLAND MONACHORUM, YELVERTON PL20 7LQ

Tel 01822 854769 **Fax** 01822 855358
Website www.thegardenhouse.org.uk
Location Signed off A386 on Plymouth side of Yelverton
Opening hours 10.30 am – 5 pm; daily; March to October
Admission fee Adults £4; OAPs £3.50; Children £1; RHS
members free

The Garden House was first developed by the late Lionel Fortescue, a retired Eton 'beak' between 1945 and 1981. The setting is awesome: a ruined abbey on the edge of Dartmoor, with stupendous views. Fortescue was responsible for much of the design and planting as we still see it in the walled garden. He was a great plantsman and insisted upon growing only the best forms and cultivars. He also believed that plants should be well fed and firmly controlled: they still flourish on the treatment and Fortescue's plantings have continued to fulfil their early promise. Over the last 20 years, however, the Garden House has developed in quite a different way under the guidance of the curator Keith Wiley. He has developed six acres of inter-connected gardens, each dedicated to a single theme. The South African garden is intended to replicate the spring flowering of the South African veldt, though mixed with some Californian annuals which pick up the same bright colours – eschscholtzias among the arctotis and osteospermums: it is probably best in July and August. Nearby is the quarry garden where natural outcrops have been covered with such plants as rock roses and creeping thymes, at its best in May and June. The Cretan cottage garden is a pan-European wildflower meadow where the native campions and ox-eye daisies are joined by such plants as *Alchemilla mollis*

and astrantias. There is an maple glade underplanted with thousands of naturalised crocus in March, followed by azaleas in April and May: the autumn colour is spectacular. Elsewhere are a lime-tree avenue, a spring garden, a herbaceous bed, a wisteria bridge, a peat garden, a bulb meadow and the prairie garden which uses a lot of grasses as well as ground orchids and *Verbena bonariensis*. But this is a garden in an active state of evolution, full of new features and stimulation at every time of the year.

Plant Highlights Plantsman's collection of plants; good herbaceous borders; alpine bank; flowering cherries; wisterias; a developing naturalistic extension with *Acer* glade, spring garden, quarry garden, wildflower meadow & South African garden.

Owned by Fortescue Garden Trust

Knightshayes Garden

TIVERTON EX16 7RG

Tel 01884 254665   **Fax** 01884 253264
Website www.nationaltrust.org.uk
Location Off A396 Tiverton – Bampton Road
Opening hours 11 am – 5.30 pm; daily; 24 March
to 4 November
Admission fee Adults £3.80; Children £1.90

Knightshayes is a garden in a wood – one of the best of its kind in the world. Much of the original canopy is there – notably some very fine oaks – but it is now supplemented by magnolias, birches, nothofagus and sorbus. The garden unveils as a series of walks and glades, with beautiful rhododendrons, camellias and rare shrubs underplanted with hellebores, erythroniums, foxgloves, cyclamen and bluebells. Closer to the house are the stately formal gardens, enclosed by immaculately clipped yew hedges. Here alpine treasures and small bulbs grow in raised beds. The old bowling lawn is filled by a vast circular pool and a single weeping pear, *Pyrus salicifolia* 'Pendula', which is pruned to thin out its canopy of branches. In the surrounding park is a very fine collection of trees, including several record breakers. The Douglas firs are particularly impressive.

Plant Highlights Woodland garden; topiary; good herbaceous borders; hellebores; cyclamen; bulbs; peat beds; centenary planting of 100 trees along visitors' entrance; tallest *Quercus cerris* (40m) in the British Isles.

Owned by The National Trust
English Heritage grade II*

Lukesland

HARFORD, IVYBRIDGE PL21 0JF

Tel 01752 893390   **Fax** 01752 896011
Location 1½ miles from Ivybridge on the Harford road
Opening hours 2 pm – 6 pm; Wednesdays,
Sundays & Bank Holiday Mondays; 15 April to 17 June
Admission fee Adults £2.90; Children free

Lukesland is a woodland garden in a stream-fed Devon valley: it offers the perfect conditions for growing rhododendrons, azaleas and many other flowering shrubs. The house and the earliest plantings date from the 1880s, but most of what we see now has been planted by the present owners since 1975. The family's policy is to try to regenerate poor or over-mature areas, so that the quality and display of plants are improved: during the 1990s, for example, the Howells planted a good selection of late-flowering rhododendrons at the north end of the pinetum. Here too, in 1992, they built a striking reverse suspension bridge, designed by the Scottish architect Sir James Dunbar-Nasmith. The gardens contain some fine species of rhododendron including the large-leafed *R. sinogrande*, *R. macabeanum*, *R. falconeri* and *R. Arizelum*. The many Exbury hybrids include 'Cornish Cross', 'Hawk Crest' and 'Jalisco'. Youngish camellias are starting to make an impact, while other good shrubs include *Drimys lanceolata*, *Michelia doltsopa*, hoherias and eucryphias. There are some very fine specimen trees: *Ginkgo biloba* at 72ft, *Davidia involucrata* var. *vilmoriniana* planted in 1936 and now a broad 56-ft specimen, and a magnificent *Magnolia campbellii* planted at the same time and now about 75ft high – its exceptionally wide spread makes it one of the largest in the country.

Marwood Hill Gardens

BARNSTAPLE EX31 4EB

Tel 01271 42528
Location Signed from A361 Barnstaple & Braunton Road
Opening hours Dawn – dusk; daily; all year except
Christmas Day
Admission fee Adults £3

Marwood Hill is a remarkable plantsman's garden, conceived on a grand scale and fast maturing, though it is still expanding along the long sheltered valley which gives such vigorous growth to its plants. It is exciting for its scale and variety, and for the energy and enthusiasm of its owner, which are an inspiration to many. There is no better place in the south-west to learn about plants of every kind, especially as all the plants are clearly labelled. It is moreover a garden of year-round interest. Late in the year, *Galanthus reginae-olgae* flowers with the last of the *Cyclamen hederaefolium*: these are followed in midwinter by many other snowdrops and *Cyclamen coum*. There is a wonderful collection of camellias at this season too – some in the open, and others (huge bushes of Reticulata Hybrids) under glass. Magnolias are numerous, including many of the Jury hybrids from New Zealand, the dark form of *M. campbellii* called 'Betty Jessel', *M. sprengeri* var. *diva*, *M. Dawsoniana*, M. × *wiesneri* and the home-grown 'Marwood Spring'. Many are underplanted with drifts of narcissi. Come the spring, and the pergola draped with twelve different wisterias starts into flower (the colour is extended by interplanted clematis and climbing roses) and the walled garden begins to make an impact with ceanothus, *Clianthus puniceus* and the poppy bush (*Dendromecon rigidum*). In early summer

the bog garden comes into its own, starting with drifts of candelabra primulas and continuing with astilbes from the National Collection: in fact the bog garden is full of colour right through until autumn. Hydrangeas are another success story: a very large number of cultivars is planted throughout the garden. As the soil is acid, the 'mopheads' come out in many shades of blue, alongside the cultivars of *Hydrangea paniculata* (Dr Smart considers 'Pink Diamond' one of the best) and *Hydrangea quercifolia* whose oak-shaped leaves change to brilliant colours in the autumn. Leaves and bark are important elements of the garden: Dr Smart has planted the birches close to the eucalyptus so that the contrasts of bark can be enjoyed together – he has planted large numbers of both *Betula* and *Eucalyptus* species. He also has a high regard for the seldom-seen *Amomyrtus lechleriana* in the walled garden. And there is a fine collection of rhododendrons, including large plants of *R. macabeanum*, *R. sinogrande*, *R. eximium*, *R. arizelum*, *R. arboreum* and *R.* 'Sir Charles Lemon'.

Owned by Dr J A Smart
NCCPG National Collections *Astilbe*; *Iris ensata*; *Tulbaghia*

Owned by Mr & Mrs B N Howell
Number of gardeners family, plus part-time help
Size 15 acres

Nicky's Rock Garden Nursery

BROADHAYES, STOCKLAND, HONITON EX14 9EH

Tel 01404 881213
Location 6 miles east of Honiton, off midpoint of north-south road between A30 & A35
Opening hours 9 am – dusk, daily. Please telephone first

This nursery is one of few in the south-west which specialise in alpines, but the owners are both distinguished members of the Alpine Garden Society. They are keen plantsmen and therefore sell a wide selection of alpines and dwarf plants for rock gardens: bulbs, conifers and shrubs. Almost everything can be seen growing in their show garden. The owners enjoy looking at the garden with visitors and talking about the problems of growing and propagating rock plants.

The Old Glebe

EGGESFORD, CHULMLEIGH EX18 7QU

Tel & Fax 01769 580632
Location Uphill (& south) of Eggesford for two-thirds of a mile; right into bridleway
Opening hours 2 pm – 6 pm; 5, 6 & 7 May for National Gardens Scheme. And by appointment
Admission fee Adults £2; Children £1

This is a great rhododendron collection, well-known to the *cognoscenti*. Nigel Wright has over 6,000 plants and 750 different

cultivars, and his nursery sells over 200 of them. It is one of the best lists in the UK. The house is an old rectory, with fine lawns, mature trees, walled herbaceous borders, a bog garden and a small lake.

Owned by Nigel Wright
Number of gardeners 1 part-time
Size 7 acres

Overbecks Museum & Garden

SHARPITOR, SALCOMBE TQ8 8LW

Tel 01548 843238
Website www.nationaltrust.org.uk
Location 2 miles south of Salcombe
Opening hours 11 am – 8 pm (or dusk, if earlier); daily; all year
Admission fee Adults £2.90; Children £1.40

Overbecks has a small, intensely planted, almost jungly garden, perched above the Salcombe estuary. The formal terraces (rather 1930s) are stuffed with interesting tender plants: *Musa basjoo*, phormiums, agapanthus, self-sown *Echium pininana* and every kind of South African daisy, all held together in a framework of hundreds of *Trachycarpus* palms.

Owned by The National Trust
English Heritage grade II

Paignton Zoo & Botanical Gardens

TOTNES ROAD, PAIGNTON TQ4 7EU

Tel 01803 697500 **Fax** 01803 523457
Website www.paigntonzoo.org.uk
Location On A385 Totnes Road, 1 mile from Paignton

Opening hours 10 am – 6 pm (or dusk, if earlier); daily;
all year
Admission fee Adults £7.50; OAPs £5.90; Children £5.40
(subject to review in April 2001)

Once a private garden devoted to blue-
flowered and blue-leaved plants, this is now
an inspiring combination of zoo, botanic
collection, public park and holiday
entertainment. Plans to increase the
commitment to conservation have begun
with six new habitats. A new tropical house
opened in 2000: tropical plants and reptiles
under the same glass roof.

Owned by Whitley Wildlife Conservation Trust

Plant World Botanic Gardens

ST MARYCHURCH ROAD, NEWTON
ABBOT TQ12 4SE

Tel 01803 872939   Fax 01803 875018
Location Follow brown tourist signs from Penn Inn
roundabout at Newton Abbot
Opening hours 9.30 am – 5 pm; daily; April to September

This plantsman's nursery sells a selection of
alpines, perennials and shrubs. There is an
illustrated seed list with fresh material from
the gardens and some interesting collected
species. The National Collection of *Primula*
extends only to the *Cortusoides* section of
the genus, but the nursery used to collect the
Capitatae and *Farinosae* too, and it still
grows many from those sections. The
mature four-acre gardens are planted out as
special habitat zones: worth a long journey
to visit in their own right.

NCCPG National Collections *Primula* (Cortusoides
section

The Plantsman Nursery

NORTH WONSON FARM,
THROWLEIGH, OKEHAMPTON
EX20 2JA

Tel 01647 231618   Fax 01647 231699
Website www.plantsman.com
Location At the northern end of Wonson village
Opening hours By appointment

This young and expanding nursery has a
most interesting list of climbers and wall
shrubs. Many are the sort one sees in
Mediterranean gardens – asarinas,
thunbergias and passion flowers, for instance
– but there are more than 450 of them.
Some are rare and unusual, grown from
gifts from such plant-collectors as Martyn
Rix. And no nursery in Europe has a more
comprehensive list of *Aristolochia* species.

NCCPG National Collections *Aristolochia*

Pleasant View Nursery & Garden

TWO MILE OAK, DENBURY, NEWTON
ABBOT TQ12 6DG

Tel 01803 813388
Location Off A381 at Two Mile Oak pub towards Denbury:
then ¾ mile on the left
Opening hours Garden: 2 pm – 5 pm; Wednesdays
& Fridays; May to September. Nursery: 10 am – 5 pm;
Wednesday – Friday; mid-March to end of September

This garden is a remarkable achievement:
the collection of trees and shrubs is
exceptionally comprehensive – enough to be
called an arboretum – and it has all been
achieved from open pasture since 1988.
Ceanothus and abelias flourish despite being

some way inland from the south coast. The nursery has lots of interesting shrubs, both for garden planting and for conservatories, with a special emphasis upon salvias from the National Collection. Pleasant View is the only place to offer some of the rarer species – *S. longispicata, S. madrensis* and the creeping California shrub *S. sonomensis*, for example.

Size 4 acres
NCCPG National Collections *Abelia; Salvia*

Powderham Castle

EXETER EX6 8JQ

Tel 01626 890243   **Fax** 01626 890729
Location Off A379 Dawlish to Exeter Road at Kenton
Opening hours 10 am – 5.30 pm; Sunday – Friday; 1 April to 28 October
Admission fee Adults £5.85; OAPs £5.35; Children £2.95. Charges include guided tour of Castle

Powderham is not a major garden, though it has some good trees – notably the cork oak (*Quercus suber*) and its Devon hybrid *Q. × lucombeana*. Nevertheless the eighteenth-century landscaped park is serenely English, the woodland garden is stupendous in March and there is a cheerful modern rose garden all along the front of the house. Work has now started (2001) on restoring the Victorian walled garden.

Owned by Earl & Countess of Devon
Number of gardeners 3
Size 60 acres, including grounds
English Heritage grade II

R D Plants

HOMELEA FARM, TYTHERLEIGH, AXMINSTER EX13 7BG

Tel 01460 220206
Location On A358, just inside the county boundary
Opening hours 9 am – 1 pm, 2 pm – 5.30 pm, February to September. Phone first (between 8.30 am and 9.30 am only)

This nursery specialises in good herbaceous plants for damp and shady places – woodlanders from all over the world. It is particularly strong on anemones and modern developments of *Helleborus orientalis* – especially scented cultivars and doubles.

RHS Garden Rosemoor

GREAT TORRINGTON EX38 8PH

Tel 01805 624067   **Fax** 01805 624717
Location 1 mile south of Torrington on B3220
Opening hours 10 am – 6 pm (but 5 pm October to March); daily; 2 January to 24 December
Admission fee Adults £4.50; Children £1; Groups (10+) £3.50. RHS members free

The Royal Horticultural Society's garden at Rosemoor is situated in the delightful setting of the Torridge Valley, nestled within extensive surrounding woodlands. After twelve years of development all of the projects envisaged in the original garden masterplan for Rosemoor are now complete. Many of the new garden areas are reaching maturity and these, together with Lady Anne's unique and delightful garden, ensure that a visit to Rosemoor will provide something for all tastes and interests, at every season of the year. Rosemoor is rich in variety: the formal garden demonstrates a wide range of plants and planting styles in a series of individual garden 'rooms', with lots of ideas to inspire visitors for their own gardens. Included are two rose gardens, for modern and shrub roses; two colour-themed gardens – the spiral garden with its soft, pastel theme and the square garden with its searing, hot coloured plantings; the ever-popular cottage and herb gardens; the *potager*, with decorative vegetable planting; a foliage garden, where leaf form and colour are dominant; a winter garden, full of colour during the colder months; and the model gardens, demonstrating three contrasting design solutions for the average domestic plot. Other attractions include the stream garden and lake; a richly planted fruit and vegetable garden; large areas of parkland and arboretum; and newly developed woodland walks.

 Plant Highlights Woodland garden; roses (ancient & modern); plantsman's collection of plants; stream and bog garden; foliage garden; colour theme gardens; fruit and vegetable gardens; herb garden; cottage garden; tallest *Eucalyptus glaucescens* (21m) in the British Isles (and seven further record trees).

Owned by The Royal Horticultural Society
Number of gardeners 16
Size 40 acres
NCCPG National Collections *Ilex*; *Cornus*

Rowden Gardens

BRENTOR, TAVISTOCK PL19 0NG

Tel 01822 810275
Location 1 mile west of North Brentor
Opening hours 10 am – 5 pm; Saturday – Sunday and Bank Holiday Mondays; April to September. And by appointment

Rowden Gardens is a nursery with a show garden attached. Its speciality is aquatic plants, and the remarkable thing about the garden is that it is made in old watercress beds – long, rectangular tanks. More than 3,000 different plants grow in the garden, which provides the propagating material for the nursery. Almost all its stock is of aquatic or moisture-loving plants: there is a good choice of *Iris ensata* cultivars, for example, many of them raised by the nursery. But Rowden is also *the* place for celandines from its National Collection of *Ranunculus ficaria*: it grows and offers for sale many more cultivars than anyone else. It is also a reliable source of unusual species and selected forms of *Persicaria*. The nursery prides itself on being an introducer of new plants. Until recently it was also a regular exhibitor at RHS shows, where its displays were always much admired for their variety.

NCCPG National Collections *Fallopia*; *Persicaria*; *Ranunculus ficaria*

Saltram

PLYMPTON, PLYMOUTH PL7 3UH

Tel 01752 336546 **Fax** 01752 336474
Website www.nationaltrust.org.uk
Location 2 miles west of Plympton
Opening hours 11 am – 4 pm on Saturdays & Sundays February & March. Then 10.30 am – 5.30 pm; Sunday – Thursday; 1 March to 4 November. Also Good Friday
Admission fee Adults £3; Children £1.50

Twenty acres of beautiful parkland, whose huge and ancient trees are underplanted with camellias and rhododendrons. Best in spring when the daffodils flower in hosts.

 Plant Highlights Rhododendrons & azaleas; camellias; parkland; handsome orangery; lime avenue; 'melancholy' walk undergoing restoration (1998); tallest *Acer palmatum* 'Osakazuki' (13m) in the British Isles.

Owned by The National Trust
English Heritage grade II*

Sherwood

NEWTON ST CYRES, EXETER EX5 5BT

Tel 01392 851216   **Fax** 01392 851870
Location 2 miles south-west of Newton St Cyres, at the end of a signed track
Opening hours 2 pm – 5 pm; Sundays; 11 March to 11 November
Admission fee Adults £2

This is an important rhododendron garden with much more than the collection of Knap Hill azaleas to see and enjoy. The magnolias are good, and there are handsome collections of buddlejas, berberis, cotoneasters and maples which take the garden right through the year.

Owned by Sir John & Lady Quicke
Number of gardeners 1½
Size 14 acres
NCCPG National Collections *Rhododendron* (Knap Hill azaleas)

Tapeley Park

INSTOW EX39 4NT

Tel 01271 42371
Location Off A39 between Barnstaple & Bideford
Opening hours 10 am – 5 pm; daily, except Saturdays; 19 March to 31 October
Admission fee Adults £3.50; OAPs £3; Children £2

Tapeley's fame rests on its fine Italianate formal garden laid out on several levels in about 1900 and planted with such tender plants as *Sophora tetraptera* and *Myrtus communis* subsp. *tarentina*. Beyond are palm trees and a rhododendron woodland: worth exploring. All parts are undergoing restoration and replanting with advice from Mary Keen and Carol Klein.

Owned by N D C I Ltd
Number of gardeners 2½
Size 35 acres
English Heritage grade II*

Thornhayes Nursery

DULFORD, CULLOMPTON EX15 2DF

Tel 01884 266746   **Fax** 01884 266739
Website www.thornhayes-nursery.co.uk
Location 10 minutes from M5, Jct28
Opening hours 8 am – 4.30 pm; Monday – Friday

This nursery (retail and wholesale) was founded in 1991 with the aim of growing a wider range of ornamental and fruit trees than was generally available in the West Country. Thornhayes has some interesting ornamental trees: they include *Fitzroya cupressoides, Betula* 'Conyngham' and good collections of sorbus, pyrus and crataegus: dendrophiles should take a closer look. Hard-to-get West Country apples for cider, cooking and eating are another speciality: these include 'Chorister Boy', 'Peter Lock' and 'Royal Somerset'.

Wylmington Hayes Gardens

WILMINGTON, HONITON EX14 9JZ

Tel 01404 831751 **Fax** 01404 831826
Location Signed off A30: turn north off A35 in Wilmington
Opening hours Parties by arrangement during last two weeks of May and first week of June to see the rhododendrons

Admission fee Adults £3

Wylmington Hayes is an Edwardian house in the Tudor style, with a formal Italian garden. Its 90 acres of ornamental woodland are planted with spectacular azaleas, rhododendrons, camellias, acers and magnolias.

Owned by Mr & Mrs P Saunders

DORSET

Both Dorset's Grade I gardens – Abbotsbury and Athelhampton – have plenty of horticultural interest to offer their visitors as well as their historic importance. Abbotsbury has an especially good collection of old trees, including several UK record-holders. Minterne and Forde, too, are good for specimen trees, while one of the tallest specimens in the British Isles of the dawn redwood (*Metasequoia glyptostroboides*) is a twin-stemmed specimen more than 25m high in Bournemouth's Central Park. Most of Dorset's leading nurseries are close to the coast – the chalk hinterland can be cold in winter – and there is a cluster of eminent nurseries on the sandy soils in the south east of the county. The National Gardens Scheme is very well supported and lists over one hundred gardens – a remarkable number for such a small county. It is sad to learn, however, that the furniture-maker John Makepiece no longer feels able to open his garden at Parnham to visitors: the income does not justify the cost in time and money. The NCCPG has a very active group in the county, but comparatively few National Collections – among them are *Hoheria, Ceanothus* and *Penstemon,* all of them benefiting from the mild climate along the Dorset coast. Kingston Maurward is a RHS Partner College: the estate once belonged to Sir Thomas Hanbury, who gave Wisley Gardens to the Royal Horticultural Society.

Abbotsbury Sub-Tropical Gardens

ABBOTSBURY, WEYMOUTH DT3 4LA

Tel 01305 871387 **Fax** 01305 871902
Location B3157, on coast, in village
Opening hours 10 am – 6 pm (dusk in winter); daily; all year. Closed 1 January, 25 & 26 December. Free to RHS members from January to February and from October to December
Admission fee Adults £4.70; OAPs £4.50; Children £3.20

Abbotsbury is a woodland garden of splendid trees and shrubs of great rarity which has enjoyed a spectacular renaissance in recent years. Palms, eucalyptus, pittosporum and camellias all grow lushly in the sheltered valley and romantic walled garden. Among the trees are many exceptionally large specimens of species that are normally too tender to grow even in southern England – including *Buxus balearica, Ilex fargesii, Photinia nussia, Picconia excelsa,* and *Pittosporum crassifolium.* As well as the collection of hoherias, the gardens' comprehensive display of large-leaved hebes was until quite recently designated a National

Collection by the NCCPG. A stylish Visitors' Centre designed as a Colonial Teahouse and an excellent nursery make for added value.

 Plant Highlights Sub-tropical plants; fine collection of trees; magnolias; candelabra primulas; rare trees; free-standing loquat *Eriobotrya japonica*; excellent collection of rare trees and shrubs; camellias; rhododendrons & azaleas; bluebells; sub-tropical rarities; tallest English oak *Quercus robur* (40m) in the British Isles; five other record trees.

Owned by Ilchester Estates
Number of gardeners 5
Size 20 acres
NCCPG National Collections *Hoheria*
English Heritage grade I

Athelhampton

DORCHESTER DT2 7LG

Tel 01305 848363   **Fax** 01305 848135
Website www.athelhampton.co.uk
Location 4 miles east of Dorchester, off A35 at Northbrook-Puddletown junction
Opening hours 10.30 am – 5 pm; Sunday – Friday; March to October. Plus Sundays from November to February, and Saturdays at Easter and August Bank Holiday
Admission fee House & garden: £5.50. Garden only: £3.95

Inigo Thomas designed these gardens about 100 years ago as the perfect complement for the perfect manor house. Sharply cut pyramids of yew, a long canal with water lilies, and rambling roses in early summer are some of the main features. The overall effect is most satisfying and harmonious.

Plant Highlights Topiary; gazebos; beautiful walls and hedges; winner of HHA/Christie's Garden of the Year Award for 1997; two *Metasequoia glyptostroboides* from the original seed.

Owned by Patrick Cooke
Number of gardeners 3
Size 10 acres
English Heritage grade I

Bennetts Water Lily Farm

WATER GARDENS, PUTTON LANE, CHICKERELL, WEYMOUTH DT3 4AF

Tel 01305 785150
Location 2 miles west of Weymouth, signed off B3157 Bridport road
Opening hours 10 am – 5 pm; Tuesday – Sunday; April to August. 10 am – 5 pm; Tuesday – Saturday; September. Open on Bank Holidays

Bennetts Water Lily Farm is the leading nursery in the south-west for aquatic plants: water lilies, pond plants and marginals in abundance. The flowering season is from to June to late September, which coincides with the tourist season. The gardens have been developed recently as a visitor attraction: thousands of water lilies and a 'Monet' bridge.

NCCPG National Collections *Nymphaea*

Chettle House

CHETTLE, BLANDFORD FORUM DT11 8DB

Tel & Fax 01258 830209
Location 6 miles north of Blandford; 1 mile west of A354
Opening hours 11 am – 5 pm; Sundays; Easter to September. Plus daily except Saturday in August. And by appointment
Admission fee Adults £2.50; Children free

Chettle House is stunning – built by Thomas Archer in the 1710s and actually improved in the 1840s: it is full of beautiful architectural detail. The gardens are old and formal in structure, but have been re-planted in the English style since about 1970. A croquet lawn fringed by herbaceous plantings fills the foreground to the park, while the borders in the main garden surround a sunken lawn. The plantings are effective, and include a variegated liriodendron, a stauntonia growing over an old yew, and some 60 clematis cultivars. A small vineyard planted with 'Bacchus' lies to one side and a walnut planted in 1957 is already nearly 60ft high. This garden is the original home of the very pretty (and popular) *Campanula persicifolia* 'Chettle Charm' which is white with a blue edge. But the really inspirational thing about the garden is that it is all maintained by the husband-and-wife owners who inherited the estate in 1967 and have devoted themselves to restoring both house and garden.

Owned by Patrick Bourke
Number of gardeners owners only
Size 4 acres

Chiffchaffs

CHAFFEYMOOR, BOURTON, GILLINGHAM SP8 5BY

Tel 01747 840841
Location At Wincanton end of Bourton, off A303
Opening hours 2 pm – 5 pm; Wednesdays & Thursdays; April to September. Plus 4 March; 1, 15, 22 & 29 April; 6, 20 & 27 May; 10 & 24 June; 8 July; 26 August; 9 September; 7 October
Admission fee Adults £2; Children 50p

A pretty cottage, with an excellent small nursery attached, and just off the A303. Started in 1978, the garden has a flowing

design, exploits a great variety of habitats and burgeons with good plants. A bluebell-lined path leads to the woodland garden, which boasts a splendid collection of rhododendrons, drifts of daffodils and candelabra primulas, and yet more carpets of bluebells. It was originally a dank and scrubby alder copse – on a spring line – but the Potts have cleared it, drained it and planted ornamental trees and shrubs, with autumn colour in mind as much as spring flowers. Here are about a dozen cultivars of *Liquidamber styraciflua* and groups of *Disanthus cercidifolius.* The nursery is open at the same times as the garden.

Owned by Mr & Mrs K R Potts
Number of gardeners part-time help
Size 3½ acres (including woodland)

Compton Acres Gardens

CANFORD CLIFFS ROAD, POOLE BH13 7ES

Tel 01202 700778   **Fax** 01202 707537
Website www.comptonacres.co.uk
Location Well signed locally
Opening hours 10 am – 6 pm; daily; March to September
Admission fee Adults £5.75; OAPs £5.25; Children £2.95

Very touristy, very Bournemouth and very 1920s, Compton Acres offers ten totally unconnected but highly entertaining gardens, all in different styles but joined by tarmac paths. They include an Egyptian Court garden, the Spanish water garden, the Roman gardens and the Canadian Woodland Walk. Best are the Italian garden, the Palm Court, the white azaleas in the watery glen which runs down to the harbour, and the stupendous Japanese Garden. The gardens are undergoing extensive renovation, and the views across Poole Harbour have been opened out again. The atmosphere is still fairly commercial, but the standards of maintenance are among the highest in any garden: no visitor could fail to be cheered up by the bravura of it all.

Owned by Red Sky Leisure Ltd
Number of gardeners 4
Size 10 acres
English Heritage grade II*

Cranborne Manor

CRANBORNE, WIMBORNE BH21 5PP

Tel 01725 517248   **Fax** 01725 517862
Website www.cranborne.co.uk
Location 10 miles north of Wimborne on B3078
Opening hours 9 am – 5 pm (7 pm in May & June); Wednesdays; mid-March to September. Plus 10 am – 5 pm on 24 June for National Gardens Scheme
Admission fee Adults £3.50; Concessions £2.50; Children 50p. But subject to review

Much of the garden at Cranborne is modern, laid out and planted by Lady Salisbury in the 1960s and 1970s, though you would never know it. The Jacobean-style features are designed to complement the old house which dates principally from the 1610s, and to remind us that the first gardener was John Tradescant the Elder. You enter the garden through a large (and excellent) garden centre, passing through a small walled kitchen garden where apple trees are trained as five-foot espaliers. Espaliered apples appear almost as a *Leitmotif* in many other places in the garden. It is fairly simply planted, though you leave through a pretty double border with windows cut into the yew hedge on one side, and on through a herb garden. Everywhere are neat yew hedges and a little topiary. There are no horticultural rarities, but bulbs

and polyanthus in spring and a cyclamen bank in autumn, and everywhere a sense of spaciousness, order and age. The classic view is of the narrow cottage-garden walk, backed by more apple-trees, leading towards the pretty flint church. Cranborne also has some fine old trees, notably beeches, limes and a vast low-branching ilex close to the house. The garden is better maintained now than a few years ago: it has clearly been taken in hand and is looking good again.

Owned by Viscount Cranborne
Number of gardeners 2½
Size 8 acres
English Heritage grade II*

Dean's Court

WIMBORNE BH21 1EE

Tel 01202 888478
Location 2 mins walk from central Wimborne
Opening hours 2 pm – 6 pm; 15 April, 6 & 27 May, 10 & 24 June, 22 July, 4, 5 & 26 August & 16 September. Plus 10 am – 6 pm on 16 April, 7 & 28 May, & 27 August
Admission fee Adults £2; OAPs £1.50; Children 50p

A very wholesome garden: everything, including 150 different herb varieties, is grown without artificial fertilisers, pesticides or herbicides. A new rose garden opened last year.

Owned by Sir Michael & Lady Hanham
Number of gardeners 4
Size 13 acres

Edmonsham House

EDMONDSHAM, WIMBORNE
BH21 5RE

Tel 01725 517207
Location Off B3081 between Cranborne & Verwood
Opening hours 2 pm – 5 pm; Wednesdays & Sundays;
April to October
Admission fee Adults £1.50; Children 50p

The walled garden is maintained organically, with borders round the sides – go in August to see the vast patches of white crinums. It is intensively cultivated and brims with interesting vegetables and fruit houses. Fine trees around the main lawns.

Owned by Mrs Julia E Smith
Number of gardeners 1, plus 3 part-time
Size 6 acres (plus one-acre walled garden)

Forde Abbey

CHARD TA20 4LU

Tel 01460 220231   **Fax** 01460 220296
Website www.fordeabbey.co.uk
Location 4 miles south of Chard
Opening hours 10 am – 4.30 pm; daily; all year
Admission fee Adults £4.20; OAPs £3.95; Children free.
RHS members free from October to April

The Gardens of Forde Abbey surround the twelfth-century Cistercian Monastery, a rambling private home since 1650, part Jacobean and part Gothic. They extend over 30 informal acres, with plants of interest and beauty throughout the year, set off by ancient and mellowed stone walls. Trees survive from 1700, although much has been planted in recent years: rhododendrons, azaleas, acers, magnolias, irises, meconopsis and candelabra primulas. But there are also mature Victorian conifers (*Sequoia sempervirens, Calocedrus decurrens*), lakes, ponds, streams, cascades, bogs and such oddities as a Beech House.

 Plant Highlights Good herbaceous borders; fine collection of trees; rock garden planted by Jack Drake; Ionic temple (Ham stone); seventeenth-century vistas opened up (2000); HHA/Christie's Garden of the Year in 1993; tallest *Cornus controversa* (16m) in UK.

Owned by The Trustees of the G D Roper settlement
Size 30 acres
English Heritage grade II*

C W Groves & Son

NURSERY & GARDEN CENTRE, WEST
BAY ROAD, BRIDPORT DT6 4BA

Tel 01308 422654   **Fax** 01308 420888
Website www.users.zetnet.co.uk/c/w/grovesandson/
Location South of town centre, above river, next to the
Crown
Opening hours 8.30 am – 5 pm; Monday – Saturday.
10.30 am – 4.30 pm; Sundays

This modern, up-to-date garden centre (rose beds, Koi carp etc.) also has a traditional nursery attached. Founded in 1866 by the present owner's great-great-grandfather, it specialises in Sweet Victorian Violets. These are available from the garden centre as well as by mail order and include a large number of rarities: *Viola* 'Gloire de Verdon', *V.* 'Princess Alexandra' and *V.* 'Pritchard's Russian', for example.

Ivy Cottage

ALLER LANE, ANSTY, DORCHESTER
DT2 7PX

Tel & Fax 01258 880053
Location Midway between Blandford & Dorchester
Opening hours 10 am – 5 pm; Thursdays; April to September. And 2 pm – 5.30 pm on 26 August for National Gardens Scheme
Admission fee Adults £2.25; Children free. But £2.50

This cottage garden has been made (and immaculately maintained) by the present owners since the mid-1960s and is crammed with interesting things, particularly moisture-loving plants. Springs and streams, combined with greensand soil, multiply the possibilities – drifts of marsh marigolds, astilbes and candelabra primulas. Many are chosen with wildlife in mind.

Owned by Anne & Alan Stevens
Number of gardeners owners only
Size 1½ acres

Kingston Lacy

WIMBORNE MINSTER BH21 4EA

Tel 01202 883402   **Fax** 01202 882402
Website www.nationaltrust.org.uk
Location 1½ miles from Wimborne on B3082 to Blandford
Opening hours 11 am – 4 pm; Saturdays & Sundays; February & March. Then 11 am – 6 pm; daily; 31 March to 4 November. Then 11 am – 4 pm; Friday – Sunday; 9 November to 23 December
Admission fee Adults £3; Children £1.50

The magnificent home of the Bankes family sits among 400 acres of parkland, filled in all directions as far as the eye can see with single specimen trees of great breadth – beech, oak and chestnut. Nearer the house are a wonderfully gloomy cherry laurel walk, a lime avenue, and a cedar avenue planted over the centuries to commemorate visits by everyone from the Duke of Wellington to the Kaiser. Next to the house is a pretty formal garden, first laid out in 1899 and still planted with the original scheme of pink begonias and blue heliotrope in summer, and pansies and wallflowers in spring. Nearby is a fern garden under a canopy of hollies, aucubas and yews: gravel paths run between irregularly shaped raised beds planted with male ferns and hart's tongues. There is little of horticultural interest apart from daffodils in spring and some pretty roses near the stables restaurant – notably 'Cardinal Hume' and 'Anna Zinkeisen' – together with some handsome trees, including a cut-leaved beech. The garden ornaments are however exceptional: they include an Egyptian obelisk (Ptolemy VII) and some first-class nineteenth-century marbles from Italy.

Plant Highlights Snowdrops; mature conifers; Victorian fernery; Dutch parterre; huge cedars of Lebanon planted by visiting royalty.

Owned by The National Trust
NCCPG National Collections Anemone nemorosa; Convallaria
English Heritage grade II

Kingston Maurward Gardens

KINGSTON MAURWARD COLLEGE, DORCHESTER DT2 8PY

Tel 01305 215000   **Fax** 01305 250001
Location 1 mile east of Dorchester from A35: signed
Opening hours 10 am – 5.30 pm; daily; 6 January to 23 December
Admission fee Adults £3.75; Children £2; Family £10

Kingston Maurwood belonged to the Hanbury family who owned La Mortola on the Riviera, and laid out the formal garden here in the Italian style in the 1920s. It has been remade in the country house style with herbaceous borders and old fashioned roses. The 'Grecian' temple was restored in 2000, and the hardy salvias in the National Collection have just been planted in a new parterre. The old kitchen garden is a splendid modern teaching garden with innumerable demonstrations of what can be grown in Dorset. Highly instructive.

Owned by Kingston Maurward College
Number of gardeners 8
Size 35 acres
NCCPG National Collections *Penstemon*; *Salvia*
English Heritage grade II*

Knoll Gardens

Stapehill Road, Wimborne
BH21 7ND

Tel 01202 873931   **Fax** 01202 870842
Website www.knollgardens.co.uk
Location Signed from B3073 at Hampreston
Opening hours 10 am – 4 pm; Wednesday – Sunday; March, October & November. 10 am – 5 pm; daily; April to September
Admission fee Adults £4; OAPs £3.50; Children £2. RHS members free in April, May, September & October

Ⓟ ⓦ🅒 ♿ ⚘ ▦ ☕ 🍴

This garden was once an intimate and enclosed collection of tender exotics – many of them Australian. It was here, too, that the first owner, John May, bred the hybrid *Phygelius × rectus* 'African Queen'. In recent years, the garden has been enormously expanded as a horticultural visitor attraction. Most impressive is a massive new rock garden of Purbeck stone, which is weathering well and already looks well-established. The modern plantings lower

down are growing together and provide much interest. In fact, this is a garden to interest the plantsman as much as the casual holiday-maker. The many different areas, winding pathways, and constantly changing views give an impression of a much larger area than its four acres. The owners continue to develop the garden and its plant collections, particularly of hardy perennials and grasses – in which the adjoining nursery specialises. There is a fine open area of lawn bottom which gives onto a gravel garden, a conifer collection, a small pond and sinuous herbaceous plantings. The garden is maintained to a high standard.

Owned by John & Janet Flude, & Neil Lucas
Size 4 acres
NCCPG National Collections *Ceanothus* (deciduous); *Phygelius*

Macpennys Nurseries

154 Burley Road, Bransgore,
Christchurch BH23 8DB

Tel 01425 672348
Location On the Burley Road, on the north-west edge of Bransgore
Opening hours 9 am – 5 pm; Monday – Saturday. 2 pm – 5 pm; Sundays. Closed at Christmas & New Year

 Ⓟ ⚘

This long-established nursery ('old-fashioned' in the best sense) has a reliable general range across the plant spectrum, plus a few rarities. It is particularly good for conifers, rhododendrons and shrubs. The large woodland garden next to the nursery is open for the National Gardens Scheme and full of interesting plants. Many have grown to a considerable size.

Mapperton Gardens

BEAMINSTER DT8 3NR

Tel 01308 862645   **Fax** 01308 863348
Website www.mapperton.com
Location 2 miles south-east of Beaminster
Opening hours 2 pm – 6 pm; daily; 1 March to 31 October
Admission fee Adults £3.50; Children (508) £1.50
(under 5, free)

Mapperton has spectacular hanging gardens that you see laid out in their entirety from the lawn beside the house. First comes an enchanting steep formal valley-garden, running down from a pinnacled orangery to a handsome pool surrounded by terracing and gardens of clipped yew. Below are two canals and finally a long dell garden, with an excellent collection of spring-flowering trees and shrubs.

Owned by The Earl & Countess of Sandwich
English Heritage grade II*

Minterne

MINTERNE MAGNA, DORCHESTER DT 7AU

Tel 01300 341370   **Fax** 01300 341747
Location On A352, 2 miles north of Cerne Abbas
Opening hours 10 am – 7 pm; daily; 1 March to 10 November
Admission fee Adults £3; Children free

A woodland garden, best in spring, and well integrated into the park around the handsome Edwardian house. The oldest rhododendrons came from Hooker's collection, but the remarkable Lord Digby (father of the present owner) supported Farrer, Forrest, Rock and Kingdon Ward, which makes Minterne one of the best

Himalayan collections. The circular walk down a greensand valley to the woodland stream and back again is ravishing: magnolias and Japanese cherries are underplanted with camellias and azaleas, while candelabra primulas and astilbes line the pools at the bottom. The fine collection of trees includes exceptional specimens of *Corylus avellana* 'Heterophylla' and *Cercidiphyllum japonicum*, while the many handkerchief trees (*Davidia involucrata*) are sensational in late May.

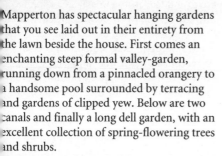 **Plant Highlights** Cherries; cyclamen; *Lathraea clandestina*; rhododendrons & azaleas; fine woodland walks; tallest *Chamaecyparis pisifera* 'Filifera' (25m) in the UK.

Owned by Lord Digby
Number of gardeners 3
Size 29 acres
English Heritage grade II

Snape Cottage

BOURTON SP8 5BY

Tel & Fax 01747 840330
Website www.snapecottagegarden.co.uk
Location At west end of Bourton, ¼ mile up Chaffeymoor Hill
Opening hours 10.30 am – 5 pm; Wednesdays; April to July, plus September
Admission fee Adults £2; Children free

This small cottage garden is crammed with several thousand plants and organically managed to attract wild life. It is therefore especially inspirational for visitors who garden with plants in a small space. Plant specialities include hellebores, pulmonarias, auriculas, geraniums, dianthus, irises and asters, but perhaps the most impressive collection is of snowdrops (*Galanthus*

Sticky Wicket

BUCKLAND NEWTON, DORCHESTER DT2 7BY

Tel & Fax 01300 345476
Location 11 miles from Dorchester & Sherborne
Opening hours 10.30 am – 8 pm; Thursdays; June to September. Plus 17 June & 19 August for National Gardens Scheme (2 pm – 8 pm)
Admission fee Adults £2.50; Children £1.50

(P) (WC) (&) (⚘) (☕)

Sticky Wicket is a highly original garden and worth revisiting frequently. The owners are both designers and conservationists, and their devotion to ecology guides their garden-making: they understand the need to attract birds, insects and other wild life. Yet it is also one of the most photographed and admired of modern gardens, because of the subtlety and integrity of Pam Lewis's colour combinations. She and her husband began the garden in 1987 but the plantings are constantly reworked, so that you find new compositions and combinations every year. Berrying trees and shrubs and those with interesting winter stems are supplemented by plants chosen for their scent, decoration and usefulness to wildlife. The planting is increasingly naturalistic and draws upon a choice of native British plants. There are four principal wildlife gardens: the Frog and Bird gardens where ponds, bird baths, nesting boxes and feeders are thickly incorporated into the design, to attract wildlife close to the house where they can be seen; the beautiful Round Garden, whose colours move from pastel tints to richer hues and back again, but where the plants are chosen for the nectar and pollen they offer to insects; and the new White Garden, where ornamental grasses and flowers in loosely planted borders echo the colours of the meadows beyond.

Plant Highlights Wide collection of interesting plants; strong ecological interest; made since 1987; good colour associations.

Owned by Peter & Pam Lewis
Size 2½ acres

species and cultivars) – over 300 different ones.

Owned by Mrs A Whitfield
Number of gardeners 1
Size ½ acre

Stapehill Abbey

STAPEHILL, WIMBORNE BH21 2EB

Tel 01202 861686   **Fax** 01202 894589
Location Signed from A31
Opening hours Not known as we went to press. In 2000 the garden was open 10 am – 5 pm; daily; Easter to September. Plus 10 am – 4 pm; Wednesday – Sunday; October to December
Admission fee Adults £7; OAPs £6.50; Children £4.50 (2000 prices)

A modern leisure development with vintage tractors to admire and lots of plants to sell. The design is rather unco-ordinated but the individual gardens are richly planted and there are some handsome features: a small rose garden, a laburnum pergola, a watergarden, a small tropical house and an extensive rock garden, more noteworthy for its design and size than for its plantings. Not a botanical collection, but a good horticultural one.

Owned by Stapehill Enterprises Ltd

Trehane Camellia Nursery

STAPEHILL ROAD, HAMPRESTON, WIMBORNE BH21 7NE

Tel & Fax 01202 873490
Location Between Ferndown & Wimborne, off A31
Opening hours 9 am – 4 pm; Monday – Friday; all year. 10 am – 4.30 pm; Saturdays & Sundays; late February to end May or by appointment

Wholesale and retail camellia growers. They have a wide choice of *Camellia* hybrids, plus a good range of magnolias, pieris, rhododendrons and blueberries.

Co Durham

Durham is too often – and wrongly – considered a horticultural wasteland, though it is true that when Viscount Ridley advised the society in the 1980s, the Royal Horticultural Society had fewer members in Durham than any other English county – less than one hundred. Things have come a long way since then. English Heritage has drawn attention to the importance of historic landscapes like Raby Castle and the Bowes Museum, and there are now five National Collections in the county – the same number as Lancashire and Hertfordshire. Horn's Garden Centre at Shotton Colliery has the National Collection of coleus (*Solenostemon* cvs.) and a large collection of *Streptocarpus* and pelargoniums too. The city of Durham itself has two outstandingly good gardens for learning about plants – the University of Durham Botanic Garden and the gardens attached to Houghall College, a RHS Partner College.

Barningham Park

BARNINGHAM, RICHMOND
DL11 7DW

Tel 01833 621202 **Fax** 01833 621298
Location 10 miles north-west of Scotch Corner off A66
Opening hours 2 pm – 5 pm; 20 May & 3 June. And parties by appointment
Admission fee Adults £2.50; Children free

This early nineteenth-century landscape runs up from the terrace to the old bowling green and down to the skating pond. Humphry Repton had a hand in it. Some Victorian ancestors planted a pinetum, then some keen horticultural Milbanks designed the splendid rock garden and diverted a stream to form cascades and pools through it. Unknown and perhaps underrated.

Owned by Sir Anthony Milbank Bt
Number of gardeners 1
Size 4 acres, plus 60 acres of woodland

The Bowes Museum Garden & Park

BARNARD CASTLE DL12 8NP

Tel 01833 690606 **Fax** 01833 637163
Website www.durham.gov.uk/bowesmuseum
Location ½ mile west of Barnard Castle town
Opening hours Dawn – dusk; daily; all year
Admission fee free

Twenty-one acres of Victorian splendour, now maintained by the trustees as a public amenity. The formal gardens around the fountain are good – a vast oval parterre remade in the French style in 1982 – and mature trees pepper the park. Almost all were planted in the 1870s: some of the conifers are particularly fine.

Owned by Trustees of the Bowes Museum
English Heritage grade II

Houghall

DURHAM DH1 3SG

Tel 0191 386 1351   **Fax** 0191 386 0419
Location Follow A177 from A1 to Durham
Opening hours 12.30 pm – 4.30 pm; daily; all year
Admission fee free

Houghall is a well-run teaching garden, originally attached to the Durham's Horticultural college but now part of an amalgamation of further education colleges called East Durham & Houghall Community College. There is much to see here: a fine arboretum (more than 500 different trees), a young pinetum, good displays of perennial plants and shrubs (one of the best in northern England), and a wildflower meadow for summer interest. Many trials are conducted here, for example on the hardiness of fuchsias: the garden staff say that 'if it grows at Houghall it will grow anywhere'.

Plant Highlights Roses (mainly modern); rock garden; plants under glass; good herbaceous borders; fine collection of trees; alpine plants; heathers; hardy fuchsias; seasonal bedding; excellent young pinetum.

Owned by Durham College of Agriculture & Horticulture
NCCPG National Collections Sorbus; Meconopsis

University of Durham Botanic Garden

HOLLINGSIDE LANE, DURHAM
DH1 3TN

Tel 0191 374 7971   **Fax** 0191 374 7478
Website www.durham.ac.uk
Location In the south of the City of Durham
Opening hours 10 am – 5 pm; daily; March to October.
9 am – 4 pm; daily; November to February

Admission fee Adults £1.50; Concessions 50p

Moved to its present site in 1970, this garden impresses with its youthful energy. The new 'American arboretum' was planted to copy natural associations fifteen years ago. A woodland garden dates from 1988, a wetland one from 1989, and 1992 saw the opening of the 'Prince Bishop's Garden' with statues transferred from the Gateshead garden festival.

Plant Highlights Roses (mainly old-fashioned); fine collection of trees; New Zealand plants; primulas; meconopsis; autumn colour; woodland plants; sculpture by Ian Hamilton Findlay.

Owned by University of Durham
Number of gardeners 3, plus volunteers

Westholme Hall

WINSTON, DARLINGTON DL2 3QL

Tel 01325 730442   **Fax** 01325 730946
Location On B6274 north towards Staindrop
Opening hours 2 pm – 6 pm; 20 May, 1 July & 26 August
Admission fee Adults £2; Children 50p

Westholme has five acres of late-Victorian gardens, recently restored and revived, around a beautiful Jacobean house. They were designed and planted for all seasons: parts are for spring display (bulbs and azaleas), and other for summer (roses and lilacs) and autumn (herbaceous borders). All is maintained by the owners' own hard work and enthusiasm. The garden is worth a long detour to see: would that it were open more often.

Owned by Mrs J H McBain
Number of gardeners owners only
Size 5 acres

ESSEX

Considering its proximity to London, where fortunes have for centuries been made and spent on country houses, Essex has few famous historic gardens: Audley End is the pre-eminent exception, and as important horticulturally as historically. It is the county's only Grade I garden. Few of the county's other historic gardens are open to the public. Essex's most famous gardener was Miss Ellen Willmott of Warley Place, Great Warley, but her house was demolished shortly after her death in 1934 and the garden (what remains of it) is now a nature reserve: arrangements to visit is made be made through Essex Wildlife Trust. It has one of Essex's few record trees, an *Umbellularia californica* 20 metres high. Low rainfall and hot summers define Essex gardening: Beth Chatto has made a study of dry gardening at her nursery near Elmstead Market. Other nurseries of exceptional interest to keen plantsmen are Glen Chantry and Langthorns Plantery. The National Gardens Scheme has a fair number of gardens opening for the Yellow Book, most of them medium-sized and good for seeing plants. There are about a dozen National Collections in the county. Writtle College near Chelmsford is a RHS Partner College, with lectures and workshops on a wide range of hands-on topics throughout the year. The garden at Hyde Hall is an interesting recent acquisition for the Royal Horticultural Society.

Amberden Hall

WIDDINGTON, SAFFRON WALDON
CB11 3ST

Tel & Fax 01799 540402
Location In Amberden, turn down Cornells Lane: house is 1 mile along
Opening hours By appointment only
Admission fee £3

This much praised modern garden around a handsome old house is open only by appointment at the moment. The single-colour borders contain a wide range of unusual plants and a fine collection of

climbing plants backed by attractive old walls.

Owned by Mr & Mrs David Lloyd
Number of gardeners ½

Audley End

SAFFRON WALDEN CB11 4JF

Tel 01799 522842/520052   **Fax** 01799 522131
Location On B1383, 1 mile west of Saffron Walden
Opening hours Garden: 11 am – 6 pm; Wednesday – Sunday, plus Bank Holiday Mondays; April to September
Admission fee Gardens: Adults £4; OAPs £3; Children £2

Beth Chatto Gardens

ELMSTEAD MARKET, COLCHESTER CO7 7DB

Tel 01206 822007   **Fax** 01206 825933
Location 7 miles east of Colchester
Opening hours 9 am – 5 pm; Monday – Saturday; March
to October; 9 am – 4 pm; Monday – Friday; November to
February. Closed on Bank Holidays
Admission fee Adults £3; Children free

Beth Chatto's garden is a superb example of modern planting, with a very wide range of different plants to see and study, and all chosen for their foliage as much as their flowers. There are two main types of planting here and it is the contrast between them which makes the garden. First there are the parts on dry gravelly soil, where Mediterranean plants flourish; second, there are the water- and bog-gardens on clay. All have been made since 1960. Around the modest house, where the soil is thin and dry, Beth Chatto planted a Mediterranean garden: cistus, *Cytisus battandieri*, salvias, euphorbias, potentillas, verbascums and a tree-like *Genista aetnensis* have come together on the warm slopes. A short walk leads down to a water-garden of remarkable luxuriance, made by damming a damp ditch to create a series of ponds in the valley. The lush and clumpy plantings are quite untypical of Essex, where rainfall averages 20in a year. Here are gunneras, astilbes, lysichitons, hostas, phormiums, water-irises, *Rheum palmatum* and the ostrich fern *Matteuccia struthiopteris*. They have a continuous background, not too intrusive, of conifers, specimen trees and shrubs – but the emphasis throughout the garden is on the herbaceous plants for which the adjoining nursery is famous. A copse has been developed as woodland garden: a canopy of young oaks underplanted with shade-lovers. Here, and in the long shady border above the water garden, are rich plantings of bulbs, woodlanders and ground-cover – aconites, cyclamen, erythroniums and dicentras. The most recent development is the gravel garden, made in 1992 on the site of the old car park, where drought-resistant sun-lovers appear to have been planted straight into gravel in a fluid sequence of island beds. But garden-making is only one of Beth Chatto's gifts: her writings and nursery have made her famous. And the standard of maintenance is impeccable.

Owned by Beth Chatto

Capability Brown landscaped the park (rather too many Canada geese) but the recent excitement at Audley End has been the rejuvenation of the formal garden behind the house. This dates from the 1830s and has 170 geometric flower beds crisply cut from the turf and planted with simple perennials for late summer effect. Work continues: the kitchen garden is now run as a joint venture with HDRA as a working organic garden. It now looks much as it would have done in late Victorian times with vegetables, fruit, herbs and flowers to supply the household. The cultivation is, of course, entirely organic. The vinehouse is one of the earliest and largest in the country, with vines nearly 200 years old.

Owned by English Heritage
English Heritage grade I

County Park Nursery

384 WINGLETYE LANE, HORNCHURCH RM11 3BU

Tel 01708 445205
Location 2½ miles from M25, Jct29. Off Wingletye Lane, in Essex Gardens, Hornchurch
Opening hours 9 am – 6 pm, Monday – Saturday; 10 am – 5 pm, Sundays; from March to October. Closed Wednesdays. Open in winter by appointment only

This small nursery specialises in Antipodean plants, many of them grown from native seed and not available from any other nursery in the UK. There is no show garden to speak of, but every tiny corner seems covered in pots of unusual plants. There are lots of hebes and parahebes, as well as New Zealand *Clematis* species, *Coprosma* and other shrubs like leptospermums. They also have a long list of podocarpus cultivars, selected by themselves for their spreading

habit and unusual leaf colours. Very interesting.

NCCPG National Collections *Coprosma*; *Parahebe*

Easton Lodge

WARWICK HOUSE, GREAT DUNMOW CM6 2BB

Tel & Fax 01371 876979
Location Signed from A120 at Great Dunmow
Opening hours 12 noon – dusk; daily; February to early March (ring for exact dates) for snowdrops. Then 12 noon – 6 pm; Friday – Sunday & Bank Holiday Mondays; Easter to October
Admission fee Adults £3.80; OAPs £3.50; Children £1.50

The garden was laid out by Harold Peto in 1902 for the Countess of Warwick (Edward VII's 'darling Daisy'), fell into to serious neglect, and has been wonderfully restored since 1993. Much remains to be done, as the owner is the first to admit, but the Lime Grove has now been cleared and the Peto shrubbery was rejuvenated last winter. This summer the paving in the Italian garden will be re-laid.

Owned by Brian Creasey

The Gibberd Garden

MARSH LANE, GILDEN WAY, HARLOW CM17 0NA

Tel 01279 442112
Location Leave Harlow on B183. Marsh Lane is on left
Opening hours 2 pm – 6 pm; Saturdays, Sundays & Bank Holidays; April to September
Admission fee Adults £3; Concessions £2; Children free

Glen Chantry

ISHAMS CHASE, WICKHAM BISHOPS CM8 3LG

Tel & Fax 01621 891342
Location Turn off B1019 just south of A12 towards
Wickham: immediately left after bridge & up track ½ mile
Opening hours 10 am – 4 pm; Fridays & Saturdays; 6 April
to 6 October
Admission fee Adults £2; Children 50p

This remarkable garden has been made from a bare hillside since 1976: the owners have an excellent eye for good plants and for how to use them. You enter past a very pretty new *potager* and through the immaculately tidy nursery, itself a plantsman's treasure-house for alpine and herbaceous plants. Then you step down into the garden, filled with endless micro-habitats, some exploiting the opportunities offered by dry, stony acid soil, and other defying it. Scree beds, peat beds, raised beds and an artificial stream are part of the story, but so is a winding pattern of ebbing and flowing island beds. Along the centre of these beds are trees and shrubs which screen the two faces from each other and make it possible to plant both sides of a path with the same colour. The owners also practice 'vertical planting', which means that season after season different displays are possible from the same patch: in one small area, for example, the spring-flowering fritillaries, erythroniums and corydalis are covered in summer by hostas, grasses and rushes. Glen Chantry is a model of what devoted plantsmanship can achieve: educational, functional and beautiful all at once. There is one formal garden near the house, white and green in summer with 'Yvonne Rabier' and 'Iceberg' roses, campanulas, lilies, eryngiums, alliums and geraniums, but the rest of the garden is fluid, however

disciplined may be the controlling hand. In fact, very little seeding around is allowed – perhaps a few plants of Martyn Rix's form of *Eryngium* 'Silver Ghost' – because the planting is intended to slow you down and stop you on your way, to admire individual plants. Besides, the standards of maintenance are immaculate.

Owned by Sue & Wol Staines
Number of gardeners owners
Size 2½ acres

This was the private garden of Sir Frederick Gibberd, the master planner of Harlow New Town. It was designed as a series of distinct rooms, and filled with sculpture, pots and architectural salvage. One of the most important architectural gardens of the twentieth century, it is being restored with aid from the Heritage Lottery Commission. There is an active Friends Organisation: details from Ken Collins on 01279 726047.

Owned by Gibberd Garden Trust
Number of gardeners 3 part-time plus volunteers
Size 7 acres

Langthorns Plantery

LITTLE CANFIELD, DUNMOW
CM6 1TD

Tel & Fax 01371 872611
Location Between Takeley & Great Dunmow, signed off A120
Opening hours 10 am – 5 pm; daily. Closed Christmas to New Year

Langthorns Plantery is a go-ahead modern nursery with an eye for good plants. Though best known for their wide range of hardy herbaceous plants, the owners apply their discriminating taste to all their stock – alpines, shrubs, trees and climbers, especially clematis. The garden is worth a visit in its own right but not always open, so check before you visit.

Olivers

OLIVERS LANE, COLCHESTER
CO2 0HJ

Tel 01206 330575   **Fax** 01206 330366
Location 3 miles south-west of Colchester between B1022 & B1026

Opening hours 2 pm – 6 pm; 6 & 7 May, and 5 August. And by appointment
Admission fee Adults £2; Children free

Quite a modern garden, started in 1968 around three small lakes, with an eye-catching walk to one side leading down to a statue of Bacchus. Good plants and planting everywhere, from the parterres by the house to the woodland where roses and rhododendrons flourish. The main borders underwent a highly successful major re-design in 1998 and are looking very good now. This is the garden of enthusiastic and energetic owners: an inspiration.

Owned by Mr & Mrs David Edwards
Number of gardeners 1

Rhodes & Rockliffe

2 NURSERY ROAD, NAZEING EN9 2JE

Tel 01992 463693   **Fax** 01992 440673
Location ½ mile west of Lower Nazeing along B194; turn right into Nursery Road
Opening hours By appointment only

David Rhodes and John Rockliffe have the finest collection of *Begonia* species and hybrids in Britain. Their occasional exhibits at Chelsea and other RHS flower shows have contributed immensely to popularising the genus in recent years. Their knowledge of begonias is prodigious – as are the size of their collection and the vigour of their plants.

NCCPG National Collections *Begonia*

RHS Garden Hyde Hall

RETTENDON, CHELMSFORD CM3 8ET

Tel 01245 400256 **Fax** 01245 401363
Location 6 miles south-east of Chelmsford, signed
from A130
Opening hours 11 am – 6 pm (5 pm in September &
October); daily; 31 March to 28 October
Admission fee Adults £3; Children (6 – 16) £1; Groups
(10+) £2.50. RHS members free

From the original six trees on a windy hill
with beautiful views to the delightful and
imaginatively planted garden of today, Hyde
Hall is the result of 40 years of dedication,
endeavour and inspiration. Home to the
National Collection of *Viburnum*, the
garden has also become well-known as a
plantsman's garden and for its superb
collection of roses. There is a particularly
good collection of modern roses from the
1970s – cultivars like 'City of Leicester' and
'Gardeners' Sunday' which are no longer
available commercially. But both modern
and old-fashioned roses are displayed here
in a new rose garden designed by Robin
Williams and completed in 2000, together
with a large number of climbers and
ramblers, many of which are pruned and
trained in interesting and unusual styles.
The sheltered woodland garden on the
northern side is a triumph of cultivation and
there are interesting examples of hardiness
throughout: *Eriobotrya japonica*, *Eucalyptus
urnigera* and *Pittosporum tenuifolium* are
grown in the open, *Buddleja officinalis* and
Crinodendron patagua against a wall of the
yard and *Feijoa sellowiana* against the house.
Hyde Hall was donated to the Society in
1993 and much work has been carried out.
The new Entrance Garden, with its
distinctive oak pergola and water feature
was extended in spring 1999 with new
plantings around the Upper Pond and Hyde

Hall Farmhouse. The long herbaceous
border has been reworked – backed by new
shelter hedges of yew and tongues of yew
which divide the border into bays. In spring,
there is a delightful mix of bulbs and
blossom throughout the garden, particularly
in the old stable-yard and Hermione's
Garden, and towards the end of the year
colour is provided in large part by
viburnums and crab apples, both of which
are particularly noted for their autumn
foliage and fruit.

Owned by Royal Horticultural Society
Number of gardeners 7, plus student(s)
Size 24 acres
NCCPG National Collections *Viburnum*

Saling Hall

GREAT SALING, BRAINTREE
CM7 5DT

Location 2 miles north of the Saling Oak on A120
Opening hours 2 pm – 5 pm; Wednesdays; May,
June & July. Plus 2 pm – 6 pm on 17 June. Groups
by appointment on weekdays
Admission fee Adults £2.50 (for National Gardens
Scheme); Children free

A thinking man's garden, Saling also
provokes thought in its visitors. The
plantsmanship is impressive, particularly the
choice and placing of trees and shrubs. Few
modern gardens are conceived on such a
scale, or mix classical and Japanese elements
so smoothly. The moods, and the lessons,
are endless.

Owned by Mr & Mrs Hugh Johnson
Size 12 acres
English Heritage grade II

GLOUCESTERSHIRE

Gloucestershire is rich in nurseries and large important gardens. Six of its nine Grade I historic gardens (a remarkable number for one county) are regularly open to the public – Batsford Park, Frampton Court, Hidcote Manor, Sezincote, Stanway House, and Westonbirt Arboretum – while a seventh, Stancombe Park, is open by appointment. Almost all the county's Grade II* gardens also welcome visitors, including Abbotswood, Berkeley Castle, Kiftsgate Court, Miserden Park, Painswick House, Rodmarton Manor, Sudeley Castle and Westbury Court. Most have important collections of plants as well as attractive design features. Indeed, almost all Gloucestershire's leading historic gardens have been graded highly precisely because of their horticultural attractions. Rich clay soils account for some of the popularity of gardening in Gloucestershire, though the inland, upland parts of the county can be very cold in winter. Among gardens centres and nurseries, the Batsford Garden Centre has a very good general range and makes a speciality of ferns, while Hunt's Court is excellent for roses of every kind. A very large number of gardens open for the National Gardens Scheme though, slightly confusingly, the southern part of the county which used to belong to Avon, is still separately organised: both continue to be very successful in persuading garden-owners to open their gardens and visitors to visit them. Permission to visit HRH The Prince of Wales's garden at Highgrove House near Tetbury may be given to garden clubs and similar organisations. In addition to the world-famous Westonbirt Arboretum, there are important collections of trees at Highnam Court, Batsford Park, and Tortworth Court: the latter is due to open as a luxury hotel in May 2001.

Abbotswood

STOW-ON-THE-WOLD, CHELTENHAM
GL54 1LE

Tel 01451 830173
Location 1 mile west of Stow-on-the-Wold
Opening hours 1.30 pm – 6 pm; 1 & 15 April,
13 & 27 May, and 10 June

Admission fee Adults £2; Children free

One of the most interesting gardens in the Cotswolds. Handsome formal gardens in front of the house: very Lutyens, very photogenic. A magnificent rock garden with a stream which meanders through alpine meadows, bogs and moraines, past dwarf azaleas, primulas, lysichitons, heaths and heathers until it disappears again. There is also a small arboretum, with some unusual cultivars dating from about 100 years ago, fascinating to browse around: it is being cleared and replanted. The kitchen garden is worth the half-mile walk on the occasions when it too is open.

Owned by Dikler Farming Co
Size 20 acres
English Heritage grade II*

Barnsley House Garden

BARNSLEY, CIRENCESTER GL7 5EE

Tel 01285 740561 **Fax** 01285 740628
Location On B4425 in Barnsley village
Opening hours 10 am – 5.30 pm; Mondays, plus Wednesday – Saturday; February to Christmas. Parties by appointment only
Admission fee Adults £3.75; OAPs £3; Children free

Rosemary Verey's own garden: compact, modern, much copying and much copied. Barnsley is interesting at all seasons, but best when the little laburnum walk and the purple alliums underneath are in flower together. Influential and, according to Charles Verey, more intimate than many anticipate.

Owned by Mr & Mrs Charles Verey
Number of gardeners 2½
Size 5½ acres

Batsford Arboretum

THE ESTATE OFFICE,
MORETON-IN-MARSH GL56 9QF

Tel 01386 701441 **Fax** 01386 701329
Website www.batsford-arboretum.co.uk
Location Off A44 between Moreton-in-Marsh & Bourton-on-the-Hill
Opening hours 10 am – 5 pm; daily; 1 March to mid-November. Last admissions 4.30 pm
Admission fee Adults £4; OAPs £3; Children £1

Batsford has an openness which makes its hillside a joy to wander through, passing from one dendrological marvel to the next. Begun in the 1880s, the Arboretum also has several oriental curiosities brought from Japan by Lord Redesdale – a large bronze Buddha and an oriental rest-house for instance. But the arboretum is mainly the work of the late Lord Dulverton, who added a large number of new plantings between 1956 and 1992. These include nearly 100 different magnolia cultivars, a comprehensive collection of Japanese cherries, some very beautiful conifers, and excellent collections of such genera as *Acer*, *Betula* and *Sorbus*. Some are already record-breakers: all are in the prime of their life, well-grown and vigorous. The underplantings of spring bulbs are worth seeing, but visit Batsford at any season and you will find much to admire and enjoy.

Plant Highlights Mature conifers; fine collection of trees; bluebells; maple glade; tallest *Betula platyphylla* (19m) in the British Isles (and 12 other tree records).

Owned by The Batsford Foundation (a Registered Charity)
Number of gardeners 3
Size 55 acres
English Heritage grade I

Berkeley Castle

BERKELEY GL13 9BQ

Tel 01453 810332
Location Off A38
Opening hours 2 pm – 5 pm; Tuesday – Sunday;
April & May. 11 am – 5 pm, Tuesday – Saturday; also
2 pm – 5 pm, Sundays; May to September. Plus Mondays
in July & August. 2 pm – 4.30 pm; Sundays; October.
11 am – 5 pm; Bank Holiday Mondays
Admission fee Garden only: Adults £2; Children £1

The grim battlements of Berkeley Castle are
host to an extensive collection of tender
plants. On three terraces are *Cestrum, Cistus*
and *Rosa banksiae* among hundreds of plant
varieties introduced by the owner's
grandmother, a sister of Ellen Willmott. An
Elizabethan-style bowling green and a
water-lily pond fit well into the overall
scheme.

Owned by R J G Berkeley
English Heritage grade II*

Bourton House

BOURTON-ON-THE-HILL,
MORETON-IN-MARSH GL56 9AE

Tel 01386 700121   **Fax** 01386 701081
Location On A44, 1½ miles west of Moreton-in-Marsh
Opening hours 10 am – 5 pm; Thursdays & Fridays;
25 May to 20 October, plus 27 & 28 May, 26 & 27 August
Admission fee Adults £3.50; Children free

First laid out by Lanning Roper in the 1960s,
but consistently improved by the present
owners, the gardens at Bourton House are
both fashionable and a delight. They include
a knot garden, a small *potager*, a raised
pond, the topiary walk, trellis work, a
croquet lawn, and borders bulging with

good colour schemes – purple-leaved
prunus with yellow roses, for instance.

Owned by Mr & Mrs Richard Paice
Number of gardeners 2, plus 3 part-time
Size 3 acres
English Heritage grade II

Dyrham Park

CHIPPENHAM SN14 8ER

Tel 0117 937 2501
Website www.nationaltrust.org.uk
Location On A46, 8 miles north of Bath
Opening hours 11 am – 5.30 pm; Friday – Tuesday;
31 March to 4 November. Closed 6 – 9 July
Admission fee Garden only £3; Children £1.50

Dyrham is fascinating for garden historians,
who can study the Kip plan and trace the
lines of the seventeenth-century formal
garden which Humphry Repton turned into
classic English parkland. It is not a Mecca for
the dedicated plantsman, but the impressive
orangery is full of colour and scent.

Owned by The National Trust
English Heritage grade II*

Ernest Wilson Memorial Garden

HIGH STREET, CHIPPING CAMPDEN
GL55 6AF

Tel 01386 841298
Location North end of Main Street
Opening hours 9 am to dusk; daily, except Christmas
day; all year
Admission fee Donations invited

A collection of plants all introduced by Ernest H. Wilson, the greatest of European plant hunters in China: Chipping Campden was his birthplace. *Acer griseum, Clematis montana* var. *rubens* and the pocket-handkerchief tree (*Davidia involucrata*) are among his best-known introductions: all are represented here.

Owned by Chipping Campden Town Council
Number of gardeners 1
Size ¼ acre

Frampton Court

FRAMPTON-ON-SEVERN GL2 7EU

Tel 01452 740267   **Fax** 01452 740698
Location Signed to Frampton-on-Severn from M5 Jct13 (3 miles)
Opening hours By appointment all year
Admission fee House & garden £4.50; Garden £1

Beautiful and mysterious garden, little changed since 1750. The Dutch water garden – a long rectangular pool – reflects the orangery of Strawberry Hill Gothic design. But do also ask to see the collection of botanical water colours known as the Frampton Flora.

Owned by Mrs Peter Clifford
Number of gardeners 1½
English Heritage grade I

Goldney Hall

LOWER CLIFTON HILL, CLIFTON, BRISTOL BS8 1BH

Tel 0117 903 4873   **Fax** 0117 903 4877
Location Top of Constitution Hill: entrance on Lower Clifton Hill
Opening hours 2 pm – 6 pm; 29 April and probably again in August (ring for dates)

Admission fee Adults £2; Concessions £1

A Bristol merchant's extravagance, nearly 300 years ago. Ten acres in the middle of the City, with an elegant orangery, a gothic folly tower and the gorgeous Goldney Grotto, which sparkles with crystalline rocks among the shells and follies, and in which the *Chronicles of Narnia* were filmed.

 Plant Highlights Plants under glass; good herbaceous borders; holm oak hedge; many varieties of fruit.

Owned by The University of Bristol
Number of gardeners 6
English Heritage grade II*

Highfield Nurseries

SCHOOL LANE, WHITMINSTER, GLOUCESTER GL2 7PL

Tel 01452 740266   **Fax** 01452 740750
Location Off A38, ½ mile from M5, Jct13
Opening hours 9 am – 4 pm, Monday – Friday. Closed Saturdays and Sundays

Highfield is a large nursery, specialising in fruit trees and bushes: it offers a good choice of the best and most reliable cultivars. It also has a good list of roses, ornamental trees, shrubs and herbaceous plants – something for everyone, in fact.

Highnam Court

HIGHNAM, GLOUCESTER GL2 8DP

Tel 01452 511303   **Fax** 01452 308251
Location Entrance on A40 roundabout
Opening hours 11 am – 5 pm; first Sunday of the month; April to September

Hidcote Manor

HIDCOTE BARTRIM, CHIPPING CAMPDEN GL55 6LR

Tel 01386 438333   **Fax** 01386 438817
Website www.nationaltrust.org.uk
Location Signed from B4632, Stratford/Broadway Road
Opening hours 11 am – 6.30 pm (5.30 pm in October
& November); daily except Tuesday & Friday; 31 March
to 4 November. Plus Tuesdays in June & July, and Good
Friday. Last admission one hour before closing
Admission fee Adults £5.70; Children £2.80. RHS
members free from April to October

(P) (WC) (占) (苗) (曲) (ₒ)

One of England's great gardens, Hidcote is an arts-and-crafts masterpiece created by the American plant-collector Major Lawrence Johnston. It was designed as a series of outdoor rooms, each with a different character and separated by walls and hedges of many different species. Hidcote therefore has a firm architectural structure – many of Lawrence Johnston's ideas came from France and Italy – combined with a great love of plants. The planting is exuberant but always considers the contrasts and harmonies which can be obtained by planting different things together. Some of the rooms are very small, like Mrs Winthrop's garden – no more than a courtyard with a potted cordyline at the centre – and others like the long walk and the great lawn give a great sense of space – though in fact the garden is no more than ten acres in size. Among the most famous features are: the mixed borders down the middle of the kitchen garden richly planted with old roses and companion plants; the red borders, which were one of the first single-colour borders in the country when first planted in 1913; the cottage garden, planted like an Edwardian flower painting where *Campanula latiloba* 'Hidcote Amethyst' is prominent; the sunken garden

where a huge circular swimming pool fills a hedged compartment; and the woodland area known as Westonbirt where Johnston planted long vistas which run from end to end, but which disappear and reappear as you follow the paths back and forth. The National Trust has just begun a programme of renewal and regeneration and it fair to say that Hidcote is now looking better than ever.

 Plant Highlights Woodland garden; topiary; roses (ancient & modern); rock garden; plantsman's collection of plants; good herbaceous borders; tallest pink acacia *Robinia × ambigua* 'Decaisneana' (19m) in the British Isles.

Owned by The National Trust
NCCPG National Collections *Paeonia*
English Heritage grade I

Admission fee Adults £2.50; Children free

Little remains of the original Highnam, laid out when the house was built in 1658. The garden was however very famous 100 years ago for the features designed or commissioned by Thomas Gambier-Perry in the middle of the nineteenth century: the terraces, the broad walk, the arboretum and, above all, the winter garden where natural stone is supplemented by Pulhamite – the largest and earliest surviving example of the artificial stone from which the rock garden at Wisley is also made. The estate was neglected for nearly 100 years, but restoration – slow and painstaking – began in 1994, so this is a garden to watch and revisit as the work continues.

Owned by Roger Head
Number of gardeners 2
Size 30 acres
English Heritage grade II*

Hodges Barn

Shipton Moyne, Tetbury GL8 8PR

Tel 01666 880202   **Fax** 01666 880373
Location 3 miles south of Tetbury on Malmesbury Road from Shipton Moyne
Opening hours 2 pm – 6 pm; 8 & 9 April, 13 & 14 May & 10 & 11 June. Plus 10 am – 5 pm; 2, 3 & 6 July
Admission fee Adults £3; Children free

This is a large garden – six acres surrounding a converted fifteenth-century columbarium – all intensively planted. The terraces, courtyards and gardens are divided into rooms (surrounded either by walls or by tapestry, laurel or yew hedges) to give year-round colour. Old-fashioned rose beds are underplanted with tulips for spring and with alliums and campanulas for summer.

There is a formal herbaceous border, a water garden and a swimming pool area with large planted pots. Shrub roses and climbers are another Hornby passion and are to be found winding up walls and trees. The plantings reflect a desire to create an informal feeling within a formal framework. The woodland garden is almost an arboretum of ornamental trees (especially birches, maples, whitebeams and many different magnolias), underplanted with spring bulbs. In summer the grass is left long in the wood and wildflowers are encouraged to naturalise. Hodges Barn is a garden of great energy and diversity.

Owned by Mrs Charles Hornby
Number of gardeners 2 part-time
Size 6 acres

Hunts Court

North Nibley, Dursley GL11 6DZ

Tel 01453 547440   **Fax** 01453 549944
Location Signed in centre of village. Or turn across front of Black Horse pub & bear left for ¼ mile
Opening hours 9 am – 5 pm; Tuesday – Saturday & Bank Holiday Mondays in spring; all year, except August. Also 17 & 24 June, 1 July and 2 & 9 September for National Gardens Scheme
Admission fee Adults £2; OAPs £1.50; Children free; RNRS members free

The garden at Hunts Court has been planted since 1976 by something of a horticultural rarity – a plant-loving farmer, and his wife. Keith and Margaret Marshall say they have 'the collector's touch of madness': the result is a garden which is charming, peaceful and educational. Their first love was old-fashioned roses, and they moved their garden fence out into the surrounding fields as the collection of Gallicas, Damasks and Hybrid Perpetuals began to grow: it is now the best in the west of England, and still expanding. The 450 cultivars include climbers, species and a few modern shrub roses. Many are underplanted by the Marshalls' next great passion – hardy geraniums and penstemons, each of which is represented by over 100 cultivars. The fence has been moved out several times now to accommodate a large collection of ornamental trees and shrubs, underplanted in turn by more unusual herbaceous plants. These are the stock plants for the thriving nursery they now run in their old stock-yard. It is surrounded by a fine plantsman's garden with something for all seasons, including good autumn colour and winter-flowering shrubs. But the Marshalls have just moved the fence again – to plant a mini-arboretum.

Owned by T K & M M Marshall
Number of gardeners 1
Size 2½ acres

Just Phlomis

SUNNINGDALE, GRANGE COURT, WESTBURY ON SEVERN GL14 1PL

Tel & Fax 01452 760268
Location 600 yards east of Northwood Green, on the left-hand side
Opening hours By appointment

The list of *Phlomis* from the National Collection holder is short by other nurseries' standards, but remarkably long for the interested plantsman – nearly 30 species and cultivars. Some are herbaceous, like the sturdy and reliable *Phlomis russeliana* and *P. tuberosa*, while others are shrubby – the pink *P. italica* will grow to two metres. But there are stunners like *P. bovei* subsp. *maroccana* and little-known species, originally from wild-collected seed, like

P. platystegia from Syria and *P. atropurpurea* from Yunnan.

NCCPG National Collections *Phlomis*

Kiftsgate Court

CHIPPING CAMPDEN GL55 6LW

Tel & Fax 01386 438777
Location 3 miles from Chipping Campden opposite Hidcote Manor
Opening hours 2 pm – 6 pm; Wednesdays, Thursdays, Sundays & Bank Holiday Mondays; April, May, August & September; plus 12 noon – 6 pm on Wednesdays, Thursdays, Saturdays & Sundays in June & July
Admission fee Adults £4: Children £1

Famous for its roses, especially the eponymous *Rosa filipes*, Kiftsgate is all about plants and the use of colour. The best example is the yellow border, where gold and orange are set off by occasional blues and purples. After some dull years, everything about Kiftsgate has revived again: new thinking, new plantings and new enthusiasm have more than restored its excellence. The latest addition (2000) is in marked contrast to the rest of the garden: the tennis court has been transformed into a contemporary water garden, full of movement and sound, by Simon Allison. Structure and form predominate here over Kiftsgate's traditional themes of colour and texture.

Owned by Mr & Mrs J Chambers
Number of gardeners 2
Size 4 acres
English Heritage grade II*

Lydney Park Gardens

LYDNEY PARK GL15 6BU

Tel 01594 842844   **Fax** 01594 842027
Location Off A48 between Lydney & Aylburton
Opening hours 11 am – 6 pm; Sundays, Wednesdays & Bank Holidays; 25 March to 3 June. Plus daily 15 to 20 April, and 27 May to 1 June
Admission fee £3, but £2 on Wednesdays; Children 50p

A remarkable collection of rhododendrons planted over the last 50 years is the backbone to this extensive woodland garden. And not just rhododendrons, but azaleas and camellias too – all are carefully planted to create distinct effects from March to June. The numbers are still growing, and include plants grown from collected seed and hybrids from distinguished breeders, many as yet unnamed, while others have yet to flower. Lydney is now recognised as one of the best rhododendron gardens in England.

Owned by Viscount Bledisloe

Miserden Park

MISERDEN, STROUD GL6 7JA

Tel 01285 821303   **Fax** 01285 821530
Location Signed from A417, or turn off B4070 between Stroud & Birdlip
Opening hours 9.30 am – 4.30 pm; Tuesday – Thursday; April to September
Admission fee Adults £3

The Cotswold house at Miserden (Jacobean, with a Lutyens addition) has wide views across the Golden Valley, while the spacious peaceful gardens lie to the side. Most were laid out in the 1920s – a charming rose garden, the long yew walk and expansive herbaceous borders – but there is also an older arboretum and an Edwardian shrubbery. In the walled garden near the entrance is a promising young nursery with a stock of interesting herbaceous plants.

Owned by Major M T N H Wills
Number of gardeners 2
Size 12 acres
English Heritage grade II*

Owlpen Manor

ULEY, DURSLEY GL11 5BZ

Tel 01453 860261   **Fax** 01453 860819
Website www.owlpen.com
Location Off B4066 near Uley
Opening hours 2 pm – 5 pm; Tuesday – Sunday & Bank Holiday Mondays; April to September
Admission fee Adults £4.50; Children £2

Owlpen is a dreamy Cotswold manor house whose loveliness depends upon its site. It also has a small terraced garden with box parterres, overgrown topiary yews and plantings of roses and herbs, most of them added since 1980 by the present owners. The aim is to suggest an earlier garden 're-ordered conservatively' in about 1700. Owlpen is perhaps not worth a special journey by keen plantsmen, but the restaurant, the setting and the house all add up to a good place for an outing.

Owned by Nicholas Mander
Number of gardeners 2
Size 2 acres
English Heritage grade II

Painswick Rococo Garden

THE STABLES, PAINSWICK HOUSE, PAINSWICK GL6 6TH

Tel 01452 813204   **Fax** 01452 814888
Website www.rococogarden.co.uk
Location Outside Painswick on B4073
Opening hours 11 am – 5 pm; Wednesday – Sunday;
10 January to 30 November. But daily from May to
September
Admission fee Adults £3.30; OAPs £3; Children £1.60

Only ten years of restoration work lie behind the unique rococo garden at Painswick which has re-emerged from back-to-nature woodland. A white Venetian gothic exedra, a Doric seat, the plunge pool, an octagonal pigeon house, a gothic gazebo called the Eagle House, a bowling green, the fish pond and a gothic alcove have all been reconstructed in their original positions thanks to the efforts of Lord Dickinson and the Painswick Rococo Gardens Trust. A remarkable garden and brilliant theatrical achievement.

Owned by Painswick Rococo Garden Trust
Number of gardeners 4
Size 6 acres
English Heritage grade II*

Rodmarton Manor

RODMARTON, CIRENCESTER GL7 6PF

Tel 01285 841253   **Fax** 01285 841298
Location Off A433 between Cirencester & Tetbury
Opening hours 2 pm – 5 pm; Wednesdays,
Saturdays & Bank Holiday Mondays; 9 May to 29 August
Admission fee Adults £3; Children free

A splendid Arts & Crafts garden, with a strong design and exuberant planting. Simon Biddulph says there are eighteen different areas within the garden, from the trough garden for alpine plants to the famous double herbaceous borders, now entirely renovated, which lead to a Cotswold summerhouse. Highly original – contemporary, but made without any contact, with Hidcote.

Plant Highlights Interesting plants; old-fashioned roses; topiary; much renovation and replanting, including the fine herbaceous borders, white border & wild garden (1998).

Owned by Simon Biddulph
English Heritage grade II*

Sezincote

MORETON-IN-MARSH GL56 9AW

Location On A44 to Evesham, 1½ miles out of
Moreton-in-Marsh
Opening hours 2 pm – 6 pm (or dusk, if earlier);
Thursdays, Fridays & Bank Holiday Mondays; January to
November
Admission fee Adults £3.50; Children £1 (under 5s free)

The house at Sezincote was the model for Brighton Pavilion, and seems inseparable from the cruciform Moghul garden that sets off its Indian façade so well: yet this brilliant formal garden was designed as recently as 1965. On the other side are sumptuous borders planted by Graham Thomas and a luscious water garden of candelabra primulas and astilbes around the Temple to Surya, the Snake Bridge and Brahmin bulls. Humphry Repton had a hand in the original landscape, but the modern gardens are even more satisfying than the classical setting.

Plant Highlights Fine collection of trees; good, bold plantings in the water garden; tallest maidenhair tree *Ginkgo biloba* (26m) in the British Isles and 5 other record trees. These include the blue-leaved noble fir *Abies procera* 'Glauca', the weeping hornbeam *Carpinus betulus* 'Pendula' and the yellow-leaved beech *Fagus sylvatica* 'Zlatia'.

Owned by Mr & Mrs D Peake
Number of gardeners 3
Size 10 acres
English Heritage grade I

Snowshill Manor

BROADWAY WR12 7JU

Tel & Fax 01386 852410
Website www.nationaltrust.org.uk
Location In Snowshill village
Opening hours 11 am – 5.30 pm; Wednesday – Sunday; 31 March to 4 November. Plus Mondays in June & July
Admission fee Gardens only: £3

The garden at Snowshill has often been praised for its changes of levels and collection of curious artefacts – an armillary sphere and a gilt figure of St George and the Dragon, for instance. Snowshill is as curious as its maker, Charles Wade, and the spooky bric-a-brac which fills his house, but many visitors find it 'charming' or 'interesting'. Snowshill was the National Trust's first all-organic garden.

Owned by The National Trust
English Heritage grade II

Special Plants

HILL FARM BARN, GREENWAYS LANE, COLD ASHTON, CHIPPENHAM SN14 8LA

Tel 01225 891686 **Fax** 01225 852528
Location Near Bath, just south of junction of A46 & A420. Not in Cold Ashton
Opening hours 10.30 am – 4 pm; daily; March to September. And by appointment. The garden is open for the National Gardens Scheme from 2 pm to 6 pm on 10 May, 14 June, 12 July, 16 August & 13 September

The collection of hardy plants at this connoisseur's nursery is excellent, but it is for her tender perennials that Derry Watkins's nursery is best known. Diascias, salvias, pelargoniums and streptocarpus are among her top lines, together with conservatory climbers and shrubs. A three-month visit to South Africa has introduced some interesting novelties – both plants and seeds are available. There are also one-day courses at the nursery in autumn. The new garden is open monthly for the National Gardens Scheme and a useful adjunct to the nursery. The Watkins bought a three-acre field in 1996 and have started to lay out about ¾ acre in a fairly modern style – not a single rose or clematis – with springs, ponds, a gravel garden, a 'black & white' garden, tender perennials and wonderful views.

Stancombe Park

DURSLEY GL11 6AU

Tel 01453 542815
Location Off the B4060 between Dursley & Wotton-under-Edge
Opening hours Groups by appointment
Admission fee Adults £3; Children (under 10) £1

Stancombe has everything: a handsome house above a wooded valley, a flower garden of wondrous prettiness, and a gothic horror of an historic Folly Garden at the valley bottom. Start at the top. Peter Coates, Lanning Roper and Nadia Jennett all worked on the rose gardens and mixed borders by the house: there is more to learn about good modern design and planting here than any garden in Gloucestershire. Then wander down the valley where the path narrows and the incline steepens to a ferny tunnel, and start the circuit of the follies, best described as an open-air ghost train journey without the ghosts. Highly recommended.

 Plant Highlights Fine collection of trees; excellent borders; fine spring bulbs; lots of roses; some interesting and unusual plants; temple restored by English Heritage (1998); new bog garden (2000) backed by two sprouting Ms for the millennium.

Owned by Mrs Basil Barlow
English Heritage grade I

Stanway House

STANWAY, CHELTENHAM GL54 5PQ

Tel 01386 584469 **Fax** 01386 584688
Location On B4077
Opening hours 2 pm – 5 pm; Tuesdays & Thursdays; August & September. And groups by appointment
Admission fee Adults £3; OAPs £2.50; Children £1

The important water-gardens are undergoing restoration. A pyramidal folly dominates the hillside behind the house. Repairs have begun on the 170-metre cascade which runs down to a long still tank known as the Canal. On the way up to the top are some interesting trees and shrubs. Worth another visit.

Owned by Lord Neidpath
Number of gardeners 1½
Size 20 acres
English Heritage grade I

Stowell Park

NORTHLEACH GL54 3LE

Tel 01285 720308 **Fax** 01285 720360
Location A429 between Cirencester & Northleach
Opening hours 2 pm – 5 pm; 20 May, 24 June & 9 September
Admission fee Adults £2.50 (£3 is September); Children free

Stowell has an historic landscape in a magnificent position, with terraced gardens and superb traditional walled gardens, stylishly developed and replanted by Lady Vestey with advice from Rosemary Verey of nearby Barnsley.

Owned by Lord Vestey
Number of gardeners 4
Size 8 acres
English Heritage grade II

Sudeley Castle & Gardens

WINCHCOMBE GL54 5JD

Tel 01242 602308 **Fax** 01242 602959
Website www.stratford.co.uk/sudeley
Location 8 miles north-east of Cheltenham B4632
Opening hours 10.30 am – 5.30 pm; daily; 3 March to 28 October
Admission fee Adults £4.70; OAPs £3.70; Children £2.50

This large commercially-run garden has features by many top garden designers: Jane

Fearnley-Whittingstall did the roses and Rosemary Verey planted some borders. There are fine old trees, magnificent Victorian topiary (mounds of green and gold yew) and a raised walk around the pleasure gardens that may be Elizabethan in origin. Popular and successful.

 Plant Highlights Topiary; roses (ancient & modern); herbs; mature conifers; good herbaceous borders; ruins of banqueting hall, now a pretty garden; new 'Victorian' kitchen garden (all organic); new wildflower meadow (2001).

Owned by Lady Ashcombe
Number of gardeners 5
Size 14 acres
English Heritage grade II*

University of Bristol Botanic Garden

BRACKEN HILL, NORTH ROAD, LEIGH WOODS, BRISTOL BS8 3PF

Tel 0117 973 3682   **Fax** 0117 973 3682
Location Take M5 Jct19 towards Clifton, left into North Road before suspension bridge
Opening hours 9 am – 5 pm; Monday – Friday; all year except public holidays. Plus 10 am – 5 pm on 24 June & 2 September for the National Gardens Scheme
Admission fee Free, except when open for National Gardens Scheme

Ⓟ ⓦⓒ 🌱 🏛

This is an educational and accessible garden that bridges the gap between botany and horticulture. The unusual climatic conditions in its position high above the river Avon have made possible some fine new plantings of South African and New Zealand plants. The collection of *Aeonium* is the most comprehensive in the UK, and the collections of *Pelargonium* species and Central American *Salvia* species are also very

good. The rare endemic *Sorbus bristoliensis* grows in a part of the garden dedicated to the flora of the Clifton Gorge. There is an active Friends groups: winter lectures, summer visits, a seed scheme and a good newsletter – all for £20.

Owned by University of Bristol
Number of gardeners 6½

Westbury Court

WESTBURY-ON-SEVERN GL14 1PD

Tel 01452 760461
Website www.nationaltrust.org.uk
Location 9 miles south-west of Gloucester on A48
Opening hours 10 am – 6 pm, Wednesday – Sunday & Bank Holiday Mondays; 1 March to 28 October.
Daily in July & August
Admission fee Adults £2.90; Children £1.40

Ⓟ ⓦⓒ ♿ 🌱 🍽

Westbury has been restored over the last 20 years to become the best example of a medium-sized seventeenth-century Dutch garden in England. A pretty pavilion, tall and slender, looks down along a long tank of water. On the walls are old apple and pear varieties. Parterres, fine modern topiary and a T-shaped tank with a statue of Neptune in the middle make up the rest of the garden, with an opulent rose garden (old varieties only) underplanted with pinks, tulips and herbs. Immaculately maintained.

Plant Highlights Topiary; roses (mainly old-fashioned); herbs; fruit; good herbaceous borders; biggest holm oak *Quercus ilex* in the British Isles; new restoration of pool & fountain as shown by Kip in 1712.

Owned by The National Trust
English Heritage grade II*

Westonbirt Arboretum

WESTONBIRT, TETBURY GL8 8QS

Tel 01666 880220   **Fax** 01666 880559
Website www.forestry.gov.uk
Location 3 miles south of Tetbury on A433
Opening hours 10 am – 8 pm (or dusk if earlier); daily;
all year. Visitor centre open 10 am – 5 pm; daily; March
to December
Admission fee Adults £4.25; OAPs £3.50; Children £1.
RHS members free. Prices will rise in October 2001

Westonbirt is the finest and largest arboretum in the British Isles: it contains one of the most important collections of trees and shrubs in the world. There are 18,000 of them, representing 4,000 species and cultivars, planted from 1829 to the present day, and covering some 600 acres of beautifully landscaped grounds. The maple glade is famous, and so are the bluebells in the part known as Silk Wood. Magnificent spring displays of rhododendrons, azaleas and magnolias, wild flowers in summer and architectural winter beauty are matched by the spectacular autumn colouring for which Westonbirt is justifiably famous. Westonbirt is also one of the best gardens in England for a winter walk but, with seventeen miles of paths, you can find quiet areas even in the third week of October when the maples are at their most colourful. The arboretum is brilliantly managed by the Forestry Commission, whose Visitor Centre is a marvel of helpfulness.

Plant Highlights 109 species of record-breaking trees, including 24 maples (*Acer* species) and 16 *Sorbus*. Other Champion trees include the red horse chestnut *Aesculus × carnea* at 27 metres; the upright birch *Betula pendula* 'Fastigiata' at

29 metres; the handkerchief tree *Davidia involucrata* at 24 metres; the home-sprung *Pinus × holfordiana* at 36 metres; and the large-leaved deciduous oak *Quercus macranthera* at 31 metres.

Owned by The Forestry Commission
Number of gardeners 8
Size 600 acres
NCCPG National Collections *Acer* (Japanese cvs.); *Salix*
English Heritage grade I

Willow Lodge

L ONGHOPE, G LOUCESTER GL17 0RA

Tel & Fax 01452 831211
Location On A40, 10 miles from Gloucester & 6 miles from Ross-on-Wye: ½ mile west of Dursley Cross
Opening hours 1 pm – 5 pm; 6, 7, 13, 14, 27 and 28 May; 10, 11, 17 & 18 June; 1, 2, 15, 16, 29 & 30 July; 5, 6, 12 & 13 August. And by appointment
Admission fee Adults £2; Children free

This garden has been entirely made by enthusiastic plantsmen since they moved here in 1987. At first they developed just an acre around the house: it remains a good garden of mixed herbaceous and shrubby plantings. Then they started to develop the adjoining field as an arboretum, underplanted with native daffodils and snowdrops. Here are some extremely interesting plants collected on their travels in China and North America – *Sinocalycanthus chinensis* for example, and several *Lespedeza* species. The stream that runs from end to end of the garden has been used to create a bog garden and a pond, alongside a large alpine bed. There is much to enjoy and learn throughout the garden.

Owned by Mr & Mrs J Wood
Number of gardeners 3
Size 4 acres

HAMPSHIRE

For such a prosperous county, Hampshire has comparatively few historic gardens of the highest importance: only Hackwood Park (not open to the public) and Highclere Park (right in the north) are listed as Grade I. But Hampshire compensates with a wealth of twentieth-century plantsman's gardens and nurseries. Indeed, the Sir Harold Hillier Gardens & Arboretum at Ampfield – the world's greatest collection of temperate trees and shrubs – is less than 50 years old and grew out of the commercial activities of Hillier's Nursery. When modern gardens like Exbury, Longstock, Spinners, Longthatch and Meon Orchard are taken into account, and some of the small specialist nurseries like Blackthorn and Langley Boxwood, Hampshire emerges as one of the best places in Europe for plants and gardens, plantsmen and gardeners. The National Gardens Scheme is extremely well represented in the county, with a very large number of gardens (over 160 last year) opening for charity. There are many good gardens which do not open often enough for us to list in this guide: Pylewell Park, Moundsmere Manor and Conholt Park among them. And deep in the New Forest, at Rhinefield, is the best late-Victorian pinetum in southern England. The Hampshire Group of the NCCPG is strong – always a good measure of the interest in gardening with plants – with 24 collection holders responsible for no less than 43 genera. And the Hampshire Gardens Trust, founded more than 20 years ago by the energy and foresight of Gilly Drummond, has been the model for every county-based gardens trust since then. Sparsholt College, between Winchester and Stockbridge, is a RHS Partner College and the venue for five RHS regional lectures in 2001; four RHS special events are also planned for the nursery garden at Spinners.

Apple Court

HORDLE LANE, HORDLE, LYMINGTON SO41 0HU

Tel 01590 642130   **Fax** 01590 694220
Website www.applecourt.com
Location South of New Forest, just north of A337 at Downton crossroads

Opening hours 9.30 am – 1 pm & 2 pm – 5 pm; daily except Wednesdays; March to September
Admission fee Adults £2; Children 50p

The display gardens attached to this hosta and hemerocallis specialist nursery are firmly designed and would be worth a visit even without plants. The white garden is especially original: at its heart is an oval-shaped lawn, surrounded by pleached hornbeams. The white plantings lie *outside* this oval of limes. Elsewhere are about 120 cultivars of *Hosta*, many of them – like the daylilies – bred in USA and offered for sale by Apple Court but by no other UK nursery. There are 120 *Hemerocallis* cultivars too, including spider and other unusual forms. Grasses are a third feature and, here too, the nursery has introduced many from across the Atlantic.

NCCPG National Collections *Hosta* (small leaved); *Rohdea japonica; Woodwardia*

Blackthorn Nursery

KILMESTON, ALRESFORD SO24 0NL

Tel 01962 771796   **Fax** 01962 771071
Location 1 mile south of Cheriton, off A272
Opening hours 9 am – 5 pm; Fridays & Saturdays; March to June

Blackthorn's plants tend to be spring beauties: the nursery's three specialities are hellebores, epimediums and daphnes, all of which they breed, as well as introducing new species. Their most striking hellebores are semi-doubles called 'Party Dress' hybrids. The list of epimediums is the best in England – over 40 different names: their rarities include a large number of collected species like *E. fargesii* Og. 93057 and *E. franchetii* 'Brimstone Beauty' Og. 87001. The daphnes are no less remarkable: over 50 different names, including such little-known hybrids as *D.* × *thauma* and no less than 7 cultivars of *D.* × *hendersonii*. Their general list of alpines and herbaceous plants is equally exciting: they have a covetable and ever-changing selection of good plants. For dedicated plantsmen, a visit to Blackthorn on an open day in February or March is one of social highlights of early spring: every fellow-plantsman in the country seems to be there too.

Bramdean House

BRAMDEAN, ALRESFORD SO24 0JU

Tel 01962 771214   **Fax** 01962 771095
Location On A272, between Winchester & Petersfield
Opening hours 2 pm – 5 pm; 15 April, 13 May, 17 June, 8 July, 12 August, 9 September, and by appointment
Admission fee Adults £2.50; Children free; for National Gardens Scheme. Otherwise Adults £4.

The gardens at Bramdean are much admired, and rightly so. Against a backdrop of mature trees, two wide mirror-image borders lead away from the back of the house. At the end of the central axis, steps lead to a one-acre walled kitchen garden whose central bed is planted with 'Catillac' pears, roses, perennials and bulbs. The vista runs yet further, through an orchard under-planted with massed daffodils to an apple-house some 300 yards from the house. The views in both directions are stunning.

Owned by Mr & Mrs H Wakefield
Number of gardeners 2
Size 6½ acres
English Heritage grade II

Braxton Gardens

BRAXTON COURTYARD, LYMORE LANE, MILFORD-ON-SEA SO41 0TX

Tel 01590 644499   **Fax** 01590 642008
Location South of Everton: follow brown tourist signs in village
Opening hours 10 am – 5 pm; daily; mid-March to October

Brandy Mount House

EAST STREET, ALRESFORD SO24 9EG

Tel 01962 732189
Location Left into East Street from Broad Street, 50 yards first right
Opening hours 11 am – 4 pm; 3, 4 & 7 February.
2 pm – 5 pm; 4 March, 8 April, 6 May, and by appointment
Admission fee Adults £2; Children free

Brandy Mount is the garden of plantsmen – but plantsmen who are also distinguished cultivators and exhibitors of alpine plants. The first surprise is to find quite such a large and secluded garden so near the centre of a busy town. Then you discover that, although the underlying soil is chalky, a great variety of the rarer shade-loving plants thrive in the rich soil under the trees – as well as the snowdrops, for which the garden is famous among galanthophiles. The herbaceous borders in the sunnier parts support many species of geranium, peonies, daphnes and spring-flowering bulbs. The planting of all these areas is informal, with wide sweeps of lawn between the borders. The vegetable area has just been re-organised as a formal *potager* with traditional box hedges and small beds to allow the owners to grow a greater variety of salad crops and more unusual vegetables, interspersed with flowering plants. Alpines have always been a speciality: they flourish around the terrace in front of the house, where there are over thirty kinds of smaller daphnes. Many alpines are also grown in troughs and sinks, which have recently been reorganised as a group and replanted as small crevice gardens. These support many rare and tricky species which are also grown in frames and in the Alpine House. There is a fine collection of European primulas, saxifrages and dwarf narcissi which are also

exhibited from time to time. This garden is fascinating, immaculately maintained, and forever changing, as the collection of rare plants grows ever larger. Strongly recommended.

Owned by Caryl & Michael Baron
Number of gardeners part-time (*very*)
Size 1¼ acres
NCCPG National Collections Daphne; *Galanthus*

Admission fee Free

This is a young garden, attached to a plant centre and farm shop. The main features are a pretty modern knot garden of germander and cotton lavender, and an old farmyard planted with roses and stylish perennials. The owners hope soon to finish a pool garden and re-instate the old parkland. The nursery stocks herbs, alpines, roses and shrubs.

Owned by J D M Aldridge
Number of gardeners 2
Size 1 acre

Broadlands

ROMSEY SO51 9LB

Tel 01794 505010   **Fax** 01794 505040
Website www.broadlands.net
Location On Romsey by-pass by town centre roundabout
Opening hours 12 noon – 5.30 pm (last admissions 4 pm); daily; 11 June to 2 September
Admission fee Adults £5.95; OAPs £4.95; Children (12 – 16) £3.95

Classic Capability Brown landscape, handsome old trees and an open park which runs slowly down to a lake and the River Test. The main horticultural interest comes from the massive taxodiums and plane-trees growing luxuriantly alongside the leat. The house majors on the estate's association with Earl Mountbatten of Burma. The shrub borders rely heavily on *Aegopodium podagraria* for their underplanting.

Plant Highlights Fine trees; tallest swamp cypress *Taxodium distichum* (36m) in the British Isles.

Owned by Lord & Lady Romsey
English Heritage grade II*

Exbury Gardens

EXBURY, SOUTHAMPTON SO4 1AZ

Tel 023 8089 1203   **Fax** 023 8089 9940
Website www.exbury.co.uk
Location 3 miles south of Beaulieu
Opening hours 10 am – 5.30 pm (or dusk if earlier); daily; 24 February to 25 November
Admission fee Adults £3.50; OAPs £3; Children £2.50. But Adults £5; OAPs £4.50; Children £4 in high season (approximately mid-March to mid-June)

Rhododendrons, rhododendrons, rhododendrons: over one million of them in 200 acres of natural woodland. More than 40 have won awards from the Royal Horticultural Society. But there are magnolias, camellias and rare trees too, many grown from the original seed introduced by famous plant collectors. A place of wonder in May. The collection of nerines which Lionel de Rothschild bred between the wars was dispersed after his death but reassembled and developed by Sir Peter Smithers in Switzerland. A few years ago he returned them to Exbury where they may be seen once again in October.

Plant Highlights Good herbaceous borders; candelabra primulas; rare trees; new grasses garden (1998); new camellia walk (1998); rose garden; water garden; daffodils; massive two-acre rock garden; *Nerine* hybrids; tallest shagbark hickory *Carya ovata* (21m) in the British Isles (and five other tree records).

Owned by Edmund de Rothschild
Number of gardeners 8
Size 200 acres
English Heritage grade II*

Fairfield House

HAMBLEDON, WATERLOOVILLE
PO7 4RY

Tel 023 9263 2431
Location East Street, Hambledon
Opening hours 2 pm – 6 pm; 8 April & 17 June, and by appointment
Admission fee Adults £2.50; Children free

Fairfield is one of the best private rose gardens in England. Old roses and climbers were the late Peter Wake's main interest and he grew them unusually well. The shrubs are trained up a cat's cradle of string drawn between five wooden posts. The results make you gasp – 'Charles de Mills' ten feet high.

Owned by Mrs Peter Wake
Number of gardeners 1½
Size 6 acres

Furzey Gardens

MINSTEAD, LYNDHURST SO43 7GL

Tel 023 8081 2464   **Fax** 023 8081 2297
Location Off A31 or A337 to Minstead
Opening hours 10 am – 5 pm (dusk in winter); daily except 25 & 26 December
Admission fee March – October: Adults £3.50; OAPs £2.80; Children £1.50. Reductions in winter

Furzey demonstrates how woodland garden effects can be created in quite small areas. Parts are a maze of narrow curving paths running between hedges of Kurume azaleas, unforgettable in April and May, but the late summer flowering of eucryphias runs them close and the autumn colours of nyssas, parrotias and enkianthus are worth a visit in October.

Owned by Furzey Gardens Charitable Trust
Number of gardeners 2 horticultural instructors with teams of students with learning difficulties
Size 8 acres

Gilbert White's House

HIGH STREET, SELBOURNE, ALTON
GU34 3JH

Tel 01420 511275   **Fax** 01420 511040
Location In centre of Selbourne, on B3006
Opening hours 11 am – 5 pm; daily; 1 January to 24 December
Admission fee Adults £4; OAPs £3.50; £1 Children

The house was bought some years ago, and the museum founded to commemorate the life and work of Gilbert White, author of *The Natural History & Antiquities of Selbourne*. The garden provides a very good example of how a person of modest means might construct a scaled-down landscaped park in the mid-eighteenth century. The orchard and vegetable garden have been restored to the same period and planted with cultivars that White himself knew and wrote about. Lawns, a rose garden, a herb garden and a flower garden complete the idyll.

Owned by Oates Memorial Trust
Number of gardeners 2, plus volunteers
Size 30 acres

Green Farm Plants

BENTLEY, FARNHAM GU10 5JX

Tel 01420 23202
Location Turn north in Bentley, past Jenkyn Place and then another for 1 mile

Opening hours 10 am – 6 pm; Wednesday – Saturday; mid-March to October

This fashionable nursery is full of interesting plants, including the results of recent collecting trips. The main groups are hardy and half-hardy perennials, with an increasing number of woodland plants and sun-loving shrubs. Piet Oudolf's provocative garden is worth a visit in its own right.

Hardy's Cottage Garden Plants

PRIORY LANE, FREEFOLK, WHITCHURCH RG28 7NT

Tel 01256 896533 **Fax** 01256 896572
Location Off B3400 Whitchurch to Overton road: 1½ miles on left, past Watership Down pub
Opening hours 10 am – 5 pm; daily; March to October. Evening visits by appointment

This family-run nursery has a large range of pretty cottage garden perennials and flowering shrubs. Its attractive exhibits have been a great feature of RHS shows in recent years – including Chelsea and Hampton Court. One of the best nurseries in southern England for a really wide choice of good plants.

Heath Lands

47 LOCKS ROAD, LOCKS HEATH, SOUTHAMPTON SO31 6NS

Tel 01489 573598 **Fax** 01489 557884
Location Locks Road is the main north-south road through the middle of Locks Heath
Opening hours 2 pm – 5.30 pm; 18 March, 15 April, 13 May & 26 August

Admission fee Adults £2; Children free

Since building his house in 1967, Dr Burwell has filled his one-acre of deep gravelly stoney soil with a wonderful choice of immaculately grown plants of every type. It is the embodiment of careful plantsmanship, a garden to go round slowly – looking, studying and thinking. Your first sight is an 80-metre line of *Paulonia tomentosa* all along the road, grown from seed in about 1970. Next comes *Garrya elliptica* trained as a small tree. Round the side of the house is a tall yew hedge, topped by a brooding topiary peacock. The design is a mixture of formal and informal, with a large number of different habitats. Under a canopy of light oak woodland thrives a shady fernery with orchids and *Rhododendron sinogrande*. *Iris confusa* flourishes against a wall of the house. Cyclamen and bulbs are everywhere. The climate is mild – the sea is only a mile or so away – so there are hedges of griselinia, a plant of *Pittosporum tenuifolium* 'Garnettii' five metres high, and *Cleyera japonica* growing in the open. In a narrow alley between tall hedges of yew and rhododendron is the National Collection of Japanese Anemones. Dr Burwell will tell you that many were imported from Japan as garden cultivars: though first described in 1695 they were not introduced until the 1840s by Robert Fortune. The collection has about 40 cultivars, including a seedling which will shortly be introduced as 'Heathlands Ruby'.

Owned by Dr John Burwell
Size 1 acre
NCCPG National Collections *Anemone* (Japanese anemones)

Highclere Castle

HIGHCLERE, NEWBURY RG15 9RN

Tel 01635 253210   **Fax** 01635 255315
Website www.highclerecastle.co.uk
Location South of Newbury off A34
Opening hours 11 am – 5 pm (3.30 pm on Saturdays);
daily; 1 July to 31 August (closed 21 & 22 July)
Admission fee Gardens only: Adults £3; Children £1

A major historic garden – when Capability
Brown landscaped it in the 1770s he left
intact the avenues and follies of the early
eighteenth century, but the park is
dominated now by hundreds of huge cedars.
Salvin's imposing house has 365 windows.
Jim Russell advised on the planting in the
walled garden, though the 'Secret Garden' is
not among his best.

Owned by The Earl of Carnarvon
Number of gardeners 2
Size 600 acres of parkland
NCCPG National Collections *Rhododendron*
English Heritage grade I

Hinton Ampner House

BRAMDEAN, ALRESFORD SO24 0LA

Tel 01962 771305   **Fax** 01962 793101
Website www.nationaltrust.org.uk
Location On A272 1 mile west of Bramdean
Opening hours 1.30 pm – 5.30 pm; Tuesdays,
Wednesdays, Saturdays, Sundays & Bank Holiday
Mondays; 18 & 25 March, then April to September
Admission fee Adults £3.40; Children £1.20

The gardens at Hinton Ampner were laid
out by the scholarly Ralph Dutton in the
middle of the twentieth century with great
regard to line, landscape and historical
propriety. Statues, buildings, axes and views
have been placed with exquisite judgement
to lead you subtly along the exact route that
Dutton intended. He was also careful to
chose plants which would do well on chalk
and then planted lots of them – using always
the best forms: among them are buddlejas,
lilacs, philadelphus, cotoneasters, weigelas
and shrub roses. It is now one of England's
best mid-twentieth-century gardens,
maintained to a high specification.

Owned by The National Trust
Number of gardeners 3
Size 20 acres
English Heritage grade II

Houghton Lodge

HOUGHTON, STOCKBRIDGE
SO20 6LQ

Tel 01264 810912   **Fax** 01264 810177
Location Off A30 at Stockbridge
Opening hours 2 pm – 5 pm; Mondays, Tuesdays,
Thursdays & Fridays. 10 am – 5 pm; Saturdays, Sundays &
Bank Holidays. March to September. And by appointment
Admission fee £5 for garden & hydroponicum. Groups at
special rates

A lovely gothic *cottage ornée* on a ledge
above the River Test, with long spacious
views down the river and across the
watermeadows. Part of BBC's 'David
Copperfield' was shot here. The owner has
just begun to restore the eighteenth-century
shrubbery: this means clearing seedling trees
to open up the view across the river and
re-planting with trees and shrubs which
were grown there 200 years ago. Houghton
also boasts the leading hydroponic
greenhouse in England, where plants are
grown in nutrient-rich solutions instead of
soil – salad vegetables and some 50 different
herbs, as well as bougainvilleas and bananas.

The garden makes a great effort to be educational and entertaining.

Owned by Martin Busk
Number of gardeners 2 part-time
Size 5 acres
English Heritage grade II*

Langley Boxwood Nursery

RAKE, LISS GU33 7JL

Tel 01730 894467
Website www.boxwood.co.uk
Location 5 miles north of Petersfield, ring for map or directions
Opening hours Monday – Friday. Saturday by appointment

These specialist growers of box have a comprehensive range of box plants for hedging, edging and topiary. There are over fifty cultivars of *Buxus* in their delightful catalogue, and some yew (*Taxus*) also. Both are available in a wide variety of topiary shapes, from simple balls to complex crowns and animals, and (given sufficient notice) they will create individual designs.

NCCPG National Collections *Buxus*

Longmead House

LONGPARISH, ANDOVER SP11 6PZ

Tel & Fax 01264 720386
Location 1½ miles from junction of A303 & B3048
Opening hours 2 pm – 6 pm; 3, 6 & 17 June. And by appointment
Admission fee Adults £1.50

Longmead House is an organic showcase: Wendy Ellicock is on the council of the Henry Doubleday Research Association. She and her husband started the garden when they left London in 1987. The wildflower meadow was one of their first endeavours, begun by planting plugs into areas cleared of turf: now it provides colour from February to November. The kitchen garden has 25 deep beds, much enriched by organic compost. There are also wildlife areas and natural corners, a deliberate result of allowing nettles and other 'weeds' to provide food for insects and mammals.

Owned by Wendy Ellicock
Number of gardeners 2
Size 2½ acres

Longthatch

LIPPEN LANE, WARNFORD, SOUTHAMPTON SO32 3LE

Tel 01730 829285
Location 1 mile south of West Meon on A32, turn right by George & Falcon, & right again. 400m on right
Opening hours 10 am – 5 pm; Wednesdays; 7 March to 25 July. And 2 pm – 5 pm; 4, 11, 18 & 25 March, 22 April, 27 & 28 May, 17 June & 22 July for National Gardens Scheme
Admission fee Adults £2.50; Children free

The Shorts have gardened at Longthatch since 1955, though in their early years they were busy with the farm around their sixteenth-century thatched cottage. They started to develop the garden seriously in 1968: it is now a great favourite among dedicated plantsmen. Over the years they have built up large collections not only of hellebores, but also of herbaceous plants (especially hardy geraniums), unusual trees and shrubs. Some of the trees they planted in the early days are now spectacularly

Longstock Water Gardens

LONGSTOCK, STOCKBRIDGE SO20 6EH

Tel 01264 810894 & 01264 810904   **Fax** 01264 810924
Location 1½ miles north-east of Longstock Village
Opening hours 2 pm – 5 pm; 1st & 3rd Sunday in the month; April to September
Admission fee Adults £3; Children 50p

Longstock has quite the most extraordinary and beautiful water garden in England, a little Venice where dozens of islands and all-but-islands are linked by an apparently endless number of small bridges and intensely planted with water-loving plants. Drifts of astilbes, primulas, kingcups, hemerocallis, musks, water irises and lilies. The ground is so soft that the islands seem to float, and a remarkable accumulation of peat has allowed such calcifuge plants as *Meconopsis betonicifolia* to flourish in this chalky valley. But the garden as a whole has a remarkable variety of habitats: parts are very dry. A seam of acid soil supports a collection of *Rhododendron orbiculare* and *R. williamsiamum* cultivars and their hybrids like 'Temple Belle'. Around the perimeter are swamp cypresses and liquidambers; further away are oaks and Scots pines. On the other side of the road lies the splendid arboretum, open at the same time and with a vast collection of well-spaced specimen trees now approaching the prime of their life. Both the water gardens and the arboretum are open only rarely, so that they can be maintained principally for the benefit of partners of John Lewis, but up at the top, along a wooded drive, is an excellent nursery which is open daily throughout the year (afternoons only on Sundays). It specialises in rare trees and shrubs, and has a constantly changing stock of interesting plants. Nearby – but you need permission to see it – is a walled garden which contains the National Collection of *Buddleja* and a beautiful rose and clematis pergola. Every part of the Longstock estate – water gardens, arboretum, nursery and walled garden – are models of their kind, beautifully maintained and in top condition.

Owned by John Lewis Partnership
Number of gardeners 3 at water garden; 3 in arboretum
Size 10 acres of water garden; 65 acres in arboretum
NCCPG National Collections *Buddleja*; *Clematis viticella*

mature. There are two central features: first an acre of woodland filled with wonderful small plants, from snowdrops and pulmonarias in winter through to cyclamen in late autumn; and, second, the River Meon which flows through the garden. This is supplemented by numerous spring-filled ponds throughout the garden, one of which helps to maintain the bog garden where *Gunnera manicata* and many other damp- and shade-loving plants flourish. The owners say that their best season is spring – *Narcissus* is another of their many special interests – but there is much to see throughout the year. Birds are encouraged – as is all wildlife, including the trout in the river and waterfall pool.

Owned by Peter & Vera Short
Number of gardeners keen owners only!
Size 3½ acres
NCCPG National Collections *Helleborus* (part)

The Manor House

UPTON GREY, BASINGSTOKE
RG25 2RD

Tel 01256 862827   **Fax** 01256 861035
Website www.gertrudejekyllgarden.co.uk
Location In Upton Grey village above & beside the church
Opening hours By appointment only: 9 am – 4 pm; weekdays
Admission fee £4, to include a copy of the guidebook; £3.50 for groups of 20+

Ros Wallinger has restored this Jekyll garden since 1984 using the original planting plans (now at Berkeley University, California). She has gone to great pains to recreate it exactly in all its Edwardian loveliness. Some of the roses were extinct here until re-introduced from private gardens in France and Italy after years of searching. The rich herbaceous borders drift from cool blues, white and

pinks at either end to hot reds, oranges and yellows in the middle. There is no better place to study Gertrude Jekyll's plantings, but what makes it so special is that it is a 'young' garden again. And the restoration continues. Read more about it in Ros Wallinger's *Gertrude Jekyll's Lost Garden* (Garden Art Press, 2000).

Owned by Mrs John Wallinger
Number of gardeners 1, plus very keen owners
Size 5 acres
English Heritage grade II

Meon Orchard

KINGSMEAD, WICKHAM, FAREHAM
PO17 5AU

Tel & Fax 01329 833253
Location Take A32 north from Wickham for 1½ miles; turn left at Roebuck; ½ mile on left
Opening hours 2 pm – 6 pm; 3 June, 29 July, 2 September. And groups by appointment
Admission fee Adults £2

This stylish garden is a plantaholic paradise. The emphasis is upon difficult and tender plants which look their best in late summer. An extraordinary number of plants survive the winter outside with a little protection: bananas, hedychiums, *Impatiens tinctoria* and *Dahlia imperialis* for example. The Smiths bought the property in 1986 and designed the garden as a series of interlinking paths and glades which radiate out and give the whole lay-out the impression of being much larger than it really is. It is not a quiet or refined garden, but exuberant and experimental, full of dramatic plants and contrasts. The fifty or so *Eucalyptus* species in their National Collection have grown quickly and give the garden an air of maturity. Cordylines, Italian cypresses and *Ligustrum japonicum*

'Rotundifolium' also recur throughout the garden and bind it together. A vast number of pots are planted out for the summer or grouped together. Some may be put in a strategic position for only a few weeks while their flowers associate well with another plant. The owners' plantsmanship is very broad and encompasses hardy plants and alpines plants too: a laburnum hedge as you come down the drive, bulbs of every kind, a quincunx of Japanese anemones, a water garden, a pond, and hundreds of hardy trees and shrubs too. This is a most imaginative and creative garden to visit for ideas about what to grow and how to display it.

Owned by Dr D J & Mrs L A Smith
Number of gardeners owners
Size 1½ acres
NCCPG National Collections *Eucalyptus*

Mottisfont Abbey

ROMSEY SO51 0LJ

Tel 01794 340757 **Fax** 01794 341492
Website www.nationaltrust.org.uk
Location 4 miles north-west of Romsey
Opening hours 11 am – 6 pm; Saturday – Wednesday; 17 March to 4 November. Plus 11 am – 8.30 pm; daily; 9 to 24 June
Admission fee £6

The park and gardens near the house are stately: Russell Page, Geoffrey Jellicoe and Norah Lindsay all worked here. A broade chalk spring surges out in the grounds and runs down to feed the River Test. One of the London planes *Platanus × hispanica* near the river has two huge trunks fused together, though no-one can work out whether the two stems are on the same roots. But it is the old rose collection in the walled garden which has made Mottisfont's name. It is Graham Thomas's best known work, a collection of all the roses he has discovered, assembled, preserved and made popular through his writings. Surely the loveliest rose garden in Britain, but expect some temporary slippage as it is thoroughly overhauled for the first time since the walled garden was planted in 1972.

 Plant Highlights Roses (mainly old-fashioned & climbers); plantsman's collection of plants; good herbaceous borders; guided walks and 'rose clinics' in season; tallest *Paulownia tomentosa* (13m) in the British Isles.

Owned by The National Trust
NCCPG National Collections *Platanus; Rosa*
English Heritage grade II

Oakleigh Nurseries

PETERSFIELD ROAD, MONKWOOD, ALRESFORD SO24 0HB

Tel 01962 773344
Website www.oakleigh-nurseries.co.uk
Location In the middle of Monkwood
Opening hours 10 am – 4.30 pm (10.30 am – 4 pm at weekends); daily; March to July, then mid-September to 31 October

Ⓟ 🏵

The main specialities of this interesting nursery are fuchsias, penstemons and epiphyllums, with a special emphasis upon pelargoniums – regal, angel, ivy-leaf, zonal, stellar, cactus and scented. But the nursery also has a line in double primroses. A new introduction for 2001 is the new angel pelargonium 'Sarah Don'. The website is excellent.

Petersfield Physic Garden

5 CHURCH ROAD, STEEP GU32 2DW

Tel 01730 233371
Website www.hants.gov.uk/leisure/attractnature.html
Location Behind 16 The High Street
Opening hours Dawn – dusk; daily except Christmas Day
Admission fee free

This is a small town garden, surrounded by walls and planted with the fruit trees, roses, herbs and other plants which were known in the seventeenth century. It is an initiative of that most energetic and successful organisation, the Hampshire Gardens Trust.

Owned by Hampshire Gardens Trust

Sir George Staunton Country Park

MIDDLE PARK WAT, HAVANT PO9 5HB

Tel 023 9245 3405   **Fax** 023 9249 8156
Location North of Havant on B2149
Opening hours Glasshouses 10 am – 5 pm (4 pm in winter); daily; all year. Park dawn to dusk
Admission fee free

The historic heart of this landscape garden is a Regency walled garden and *ferme ornée*, but the local authority has also restored and developed the Victorian glasshouses as an educational resource. Here you can see useful plants like tea, coffee, pineapple, coconut palms, papyrus and rice plants, as well as such ornamentals as *Victoria amazonica*, passion flowers, sarracenias, *Nepenthes* and strelitzias.

Owned by Hampshire County Council
English Heritage grade II*

Spinners

BOLDRE, LYMINGTON SO41 5QE

Tel 01590 673347
Location Signed off A337 between Brockenhurst & Lymington
Opening hours 10 am – 5 pm; Tuesday – Saturday; all year. Other days by appointment
Admission fee £2 from 14 April to 14 September; free at other times

Only two acres, but what a garden! Spinners is a plantsman's paradise, where the enthusiast can spend many happy hours browsing at any time of the year. The habitat plantings and plant associations are particularly interesting to study. Much of the garden is light woodland, so it has good collections of hydrangeas, lilies, hostas, rodgersias and ferns. Peter Chappell's nursery sells an extraordinary range of good plants: you always come away with a bootful of novelties. The trilliums are of course one of the nursery's specialities: they include such rarities as *T. chloropetalum* var. *giganteum* (which has an Award of Garden Merit from the RHS) and *T. parviflorum*. The list of magnolias is perhaps even more impressive: about 90 cultivars, including a great range of Acuminata Hybrids, Gresham hybrids and the new *M. stellata* × *liliiflora* hybrids, as well as such introductions as *M. dawsoniana* 'Chyverton Red' and *M.* × *loebneri* 'Donna'.

Plant Highlights Woodland garden; an important plantsman's garden; fine collection of trees; rhododendrons; magnolias; woodland plants; rarities and novelties; new peat beds & bog garden;

The Sir Harold Hillier Gardens & Arboretum

JERMYNS LANE, AMPFIELD, ROMSEY SO51 0QA

Tel 01794 368787   **Fax** 01794 368027
Website www.hillier.hants.gov.uk/
Location Signed from A3090 & A3057
Opening hours 10.30 am – 6 pm (dusk if earlier); every day except Bank & Public Holidays over Christmas
Admission fee Adults £4.25; Concessions £3.75; Children (under 16) free. RHS members free

This is quite the most important modern arboretum in UK. The gardens have the greatest collection of wild and cultivated woody plants in the world: over 12,000 taxa in 180 acres, totalling 40,000 plants. The arboretum was established in 1953 by the late Sir Harold Hillier: Hillier's Nursery aimed at the time to offer for sale every cultivar of every tree or shrub that was hardy in the British Isles. Sir Harold himself was an active importer and collector of new species from all over the world, at a time (of relative economic depression) when few British horticulturists had the impetus to look outside the UK for plants of any kind. Every part of the arboretum is an education and a pleasure, whatever the season or weather. It has so many unique features that the visitor needs all day to see more than a fraction of its riches: the collection of poplar trees called the Populetum; more than 100 pines (*Pinus* species), including the 'big cone' pine *P. coulteri* whose cones may weigh as much as two kilos; a maple valley; the largest Winter Garden of its kind in Europe and a Gurkha Memorial Garden. But it is the sheer number of trees and shrubs here that makes the most lasting impression: every time you visit, and wherever you walk, you see interesting plants that you have never seen before. The labelling is exemplary and helpful guidebooks are available. Hilliers' nursery shares a car park with the arboretum. Details of seasonal special events, workshops, evening talks, guided tours and children's activities can be obtained on request.

Plant Highlights A plantsman's collection of trees and shrubs; mature conifers; also good herbaceous plants; mixed borders; new winter garden (1998); new all-ability access path (2000); 51 record trees, including 11 *Sorbus*.

Owned by Hampshire County Council
Size 180 acres
NCCPG National Collections Carpinus; Cornus; Corylus; Cotoneaster; Hamamelis; Ligustrum; Lithocarpus; Photinia; Pinus; (excl. dwarf cvs.); Quercus; 'Hillier' plants

biggest *Eucalyptus perriniana* in the British Isles.

Owned by Diana & Peter Chappell
Number of gardeners a little part-time help
Size 2 acres
NCCPG National Collections *Trillium*

Steven Bailey Ltd

SILVER STREET, SWAY, LYMINGTON SO41 6ZA

Tel 01590 682227   **Fax** 01590 683765
Location East of Hordle, not in Sway
Opening hours 10 am – 4 pm; Monday – Friday; all year. Plus Saturdays & Sundays from March to June. And Saturdays in December

This long-established nursery built its reputation on breeding and introducing carnations and pinks. *Dianthus* 'Michael Saunders' and 'Sandra Neal' are among several excellent cultivars to which the RHS has awarded its Award of Garden Merit kitemark but which are available only from this nursery. Its exhibits have for long been a feature of RHS shows. The nursery shop has a selection of bedding and summer pot plants, alstroemerias and seasonal flowering perennials.

Stratfield Saye House

STRATFIELD SAYE, BASINGSTOKE RG7 2BT

Tel 01256 882882   **Fax** 01256 882345
Location 1 mile west of A33 between Reading & Basingstoke
Opening hours 11.30 am – 5 pm (last admissions 3 pm); 26 to 28 May, then Wednesday – Sunday from June to August. Plus groups by arrangement

Admission fee Garden only: £2.50

Not a great garden, but there are some fine incidents: a huge kitchen garden, a large and cheerful rose garden, rhododendrons in the park, and magnificent trees, including wellingtonias, named after the Iron Duke.

Plant Highlights Roses (mainly modern); mature conifers; good herbaceous borders; camellia house in walled garden; American garden; tallest Hungarian oak *Quercus frainetto* (33m) in the British Isles.

Owned by The Duke of Wellington
English Heritage grade II

Tudor House Garden

BUGLE STREET, SOUTHAMPTON SO14 2AD

Tel 023 8063 5904   **Fax** 023 8033 9601
Website www.southampton.gov.uk/leisure/heritage
Location Bugle Street runs parallel to the High Street in the old town
Opening hours 10 am – 12 noon and 1 pm – 5 pm (4 pm on Saturdays); weekdays. Plus 2 pm – 5 pm on Sundays. April to October. But 10 am – 4 pm on weekdays; 10 am – 12 noon and 1 pm – 4 pm on Saturdays; and 2 pm – 5 pm on Sundays for the rest of the year.
Admission fee free

Sylvia Landsberg's unique reconstruction of a Tudor garden has a knot garden, a fountain, a secret garden and contemporary plantings of herbs and flowering plants all crammed into a tiny area. Some call it a pastiche, others a living dictionary of Tudor garden language.

Owned by Southampton City Council
Size 100ft by 100ft

Water Meadow Nursery & Herb Farm

CHERITON, ALRESFORD SO24 0QB

Tel 01962 771895   **Fax** 01962 771985
Website www.plantaholic.co.uk
Location Just off the A272, on the B3046 to Alresford
Opening hours 10 am – 5 pm; Wednesday – Saturday;
7 March to 28 July. August to November, by appointment

This nursery offers a good list of waterlilies – *Nymphaea* cultivars, of which they have seventy – and oriental poppies, which indicates that it is equally good for plants for wet situations and dry banks. Many of the hardy plants and herbs in the general list are unusual. The display garden is beautifully laid out – they offer a design and landscaping service – and open several times from May to July to show off its collection of more than 100 cultivars of *Papaver orientale*.

NCCPG National Collections *Papaver orientale*

West Green House

HARTLEY WINTNEY, BASINGSTOKE RG27 8JB

Tel 01252 844611
Location In West Green village
Opening hours 11 am – 4.30 pm; Thursday – Sunday & Bank Holiday Monday; May to August. Also for the National Trust
Admission fee Adults £4; Children £1

Marylyn Abbott is restoring and remaking the garden at West Green with all the energy she showed in the garden she made in her native Australia. Formality, variety, invention and sheer beauty are here in abundance. The *potager* is especially stylish. Visit it, if you can, and see one of the greatest modern gardens come to life again.

Owned by Marylyn Abbott
Number of gardeners 3
Size 8 acres

White Windows

LONGPARISH, ANDOVER SP11 6PB

Tel & Fax 01264 720222
Location In village centre
Opening hours 2 pm – 6 pm; by appointment from April to September on Wednesdays. And on 15 & 16 April & 23 September for National Gardens Scheme
Admission fee Adults £2; Children free

White Windows is one of the best small modern plantsman's gardens on chalk, remarkable for the way Jane Sterndale-Bennett, Chairman of the Hardy Plant Society, arranges her material. Layer upon layer, White Windows bulges with good plants, well grown and controlled. Leaves and stems are as important as flowers, especially in the combinations and contrasts of colour – gold and yellow, blue and silver, and crimsons, pinks and purples. Much use is made of evergreens and variegated plants. Perhaps the most luxuriant chalk garden in Hampshire and all made since 1979.

Owned by Mrs J Sterndale-Bennett
Number of gardeners owner only
Size 0.7 acres
NCCPG National Collections *Helleborus* (part)

HEREFORDSHIRE

There is, of course, no such county as Herefordshire – not any more. It was dissolved in 1974, when the county was linked to its neighbour as 'Hereford & Worcester'. This was never a popular union, and Herefordshire people were always quick to point out that they retained their own identity and Lord Lieutenant. Herefordshire is now a District Council but, so distinct does it consider itself, that we are listing it in this book as a county again. It is a pity that so few of its historic gardens are open to the public. Hergest Croft has by far the most important collection of trees, with a large number of 'record breakers' among them: Eastnor Castle also has some fine trees, the largest of their kind in England. There are comparatively few top-class modern gardens – Elton Hall and the Lance Hattatt Design Garden are memorable exceptions (as is Sir Roy Strong's private garden at Much Birch) – and the county does not do conspicuously well for the National Gardens Scheme. Likewise, it has comparatively few National Collections and National Collection holders and no RHS Partner Colleges or Partner Nurseries. But good nurseries exist – Kenchester Water Gardens and Rickard's Hardy Ferns are two of the best – and the extensive fruit orchards testify to the county's suitability for horticulture. The NCCPG group has worked with the Marcher Apple Network to identify old trees, propagate them and establish new orchards to preserve them (further details from John Aldridge on 01432 820304).

Abbey Dore Court Garden

ABBEY DORE, HEREFORD HR2 0AD

Tel 01981 240419
Location 3 miles west of A465, midway between Hereford & Abergavenny
Opening hours 11 am – 6 pm; daily except Mondays & Wednesdays (open Bank Holidays); 30 March to 30 September
Admission fee Adults £2.50; Children 50p

This is a splendid plantsman's garden on a damp cold site, with fine borders leading down to the ferny river walk. Mrs Ward says her 'rambling garden' has 'stopped getting any bigger', but the truth is that the garden grows, changes and improves with every visit: very exciting. There may be changes to the visiting arrangements during 2001, so please telephone to check before leaving home.

Owned by Mrs Charis Ward
Number of gardeners 1
Size 5 acres

The Bannut

BRINGSTY WR6 5TA

Tel & Fax 01885 482206
Location On the A44, 2½ miles east of Bromyard
Opening hours 2 pm – 5 pm; Wednesdays,
Sundays & Bank Holiday Mondays; Easter to September
Admission fee Adults £2; Children £1

Unlike many plantsman's gardens, the
plants at The Bannut have been used to
great decorative effect. The best example is
the knot garden made from the contrasting
leaf colours of different heathers, though the
Everetts are fond of all heathers and grow a
large number of different cultivars in the
summer heather garden. They are, however,
interested in all types of plants and how to
display them in the garden. The beds and
borders are planted with colour harmonies
and contrasts, mainly of herbaceous plants
near the modern house, but with more
shrubs towards the little copse where
cowslips flower in spring. The standard of
maintenance throughout is excellent.

Owned by Maurice & Daphne Everett
Number of gardeners owners, plus very part-time help
Size 2½ acres

Berrington Hall

LEOMINSTER HR6 0DW

Tel 01568 615721   **Fax** 01568 613263
Website www.nationaltrust.org.uk
Location On A49, 3 miles north of Leominster
Opening hours 12 pm – 5 pm (4.30 pm in October);
Saturday – Wednesday, plus Good Friday; April to October
Admission fee £2

This majestic park is classic Capability
Brown. The National Trust has laid out a
one-mile parkland walk which takes in the
best vantage points and shows you how the
landscape would have looked when young.
In the old walled garden, a comprehensive
collection of Hereford Pomona is
supplemented by old pear varieties, quinces
and medlars.

Owned by The National Trust
English Heritage grade II*

Bryan's Ground

STAPLETON, PRESTEIGNE LD8 2LP

Tel 01544 260001   **Fax** 01544 260015
Location On minor road between Stapleton & Kinsham
Opening hours 2 pm – 5 pm; 29 May & 3 July for National
Gardens Scheme. Plus groups by appointment between
21 May & 13 July
Admission fee Adults £2.50; Children £1

A young garden: incredibly, the owners
moved here as recently as November 1993.
They have made wonderfully good use of
the inherited structure (yew hedges and
mature trees around the Surrey stockbroker
house) and filled it with good plants. Recent
additions include an auricula theatre, a
belvedere, a mirror pool and a developing
four-acre arboretum. Full of original ideas,
Bryan's Ground is already an influential and
fashionable garden. David Wheeler was the
founding editor of the influential gardening
quarterly *Hortus* which Simon Dorrell now
edits.

Owned by David Wheeler & Simon Dorrell
Number of gardeners 2
Size 7 acres

Dinmore Manor

HEREFORD HR4 8EE

Tel 01432 830322   Fax 01432 830503
Location 6 miles north of Hereford on A49
Opening hours 10 am – 5.30 pm; daily; all year
Admission fee Adults £3; Children under 14 free

Dinmore's gardens include a 1920s rock garden which has been planted with dwarf conifers and Japanese maples. The 1200-year-old yew is an impressive sight.

Owned by Dinmore Manor Estate Ltd

Eastnor Castle

EASTNOR, LEDBURY HR8 1RL

Tel 01531 633160   Fax 01531 631776
Website www.eastnorcastle.com
Location 2 miles east of Ledbury on A438 Tewkesbury road
Opening hours 11 am – 5 pm; Sundays & Bank Holiday Mondays; 15 April to 7 October. Also daily except Saturdays in July & August
Admission fee Adults £3; Children £2

Eastnor is all about trees. The arboretum planted by Lord Somers from 1852 and 1883 is now mature, and full of champion specimens. Many are rare, including a tall American beech (*Fagus grandifolia*) and an enormous red hickory (*Carya ovalis*). It is however the conifers which dominate the setting for the neo-Norman castle, largely because they were planted so thickly and in such great numbers. Michael Hadfield wrote that Eastnor was 'embowered by vast conifers – plantations which spill out into the surrounding hills and fields'. Quite apart from the many hundreds of cedars, the record-breaking specimens include the Shensi fir (*Abies chensiensis*), the purple-coned fir (*Picea purpurea*) from south-east China, and *Pinus hartwegii* from Mexico. The rest of the garden is less interesting, but tree-lovers will find Eastnor a real treat.

 Plant Highlights Mature conifers; fine collection of trees; spring bulbs; tallest deodar *Cedrus deodara* (38m) in the British Isles, plus eleven more record trees.

Owned by Mr James & The Hon Mrs Hervey-Bathurst
Number of gardeners 1
Size 40 acres
English Heritage grade II*

Elton Hall

LUDLOW SY8 2HQ

Tel 01568 770218   Fax 01568 770753
Location Between Wigmore & Ludlow
Opening hours 2 pm – 6 pm; 22 June & 28 September for National Gardens Scheme, and 2 September for Plant Fair. And by appointment for clubs and groups
Admission fee Adults £2

Into this historic landscape (home 200 years ago to Thomas Knight, President of the not-yet-Royal Horticultural Society) the Hepworths and their gardener Anthony Brooks have since about 1990 set a remarkably original and beautiful new garden. Huge herbaceous borders, clear design, rare plants and great sensitivity to form and colour are the essence of it. But what makes it exceptional is the range of quirky follies and fancies with which the garden is strewn – the Tortoise Fort, for instance, and the Moorish sheep palace. Last year they added a gazebo and a hermitage.

Owned by Mr & Mrs James Hepworth
NCCPG National Collections *Echinacea; Rudbeckia*

The Lance Hattatt Design Garden

WEOBLEY HR4 8RN

Tel & Fax 01544 318468
Location 1 mile from Weobley: off Wormsley road, signed Ledgemoor & second right, first house on left
Opening hours 2 pm – 5 pm; Wednesday – Sundays; April to September
Admission fee Adults £3. Unsuitable for children

The Lance Hattatt Design Garden is what we used to know as Arrow Cottage, a name which Lance Hattatt says he felt to be misleading: he specialises in 'contemporary garden design in the best English tradition' and believes that the new name is more appropriate. The garden is a good example of a modern design where a series of gardens in different styles exhibits a fair measure of plantsmanship. But there is still a problem of naming: though all are to some extent explained, it may be difficult for visitors to see the connection between the names and the gardens. Akademia, Luxor, Andrassy, Indigo Yard, Solomon and Easter Island are just some of them. It should be said, however, that all are maintained to the highest standard. Moreover, the keen plantsman will find *Iris confusa* 'Martyn Rix' flourishing outside, and pots of *Agapanthus africanus* along the rill in summer. Few such gardens combine plantsmanship and artistry so well: it's just a pity about all those existentialist names.

Owned by Jane & Lance Hattatt
Number of gardeners 1½
Size 2 acres

Hergest Croft Gardens

KINGTON HR5 3EG

Tel 01544 230160   **Fax** 01544 230160
Website www.hergest.co.uk
Location Signed from A44
Opening hours 1.30 pm – 6 pm; daily; April to October
Admission fee Adults £5; Children free

Hergest Croft is an extremely important woodland garden and arboretum around a whopping Edwardian house. There is no end to the garden's marvels: huge conifers, magnificent birches, scores of interesting oaks, many acres of billowing rhododendrons. But it is also worth visiting for its good herbaceous borders, alpine collections, autumn gentians and kitchen garden, all on a scale that most of us have forgotten. There is also an informative website.

Plant Highlights Roses (mainly old-fashioned); fruit; good herbaceous borders; fine collection of trees; rhododendrons; tallest *Cercidiphyllum japonicum* (25m), *Toona sinensis* (27m) and *Corylus colurna* (27m) in the British Isles, among 17 record trees.

Owned by W L Banks
Number of gardeners 6
Size 70 acres
NCCPG National Collections *Acer; Betula; Zelkova*
English Heritage grade II*

How Caple Court

HOW CAPLE, HEREFORD HR1 4SX

Tel 01989 740626   **Fax** 01989 740611
Location Signed on B4224 & A449 junction
Opening hours 10 am – 5 pm; daily; Easter to September
Admission fee Adults £2.50; Children free

Spectacular formal gardens laid out about 100 years ago (some Italianate, others more Arts & Crafts), and now undergoing restoration. Pergolas, loggias, dramatic terraces and *giardini segreti* with stunning views across a lushly wooded valley. How Caple is a garden of national importance, but little known even locally.

Owned by Mr & Mrs Roger Lee
Number of gardeners 1 part-time
Size 11 acres

Kenchester Water Gardens

CHURCH ROAD, LYDE, HEREFORD HR1 3AB

Tel 01432 270981   **Fax** 01432 342243
Location On A49 between Hereford & Leominster
Opening hours 9 am – 6 pm (5.30 pm from October to March); daily; all year. 10.30 am – 4.30 pm on Sundays. Closed Christmas Day

The gardens and the nursery at Kenchester are equally important for anyone interested in water-plants. The range of plants grown and offered for sale is excellent, and includes nearly 210 cultivars of *Nymphaea*, of which they have a National Collection. The gardens have pools and ponds over a large area – well worth a longish visit. This is a dynamic nursery which is getting bigger and better all the time.

Size 6 acres
NCCPG National Collections *Nymphaea*

Kingstone Cottage Plants

WESTON UNDER PENYARD, ROSS-ON-WYE HR9 7PH

Tel 01989 565267
Location North of Weston under Penyard, on the road to Rudhall
Opening hours 10 am – 5 pm; Monday – Friday; 7 May to 6 July
Admission fee Adults £1 for National Gardens Scheme

The main feature of this garden is its National Collection of old *Dianthus* cultivars which flower in early summer. This is the place to see such rarities as *D.* 'Fenbow Nutmeg Clove' and *D.* 'Cranborne Seedling'. Mr & Mrs Hughes also sell plants which they have propagated from their collection – the best way to promote a wider interest in old cultivars and guarantee their future survival.

Owned by Michael & Sophie Hughes
NCCPG National Collections *Dianthus*

Lakeside

GAINES ROAD, WHITBOURNE, WORCESTER WR6 5RD

Tel 01886 821119
Location 9 miles west of Worcester off A44 at County boundary sign
Opening hours Parties of 10+ by appointment only
Admission fee Adults £2; Children free

These six acres were dramatically planted by Chris Philip, who founded *The RHS Plant Finder*. Tender plants flourish against the old kitchen garden walls. Daffodils bred by Michael Jefferson-Brown run down to the lake, where clean-limbed alders stretch gothically heavenwards. Throughout the garden are good plants, used well: Lakeside is an inspiration to new gardeners, and a place from which all can learn.

Owned by Denys Gueroult
Size 6 acres

Marston Exotics

BRAMPTON LANE, MADLEY,
HEREFORD HR2 9LX

Tel 01981 251140
Location 7 miles south of Hereford
Opening hours 8 am – 4.30 pm; Monday – Friday; all year.
1 pm – 5 pm; Saturday – Sunday; March to October.
11 am – 5 pm; Bank Holidays

Marston Exotics is the leading nursery for carnivorous plants in the UK – perhaps in Europe. The range is formidable: the list of sarracenias, droseras, and pinguiculas is extremely comprehensive. Marston Exotics have been regular exhibitors at RHS shows over many years and have done a lot of work on the selection and hybridisation of the genus. Their National Collection of *sarracenias* has about seven species and over 60 cultivars.

Old Court Nurseries

WALWYN ROAD, COLWALL,
MALVERN WR13 6QE

Tel 01684 540416   **Fax** 01684 565314
Website www.autumnasters.co.uk
Location 3 mile west of Great Malvern; 5 miles east of Ledbury on B4218
Opening hours 11 am – 5 pm; Wednesday – Sunday;
April to October. 11 am – 5 pm; daily; September to

mid-October. 11 am – 5 pm; Wednesday to Sunday;
mid-to-end October

Old Court Nurseries are holders of National Collection of Michaelmas daisies (*Aster*). This is their speciality: the extensive collection is fully described in Paul Picton's excellent book *Gardener's Guide to Growing Asters* (1999). But there are also many other interesting perennials and cottage garden-type plants here. The garden is worth a visit in its own right, especially when the Michaelmas daisies are in flower: then the banks of colour, graded for height, recall the grandest of Edwardian gardens.

NCCPG National Collections Aster (autumn-flowering)

Queen's Wood Arboretum & Country Park

DINMORE HILL, LEOMINSTER
HR6 0PY

Tel 01568 797052   **Fax** 01568 879305
Location Midway between Leominster & Hereford on A49
Opening hours 9 am – dusk; daily; all year
Admission fee free, but small charge for parking

A vigorous young arboretum, planted over the last 40 years with public amenity in mind. Wonderful for walking, whatever the season, and well run in a friendly, efficient manner so that visitors get the most from it. They rangers say that spring and autumn are the best time for colour, but there are lots of early purple orchids and spotted orchids in summer too.

Owned by Hereford Council
Number of gardeners 4
Size 60 acres

Rushfields of Ledbury

ROSS ROAD, LEDBURY HR8 2LP

Tel 01531 632004   **Fax** 01531 633454
Website www.rushfields.co.uk
Location ½ mile south-west of Ledbury off A449
Opening hours 11 am – 5 pm; Wednesday – Saturday;
and by appointment

Rushfields specialise in 'choice garden plants', most of them herbaceous. They are particularly good for hellebores, of which they have been developing their own Helen Ballard strains. Other specialities include geraniums, euphorbias, penstemons and monardas, but the nursery is a good place to see and buy a wide range of well-chosen herbaceous plants.

HERTFORDSHIRE

Hertfordshire has two great historic gardens (Hatfield House and St Paul's Walden Bury) which are open to the public, and a couple of lesser ones (Ashridge and Knebworth) but few of the others admit visitors. Nor does Hertfordshire have as many good modern gardens as its proximity to London might suggest. Both the Beale Arboretum and the Gardens of the Rose are less than fifty years old, and of interest mainly for their specialist collections of trees and roses. The only garden with really good herbaceous plantings is Benington Lordship. There is a sprinkling of fine trees at such gardens as Bayfordbury (sometimes open for the National Gardens Scheme) and Aldenham – both relics of keen gardening owners in the past – but no old-established arboretum or pinetum of special merit. The National Gardens Scheme can muster only about two-thirds of the number of gardens which open for charity in such a county as Northamptonshire and there are only five National Collections in the county – less than in the Isle of Wight. But Hertfordshire has some good nurseries and a large number of excellent garden centres. The presence of the Royal National Rose Society and its spectacular display gardens is a considerable asset to the St Albans area, as is the nearby horticultural college at Oaklands. Nevertheless, it remains difficult to explain why a county so close to London should not be endowed with horticultural wealth on anything like the scale of Surrey or Kent.

Aylett Nurseries Ltd

NORTH ORBITAL ROAD, LONDON COLNEY, ST ALBANS AL2 1DH

Tel 01727 822255 **Fax** 01727 823024
Location On A414, on left-hand side when driving towards Hatfield
Opening hours 8.30 am – 5.30 pm; Monday – Friday. 8.30 am – 5 pm; Saturdays. 9.30 am – 5 pm; Bank Holidays. 10.30 am – 4.30 pm; Sundays

This huge (and very busy) general garden centre has a prime trading position with a vast range of plants and every imaginable sundry. It also offers a design service and delivery. But Ayletts also has a speciality – its award-winning dahlias which have been a feature of RHS shows for many years. The growing fields are a mile or so from the nursery and well worth a visit in late summer or early autumn. All the different classes of dahlia hybrids are represented in both quantity and quality.

The Gardens of the Rose

CHISWELL GREEN, ST ALBANS AL2 3NR

Tel 01727 850461 **Fax** 01727 850360
Website www.roses.co.uk
Location 1 mile from junction of M1 & M25; 2 miles south of St Albans
Opening hours 9 am – 5 pm (10 am – 6 pm on Sundays & Bank Holidays); daily; 2 June to 30 – September
Admission fee Adults £4; OAPs £3.50; Children £1.50; Members free

This is the most comprehensive rose garden in Britain, and the best in which to learn about roses of all kinds. Its design and layout is something of a 1960s hangover – lots of beds cut out of the turf and filled with bushes of a single cultivar. This was the way that roses were commonly grown until about 1980, and it is fair to say that the Royal National Rose Society has not made enough effort to underplant their garden with other plants: this would enable them to open earlier in the season and attract garden visitors in the peak garden visiting months of April and May. Every class of rose is well represented in the gardens. The old roses – Gallicas, Damasks and Mosses – are concentrated in a garden with sweeping curves designed by Graham Stuart Thomas. Elsewhere are collections of Bourbons and Hybrid Perpetuals. The greatest impact comes from the Hybrid Teas, Floribundas and climbing roses: the view down the central avenue from the house in which the Society has its offices is one of the greatest sights among all English gardens. It is a paved walk down to a pool, backed by a pergola of climbing roses and flanked with modern roses in every imaginable colour. We carry a photograph of this outstanding modern garden on the cover of this book. It celebrates quite unashamedly the glory of the rose as a good value, easy-to-grow plant that gives greater beauty over a longer period than any other. Yet further parts of the garden are devoted to wild species of roses, ground cover roses, miniatures and special types such as those which have received leading awards from the Rose Society's trials. Some 600 unnamed cultivars at any one time are undergoing trialling, a process which lasts three years. The greatest excitement of recent years was the first appearance of the bluest rose ever seen – 'Rhapsody in Blue' – which will be introduced in 2002. In the main garden itself are 30,000 rose bushes and 1,750 cultivars: no place can beat the Gardens of the Rose in June and July for colour and fragrance. The Rose Society has ambitious plans to expand its gardens to some 60 acres. These began with the opening of the Peace Garden in 1995 (designed to show the importance of the 'Peace' rose in the history of modern rose breeding) but were held up pending a planning appeal. Planning permission to develop the garden has at last been received, and the society hopes to start on the expansion shortly, but inevitably the new development does depend upon funding.

Owned by The Royal National Rose Society
Number of gardeners 7
Size 27 acres
NCCPG National Collections *Rosa* (species & cultivars)

Beale Arboretum

WEST LODGE PARK, COCKFOSTERS
ROAD, HADLEY WOOD, BARNET
EN4 0PY

Tel 020 8441 5159 x 304   **Fax** 020 8449 9916
Location A111 halfway between M25 Jct24
& Cockfosters station
Opening hours 2 pm – 5 pm; Wednesdays;
April to October. Plus: 21 May & 29 October for
National Gardens Scheme
Admission fee £2 on Wednesdays; £2.50 for
National Gardens Scheme. Children free

The Beale Arboretum, first planted in 1975,
is about to double its size from ten acres to
twenty over the next five years. It is already
an exceptional collection: young trees have
been planted among much older specimens
– Victorian cedars and redwoods – with a
view to the overall effect. There are fine
collections of oaks, hornbeams,
liquidambers and nyssas, as well as shrubby
eleagnus and underplantings of
rhododendrons. Little known as yet, the
Beale Arboretum is undoubtedly to be
reckoned among the great late-twentieth-
century arboreta.

Plant Highlights Woodland garden;
mature conifers; a fine collection of
young trees; oaks; liquidambers; hornbeams;
300-year-old specimen of *Arbutus unedo*.

Owned by Trevor Beale
Number of gardeners 2
Size 20 acres
NCCPG National Collections *Carpinus*; *Eleagnus*

Benington Lordship

BENINGTON, STEVENAGE SG2 7BS

Tel 01438 869228   **Fax** 01438 869622
Website www.beningtonlordship.co.uk
Location Off A602 Stevenage to Hertford, in Benington
village
Opening hours 12 noon – 5 pm; Wednesdays; April to
September. 2 pm – 5 pm; Sundays; April to August. Also
open for snowdrops 12 noon – 4 pm from 3 to 17 February
Admission fee Adults £3; Children free

Benington Lordship is a Georgian house
with an Edwardian add-on, a mock Norman
gateway and the ruins of a real Norman
castle in the grounds. The extensive gardens
have been revived and replanted in recent
years without destroying the older features:
a Pulhamite folly, an Edwardian rock garden
and a sense of spacious parkland. But the
highlight of a visit today is the stupendous
double herbaceous border that Mrs Bott
has planted in gentle pastel shades: the best
we know.

Owned by C H A Bott
Number of gardeners 2
Size 7 acres
English Heritage grade II

Hill House

STANSTEAD ABBOTS, WARE
SG12 8BX

Tel 01920 870013
Location Next to the Parish Church in Capell Lane
Opening hours 2 pm – 5 pm on 29 April. 2 pm – 5.30 pm
on 3 & 10 June. Groups at other times by appointment
Admission fee Adults £2.50; Children 50p

Outstanding plantings in the old kitchen
garden include colour borders of purple and

Hatfield House

HATFIELD AL9 5NQ

Tel 01707 287010 **Fax** 01707 275719
Location Off A1(M) Jct4
Opening hours 24 March to 23 September. West gardens:
11 am – 6 pm; daily except Mondays. East gardens:
11 am – 6 pm, Fridays ('Connoisseur's Days')
Admission fee House, park & garden: Adults £6.60, but
£10 on Fridays

The gardens at Hatfield are mainly late nineteenth- and twentieth-century. An 1890s parterre called the East Garden is the outstanding feature: in 1977 Lady Salisbury enclosed it on either side with avenues of evergreen oaks – they are grown on two-metre stems and clipped like lollipops – and replanted the formal beds. Two years later she started on the Knot Garden, an historical recreation in front of the old palace. The designs are extracted from traditional English patterns in such herbaries as Parkinson's. Four central beds surround a small pool: the corners of the beds are marked by pyramids of box. Three are knots; the fourth is a gravel maze, to remind us that Hatfield already had a maze when Queen Elizabeth I visited it. The Elizabethan fruit garden is represented by pomegranates which are put out in the summer, another link to the earliest gardens at Hatfield. The planting is true to the period too: every plant is one that would have been introduced to England before 1620. They include clove carnations, ancient roses and a collection of historical tulips given to Lady Salisbury by the *Hortus Bulborum* in Holland. Lady Salisbury has tried to re-make the gardens as they might have been, and bring them back into sympathy with the great unchanging house. 'It is my dream' she wrote 'that one day they will become again a place of fancies and conceits, where not only pleasure and peace can be found but a measure of surprise and mystery'.

Owned by The Marquess of Salisbury
Number of gardeners 6
Size 42 acres
English Heritage grade I

gold, weeping pears, and vegetables all as neat as imaginable. Pretty woodland garden and lush growth around the small lake.

Owned by Mr & Mrs Ronald Pilkington
Number of gardeners 1
Size 8 acres

Hopleys

HIGH STREET, MUCH HADHAM
SG10 6BU

Tel 01279 842509   **Fax** 01279 843784
Website www.hopleys.co.uk
Location 50 yards north of The Bull pub
Opening hours 9 am (2 pm on Sundays) – 5 pm; daily except Tuesdays. Closed in January & February

Hopleys has a fine four-acre garden with some excellent plants (especially conifers), but the nursery is its principal draw. It offers an extensive choice of hardy shrubs and perennials, with many half-hardy plants too – being particularly strong on diascias, osteospermums, penstemons and salvias. Since its foundation in 1968, the nursery has been responsible for numerous introductions: the most famous are *Lavatera* 'Barnsley' and *Potentilla fruticosa* 'Red Ace'. The tradition continues with its new *Abelia* × *grandiflora* 'Hopleys'. The website is excellent – very comprehensive and informative.

Knebworth House

KNEBWORTH, STEVENAGE SG3 6PY

Tel 01438 812661   **Fax** 01438 811908
Website www.knebworthhouse.com
Location Off A1(M) Jct7
Opening hours 11 am – 5.30 pm; daily; 7 to 22 April, 26 May to 3 June and 7 July to 4 September.

Plus weekends and Bank Holidays from 28 April to 20 May and weekends only from 9 June to 1 July and from 8 to 30 September
Admission fee £5.50

Most of the garden was laid out by Lutyens, who married a daughter of the house. It has been well restored over the last 15 years with Jekyll plantings where appropriate. Inventive and harmonious, few gardens make such good use of space and perspective.

Owned by The Hon Henry Lytton Cobbold
Number of gardeners 4
Size 25 acres
English Heritage grade II*

St Paul's Walden Bury

WHITWELL, HITCHIN SG4 8BP

Tel 01438 871218   **Fax** 01438 871229
Location B651 5 miles south of Hitchin
Opening hours For NGS, and groups by arrangement

St Paul's Walden Bury is highly important as a unique example of the French eighteenth-century style – three hedged *allées* lead off into the woodland towards temples, statues and pools. The present owner's father (the Queen Mother's brother) was a past President of the Royal Horticultural Society, and was able to blend rhododendrons, azaleas, maples and magnolias (plus much more besides) into parts of the woodland. It is therefore a garden that appeals to historians, plantsmen and artists alike.

Owned by St Paul's Walden Bury Estate Co
English Heritage grade I

The Van Hage Garden Company

GREAT AMWELL, WARE SG12 9RP

Tel 01920 870811 **Fax** 01920 871861
Website www.vanhage.co.uk
Location On A1170
Opening hours 9 am – 6 pm; Monday – Saturday.
10.30 am – 4.30 pm; Sundays. Opens at 9.30 am on
Mondays

This long-established and award-winning garden centre is particularly strong on house plants, though it offers a large choice of hardy plants too. Van Hage are also seed merchants: they sell their own flower and vegetable seed, including the record-breaking carrot 'Flak' and some untreated seed which is suitable for organic gardeners. They have two other garden centres, one at Chenies near Rickmansworth and the other at Bragbury End on the south-east edge of Stevenage.

ISLE OF WIGHT

The Isle of Wight ('the island' to its residents) may be small and deficient in wealth-creating industries, but it has two exceptional gardens: the nineteenth-century royal palace of Osborne which overlooks the Solent on the northern shores of the island, and the modern botanic garden at Ventnor on the sunny southern side. It also has some fine plantsman's gardens (most notably John Harrison's at North Court), an active Historic Gardens Trust and NCCPG group, several National Collections and some good nurseries. In addition to those listed below, there is a magnificent choice of daylilies available from A la Carte Daylilies (Little Hermitage, St Catherine's Down, Ventnor PO38 2PU – by appointment only), including many of the new American hybrids: the nursery has two National Collections of *Hemerocallis*, large flowered cultivars which have received awards since 1960, and miniature and small-flowered cultivars. Another National Collection is held by Springbank Nurseries (Winford Road, Newchurch, Sandown PO36 0JX), whose nerines have won several awards at RHS shows in recent years and extend to over 600 cultivars.

Barton Manor

WHIPPINGHAM, EAST COWES
PO32 6LB

Tel 01983 292835   **Fax** 01983 293923
Location Next to Osborne House on East Cowes Road (A3021)
Opening hours 10 am – 5 pm; 3 June, 1 July, 5 August, 2 September. Closes at 7 pm in September
Admission fee Adults £3; OAPs £2; Children £1

Laid out by Prince Albert, Barton was for many years part of the Osborne estate. He planted some of the best trees, including the cork plantation near the house. The collection of kniphofias is the main modern attraction for garden-visitors: many are available by mail order.

Owned by R Stigwood
Size 26 acres
NCCPG National Collections *Kniphofia*

Deacon's Nursery

MOOR VIEW, GODSHILL PO38 3HW

Tel 01983 840750/522243   **Fax** 01983 523575
Location Moor View is next to school, down School Crescent
Opening hours 8 am – 4 pm (2 pm on Saturdays); Monday – Friday; October to April. 8 am – 6 pm (4 pm on Saturdays); Monday – Friday; April to October

Deacon's is one of the leading fruit-tree nurseries in England, with tree and soft fruit of every size and variety. The very comprehensive list includes over 300 apple cultivars, many which are not listed elsewhere – including such regional specialities as 'Devonshire Crimson Queen' and 'Welsh Russet'. All rootstocks are of virus-free origin.

Mottistone Manor

NEWPORT PO30 4ED

Tel 01983 740012
Website www.nationaltrust.org.uk
Location On B3399 west of Brighstone
Opening hours 2 pm – 5.30 pm; Wednesdays, Sundays and Bank Holiday Mondays; 25 March to 28 October
Admission fee £2.50

Mottistone has a cleverly designed modern garden on a difficult site – steep and narrow. Much has been terraced and enclosed to allow a rose garden and good herbaceous borders. Most of the rest is given to a wide variety of fruit trees, trained to make avenues and underplanted with vegetables or spring bulbs. It is a model for this type of planting, and made long before the current fashion for ornamental *potagers*.

Owned by The National Trust

North Court

SHORWELL PO30 3JG

Tel & Fax 01983 740415
Location 4 miles south-west of Newport, off B3323
Opening hours For National Gardens Scheme & by appointment

The Harrison family which owns North Court inherited fine grounds with some magnificent trees and a clear stream at the bottom. John Harrison has extensively replanted it with a plantsman's enthusiasm and a special interest in tender exotica. Definitely a garden to watch in future.

Owned by Mr & Mrs John Harrison

Nunwell House

BRADING, RYDE PO36 0JQ

Tel 01983 407240
Location Signed off A3055, 1 mile to the west of Brading
Opening hours 1 pm – 5 pm; 28 & 29 May; then Monday – Wednesday from 3 July to 6 September. Plus 2 pm – 5 pm on 3 June for National Gardens Scheme
Admission fee Gardens only: £2.50

This pretty garden was largely replanted by Vernon Russell-Smith about 30 years ago: he also planted a small arboretum. The present owners have added some highly attractive garden ornaments and are restoring the fabric and the plantings after some years of neglect. The double herbaceous borders are excellent. Work continues.

Owned by Colonel & Mrs J A Aylmer
Number of gardeners owners, plus ½
Size 6 acres
English Heritage grade II

Ventnor Botanic Garden

UNDERCLIFF DRIVE, VENTNOR PO38 1UL

Tel 01983 855397 **Fax** 01983 856154
Website www.botanic.co.uk
Location 1½ miles west of Ventnor on A3055
Opening hours Dawn – dusk; daily; all year. Temperate House & Visitor Centre open 10 am – 5 pm from 5 March to 28 October, and 11 am to 4 pm on Saturdays & Sundays at other times
Admission fee Garden: free. Temperate House: 50p (20p for children) Parking charges

Originally an offshoot of Hillier's Nursery, the Ventnor Botanic Garden is devoted to exotic plants. It is not strictly a *botanic* garden, but it has a remarkable collection. Many of the plants – perhaps most – are from the southern hemisphere but flourish in the unique microclimate of the 'Undercliff': widdringtonias from Zimbabwe and Tasmanian olearias, for instance, as well as astelias, *Sophora microphylla* and *Griselinia lucida* from New Zealand. *Geranium maderense* has naturalised on the sunny slopes and so has an amazing colony of 4-metre *Echium pininana*. Elsewhere are such Mediterranean natives as acanthus, cistus and *Coronilla valentina*, and a remarkable area called the Palm Garden, where stately foliage-plants like yuccas, cordylines, phormiums and beschornerias are underplanted with watsonias, cannas and kniphofias. Almost destroyed by the gales of 1987 and 1990, the collections were rapidly re-made and the garden now looks wonderfully vigorous again. This year will see some extensive re-landscaping of the Mediterranean garden. The energetic head gardener has a splendid eye for planting. A magnificent new visitor centre opened recently: it offers the venue for exhibitions and a programme of events as well as a restaurant for visitors. The nursery sells some very interesting and often tender plants which are surplus to the garden's own requirements. Most are seed-raised and come from all around the world wherever there is a Mediterranean-type climate.

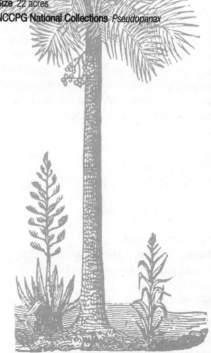

Plant Highlights Sub-tropical plants; plantsman's collection of plants; good herbaceous borders; palms; olives; bananas; medicinal herbs from all over the world; new xerophytic garden (1998); largest collection of New Zealand plants in UK.

Owned by Isle of Wight Council
Number of gardeners 8
Size 22 acres
NCCPG National Collections *Pseudopanax*

Osborne House

EAST COWES PO32 0JY

Tel 01983 200022 **Fax** 01983 281380
Location Follow the brown tourist signs
Opening hours 10 am – 6 pm (5 pm in October); daily;
April to October
Admission fee Garden only: Adults £3.80; Concessions
£2.80; Children £1.90

Prince Albert laid out the stupendous
Italianate terraces between this elegant
Florentine palace and the parkland below.
Starting in 1847, he embellished the terraces
with balustrades, urns, steps, statues and
fountains, all based on designs he had seen
in northern and central Italy. The seasonal
displays of massed bedding are still
impressive. In the park are many fine trees,
including a great avenue of cedars and a
fastigiate form of *Cupressus macrocarpa*
planted by Queen Victoria. The kitchen
garden has recently been restored to use:
English Heritage has repaired the wall and
the old glasshouse, reinstated the original
paths, started to train fruit trees against the
walls (including 'Lane's Prince Albert'
apples), and filled the beds with vegetables
and flowers for cutting.

Owned by English Heritage
Size 50 acres
English Heritage grade II*

KENT

Kent is thick with good gardens and nurseries: the Garden of England has the oldest market gardens in the country. These were developed in the sixteenth century to supply fresh fruit and vegetables to the fast-growing population of London: the men of Kent filled their barges up with the capital's night soil on the return journey and applied this bounty to their orchards. Kent has long been a rich county, not only because of its soil and climate, but also because many Londoners have traditionally spent the fortunes they made in the City on the acquisition of houses and gardens there. The exceptional number of arboreta and record-sized trees in Kent testifies to its long tradition of ornamental gardening. Not only does it have an exceptional number of important historic gardens, but all six of those which are rated Grade I by English Heritage are open regularly to the public – Godington, Hever, Knole, Penshurst, Scotney and Sissinghurst. Many of the other graded gardens are also open throughout the summer. But the historic gardens are supplemented by fine modern ones with important horticultural collections: the national pinetum at Bedgebury, for example, and the stupendous fruit collections at Brogdale – both of them, incidentally, gardens which offer free access to RHS members throughout their open season. The three other free-access gardens – Yalding, Broadview and Cabbages & Kings – are important examples respectively of organic gardening, a teaching garden and good modern design. The National Gardens Scheme thrives in Kent: some 170 gardens great and small open for its charitable purposes, one of the largest number in the whole country. Gardens and gardening flourish in every town and village: a great number of good garden centres and nurseries exist to satisfy the demand for plants. The nurseries include some of the leading specialists in their field: Brenda Hyatt, for example, has won many awards over the years for her auriculas, while Downderry Nursery (another regular at RHS shows in season) has National Collections of lavender and rosemary. It is however a matter for regret that the sempervivum specialist Alan C. Smith of Keston decided to retire at the end of last year: he grew over 1,000 cultivars and his exhibits at RHS shows were a revelation to many. The RHS runs lectures at Bedgebury and Cabbages & Kings and, in particular, at Hadlow College which is one of its Partner Colleges.

Bedgebury National Pinetum

GOUDHURST, CRANBROOK TN17 2SL

Tel 01580 211044 **Fax** 01580 212423
Location 1 mile east of A21 at Flimwell on B2079
Opening hours 10 am – dusk; daily; all year
Admission fee Adults £3; OAPs £2.50; Children £1.50

Bedgebury Pinetum is the national conifer collection: the International Dendrological Research Institute considers it the best conifer collection in the world. It was founded as a joint venture between the Forestry Commission and the Royal Botanic Gardens at Kew: the first plants for the pinetum were raised at Kew in 1921 and planted out at Bedgebury four years later. The collection boasts of over 1,500 different species or cultivars and stretches across 300 acres of landscaped woodland around a series of lakes and streams. But Bedgebury is not just for conifer lovers. The woodland garden is also well known for its deciduous trees: it has fine collections of oaks and maples, azaleas and rhododendrons. A new Japanese glade was added in 1996. Bedgebury is also good for its autumn colour and one of the best places we know for a winter walk.

 Plant Highlights Mature conifers; rhododendrons; fungi; new Japanese maple glade; eighteen record tree species, including two broadleaves.

Owned by Forestry Commission
Number of gardeners 6
Size 250 acres
NCCPG National Collections *Chamaecyparis lawsoniana* cvs.; *Juniperus*; *Taxus*; *Thuja*; × *Cupressocyparis*
English Heritage grade II*

Belmont Park

BELMONT, THROWLEY, FAVERSHAM ME13 0HH

Tel 01795 890202
Location Signed from A251 at Badlesmere
Opening hours 2 pm – 5 pm; Saturdays, Sundays & Bank Holiday Mondays; 23 April to 30 September
Admission fee Garden: Adults £2.75; Children £1

Quiet parkland and the relics of a 200-year-old arboretum surround this handsome Samuel Wyatt house. The pleasure gardens are so obviously for the pleasure of the owners, not for display, that they add considerably to the sense of domesticity: a rock garden, a rose garden, and a Coronation Avenue planted in 1953 of chestnut and walnut. The old kitchen garden has been restored for the millennium.

Owned by The Harris (Belmont) Charity
Number of gardeners 3
Size 40 acres
English Heritage grade II

J Bradshaw & Son

BUSHEYFIELDS NURSERY, HERNE, HERNE BAY CT6 7LJ

Tel & Fax 01227 375415
Location 2 miles south of Herne on A291
Opening hours 10 am – 5 pm; Tuesday – Saturday & Bank Holidays; March to October

This small family nursery (established in 1910) specialises in clematis, honeysuckles and other climbing wall-plants – ivies, roses, passion-flowers and shrubs which adapt well to walls. Until recently, the nursery had National Collections of climbing honeysuckles (*Lonicera*) and *Clematis*

montana cultivars, and this interest is reflected in its excellent list. Many of the species and cultivars it offers are unique to it and not available elsewhere in the British Isles – *Lonicera prolifera* and *L. periclymenum* 'Liden', for example.

Broadview Gardens

HADLOW, TONBRIDGE TN11 0AL

Tel 01732 850551   **Fax** 01732 853207
Location Signed from A26, 3 miles north-east of Tonbridge
Opening hours 10 am – 5 pm; daily; April to October
Admission fee Adults £2; Children free. RHS members free in September & October

These new gardens attached to Hadlow College include a series of model designs and plantings which are intended to help students to learn the skills of garden design and horticulture. They are, of course, extremely interesting and inspiring for ordinary visitors: they include a sub-tropical garden, a low-maintenance garden, long herbaceous borders, a Japanese garden and a cottage garden. The college also has a good garden centre.

Owned by Hadlow College
Size 8 acres
NCCPG National Collections *Anemone* (Japanese); *Helleborus*

Brogdale

BROGDALE ROAD, FAVERSHAM ME13 8XZ

Tel 01795 535286   **Fax** 01795 531710
Location 1 mile south-west of Faversham

Opening hours 9.30 am – 5.30 pm; daily; spring & summer. 10 am – 4.30 pm; daily; winter. Closed on Mondays & Tuesdays from 1 December to 25 March
Admission fee Adults £3; OAPs £2.50; Children £1.50. RHS members free all year

Brogdale describes itself as 'a living museum' and claims to have the largest collection of fruit cultivars in the world: more than 2,300 apples, 400 pears and 360 plums. There are demonstrations, exhibitions, workshops and events throughout the year. Fruit from the collections is sold, and scion wood supplied.

Owned by Brogdale Horticultural Trust
Size 30 acres
NCCPG National Collections *Corylus*; (cobnuts & filberts); *Fragaria*; × *ananassa*; *Malus* (apples, ornamental cvs. & cider apples); *Prunus* (cherry); *Prunus* (plums); *Pyrus*; *Ribes grossularia* (gooseberries); *Ribes nigrum* (blackcurrants); *Ribes sativum* (currants other than blackcurrants); *Vitis vinifera*

Chartwell

WESTERHAM TN16 1PS

Tel 01732 866368   **Fax** 01732 868193
Website www.nationaltrust.org.uk
Location A25 to Westerham then signed from B2026
Opening hours 11 am – 5 pm; Wednesday – Sunday & Bank Holiday Mondays (plus Tuesdays in July & August); 31 March to 4 November
Admission fee House & Gardens: Adults £5.60; Children £2.80

The spacious and extensive gardens are well laid out and planted in a slightly old-fashioned style. One of the rose gardens has the variety 'Winston Churchill' but every part has a deep sense of history and all is maintained to a very high standard.

Owned by The National Trust
English Heritage grade II*

Church Hill Cottage Gardens

CHARING HEATH, ASHFORD
TN27 0BU

Tel 01233 712522
Location Church Hill is in the middle of Charing Heath
Opening hours 10 am – 5 pm; Tuesday – Sunday
& Bank Holidays; February to November

This is a true cottage garden nursery. It specialises in hardy herbaceous perennials, but there are many dianthus, alpines, hostas, violas, ferns and shrubs to choose from too. The garden has six distinct areas and some island beds but is unified by the profusion of cottage plants, bulbs, alpine and herbaceous plantings in each of them. Ornamental trees like birches give added structure, and there is a pretty woodland area with yet more interesting plantings.

Copton Ash Gardens

105 ASHFORD ROAD, FAVERSHAM
ME13 8XW

Tel 01795 535919
Location On A251, opposite M2 eastbound exit
Opening hours 2 pm – 6 pm; Tuesday – Sundays. And by appointment
Admission fee free to nursery visitors

This is a first-rate plantsman's garden, attached to a nursery specialising in real rarities. Started in 1978, the garden now has over 3,000 different plants growing in 1½ acres – the fruit of Tim Ingram's constant quest for new things to try out. His interests can be seen in the large collection of rare Mediterranean plants, a fascinating collection of *Umbelliferae* (many of them new to cultivation) and good plants from the Southern Hemisphere which he tests for hardiness. The nursery is excellent, offering the best of these rarities, and with a catalogue that is based on Tim Ingram's own observations, not the recycled nursery-speak of others.

Owned by Tim Ingram

Doddington Place Gardens

SITTINGBOURNE ME9 0BB

Tel & Fax 01795 886101
Location Follow brown tourist signs from A2
Opening hours 10.30 am – 5 pm; Tuesday – Thursday
& Bank Holiday Mondays; Easter to September.
And 2 pm – 5 pm on Sundays
Admission fee Adults £3; Children 50p

The house and garden both date back to the 1860s: Markham Nesfield had a hand in the original formal gardens. The handsome *Sequoiadendron giganteum* and billowing yew hedges are also nineteenth-century, but this is a garden to which every generation has added something. From the Edwardian era dates the rock garden of local stone: cyclamen have naturalised all through it. The woodland garden was developed in the 1960s on a small outcrop of greensand: rhododendrons, camellias, styrax, eucryphias and maples flourish here as nowhere nearby. More recent are a paved rose garden (*very* pretty), an avenue of *Sorbus aucuparia* 'Beissneri' planted for its winter bark, and excellent colour borders (red and white). And the present owners are adding architectural features and new plantings with great verve.

Owned by Mr R Oldfield
Number of gardeners 2, plus 2 part-time
Size 10 acres
English Heritage grade II

Downderry Nursery

PILLAR BOX LANE, HADLEY,
TONBRIDGE TN11 9SW

Tel 01732 810081 **Fax** 01732 811398
Location Follow Tourist signs off A26 north-east
of Hadlow
Opening hours 10 am – 5 pm; daily; May to November

This nursery in an old walled garden has the widest imaginable list of lavender and rosemary cultivars. Almost all the species are here, including the most unusual ones, and a wide number of hybrids and selections, some of them bred or chosen by the owner Dr Charlesworth himself. His exhibits at the major RHS summer shows have been a source of inspiration to many gardeners, and hurried them to visit his nursery, where he has also begun to make a display garden. Customers speak well of the quality of his plants.

NCCPG National Collections *Lavandula*; *Rosmarinus*

Edenbridge House

MAIN ROAD, EDENBRIDGE TN8 6SJ

Tel 01732 862122 **Fax** 01732 978385
Location On B2026, 1½ miles north of Edenbridge
Opening hours 2 pm – 6 pm; 15 & 29 April, 6 & 13 May, 10 June, 8 & 15 July, & 23 September. Plus 1 pm – 5 pm on 16 May & 19 September, and 6 pm – 9 pm on 13 June. And groups by appointment
Admission fee Adults £2; Children 25p

This 1920s garden has been renewed and replanted by the present owner as a series of garden rooms to offer something of interest at every season. The spacious terraces are home to a rich mix of tender plants, many of them put out in pots for the summer months. A stream with bog plants along its edges runs down to a small pool. In the kitchen garden is a fine greenhouse and small collection of ornamental trees, as well as apples and an appetising vegetable garden.

Owned by Mrs M T Lloyd
Number of gardeners owners plus 3 part-timers
Size 5 acres

Emmetts Garden

IDE HILL, SEVENOAKS TN14 6AY

Tel 01732 750367 **Fax** 01732 750490
Website www.nationaltrust.org.uk
Location Between Sundridge & Ide Hill off B2042
Opening hours 11 am – 5.30 pm (last ticket 4.30 pm); Wednesday – Sunday & Bank Holiday Mondays; 31 March to 3 June. Then Wednesdays, Saturdays, Sundays & Bank Holidays from 6 June to 4 November
Admission fee Adults £3.40; Children £1.70

A stiff walk up from the carpark brings you to this windswept hilltop garden, laid out in Edwardian times and maintained on a slim budget. The formal Italianate rose garden is pretty in July, but better still is the informal woodland garden laid out with trees and shrubs in the William Robinson style. Best in bluebell time.

Owned by The National Trust
English Heritage grade II

Godington Park

ASHFORD TN23 3BP

Tel & Fax 01233 632652
Location Godington Lane, Potters Corner A20
Opening hours 2 pm – 5.30 pm; Thursday – Monday;
17 March to 7 October. House open 14 April to
15 October.
Admission fee Adults £2; Children £1

Godington is the prettiest house in Kent, a
Jacobean mansion reworked in the 1920s by
Sir Reginald Blomfield who advised on the
garden for over 20 years. The charming
Italian garden is his: statues, loggia,
summerhouse, box-edged quincunx and
Italian cypresses. The magnificent yew hedge
– said to be the longest in the country –
dates from his first plantings in the 1900s:
Dutch gables have been cut along its top to
match the architecture of the house.
Elsewhere are an avenue of sorbus and
cherry, a sunken pool, a formal rose garden,
herbaceous borders, sweeping lawns and an
eighteenth-century park. The trees include a
pair of *Prunus* 'Tai Haku' (one of them
reputed to be the largest in the country) and
a vast specimen of the tulip tree
(*Liriodendron tulipifera*). Planting continues:
the owners are keen plantsmen and have for
many years been making the woodland
garden. Part of the walled garden has just
been planted as a wildflower mix with
common arable flowers, like cornflowers,
corn marigold and corn cockle. Meanwhile
the Delphinium Society has planted a border
with rare cultivars and there is a growing
collection of *Clematis montana* cultivars,
taken over from the Kent nursery of
J Bradshaw & Sons. And the reason that the
garden opens several weeks before the house
is so that visitors can see the daffodils and
fritillaries: the owners have their priorities
right.

Owned by The Godington House Preservation Trust
Number of gardeners 3
Size 12 acres
English Heritage grade I

Goodnestone Park

WINGHAM, CANTERBURY CT3 1PL

Tel 01304 840107
Location Follow brown tourist signs from B2046
Opening hours 11 am – 5 pm; Mondays, Wednesday
– Friday; 26 March to 26 October. Plus 12 noon – 6 pm on
Sundays from 2 April to 15 October
Admission fee Adults £3; OAPs £2.50; Children (under 12)
30p; Disabled in wheelchairs £1; Group (20+) £2.50;
Guided Group £3.50

Goodnestone is a handsome Palladian
building. Jane Austen's brother married a
daughter of the house: she will have known
the fine chestnut avenue dating from about
1800 and the eighteenth-century parkland
beyond. Later came the formal nineteenth-
century terraces around the house, a 1930s
woodland garden (maples, camellias,
azaleas), a 1980s holly walk, and good mixed
plantings in the old kitchen garden. A
formal parterre in early eighteenth-century
style has just been replanted in front of the
house, to celebrate the millennium. Now the
woodland garden is being expanded to take
in another three acres which will be planted
as an arboretum from 2001 onwards. It is
inspired by the passionate plantsmanship
which has imbued the present owners since
they first started to garden here nearly 50
years ago. Much of the garden is accessible
by wheelchair, but not all.

Owned by Lord & Lady FitzWalter
Size 14 acres
English Heritage grade II*

Great Comp

ST MARY'S PLATT, BOROUGH GREEN,
SEVENOAKS TN15 8QS

Tel 01732 886154
Location 2 miles east of Borough Green: take B2016
off A20
Opening hours 11 am – 6 pm; daily; April to October
Admission fee Adults £3.50; Children £1

Great Comp is a monument to the energy
and enthusiasm of Eric Cameron who has
built up the garden over the last 40 years.
The plant content is of considerable
horticultural interest and includes some 30
magnolia cultivars and a good range of
rhododendrons, conifers, heathers and
herbaceous plants: over 3,000 different
plants in all. But the most interesting thing
about the garden is the way in which large
areas have been planted for minimum
maintenance. There is much to learn and
admire here.

Owned by Great Comp Charitable Trust

Groombridge Place Gardens

GROOMBRIDGE, TUNBRIDGE WELLS
TN3 9QG

Tel 01892 863999   **Fax** 01892 863996
Location On B2110, 4 miles south-west of
Tunbridge Wells
Opening hours 9 am – 6 pm; daily; 1 April to
28 October (provisionally)
Admission fee Adults £7.70; OAPs & Children £6.60

This old/new garden was up for sale as we
went for print. It is to be hoped that the new
owners will continue to open it to visitors,
because Groombridge has lots to offer: a
drunken garden where the yews lean at tipsy
angles, an oriental garden, a 'draughtsman's
garden' and a chessboard garden. Best of all
are the brilliant colour plantings, among the
best we know. Some visitors have felt in the
past that the entry price was quite steep for
what they got: new owners, please note.

Hever Castle

EDENBRIDGE TN8 7NG

Tel 01732 865224   **Fax** 01732 866796
Website www.hevercastle.co.uk
Location 3 miles south-east of Edenbridge, signed from
M25 Jct 6
Opening hours 11 am – 5 pm (4 pm in winter); daily;
March to November
Admission fee Adults £6.30; OAPs £5.40; Children £4.20

Hever is one of the most important
Edwardian gardens in England. The pretty
moated castle sits in a park of oaks and firs
(underplanted with rhododendrons) with a
yew maze and formal neo-Tudor garden to
one side. The best part is a spectacular
five-acre Italian garden where a long pergola
(cool dripping fountains all along) leads past
a series of exquisite Italian gardens, stuffed
with outstanding sculptures, urns,
sarcophagi and other loot brought by
William Waldorf Astor from Rome; it finally
bursts onto a theatrical terrace and a 35-acre
lake, hand-dug by 800 workmen in less than
two years.

Plant Highlights Woodland garden;
topiary; 3,000 roses (old-fashioned and
modern, with some climbers too);
rhododendrons & azaleas; snowdrops;
crocus; daffodils; bluebells; tulips; dahlias;
autumn colour; Christie's/HHA Garden of
the Year in 1995.

Owned by Broadland Properties Ltd
Number of gardeners 10
Size 40 acres
English Heritage grade I

Hole Park

ROLVENDEN, CRANBROOK TN17 4JB

Tel 01580 241344 **Fax** 01580 241882
Location Off B2086 between Rolvenden & Cranbrook
Opening hours 2 pm – 6 pm; 8, 15, 22 & 29 April;
6, 20 & 27 May; 17 June; 14 & 21 October. Plus
Wednesdays from April to June and in October.
Guided tours and groups by appointment
Admission fee Adults £3; Children 50p

This great garden is far too little known. The
drive runs under an avenue of horse
chestnuts through classical parkland. The
pleasure garden is Edwardian in origin, but
has been revived and replanted by the
present owner. Solid hedges and clipped
specimens of yew are everywhere: backing
the excellent herbaceous borders, around
the waterlily pond and framing a croquet
lawn with standard wisterias. The flowery
woodlands have palm trees in the dell, while
the lake is surrounded by orange azaleas and
purple rhododendrons. Bluebells, daffodils
and wonderful views are added delights.

Owned by David Barham
Number of gardeners 2
Size 15 acres

Iden Croft Herbs

FRITTENDEN ROAD, STAPLEHURST
TN12 0DH

Tel 01580 891432
Opening hours 9 am – 5 pm; Monday – Saturday; all year.
11 am – 5 pm; Sundays & Bank Holidays; March to
September only

The owners have developed this substantial
nursery over the last 30 years and planted a
series of demonstration gardens. These
incorporate a sixteenth-century walled
garden, originally attached to Staplehurst
Manor. Other gardens include a cottage
garden near the café, and a 'sensory garden'
which shows how herbs may be arranged
and appreciated for their scent, colour,
shape, form and texture. The intention is to
provide design and planting ideas for all
visitors, whatever the size of their garden.
Insects and birds are encouraged and the
catalogue which the nursery produces lists
plants under both their Latin and common
English names.

NCCPG National Collections *Mentha; Origanum*

Ightham Moat

THE NATIONAL TRUST, IVY HATCH,
SEVENOAKS TN15 0NT

Tel 01732 810378 **Fax** 01732 811029
Website www.nationaltrust.org.uk
Location Signed from A25 in Ightham village
Opening hours 11 am – 5.30 pm; daily except Tuesdays
& Saturdays; 1 April to 4 November
Admission fee Adults £5; Children £2.50

Ightham is a moated Mediaeval manor in a
wooded Kentish valley, with borders of
pinks, old roses and lilies. These were

remade about a hundred years ago in a dreamily English style. In the woodland parts are thicketed rhododendrons.

Owned by The National Trust
English Heritage grade II

Keepers Nursery

GALLANTS COURT, EAST FARLEIGH, MAIDSTONE ME15 0LE

Tel & Fax 01622 726465
Opening hours By appointment at all reasonable times

Less than twenty years old, Keepers is now the leading fruit tree nursery in the UK. It offers over 600 cultivars – apples, pears, plums and cherries, as well as the more unusual fruits like quince, medlars and mulberries. The owners have an excellent on-line ordering facility and a wide choice of rootstocks. They claim – proudly and correctly – to have made a significant contribution to the conservation of old cultivars of fruit. More than 100 of their apples are not available from any other commercial source: two which the editor of *The RHS Garden Finder* can personally recommend are 'Mollie's Delicious' and 'Carswell's Orange'.

Ladham House

GOUDHURST TN17 1DB

Tel 01580 211203
Location Left at Chequers Inn on Cranbrook road, then right to Curtisden Green
Opening hours 1.30 pm – 5.30 pm; 22 April & 20 May. And by appointment
Admission fee Adults £2.50; Children (under 12) 50p

Ladham was laid out by a botanist Master of the Rolls in the mid-nineteenth century, and has been enthusiastically restored and updated by the present owner. There is a good mixture of new plantings and old: the latter include the deep red form of *Magnolia campbellii* which has been named 'Betty Jessel' and is now available commercially.

Owned by Mr & Mrs Alastair Jessel
Number of gardeners 2
Size 10 acres

Leeds Castle

MAIDSTONE ME17 1PL

Tel 01622 765400   **Fax** 01622 735616
Website www.leeds-castle.co.uk
Location Jct8 off the M20
Opening hours 10 am – 5 pm, March to October (but closed on 30 June & 7 July); 10 am – 3 pm, November to February
Admission fee Park & gardens: Adults £8.50; OAPs & Students £7; Children £5.20

More a romantic castle than a garden, Leeds is best seen across the lake (the 'Great Water') which Russell Page created in the 1930s. Page also designed and planted the Culpeper Garden, which takes its name partly from Sir Thomas Colepeper, who bought the castle in 1632, and partly from Nicholas Culpeper, the seventeenth-century herbalist. It could be said that the Culpeper Garden does not show the twentieth century's greatest garden designer at his best: informal plantings of old garden flowers – roses, pinks, lavender, poppies and lupins. Here too is the National Collection of bergamot (*Monarda*) cultivars. The latest development – open in 1999 – is the 'Lady Baillie Garden', a series of sheltered terraces between the Culpeper Garden and the lake. In this part of the garden the planting is more Mediterranean in character. The nearby maze, planted in 1988, is fun to visit: it resembles a topiary castle with towers and bastions and, when you get to its centre, you find the entrance to an underground grotto. The 'wood garden' is planted with rhododendrons and azaleas and underplanted with daffodils and anemones and there are further rhododendrons to the west of the moat. Leeds is run by a high profile charitable trust with a big advertising budget, which may help to explain the high entry charges. Are they worth it for someone who is principally interested in gardens and plants? The answer – paradoxically – is yes, provided you also visit the castle (extra fee payable) and some of the many other attractions here. The owners say you need at least three hours to experience and enjoy them properly.

 Plant Highlights Woodland garden; roses (mainly old-fashioned); herbs; good herbaceous borders; tallest *Acer cappadocicum* 'Aureum' (23m) in the British Isles.

Owned by Leeds Castle Foundation
NCCPG National Collections *Monarda*
English Heritage grade II*

Long Barn

LONG BARN ROAD, WEALD, SEVENOAKS TN14 6NH

Location 3 miles south of Sevenoaks; end of village
Opening hours 2 pm – 5 pm; 17 June, 15 July
Admission fee Adults £2; OAPs £1.50; Children 50p

Notable as the first English garden of Harold Nicholson and Vita Sackville-West, Long Barn has been restored and developed over fifteen years by the present owners. Within the original architecture the terraced garden

has been extensively replanted and new features added to extend the variety of its rooms. The strong designs and exuberant plantings of Sissinghurst are all there in embryo.

Owned by Mr & Mrs Brandon Gough
English Heritage grade II*

Madrona Nursery

PLUCKLEY ROAD, BETHERSDEN TN26 3DD

Tel 01233 820100   **Fax** 01233 820091
Location Half way between Bethersden village & Pluckley railway station
Opening hours 10 am – 5 pm; Saturday – Tuesday; mid-March to end October

This is a first-rate general nursery, with a good choice of the more unusual (and better) cultivars across the range. Trees and shrubs are perhaps its main speciality – it is particularly strong on hydrangeas, *Aesculus* and unusual conifers like Prince Albert's yew (*Saxegothea conspicua*) – but Madrona also offers a fine choice of herbaceous perennials. All are well-grown and well-displayed: a thoroughly satisfying nursery to visit.

Marle Place Gardens

BRENCHLEY, TONBRIDGE TN12 7HS

Tel 01892 722304   **Fax** 01892 724099
Location Follow tourist signs from Brenchley
Opening hours 10 am – 5 pm; daily; April to September. And by appointment
Admission fee Adults £3.50; Concessions £3

The gardens around the Elizabethan house are mainly formal: they were well designed and imaginatively planted in the 1930s. The sunken garden, laid out with scented plants, is particularly charming. The Victorian greenhouse (recently restored) now has a collection of orchids in it. Other modern additions include some fun sculpture, a 'mosaic terrace', avenues running into the woodland and a young nut plat. And all around are orchards of Kentish apples.

Owned by Mrs L Williams
Number of gardeners 2
Size 15 acres
NCCPG National Collections Santolina; Calamintha

Penshurst Place

PENSHURST, TONBRIDGE TN11 8DG

Tel 01892 870307 **Fax** 01892 879866
Website www.seetb.org.uk/penshurst/
Location Follow brown tourist signs from Tonbridge
Opening hours 11 am – 6 pm, Saturday & Sunday, 4 to 31 March; then daily, 1 April to 31 October
Admission fee Gardens only: Adult £4.50; OAPs £4; Children £3.50

This is an historic garden of great importance: a garden with substantial genuine Tudor remains. Much of what we see now was developed in the mid-nineteenth century as a re-creation of the ideal Elizabethan garden, divided into small self-contained garden rooms each with its own style and character. They have been well restored and developed in recent years. A vast Italianate parterre dominates the immediate pleasure garden: it is planted with scarlet polyantha roses – another is planted as a Union Jack. There are borders by Lanning Roper and John Codrington, a 100-yard bed of peonies, and a garden for the blind, bought off the peg at the Chelsea

Flower Show in 1994. One impressive statistic: the garden has over one mile of yew hedging.

Owned by Viscount De L'Isle
English Heritage grade I

Plaxtol Nurseries

THE SPOUTE, PLAXTOL, SEVENOAKS TN15 0QR

Tel & Fax 01732 810550
Location On the east side of Plaxtol, off A227
Opening hours Nursery open 10 am – 5 pm, daily. Closed for a fortnight after Christmas. Gardens open by appointment

This excellent family-run garden nursery offers about 1,500 different plants, with an emphasis on flowers and foliage for flower arrangers. The main garden reflects this interest and sets out to produce the effects that you would achieve in different flower arrangement: a series of small garden rooms in widely contrasting styles. There is also a small garden made in the Japanese style: the family's other speciality is Japanese plants and garden ornaments. The nursery has a good website.

Port Lympne

LYMPNE, HYTHE CT21 4PD

Tel 01303 264647 **Fax** 01303 264944
Location Exit 11 on M20 & follow brown tourist signs
Opening hours 10 am onwards; daily except 24 December. Last admissions 4 pm in summer and 3 pm in winter
Admission fee Adults £9.80; OAPs & Children £7.80

More than a zoo, Port Lympne is a stylish and luxurious house, with a seriously important twentieth-century garden. It was laid out by Philip Tilden for Sir Philip Sassoon in 1911 on the steepest of slopes above Romney Marshes and worked on by Russell Page in the 1950s. The modern approach too is nothing if not dramatic – an absolutely straight 100-yard walk lined with hydrangeas which brings you suddenly to the top of the stupendous long stone staircase known as the Trojan stairs. Around the front door is a forecourt with thirteen statues acquired from the sale at Stowe, in Buckinghamshire in 1921: castellations in the yew hedges give views to the south. The slopes are terraced into five levels and include a vineyard and 'figyard'. The chess board garden – oblong rather than square – has squares of grass and gravel contrasted with beds for bulbs and annual displays: it is matched by a 'striped' garden on the other side of the main terrace. Down one side are the Long Borders, planted as mixtures of shrubs and perennials, and leading to the magnolia walk, the bowling green, the rose terrace, the dahlia terrace and the herbaceous border. Standards of maintenance remain high: a good garden for grandparents who want to see something more than animals.

Owned by Howletts & Port Lympne Estates Ltd
Number of gardeners 6
Size 15½ acres

Riverhill House Gardens

SEVENOAKS TN15 0RR

Tel 01732 452557 **Fax** 01732 458802
Location 2 miles south of Sevenoaks on A225
Opening hours 12 noon – 6 pm; Wednesdays & Sundays, plus Bank Holiday weekends; April to June

Admission fee Garden only: Adults £3; Children 50p. House open by appointment to groups

Riverhill is a handsome Queen Anne house with grand views over the Weald: the garden suffered badly in the Great Storm of 1987. In the middle of the nineteenth century it belonged to John Rogers the botanist, who planted many of the surviving conifers and specimen trees. The vast billowing rhododendrons include original introductions by Hooker and Fortune. Rogers's descendants made the rock garden and rose walk.

 Plant Highlights Rhododendrons & azaleas; mature conifers; bluebells; tallest *Magnolia × soulangeana* (13m) in the British Isles.

Owned by The Rogers Family
Number of gardeners 1
Size 8 acres
English Heritage grade II

Rosewood Daylilies

70 DEANSWAY AVENUE, STURRY, CANTERBURY CT2 0NN

Tel 01227 711071
Location Off to the right of Herne Bay Road, the main road leading north out of Sturry
Opening hours By appointment

Here is a splendid place to see daylilies, especially those bred and introduced since 1970. These include many of the hundreds of modern American hybrids: the owners trial new cultivars and then offer the best for sale. The nursery's list grows every year: a lot of cultivars with an RHS Award of Garden Merit have recently been added. It also offers a range of companion plants: agapanthus, crocosmias, and hardy geraniums.

Scotney Castle

LAMBERHURST, TUNBRIDGE WELLS
TN3 8JN

Tel 01892 891081   **Fax** 01892 890110
Website www.nationaltrust.org.uk
Location On A21, south of Lamberhurst
Opening hours noon – 5 pm; 17, 18, 24 & 25 March.
11 am – 6 pm (but 2 pm – 6 pm on Saturdays & Sundays);
Wednesday – Sunday; 31 March to 4 November. Plus
12 noon – 6 pm on Bank Holiday Mondays & preceding
Sundays
Admission fee Adults £4.40; Children £2.20

The house was built by Salvin in the late
1830s: the quarry where they extracted the
stone for building it is now a sheltered
woodland dell. During the nineteenth
century, many specimen trees were added
to the parkland – cypresses, cedars and
wellingtonias which, provided they survived
the gales of 1988, still give structure to the
gardens in their maturity. But the slopes
between the house and the moated and
abandoned castle at the bottom are now
covered with ornamental trees and shrubs
planted by Christopher Hussey in the 1950s
– among them are many rhododendrons,
azaleas, hydrangeas, kalmias and maples.
The ruined castle is now the focus of the
whole picturesque composition and the way
it has been richly draped in wisteria, clematis,
honeysuckles and roses is both romantic and
photogenic. Among the ruins are a herb
garden and a cottage garden designed by
Lanning Roper in about 1970, surprisingly
appropriate and effective. The views of the
castle as you meander round the edge of the
moat are little short of miraculous.

Plant Highlights Woodland garden;
plantsman's collection of plants;
rhododendrons; azaleas; water lilies;
wisteria; good autumn colour; plantings in
ruins of fourteenth-century castle.

Owned by The National Trust
English Heritage grade I

Sissinghurst Castle

SISSINGHURST, CRANBROOK
TN17 2AB

Tel 01580 715330   **Fax** 01580 713911
Website www.nationaltrust.org.uk
Location 1 mile east of Sissinghurst village, ½ mile off
A262. Cross-country footpath from village
Opening hours 1 pm – 6.30 pm (5.30 pm on Good Friday,
Saturdays & Sundays); Tuesday – Sunday; 31 March to
14 October. Timed ticket system: immediate entry
guaranteed after 4 pm Tuesday – Friday
Admission fee Adults £6.50; Children £3

So important, influential and well-known is
Sissinghurst that it comes as a shock to
realise that Harold Nicolson and Vita
Sackville-West began to make the garden
there as recently as 1930. Her writings made
it famous right from the beginning so that it
is possible to trace the history of such
features as the white garden in her many
books still in print. Harold Nicolson was a
careful designer who understood the
importance of line and measure: he was very
much a classicist in taste. Vita Sackville-
West was a romantic, exuberant poetic
plantswoman. It was the combination of
these two complementary talents that made
the garden a source of wonder and
inspiration. Sissinghurst is now part of every
English gardener's education, and one to
which it is important to return time and
again. The garden is always changing and
developing. It was the Nicolsons' intention
that the garden should continue to develop
after they gave it to the National Trust, and
this principle – that the garden must be kept

up to date with new plants – is inherent in the way that it has been managed. The design is unaltered and unalterable, and the plantings continue to be governed by the Gertrude Jekyll principles of which Sissinghurst is a supremely beautiful interpretation. But the plants are always changing and Sissinghurst therefore remains an influential plantsman's garden too. There is a timed ticket system to restrict visitors to 400 at a time, which may mean waiting. It is best visited out of season on a weekday, late in the afternoon, in April, September and October.

Owned by The National Trust
English Heritage grade I

Squerryes Court

WESTERHAM TN16 1SJ

Tel 01959 562345 **Fax** 01959 565949
Location ½ mile from A25, signed from Westerham
Opening hours 12 noon – 5.30 pm; Wednesdays, Saturdays, Sundays & Bank Holiday Mondays; April to September
Admission fee Garden only: Adults £2.50; OAPs £2.20; Children £1.50

The gardens have been excellently restored with advice from Tom Wright since 1987, guided by a Kip plan of the original garden made in 1719, before they were landscaped in the 1760s. The main feature is a formal garden behind the house, where box-edged beds are filled with santolina, lavender, sage and other sweet-smelling herbs. Beyond are beautifully planted Edwardian borders, rose gardens, shrub borders with rhododendrons and azaleas and the eighteenth-century park. The modern design and planting are inevitably a compromise, but Squerryes is place of great beauty and variety, especially in early summer.

Owned by J & A Warde
Number of gardeners 1, plus 2 part-time
Size 25 acres
English Heritage grade II

Starborough Nursery

STARBOROUGH ROAD, MARSH GREEN, EDENBRIDGE TN8 5RB

Tel 01732 865614 **Fax** 01732 862166
Location On B2028 Edenbridge to Lingfield Road
Opening hours 9.30 am – 4 pm; Monday – Saturday. Closed Wednesdays in January, July & August

Starborough has for long been an important nursery for trees and shrubs and, since it took over G Reuthe Ltd, in the 1990s, for rhododendrons and azaleas too. It is a regular exhibitor at RHS shows, where its displays of *Hamamelis* are particularly admired in mid-winter. The list of *Hamamelis* for sale includes several cultivars stocked by no other UK nursery.

Stoneacre

OTHAM, MAIDSTONE ME15 8RS

Tel 01622 862871 **Fax** 01622 862157
Website www.nationaltrust.org.uk
Location 1 mile south of A20; north end of Otham village
Opening hours 2 pm – 6 pm; Wednesdays & Saturdays; 4 April to 31 October
Admission fee Adults £2.60; Children £1.30

Stoneacre is particularly interesting because the tenant until 2000 was Rosemary Alexander, Principal of the English Gardening School at the Chelsea Physic Garden. It was where she worked out her ideas and showed her students how the principles of design and planting look 'on the ground'. The new tenants intend to preserve and develop the garden still further. It is one of the most exciting new gardens we know, and in perfect harmony with the Tudorised house.

Owned by The National Trust

Tile Barn Nursery

STANDEN STREET, IDEN GREEN, BENENDEN TN17 4LB

Tel & Fax 01580 240221
Location 2 miles south of Benenden; turn left at crossroads in Iden Green
Opening hours 9 am – 5 pm, Wednesday – Saturday

This is a splendid garden-nursery devoted to one genus – *Cyclamen*. Cyclamen are everywhere: they have spread through the lawns and into the drive, as well as under the shelter trees, shrubs and hedges. In the glasshouses are rows and rows of every imaginable hardy species and cultivar of cyclamen of different ages, all pot-grown and all of flowering size – a wonderful sight from August to April. Visitors will also find pots of some other unusual bulbs species, particularly the smaller, daintier colchicums, crocus, fritillarias, snowflakes and narcissus.

NCCPG National Collections *Cyclamen*

Walmer Castle

KINGSDOWN ROAD, WALMER, DEAL CT14 7LJ

Tel 01304 364288
Location Follow brown tourist signs
Opening hours 10 am – 6 pm (5 pm in October, and 4 pm from November to March); Wednesday – Sunday; all year. Closed January, February, 24 to 26 December and when the Lord Warden is in residence
Admission fee Adults £4.80; Concessions £3.60; Children £2.40

The gardens at Walmer Castle are well worth a visit, partly for their horticultural interest and partly for their many historical associations – William Pitt, the Duke of Wellington and Winston Churchill were all Wardens of the Cinque Ports. The castle looks onto the Broad Walk, 100m long, on either side of a wide path backed by massive mature yew hedges (3m tall and 2m wide), and lined with fine herbaceous borders. Beyond are a croquet lawn, magnificent nineteenth-century terraces, and Penelope Hobhouse's new Queen Elizabeth the Queen Mother's Garden. To the north of the Broad Walk is the Kitchen Garden – an enclosed orchard with espaliered fruit trees, a cutting garden and glasshouses. Further away are drifts of daffodils, a lawnful of specimen trees planted by famous visitors from the nineteenth century onwards, a wildflower meadow, a thickly wooded quarry and a holm oak avenue planted in 1866.

Owned by English Heritage
Number of gardeners 4
Size 8 acres
English Heritage grade II

Yalding Organic Gardens

YALDING, MAIDSTONE ME18 6EX

Tel & Fax 01622 814650
Website www.hdra.org.uk
Location On B2162, ½ mile south of village
Opening hours 10 am – 5 pm; Wednesday – Sunday; May to September. Also weekends in April & October and all Bank Holiday Mondays
Admission fee Adults £3; Children free. RHS members free

Yalding has a series of fourteen historically themed gardens run organically by the HDRA. They illustrate different gardening styles from the thirteenth century to the present day. They include an apothecary's garden in the thirteenth-century style, a late-nineteenth-century artisan's garden and a post-war allotment: all very stylish and educational. Others show the influence of William Cobbett and Gertrude Jekyll through the centuries. There is a central hop-pole pergola – a good example of how design features should come out of their surrounding landscape. A recent addition is a tall wooden henge.

Owned by Henry Doubleday Research Association
Number of gardeners 4
Size 5 acres

LANCASHIRE, GREATER MANCHESTER & MERSEYSIDE

There are few historic gardens in this industrial corner of the north-west, but several public parks whose importance is both historical and contemporary: Sefton Park in Liverpool was designed by Edouard André, Birkenhead Park by Sir Joseph Paxton, and Heaton Park in Manchester by William Emes. The public gardens at the seaside resorts of Blackpool and Southport are famous for their summer displays. Few private gardens are open to the public, though the National Gardens Scheme has in several villages managed to persuade a cluster of gardens to open simultaneously and make up a good afternoon's visiting. Myerscough College near Preston is a RHS Partner College, with about fifteen lectures and workshops all through the year. It also has a National Collection of *Eryngium*. There is a handful of other National Collections in the three counties, but this is not a corner of England with any established interest in plants apart, perhaps, from alpines: Reginald Kaye at Carnforth and Holden Clough near Clitheroe are both long-established nurseries specialising in plants for cold climates.

Bank House

BORWICK, CARNFORTH LA6 1JR

Tel 01524 732768
Location 2 miles north-east of Carnforth off A6
Opening hours 2 pm – 6 pm; 1 July
Admission fee Adults £1.50; Children free

Bank House is a successful private garden made over the last 30 years by the present owners. It manages to shoe-horn such features as a woodland garden, gravel garden, old-fashioned rose collection and a mini-arboretum into two acres. But it works.

Owned by Mr & Mrs R G McBurnie
Number of gardeners owners
Size 2 acres

Catforth Gardens

ROOTS LANE, CATFORTH, PRESTON
PR4 0JB

Tel 01772 690561
Location M6 Jct32, then north up A6 & follow brown tourist signs
Opening hours Farm gardens open 10.30 am – 5 pm; daily; mid March – mid September. Bungalow gardens open same times & dates but only Thursday – Sunday
Admission fee Adults £2.50; OAPs £2; Children 50p. RHS members free from April to August

Catforth Gardens incorporate the gardens of two separate but adjoining houses, those of Cherry Tree Lodge and Willow Bridge Farm. The garden around Cherry Tree Lodge is planted with trees, shrubs and herbaceous plants to give year-round colour. Rock gardens, bog gardens, ponds, woodland and island beds support a wide variety of plants, and it is home to a National Collection of *Geranium*. Willow Bridge Farm has a cottagey garden, but its main features lie in the large paddock garden, designed as a summer flower and water garden with sweeping herbaceous beds, roses, ponds and dry banks. Both gardens contain a wide variety of plants, many rare and unusual, and the nurseries specialise in the herbaceous plants which grow in them.

Owned by Judith & Tony Bradshaw
NCCPG National Collections *Geranium*

Croxteth Hall & Country Park

CROXTETH HALL LANE, LIVERPOOL
L12 0HB

Tel 0151 228 5311   **Fax** 0151 228 2817
Location Muirhead Avenue East

Opening hours 11 am – 5 pm; daily; April to September
Admission fee Adults £1.10; OAPs & Children 60p for walled garden. Grounds free

Very much a public amenity, Croxteth Hall has a fine woodland trail along the River Alt, but the main interest for gardeners is the Victorian walled garden. This aims to show visitors what they can achieve at home. There are lines of trained fruit trees, growing either against the walls or free-standing, a large vegetable garden (lots of varieties grown from the HDRA), an area for soft fruit, a herb garden, and a mushroom house – to remind people how mushrooms were once cultivated in grand gardens. These are interplanted with more ornamental features – a bedding display, a rose garden, some herbaceous borders and the collection of fuchsias. There are also working greenhouses and some bee hives, which add to the garden's interest.

 Plant Highlights Herbs; plants under glass; fruit; good herbaceous borders.

Owned by City of Liverpool
NCCPG National Collections *Fuchsia*
English Heritage grade II

Dunham Massey

ALTRINCHAM WA14 4SJ

Tel 0161 941 1025   **Fax** 0161 946 9291
Website www.nationaltrust.org.uk
Location 3 miles south-west of Altrincham off A56, well signed (Dunham Massey Hall & Park)
Opening hours 11 am – 5.30 pm (4.30 from 1 October); daily; 31 March to 4 November
Admission fee Gardens only: Adults £3.20; Children £1.60

Dunham Massey's 250 acres include an ancient deer park, a mediaeval moat made into a lake in the eighteenth century, an

Elizabethan mount, an eighteenth-century orangery and some early landscape avenues. All remain as features of the grounds, but the National Trust has decided to major on its even more interesting Victorian relics – evergreen shrubberies, ferns and colourful bedding-out schemes. Even that does not preclude the Trust from planting the most modern forms, such as the hybrids of *Rhododendron yakushimanum* and latest *R. occidentale* azalea hybrids. The result is a potent cross-section of historical and modern styles with a solid core of Victorian excellence, while the standard of maintenance is one of the highest in any National Trust garden.

 Plant Highlights Topiary; good herbaceous borders; hydrangeas; skimmias; Edwardian parterre.

Owned by The National Trust
English Heritage grade II*

Fletcher Moss Botanical Gardens

MILL GATE LANE, DIDSBURY M20 8SD

Tel 0161 434 1877
Location In East Didsbury, off A5145
Opening hours 8 am (9 am at weekends & Bank Holidays) – dusk; daily; all year
Admission fee Free

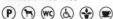

Fletcher Moss is a model municipal botanic garden, beautifully maintained but open free to the public. In the rock garden, which is substantially constructed on three levels with a pool at the bottom, is a rich collection of alpine plants, small conifers, maples and aquatics. The woodland areas have excellent autumn colour, almost as good as in spring.

Owned by Manchester City Council

Hoghton Tower

HOGHTON, PRESTON PR5 0SH

Tel 01254 852986   **Fax** 01254 852109
Location A675 midway between Preston & Blackburn
Opening hours 11 am – 4 pm; Monday – Thursday; July to September. 1 pm – 5 pm; Sundays; July to September. Also Bank Holiday Mondays from Easter to August
Admission fee Adults £3; Children (under 5) free

A series of spacious courtyards and walled gardens surround this fierce castellated house which is approached up a long avenue. Its garden is not among the greatest, but the setting is impressive and there are fine spring walks in the rhododendron woods below. There are plans to restore the rose garden this year.

Owned by Sir Bernard de Hoghton Bt
English Heritage grade II

Holden Clough Nursery

HOLDEN, BOLTON BY BOWLAND, CLITHEROE BB7 4PF

Tel & Fax 01200 447615
Website www.holdencloughnursery.co.uk
Location 8 miles north-east of Clitheroe, off A59
Opening hours 9 am – 5 pm; Monday – Saturday: all year. Plus 1.30 pm – 5 pm on certain Sundays in April & May. Other times by appointment

This long-established working nursery (founded in 1927) has a large range of interesting alpines, perennials, dwarf conifers, shrubs, ferns, grasses and foliage plants. It is well-known at shows, all over the country. One of its best introductions is the hardy and vigorous hybrid *Iris* 'Holden Clough'.

Leighton Hall

CARNFORTH LA5 9ST

Tel 01524 734474 **Fax** 01524 720357
Location Signed from A6 junction with M6
Opening hours 2 pm – 5 pm; daily except Saturday &
Monday; May to September. Open at 11.30 am in August
Admission fee Adults £4; OAPs £3.50

The handsome semi-castellated house at
Leighton is set in lush parkland with the
Lakeland fells as a backdrop: the Victorian
conservatory to the side of the house has just
been restored. The main garden features are
in the nineteenth-century walled garden,
whose formal paths contrast with the
exuberant informality of the planting. Here
are herbaceous borders, a herb garden, fruit
trees, a vegetable plot and masses of climbing
roses – as well as the unusual gravel maze.

Owned by R G Reynolds

Rufford Old Hall

RUFFORD, ORMSKIRK L40 1SG

Tel & Fax 01704 821254
Website www.nationaltrust.org.uk
Location 7 miles north of Ormskirk on A59
Opening hours 12 noon – 5 pm; Saturday – Wednesday;
31 March to 4 November
Admission fee Garden only: Adults £2; Children £1

One of the National Trust's most successful
re-creations, the gardens are laid out in the
Regency style around a remarkable
fifteenth-century timber-framed house.

Owned by The National Trust

LEICESTERSHIRE

One of the reasons why there are so few historic gardens in Leicestershire (no Grade I and only two Grade II* gardens) is that much of the county was open and unenclosed until the latter half of the eighteenth century. Even today, it is not as rich in interesting gardens as its neighbours Northamptonshire and Warwickshire. However the National Gardens Scheme offers a respectable number of gardens to visit in its Yellow Book, and there are interesting plantsman's collections at Wartnaby and Long Close, as well as the excellent University of Leicester Botanic Garden. Leicestershire has some good garden centres, and a handful of first-rate specialist nurseries, notably Bluebell Nursery near Ashby-de-la-Zouche which is an RHS Partner Nursery and has a splendid young arboretum. Brooksby College is a RHS Partner College with a fine teaching garden and collection of plants: it offers about 20 lectures, workshops and demonstrations to the public throughout the year. It also has two recently confirmed National Collections: *Liriope* and *Ophiopogon*. Contrary to local belief, there is no such county as Rutland: it was dissolved in 1974 and absorbed into Leicestershire, where it remains.

Barnsdale Plants and Gardens

THE AVENUE, EXTON, OAKHAM LE15 8AH

Tel 01572 813200   **Fax** 01572 813346
Location The Avenue is on the south west edge of Exton
Opening hours 10 am – 5 pm (last entry 3 pm); daily; March to October. 10 am – 4 pm; weekends only; November to February. Closed for two weeks at Christmas & New Year.
Admission fee Adults £5; Groups £4; Children free. RHS members free

Barnsdale was famous for twenty years as Geoff Hamilton's *BBC Gardener's World* garden. Within it are 37 individual small gardens, laid out and maintained with the same intention – to encourage people to make the most of their opportunities as garden-owners. The gardens are of every kind. Some have descriptive names like the Tranquil Garden and the Town Paradise: others are more specific like the Plantsman's Garden, the Fruit Orchard, the Rose Garden, the Stream and Bog Garden. But for many visitors the most interesting are those which match their own particular circumstances and inspire them to be better gardeners – the First Time Garden, the Small Town Garden, the Ornamental Kitchen Garden and the Allotment Garden. All are maintained to the highest standard and continue to educate, delight and inspire. The attached nursery sells over 1,500 different plants, often in small quantities. Run by

Geoff Hamilton's son, its policy is to offer the widest possible choice of good plants to its customers.

Owned by Mrs Sue Hamilton
Number of gardeners 7
Size 8 acres

Belvoir Castle

BELVOIR, GRANTHAM NG32 1PD

Tel 01476 870262   **Fax** 01476 870443
Website www.country-focus.co.uk/belvoir/castle
Location 6 miles west of Grantham
Opening hours 11 am – 5 pm; daily; 13, 17, 22 & 23 April;
May to September. Then Sundays only in October. Spring
garden open 22 April, 1 & 29 July, and 30 September
Admission fee Castle & gardens: Adults £6; OAPs £5.50;
Children £3.50

Belvoir has formal gardens along the Victorian terraces beneath the castle, and a Broad Walk overlooking the nineteenth-century rose garden. Some way off is a hedged enclosure with seven statues by Colley Cibber. The Spring Garden, a pretty woodland garden, has recently been restored to its early nineteenth-century form and is open by appointment to groups at any time of the year.

Plant Highlights Woodland garden; roses (mainly modern); tallest bird cherry *Prunus avium* (28m) and yew tree *Taxus baccata* (29m) in the British Isles.

Owned by The Duke of Rutland
Number of gardeners 4
English Heritage grade II

Goscote Nurseries Ltd

SYSTON ROAD, COSSINGTON
LE7 4UZ

Tel 01509 812121   **Fax** 01509 814231
Location 5 miles north of Leicester, on B5328
Opening hours 9 am – 5 pm; Monday – Saturday.
10 am – 5 pm; Sundays. Closes at 4.30 pm in winter

Goscote has a wide range of reasonably-priced plants of all types – more than 1,500 are produced on site. They offer an extensive collection of trees and shrubs, including acers, azaleas, clematis, conifers and rhododendrons, many of them rare or unusual but suitable to the cold Midlands. Plants can also be seen in the show gardens, laid out as island beds. The website is helpful and comprehensive.

The Herb Nursery

THISTLETON, OAKHAM LE15 7RE

Tel 01572 767658   **Fax** 01572 768021
Location In the middle of the village
Opening hours 9 am – 6 pm (or dusk); daily; closed from
Christmas to New Year

This family-run nursery lists nearly 500 herbs and wildflower plants, with a special emphasis upon lavender, mint and thyme. The range of scented-leaf pelargoniums is good, and there is a fair range of cottage garden plants. Local gardeners speak well of it.

Kayes Garden Nursery

1700 MELTON ROAD, REARSBY,
LEICESTER LE7 4YR

Tel 01664 424578
Location On A607, north-east of Leicester
Opening hours 10 am – 5 pm (but 12 noon on Sundays);
Tuesday – Sunday; March to October. 10 am – 4 pm;
Fridays & Saturdays, November to February

This popular nursery has an excellent,
mature display garden, about 1½ acres in
size and densely planted with a wide range
of interesting plants. It also opens for the
National Gardens Scheme. The nursery's
own specialities are hardy herbaceous plants,
grasses, aquatics and climbers. Hazel Kaye
has a plantsman's eye for quality, and the list
includes many of the best forms of a wide
range of plants.

Long Close

60 MAIN STREET, WOODHOUSE
EAVES, LOUGHBOROUGH LE12 8RZ

Tel 01509 890616 (daytime)
Location 4 miles south of Loughborough
Opening hours 9.30 am – 1 pm and 2 pm – 5.30 pm;
Monday – Saturday; March to July
Admission fee Adults £2.50; Children free. Tickets from
Pene Crafts Gift Shop, opposite. Groups by appointment

This is a plantsman's garden, made by the
owner's mother over many years, and now
magnificently mature. Many of the plants
might be thought too tender for
Leicestershire. The woodland garden is very
fine, underplanted with magnolias, camellias
and massed rhododendrons and azaleas.
Elsewhere are good herbaceous plantings,
waterlily ponds and a *potager*. The adjacent

wildflower meadow is also pretty in late
spring.

Owned by John Oakland & Pene Johnson
Size 5 acres

Philip Tivey & Son

28 WANLIP ROAD, SYSTON LE7 1PA

Tel 0116 269 2968
Location About 200 yards west of junction with Station
Road
Opening hours 9 am – 5 pm; Monday – Friday.
9 am – 3 pm; Saturdays

These growers of dahlias are well-regarded
by specialists. They also have a good list of
Korean and hardy chrysanthemums.

University of Leicester Botanic Garden

BEAUMONT HALL, STOUGHTON
DRIVE, OADBY LE2 2NA

Tel 0116 271 7725
Location 3 miles south of Leicester on A6 London Road
opposite Racecourse: badly signed
Opening hours 10 am – 4 pm (3.30 pm Friday);
Monday – Friday; all year except Bank Holidays. Guided
tours by appointment: 0116 271 2933
Admission fee free

The University of Leicester Botanic Garden
moved to its present site in 1947. It fills the
grounds surrounding four houses which
were built early in the twentieth century and
are now used as student residences. The four
(once separate) gardens have been merged
into a single entity, the University Botanic
Garden with some sixteen acres. They now

support a wide variety of plants from historic trees to an 1980s ecological meadow. A pretty Edwardian pergola draped with roses, a well-planted rock-garden and a splendid display of hardy fuchsias from the National Collection all add to its interest. In 1997 the garden opened an out-station at Knighton, known as the Attenborough Arboretum. Though its plantings are still few and the trees very young, it is intended to show the native tree flora of England and to display it in historical sequence of arrival – ending with beech (*Fagus sylvatica*) after the last ice age.

 Plant Highlights Roses (ancient & modern); rock garden; rhododendrons & azaleas; plants under glass; mature conifers; cacti; succulents; heathers; fuchsias; tallest red hawthorn *Crataegus laevigata* 'Paul's Scarlet' (12m) in the British Isles.

Owned by The University of Leicester
Size 16 acres
NCCPG National Collections *Aubrieta*; *Chamaecyparis lawsoniana*; *Fuchsia*; *Hesperis*; *Skimmia*

Warren Hills Cottage

WARREN HILLS ROAD, COALVILLE
LE67 4UY

Tel 01530 812350
Location On B587 between Copt Oak & Whitwick Road
Opening hours 12 noon – 5 pm; 25 March, 15 April, 27 May, 8 July & 16 September. And by appointment
Admission fee Adults £1.50; Children 50p

(P) (WC) (&) (⚘)

This young garden is attached to a small nursery specialising in herbaceous plants. It has been landscaped and planted to provide year-round interest. The owners hope to establish a National Collection of *Astrantia* soon. They also run practical short courses with Steve Pole of Brooksby College. A garden to watch.

Owned by Mr & Mrs G Waters
Number of gardeners 2 part-time
Size 2 acres

Wartnaby Gardens

WARTNABY, MELTON MOWBRAY
LE14 3HY

Tel 01664 822549 **Fax** 01664 822231
Location 3 miles north of Melton Mowbray on A606. Left at A6 Kettley then 1 mile
Opening hours 11 am – 4 pm; 29 April, 20 May & 24 June and by appointment (not mid-week)
Admission fee Adults £2.50; Children free

(P) (⚘) (WC) (&) (⚘) (⚏) (☕)

Wartnaby is the garden of someone who loves roses and is prepared to make them one of the principal elements of her garden design: the result is one of the best modern examples of how to grow roses in mixed borders. Even in the so-called rose garden, the roses do not dominate: they are interplanted instead with other shrubs, like ceanothus, hebes and tree peonies, and underplanted with geraniums and bulbs. Foliage, shapes, colours and textures take over when the roses are not in flower. The long central path in the substantial kitchen garden is flanked by massed plantings of hybrid musks, including 'Felicia', 'Prosperity' and 'Pink Prosperity', underplanted with the grey-leaved *Stachys byzantina* and *Lychnis flos-jovis*, and edged with lavender and box. Wartnaby is a garden of enormous interest an charm: if only it were open more often!

Owned by Lady King

Whatton House

LONG WHATTON, LOUGHBOROUGH
LE12 5BG

Tel 01509 842225 **Fax** 01509 842268
Location Jct24, Kegworth A6 towards Hathern
Opening hours 2 pm – 6 pm; 15 April, 3 June & 8 July.
And parties by arrangement
Admission fee Adults £2.50; OAPs & Children £1.50

ⓟ ⓱ ⓦⓒ ⓰ ⊕ ☕

Fifteen acres attached to a garden centre.
Most of the features date from about 1900
but there has been much replanting in
recent years. Two rose gardens, fine
herbaceous borders and some magnificent
specimen trees are among the attractions.
The Chinese garden sports some
extraordinary mythological figures – among
them a cock and hen, storks, an eagle on a
globe, a Shishi dog and a cauldron with
three wise men on top. There is also a
mysterious 'bogey hole'.

Owned by Lord Crawshaw
Number of gardeners 1
Size 15 acres
English Heritage grade II

LINCOLNSHIRE

Lincolnshire, with which we include what was for a while south Humberside, has long been known for its horticulture industry based on bulb-growing, and it still has a high number of producers, both wholesale and retail. Their show-garden at Springfields, together with its trade fairs and flower-parades, is one of the great attractions of Lincolnshire in spring. The county has its fair share of important historic gardens: Belton House and Grimsthorpe Castle are both open to the public, though the third Grade I garden at Brocklesby Park (Capability Brown, Humphry Repton, and Reginald Blomfield all worked there) remains strictly private. The National Gardens Scheme has a fair number of gardens opening for charity and the county is blessed with several specialist nurseries of national importance. In addition to the alpine experts Potterton and Martin near Caistor, there are two nurseries with significant National Collections – the fuchsia enthusiast Kathleen Muncaster on the north-west outskirts of Gainsborough and the auricula specialists Martin Nest Nurseries to the east of the same town. RHS members have free access to Normanby Hall Country Park, one of the most interesting restoration projects on the East Coast of England.

Baytree Nurseries

HIGH ROAD, WESTON, SPALDING
PE12 6JU

Tel 01406 370242 **Fax** 01406 372829
Website www.baytree-gardencentre.com
Location 1½ miles east of Spalding, on A151
Opening hours 9 am – 6 pm; summer. 9 am – 5 pm; winter. Closed for Easter Day, Christmas Day & Boxing Day

(P) (WC) (⚘) (🍴)

Baytree won the Garden Centre of Excellence Award some years ago: last year it also won the growers' Retailer of the Year Award. It indicates that a visit offers more than just an opportunity to buy plants: Baytree's 16 acres include a pets and aquatic department, a leisure complex devoted to selling garden furniture and an owl centre. But it also aims to carry the largest selection of bulbs available at retail level anywhere in the country and a very large stock of plants, many of them grown on-site. Roses are a speciality: Baytree lists over 300 cultivars including some which it has bred and introduced itself.

Belton House

GRANTHAM NG32 2LS

Tel 01476 566116 **Fax** 01476 579071
Website www.nationaltrust.org.uk
Location 3 miles north-east of Grantham on the A607

Opening hours 11 am – 5.30 pm; Wednesday – Sunday plus Bank Holiday Mondays; 1 April to 29 October. Closed Good Friday
Admission fee Adults £5.40; Children £2.70

Grandeur and amenity go hand in hand at Belton. There are 1,000 acres of wooded deer park, a Wyattville orangery, a Dutch garden and an Italian garden with statues and parterres. But the adventure playground and other facilities make it popular with all ages.

 Plant Highlights Woodland garden; topiary; snowdrops; daffodils; bluebells; good herbaceous borders; biggest sugar maple *Acer saccharum* in the British Isles.

Owned by The National Trust
English Heritage grade I

Doddington Hall

DODDINGTON, LINCOLN LN6 4RU

Tel 01522 694308   **Fax** 01522 682584
Location Signed off the A46 Lincoln bypass
Opening hours Garden only: 2 pm – 6 pm; Sundays; 4 February to 29 April. House & garden: Wednesdays, Sundays & Bank Holiday Mondays; May to September
Admission fee Garden only: £3; Children £1.50

Doddington is a ravishing Elizabethan house around which successive generations have made a successful Tudor-style garden. The owners keep it simple and open at the front, but in the walled garden (thickly and richly planted) are Edwardian knots and parterres, a modern herb garden and pleached hornbeams. Wonderfully harmonious and strongly recommended in early summer.

Owned by Anthony Jarvis
Number of gardeners 2, plus volunteers
Size 6 acres
English Heritage grade II*

Grimsthorpe Castle

GRIMSTHORPE, BOURNE PE10 0NB

Tel 01778 591205   **Fax** 01778 591259
Website www.grimsthorpe.co.uk
Location On A151, 4 miles north-west of Bourne
Opening hours 11 am – 6 pm; Thursdays, Sundays & Bank Holidays; April to September. Plus daily in August except Friday & Saturday
Admission fee Adults £3; Concessions £2; Children £1.50

Capability Brown made the lake in 1771: the Victorians added the Italian garden, still maintained with summer bedding among the topiary, urns and sculptures. The most interesting horticultural feature is a formal vegetable garden, made in the 1960s before the craze for *potagers*, right below the Italian garden.

Owned by Grimsthorpe & Drummond Castle Trust Ltd
Number of gardeners 4
Size 27 acres
English Heritage grade I

Gunby Hall

GUNBY, SPILSBY PE23 5SS

Tel 01909 486411
Website www.nationaltrust.org.uk
Location 2½ miles north-west of Burgh-le-Marsh
Opening hours 2 pm – 6 pm; Wednesdays (plus Thursdays for garden only); 4 April to 30 September
Admission fee Garden only: Adults £2.50, Children £1

Ignore the parkland and make for the two walled gardens. Here is all the action: rich herbaceous borders, an arched apple walk, shrub roses, herbs and vegetables.

Owned by The National Trust
English Heritage grade II

Hall Farm & Nursery

HARPSWELL, GAINSBOROUGH
DN21 5UU

Tel 01427 668412 **Fax** 01427 667478
Website http://aol.members.com/hfnursery
Location On A361, 7 miles east of Gainsborough
Opening hours 10 am – 5 pm (or dusk, if earlier); daily;
all year except Christmas week. For National Gardens
Scheme: 10 am – 5.30 pm on 2 September
Admission fee Adults £2; Children 50p on National
Gardens Scheme day, otherwise free

This small, modern garden is intensely
planted and beautifully maintained as an
adjunct to the nursery, and for the owners'
pleasure. There are plants of every kind
– trees, shrubs, bulbs and herbaceous
plant – but over 100 different roses. Last
year they added a gravel garden. The
National Gardens Scheme day in September
is a 'free seed collection' day!

Owned by Pam & Mark Tatam
Size 1 acre

Hippopottering Nursery

ORCHARD HOUSE, BRACKENHILL
ROAD, EAST LOUND, HAXEY,
DONCASTER DN9 2LR

Tel & Fax 01427 752185
Location Off A161 at Haxey on Owston Ferry road to
East Lound
Opening hours By appointment

Hippopottering Nursery – the name has its
origins in a family joke – are specialists in
Japanese maples. They offer everything from
selected colourful seedlings and bonsai
material to mature specimens. Cultivars are
selected from their collection of over 120;

they also sell rootstocks. Their website
www.hippopottering.com should be up and
running by March 2001.

Kathleen Muncaster Fuchsias

18 FIELD LANE, MORTON,
GAINSBOROUGH DN21 3BY

Tel 01427 612329
Website www.kathleenmuncasterfuchsias.co.uk
Location North-west of Gainsborough: Field Lane is off
the minor road to Walkerith
Opening hours 10 am – dusk, February to mid-July.
Phone first at other times

This is the nursery of a fuchsia specialist
who began as an amateur and now has a
National Collection of hardy cultivars and
one of the largest nurseries in the country
which specialises in the genus. The hardy
fuchsias can be seen in the garden, together
with the stock plants: almost all the
glasshouses may also be visited. The list is
impressive, though not all the cultivars in
the collection are propagated regularly – ask
if they have a cutting available. They
introduce new fuchsias every year: 2001's
introductions include two with semi-erect
flowers (pale pink 'Harlow Perfection' and
pink-edged white 'Sharonelle'), the long-
tubed 'Scarlet Cascade' and one with
green-tipped sepals called 'Eileen Storey',
which is a great improvement on its
ancestor 'Estelle Marie'.

NCCPG National Collections Fuchsia (hardy)

Martin Nest Nurseries

GRANGE COTTAGE, HEMSWELL,
GAINSBOROUGH DN21 5UP

Tel 01427 668369 **Fax** 01427 668080
Location 6 miles east of Gainsborough on A631
Opening hours 10 am – 4 pm, daily
Ⓟ 🌳

Martin Nest Nurseries are wholesalers and retailers with a good business-like range of tough pot-grown hardy alpine plants. Primulas and auriculas are their speciality: some of their cultivars are unique to them. Visitors may be shown the National Collection of *Primula auricula* cultivars on request.

NCCPG National Collections *Primula auricula*

Normanby Hall Country Park

NORMANBY, SCUNTHORPE
DN15 9HU

Tel 01724 720588 **Fax** 01724 721248
Location 3 miles north of Scunthorpe
Opening hours 10.30 am – 5 pm; daily; all year. Closed 1 January, 25 & 26 December
Admission fee Adults £2.90; Concessions £1.90. RHS members free from April to September

The Victorian Walled Garden (actually built in 1817, before Queen Victoria was even born) has been restored and planted – with help from the Lottery – as a living museum of nineteenth-century horticulture. Old varieties of fruit and vegetables are grown organically. The glasshouses have recently been rebuilt to house peaches and other fruit. Ferns and exotic ornamentals fill a display house. There are plans to make a bog garden this spring along the base of the ha-ha (400ft long) and plant up the woodland garden in the Victorian style. Five RHS special events will take place at Normanby Hall Country Park during 2001: details from 020 7821 3408.

Owned by North Lincolnshire Council
Number of gardeners 4
Size 1 acre, plus 39 outside the walled garden

Potterton and Martin

MOORTOWN ROAD, NETTLETON,
CAISTOR LN7 6HX

Tel 01472 851714 **Fax** 01472 852580
Location On B1205: leave A46 at Nettleton
Opening hours 9 am – 4.30 pm; daily

This alpine and rock plant specialist has an interesting and extensive range of plants for sale, running from the easy to the unusual. All are propagated on-site, and most can be seen in the extensive display garden. The nursery holds many Chelsea gold medals, and has won the RHS Farrer Trophy (best alpine display) on several occasions. Satisfied customers praise not only the nursery's wide choice of plants, but also its cultivation skills and reasonable pricing policy.

Springfields Show Gardens

SPALDING PE12 6ET

Tel 01775 724843   **Fax** 01775 711209
Website www3.mistral.co.uk/springfields
Location 1 mile from Spalding, off new bypass
Opening hours 10 am – 6 pm; daily; 16 March to 13 May
Admission fee Adults £3.50; OAPs £3; Children free

Originally (in 1966) a display garden for the Lincolnshire bulb trade, Springfields now offers fun and colour all through the season, with roses providing the midsummer display and bold bedding taking over until the autumn frosts. But it is still the bulbs which make the greatest impression – daffodils, tulips, hyacinths and many others, all donated by the industry. There are plans to develop and upgrade the garden as a major tourist attraction incorporating some retailing, but this depends upon a planning decision which is not expected until later in the year. Meanwhile Springfields remains a real eyeful of a garden, splendidly maintained.

Plant Highlights Woodland garden; roses (mainly modern); millions of bulbs.

Owned by Springfields Horticultural Society Ltd
Size 25 acres

LONDON

London gardeners are much more fortunate than they would have you believe. They have a micro-climate which enables them to grow plants that would not be hardy anywhere except in the mildest corners of the south-west, and they enjoy a good choice of suitably stylish plants from garden centres and other outlets within the city itself. Some of the world's greatest gardens are within a short journey: among them are the Chelsea Physic Garden, Chiswick House, the Royal Botanic Gardens at Kew, Richmond Park and Syon Park. The Royal Parks Agency manages the inner-city green spaces like Hyde Park and Regents Park with immense horticultural skill: almost all the parks contain acres of well-kept grass and trees of record size. London is of course the seat of the Royal Horticultural Society: the Chelsea Flower Show is traditionally regarded as the start of the London summer season. The Hampton Court Palace Flower show in July is, if possible, even more of a Londoners' show, while the regular London shows at the RHS's own halls in Westminster are attended by thousands of London gardeners keen to see plants and buy them. Nowhere has so many lectures and other educational garden events as London does. The RHS's Partner College at Capel Manor has a long programme of lectures, demonstrations and workshops throughout the year. The RHS Partner Nursery at the Palm Centre in Ham has a RHS special event in March. Many of the specialist plant societies have their shows and administrative offices in London, too: if you want to see plants as diverse as orchids, carnations, vegetables, daffodils or camellias, London is the place to do so. The National Gardens Scheme thrives there; the Museum of Garden History is based there – just across the river from the Houses of Parliament; the Association of Gardens Trusts has its office in London – and so does the Institute of Horticulture. The London Historic Parks & Gardens Trust is one of the country's most successful conservation societies. The greater part of the RHS's Lindley Library – Britain's largest collection of horticultural books and primary sources about gardening – is based in London. Perhaps the only thing that a Londoner cannot do is to garden on a large scale. That apart, there is no better place to be a garden-lover.

26 Thompson Road

DULWICH SE22 9JR

Tel & Fax 020 8693 5002
Location Dulwich
Opening hours 2.30 pm – 6 pm; 29 April & 16 September
Admission fee Adults £2; Concessions £1

The actor Anthony Noel's garden in Fulham was widely praised – and rightly so. His new garden in Dulwich shows what is possible in a small (38 × 16ft) north-facing site. The garden – like his designing style, he says – has moved with the times, and 'shows a new simplicity and under-stated feeling of luxury'. And quiet self-confidence, too: he describes himself now as an author and garden designer.

Owned by Anthony Noel

Cannizaro Park

WEST SIDE COMMON, WIMBLEDON SW19

Tel 020 8946 7349
Location West side of Wimbledon Common
Opening hours 8 am – sunset, Monday – Friday; 9 am – sunset, Saturday, Sunday & Bank Holidays; all year
Admission fee free

Cannizaro is well-known among connoisseurs for its azaleas, planted about 40 years ago and a magnificent spectacle when in full flower. It is one of the best woodland gardens of its type in the country.

Plant Highlights Woodland garden; mature conifers; azaleas; magnolias; tallest *Sassafras albidum* (17m) in the British Isles.

Owned by London Borough of Merton
Size 39 acres
English Heritage grade II*

Capel Manor

BULLSMOOR LANE, ENFIELD EN1 4RQ

Tel 020 8366 4442   **Fax** 01992 717544
Website www.capelmanorcollege.co.uk
Location A10 by Jct25 on M25
Opening hours 11 am – 6 pm (or dusk if sooner); daily; March to October. But closed on Saturdays in March & October. Ring for open weekdays from November to February
Admission fee £4 Adults; £3.50 OAPs; £2 Children

There are three main areas at this high-profile demonstration garden attached to a horticultural college 'where the City meets the Countryside'. First there is the National Gardening Centre, where dozens of small model gardens are designed and planted to give people state-of-the-art ideas for their own gardens. Second, there are the trial grounds run by *Gardening Which?*, where this influential monthly magazine carries out all its trials and experiments, long-term and seasonal. Third, there is the series of themed gardens laid out for students to learn from: a walled garden, a herb garden, a knot garden, a disabled person's garden, a shade garden, an Italianate holly maze, a pergola, a Japanese garden, alpine beds and some historical recreations. Whatever your interests and whatever the time of the year, Capel Manor is a garden which educates and delights. And it is brilliant for new ideas, especially for small gardens.

Owned by Capel Manor Corporation
Number of gardeners 8
Size 30 acres
NCCPG National Collections *Achillea*; *Sarcococca*

Chelsea Physic Garden

66 ROYAL HOSPITAL ROAD, CHELSEA
SW3 4HS

Tel 020 7352 5646   **Fax** 020 7376 3910
Website www.cpgarden.demon.co.uk
Location Chelsea
Opening hours 11 am – 3 pm; 4 & 11 February for
snowdrops. 12 noon – 5 pm, Wednesdays; 2 pm – 6 pm,
Sundays; 1 April to 28 October. Plus 21 to 25 May for
Chelsea Flower Show and 18 to 22 June for Chelsea
Festival
Admission fee Adults £4; Concessions £2

This oasis of peace between Royal Hospital
Road and the Chelsea Embankment started
life in 1673 as a pharmacological collection,
and has kept its original design – hence the
word 'Physic' in its name. But it also has the
oldest rock garden in Europe, the largest
olive tree in Britain, extensive botanical order
beds, a vast number of rare and interesting
plants, and probably the last known
specimen of the 1920s white Hybrid Tea
rose 'Marcia Stanhope'. An historical walk
emphasises the importance of the garden
through the ages by drawing attention to the
number of plants first introduced to Britain
by the garden and its curators. The website
is a bit of a turn-off, though – so full of
arty-smarty gimmicks that it takes ages to
download the underlying information.

Plant Highlights Herbs; plants under
glass; good herbaceous borders;
eighteenth-century rock garden; new
Pharmaceutical Garden (1999); large olive
tree growing outside.

Owned by Chelsea Physic Garden Company
Number of gardeners 5
Size 4 acres (nearly)
NCCPG National Collections Cistus
English Heritage grade I

Chiswick House

BURLINGTON LANE, CHISWICK
W4 2RP

Tel 020 8742 1225
Location South-west London on A4 & A316
Opening hours 8 am – dusk; daily; all year
Admission fee free

Laid out by Bridgeman and Kent for Lord
Burlington, Chiswick is the best baroque
garden in southern England, and the
exquisite house is pure Palladian. The
bachelor Duke of Devonshire added an
Italian renaissance garden early in the
nineteenth century, and a Camellia House
with slate benches and huge bushes, mainly
of old Japonica hybrids. But it is the lay-out
and buildings which are so exceptional: the
Ionic temple, the Inigo Jones gateway, the
obelisk and the statues. Forget the dogs and
the joggers – almost all free-entry gardens
have a municipal heart – but explore the
pattes d'oie, *allées* and ilex groves of the main
garden on a hot July morning and you
might be doing a Grand Tour of Italy 250
years ago.

Owned by London Borough of Hounslow
Number of gardeners 8
Size 40 acres
English Heritage grade I

Clifton Nurseries

CLIFTON VILLAS, LITTLE VENICE
W9 2PH

Tel 020 7289 6851
Website www.clifton.co.uk
Location Little Venice
Opening hours 8.30 am – 6 pm; Monday – Saturday:
10.30 am – 4.30 pm; Sundays: March to September.

8.30 am – 5.30 pm; Monday – Saturday: 10 am – 4 pm; Sundays: October to February

Clifton nurseries were founded about 100 years ago and have grown to become one of the smartest and most stylish sources of good plants and designer sundries for Londoners. They concentrate on town gardens, with containers, statuary, climbers and shrubs in specimen sizes, indoor and conservatory plants. Topiary is one of their specialities: so are mature plants for instant gratification.

Fenton House

HAMPSTEAD GROVE, HAMPSTEAD NW3 6RT

Tel 020 7435 3471
Website www.nationaltrust.org.uk
Location Entrances in Hampstead Grove near Hampstead Underground station
Opening hours 2 pm – 5 pm; Saturdays & Sundays; 3 to 25 March. Then 2 pm – 5 pm; Wednesday – Sunday plus Bank Holiday Mondays but not Good Friday; 31 March – 4 November. Opens at 11 am on Saturdays, Sundays & Bank Holiday Mondays
Admission fee Adults £4.30; Children £2.10

Fenton House has a country garden in Hampstead, with neat, terraced gardens near the house, and a rather more informal deign at the bottom. It is not outstandingly flowerful, but the hedges are good and plants are firmly trained: definitely worth knowing, and very popular with visitors.

Owned by The National Trust

Fulham Palace Garden Centre

BISHOPS AVENUE, FULHAM SW6 6EE

Tel 020 7736 9820   **Fax** 020 7371 8468
Website www.fulhamgardencentre.com
Location Off Fulham Palace Road
Opening hours 9.30 am – 5.30 pm, Monday – Thursday; 9.30 am – 6 pm, Friday – Saturday; 10 am – 5 pm, Sundays. Shuts earlier in winter months

Fulham Palace Garden Centre has everything for the town gardener, including specimen-sized plants, topiary and a good range of containers. The general range includes herbs, vegetables, fruit trees, herbaceous plants, climbers, ferns, grasses, olives, figs and oranges. The nursery will deliver seven days a week in London and further afield. It is owned by Fairbridge, the charity which arranges training for inner-city children.

Ham House

RICHMOND TW10 7RS

Tel 020 8940 1950   **Fax** 020 8332 6903
Website www.nationaltrust.org.uk
Location On River Thames, signed from A307
Opening hours 11 am – 6 pm (or dusk, if earlier); Saturday – Wednesday; all year except 1 January & 25/26 December
Admission fee Adults £2

Ham is a modern re-creation of the original seventeenth-century garden. It is not a literal copy, but more of a free-handed re-interpretation. The best part is a grand series of hornbeam enclosures with white summerhouses and seats. There are plans to

Hampton Court Palace

HAMPTON COURT KT8 9AU

Tel 020 8781 9500
Website www.hrp.org.uk
Location North side of Kingston bridge over the Thames on A308 Jct with A309
Opening hours Park: dawn – dusk; daily; all year. King's Privy Garden: 9.30 am – 6 pm (4.30 pm from October to March). Opens at 10.15 am on Mondays
Admission fee Privy Garden: Adults £2.50; Children £1.30. Maze: Adults £2.30; Children £1.50

William III was responsible for the main features at Hampton Court today. His Privy Garden has recently been reconstructed as it was in 1702 and remains the outstanding example of a successful historic restoration from the 1990s. Even the planting is accurate – roses, fritillaries and other flowering plants chosen and cultivated exactly as they would have been 300 years ago. Note how widely spaced they are in their slightly raised beds, an exact copy of horticultural practices of the time. Next to the vast Privy Garden is the Pond Garden, a sunken formal garden with magnificent displays of bedding – tulips in spring and tender perennials in summer. Nearby is the Great Vine – actually 'Black Hamburgh' – planted in 1768 on the advice of Capability Brown: it is the world's oldest known vine and produces 500–700lbs of grapes every year. To one side of the Privy Garden lies the great formal East Garden. Its central feature is the Long Water which cuts right through the deer park: the Hampton Court Palace Flower Show (organised by the Royal Horticultural Society) takes place astride its banks from 3 to 8 July: tickets may be purchased in advance on 0870 906 3790. The garden at the palace end of the long water was laid out as a parterre by William III with

twelve marble fountains: Queen Anne added the semi-circular canals in 1710. On the other side of the palace are the wilderness gardens, extending over a considerable area, and a mass of naturalised daffodils in spring. Here too is the famous Hampton Court Maze, which covers about one third of an acre and has yew hedges totalling nearly half a mile. Parents, please note that it is not a difficult maze to get in and out of safely. Other areas in the Wilderness also have considerable horticultural interest, including the rose garden, a herbaceous garden, and walls covered with climbing plants. Hampton Court is large and you need several hours to appreciate all the gardens, their different styles and what they offer. The website is excellent – educational and helpful.

Owned by Historic Royal Palaces
Number of gardeners 40
Size 60 acres of formal gardens & 600 acres of deer park
NCCPG National Collections Heliotropium
English Heritage grade I

re-develop this and some of the other areas to make them resemble the original gardens more closely.

Owned by The National Trust
English Heritage grade II*

Isabella Plantation

RICHMOND PARK, RICHMOND
TW10 5HS

Tel 020 8948 3209 **Fax** 020 8332 2730
Location Richmond Park
Opening hours Dawn – dusk; daily; all year
Admission fee free

The Isabella Plantation in Richmond Park is at last getting the recognition it deserves: the 42 acres of rhododendrons and azaleas under a mature deciduous canopy are one of the best woodland gardens in the country. They are probably at their own best in late April and May, when the azaleas are accompanied by lush streamside plantings of candelabra primulas, ferns and hostas. And it all gets better still: a new bog garden was opened last year.

Owned by The Royal Parks Agency
Number of gardeners 5
Size 43 acres
NCCPG National Collections Rhododendron (Kurume azaleas, the Wilson 50)
English Heritage grade I

Kenwood

HAMPSTEAD LANE, HAMPSTEAD
NW3 7JR

Location North side of Hampstead Heath
Opening hours 8 am to dusk (8.30 pm if sooner); daily; all year

Admission fee free (to park)

These 100 acres of superb eighteenth century parkland around two glittering lakes were recently half-restored to Repton's original designs. There are splendid large plantings of rhododendrons, fine azaleas, and wonderful landscaped views to London and Westminster, but rather more could be done horticulturally.

Owned by English Heritage
English Heritage grade II*

Museum of Garden History

LAMBETH PALACE ROAD, LAMBETH
SE1 7LB

Tel 020 7401 8865 **Fax** 020 7401 8869
Website www.museumgardenhistory.org
Location Between Lambeth Bridge & Lambeth Palace
Opening hours 10.30 am – 5 pm; daily; all year
Admission fee Donation (£2.50 suggested)

The garden is small, and secondary to the Museum's fascinating collections and excellent exhibitions. Nevertheless it is neatly designed and planted – with a fair degree of historical correctness – as a seventeenth-century knot garden, using plants associated with the Tradescants. A garden for contemplation. But the events, exhibitions, lectures and courses are well worth knowing about.

Owned by The Tradescant Trust

Royal Botanic Gardens, Kew

KEW, RICHMOND TW9 3AB

Tel 020 8940 1171
Website www.rbgkew.org.uk
Location Kew Green, south of Kew bridge, or Underground Station
Opening hours 9.30 am – 6.30 pm (7.30 pm at weekends), but closes at 5.30 pm from 10 February to 24 March, at 6 pm from 3 September to 27 October, and at 4.15 pm from 28 October; daily; all year except Christmas & New Year's Day
Admission fee Adults £5; Concessions £3.50; Children £2.50 (under 5 free)

Kew Gardens are enormous – the guide book advises that they take a whole day to visit – and have one of the largest collection of plants in the world. The emphasis is upon species rather than garden cultivars, but there is an immense amount for gardeners to see and admire and – of course – to learn from. There are also seasonal features like the winter garden and historic areas like the Queen's garden behind Kew Palace which was designed in the 1960s as a reconstructed seventeenth-century garden. Nor should the famous pagoda and Japanese landscape gardens be forgotten. There are many horticulturally themed gardens. The azalea garden divides azaleas into twelve distinct horticultural groups, e.g. the Ghent hybrids and the Knap Hill hybrids, and arranges them all systematically in historic order. The bamboo garden has over 120 cultivars arranged to maximise the contrast between their forms and leaf shapes. The berberis dell is a unique feature with a comprehensive collection of berberis and mahonia – the tallest is a five-metre specimen of *Berberis lycoides*. Kew has one of the best bluebell woods in the London area, behind Queen Charlotte's cottage. The grass garden has over 550 species and is being added to continuously: although the scientific purpose is to display the diversity and importance of grasses, the garden is arranged ornamentally. The holly walk was laid out in 1874 by Sir Joseph Hooker: the original specimens are therefore over 130 years old and as high as 30 metres. The collection has over 600 hollies. The juniper collection is the largest in Europe. The lilac garden ('Go down to Kew in lilac time') was renovated in 1993 and has over 100 specimens in ten separate beds. The rhododendron dell (700 plants) includes some unique Kew hybrids as well as hardy species. The rose garden was created in 1923 and is very popular in high summer: it has roses of all types and an area which illustrates the history of roses in cultivation. There is also a rose pergola running through the order beds, which were originally designed as a living library of flowering plants systematically arranged for students of botany. The pinetum has an important collection of conifers and there are many record breakers among the deciduous species at Kew too. The rock garden was rebuilt in the 1980s to include more micro-habitats. It has over 2,500 different plants roughly arranged in geographical areas, e.g. the mountains of Europe, the Mediterranean and Patagonia. The glasshouses also contain a vast collection of plants. The palm house was built in the 1840s to house tropical trees and shrubs – these include coconuts, bananas, bread-fruit, mangoes and paw-paws. The Princess of Wales conservatory opened in 1987 and has ten distinct climatic zones ranging from arid to moist tropical: here are such plants as ginger, pineapple and orchids. The temperate house is set out geographically: among its most striking plants are proteas from South Africa. In the hot and humid waterlily house are tropical *Nymphaea* and *Victoria cruziana*, as well as such economic plants as rice and lemon grass. The alpine house was opened in 1981 and its systems of refrigeration and ventilation enable Kew to grow plants which would not otherwise survive the damp, mild climate of England. Other glasshouses to visit include the evolution house, which tells the story of plant evolution over the last 3,500 million years and the unique filmy fern house. Kew has every imaginable facility for visits by schools, groups, tourists and students of botany. In summer it also has very good bedding-out schemes, but the garden is somewhat bedevilled by Canada geese, which foul the grass, and by aircraft noise.

Plant Highlights Woodland garden; sub-tropical plants; snowdrops; roses of every kind; rock garden; plantsman's collection of plants; herbs; plants under glass; fruit; mature conifers; good herbaceous borders; fine collection of trees; alpine plants; heather gardens; 138 record trees – more than any other garden in the British Isles – including 38 different oaks (*Quercus sp.*).

Owned by Trustees of the Royal Botanic Gardens
Size 300 acres
English Heritage grade I

Myddelton House

BULLS CROSS, ENFIELD EN2 9HG

Tel 01992 717711 **Fax** 01992 651406
Location Off A10 onto Bullsmoor Lane: signed at Bulls Cross. Or train to Turkey Street Station
Opening hours 10 am – 4.30 pm; weekdays except Christmas Holidays; all year. 2 pm – 5 pm; Sundays & Bank Holidays; Easter to October. Plus 27 February, 28 May & 30 July for National Gardens Scheme
Admission fee Adults £1.90; Concessions £1.30

Holy ground for plantsmen with a sense of history, E A Bowles' garden was abandoned for 30 years: Lee Valley Regional Park Authority has started to restore it. Thousands of naturalised bulbs have survived: snowdrops, crocus and narcissi in spring and cyclamen, colchicums and sternbergias in autumn too. The large wisteria planted in 1903 has also survived, while the rose garden has been replanted with varieties that Bowles grew. The iris borders are spectacular in May but it is true to say that, as with all plantsman's gardens, there is much to see throughout the year. A current project is to restore the Lunatic Asylum, Bowles's collection of freak plants like the double-flowered (but non-berrying) blackberry *Rubus ulmifolius* 'Bellidifolius'. The RHS thought so highly of this part of the garden that, even in the cash-strapped 1950s, it propagated the plants and created its own Lunatic Asylum corner at Wisley. And the Lee Valley Regional Park Authority has just re-acquired the kitchen garden and have plans to restore it too. There is a friends' group called the E A Bowles of Myddelton House Society which has an active programme of events: details from Mr A Pettitt, 2(A) Plough Hill, Cuffley, Potters Bar, Hertfordshire EN6 4DR or from michaelkingdom@aol.com

Owned by Lee Valley Regional Park Authority
NCCPG National Collections *Iris*
English Heritage grade II

Osterley Park

ISLEWORTH TW7 4RB

Tel & Fax 020 8568 7714
Website www.nationaltrust.org.uk
Location 5 miles west of central London on A4
Opening hours 9 am – 7.30 pm (or dusk, if earlier); daily; all year
Admission fee Park & pleasure grounds free

Osterley is a classical eighteenth-century landscape with a fine temple and semi-circular conservatory by Robert Adam and some good trees – especially cedars and oaks.

 Plant Highlights Woodland garden; herbs; fruit; fine rare oaks; autumn colour; tallest variegated chestnut *Castanea sativa* 'Albomarginata' (16m) in the British Isles.

Owned by The National Trust
English Heritage grade II*

Queen Mary's Gardens

INNER CIRCLE, REGENT'S PARK NW1 4NR

Tel 020 7486 7905
Location In the middle of Regent's Park
Opening hours Dawn – dusk; daily; all year
Admission fee free

Queen Mary's Gardens are contained within Regent's Park's Inner Circle. Originally a display garden for the Royal Botanic Society (a nineteenth-century rival to the Royal

Horticultural Society: Robert Marnock and William Robinson both worked there), the Japanese garden, the lake and the mound made from the excavations all date from the 1850s. The horticultural interest comes from the excellent herbaceous borders, tender bedding plants, displays of annuals and spring bulbs. Above all, Queen Mary's Gardens are known for their rose gardens, where large beds are planted each with just one cultivar – mainly modern Hybrid Teas and Floribundas, though there are English roses and old-fashioned ones too, often in mixed borders. At one end is a circular catenary of climbing and rambling roses around yet more beds of bright modern roses: a spectacular sight in early June – roses flower earlier in the London parks than anywhere else in England, and are worth a visit at any time after about the middle of May.

Owned by Royal Parks Agency

Syon Park

BRENTFORD TW8 8JF

Tel 020 8560 0883 **Fax** 020 8568 0936
Website www.syonpark.co.uk
Location Between Brentford & Isleworth, north bank of Thames

Opening hours 10 am – 5.30 pm, or sunset if earlier; daily except 25 & 26 December; all year
Admission fee Adults £3; Concessions £2.50

Syon is a mixture of eighteenth-century landscape, nineteenth-century horticultural seriousness, twentieth-century plantsmanship and twentyfirst-century theme park. The Great Conservatory was designed by Charles Fowler in the 1820s: the formal terraces followed in the 1830s. But one of the nicest details about Syon is the way the water meadows along the banks of the Thames are still grazed by cows: it creates a unique rural prospect so close to the heart of London. There are fine trees too, the relic of a botanical collection dating back to the 1820s: some, including four species of oak, are record-breakers. Syon Park also has a tropical butterfly house.

Plant Highlights Spectacular Great Conservatory; woodland garden; mature conifers; good herbaceous borders; fine collection of trees; cacti; ferns; new walk around lake; tallest *Catalpa ovata* (22m) in the British Isles (and fourteen further record trees).

Owned by The Duke of Northumberland
Number of gardeners 8
Size 40 acres
English Heritage grade I

NORFOLK

Norfolk has a large number of important historic gardens. Only a few are open to the public, but they include Blickling, Felbrigg, Holkham, Sheringham and the royal gardens at Sandringham – an impressive list. The garden with the finest collection of trees is Ryston Hall, but it is not open to the public. The same is true of Talbot Manor, which was planted from about 1950 onwards by the late Maurice Mason with advice from Sir Harold Hillier. Nevertheless, the National Gardens Scheme does fairly well in Norfolk and the county also has a good number of first-rate nurseries: Peter Beales Roses, Norfolk Lavender, P W Plants, Reads Nursery and the Romantic Garden Nursery are all of national importance and Bressingham Plant Centre was largely responsible for the enormous renewal of interest in herbaceous plants from about 1970 onwards. There are eleven National Collections in the county, including a collection of *Elaeagnus* which is spread among several members of the Norfolk Group of the NCCPG. The Royal Horticultural Society has good links with Norfolk: P W Plants is a RHS Partner Nursery, while Fairhaven Woodland & Water Garden and East Ruston Old Vicarage are RHS Free Access gardens. Many people consider that East Ruston Old Vicarage is the most important new garden to have been made in the UK during the last few years. And there is no doubt that both the Dell garden and Foggy Bottom at Bressingham have also been immensely influential.

African Violet & Garden Centre

STATION ROAD, TERRINGTON ST CLEMENT, KING'S LYNN PE34 4PL

Tel 01553 828374   **Fax** 01553 828376
Location 3 miles west of King's Lynn, beside A17
Opening hours 9 am – 5 pm; daily; all year. Opens at 10 am on Sundays. Closed for New Year's Day, Christmas Day & Boxing Day

This nursery built its reputation on African violets, and its Chelsea exhibits have been memorable. Though it is now moving into other retail areas, it still has a fair selection on offer and displays to admire.

Blickling Hall

BLICKLING, NORWICH NR11 6NF

Tel 01263 738030   **Fax** 01263 731660
Website www.nationaltrust.org.uk
Location 1 mile west of Aysham on B1354

Opening hours 10.15 am – 5.15 pm;
Wednesday – Sunday & Bank Holiday Mondays; 8 April to
29 October. Plus Tuesdays in August. 11 am – 4 pm;
Thursday – Sunday; November & December
Admission fee Adults £3.80; Children £1.90

Blickling is the garden with everything:
a Jacobean mansion, handsomely
symmetrical; an early landscape layout (the
Doric Temple was built in about 1735); a
pretty conservatory by Samuel Wyatt; a large
mid-nineteenth-century parterre by Nesfield
(note the topiary pillars); and 1930s
herbaceous colour plantings by Nancy
Lindsey (her masterpiece). And there are
sheets of bluebells in the woods.

Plant Highlights Woodland garden;
rhododendrons & azaleas; good
herbaceous borders; bluebells; herbaceous
borders at peak July/August.

Owned by The National Trust
English Heritage grade II*

Bradenham Hall

BRADENHAM, THETFORD IP25 7QR

Tel 01362 687243   **Fax** 01362 687669
Location West of East Dereham, north of Bradenham
Opening hours 2 pm – 5.30 pm; 2nd, 4th & 5th Sundays
of month; April to September
Admission fee Adults £3; Children free

This is an exceptional plant-lover's garden
for all seasons, made over the last 40 years in
a windy, open position at the top of what
passes in Norfolk for a hill. The first thing
you notice is that the house (early Georgian)
and garden walls are covered with unusual
shrubs, climbers and fruit. The flower
gardens are formally designed and richly
planted within beautiful yew hedges: formal

rose gardens, a paved garden, and herbaceous
and shrub borders. The arboretum has a
remarkable collection of trees – more than
800 different species and forms, many of
them rare or very rare. All are labelled. The
walled kitchen gardens are traditionally
managed, with vegetables, cut flowers,
mixed borders, and two glasshouses. In
spring, the parkland and arboretum are
filled with daffodils – massed plantings of
more than 90 carefully chosen and graded
cultivars. A delight and an education.

Owned by Chris & Panda Allhusen
Number of gardeners 3
Size 21 acres

Bressingham Plant Centre

BRESSINGHAM, DISS IP22 2AB

Tel 01379 687464
Website www.blooms-online.com
Location On A1066 3 miles west of Diss
Opening hours 9 am – 5.30 pm; daily except Christmas
and Boxing Day

The plant centre at Bressingham is the
flagship of the Blooms' site, though no
longer so closely associated with the Bloom
family as it used to be. The retail range is
strong on hardy perennials and shrubs,
conifers and heathers, with a wide range
of almost every type of garden plant. The
owners are not just focused on plants,
though: they say they 'also stock a wide
range of gifts and lifestyle products'. The
company also has other garden centres, for
example at Dorney Court in Berkshire and
Elton Hall in Cambridgeshire.

Chanticleer

DEREHAM ROAD, OVINGTON,
WATTON, THETFORD IP25 6SA

Tel 01953 881194
Location On A1075, 2 miles from Watton on the Dereham road
Opening hours 10 am – 4 pm; 16 & 17 June, 4 & 5 August. And groups by appointment
Admission fee Adults £2; OAPs £1; Children free

Chanticleer is a former public house, converted to a private dwelling in the 1920s and since extended. The present owners have lived and gardened there for twenty years, originally in just under two acres, but then with three further acres for a small flock of Jacob sheep, Vietnamese pot-bellied pigs, goats, geese, chickens and ducks. The main garden includes a kitchen garden, greenhouses, orchard, herb garden and a large wildlife garden with a pond: all are managed organically. Great emphasis is placed on working with nature: the wildlife garden is frequented by birds, insects and small mammals, including breeding water voles. Most native shrubs and trees are represented, as are many wild flowers – including two species of orchids, which have colonised parts of the wildlife area.

Owned by Mr & Mrs T Rands
Number of gardeners owners only
Size 5 acres

Dell Garden

BRESSINGHAM, DISS IP22 2AB

Tel 01379 688585 **Fax** 01379 688340
Location On A1066, 3 miles west of Diss
Opening hours 10.30 am – 5.30 pm (4.30 pm in October); daily; April to October

Admission fee Adults £10; OAPs £9; Children £7. Please note that this admission price includes joint entrance to Foggy Bottom garden & the Bressingham Steam Experience plus a £5 voucher redeemable against Blooms Heritage Collection plants. Unfortunately, Foggy Bottom is only open 12.30pm – 4.30pm, Tuesday – Friday, Sundays & Bank Holiday Mondays

There is no better place to learn about herbaceous plants – what they look like, how they grow and how to place them. The Dell is a six-acre complex of about fifty island beds, which act as a trial ground and conservation resource for the herbaceous and alpine plants (over 5,000 of them) for which Alan Bloom is famous. There is a new Summer Garden opening in 2001 which has been designed by Adrian Bloom to provide a new and more dramatic entrance to the garden. It has a stunning display of *Crocosmia* and *Miscanthus* cultivars interplanted with other perennials. The Blooms are keen to emphasise that the Dell Garden is not a museum piece but a carefully tended collection of perennials, developing and growing all the time.

Owned by Alan Bloom
Number of gardeners 2
Size 6 acres

East Lode

NURSERY LANE, HOCKWOLD,
THETFORD IP26 4ND

Tel 01842 827096
Location Down Church Lane in Hockwold, left at iron seat, then first house on right
Opening hours By arrangement
Admission fee Adults £2

This is half-acre cottage garden is absolutely full of interest – shrubs, roses, clematis, and

East Ruston Old Vicarage

EAST RUSTON, NORWICH NR12 9HN

Tel 01602 632432 **Fax** 01692 651246

Website www.e-ruston-oldvicaragegardens.co.uk

Location Turn off A149 near Stalham – signed Walcott, Bacton. Left at junction. On right after 2 miles

Opening hours 2 pm – 5.30 pm; Wednesdays, Fridays, Sundays & Bank Holidays; 1 April to 26 October

Admission fee Adults £3.50; Children £1. RHS members free in September & October

(P) (WC) (symbol) (symbol)

This fine modern garden has been conceived on the grand scale. The owners, Graham Robeson and Alan Gray, combine the rare qualities of superb architectural design and exceptional plantsmanship. The house was built by a Surrey architect in 1913 in the Arts and Crafts style, which is uncommon in Norfolk. When the owners started to make their garden in 1988, it sat in an empty field. It was then that they planted the shelter belts, almost all tough evergreens. One of the most exciting things about the garden is to see so many tender exotics growing happily outside – literally thousands of them – which would not have been possible without the shelter belts. This is helped by the garden's location close to the North Sea, with its maritime influence. The garden has been designed as a series of 'rooms', getting larger the further you move from the house. There are fine views borrowed from the landscape on two local churches and a whimsical porthole view of Happisburgh lighthouse. The 19 acres feature superb long borders abundantly and richly planted, a box parterre annually bedded out with unusual and original plant combinations, a gravelled forecourt with large groups of *Aeonium* 'Zwartkop' and various echeverias, a sunken garden containing many varieties

including a large group of *Lobelia tupa*, and the newly reloc- ated and much extended exotic garden with fabulously bold plantings of palms, bananas, shrubby salvias and many tender exotics which are propagated on the premises. Much thought has gone into the design and preparation of beds for plants. The Mediterranean garden, for example, faces south and has a lot of brickwork and paving to preserve the warmth which plants need to survive. The beds are heavily mulched with gravel, and the result is that there are many plants surviving which are typical of the Mediterranean *maquis*, the Californian chaparral and Australasia – clouds of yellow Australian mimosa, a very dark blue rosemary from the Mediterranean and *Beschorneria yuccoides* from Mexico. Even more impressive is the newly planted desert wash, made from nearly 200 tons of flints of varying sizes and covering at least an acre. It is intended to imitate the Arizona desert where the only rainfall is one of tumultuous thunderstorms every year. The plantings include some great specimens of palm trees, *Trithrinax campestris* from Argentina and *Brahea armata*, the Mexican blue palm, plus many agaves and aloes, some of which were grown from imported seed by the owners. East Ruston also has a pretty no-nonsense vegetable garden, a cutting garden, woodland walks, wildflower meadows, a walled garden and a spectacular corn field, brimming with field poppies, cornflowers and corn marigold. We carry a photograph of a herbaceous border in this outstanding modern garden on the cover of this book.

Owned by Graham Robeson & Alan Gray

Size 19 acres

Elsing Hall

ELSING, DEREHAM NR20 3DX

Tel & Fax 01362 637224
Location B1110 to North Tuddenham, then follow signs
Opening hours 2 pm – 6 pm; Sundays; June to September; and by appointment
Admission fee Adults £3; Children free

David and Shirley Cargill bought Elsing Hall in 1984 and started to plant roses: their taste is both catholic and voracious. On the terracing in front of the house are cultivars as distinct as the shrub rose 'Centenaire de Lourdes' (a great favourite in France, but all too seldom seen in England), the lanky purple moss-rose 'William Lobb', pink 'Fimbriata' whose petals are fringed like a carnation's, the sumptuous 'Ardoisée de Lyon', and dainty white 'Katharina Zeimet'. Now the Cargills grow more than 500 different roses, and the number rises annually. They have a relaxed approach to the demands of maintenance, since most roses flourish on benign neglect and go on flowering year after year with little or no attention. The Cargills understand that there are better ways of passing your time as a gardener than following the conventional routines of spraying, pruning and training. There is no better place than Elsing Hall to enjoy the wild romantic way of growing roses. This is liberation gardening. Giant hogweeds seed around the front door; their outsize stateliness quite appropriate to the scale of the gabled hall. The huge grey thistle *Onopordon arabicum* self-seeds in the lawn below and is spared by the mower. But Elsing Hall is much more than a rose garden. The Cargills are enthusiastic plantsmen: their garden is a celebration of the sheer variety of the plant kingdom. Alongside the moat are bamboos, *Caltha polypetala*, a

patch of *Matteuccia struthiopteris* under a huge weeping ash, skunk cabbages, *Ligularia dentata* 'Desdemona', *Gunnera manicata* and *G. tinctoria* too: all are vigorous plants, lush growers, nudging each other for space. Some of their more recent additions – the garden is expanding all the time – include an avenue of ginkgos, a collection of willows, a small arboretum of trees chosen for their coloured bark, a formal garden with 64 yew pyramids and an old church steeple in the middle, a lime tunnel, and an autumn garden inspired by Piet Oudolf's use of autumn colour in his garden in Holland. heir latest project is a small 'theatre garden' with arches of variegated holly.

 **Plant Highlights** Roses (mainly old-fashioned); fruit; fine collection of trees; kitchen garden; enlarged collection of old roses (1998); many rare trees planted (1999).

Owned by Mr & Mrs D H Cargill

many unusual plants – all put together in the cottage garden style. Mrs Mansey fills it with colour throughout the year: many hellebores in spring, roses in summer, evergreens and silvers for autumn and winter, and tremendous underplantings of bulbs. There is a small pond, a greenhouse, some scree beds and a conservatory. It is also intended to be a haven for bees, birds and butterflies.

Owned by Mrs P Mansey
Number of gardeners 1
Size ½ acre

Fairhaven Woodland & Water Garden

SOUTH WALSHAM, NORWICH NR13 6EA

Tel & Fax 01603 270449
Location 9 miles north-east of Norwich on the B1140
Opening hours 10 am – 5 pm; daily; all year except 25 December. Closes 9 pm on Wednesdays & Thursdays from May to August
Admission fee Adults £3.50; OAPs £3; Children £1.25. RHS members free in April, May & October

Ⓟ 🐦 ⓌⒸ �&. 🌳 🏛 ☕

This is a vast woodland garden of naturalised rhododendrons under a canopy of ancient oaks – one vast pollarded specimen known as the King Oak is estimated to be 900 years old. Then, in the 1960s, Lord Fairhaven laid two fairly narrow paths straight across a section of boggy Broads where sheets of candelabra primulas flourish in alder woodland. On the drier ground he planted masses of rhododendrons and azaleas among the naturalised *R. ponticum*. The garden is at its loveliest at the end of May, when the rhododendrons and candelabras are reflected in the still waters of the Broads. It is a bit short on follow-up

later in the year, though there are effective plantings of *Osmunda regalis*, ligularias and gunneras. Many visitors use it as an access to South Walsham Broad, so that even in high season the horticultural visitor may be almost alone in the woodland garden. Good for wild life, too.

Owned by Fairhaven Garden Trust
Number of gardeners 3
Size 90 acres

Felbrigg Hall

ROUGHTON, NORWICH NR11 8PR

Tel 01263 837444   **Fax** 01263 837032
Website www.nationaltrust.org.uk
Location Entrance off B1436, signed from A148 & A140
Opening hours 11 am – 5.30 pm; Saturday – Wednesday; 31 March to 4 November
Admission fee Adults £2.20; Children £1.10

 Ⓟ ⓌⒸ &. 🌳 🏛 ☕

There are fine trees in the park, but the best bit of Felbrigg is the walled kitchen garden, oriented on a large brick dovecote flanked by Victorian vineries. Fruit trees are trained against the walls (figs, pears, plums) and the garden laid to neatly grown vegetables with herbaceous borders along the box-edged gravel paths.

Owned by The National Trust
NCCPG National Collections Colchicum
English Heritage grade II*

Foggy Bottom

BRESSINGHAM, DISS IP22 2AA

Tel 01379 688585   **Fax** 01379 688340
Location On A1066, 3 miles west of Diss
Opening hours 12.30 pm – 4.30 pm; Tuesday – Friday, plus Sundays; April to October

Admission fee Adults £10; OAPs £9; Children £7. Please note that admission price includes joint entrance to the Dell Garden & the Bressingham Steam Experience plus a £5 voucher redeemable against Blooms Heritage Collection plants

Adrian Bloom started planting Foggy Bottom over twenty-five years ago as a garden for year-round seasonal colour and interest. Its centre-piece was his unique collection of conifers, collected from all over the world and tested for English conditions. They were, for many years, the dominant plants in the garden, and he used them to show off the innumerable contrasts of form, colour, texture and shape between different cultivars. Then he began to use them in other plant combinations – with ornamental grasses, perennials and shrubs – chosen to give a succession of colour, texture and other interest throughout the year. Finally, last year, he decided to overhaul it completely, and this overhaul amounted to a complete re-design. Some conifers were moved to other parts of the garden: others were heavily pruned. Some overgrown specimens were removed completely to make way for new planting schemes of shrubs, heathers, ornamental grasses and new young conifers. These new plantings are surrounded by an amphitheatre of mature beds. Adrian Bloom has also added a new woodland glade where shade- and moisture-loving plants surround a large pond. The net result is that Foggy Bottom continues to be an inspirational source of ideas for the smaller garden, but is now a Year 2000 garden instead of a 1975 one. We carry an old photograph of this outstanding modern garden on the cover of this book.

Owned by Mr & Mrs Adrian Bloom
Number of gardeners 2
Size 6 acres

Hoecroft Plants

SEVERALS GRANGE, HOLT ROAD,
WOOD NORTON, DEREHAM
NR20 5BL

Tel 01362 684206
Location 2 miles north of Guist on B1110 (not in West Norton village)
Opening hours 10 am – 4 pm; Thursday – Sunday; April to September

Hoecroft is a small but well-known specialist nursery which began by concentrating upon variegated and coloured foliage plants. These range from the smallest alpines to large shrubs. Perhaps more prominent now is its list of ornamental grasses, rushes, sedges and bamboos: it offers over 250 different cultivars, which may be seen in the attached display garden.

Holkham Hall

HOLKHAM, WELLS-NEXT-THE-SEA
NR23 1AB

Tel 01328 710227 **Fax** 01328 711707
Location Off A149, 2 miles west of Wells
Opening hours 1 pm – 5 pm; Sunday – Thursday; 29 May to 30 September. Plus 11.30 am – 5 pm on 15 & 16 April, 6, 7, 27 & 28 May, 26 & 27 August. Park open from 9 am, Sunday to Friday, in summer; Monday to Friday in winter
Admission fee Park free

Holkham is a big landscape garden, worked on by Kent, Brown and Repton. Formal terraces were added in the 1850s. In the eighteenth-century walled garden are several demonstration gardens (including areas of herbs, roses and perennials), a nursery and a fig house undergoing restoration.

Owned by The Earl of Leicester
English Heritage grade I

Hoveton Hall

WROXHAM, NORWICH NR12 8RJ

Tel 01603 782798   **Fax** 01603 784564
Location 9 miles from Norwich: brown tourist signs from A1151
Opening hours Not known as we went to press. In 2000 the garden was open from 11 am to 5.30 pm; Wednesdays, Fridays, Sundays & Bank Holiday Mondays; Easter to mid-September
Admission fee Adults £3; Wheelchair-bound £2; Children £1 (2000 prices)

The gardens are laid out around a series of streams, with beautiful waterside plantings and candelabra primulas. The walled garden, built as late as 1936, is set out for growing fruit and vegetable in the traditional way, with fine herbaceous borders too.

Owned by Mr & Mrs Andrew Buxton

Lynford Arboretum

MUNFORD, THETFORD IP26 5HW

Location Turn right off A1065 just north of Munford
Opening hours Dawn – dusk; daily; all year
Admission fee free

The Lynford Arboretum was started in 1947 by students at the Forester Training School who at that time occupied nearby Lynford Hall. They planted about 100 species of conifers and broadleaves, some in forestry plots but mostly as individual specimens within the parkland and policies surrounding the house. The soil is thin and sandy, but some of those original plantings

are already handsome specimens, including a *Nothofagus obliqua* and a *Pinus banksiana* each 20m tall. Rather simply maintained by the Forestry Commission, the arboretum has considerable potential for development. Lynford Hall is now an hotel: the extensive formal garden (rather gone back) was laid out by William Burn in the 1860s and was famous for its bedding until 1914. Beyond is a curving lake. Rather surprisingly, the Forestry Commission does not permit dogs in the arboretum.

Owned by Forestry Agency

Mannington Gardens

MANNINGTON HALL, NORWICH NR11 7BB

Tel 01263 584175   **Fax** 01263 761214
Location Signed from B1149 at Saxthorpe
Opening hours 12 noon – 5 pm; Sundays; May – September. And 11 am – 5 pm; Wednesday – Friday; June – August
Admission fee Adults £3; Concessions £2.50; Children free (2000 prices)

Mannington has a moated house, two lakes, a scented garden and handsome herbaceous borders, but the best part is the Heritage Rose Garden, made in association with Peter Beales, where thousands of old-fashioned roses are planted to illustrate the history of roses in cultivation.

Plant Highlights Roses (mainly old-fashioned & climbers); natural surroundings; colour borders; lakes; wildflowers.

Owned by Lord Walpole
Number of gardeners 3½
Size 20 acres
English Heritage grade II

Norfolk Lavender

CALEY MILL, HEACHAM, KING'S LYNN
PE31 7JE

Tel 01485 570384   **Fax** 01485 571176
Location On A149, 13 miles north of Kings Lynn
Opening hours 9.30 am – 6 pm; summer.
10.30 am – 4 pm; winter. Closed for about 2 weeks at
Christmas & New Year

This family-run nursery has grown into
quite a business, and can be crowded when
the fields of lavender (100 acres) flower in
stripes across the surrounding fields. The
nursery sells lavender (hardy and tender,
bare root and potted), lavender products
and other scented plants. Of most interest to
the horticulturally aware will be the National
Collection of *Lavandula* cultivars. And all
will enjoy the four-acre 'fragrant meadow'
of plants chosen for their aromatic qualities.

NCCPG National Collections *Lavandula* (sect. Lavandula,
Dentata, Pterostoechas & Stoechas)

Oxburgh Hall

OXBOROUGH, KING'S LYNN PE33 9PS

Tel 01366 328258   **Fax** 01366 328066
Website www.nationaltrust.org.uk
Location 7 miles south-west of Swaffham on Stoke Ferry
road
Opening hours 11 am – 4 pm; Saturdays & Sundays; 3 to
25 March. Then 11 am – 5.30 pm; Saturday – Wednesday;
31 March to 4 November. Daily in August
Admission fee Adults £2.60; Children £1.30

The baroque nineteenth-century parterre
has been replanted by the National Trust
with such herbs as rue and santolina making
permanent companions for annuals and
bedding plants. Good fruit trees in the

walled garden: medlars, quinces and
mulberries. Not a great garden, but a good
one.

Owned by The National Trust
English Heritage grade II

P W Plants

SUNNYSIDE, HEATH ROAD,
KENNINGHALL NR16 2DS

Tel & Fax 01953 888212
Location South-west of Norwich, just off B1113
Opening hours 9 am – 5 pm; Fridays; and last Saturday of
the month

This nursery offers a wide range of plants
chosen for their general garden-worthiness,
interesting foliage and shape. They are
perhaps best known for their bamboos,
which have won them many medals at RHS
shows, but they also stock grasses, shrubs,
perennials and climbers. Most can be seen
growing in their display gardens.

Peter Beales Roses

LONDON ROAD, ATTLEBOROUGH
NR17 1AY

Tel 01953 454707
Location 2 miles south of Attleborough: leave A11 at
Breckland Lodge
Opening hours 9 am – 5 pm (4 pm in January);
Monday – Friday. 9 am – 4.30 pm; Saturdays.
10 am – 4 pm; Sundays

There is a small display garden attached to
this well-known rose nursery: parts are
better maintained than others. A good range
of older and classic roses is offered for sale,
both at the nursery and from its mail-order

catalogue which lists over 1000 species and cultivars, many not available elsewhere in the UK.

NCCPG National Collections *Rosa* (species)

Plantation Garden

4 EARLHAM ROAD, NORWICH
NR2 3DB

Tel 01603 455223
Location Between The Crofters Hotel & The Beeches Hotel, near Roman Catholic Cathedral
Opening hours dawn-dusk; daily; all year
Admission fee Adults £1.50; Children free. Honesty box

The Plantation Garden was made in an abandoned chalk quarry by Henry Trevor, a successful Norwich businessman, between around 1856 until his death in 1897. In the ensuing years the garden passed through various hands until, in 1980, it was totally overgrown and abandoned. In that year it was rediscovered and the Plantation Garden Preservation Trust formed to save and restore the garden. The area, nearly 3 acres in all, contains many features including woodland walkways, flower beds, lawns, a gothic fountain, Italianate terrace, 'Mediaeval' terrace wall and rustic bridge. There are many unique aspects to this very idiosyncratic garden making it a haven of peace and tranquillity – a refuge from the hurly-burly of modern life and a glimpse into a bygone age. Sir Roy Strong is patron of the Trust and points out that the garden is 'something of a rarity, for in most cases it is usually only the grandest of gardens which survive from earlier periods'.

Owned by The Plantation Garden Preservation Trust
Number of gardeners 1, plus volunteers
Size 3 acres
English Heritage grade II

Raveningham Hall Gardens

RAVENINGHAM, NORWICH
NR14 6NS

Tel 01508 548480   **Fax** 01508 548958
Location Signed off A146 at Hales
Opening hours 2 pm – 5.30 pm on Sundays, Wednesdays & Bank Holiday Mondays; April to September
Admission fee Adults £2.50; OAPs £2; Children free

The house at Raveningham is partly Georgian and partly twentieth-century: the fourteenth-century church of St Andrew near the house is an integral part of the landscape. Both are set in a splendid eighteenth-century park and enhanced by nineteenth-century tree plantings. Despite all this history, the main attraction now is the modern plantings. These were largely the work of Priscilla, Lady Bacon, who collected rare plants and arranged them beautifully in areas like the long herbaceous border. She was also a keen dendrologist and planted the young arboretum. In the working walled garden (very pretty) are a herb garden, orchard and glasshouse. It is good to see this excellent modern garden open more often to the public again.

Owned by Sir Nicholas Bacon Bt
English Heritage grade II

Reads Nursery

HALES HALL, LODDON NR14 6QW

Tel 01508 548395   **Fax** 01508 548040
Website www.readsnursery.co.uk
Location Off A146, 1 mile south of Loddon

Opening hours 10 am – 5 pm (4 pm in winter); Tuesday – Saturday; all year. Plus 11 am – 4 pm; Sundays & Bank Holiday Mondays; April to October

This important and long-established family nursery specialises in citrus fruit-trees and conservatory plants. Its extensive list of *Citrus* cultivars is based upon the centuries-old collection made by Rivers of Sawbridgeworth. Rivers were famous fruit-breeders in the nineteenth century, and their citrus trees supplied the scions needed to start the California fruit industry. Reads acquired their stock when Rivers closed in 1983. They also grow and sell over seventy different grape cultivars, including many more English-raised vines than any other nursery: this is the place to find such Victorian delicacies as 'Lady Downe's Seedling' and 'Mrs Pince's Black Muscat'. Their list of figs is equally extensive, and unparalleled among UK nurserymen: 'Goutte d'Or', 'Malcolm's Giant' and 'White Ischia' are among their specialities. But they also stock a large number of proper traditional conservatory plants – abutilons, bougainvilleas, brugmansias, gardenias, jasmines, passionflowers, sparmannias and hundreds more.

NCCPG National Collections *Citrus*; *Ficus*; *Vitis vinifera* (grapes)

The Romantic Garden Nursery

SWANNINGTON, NORWICH
NR9 5NW

Tel 01603 261488 **Fax** 01603 864231
Website www.romantic-garden.demon.co.uk
Location 7 miles north-west of Norwich

Opening hours 10 am – 5 pm; Wednesdays, Fridays & Saturdays

The Romantic Garden Nursery sells topiary: ornamental standards, bobbles and pyramids in *Cupressus* and *Ilex*, as well as box in animal and other shapes. It is a specialist nursery holding one of the largest selections of topiary and ornamental standards in the country. It offers topiary packages too – these include a layout together with the necessary plants – and a range of wire frames for growing and shaping your own topiary. Clematis and half-hardy plants are also available.

Sandringham House

SANDRINGHAM, KING'S LYNN
PE35 6EN

Tel 01553 772675 **Fax** 01485 541571
Website www.sandringhamestate.co.uk
Location Signed from A148
Opening hours 10.30 am – 5 pm; daily; 14 April to 17 July and 1 August to 28 October
Admission fee Adults £6; OAPs £4.50; Children £3.50

The best of the royal gardens. The woodland and lakes are rich with ornamental plantings, and the splendid herbaceous borders were designed by Geoffrey Jellicoe, but it is the scale of it all that most impresses, and the grandeur too.

Owned by H M The Queen
Number of gardeners 8
Size 60 acres
English Heritage grade II*

Sheringham Park

GARDENER'S COTTAGE, SHERINGHAM
PARK, SHERINGHAM NR26 8TB

Tel & Fax 01263 823778
Website www.nationaltrust.org.uk
Location Jct of A148 & B1157
Opening hours Dawn – dusk; daily; all year
Admission fee Cars £2.70

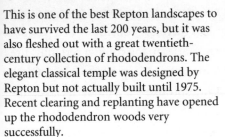

This is one of the best Repton landscapes to have survived the last 200 years, but it was also fleshed out with a great twentieth-century collection of rhododendrons. The elegant classical temple was designed by Repton but not actually built until 1975. Recent clearing and replanting have opened up the rhododendron woods very successfully.

Owned by The National Trust
English Heritage grade II*

Thorncroft Clematis Nursery

THE LINGS, REYMERSTON, NORWICH
NR9 4QG

Tel 01953 850407   **Fax** 01953 851788
Location Between Dereham & Wymondham on B1135
Opening hours 10 am – 4.30 pm, daily, March to October. Closed Wednesdays. By appointment only in winter

This family-run specialist nursery began as a hobby and has now developed into a substantial business. Over 300 clematis cultivars grow in the display garden attached to the nursery. Here the owners have set out some of the many ways that clematis may be grown – in borders and island beds, over shrub roses, through ornamental trees and in containers. There is also a formal sunken garden with clipped box hedges and classical obelisks (covered by yet more clematis, and roses). The nursery does not stock all 300 clematis cultivars, but prefers to list those it regards as best: these are selected for such qualities as their length of flowering, colour, form, quantity of bloom, strength of growth and so on.

NORTHAMPTONSHIRE

Despite its industrial importance and proximity to London, Northamptonshire is still a county of large estates. Three of the four Grade I historic gardens are open to the public (Althorp, Boughton House and Castle Ashby), while the fourth (Drayton) is occasionally open to groups from bodies like the Garden History Society. Althorp and Boughton also have good arboreta, each with a few champion trees. The National Gardens Scheme does well in Northamptonshire: it is particularly successful in persuading groups of gardens, as many as eight or nine in a village, to open together on the same day. It is therefore something of a paradox that there appears to be comparatively few nurseries in the county: certainly, the Royal Horticultural Society has no Partner Nurseries in Northamptonshire. On the other hand, its only Free Access garden – Cottesbrooke – is a modern classic, an historic landscape with a really good horticultural garden inserted into it.

Althorp

ALTHORP, NORTHAMPTON NN7 4HQ

Tel 01604 770107 **Fax** 01604 770042
Website www.althorp.com
Location Signed from M1, Jct16
Opening hours 9 am – 5 pm; daily; 1 July to 30 August
Admission fee Tickets in advance only from 0870 167 9000

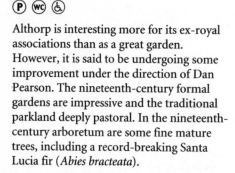

Althorp is interesting more for its ex-royal associations than as a great garden. However, it is said to be undergoing some improvement under the direction of Dan Pearson. The nineteenth-century formal gardens are impressive and the traditional parkland deeply pastoral. In the nineteenth-century arboretum are some fine mature trees, including a record-breaking Santa Lucia fir (*Abies bracteata*).

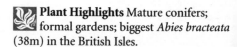

Plant Highlights Mature conifers; formal gardens; biggest *Abies bracteata* (38m) in the British Isles.

Owned by Earl Spencer
English Heritage grade I

Boughton House

KETTERING NN14 1BJ

Tel 01536 515731 **Fax** 01536 417255
Website www.boughtonhouse.org.uk
Location A43, three miles north of Kettering, signed through Geddington
Opening hours 1 pm – 5 pm; Saturday – Thursday; 1 May to 1 September. Plus Fridays in August
Admission fee Adults £1.50; OAPs & Children £1

Boughton has a seriously important landscaped park (350 acres) dating from the early eighteenth century. The lay-out is intact, and some of the plantings too – one of the lime avenues was planted in 1715. The original landscaping features have been purposefully restored over the last twenty years or so: rides, avenues, *allées*, lakes, canals and prospects. There is little of horticultural interest (even though Valerie Finnis lives in a wing of the house), but the sense of history is strongly felt. Boughton House also has a good website.

 Plant Highlights Roses (mainly modern); good herbaceous borders.

Owned by The Duke & Duchess of Buccleuch & The Living Landscape Trust
Number of gardeners 5
Size 20 acres
English Heritage grade I

Canons Ashby House

DAVENTRY NN11 3SD

Tel 01327 860044   **Fax** 01327 860168
Website www.nationaltrust.org.uk
Location Signed from A5 & A422
Opening hours 12 noon – 5.30 pm (4.30 pm in October); Saturday – Wednesday; April to October
Admission fee Adults £1 (garden only)

Canons Ashby is a rare survivor among gardens. The Drydens, who owned it, never really took to the landscape movement. The early eighteenth-century layout is intact and has been carefully restored by the National Trust. The terraces below the house (*very* pretty) are planted with clipped Portugal laurel (*Prunus lusitanica*) and period fruit trees. A place to contemplate old Tory values.

Owned by The National Trust
English Heritage grade II*

Castle Ashby Gardens

CASTLE ASHBY, NORTHAMPTON NN7 1LQ

Tel & Fax 01604 696187
Website www.thelodge.u-net.com/gardens
Location Off A428 between Northampton & Bedford
Opening hours 10 am – 6 pm; daily; all year
Admission fee Adults £2.50; OAPs & Children £1.50

Much thought and money has recently been spent on restoring the gardens at Castle Ashby. The Italian formal gardens were among the first to be renewed, and the arboretum has been restocked. There are stylish terraces, an orangery and greenhouses built by Sir Matthew Digby Wyatt in the 1860s but perhaps the best thing about Castle Ashby is the park – 200 acres of it, designed by Capability Brown.

Owned by Marquess of Northampton
Number of gardeners 3
Size 20 acres
English Heritage grade I

Coton Manor

GUILSBOROUGH, NORTHAMPTON NN6 8RQ

Tel 01604 740219   **Fax** 01604 740838
Website www.cotonmanor.co.uk
Location Signed from A5199 (formerly A50) & A428
Opening hours 12 noon – 5.30 pm; Wednesday – Sunday & Bank Holiday Mondays; April to September
Admission fee Adults £3.50; OAPs £3; Children £2

The Pasley-Tylers have lived at Coton since the 1920s, and every generation has left its mark upon the garden. Among the best features are a rose garden, a herb garden, a woodland garden, colour plantings (including a wonderful crimson and pink border), a Mediterranean bank, a five-acre bluebell wood, an apple orchard with eighty English cultivars, and a wildflower meadow. Water is everywhere: pools, streams and ponds support hostas, primulas and the black-and-yellow flowers of *Kirengeshoma palmata*. There are surprises too: one might suppose that the sweet-scented *Trachelospermum asiaticum* and long-flowering *Fremontodendron californicum* were too tender for Northamptonshire, but they both grow against the walls of the house. Recent plantings include a herb garden and a rose garden with pink 'Mary Rose' and white 'Iceberg'. The whole garden comes together nicely because the plants are chosen for their overall contribution as well as their intrinsic merits. The standard of maintenance is excellent, while the presence of a few ornamental birds adds another quite dimension to a visit.

Owned by Ian Pasley-Tyler
Number of gardeners 4
Size 10 acres

Cottesbrooke Hall

NORTHAMPTON NN6 8PF

Tel 01604 505808　**Fax** 01604 505619
Location 10 miles north of Northampton
Opening hours 2 pm – 5 pm; Thursdays, Bank Holiday Mondays & the preceding Sundays; Easter to September. Plus 2 pm – 5 pm; Tuesdays, Wednesdays & Fridays; June to September
Admission fee Garden only: Adults £3; Children £1.50. RHS members free

Cottesbrooke is the garden with everything: a two-mile drive, majestic parkland, a classical bridge, a fabulously pretty house, an eighteenth-century park, lakes, waterfalls, bluebell woods, rhododendrons, acres of daffodils, twenty-seven cultivars of naturalised snowdrops, half-a-dozen garden rooms, Scheemaker's statues from Stowe, an armillary garden, pergolas, *allées*, 300-year old cedars, new developments every year, immaculate maintenance, an enlightened owner, plants a-plenty, and the signatures of Geoffrey Jellicoe and Sylvia Crowe among the designers who have helped to develop it. And free entry for RHS members.

Owned by Captain & Mrs John Macdonald-Buchanan
English Heritage grade II

Holdenby House Gardens

HOLDENBY, NORTHAMPTON NN6 8DJ

Tel 01604 770074　**Fax** 01604 770962
Website www.holdenby.com
Location 6 miles north-west of Northampton, off A5199 or A428
Opening hours 1 pm – 5 pm; Sunday – Friday; July & August. Plus Sundays from Easter to 30 September. Closes at 6 pm on Bank Holiday Sundays & Mondays
Admission fee Adults £3; OAPs £2.50; Children £1.75

The outlines of the garden at Holdenby are Elizabethan: a bowling alley, some parterres and terraces which were built in 1580 to impress Queen Elizabeth on one of her progresses through England. They explain why Holdenby is so highly regarded as an historical garden. What we see now is modern and pretty. The Elizabethan-style garden was planted by Rosemary Verey, using only those plants which were available in 1580. Rupert Goldby planted the 'fragrant border' and there is a charming 'silver border' made to hold the owners' ever-growing collection of silver- and grey-leaved plants.

Plant Highlights Roses (mainly old-fashioned); herbs; good herbaceous borders; Elizabethan-style garden; fragrant and silver borders.

Owned by Mr & Mrs James Lowther
Number of gardeners 3
Size 15 acres
English Heritage grade II*

Kelmarsh Hall

NORTHAMPTON NN6 9LU

Tel 01604 686485 **Fax** 01604 686543
Location On A508 at crossroads in Kelmarsh
Opening hours 2 pm – 5 pm; Tuesdays, Thursdays & Sundays; Easter to 31 August. Opens at 2.30 pm on Sundays
Admission fee Adults £2

Ⓟ 🐕 ⓦⒸ

Kelmarsh is a handsome Palladian house: it looks out over formal parkland which was designed by Geoffrey Jellicoe in 1936. The view extends across a meadow lined with red chestnuts to a lake before wilder, open semi-parkland carries the eye to the horizon. Most of the horticultural interest is off to the side, around the outside of a triangular walled garden which remains tantalisingly closed to visitors. First come lumpy box hedges, pleached limes and a pretty sunken garden, designed as a quincunx and planted with white flowers. Further on, *Tropaeolum speciosum* clambers through the yew hedges which flank a sequence of narrow, intimate beds (hitherto planted with rather ordinary plants, but currently undergoing restoration). Some of the yew hedges have been breached by cutting the yew trees back to the trunks and letting them grow into curious hump-backed shapes – a very effective and unique feature of the garden. At the furthest extremity, the narrow path bursts out into a fan-shaped old-fashioned rose garden, rather recently re-made, with a splendid view of the parish church across a paddock. This is a fine garden, which will be interesting to watch as it develops in years to come.

Owned by Kelmarsh Hall Estate Preservation Trust
Number of gardeners 4
Size 14 acres

The Menagerie

NEWPORT PAGNELL ROAD, HORTON NN7 2BX

Tel & Fax 01604 870957
Location One mile south of Horton on the B526
Opening hours 2 pm – 5 pm; Mondays & Thursdays; April to September. Plus 2 pm – 6 pm on the last Sunday of those months
Admission fee Adults £3.50; Children £1.50

Ⓟ ⓦⒸ 🌳

This folly was built in the 1750s for the 2nd Earl of Halifax by Thomas Wright of Durham. In the 1970s, it was restored by the architectural historian Gervase Jackson-Stops: his companion Ian Kirby started to make the garden about ten years later. Several baroque avenues splay out from the house. One runs up to a mount, two of them lead to a fountain. The modern follies include two thatched arbours, one circular and classical, the other triangular and gothic. Orpheus plays to the animals in the grotto, which is encrusted with shells and minerals. The plantings are bold and romantic. Vernon Russell-Smith designed the rose garden: a bog garden and a collection of native plants complete the picture.

Owned by Alexander Myers
Number of gardeners 2
Size 4 acres

Old Rectory

SUDBOROUGH NN14 3BX

Tel 01832 733247   **Fax** 01832 733832
Location In village centre, by church, off A6116
Opening hours 10 am to 4 pm; Tuesdays; April to September. Plus Saturdays, Sundays & Bank Holiday Mondays from April to June. And by appointment
Admission fee Adults £3; Children free

This immaculately maintained modern garden has been made around a handsome Georgian rectory with a bit of advice from Rosemary Verey and Rupert Goldby. In front of the house, on the edge of the lawn, is a handsome and ancient *Robinia pseudaccacia*: everything else is fairly recent and extremely well grown The garden is thickly and thoughtfully planted so that every season is rich in interest. Few of the plants are rare, but all are well chosen – some for their flowers, some for their foliage and others because they look good in mixed groups. Roses are much in evidence throughout the garden and in a dedicated rose garden. The best feature is an extensive and very pretty *potager*, which has an infinite number of box-edged beds and fairly narrow brick paths between them. Clematis and roses cover the framework of a tunnel: they are joined, in season, by ornamental gourds which are encouraged to grow up the same structure. The fruit trees are trained in many different ways and good use is made of flowers in pots to ensure that the *potager* has colour at all seasons.

Owned by Mr & Mrs A P Huntington
Size 3 acres

Rockingham Castle

MARKET HARBOROUGH LE16 8TH

Tel 01586 770240   **Fax** 01586 771692
Website www.rockinghamcastle.com
Location 2 miles north of Corby on A6003
Opening hours 1 pm (but 11.30 am on Sundays & Bank Holidays) – 5 pm; Sundays, Thursdays, Bank Holiday Mondays & following Tuesdays (plus all Tuesdays in August); April to September
Admission fee £3

Rockingham has centuries of garden history in its layout: the park was landscaped in the eighteenth century but goes back to the thirteenth century as a deer park. The formal circular rose garden on the site of the old keep was added in the nineteenth century: it is surrounded by a billowing yew hedge 400 years old. The wild garden in a ravine was replanted 20 years ago as a mini-arboretum: all the modern plantings are very effective.

Owned by James Saunders Watson
Number of gardeners 3
Size 12 acres
English Heritage grade II*

Sulgrave Manor

SULGRAVE, BANBURY OX17 2SD

Tel 01295 760205   **Fax** 01295 768056
Website www.stratford.co.uk/sulgrave
Location 7 miles from Banbury
Opening hours 10.30 am – 1 pm (but mornings by appointment only on weekdays except in August) & 2 pm – 5.30 pm (4.30 pm in March, November & December); daily except Wednesdays (but weekends only in March, November & December); 1 March to 24 December, plus 27 to 31 December

Admission fee Adults £4; Children £2. But Adults £4.50;
Children £2.25 for special events

There are two reasons for visiting Sulgrave.
The first is that it belonged to George
Washington's family or, at least, to his
ancestors. This places the Great American
firmly among the English landed gentry. The
second is that, after the estate was
underwritten by the Colonial Dames in
1924, Sir Reginald Blomfield was called in to
design a period garden. In his day, Blomfield
was one of England's foremost architect-
designers, and the garden he made for
Sulgrave is formally laid out in the
seventeenth-century style, to complement
the old house. The plantings are suitably
olde worlde, and the standard of
maintenance unsurpassed.

Owned by Sulgrave Manor Board
Number of gardeners 2
Size 5 acres
English Heritage grade II

NORTHUMBERLAND AND TYNE & WEAR

Northumberland and Tyne & Wear are two sides of the same historical phenomenon: men made their fortunes in Newcastle or Sunderland, both now in Tyne & Wear, and then moved away to build houses and plant gardens in Northumberland. Belsay, Cragside and Lindisfarne all owe their gardens to this social pattern. Belsay is a Grade I garden: the only other one in Northumberland is Alnwick, where the Duchess of Northumberland has plans to develop an extensive (and expensive) new water garden. The greatest late nineteenth-century garden in Northumberland is Cragside, which now has a collection of champion conifers. There are record-breakers too at Alnwick, and a good arboretum at Howick, where many new plantings have also been made in recent years. The National Gardens Scheme does not have a large portfolio of gardens in Northumberland and Tyne & Wear, but there are several first-rate nurseries in the two counties, including Halls of Heddon, Herterton House and Hexham Herbs. The real interests of ordinary gardeners in Northumberland and Tyne & Wear are quite different: alpines and leeks. Both the Alpine Garden Society and the Scottish Rock Garden Club are well supported here, while the National Pot Leek Society could be described as a uniquely Geordie success story.

Bede's World Herb Garden

CHURCH BANK, JARROW NE32 3DY

Tel 0191 489 2196   **Fax** 0191 428 2361
Website www.bedesworld.co.uk
Location Signed from A185
Opening hours Dawn to dusk; daily; all year
Admission fee Garden only: free

(P) (WC) (&) (♣) (⊞) (⊕)

Bede's World is an educational experience: one of its main parts is an 'Anglo-Saxon farm'. But there is also a herb garden based on ninth-century descriptions: a small part of an ambitious enterprise which seeks to impart a feeling for the Anglo-Saxon world. In front of the new museum are four raised beds planted as a late-mediaeval formal garden.

Owned by Jarrow 700 AD Ltd

Bide-a-Wee Cottage

STANTON, NETHERWITTON, MORPETH NE65 8PR

Tel 01670 772262
Location 7 miles north-west of Morpeth
Opening hours 1.30 pm – 5 pm; Wednesdays
& Saturdays; 28 April to 1 September. Parties by
arrangement at other times
Admission fee £2

The situation of the garden at Bide-a-Wee Cottage is extraordinary: most of the garden is hidden in a disused quarry on the edge of a 500ft ridge. The unusual site means that there are enormous variations within its two acres – variations of aspect, topography, soil-type and moisture. Mark Robson has seized on this natural diversity to plant a remarkably wide spectrum of plants. In the wet shaded quarry bottom, by the ponds, are swathes of primulas, rodgersias, ostrich ferns, sensitive ferns and gunneras. Away from the water, on the north-facing slopes of the quarry and in the shade of trees, are meconopsis, rhododendrons and gentians. Quite a different type of plant grows on the south-facing slopes: abutilons, agapanthus, eremurus and eryngiums for example. Throughout the garden, the natural rock walls are contrasted with hedges and complemented by evergreens – conifers, rhododendrons and grasses. Then more ephemeral perennials and wild flowers are woven into the design, as are the more unusual plants that are the hallmark of a plantsman. Robson describes his garden as 'bold perennial plantings linked with a network of winding paths and steps, all associated with dramatic changes of level'. These are designed to create views across the garden or down onto lower levels, as well as into the countryside beyond. To the east, above the quarry, drifts of late-flowering perennials (including lythrum, eupatorium and helianthus) melt into the half-acre wildflower meadow that is also home to the beehives. Then the garden opens out and blends into the rough landscape of Northumberland – tough grassland grazed by sheep.

Owned by Mark Robson
Size 2 acres

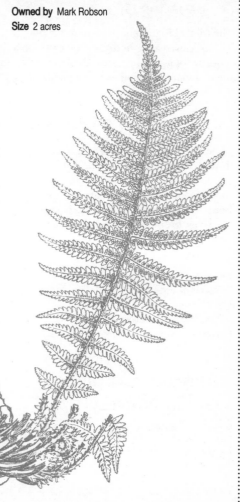

Belsay Hall

BELSAY, NEWCASTLE-UPON-TYNE
NE20 0DX

Tel 01661 881636   **Fax** 01661 881043
Location At Belsay on A696 Ponteland to Jedburgh road
Opening hours 10 am – 6 pm (5 pm in October and 4 pm from November to March); daily except 1 January & 24 – 26 December
Admission fee Adults £3.90; Concessions £2.90; Children £2

The wildly Picturesque gardens at Belsay include eleven acres of disused quarry with a sequence of gloomy chasms and a microclimate which allows such plants as *Trachycarpus* palms and eucryphias to flourish in a cold upland site. The house is very plain – inspired by ancient Athens – but underpinned by fine formal terraces where the gardeners arrange magnificent displays of bedding. Down the valley are splendid woods planted with hardy hybrid rhododendrons: elsewhere are fine weed-free lawns, intensive modern herbaceous plantings, brooding conifers and the ruins of Belsay Castle. The standard of maintenance is superb.

Owned by English Heritage
Number of gardeners 4
Size 40 acres
NCCPG National Collections *Iris*
English Heritage grade I

Birkheads Cottage Garden Nursery

BIRKHEADS LANE, CAUSEY ARCH,
SUNNISIDE, NEWCASTLE-UPON-TYNE
NE16 5EL

Tel 0378 447920   **Fax** 01207 232262

Website www.birkheadscottagegardennursery.co.uk
Location Brown sign on A6076 between Sunniside & Stanley
Opening hours By appointment. Evening visits recommended for parties and guided walks on the first Wednesday of the month

This small nursery offers a varied and informed selection of alpines, perennials and shrubs: the owner is a garden designer with a passion for plants. There are over 4,500 different plants growing in the adjoining garden: this is an remarkable number by any standards. Other features in the garden include a formal topiary garden made in the nineteenth century, a gravel garden with herbaceous beds, some rock gardens; a wildlife pond and wildflower garden, a mini arboretum and a grass garden.

Chillingham Castle

CHILLINGHAM NE66 5NJ

Tel 01668 215359   **Fax** 01668 215463
Location Off A1 between Alnwick & Berwick

Chillingham has made great efforts to smarten up for visitors. The results are very encouraging: a nineteenth-century Italianate garden by Wyattville, a modern herbaceous border in the old walled garden and splendid hardy hybrid rhododendrons in the woodland walks which surround the lake. Chillingham itself is a formidable mediaeval castle with amazing views down long eighteenth-century rides. There is an exhibition of old photographs in the castle which show the garden more than 100 years ago.

Owned by Sir Humphry Wakefield Bt
English Heritage grade II

Cragside

ROTHBURY, MORPETH NE65 7PX

Tel 01669 620333
Website www.nationaltrust.org.uk
Location 15 miles north-west of Morpeth off A697 & B6341
Opening hours 10.30 am – 7 pm (last admissions 5.30 pm). Tuesday – Sunday; 31 March to 4 November. Plus Bank Holiday Mondays. Plus 11 am – 4 pm; Wednesday – Sunday; 7 November to 16 December
Admission fee Adults £4.20; Children £2.10

There are two gardens at Cragside. The newly-acquired Italianate formal garden has splendid carpet bedding, ferneries and a fruit house with rotating pots. Even more impressive are the rhododendron woods – hundreds and hundreds of acres of nineteenth-century hybrids, plus trusty *R. ponticum* and *R. luteum*, breathtaking in late May.

Plant Highlights Roses (mainly old-fashioned); rock garden; fruit; mature conifers; massive rock garden; tallest *Abies nordmanniana* (50m), *Cupressus nootkatensis* (33m) and *Picea glauca* (28m) in the British Isles.

Owned by The National Trust
English Heritage grade II*

Halls of Heddon

WEST HEDDON NURSERIES,
HEDDON ON THE WALL,
NEWCASTLE-UPON-TYNE NE15 0JS

Tel 01661 852445
Website www.hallsofheddon.co.uk
Location 1 mile north-west of Heddon, off the B6318

Opening hours 9 am – 5 pm, Monday – Saturday; 10 am – 5 pm, Sundays

Halls produced their first dahlia and chrysanthemum catalogue in 1931: now they offer cultivars for many purposes, including showing, cutting, garden display and greenhouse cultivation. Their extensive list includes many cultivars which are unique to them – not offered by any other nursery. Their magnificent show fields are open from September until the plants are cut down by the frosts: they have over 10,000 plants on display. The garden centre carries a general range.

Herterton House Gardens & Nursery

HARTINGTON, CAMBO NE61 4BN

Tel 01670 774278
Location 2 miles north of Cambo (B6342)
Opening hours 1.30 pm – 5.30 pm; daily except Tuesdays & Thursdays; April to September. For National Gardens Scheme on 19 June, 17 July & 7 August
Admission fee Adults £2.40; Children £1

This excellent plantsman's garden is (rather unusually) firmly designed and meticulously planted. It is also attached to a small nursery – so firmly attached, in fact, that it is difficult to say whether this is a garden with a nursery or a nursery with a garden. The knot garden is famous, and much photographed, full of herbs and pharmacological plants. More impressive still are the herbaceous plantings, all weaving through each other in beautifully co-ordinated colours. In the gazebo at the top are photographs showing how the garden has developed, expanded, grown up and intensified over the years: a most inspirational display. There are further plans for the future: the Lawleys may decide to add a new parterre to the 'fancy garden' later this year.

Owned by Mr & Mrs Frank Lawley

Hexham Herbs & Hardy Plants

CHESTERS WALLED GARDEN, CHOLLERFORD, HEXHAM NE46 4BQ

Tel 01434 681483
Location 6 miles north of Hexham, off B6318 near Chollerford
Opening hours 10 am – 5 pm; daily; April to October. Telephone for winter opening times
Admission fee Adults £1.50; Children (under 10) free

This energetic and successful small modern nursery garden is strategically placed near the fort at Chesters. The herb collection is remarkable (over 1,000 cultivars) and the design within a two-acre brick-walled garden is charming. Dye plants, a Mediterranean garden, an astilbe bed and a knot garden are just some of the features. In addition to their National Collections of *Origanum* and *Thymus*, the nursery has a very good collection of *Rosmarinus* cultivars. The original name of the nursery was 'Hexham Herbs', and the addition last winter of '& Hardy Plants' indicates a widening of its market. The garden has over 3,000 different plant cultivars growing in it, and the owners aim to propagate and sell them all in rotation, which means that if they do not have something just at the moment, you should be able to buy it from them in the future.

Owned by Mrs S White
NCCPG National Collections *Origanum*; *Thymus*

Howick Hall

ALNWICK NE66 3LB

Tel & Fax 01665 577285
Location Off B1399 between Longhoughton & Craster
Opening hours 1 pm – 6 pm; daily; April to October
Admission fee Adults £2; OAPs & Children £1

Rather an un-Northumbrian garden, because its closeness to the sea makes possible the cultivation of such tender plants as *Carpenteria* and *Ceanothus*. Formal terraces below the house are well planted, but the great joy of the garden at Howick is a small woodland which has acid soil. This was planted in the 1930s with a fine collection of rhododendrons and camellias: other plants are still being added. The result looks more west coast than east.

 **Plant Highlights** Roses (mainly old-fashioned); rhododendrons & azaleas; plantsman's collection of plants; mature conifers; spring bulbs; eucryphias; much new planting; biggest stone pine *Pinus pinea* in the British Isles.

Owned by Howick Trustees Ltd
Number of gardeners 5
English Heritage grade II

Kirkley Hall Gardens

PONTELAND NE20 0AQ

Tel 01661 860808   **Fax** 01661 860047
Location Signed in Ponteland
Opening hours 10 am – 5 pm; daily; all year
Admission fee free to visitors to the plant centre

The three-acre walled garden at Kirkley Hall is one of the best in the north of England in which to learn how to garden. The emphasis is on plants – their selection, cultivation and enjoyment. Along the front of the house are colourful containers in the modern style, and traditional bedding-out: a rising star among gardens.

Owned by Northumberland College at Kirkley Hall
Number of gardeners 3
Size 10 acres
NCCPG National Collections *Fagus*

Longframlington Gardens

SWARLAND ROAD,
LONGFRAMLINGTON, MORPETH
NE65 8BE

Tel & Fax 01665 570382
Website www.longframlinghamgardens.co.uk
Location Take B6345 1 mile east of Longframlingham, then right down no through road for ¾ mile
Opening hours 9 am – 7 pm (or dusk); daily; all year. Closed Christmas & New Year
Admission fee Adults £3.50. Nursery free

This is a very young garden (started in 1998), with lots of ambition. Hazel Huddleston's plan is to plant an arboretum for year-round interest and to run it alongside her (equally young) plant centre and nursery – which she describes as 'probably the best in the north of England'. Her hope is that Longframlington will become 'a garden of national distinction' as well as 'a garden for today and the future'. The main problem at this stage is to acquire sufficient shelter on the green-field site to allow ornamentals to grow and establish well. The nursery is said to offer over 2,500 different plants, all of them suitable for the cold Northumberland climate. Four RHS special events will take place here during 2001: details from 020 7821 3408.

Owned by Hazel Huddleston
Size 12 acres

Seaton Delaval Hall

SEATON SLUICE, WHITLEY BAY
NE26 4QR

Tel 0191 237 1493
Location ½ mile from coast between Whitley Bay & Blyth
Opening hours 2 pm – 6 pm; Wednesdays & Sundays; June to September. Plus Bank Holidays in May
Admission fee Adults £3; OAPs £2.50; Children £1

The garden is modern: one of Jim Russell's earliest works, it dates from 1948. Parterres and topiary of yew and box are used to enclose old-fashioned roses, handsome ornaments and a fountain: a fair match for the sumptuous house – Vanburgh's masterpiece. The horticultural interest comes from a fine weeping ash, good plantings of rhododendrons and azaleas, and a laburnum walk.

Owned by Lord Hastings
English Heritage grade II*

St Luke's Cottage

NORTH ROAD, WOOLEY, HEXHAM
NE46 1TN

Tel 01434 673445
Location 3 miles south of Hexham (A69); 3 miles east of A68
Opening hours By appointment
Admission fee Donation to Multiple Sclerosis Society

Alan Furness is a long-standing member (and officer) of the Alpine Garden Society, that most august of specialist horticultural societies. His garden in a cold, upland valley of the north Durham moors illustrates the enormous opportunities for growing alpine plants which such a position offers. Within his garden are a wide range of specially constructed habitats to suit a wide range of plants: a large limestone scree, and one for acid-loving plants; several high humus beds and meadow beds; a tufa rock bed; a pond, a bog and several damp areas; and three alpine houses. The whole garden is both a revelation and an inspiration.

Owned by Mr & Mrs Alan Furness
Size ¾ acre
NCCPG National Collections Celmisia (species)

Wallington

CAMBO, MORPETH NE61 4AR

Tel 01670 774283
Website www.nationaltrust.org.uk
Location 6 miles north-west of Belsay (A696)

Opening hours Walled garden: 10 am – 7 pm; daily except Tuesdays; all year. Closes at 6 pm in October and 4 pm in winter. Grounds open daily in daylight hours
Admission fee Adults £4

There are three reasons to visit Wallington. First, because Capability Brown was born in nearby Kirkharle. Second, to gawp at the ancient tree-like specimen of *Fuchsia* 'Rose of Castille' in the conservatory. Third, to admire the modern mixed borders (*very* Graham Thomas) in the long, irregular, walled garden, in a sheltered valley far from the house. Worth the journey for any of them, but prepare for a longish walk to the walled garden.

Plant Highlights Woodland garden; roses (mainly old-fashioned & climbers); rhododendrons & azaleas; plants under glass; daffodils; good herbaceous borders; tallest *Sorbus discolor* (7m) in the British Isles.

Owned by The National Trust
NCCPG National Collections Sambucus
English Heritage grade II*

NOTTINGHAMSHIRE

For a county of such historic importance, Nottinghamshire has comparatively few historic gardens. Clumber Park has lost the house that was once at its centre, and Newstead Abbey has long lost its most famous owner, Lord Byron. Nevertheless there are some interesting nineteenth-century gardens in Nottinghamshire, including the curious little arboretum at Papplewick Pumping Station. One of the best civic parks in England is the twenty-acre Nottingham Arboretum, which opened in 1852: the architect Sir Joseph Paxton and the nurseryman Samuel Curtis were both involved in its design and planting. Nowadays there are few nurseries of national importance in the county, and no RHS Partner Nurseries. Nevertheless, the *RHS Plant Finder* had its origins in the list of nurseries prepared by the Nottingham Group of the Hardy Plant Society in the 1970s and early 1980s. The county also has some twelve National Collections. The National Gardens Scheme lists a fair number of gardens of all sizes which open in Nottinghamshire for charity: the RHS Free Access garden at Felley Priory is one of exceptional interest and beauty, and a good example of what can be achieved on an unpromising site in only a few years. One further sight should not be missed – the incredible hulk of the Major Oak, also known as Robin Hood's Oak, in Sherwood Forest.

Clumber Park

THE ESTATE OFFICE, WORKSOP
S80 3AZ

Tel 01909 476592 **Fax** 01909 500721
Website www.nationaltrust.org.uk
Location Off A614 Nottingham Road, 4 miles south of Worksop
Opening hours Park: dawn to dusk; every day; all year, but closed on 14 July, 18 August & 25 December. Walled garden, vineries and garden tool museum: 10.30 am – 5 pm on Wednesdays & Thursdays and 10.30 – 6 pm on Saturdays, Sundays & Bank Holidays; April to October

Admission fee Park: free. Walled garden: Adults 70p, Children 30p. Car parking £3 (free to National Trust members)

Clumber has 3,800 acres of thickly wooded parkland with a Gothic chapel, classical bridge, temples, an avenue of cedars, a heroic double avenue of limes and masses of rhododendrons. There are good conservatories and a garden tools exhibition in the old walled garden. The scale is enormous: very impressive.

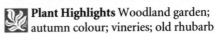 **Plant Highlights** Woodland garden; autumn colour; vineries; old rhubarb

Felley Priory

UNDERWOOD NG16 5FL

Tel 01773 810230   **Fax** 01773 580440
Location ½ mile west of M1 Jct27, on A608
Opening hours 9 am – 12.30 pm; Tuesdays,
Wednesdays & Fridays; all year. Plus 9 am – 4 pm;
2nd & 4th Wednesday of every month; March to October.
And 11 am – 4 pm; every 3rd Sunday of month; March to
October. 11 am – 4 pm on 8 April for National Gardens
Scheme. NCCPG plants fairs 12 noon – 4 pm; 4 June &
1 October
Admission fee Adults £2; Children free

Parts of the house at Felley Priory – a
wonderfully dark red sandstone
building – date back to 1557. One link with
the sixteenth century is a venerable pear-tree
which grows against the house: the Royal
Horticultural Society has identified it as
'Jargonelle', an ancient cultivar well-known
before 1600. Mrs Chaworth-Musters started
work on the garden in 1976 and was, from
the start, an adventurous gardener, willing
to try plants which might be considered
doubtfully hardy at 600ft so far inland. The
results are astonishing. Against the garden
walls are *Buddleja colvilei*, nandinas,
eucryphias, several hebes and *Drimys
winteri*: elsewhere in the garden are
Podocarpus salignus and *Correa
backhouseana*. Felley Priory is an excellent
garden for garden plants, with a very large
number of interesting ones in flower at every
season – enough to start a nursery where
everything is propagated from the garden.
Shrubs are a major interest, and Felley has
good collections of magnolias, cornus,
hydrangeas, *Paeonia suffruticosa* and
viburnums. Bulbs are planted in great
numbers: as well as snowdrops and
cyclamen there are massive displays of
daffodils in spring. The handsome yew

hedges are little more than twenty years old,
yet they fill the garden with their bulk: some
have been turned into objects of topiary,
with curvy tops and bobbles. In the rose
garden is a good display of well-grown
old-fashioned roses: some were imported
directly from French nurseries. The rarities
include a pink-and-white form of *Rosa
multiflora* which was collected in Korea by
Jamie Compton. The mediaeval garden
harks back to the original priory which was
lost at the time of the Reformation: it is
planted with plants that were known in the
fifteenth century – among them are lilies,
roses, violas, columbines, irises, tulips and
Phillyrea latifolia. Everything at Felley is
charming, stylish and well-grown: and the
garden gets better all the time.

Owned by The Hon Mrs Chaworth-Musters
Size 2½ acres

cultivars; superb trees; tallest *Ilex aquifolium* 'Laurifolia' (20m) in the British Isles.

Owned by The National Trust
English Heritage grade I

Hodsock Priory

BLYTH, WORKSOP S81 0TY

Tel 01909 591204   **Fax** 01909 591578
Website www.snowdrops.co.uk
Location Signed off the B6045 between Blyth & Worksop
Opening hours 10 am – 4 pm; daily; 3 February to 4 March
Admission fee Adults £3; Children 50p

The gardens at Hodsock are best in summer, but the owners choose to open them in February instead so that visitors can see a remarkable winter feature – snowdrops. There are thousands and thousands of them: they planted another 250,000 to celebrate the millennium alone and attracted more than 32,000 visitors last year. The Buchanans have also been planting lots of other winter-flowering plants: *Cyclamen coum*, sarcococcas, daphnes and winter-flowering loniceras.

Plant Highlights Snowdrops; aconites; hellebores; hepaticas; large *Catalpa* (Indian bean tree).

Owned by Sir Andrew & Lady Buchanan
Number of gardeners 1 full-time, 3 part-time
Size 5 acres plus woodland

Holme Pierrepont Hall

HOLME PIERREPONT, NOTTINGHAM NG12 2LD

Tel & Fax 0115 933 2371
Website www.holmepierreponthall.com
Location 3 miles east of Trent Bridge
Opening hours 2 pm – 5.30 pm; Easter, Spring & Summer Bank Holiday Sundays & Mondays; Thursdays in June; Wednesdays & Thursdays in July; Tuesday – Thursday in August
Admission fee House & gardens £3.50; Gardens £1.50

The house at Holme Pierrepont is both beautiful and historic. The main attraction of the garden is a large courtyard garden, designed in 1875, whose box parterre is filled with modern plantings. But there are fine recent additions too: an old rose collection, splendid herbaceous borders and interesting fruit trees. The rare English tulip *Tulipa sylvestris* grows wild in a remote part of the estate.

Owned by Mr & Mrs Robin Brackenbury
English Heritage grade II

Mill Hill Plants

MILL HILL HOUSE, ELSTON LANE, EAST STOKE, NEWARK NG23 5QJ

Tel 01636 525460
Website http://come.to/mill.hill.plants&garden
Location 5 miles south-west of Newark. Leave A46 at East Stoke, for Elston; ½ mile down, on right
Opening hours 10 am – 6 pm; Wednesday – Sunday & Bank Holiday Mondays; March to September. Friday – Sunday in October. Closed November to February

This nursery offers a wide range of hardy perennials, including bearded irises which are also available by mail order. The half-acre display garden is planted for year-round interest and opens for the National Gardens Scheme.

NCCPG National Collections *Berberis*

Naturescape

COACH GAP LANE, LANGAR
NG13 9HP

Tel 01949 851045/860592 **Fax** 01949 850431
Location Signed off A46 & A52
Opening hours 11 am – 5.30 pm; daily; April
to September

Naturescape is a significant nursery, specialising in British wild plants. These include wild flowers, bulbs, native shrubs and trees, pond and marsh species and cottage-garden favourites: many are available both as plants and as seeds. The principle behind the nursery is the realisation that many garden-owners want to attract wildlife to their gardens, and that growing native plant species is the best way to do so. The visitor centre opened in 1990 and is set in a wildlife garden showing different habitats. Meadows, hedges, ponds, woodland edges and wetlands are supplemented by cottage gardens and such features as a bee garden.

Newstead Abbey

NEWSTEAD ABBEY PARK NG15 8GE

Tel 01623 455900 **Fax** 01623 455904
Website newsteadabbey.co.uk
Location 4 miles south of Mansfield on A60; 12 miles
north of Nottingham

Opening hours 9 am -dusk; daily; all year except the last
Friday in November
Admission fee Adults £2; Concessions £1.50

Chiefly of interest for being the debt-ridden estate which Lord Byron the poet inherited and had to sell, Newstead has a good modern garden. Features include a Spanish garden, a tropical garden, an iris garden, a rose garden, a heather garden, ponds and lakes. Best are the Japanese garden and substantial rockery. The Council has restored and replanted it all extensively as a public amenity: lots of cheerful roses and summer bedding.

Owned by Nottingham City Council
Number of gardeners 5
Size 300 acres of parkland
English Heritage grade I

Salley Gardens

SIMKINS FARM, ADBOLTON LANE,
WEST BRIDGFORD NG2 5AS

Tel 0115 923 3878
Location Just off the A52 from Nottingham to Grantham
Opening hours By appointment

Salley Gardens is a nursery which concentrates upon plants which are especially beneficial to mankind: all are organically grown. They include dye and beverage plants, and culinary and aromatic herbs and spices. The main emphasis however is on plants with medicinal properties. Three major herbal traditions are represented: North American, European, and Traditional Chinese Medicine. Plants used in homoeopathy, ayurveda, and conventional medicine are also listed.

OXFORDSHIRE

Oxfordshire is one of the best counties for keen gardeners. The natives may grumble about the cold, wet, heavy, clay soils of the Thames Valley, but they have some of the best English gardens, ancient and modern, to show what those soils can do for them. There are no less than nine Grade I historic gardens in the county, and all are open to the public. Both the Oxford Botanic Garden and its country offshoot the Harcourt Arboretum at Nuneham Courtenay have seriously important plant collections, laid out to attract the ordinary garden-owner. It is in these two collections, too, that many of the county's record-breaking trees grow. Several twentieth-century gardens have been laid out on a grand scale, including Sutton Courtenay, Buscot, Garsington, Waterperry and Pusey – the latter, alas, no longer open to the public. But the county also has a host of good small gardens: it has long been a matter for pride that Oxfordshire should have more gardens open for the National Gardens Scheme and raise more money for its charities than any other English county. Nevertheless it has only a handful of National Collections and comparatively few first-rate nurseries – Mattocks Roses, now part of the Notcutt chain, is perhaps the best known. It is as if Oxford were relying for its horticultural reputation more upon its past achievements than its present – rather like its university, some would say. Nevertheless it was at Oxford University that the Garden History Society was born, thanks to the energy and acumen of Mavis Batey. And the many college gardens which open to the public are another of the city's gifts to garden-lovers: Robin Lane-Fox looks after the Fellows' garden at New College. The Royal Horticultural Society has arranged free access for its members, albeit for only one month of the year, to a great teaching garden – Waterperry.

Blenheim Palace

WOODSTOCK, OXFORD OX20 1PX

Tel 01993 811091 **Fax** 01993 813527
Website www.blenheimpalace.com
Location 8 miles north of Oxford
Opening hours 10.30 am – 5.30 pm; daily; 13 March to 31 October

Admission fee Park & gardens: Adults £5.50; Children £2.75. Maze extra: £1.50 for adults & £1 for children

Blenheim is the grandest of grand gardens. Vanburgh, Bridgeman, Hawksmoor and Wise worked here: the grand bridge, the triumphal arch and the column of victory all date from the 1720s. The huge (2,000 acre)

park was landscaped by Capability Brown. Achille Duchêne redesigned the formal gardens in the 1920s: the water terraces centre on a Bernini fountain and took five years to build. The Italian garden focuses on the neo-classical mermaid fountain and is decked with orange trees in summer. There is a pretty Victorian rose garden and, further away from the house, a maze and a lavender garden. The arboretum has some interesting trees, including four fine upright incense cedars (*Calocedrus decurrens*): in 1908, Winston Churchill proposed to his wife here.

 Plant Highlights Formal gardens; new maze.

Owned by The Duke of Marlborough
English Heritage grade I

Brook Cottage

WELL LANE, ALKERTON, BANBURY OX15 6NL

Tel 01295 670303   **Fax** 01295 730362
Location 6 miles west of Banbury, ½ mile off A422
Opening hours 9 am – 6 pm; Monday – Friday; Easter Monday to 31 October. Groups, evening & weekend visits by appointment
Admission fee Adults £3; OAPs £2; Children free

This first-rate modern garden has been made by the present owner since 1964 on 4 acres of sloping pasture. It has good plants and good plantings but, above all, a good sense of colour and form. Beautiful flowering trees in spring are followed by opulent old roses in summer and fine autumn colour. A recent addition is a border of blue and white agapanthus interspersed with kniphofias in shades of lemon and lime. The yellow border is backed by a hedge of copper beech, while

the white border is brought to life by a dark hedge of yew. But the garden is always changing and improving.

Owned by Mrs D M Hodges
Number of gardeners 1, plus some part-time help
Size 4 acres

Broughton Castle

BANBURY OX15 5EB

Tel & Fax 01295 276070
Website www.broughtoncastle.demon.co.uk
Location 2½ miles west of Banbury on the B4035
Opening hours 2 pm – 5 pm; Wednesdays & Sundays; 18 May to 14 September. Plus Thursdays in July & August and Bank Holiday Sundays and Bank Holiday Mondays (including Easter)
Admission fee Castle & gardens: Adults £4; OAPs & Students £3.50; Children £2

The garden at Broughton Castle dates back to the 19th century: the neat knot garden with roses and lavender (best seen from the house) was designed by Lady Algernon Gordon-Lennox in the 1890s. The modern garden was established in 1970 with advice from Lanning Roper. It has two fine colour-themed borders. The blue-yellow-white border has roses like the pale yellow 'Mermaid', mid-yellow 'Golden Wings' and white 'Schneezwerg' growing with berberis, philadelphus and blue campanulas. The pink-and-silver one has shrub roses like 'Fantin Latour', 'Fritz Nobis' and *Rosa glauca*. The garden is probably at its best towards the end of June when all the roses are in full flower.

Owned by Lord Saye
English Heritage grade II*

Buscot Park

FARINGDON SN7 8BU

Tel 01367 240786 **Fax** 01367 241794
Website www.faringdon-coll.com
Location On A417 west of Faringdon
Opening hours Garden only: Monday – Friday (but not
Bank Holidays). 2 April to 28 September
Admission fee Adults £3.30 (garden only)

There are three fairly distinct gardens at Buscot. You enter through the newest – a series of colour plantings and horticultural features created by the National Trust over the last twenty years. Here is the 'Parents' Walk', a lush double herbaceous border designed by Peter Coats in the 1980s: it uses a lot of yellow foliage and contrasts it with purple, to create a sense of lightness and brightness even on the dullest of days. Next to it is the old kitchen garden which Tim Rees turned into a 'four seasons' garden in the early 1990s: each of the quadrants has plantings to represent one of the four seasons. It also has prettily trained fruit trees, vegetables as climbing used plants and gooseberries grown as standards. You climb out of the walled garden, up a steep staircase lined with yews and walk past the front of the house on your way to the second of the gardens: a perfect *patte d'oie*, focused on the archway which leads into the service courtyard – it is pleasant to think that Lord Faringdon (who commissioned it in the 1890s) and his family used to go in and out of the kitchens on their way to the garden. The temptation is to explore all three avenues of the *patte d'oie* at once, but they are linked by cross-paths which run between further gardens cut out of the woodland: these include a circular sunken garden furnished in summer with orange- and lemon-trees in pots, and a pretty

white-and-green garden which is known as the 'swinging garden' because of the swinging seats which surround it. But the third and best-known garden at Buscot is Harold Peto's water-garden, which dates from the 1900s and stretches down over hundreds of yards in a series of steps and then along a long, narrow, straight canal punctuated towards the end by a chunky Italianate bridge until it bursts out into the view of the lake at the bottom. The canal – little more than a rill really, and narrow enough to jump over in places – is framed first by Irish yews and then by clipped box hedges. It has an amazing dynamism and strength of design which makes it an entirely self-contained garden. The only downside to a visit is that the lake is actually the furthest point of the garden, and there is then no other way out except to re-trace your steps across the park and through the modern gardens. But actually Peter Coats's borders look even better as you approach them again from outside the walled gardens. And a word of warning: Buscot is a big garden, so allow lots of time for your visit.

Plant Highlights Topiary; roses (mainly old-fashioned); fruit; good herbaceous borders; tallest *Pinus nigra* var. *cebennensis* (32m) in the British Isles.

Owned by The National Trust
English Heritage grade II*

Greenways

40 OSLER ROAD, HEADINGTON,
OXFORD OX3 9BJ

Tel 01865 767680 (after dark) **Fax** 01865 767922
Location Osler Road is off London Road, within Ring road
Opening hours 2 pm – 6 pm; 13 May; 17 July; 12 August.
And groups by appointment
Admission fee Adults £2; Children free

This garden is totally different. The Cootes
have emphasised the Provençal looks of the
house by planting a rich Mediterranean
garden – glittering evergreens, terracotta
pots, old oil jars, gravel, parterres – with an
exuberance of tender plants including olives,
daturas, yuccas, oleanders, acanthus and
Albizia julibrissin. It is quite the most stylish
small garden we know, and intensively
maintained to the highest standard.

Owned by Mr & Mrs N H N Coote
Number of gardeners owners
Size ¾ acre

Harcourt Arboretum

NUNEHAM COURTENAY OX44 9PQ

Tel 01865 343501 **Fax** 01865 341828
Location On A423, just south of village of Nuneham
Courtenay
Opening hours 10 am – 5 pm; daily; May to October.
10 am – 4.30 pm; Monday – Friday; November to April.
Closed over the Easter weekend & 22 December to
4 January 2002
Admission fee free: £2 for car park

Though it belongs to the University of
Oxford Botanic Garden, Harcourt
Arboretum is best regarded as a stand-alone
woodland garden with a distinct history and
character. It has been developed since 1950

around a nucleus of magnificent American
conifers planted c.1840 in a corner of the
Nuneham Courtenay estate. The new
plantings include 'plants from high places'
(geographically arranged), conservation
areas, an extensive glade of ornamental
maples, and fine modern features like a
collection of *Nothofagus.* The labelling is
fairly good and there are useful information
boards in front of specimens of particular
interest. It is perhaps best visited in May,
when the mature oak woodland which
surrounds the conifers is filled with vast
oceans of bluebells.

Owned by University of Oxford
Number of gardeners 3
Size 80 acres

Kelmscott Manor

KELMSCOTT, LECHLADE GL7 3HJ

Tel 01367 252486 **Fax** 01367 253754
Location Signed from B4449 & A4095
Opening hours 11 am – 1 pm and 2 pm – 5 pm;
Wednesdays; April to September. Plus 2 pm – 5 pm on the
3rd Saturday of the month in April, May, June & September
and 1st & 3rd Saturdays in July & August
Admission fee Adults £7; Students £3.50. Gardens only:
Adults £2; Children free

William Morris's garden is being remodelled
and restored. Worth a visit if you are
interested in the Arts & Crafts movement:
the price of a ticket includes a tour of the
house.

Owned by The Society of Antiquaries of London
Number of gardeners 1 part-time
Size 3¼ acres
English Heritage grade II

Lime Close

35 HENLEY'S LANE, DRAYTON, ABINGDON OX14 4HU

Tel & Fax 01235 531231
Location Off main road through Drayton
Opening hours 2 pm – 6 pm; 29 April & 3 June
Admission fee Adults £2; Children 50p

This modern garden has been much praised, and deservedly, for its wide range of plants and the way in which they are grouped. As well as rare trees, shrubs, perennials and bulbs, it can boast a recently-planted shade border, a pond, a pergola, some unusual topiary, an ornamental kitchen garden, a herb garden designed by Rosemary Verey and a wonderful selection of raised beds and troughs planted by the owner's aunt Miss Christie-Miller.

Owned by Marie-Christine de Laubarède
Size 3 acres

The Manor House

STANTON HARCOURT, WITNEY OX8 1RJ

Tel 01865 881928   **Fax** 01865 880117
Location In village
Opening hours 2 pm – 6 pm; 15, 16, 26 & 29 April; 3, 6, 7, 17, 20, 24, 27 & 28 May; 14, 17 & 28 June; 1, 5, 8, 19 & 22 July; 2, 5, 16, 19, 23 & 26 August; 6, 9, 20 & 23 September
Admission fee Garden only: Adults £3; OAPs & Children £2

The remarkable late-mediaeval manorhouse at Stanton Harcourt is surrounded by Edwardian gardens in the Elizabethan style. Parts are romantically overgrown. Others have been spruced up in contemporary taste with David Austin roses and espaliered fruit trees.

Owned by The Hon Mrs Gascoigne
Size 12 acres

Mattocks Roses

NUNEHAM COURTENAY, OXFORD OX44 9PY

Tel 01865 343265   **Fax** 01865 343166
Website www.mattocks.co.uk
Location On B4015, Roundabout Golden Ball (A4074)
Opening hours 9 am – 5.30 pm (5 pm in winter); Monday – Saturday. 11 am – 5 pm; Sundays

This is one of the oldest nurseries in England, founded in 1875 and now part of the Notcutts empire. Mattocks have been particularly successful in promoting their 'County' series of ground-cover roses. They offer a large choice of all kinds of roses, and on-line ordering too. One of their specialities, bred by John Mattock and introduced in 1973, is the yellow repeat-flowering climber 'Dreaming Spires'.

Old Rectory

FARNBOROUGH, WANTAGE OX12 8NX

Tel 01488 638298
Location In village, opposite church
Opening hours 2 pm – 6 pm; 1 April, 13 May & 24 June. And by written appointment (£5 – which includes tea, coffee & cakes)
Admission fee Adults £2 for National Gardens Scheme

This excellent modern garden has been made by the owners on a high, cold, windy site over the last 25 years. Lots of hedges and thick planting were the keys to survival, but the effect now is of shelter and luxuriance.

Splendid double herbaceous border and clever colour plantings.

Owned by Mr & Mrs Michael Todhunter

Oxford Botanic Garden

ROSE LANE, OXFORD OX1 4AX

Tel 01865 286690   **Fax** 01865 286693
Location East end of High Street next to river
Opening hours 9 am – 5 pm (4.30 pm from October to March); daily; all year except Good Friday & Christmas Day. Glasshouses open 10 am – 4 pm
Admission fee Donation box: £2 from April to August

This is the oldest botanic garden in England, first laid out in 1621: the handsome gateways were added a few years later. It has kept its original rectangular design and many of the statues and garden ornaments. It also has a calm that is far from the bustle outside and has proved a refuge for generations of undergraduates. There are good and representative collections of almost every type of plant, including a grass garden, ferns, carnivorous plants, a water garden, fernery, orangery and several conservatories. Everything is well-labelled, of course, and designed not only as a living collection of plants for the university botanists but, much more generally, as an educational resource. In recent years the area outside the walled garden has been developed as a garden to inspire gardeners: here are a new water garden, rock garden, herbaceous border and autumn border. The palm house was re-designed last year so that visiting schoolchildren could enjoy 'the ultimate rainforest experience'.

Owned by University of Oxford
Number of gardeners 10
Size 4½ acres
NCCPG National Collections *Euphorbia*
English Heritage grade I

Rousham House

STEEPLE ASTON, BICESTER OX6 3QX

Tel & Fax 01869 347110
Website www.information-britain.co.uk
Location A4260 then off the B4030
Opening hours 10 am – 4.30 pm; daily; all year
Admission fee Adults £3. No Children under 15

Rousham is the most perfect surviving example of William Kent's landscaping: *Kentissimo*, according to Horace Walpole. The main axis brings you to Scheemakers's statue of a lion devouring a horse, high above the infant River Cherwell. Follow the correct circuit: the serpentine landscape lies away to the side. Here are Venus's Vale, the Cold Bath and Townsend's Building, from which a lime walk will lead you to the Praeneste. Rousham is an Arcadian experience. The pretty herbaceous border in the walled garden and the modern rose garden by the dovecote seem almost an irrelevance.

Owned by C Cottrell-Dormer
Number of gardeners 4
Size 25 acres
English Heritage grade I

The Skippet

MOUNT SKIPPET, RAMSDEN, WITNEY OX7 3AP

Tel 01993 868253
Location Turn off B4022 towards Finstock & immediately right again. After 500 yards, turn left
Opening hours By appointment for individuals & groups
Admission fee Donation to charity

The Skippet is a Cotswold stone house, converted from four cottages by Dr Rogers's father in the 1920s. It has magnificent empty views and yet is almost entirely secluded. Against the walls of the house grow many climbers and wall-plants, including such tender plants as *Abutilon* 'Canary Bird' and *Solanum rantonnetii*. Adventurous plantsmen are always willing to try out plants which should not survive the winter's cold or wetness, and so The Skippet also has *Cuphea cyanaea* and many other abutilons flourishing outside. Though there are plants of every kind in the garden, from trees to bog plants, it is above all an alpine plantsman's collection, brimful with rarities in pots, troughs, screes, and raised beds. Every square inch is cultivated, which means that it has much of interest on every day of the year. Dr Rogers will be ninety years old during the year, and says that the first visitors to come on his birthday (date not disclosed) will be given a special present (in a pot, of course). But he is immensely generous to all visitors: 'tell them I *want* them to take cuttings', he says.

Owned by Dr M A T Rogers
Number of gardeners ½
Size 2 acres

Stansfield

49 HIGH STREET,
STANFORD-IN-THE-VALE SN7 8NQ

Tel 01367 710340
Location Off A417 opposite Vale garage
Opening hours 10 am – 4 pm; first Tuesday of month; April to September. And 2 pm – 6 pm on 10 June for National Gardens Scheme. And by appointment
Admission fee Adults £1.50; Children free

Stansfield is a modern plantsman's garden, and a fascinating model of what an enthusiastic collector and cultivator of plants can achieve in a few years. Over 2,000

different plants grow in just over one acre. The special features include troughs, screes, open borders and endless micro-habitats. Fascinating.

Owned by Mr & Mrs D Keeble
Number of gardeners owners

Stonor

HENLEY-ON-THAMES RG9 6HF

Tel & Fax 01491 638587
Website www.stonor.com
Location 5 miles north of Henley-on-Thames
Opening hours 2 pm – 5.30 pm; Sundays & Bank Holiday Mondays from April to September; Wednesdays in July & August
Admission fee £2.50 (in 2000)

Stonor fills a hillside and can all be seen from the road below: classical parkland (with a deer park, too), the Elizabethan house, lawns, terraces, a seventeenth-century walled garden, and finally the wood with wonderful views at the top. Nothing appears to have changed for 200 years: the effect is miraculous.

Owned by Lord Camoys
English Heritage grade I

Waterperry Gardens

WHEATLEY, OXFORD OX33 1JZ

Tel 01844 339226   **Fax** 01844 339883
Location Jct8 or 8a on M40, well signed locally
Opening hours 9 am – 5 pm (4.30 pm from November to March); daily; all year except Christmas/New Year period
Admission fee April to October: Adults £3.40; OAPs £2.90; Children £1.90. November to March: all £1.60. RHS members free in September

The garden at Waterperry is extensive, well-maintained and full of interesting plants. Much of it has been redesigned and replanted in recent years, with some fine formal features and pleasing plant combinations. The glasshouse in the walled garden is notable for a large specimen citrus and Mediterranean plants. A wide range of soft fruit is also grown, while the densely planted clay bank is a good place to study shade-loving plants. The new formal garden is particularly neatly designed and colourfully planted: nearby are some interesting ways of training apples and climbing roses. But the main part of the garden is the extensive shrub borders, alpine beds, and herbaceous borders: Waterperry offers much to enjoy and learn from at every season.

Owned by School of Economic Science
Number of gardeners 3½
Size 7 acres
NCCPG National Collections Saxifraga

Westwell Manor

BURFORD OX18 4JT

Location 2 miles from A40, west of Burford roundabout
Opening hours 2 pm – 6.30 pm; 1 July. And by prior appointment for serious horticultural groups of more than 20
Admission fee Adults £3; Children 50p

Westwell is a large and peaceful Cotswold garden with several distinct 'rooms'. The features include rills, a water garden, herbaceous borders, an orchard, a lavender meadow, lots of hazel and willow fencing, a vegetable garden, a moonlight garden, lots of old roses and a clematis walk.

Owned by Mr & Mrs T H Gibson
Number of gardeners 3
Size 7 acres

SHROPSHIRE

Shropshire has the reputation of being a remote and quasi-feudal county. It is certainly true that very few of its historic gardens are ever open to the public. Hawkstone is the most notable exception, but this – the county's only Grade I garden – is now in multiple occupation: nevertheless its principal parts are still highly visitable and also have the best collection of trees, mainly conifers, in Shropshire. Among twentieth-century gardens, Hodnet Hall is of national importance, and a sizeable achievement by modern standards. Three more recent gardens are also outstanding each in its own way – Burford House, the David Austin rose gardens and Wollerton Old Hall. Wollerton is a RHS Free Access garden, though the concession does not apply in the peak months of summer. The Royal Horticultural Society also has two good Partner Nurseries – Hall Farm and Lingen – in a county which is actually rather short on nurseries of any kind. Nevertheless, there are twelve National Collections in Shropshire; and the National Gardens Scheme is well supported, mainly by gardens which are large or medium-sized.

Attingham Park

THE NATIONAL TRUST, ATTINGHAM PARK, SHREWSBURY SY4 4TP

Tel 01743 709203   Fax 01743 709352
Website www.nationaltrust.org.uk
Location 5 miles south-east of Shrewsbury on B4380
Opening hours 9 am – 8 pm (5 pm from November to March); daily; all year except Christmas Day
Admission fee Adults £2; Children £1

No garden to speak of, but the classical late eighteenth-century parkland round the vast Georgian house is a joy to walk around at any time of the year.

Owned by The National Trust
English Heritage grade II*

Benthall Hall

BROSELEY TF12 5RX

Tel & Fax 01952 882159
Website www.nationaltrust.org.uk
Location 1 mile north-west of Broseley (B4375)
Opening hours 1.30 pm – 5.30 pm; Wednesdays, Sundays & Bank Holiday Mondays; April to September
Admission fee Adults £2.25; Children £1.10

Smallish, but well restored with a Graham Thomas rose garden. Home of the nineteenth-century botanist George Maw. His Mediterranean collection is still the backbone of the garden – crocus naturalised everywhere.

Owned by The National Trust

Burford House Gardens

TREASURES OF TENBURY, TENBURY
WELLS WR15 8HQ

Tel 01584 810777   **Fax** 01584 810673
Location A456 between Tenbury Wells & Ludlow
Opening hours 10 am – 5 pm (dusk in winter); daily; all
year. Closed 1 January, 25 & 26 December
Admission fee Adults £3.50; Children £1; Groups (10+) £3
(by prior arrangement)

This glamorous seven-acre garden, made to
complement a stylish Georgian house, is
now beautiful and mature. The fluid design
is enhanced by interesting plants,
imaginatively used and comprehensively
labelled. There are good roses and
herbaceous borders, and a magnificent series
of water gardens, but Burford means
Clematis – over 350 varieties – cleverly
trained, grown and displayed among shrubs
and in the new Clematis Maze near the
coach house. Charles Cheshire is starting to
renew and reorder some of the planting, and
the results so far are excellent. There are new
developments on the other side of the river:
bulbs and wild flower plantings in
particular.

Owned by Treasures of Tenbury Ltd
Size 7 acres
NCCPG National Collections *Clematis*

David Austin Roses

BOWLING GREEN LANE,
ALBRIGHTON, WOLVERHAMPTON
WV7 3HB

Tel 01902 376300   **Fax** 01902 372142
Website www.davidaustinroses.com
Location Signed in village

Opening hours 9 am – 5 pm; Monday – Friday.
10 am – 6 pm (or dusk if earlier); Saturdays & Sundays. All
year except 25 December to 2 January. Open for National
Gardens Scheme on 24 June
Admission fee free

David Austin has developed an entirely new
strain of 'English' roses which combine the
shape and scent of old-fashioned roses with
the colours, health and floriferousness of
modern types. The display gardens adjoining
his nursery are impressive: five different
sections, each extensive and thickly planted
with old-fashioned roses and his own
hybrids – nearly 1,000 different cultivars of
English roses, nineteenth-century roses,
climbers, ramblers and species. In late June
and early July it is a place of magic beauty.
The garden is maintained to an extremely
high standard: all the roses look happy and
healthy, and flower profusely. Sculptures by
David Austin's wife add a further dimension
to a visit. Several new roses are introduced
every year at Chelsea. A new plant centre
will open in spring 2001. Groups are
sometimes allowed to see the breeding
houses and trial grounds.

Owned by David Austin
Number of gardeners 1
Size 2 acres

Hall Farm Nursery

VICARAGE LANE, KINNERLEY,
OSWESTRY SY10 8DH

Tel & Fax 01691 682135
Location 2 miles from A5, between Shrewsbury
& Oswestry
Opening hours 10 am – 5 pm; Tuesday – Saturday;
1 March to 6 October

This RHS Partner Nursery carries a good range of fashionable herbaceous perennials, including a great number of geraniums and ornamental grasses. Pulmonarias, hostas, astrantias, bog plants, sempervivums and aeoniums are other specialities. All its plants are grown and propagated on site: requests for cultural advice are therefore welcome. The display borders around the nursery are attractive and well maintained. Four RHS special events will take place here during 2001: details from 020 7821 3408.

rocks, and ornamental follies which fill the whole estate, once more than 700 acres in extent. It is the contrasts which make this landscape unique: the mosses, ferns, and dampness of these dark gullies turn suddenly into dramatic cliffs, tunnels, crags and bridges, while the peaks of the precipitous outcrops offer views across thirteen counties. But allow lots of time for your visit – the owner recommends at least three hours.

Owned by M C Boler
English Heritage grade I

Hawkstone Historic Park & Follies

WESTON UNDER REDCASTLE, SHREWSBURY SY4 5UY

Tel 01939 200611 **Fax** 01939 200311
Location Off the A49 between Shrewsbury & Whitchurch
Opening hours Gardens open at 10.30 am, but 10 am at weekends. Last admissions are 2.30 pm in January & February; 3 pm in March; 4 pm from 31 March to 1 July and from 1 September to 28 October; 5 pm between 2 July & 31 August. Open weekends only from January to March; Wednesday – Sunday & Bank Holiday Mondays from 31 March to 1 July & 1 September to 28 October; daily between 2 July & 31 August; & closed between 29 October and 31 December
Admission fee Adults £5; OAPs £3.50; Children £2.50. Reduced prices on all weekdays and at winter weekends

Sir Rowland Hill began landscaping Hawkstone in the 1750s, but most of what remains was initiated by his elder son Sir Richard and completed by his grandson, another Sir Rowland Hill, best known for inventing the postage stamp. It is a fine example of the 'sublime' movement, which sought to create contrasts of emotion in the natural landscape. Hawkstone has deep ravines and gloomy chasms, accompanied by dizzying pinnacles, soaring sandstone

Hillview Hardy Plants

WORFIELD, BRIDGNORTH WV15 5NT

Tel & Fax 01746 716454
Location Between Worfield & Albrighton, off B4176
Opening hours 9 am – 5 pm, Monday – Saturday, March to mid-October. And by appointment

This is a good nursery for hardy herbaceous perennials. Its range of primulas and auriculas, aquilegias and South African plants is especially noteworthy. Guided tours of the nursery can be arranged for groups.

Hodnet Hall Gardens

HODNET, MARKET DRAYTON TF9 3NN

Tel 01630 685202 **Fax** 01630 685853
Location Near junction of A53 & A442
Opening hours 12 noon – 5 pm; Tuesday – Sunday & Bank Holiday Mondays; April to September
Admission fee Adults £3.25; OAPs £2.75; Children £1.20

In the 1950s, *The RHS Journal* (forerunner of *The Garden*) described Hodnet as a 'small modern garden'. Now it has more than 60 acres of woodland garden around a chain of ornamental pools. The woodlands are planted with exotic trees like magnolias, maples and davidias against a background of native oaks, sycamores, lime and beech. Underneath are rhododendrons, azaleas, camellias, prunus and berberis, themselves underplanted when they flower in spring with a wide variety of herbaceous plants, especially hostas, primulas, daffodils and bluebells. The spacious mixed borders near the house are particularly interesting in July, when they are complemented by the beds of old-fashioned roses and modern floribundas. But Hodnet is a garden for everyone and every season – good in late summer too, when the hydrangeas and astilbes flower. Allow lots of time for a thorough visit to one of the greatest twentieth-century gardens.

 Plant Highlights Woodland garden; roses (mainly old-fashioned); good herbaceous borders; camellias; primulas; rhododendrons; HHA/Christie's Garden of the Year in 1985.

Owned by A E H Heber-Percy
Number of gardeners 4
Size 60+ acres
English Heritage grade II

Lingen Nursery & Gardens

LINGEN, BUCKNELL SY7 0DY

Tel 01544 267720
Location Lingen village is signed off the A4113 & A4362, north-east of Presteigne
Opening hours 10 am – 5 pm; February to October. Tea room open from April to September

This RHS Partner Nursery specialises in unusual alpine and herbaceous plants. In addition to his two National Collections, the owner has put together notable collections of auriculas and penstemons (both alpine and herbaceous) and has a number of interesting aquilegias and irises too. But it is true to say that you will not visit Lingen without seeing a plant that you have never seen before. The gardens are worth a visit in their own right: one acre is intensively planted with a rock garden and cottage garden, supplemented by an alpine house and raised beds, while two further acres are now under development. Two RHS special events will take place here during 2001: details from 020 7821 3408.

Owned by Kim Davis
NCCPG National Collections *Iris sibirica*; *Campanula*

Lower Hall

WORFIELD, BRIDGNORTH WV15 5LH

Tel 01746 716607   **Fax** 01746 716325
Location In centre of village of Worfield
Opening hours 17 June for National Gardens Scheme. 30 June & 1 July for Worfield church. And by appointment
Admission fee Adults £3; Children free

Lanning Roper helped to get this splendid garden going in the 1960s. It bestrides the River Worfe and every part has a distinct character. There are lush streamside plantings, infinite colour schemes, and a woodland area at the bottom. These contrast with formal designs, straight brick paths, a pergola and more colour themes in the old walled garden. It is one of the best gardens to be made since World War II, and neatly kept.

Owned by C F Dumbell
Number of gardeners 1
Size 4¼ acres

Preen Manor

CHURCH PREEN, CHURCH STRETTON
SY6 7LQ

Tel 01694 771207
Location Signed from B4371 Much Wenlock/Church
Stretton
Opening hours 2 pm – 6 pm; 13 May, 14 June;
12 & 26 July; 7 October (closes at 4.30 pm for Harvest
Thanksgiving). And parties by appointment
Admission fee Adults £3; Children 50p

Preen has a stylish new garden with some
original ideas to complement the historic
old site. These include a chess garden, a
collection of plants in handsome old pots,
a pebble garden, a fern garden and that
symbol of the 1990s – a gravel garden.
Down in the woodland garden are
rhododendrons and candelabra primulas.
And it gets better every year.

Owned by Philip Trevor-Jones
Number of gardeners 2½
Size 6 acres, plus woodland

Ruthall Manor

DITTON PRIORS, BRIDGNORTH
WV16 6TN

Tel 01746 712608
Location Take Weston road from church then 2nd left
Opening hours For National Gardens Scheme

This one-acre plantsman's garden, some
800ft up, has been made over the last 20
years. It has good trees, rare shrubs, lots of
ground cover, and a pretty pool with
aquatics and marginals.

Owned by Mr & Mrs G T Clarke

Swallow Hayes

RECTORY ROAD, ALBRIGHTON,
WOLVERHAMPTON WV7 3EP

Tel 01902 372624
Location M54, Jct3, then A41 towards
Wolverhampton & first right after garden centre
Opening hours 10.30 am – dusk on 21 January.
2 pm – 5 pm on 1 April, 6 & 27 May, and 7 October. And
groups by appointment
Admission fee Adults £2; Children 10p

Swallow Hayes is a plantswoman's garden
(3,000 plants) entirely made since 1968 and
a model of its kind, where ground cover
helps to minimise labour and maximise
enjoyment. The garden started life as a
stock-ground and trial-ground for the
owner's wholesale nursery. Mrs Edwards has
more than 100 different cultivars of
Geranium in a garden which is packed with
different micro-habitats, each of them
themed and exploited as fully as possible.
There is much to see and enjoy at every
time of the year – hence the National
Collection of winter-flowering witch-hazels
Hamamelis of which there are over 50
cultivars.

Owned by Mrs P Edwards
Number of gardeners owner, plus some very part-time
help
Size 2 acres
NCCPG National Collections *Hamamelis*; *Lupinus*
(Russell strains)

Wollerton Old Hall

WOLLERTON, MARKET DRAYTON
TF9 3NA

Tel 01630 685760 **Fax** 01630 685583
Location Follow brown tourist signs from A53 in Hodnet
Opening hours 12 noon – 5 pm; Fridays, Sundays & Bank
Holidays; 13 April to 31 August. Plus Fridays in September
Admission fee Adults £3.50; Children £1. RHS members
free in April, May & September

Commenced in 1984, this outstanding
garden creation seeks to combine
horticultural excellence with unrestrained
planting of perennials, careful colour design
with strong contrasts, and intimacy with
strong design structure. As the site is
centuries old, the dominant theme is of
linear formality but this gradually gives way
to total informality where the garden meets
the Shropshire countryside.

Owned by Mr & Mrs John Jenkins
Number of gardeners 2
Size 3 acres

SOMERSET

Like its neighbour Devon, Somerset is rich in both gardens and nurseries: it is a
county where gardeners are well served. Four of its five Grade I historic
gardens – Dunster, East Lambrook, Hestercombe and Montacute – are regularly
open to the public. Somerset also has an exceptional number of good small and
medium-sized gardens, often made by the present owners – as witness the large
number (in quite a small county) which open in aid of the National Gardens
Scheme. The mild climate – warm and wet – and the rich soils are famous for cider
and dairying: these also induce good growth in gardens. It has long been recognised
that along the coast – at Porlock and Cannington, for example – plants flourish
which would not survive in any but the mildest parts of Devon and Cornwall.
Nevertheless the county has no arboreta of note and few trees which are thought to
be among the tallest or largest of their kind. Somerset has many nurseries
and among them are a significant number of national or international importance:
Avon Bulbs and Broadleigh Gardens for bulbs, Kelways for peonies, Mallet Court
for rare trees, PMA Plants for Japanese maples, Thornleigh for fruit trees. Another
which we have not been able to include in this edition is Michael Michieli's Ashfield
Court Nurseries near North Petherton, which has a remarkable collection of
Verbena cultivars – over 100 of them. And, though not mentioned in the *RHS Plant
Finder* – she has a reputation for reticence – Patricia Marrow's Kingsdon Nursery at
Somerton has long enjoyed renown for first-rate plants of the sort you cannot find
elsewhere. Somerset also has a large number (over 20) of National Collections,
which is always a good indicator of the general level of interest in gardening.
And it has long been well served by the county horticultural college at Cannington,
which is one of the leading centres in all England for the teaching of amenity
horticulture. Cannington is also an RHS Partner College, with a programme of
public lectures, demonstrations and workshops all through the year.

The American Museum

CLAVERTON MANOR, BATH
BA2 7BD

Tel 01225 460503 **Fax** 01225 480726
Location Off A36 south of Bath
Opening hours 1 pm – 6 pm, Tuesday – Friday; 12 noon – 6 pm, Saturdays, Sundays & Bank Holiday Mondays; 24 March to 4 November
Admission fee Adults £3; OAPs £2.50; Children £2. Private tours by prior arrangement

The fifteen enchanting acres of garden at Claverton Manor were created by two artistic Americans, Dallas Pratt and John Judkyn, from about 1960 onwards. They bought the handsome classical house, built in 1820, to hold their collection of early American domestic arts and artefacts: the American Museum is now the largest of its kind outside the USA and well worth a visit. The house has a stunning situation with wide views across to the west-facing slopes of the Avon valley, yet sheltered and screened from all but the prettiest eye-catchers on the other side. Tea is served on the terrace in front of the house, next to the little Colonial herb garden ('Colonial' = pre-1778). Sloping lawns lead to the Mount Vernon garden, a box-edged re-creation of George Washington's own original. The first enclosure has beds of old roses: the main section is a herbaceous garden. Despite a little historical latitude with the choice of eighteenth-century plants, it is all very neat and instructive, and prettily enclosed by white picket fencing. Also of horticultural interest is a young arboretum which opened in 1985 on the slopes below. This celebration of hardy American trees and shrubs adds up to a fine well-labelled collection, and includes (among many other rarities) *Alnus rhombifolia*, *Salix mackenziana* and *Philadelphus insignis*. Also

worth discovering are a ferny dell at the bottom of the arboretum and a collection of American apple cultivars, with such names as 'Smokehouse' and 'Sheep's Nose'. The American Museum is a well-endowed foundation and its gardens are very well maintained, which adds enormously to the pleasure of a visit, though rabbits are a problem.

Owned by Trustees of the American Museum in Britain
English Heritage grade II

Ammerdown Park

KILMERSDOWN, RADSTOCK, BATH
BA3 5SH

Tel 01761 432227 **Fax** 01761 433094
Location West of Terry Hill crossroads: A362/A366
Opening hours 11 am – 5 pm; 16 April, 7 & 28 May, 27 August
Admission fee Adults £3; £1 OAPs; Children free

Ammerdown's lay-out is Lutyens at his most ingenious. The lie of the land precludes right angles, but long straight views cover up the irregularities. It has some nice plants, particularly trees, but the design is everything and there are good spring bulbs. A restoration plan has recently got under way.

Owned by The Hon Andrew Joliffe
English Heritage grade II*

Avon Bulbs

BURNT HOUSE FARM,
MID-LAMBROOK, SOUTH PETHERTON
TA13 5HE

Tel & Fax 01460 242177
Website www.avonbulbs.co.uk

Location Turn south, down no through road, halfway between West Lambrook & East Lambrook

Opening hours 9 am – 4.30 pm; Thursday – Saturday; mid-February to end March and mid-September to end October

Avon Bulbs offers an impressive variety of bulbs (and close relatives) of all sizes, types and seasons – mainly by mail order. The nursery is well-run and the plants are beautifully grown. It is well worth a visit early in the year to see the wide range of its stock, including much which is not listed in the catalogue. The opening hours are limited because of the seasonal nature of the business and the nursery's show commitments. It is a good idea to check with them before visiting.

Barrington Court

BARRINGTON, ILMINSTER TA19 0NQ

Tel 01460 241480

Website www.nationaltrust.org.uk

Location In Barrington village

Opening hours 11 am – 4.30 pm; Thursday – Sunday; March & October. 11 am – 5.30 pm; Saturday – Thursday; April to September and daily in July & August

Admission fee Adults £5; Children £2.50

There is still an Edwardian opulence about Barrington. Massive plantings of irises, lilies and rich dark dahlias. And good design detail too: the patterns of the brick paving are a study in themselves.

Owned by The National Trust

English Heritage grade II*

Bath Botanic Gardens

ROYAL VICTORIA PARK, BATH

Tel 01225 448433   **Fax** 01225 480072

Location West of city centre by Upper Bristol Road

Opening hours 9 am – dusk; daily; all year except Christmas Day

Admission fee free

Bath's Botanic Gardens were founded in 1887, extended in 1926 and again in 1987. It has nine acres of trees, shrubs, borders, limestone-loving plants and scented walks. It has never been attached to a university or institute, so it is more of a horticultural collection than a botanic garden, and public amenity is its main function. The central feature is a rocky pool designed in the Japanese style, surrounded by venerable not-so-dwarf maples. Standards are high, maintenance is good, and the seasonal highlights of bulbs and bedding are among the best. The excellent guidebook is a model of visitor-friendliness.

Plant Highlights Rock garden; fine collection of trees; autumn colour; fine bedding displays; good *Scilla* collection; tallest tree of heaven *Ailanthus altissima* (31m) and tallest hornbeam *Carpinus betulus* (27m) in England (and eleven other record trees).

Owned by Bath City Council

Blackmore & Langdon

STANTON NURSERIES, PENSFORD, BRISTOL BS18 4JL

Tel & Fax 01275 332300

Location 8 miles south of Bristol on B3130, between A37 Wells road & A38

Opening hours 9 am – 5 pm; Monday – Saturday.
10 am – 4 pm; Sundays

This family business, started in 1901 and still run by the founder's grandchildren, is celebrating its centenary this year. Blackmore & Langdon has a long tradition of breeding and growing showy border plants – huge begonias and tall delphiniums, in particular. The nursery's immaculately grown flowers have been a feature of RHS Flowers Shows – and especially the Chelsea Flower Show – for many years. What is not so well known is that the nursery also produces phlox, aquilegias and polyanthus. And all its plants are grown on site.

Broadleigh Gardens

BISHOPS HULL, TAUNTON TA4 1AE

Tel 01823 286231   **Fax** 01823 232464
Website www.broadleighbulbs.co.uk
Location At Barr, 1½ miles north-west of Bishops Hull
Opening hours 9 am – 4 pm; Monday – Friday. Viewing and collection by prior arrangement
Admission fee Charity donation

This nursery, with strong RHS connections, is best known for its small bulbs, though it now grows almost as many foliage and woodland perennials. Look out for the crocosmias, snowdrops, the many miniature narcissus and species tulips, and Broadleigh's own Pacific Coast hybrid irises. The nursery and three-acre garden are open for viewing only by prior arrangement.

NCCPG National Collections Narcissus (miniature)

Cannington College Heritage Garden

CANNINGTON, BRIDGWATER
TA5 2LS

Tel 01278 655000   **Fax** 01278 655055
Website www.cannington.ac.uk
Location 3 miles west of Bridgwater on A39
Opening hours 9 am – 5 pm; daily; April to October
Admission fee Adults £2; OAPs & Children £1.50

There have been changes at Cannington's Heritage Gardens recently: gone is the nursery, gone are the plant sales, and gone are the four National Collections. But the gardens are still worth visiting and the college can still claim to have one of the largest collections of rare and unusual plants in the south-west of England, with '10,000 named plant varieties'. This makes it highly attractive to all plantsmen and gardeners, whatever their particular interest. Originally intended as a teaching resource (Cannington was for long the leading West Country college for ornamental horticulture), the garden was strongly promoted in the 1980s for its visitor attractions. Within a mediaeval wall next to Cannington Court are five individual walled gardens, each planted with its own botanical theme. One has Australian plants, another Mediterranean. The collections are indeed very extensive and beautifully displayed and, although the collections of tender *Abutilon*, *Argyranthemum* and *Osteospermum* cultivars are much smaller than before, the garden still has a good number of different *Wisteria* cultivars.

Owned by Cannington College

Cothay Manor

GREENHAM, WELLINGTON TA21 0JR

Tel 01823 672283   **Fax** 01823 672345
Location Off A38, 1½ miles from Greenham
Opening hours 2 pm – 6 pm; Wednesdays, Thursdays, Sundays & Bank Holiday Mondays; May to September. Group (20+) by appointment
Admission fee £3.50

Cothay is an exciting old/new garden on either side of the River Tone. The seven acres of formal gardens designed in the 1920s by Reggie Cooper (a friend of Lawrence Johnston, and Harold & Vita too) have now been completely replanted, room by room, colour by colour, since the Robbs came here in 1993. Cothay makes a model study of how a garden can be rejuvenated. It is now in the prime of life, brimming with vigour. New for 2001 is an avenue of the mop-headed acacia (*Robinia pseudacacia* 'Umbraculifera') 100 yards long, underplanted with nepeta and 1,000 white tulips: it should be spectacular in May.

Owned by Mr & Mrs Alastair Robb
Number of gardeners 1½
Size 7 acres formal; 5 acres of new trees
English Heritage grade II*

Crowe Hall

WIDCOMBE HILL, BATH BA2 6AR

Tel 01225 310322
Location Off A36 up Widcombe Hill
Opening hours 2 pm – 6 pm; 18 March, 22 April, 13 May, 10 June, 15 July & by appointment
Admission fee Adults £2; Children £1

Crowe Hall is a most extraordinary and exciting garden. It looks straight out at the Capability Brown landscape at Prior Park, and 'borrows' it. Below the house is an Italianate terrace, which leads to a ferny rock garden (real rocky outcrops here) and down into a modern garden in the woodland. Recent developments include a 'Sauce' garden, in memory of Lady Barratt, a former owner, and a 'Hercules' garden.

Owned by John Barratt
English Heritage grade II

Dunster Castle

MINEHEAD TA24 6SL

Tel 01643 821314   **Fax** 01643 823000
Website www.nationaltrust.org.uk
Location 3 miles south-east of Minehead on A39
Opening hours 11 am – 4 pm; daily; January to March, and 29 September to December. 10 am – 5 pm; daily; April to 28 September. Closed 25 – 29 December
Admission fee Adults £3; Children £1.50

Dunster is a Victorian woodland on a steep slope, terraced in places and planted with tender exotica – mimosa, *Beschorneria* and a 150-year-old lemon tree in an unheated conservatory.

Plant Highlights Woodland garden; sub-tropical plants; *Arbutus* grove; tallest *Taxodium ascendens* (23m) in the British Isles.

Owned by The National Trust
NCCPG National Collections *Arbutus*
English Heritage grade I

East Lambrook Manor

EAST LAMBROOK, SOUTH PETHERTON
TA13 5HL

Tel 01460 240328　**Fax** 01460 242344
Website www.eastlambrook.com
Location Signed from A303 at South Petherton
Opening hours 10 am – 5 pm; daily; February to October.
Plus 20 May & 24 June for National Gardens Scheme
Admission fee Adults £2.95; OAPs £2.50;
Children & Students £1

East Lambrook is the archetypal super-cottage garden, made by Margery Fish, the popular gardening writer, and charmingly restored in recent years. Margery Fish was an important influence in British gardening in the 1950s and 1960s. She learnt about gardening not from books but from her own observation of plants, so that she developed her own style of gardening – unselfconscious, rich and free. As a journalist, she knew how to communicate, and her books about the garden she made at East Lambrook have been very influential. The new owners are continuing the work of restoration. They have returned Margery Fish's nursery to its original site, made a special bed for the National Collection of *Geranium* and restored the malthouse. They also run courses for gardeners all through the year. There will be a special open day on 3 June when Andrew Norton, who used to live at East Lambrook, will be talking about the National Collection of geraniums.

Owned by Marianne & Robert Williams
Number of gardeners 3
Size 2 acres
NCCPG National Collections *Geranium*
English Heritage grade I

Elworthy Cottage Plants

ELWORTHY COTTAGE, ELWORTHY,
LYDEARD ST LAWRENCE, TAUNTON
TA4 3PX

Tel 01984 656427
Location 10 miles north-west of Taunton, on B3188 in Elworthy village centre
Opening hours 10 am – 4 pm, Tuesdays, Thursdays and Fridays, mid-March to the end of September. And by appointment

Elworthy offers a pleasant selection of perennials and cottage garden plants, including quite a number which are uncommon or hard-to-find, as well as old favourites. The nursery is strong on geraniums (over 200), clematis (over 90), pulmonarias (over 50), violas (over 40), as well as crocosmias and grasses. Some of the plants the nursery offers are not available from any other source – *Geranium argenteum*, for example. It has also introduced a number of new plants, including *Geranium × oxonianum* 'Elworthy Misty'. Most of the plants can be seen growing in the display garden, which is neatly laid out with island beds and themed colours for year-round interest.

Gaulden Manor

TOLLAND, LYDEARD ST LAWRENCE
TA4 3PN

Tel 01984 667213
Location 1 mile east of Tolland church, off B3224
Opening hours 2 pm – 5 pm; Sundays & Thursdays; 3 June to 27 August. And groups by appointment at other times
Admission fee £3

Gaulden is a modern garden, well designed and well planted. It has a series of small garden rooms, each devoted to a different theme (roses, herbs etc.) which makes it seem much larger than it really is. The stream garden – very pretty – is below the monks' pond, its sides planted with candelabra primulas, ferns and gunneras.

Owned by James Starkie
Size 2 acres

Greencombe Gardens

PORLOCK TA24 8NU

Tel 01643 862363
Location ½ mile west of Porlock on left of road to Porlock Weir
Opening hours 2 pm – 6 pm; Saturday – Wednesday; April to July and October to November
Admission fee Adults £3.50; Children (under 16) 50p

Greencombe is an organic showpiece of international renown. The garden stretches across a sheltered hillside which looks up to the tree-covered slopes of Exmoor behind and down across ancient fields to Porlock Bay and an uninterrupted view of the sea. It is a woodland garden, long and narrow, with a rich underplanting of ornamental plants beneath an outstanding canopy of oaks, hollies, conifers and sweet chestnuts. Camellias, rhododendrons, azaleas, maples, lilies, roses, clematis, and hydrangeas are in turn underplanted with many ferns and the garden's four National Collections – *Erythronium* which are small mountain lilies, *Vaccinium* which the curator Joan Loraine calls 'Whortleberries Worldwide', *Gaultheria* which she refers to as 'whortleberries for bears', and *Polystichum* the 'thumbs-up' fern. The garden is completely organic, with compost heaps and leaf mould pits on show, and a riot of birds,

butterflies and lesser insects. But, like all good plantsman's gardens, Greencombe is absolutely stuffed with interesting plants and has lots to interest the visitor at every time of the year.

Owned by Greencombe Garden Trust
Number of gardeners 2 part-time
Size 3½ acres
NCCPG National Collections *Erythronium*; *Gaultheria*; *Polystichum*; *Vaccinium*

Hadspen Garden

CASTLE CARY BA7 7NG

Tel & Fax 01749 813707
Website www.hadspengarden.co.uk
Location 2 miles east of Castle Cary on A371
Opening hours 10 am – 5 pm; Thursday – Sunday & Bank Holiday Mondays; March to September
Admission fee Adults £3; Children 50p

Part garden, part nursery specialising in colour-plantings and unusual plants. Little remains of Penelope Hobhouse's first garden: the Popes have remade it in the modern idiom, using a wide range of rare plants to create decorative effects. Most visitors speak highly of it: certainly, the Popes' book *Colour by Design*, published by Conran Octopus and based on their work at Hadspen, was one of the best new gardening books of recent years. This year they are planning a major display of tulips: some 7,000 in all (130 cultivars) flowering from March to May and probably at their peak at Easter.

Owned by N & S Pope
Number of gardeners 2½
Size 5 acres
NCCPG National Collections *Rodgersia*

Hestercombe Gardens

CHEDDON FITZPAINE, TAUNTON
TA2 8LQ

Tel 01823 413923   **Fax** 01823 413747
Website www.hestercombegardens.com
Location 4 miles north of Taunton
Opening hours 10 am – 5 pm; daily; all year
Admission fee Adults £4; OAPs £3.80; Children £1

Ignore the house – a Victorian mansion now used as Council offices – and look at the famously restored garden. Lutyens's hallmarks are everywhere: iris-choked rills, pergolas, seats, relieved staircases and pools where reflections twinkle on recessed apses. Gertrude Jekyll's planting is bold and simple, which adds to the vigour. The combination of Lutyens design and Jekyll plants is extremely photogenic: Hestercombe is a highly rewarding garden to learn about symmetry, balance and proportion. The secret landscape garden which Copleston Warre Bampfylde laid out in the late eighteenth century re-opened in 1997: 40 acres of lakes, temples, combes and woodlands which have not been seen for over 100 years.

Owned by Hestercombe Gardens Project Ltd
Number of gardeners 8
Size 50 acres
English Heritage grade I

Kelways Ltd

BARRYMORE FARM, LANGPORT
TA10 9EZ

Tel 01458 250521
Location On B3153, just east of Langport

Opening hours 9 am – 5 pm; Monday – Friday.
10 am – 4 pm; Saturday – Sunday

Long famous for its herbaceous and tree peonies, Kelways also has a large range of irises, and an expanding range of perennials, shrubs and bedding plants. The nursery has undergone a number of changes in recent years. An orchid house displays and sells English-grown orchids.

NCCPG National Collections Paeonia lactiflora

Lower Severalls Gardens & Nursery

CREWKERNE TA18 7NX

Tel 01460 73234   **Fax** 01460 76105
Location 1 mile east of Crewkerne
Opening hours 10 am – 5 pm; daily; 2 March to 20 October. Closed Thursdays & Sundays, but open 2 pm – 5 pm on Sundays in May & June

Both the garden and nursery started in 1985. At first, the nursery specialised in herbs, of which it still has a wide range. However, there are also good selections of hardy geraniums and salvias. The garden is set in front of an eighteenth-century farmhouse: it has fine herbaceous borders, island beds and an area for bog plants.

Size 3 acres

Lytes Cary Manor

CHARLTON MACKRELL, SOMERTON
TA11 7HU

Tel & Fax 01458 223297
Website www.nationaltrust.org.uk
Location Near A303 junction with A372 & A37

Opening hours 2 pm – 6 pm; Mondays, Wednesdays & Saturdays; 2 April to 31 October. Plus Fridays from June to August
Admission fee Adults £4.50; Children £2.20

Lytes Cary has a neo-Elizabethan garden to go with the prettiest of manor houses: yew hedges, hornbeam walks, alleys and lawns, medlars, quinces and a simple Elizabethan flower border.

Owned by The National Trust
English Heritage grade II

Mallet Court Nursery

CURRY MALLET, TAUNTON TA3 6SY

Tel 01823 480748   **Fax** 01823 481009
Location In middle of village
Opening hours 10 am – 4 pm; Mondays to Fridays. Other days by appointment

This is a wonderful specialist tree nursery with an excellent list of unusual trees. Its displays at RHS flower shows, including Chelsea and Hampton Court, have been a delight and a revelation over many years now. Many of the species it sells are offered by no other nursery anywhere in the world. It is particularly good for *Quercus* and *Acer*, and strong on species from China and Korea, but the nursery's list is full of species of every imaginable genus of rare trees. Every dendrophile in Britain knows of it and buys from it: the array of plants to be seen at the nursery is itself an education.

The Manor House

WALTON-IN-GORDANO, CLEVEDON BS21 7AN

Tel 01275 872067
Location North side of B3124 on Clevedon side of Walton-in-Gordano
Opening hours 10 am – 4 pm; Thursday; May & June. Plus 2 pm – 6 pm on 1 July. And by appointment, at any time
Admission fee Adults £2; Children free

This is a really interesting plantsman's garden on a substantial scale, offering something for every taste, from autumn-flowering bulbs to rare conifers. Many of the trees and shrubs are grown from seeds brought back from the travels of Caryl Wills' parents, but it is not just the range of the Wills's parents' interests which is breath-taking: they also use their plants to create endless contrasts and harmonies of colour, form light and shade. Moreover – as with all good plant collections – there is always much for the visitor to learn and enjoy, whatever the season. The garden is beautifully maintained, too.

Owned by Mr & Mrs Caryl Wills

Mill Cottage Plants

HENLEY MILL, WOOKEY BA5 1AP

Tel & Fax 01749 676966
Location 2 miles from Wells, off A371. Left into Henley Lane, then 50 yards on left
Opening hours 10 am – 5.30 pm, Wednesdays, March to September

The nursery grows a selection of unusual perennials, including a wide range of geraniums, hellebores, oriental poppies, dierams, ferns and grasses. It also has a good line in rare hydrangea cultivars. The two-and-a-half-acre garden is well worth seeing, though it is best to ask if you can visit it in advance of your visit. Groups are especially welcome.

Milton Lodge

OLD BRISTOL ROAD, WELLS
BA5 3AQ

Tel 01749 672168
Location Old Bristol road off of A39
Opening hours 2 pm – 5 pm; Tuesdays, Wednesdays, Sundays & Bank Holidays; Easter to 31 October
Admission fee Adults £2.50; Children (under 14) free. Groups by arrangement

This impressive Edwardian garden is terraced down a hillside against a backdrop of Wells Cathedral. Most of the plantings are modern, and look good against the bulky yew hedges. In a combe, across the main road, is an eight-acre arboretum which has also been replanted in recent years. Both parts are full of interesting plants, excellently maintained and constantly improving. From May to August teas are available on Sundays.

Plant Highlights Roses (mainly modern); good herbaceous borders; fine collection of trees; tallest *Populus alba* (20m) in the British Isles.

Owned by D C Tudway Quilter
English Heritage grade II

Montacute House

MONTACUTE, YEOVIL TA15 6XP

Tel 01935 823289

Website www.nationaltrust.org.uk
Location In Montacute village
Opening hours 11 am – 5.30 pm (dusk if earlier); daily except Tuesday; 31 March to 4 November. Then 11.30 am – 4 pm; Wednesday – Sunday; 7 November to March 2002
Admission fee Adults £3.30; Children £1.60. Reduced rates in winter

The garden at Montacute is subsidiary to the amazing Elizabethan mansion, apart from a border started by Vita Sackville-West, worked over by Phyllis Reiss and finished by Graham Thomas. But it cannot be beaten for its sense of English renaissance grandeur.

Owned by The National Trust
English Heritage grade I

National Collection of Passiflora

GREENHOLM NURSERIES LTD,
KINGSTON SEYMOUR, CLEVEDON
BS21 6XS

Tel 01934 833350   **Fax** 01934 877255
Website www.passiflora-uk.co.uk
Location In the middle of Kingston Seymour, just to the west of the M5
Opening hours 9 am – 1 p & 2 pm – 5 pm; Monday – Saturday

This nursery is testimony to John Vanderplank's commitment to these Central and South American climbing plants. It is a good example of what an enthusiast can achieve single-handed in promoting enthusiasm for a genus by raising its profile and making it more widely grown and popular. One glance at the *RHS Plant Finder* makes clear the measure of that achievement:

over 100 species and forms are listed by this nursery and by no-one else. Vanderplank has collected many in the wild: his regular exhibits at RHS flower shows (often in the NCCPG tent at Hampton Court) invariably contain several new species, as yet unnamed. Naturally his nursery is of international importance, and he supplies material to pharmaceutical companies and botanical institutes studying the chemical make-up of plants. The catalogue (it also exists on-line) is detailed, and includes precise temperature and cultivation requirements.

NCCPG National Collections Passiflora

P M A Plant Specialities

JUNKER'S NURSERY, LOWER MEAD, WEST HATCH, TAUNTON TA3 5RN

Tel 01823 480774   **Fax** 01823 481046
Website www.junker.co.uk
Location ½ mile south-west of West Hatch
Opening hours By appointment only

P M A has some interesting container-grown trees and shrubs. It is particularly strong on Japanese and snakebark acers, daphnes, magnolias and the ornamental tree *Cornus*. Some plants are available in larger sizes for instant impact.

Prior Park

BATH BA2 5AH

Tel 01225 833422
Website www.nationaltrust.org.uk
Location 1½ miles south of Bath city centre
Opening hours 12 noon – 5.30 pm;
Wednesday – Monday; February 2001 – February 2002.
12 noon – 5.30 pm (or dusk, if earlier); Friday to Sunday;
1 – 24 & 27 – 31 December 2001 & all January 2002.
Opens at 11 am from Easter Saturday to 30 September
Admission fee Adults £4; Children £2

The classical landscape at Prior Park was laid out between 1734 and 1764 by a property developer called Ralph Allen, who was a friend of Pope and Burlington. Pope advised extensively on the original lay-out and buildings before Capability Brown gave them a make-over in the early 1760s. The park is no more than 28 acres, stretching from the extremely handsome Palladian house at the top of the steep valley to the Palladian bridge right at the bottom, which is the focus of the entire landscape. It is reached by a rugged and slippery path through the woods on either side, quite unfitted for wheelchairs and buggies and only suitable for the sure-footed and confident. There is nothing of horticultural interest, but some fine trees – mainly beech, with some yew, sycamore and seedling ashes – underplanted with ferns and laurels. Nevertheless it is hard to imagine a more elegant landscape than this one, which uses the busy and fashionable city of Bath as its background. Photographers may wish to visit it early in the afternoon, when the sun shines on the Palladian bridge. There is one snag, however: the Trust can offer no on-site parking. Badgerline runs buses (Nos. 2 & 4) from the bus station or Dorchester Place, every ten minutes. Otherwise you could try parking at the top of the hill, in Avenue Road.

Owned by The National Trust
English Heritage grade I

Sam Oldham

RYLANDS NURSERIES, WELLINGTON
TA21 9QB

Tel 01823 664499 **Fax** 01823 666009
Location At Bagley Green, just north of A38
Opening hours daily; all year

Sam Oldham is a chrysanthemum specialist who has made quite an impact on recent RHS flower shows. Large-flowered, sprays, spiders and a good list of novelties are offered in a wide choice of colours.

Scotts Nurseries Ltd

MERRIOTT TA16 5PL

Tel 01460 72306
Location 2 miles north of Crewkerne between the A30 & the A303
Opening hours 8 am – 5 pm; Monday – Friday. 9 am – 5 pm; Saturdays. 10.30 am – 4.30 pm; Sundays

Scotts of Merriott is a first-rate, long-established and respected nursery-cum-garden centre, offering a very wide range of field- and container-grown plants. It is particularly strong on old-fashioned roses, ornamental trees, top fruit and shrubs.

Sherborne Garden

PEAR TREE HOUSE, LITTON BA3 4PP

Tel 01761 241220
Location On B3114, ½ mile west of Litton village
Opening hours 11 am – 6 pm; Mondays; June to October. Plus 10 June & 14 July for the National Gardens Scheme
Admission fee Adults £2; Children free. Groups welcome by appointment

This plantsman's garden started in a modest enough way in 1964 but now extends to more than four acres. It is very thickly planted, but almost wild at the edges where it merges into the countryside. The owners are particularly interested in trees and plant them closely in groups for comparison: hence the 'prickly wood' (of hollies), the larch wood and the pinetum. But there is much more than trees and it is a garden to dawdle in and learn from.

Owned by Mr & Mrs John Southwell
Number of gardeners 1, very part-time
Size 4½ acres

Tintinhull House

TINTINHULL, YEOVIL BA22 8PZ

Tel 01935 822545
Website www.nationaltrust.org.uk
Location In Tintinhull village
Opening hours 12 noon – 6 pm; Wednesdays – Sunday; April to September
Admission fee Adults £3.80; Children £1.80

This small garden – less than two acres – is the most famous example of a Jekyll-style garden on a small scale. It combines great design with a wide range of plants and the most skilful use of colour combinations in planting them. The garden looks larger than it really is because it has been divided into a sequence of small rooms of different size, all of them hedged or walled. Perhaps the most famous part of the garden is the largest, around a formal rectangular pool in front of a pillared summerhouse. The borders on either side are in complete contrast to each other: one is made in the bright bold colours of scarlet, yellow, orange and white, while the other is dominated by pastel pinks, mauves, blues and pale yellows. Yet they are also mirror images of each other because each uses grey-leaved plants and striking leaf shapes as well as colour. No garden employs such a wide palette of plants so rigorously as elements of design. But please note – there are no plant-labels: they would spoil the dream.

Owned by The National Trust

English Heritage grade II

Wayford Manor

CREWKERNE TA18 8QG

Tel 01460 73253 **Fax** 01460 76365

Location 3 miles south-west of Crewkerne off A30 or B3165

Opening hours 2 pm – 6 pm; 15 April, 6 & 27 May, and 17 June, for National Gardens Scheme. Parties by appointment

Admission fee Adults £2; Children 50p

Wayford is one of the best gardens designed by Harold Peto: terraces and courtyards, pools and arbours, balustrades and staircases, Tuscan and Byzantine. Down in the wild garden is an extensive collection of mature acers and magnolias, as well as many rhododendrons, bog plants and daffodils. The whole garden is presently being restored by the enthusiastic and knowledgeable owners. Last year, they reinstated the pergola with Tuscan columns as Peto originally designed it.

Plant Highlights Good herbaceous borders; rhododendrons; spring bulbs; maples; tallest *Photinia davidiana* (13m) in the British Isles.

Owned by Mr & Mrs R L Goffe

Number of gardeners 1

Size 4 acres

English Heritage grade II

STAFFORDSHIRE

Staffordshire has three historic gardens to which English Heritage has accorded Grade I status: Alton Towers, Biddulph Grange and Shugborough. All are open to the public. The county is not, however, a magnet for garden-visitors with horticultural interests. The Dorothy Clive Garden is the only really first-rate garden in Staffordshire to have come out of the twentieth century. The National Garden Scheme has comparatively little success within the county and there are no nurseries of national standing. Why this should be remains a puzzle: the county is fairly wealthy, its soils are fertile, and its climate is not too subject to extremes. But it is one of the few counties in England which has no National Collections, a fairly good indicator of the low level of interest in plants and gardens in any part of the country. Staffordshire's historic gardens trust is however very active and its historic gardens are well-visited – Shugborough, Weston and Trentham have all enjoyed long traditions of popular participation in their public programmes events. There are few arboreta of note, however, and practically no record-sized trees anywhere in the county. Even the Royal Horticultural Society seems unable to stir up enthusiasm for gardening: Staffordshire is one of the few counties where it has no partnership arrangement with any nursery, garden or college.

Alton Towers

ALTON, STOKE-ON-TRENT ST10 4DB

Tel 0870 5204060 **Fax** 01538 704099
Website www.alton-towers.co.uk
Location Signed for miles around
Opening hours 9.30 am – 5/6/7 pm depending on season; daily; March to October
Admission fee Tickets vary in cost according to season but are always fairly expensive: Alton offers much more than gardens to visit

Alton has 300 acres of dotty and exuberant display, best seen from the cable-car. Ignore the theme park: the gardens are by and large detached from the razzmatazz. There are splendid Victorian conifers and gaudy bedding, magnificently done. The highlights include a Swiss Cottage, a Roman bridge, a Chinese pagoda, a flag tower, and a corkscrew fountain. It is seriously important to garden historians and excellent entertainment still – but not for contemplative souls. Best in term time.

Owned by Tussauds Group
English Heritage grade I

Biddulph Grange

BIDDULPH, STOKE-ON-TRENT ST8 7SD

Tel 01782 517999   **Fax** 01782 510624
Website www.nationaltrust.org.uk
Location ½ mile north of Biddulph, 3½ miles south-east
of Congleton
Opening hours 12 noon – 6 pm, Wednesday – Friday
(closed Good Friday); 11 am – 6 pm; Saturdays, Sundays
& Bank Holiday Mondays; 28 March to 4 November. Also
12 noon – 4 pm; Saturdays & Sundays; 10 November
to 16 December
Admission fee Adults £4.40; Children £2.30 (but £2 & £1
respectively in November & December)

National Trust has restored it energetically
since 1988 and many of the quirkier features
are as good as ever again. The trees survived
best: some of the conifers are very large
handsome specimens in the prime of middle
age now.

Owned by The National Trust
English Heritage grade I

Biddulph was made in the middle of the
nineteenth century by James Bateman –
an important amateur garden designer,
plantsman and writer. His garden has
dozens of different microclimates,
compartments, follies and whimsies: it is, in
fact, the earliest example of a garden being
divided into a series of smaller rooms, each
designed and planted to a different theme.
Some are so original and inventive that they
still strike us as frankly rather wacky – the
Brahmin garden, for example, which is
dominated by a golden cow, or the stumpery
where a large tree that had been felled or dug
out in another part of the garden would be
replanted upside-down, with its roots eight
or ten feet up in the air. Others are the
Egyptian courtyard with its own pyramid, a
bowling green and quoits ground, the
Chinese garden (surprisingly large and
beautiful, with a joss house, temple and
section of the Great Wall) and the ferny
Scottish glen. Elsewhere are areas devoted to
collections of plants – a wellingtonia avenue,
a pinetum and the dahlia walk. The estate
suffered years of neglect when the house
(fairly ugly, mid-Victorian and
neo-Jacobean) was used as a hospital but the

Dorothy Clive Garden

WILLOUGHBRIDGE, MARKET
DRAYTON TF9 4EU

Tel 01630 647237   **Fax** 01630 647902
Website www.dorothyclivegarden.co.uk
Location A51, midway between Nantwich & Stone
Opening hours 10 am – 5.30 pm; daily; April to October
Admission fee Adults £3.20; OAPs & Groups (20+) £2.70;
Children £1

Meticulously maintained and still
expanding, this garden was begun in 1940
but seems ageless. It was made on an
unpromising site, a cold windy hilltop, but
advice on plants and planting came from
Frank Knight, then director of Wisley. The
layout is informal, yet full of incidents, each
with a distinct character: they include a
superb woodland garden, an alpine scree, a
damp garden, a conifer collection and
spectacular summer flower borders. The
Dorothy Clive Garden is best perhaps in
May, when the woodland quarry is brilliant
with rhododendrons. But the scree
(replanted in 1998) and rock garden
(reflected in the lake) are hard to beat at any
season. And, since it has many well-grown
but unusual plants of all kinds, there is
always much to see whatever the season.

Owned by Willoughbridge Garden Trust
Number of gardeners 3
Size 8 acres

Moseley Old Hall

THE NATIONAL TRUST, MOSELEY
OLD HALL LANE, FORDHOUSES
WV10 7HY

Tel & Fax 01902 782808
Website www.nationaltrust.org.uk

Location South of M54 between A449 & A460
Opening hours 1.30 pm – 5.30 pm (but 11 am to 5 pm on
Bank Holiday Mondays); Wednesdays, Saturdays, Sundays,
Bank Holiday Mondays & the following Tuesdays;
24 March to 4 November
Admission fee Adults £4.10

This is a modern reconstruction of a
seventeenth-century town garden: neat box
parterres, a nut walk and an arched pergola
hung with clematis. The plantings are all of
a period: quietly inspirational.

 Plant Highlights Topiary; snowdrops;
herbs.

Owned by The National Trust

Oulton House

OULTON, STONE ST15 8UR

Tel 01785 813556
Location From Stone take Oulton Road and turn left after
Oulton sign. 3rd driveway on right
Opening hours By appointment, April to July
Admission fee Adults £2; Children 75p

This three-acre garden has been made by
Mrs Fairbairn over many years, essentially
for private enjoyment not for public display.
It is full of good plants – roses,
rhododendrons, geraniums and clematis –
arranged in colour groupings.

Owned by Mr & Mrs W A Fairbairn
Number of gardeners owners, plus part-time help
Size 3½ acres

Shugborough Hall

C/O THE ESTATE OFFICE, MILFORD, STAFFORD ST17 0XB

Tel 01889 881388   **Fax** 01889 881323
Website www.nationaltrust.org.uk
Location Signed from Jct13 M6
Opening hours 11 am – 5 pm; Tuesday-Sunday & Bank Holiday Mondays; 31 March to 30 September, plus Sundays in October. And parties by appointment. Last admissions 4.15 pm
Admission fee Vehicles £2; Coaches free

This classical and neo-classical landscape has Chinese additions; a handsome Nesfield terrace dominated by dumplings of clipped golden yew; 50 oaks in the new arboretum; and a rose garden restored by Graham Thomas. All very popular with the locals.

Plant Highlights Woodland garden; roses (mainly old-fashioned); good herbaceous borders.

Owned by The National Trust
English Heritage grade I

Trentham Gardens

STONE ROAD, STOKE-ON-TRENT ST4 8AX

Tel 01782 657341
Location Signed from M6
Opening hours 10 am – 5 pm (4 pm in winter); daily; all year
Admission fee Adults £1; Children 50p

The future of this, the grandest of grand Victorian gardens, lay in the balance as we went to press. The owners were awaiting the result of an application for re-development. It is to be hoped that its essential amenities will be preserved for posterity: the terraces were designed by Barry and Nesfield, and set within a Capability Brown park. Until recently, colourful summer bedding recalled its nineteenth-century heyday. Even that has gone now.

Owned by Trentham Leisure Ltd
English Heritage grade II*

Weston Park

WESTON-UNDER-LIZARD, SHIFNAL TF11 8LE

Tel 01952 852100   **Fax** 01952 850430
Website www.weston-park.com
Location Off the A5 to Telford
Opening hours 11 am – 7 pm (last admissions 5 pm); Easter, then every weekend until 30 June. Thereafter, daily until 3 September and every weekend until 17 September. Closed 6 June, 14 July, 4 August and 17 to 20 August
Admission fee Adults £2.50; OAPs £2; Children £1.50

Weston has a fine eighteenth-century landscape (Capability Brown worked there) and a nineteenth-century Italianate parterre, a temple of Diana and a handsome orangery by James Paine. It is not of major horticultural interest, but best for its fine collection of trees, some of them record-breakers, and the collection of *Nothofagus* planted by the late Lord Bradford.

Owned by The Weston Park Foundation
Number of gardeners 3
English Heritage grade II*

SUFFOLK

Suffolk has comparatively few historic gardens of national importance but, such as they are, they are of great interest to the garden-lover. Both Helmingham and Shrubland are rated as Grade I gardens, while Euston, Ickworth and Somerleyton are all Grade II*. There is a particularly fine collection of trees at East Bergholt Place, which has recently opened up as a visitor-friendly garden with a good general nursery attached. Suffolk is a rich county but was, until recently, rather cut off from London and its markets, which may help in part to explain why it has so many good nurseries. Notcutts is one of the largest quality nurseries in the country, with a long and distinguished history of plant introductions and exhibits at RHS flower shows. The leading seedsmen Thompson & Morgan have been at Ipswich for over a hundred years: their trial grounds may also be visited in season. But it is the sheer number of good small modern nurseries which is so surprising: we list Goldbrook, Mills Farm, Paradise Centre, Park Green and Rougham Hall among others – but Gardiner's Hall Plants at Braiseworth (over 3,000 different plants) and North Green Snowdrops (sent 'in the green') are also worth knowing. There are many good modern gardens like Wyken Hall (made by RHS Council member Sir Kenneth Carlisle), and others which we do not list, including the Blakenham Woodland Garden at Little Blakenham (made by the late Lord Blakenham, Treasurer of the RHS). The National Garden Scheme does well in the county and there is an active historic gardens trust too. The NCCPG is represented by about a dozen National Collections, including some horticulturally important genera like lilacs (*Syringa*), delphiniums and fuchsias. Otley College near Ipswich is a RHS Partner College, with lectures, workshops and garden walks throughout the year: further details from 020 7821 3408.

Euston Hall

EUSTON, THETFORD IP24 2QP

Tel 01842 766366   **Fax** 01842 766764
Location On A1088 3 miles south of Thetford & 12 miles north of Bury St Edmunds

Opening hours 2.30 pm – 5 pm; Thursdays; 7 June to 27 September, plus 24 June & 2 September. NCCPG Plant Sale on 27 May
Admission fee £1.50

The classical eighteenth-century landscaping at Euston is very beautiful. William Kent made the serpentine lake, though it was later

East Bergholt Place

EAST BERGHOLT CO7 6UP

Tel & Fax 01206 299224
Location 2 miles east of A12, on B1070, ENE of East Bergholt
Opening hours 10 am – 5 pm; daily; March to September, except for the Charity days: (2 pm – 5 pm; 1, 16 & 29 April, 13 & 28 May, 3 June & 21 October)
Admission fee Adults £2.50; Children free

East Bergholt has fifteen acres of wonderful woodland garden planted by Charles Eley, the present owner's great-grandfather, at the start of the twentieth century. It is the home of *Malus × pupurea* 'Eleyi' and has been called a 'Cornish Garden in Suffolk'. Unfortunately, not all of it is always open to the public, except on charity open days. At other times visitors can see a collection of trees known as the 'Swale', around a gentle valley with a small brook running down the middle. Many of the older trees and shrubs were grown from original collections by George Forrest: others represent modern plantings and re-plantings. The collection is well-labelled and well-maintained – a fine place to see a wide range of trees and shrubs. Good specimens include a very handsome variegated cherry-laurel *Prunus laurocerasus* 'Castlewellan' five metres high, a magnificent *Quercus castaneifolia* and a fine three-stemmed *Davidia involucrata* var. *vilmoriniana*. Some are record-breakers, including a *Lithocarpus densiflorus* twelve metres tall. The valley is sheltered by hedges of holly and yew and a mature collection of hardy rhododendrons. And it is good for insects and wildlife too. Restoration and replanting continue. The much-praised nursery in the walled garden has a good general stock, almost all of it bought in.

Owned by Mr & Mrs Rupert Eley
Number of gardeners 1
Size 15 acres

modified by Capability Brown. Kent also built the elegant banqueting house. There are avenues of beech and lime, and clumps, spinneys and belts of mature trees. The formal terraces by the house lead to herbaceous borders and rose gardens. It all adds up to a most satisfying composition where horticulture plays second fiddle to landscaping.

Owned by The Duke of Grafton
Number of gardeners 2
Size 70 acres
English Heritage grade II*

Fisk's Clematis Nursery

WESTLETON, SAXMUNDHAM
IP17 3AJ

This distinguished clematis nursery has just closed down. It gave great pleasure to gardeners and mounted beautiful exhibits at the Chelsea Flower Show for over 30 years.

Goldbrook Plants

HOXNE, EYE IP21 5AN

Tel & Fax 01379 668770
Location On south-east edge of Hoxne
Opening hours 10 am – 5 pm; Thursday – Sunday. Other days by appointment. Closed January and around Chelsea & Hampton Court Shows

Goldbrook's exhibits at Chelsea and other RHS flower shows have won them much praise – and an impressive run of gold medals. Their collection of hostas is quite exceptional – over 900 cultivars, of which a great many are available from no other nursery. The same is true of their hemerocallis. Look out for their US introductions too – many of the hemerocallis

bear the prefix 'Siloam' (e.g. *H.* 'Siloam Fairy Tale') – while the hostas they have raised themselves are often prefixed by 'Goldbrook'.

Haughley Park

STOWMARKET IP14 3JY

Tel 01359 240701   **Fax** 01359 240546
Location Signed from A14
Opening hours 2 pm – 5.30 pm; Tuesdays; May to September, plus 29 April & 6 May for bluebells
Admission fee Adults £2; Children £1

Haughley has a Jacobean mansion with well-kept modern flower gardens and fine trees (especially *Davidia involucrata*). In the walled garden are vegetables, trained fruit trees, a rose arbour and other ornamental features. But the acres of lily-of-the-valley and bluebells in the woodland garden are worth the journey no matter how far. There is a choice of three woodland walks, from 1½ to 2½ miles long: the camellias are good in May and the rhododendrons in June. In the West Woods, the owners have been carrying out an interesting experiment since the great gale of 1987. This arises from the different way in which each part was subsequently managed. Some areas were undamaged and remain 'natural'; one area of damaged woodland has been left in place to recover naturally; one area had the stumps left in place to shoot as coppice timber and several areas were cleared and replanted between 1992 and 1996.

 Plant Highlights Woodland garden; rhododendrons & azaleas; good herbaceous borders; bluebells; lily-of-the-valley; 1,000-year-old oak.

Owned by R J Williams
Number of gardeners 4
Size 8 acres, plus 265 acres of park

Helmingham Hall

STOWMARKET IP14 6EF

Tel 01473 890363 **Fax** 01473 890776
Website www.helmingham.com
Location 9 miles north of Ipswich on B1077
Opening hours 2 pm – 6 pm; Sundays; 29 April to
9 September; plus individuals & groups on Wednesday
afternoons by prior arrangement
Admission fee Adults £3.75; Children £2

A visit to Helmingham is a step back into history, to a time of ancient certainties, order and peace. The Tollemaches have lived here since 1487. The house is a moated manor, half-timbered when built in 1480, but given a cladding of bricks and tiles in the eighteenth century. It is set in the most spacious 400-acre deer-park, loosely studded with vast centennial oaks grown to their full spread. Helmingham's formal garden lies beyond the moat to the south of the house. It is surrounded by 60 hybrid musks, lightly pruned and allowed to billow out, to fill the beds. The entire garden, about 100 yards long, is edged with Hidcote lavender, underplanted with variegated London Pride, and complemented by *Campanula lactiflora*, alstroemerias, foxgloves and peonies. This is gardening on a large scale, and makes its impact through simplicity and repetition: it is immensely grand. Beyond the formal garden is the walled garden proper, built of brick in 1745. On either side of the central grassy path runs a broad and stately double herbaceous border perhaps 120 yards long. Climbing roses are tied to straining wires all along its back: they include 'Guinée', 'Long John Silver', and *Rosa multiflora* var. *cathayensis*. The roses are underplanted with herbaceous plantings chosen to blend with the soft colours of the roses: pinks, blues, mauves, whites and the palest of

creamy-yellows. Not until the main rose-flowering has finished in mid-August do yellows, bronzes, oranges and reds come to the fore. A spring border runs the whole way along one of the outer walls of the walled garden and is planted mainly with irises, tulips and peonies, backed by more climbing roses, vines, clematis, chaenomeles, ceanothus and myrtle from Queen Victoria's wedding posy. Nearer the house is a new series of knot gardens planted in 1982, which look as if they have been here for hundreds of years. The knots include the Tollemaches' heraldic device, a fret or interlacing pattern of bands, which has been made to interweave by pruning the strips of box at different levels. It leads to another rose garden: albas and species roses, centifolias and mosses, a large choice of gallicas and so on, underplanted with spring bulbs, white foxgloves, *Campanula persicifolia*, *Alchemilla mollis*, purple violas and geraniums. One reason why the garden is so successful is that the roses and their companion plantings all fall within a narrow colour range: it is a discipline from which every garden-owner can learn. But everything here is carefully thought through and controlled: you see this firmness too in the immaculately edged lawns and weedless borders. Everywhere at Helmingham, order prevails over anarchy.

Owned by Lord Tollemache
English Heritage grade I

Ickworth

NATIONAL TRUST OFFICE,
HORRINGER, BURY ST EDMUNDS
IP29 5QE

Tel 01284 735270 **Fax** 01284 735175
Website www.nationaltrust.org.uk
Location 3 miles south-west of Bury St Edmunds
Opening hours 10 am – 5 pm (4 pm in winter); daily; all year. Closed at weekends from 29 October to 31 March 2002
Admission fee Adults £2.50

Ickworth is an extraordinary garden for an extraordinary house: the main borders follow the curves of the house. There are also an Italian garden in front of the house, and long vistas in the park, but the old kitchen garden is bare.

Plant Highlights Autumn colour; Italian garden; Victorian 'stumpery'; new display of lemon trees in orangery (1998); tallest *Quercus pubescens* (29m) in the British Isles.

Owned by The National Trust
NCCPG National Collections *Buxus*
English Heritage grade II*

Mills Farm Plants and Gardens

NORWICH ROAD, MENDLESHAM
IP14 5NQ

Tel & Fax 01449 766425
Website www.millsfarmplants.co.uk
Location On A1240 just south of Mendlesham village turning
Opening hours 9 am – 5.30 pm; daily. Closed Tuesdays and all January

Mills Farm specialises in *Dianthus* (new and old hybrids, species and rock garden types) and roses: there is a list for each genus. The roses are mostly old-fashioned varieties, in a well-chosen selection – about 100 different cultivars. The nursery also lists about 500 herbaceous perennials – not a large number by the standard of most plantsman's nurseries. The owners claim to have one of the widest commercial collection of pinks (*Dianthus*) in the UK. They also breed their own and have introduced quite a number of *Dianthus* cultivars with the prefix 'Mendlesham', including 'Mendlesham Frilly', 'Mendlesham Glow' and 'Mendlesham Maid'. The garden is well worth visiting in its own right – designed entirely for the owners' pleasure as a formal and restrained place for contemplation, with a limited colour palette and the sound of falling water. It is surrounded by yew hedges and planted so that something provides flowers throughout the year. Everything has good, strong foliage, too.

Notcutts Nurseries

IPSWICH ROAD, WOODBRIDGE
IP12 4AF

Tel 01394 383344 **Fax** 01394 445307
Website www.notcutts.co.uk
Location On the Ipswich Road
Opening hours 9 am – 6 pm; Monday – Saturday. 10.30 am – 4.30 pm; Sundays

Notcutts are large wholesale nurseries with a garden centre chain and branches in Norwich, Oxford (Mattocks roses), Staines, Peterborough, St Albans, Bagshot, Maidstone, Tunbridge Wells, Cranleigh, Booker, Solihull and Ardleigh. They underwent quite a period of expansion in the 1990s and are now in the middle of a restructuring which could have implications for the future. The company as a whole is strongest on flowering shrubs and trees and their large beautifully colour-co-ordinated displays of these at the Chelsea Flower Show have been a source of wonder and praise for many years. But they offer every type of plant in all their branches and the quality of their stock is first class. Staff are also extremely helpful and knowledgeable. It is difficult for even the most experienced gardener not to come away from a visit to a branch of Notcutts without several new additions to his garden.

NCCPG National Collections *Hibiscus syiacus* cvs.

Paradise Centre

TWINSTEAD ROAD, LAMARSH, BURES
CO8 5EX

Tel & Fax 01787 269449
Website www.paradisecentre.com
Location Signed in village
Opening hours 10 am – 5 pm; Saturday – Sunday & Bank Holidays; Easter to October. By appointment at other times

This garden-nursery specialises in bulbs, herbaceous plants and shade- and damp-lovers, almost all of which are grown at the nursery. The adjoining gardens are superb: five acres of light woodland with thousands and thousands of bulbs giving colour at every season. Many are unusual. There is also a natural spring, whose water provides an ideal habitat for *Gunnera manicata*, lysichitons and other damp-loving plants.

Park Green Nurseries

WETHERINGSETT, STOWMARKET
IP14 5QH

Tel 01728 860139   **Fax** 01728 861277
Website www.parkgreen.co.uk
Location 6 miles north-east of Stowmarket
Opening hours 10 am – 5 pm; daily; March to September

This nursery specialises in *Hemerocallis*, astilbes, ornamental grasses and other hardy perennial plants, but its most important line is hostas. It stocks over 200 different cultivars and introduces new ones every year. Recent releases include *Hosta* 'Delia', *H.* 'Knaves Green', *H.* 'Sarah Kennedy' and *H.* 'Gay Search'.

Rougham Hall Nurseries

ROUGHAM, BURY ST EDMUNDS
IP30 9LZ

Tel 01359 270577   **Fax** 01359 271149
Location Off the west-bound carriageway of the A14
Opening hours 10 am – 4 pm; daily; March to October

Rougham Hall Nurseries – always very popular when they come to RHS flower shows – are breeders, introducers and growers of an extensive and interesting range of perennials. Their selection of asters is particularly good, as is their list of delphiniums, of which they have a National Collection. Their other National Collection is of gooseberries: they have by far the most extensive list anywhere in the world. The whole history of this most highly prized of dessert fruits is contained within the hundreds of cultivars which they list. The range is always increasing, too: it is worthwhile enquiring if they do not appear to have one that you are looking for.

NCCPG National Collections Delphinium; Ribes (gooseberries)

Shrubland Park Gardens

CODDENHAM, IPSWICH IP6 9QP

Tel 01473 830221   **Fax** 01473 832202
Location Between Claydon & Coddenham: come by A14 or A140
Opening hours 2 pm – 5 pm; Sundays & Bank Holiday Mondays; 15 April to 23 September
Admission fee Adults £3; OAPs & Children £2

This grand Victorian garden was designed by Charles Barry and has been famous ever since for the spectacular Italianate staircase which connects the terrace around the house with the formal gardens below. William Robinson later helped with the planting, both around the formal garden and in the park and woodland gardens beyond. Much restoration and recovery has been completed in recent years: Shrubland is getting better and better.

Owned by Lord de Saumarez
Number of gardeners 5
Size 40 acres
English Heritage grade I

Siskin Plants

DAVEY LANE, CHARSFIELD, WOODBRIDGE IP13 7QG

Tel & Fax 01473 737567
Website www.siskinplants.co.uk
Location At northern end of village of Charsfield

Opening hours 10 am – 5 pm; Thursday – Saturday; March to October

Siskins have a particularly good line in dwarf shrubs, alpine plants, and sempervivums. But their big speciality is the dwarf-growing hebes in their National Collection, which currently contains over 100 distinct species and cultivars.

NCCPG National Collections Hebe (dwarf)

Somerleyton Hall

SOMERLEYTON, LOWESTOFT NR32 5QQ

Tel 01502 730224   **Fax** 01502 732143
Website www.somerleyton.co.uk
Location 4 miles north-west of Lowestoft on B1074
Opening hours 12.30 pm – 5.30 pm; Thursdays, Sundays & Bank Holidays, plus Tuesdays & Wednesdays in July & August; April to October
Admission fee Adults £5.20; OAPs £5; Children £2.60

Somerleyton is a splendid place to visit: there much for the garden- and plant-lover to see and enjoy. In front of the house (palatial, Victorian) is an extremely grand formal grden. Nesfield laid out the terraces and the yew maze, which was planted in 1846: it is not too difficult to get to the centre – only 400 yards from the entrance, provided you make no mistakes on the way. The gardens are full of topiary and good statuary, including a great equatorial sundial, encircled by signs of the Zodiac. Near the house are quantities of roses, herbaceous borders and seasonal bedding. Further afield are large plantings of rhododendrons and azaleas. Though none is actually a record-breaker, Somerleyton has some very fine specimen trees, including a giant redwood (*Sequoiadendron giganteum*),

Eucalyptus gunnii, Monterey pine (*Pinus radiata*), Atlas cedar (*Cedrus atlantica*) and a particularly good maidenhair tree (*Ginkgo biloba*). There has been much replanting since the hurricane of 1987 and the new plantings are already making quite an impact. The walled garden was once the kitchen garden but is now planted with flowers: on the walls are many different climbers including roses, clematis, figs, climbing hydrangeas and such wall-shrubs as *Hoheria sexstylosa*. The glasshouses and peach-cases were designed by Sir Joseph Paxton, architect of the Crystal Palace with his characteristic ridge-and-furrow roofs. They are now planted with tender ornamentals like Meyer's lemon, abutilons, *Cassia corymbosa* and the sweetly-scented *Dregea sinensis*. An old boiler house has a collection of old garden equipment in it. Other good features include an elegant, long, metal pergola with lots of different wisterias and a new avenue of lime trees along the driveway, planted in 1981. The whole estate is well-kept and well-run for visitors' enjoyment.

Owned by Lord & Lady Somerleyton
Number of gardeners 4½
Size 12 acres
English Heritage grade II*

Wyken Hall

STANTON, BURY ST EDMUNDS
IP31 2DW

Tel 01359 250287   **Fax** 01359 252256
Location 9 miles north-east from Bury St Edmunds; brown signs from A143 at Ixworth to Wyken Vineyards
Opening hours 10 am – 6 pm; Wednesday – Friday, & Sundays & Bank Holiday Mondays; 1 April to 1 October. Plus 9 June for National Gardens Scheme
Admission fee Adults £2.50; OAPs £2; Children free

The garden at Wyken is ingeniously designed: a series of old-style gardens to complement the Elizabethan house. These include a knot garden, a herb garden, a traditional English kitchen garden, wildflower meadows, a nuttery and a copper beech maze. All are in scale with the house and the farmland around. Stylish and well maintained, this is one of the best modern private gardens in the country. The restaurant gets three stars in the Good Food Guide.

Plant Highlights Woodland garden; roses (ancient & modern); plantsman's collection of plants; herbs; fruit; good shrubs; good herbaceous borders; new shrub border (1999); new pond (2000); award-winning seven-acre vineyard.

Owned by Sir Kenneth & Lady Carlisle
Number of gardeners 2
Size 4 acres

SURREY

A Martian could be excused for thinking that Surrey was the centre of the horticultural universe. It is the county with everything that gardeners could ever want. Its six Grade I gardens include two very important landscapes – Claremont and Painshill – and two highly influential twentieth-century gardens – Munstead Wood and the Savill Garden. Because of its closeness to London, it has become a very rich county during the last 100 years, which means that people have the time and money to garden on a large scale. The National Gardens Scheme does extremely well in Surrey, with a large number of medium-sized gardens opening for charity, as well as a handful of intensely cultivated smaller gardens. It is the county where the National Gardens Scheme has its headquarters and where its chairman lives – her garden at Vale End is itself open to the public. Surrey has many of the country's best known nurseries – the light soils being poor for agriculture but excellent for growing plants: the floral mile along the A30 is a famous landmark, where some of the trees and shrubs in the old Waterer nurseries have grown to exceptional size. There are good trees too – and many record-breakers – at Winkworth Arboretum, the Savill Garden and the RHS Garden Wisley. Surrey still has a large number of first-class nurseries: we include the important Knap Hill Nursery, Millais Nurseries and the newer stars Brian & Heather Hiley, and Toobees Exotics. There are other nurseries which we do not have space to list but which are well worth visiting – Secretts near Godalming, Lincluden at Bisley and Pantiles at Chertsey for example. The Surrey Gardens Trust and the Surrey group of the NCCPG are both very active in the county: the NCCPG has its base at Wisley. There are over thirty National Collections in Surrey, including seven at Wisley and eight at the Savill Garden. And of course the Royal Horticultural Society's own flagship garden at Wisley dominates every aspect of gardens and gardening in the county: as many as 20 per cent of the society's members live in Surrey.

Brook Lodge Farm Cottage

BLACKBROOK, DORKING RH5 4DT

Tel 01306 888368
Location Signed from A24 past Plough Inn in Blackbrook
Opening hours 2 pm – 5 pm; 17 & 20 June, 15 & 18 July, 12 & 15 August, 5 September. And by appointment
Admission fee Adults £2; Children free

Planted by the present owner over many years, this garden has matured into a fine plantsman's garden with much variety: shrub roses, a rockery, a woodland walk, herbaceous borders and a cottage garden.

Owned by Mrs Basil Kingham
Number of gardeners 2
Size 3½ acres

Cadenza

BUTTERFLY WALK, WARLINGHAM CR3 9JA

Tel 01883 623565
Location M25 Jct6; north up A22 for 4 miles; fourth exit at large roundabout; uphill & turn right
Opening hours By appointment only
Admission fee free

This is the private garden of keen plantsmen. Their special interest is small bulbs, and they have one of England's most interesting collections of hardy cyclamen.

Owned by Mr & Mrs Ronald Frank
Number of gardeners part-time help
Size ¾ acre

Chilworth Manor

CHILWORTH, GUILDFORD GU4 8NL

Tel 01483 561414
Location In middle of village, up Blacksmiths Lane
Opening hours 2 pm – 6 pm; 2 to 28 March, 12 to 16 May, 9 to 13 June, 14 to 18 July. And by appointment
Admission fee £2

This is a remarkable garden, tiered up over seven distinct levels. The top three date from about 1700 and are walled around with beautiful brickwork. There are good climbers and shrubs against the walls, and a bog garden in the woods at the bottom. The main herbaceous border has recently been replanted by a Dutch designer. There are regular sculpture exhibitions, and on 12 July there is also an evening opening from 6 pm to 8 pm: £2.50, to include a glass of wine.

 Plant Highlights Woodland garden; good herbaceous borders; rhododendrons; interesting new shrub plantings; flower arrangements in the house; tallest *Ilex aquifolium* 'Bacciflava' (10.5m) and largest *Ilex aquifolium* 'Pendula' in the British Isles.

Owned by Lady Heald
Number of gardeners 1

Clandon Park

WEST CLANDON, GUILDFORD GU4 7RQ

Tel 01483 222482   **Fax** 01483 223479
Website www.nationaltrust.org.uk
Location Off the A247 at West Clandon
Opening hours 11 am – 5 pm; daily; all year
Admission fee free

Capability Brown's magnificent mature beeches are now underplanted with sombre Victorian shrubberies and slabs of comfrey, bergenias and *Geranium macrorrhizum* – the apotheosis of National Trust ground cover. There is a modern pastiche of a Dutch garden in front of the house but the daffodils in spring are breathtaking.

Owned by The National Trust
English Heritage grade II

Claremont Landscape Garden

PORTSMOUTH ROAD, ESHER
KT10 9JG

Tel 01372 469421
Website www.nationaltrust.org.uk
Location On southern edge of town (A307)
Opening hours 10 am – 6 pm, but dusk from November to March and 7 pm on Saturdays, Sundays & Bank Holiday Mondays from April to October (sunset, if earlier); all year. Closed 1 January, 10–11 July and 25 December. Closed at 2 pm on 12 – 15 July
Admission fee Adults £3.50

This vast historic landscape – now much reduced – was worked over by Vanbrugh, Bridgeman, Kent and Capability Brown and has been energetically restored in recent years. The elegant green theatre is best seen flanked by spreading cedars from across the dark lake. Very popular locally, it is apt to get crowded at summer weekends.

Plant Highlights Laurel lawns; tallest service tree *Sorbus domestica* (23m) in the British Isles, and two further record trees.

Owned by The National Trust
English Heritage grade I

Hannah Peschar Sculpture Garden

BLACK AND WHITE COTTAGE,
STANDON LANE, OCKLEY RH5 5QR

Tel 01306 627269   **Fax** 01306 627662
Location Turn off A29 down Cathill Lane, left at T junction, over bridge and drive is 400 yards on right
Opening hours 11 am – 6 pm; Fridays & Saturdays. 2 pm – 5 pm; Sundays & Bank Holidays. May to October. And by appointment
Admission fee Adults £7; Concessions £5; Children £4

The lush water-gardens and woodlands surrounding a black-and-white cottage are the setting for this remarkable and ever-changing collection of contemporary British sculpture. There are pools and a stream, and surprisingly few flowers – the structure of the background is more important for sculpture than any transient colour. Nevertheless, an earlier owner was the distinguished horticulturist Dick Trotter, Mr Bowles's 'nephew Dick' and sometime Treasurer of the RHS.

Owned by Hannah Peschar
Number of gardeners 1
Size 10 acres

Hatchlands

EAST CLANDON, GUILDFORD
GU4 7RQ

Tel 01483 222482   **Fax** 01483 223479
Website www.nationaltrust.org.uk
Location Off A246 Guildford to Leatherhead
Opening hours 2 pm – 5.30 pm; Tuesday – Thursday, Sundays & Bank Holiday Mondays; April to October. Also Fridays in August. Park walks in Repton Park open daily 11 am – 6 pm from April to October

Admission fee Adults £1.80

Apart from the Jekyll garden (roses, lupins, box and columbines) Hatchlands is an eighteenth-century landscape with parkland. But the garden buildings are charming and the National Trust has made good progress with restoration and replanting.

Owned by The National Trust

Herons Bonsai Ltd

WIRE MILL LANE, NEWCHAPEL, LINGFIELD RH7 6HJ

Tel 01342 832657
Location Turn left off the A22, ½ mile south of junction with B2028
Opening hours 9.30 am – 5.30 pm; Monday – Saturday. 10.30 am – 4.30 pm on Sundays. Closes at dusk in winter months

This bonsai nursery has a string of gold medals behind it from Chelsea Flower Shows. As well as trees for indoors and outdoors, there are pots, tools and accessories (retail and wholesale). They also run bonsai classes and offer Japanese garden design.

Brian & Heather Hiley

25 LITTLE WOODCOTE ESTATE, WALLINGTON SM5 4AU

Tel 020 8647 9679
Location ¾ mile south of Carshalton on the Hill, along Boundary Road
Opening hours 9 am – 5 pm; Wednesday – Saturday

The Hileys offer a stylish collection of tender perennials and shrubs: the salvias are particularly good. Among the hardy perennials the penstemons stand out. The Hileys are regulars at RHS shows where their brilliant exhibits have gained the recognition they deserve.

Hydon Nurseries

CLOCK BARN LANE, HYDON HEATH, GODALMING GU8 4AZ

Tel 01483 860252   Fax 01483 419937
Location 2 miles east of A3, Milford exit. Near Cheshire Home
Opening hours 8 am – 5 pm, Monday – Friday, and Saturdays in season. Closed for lunch 12.45 pm – 2 pm

These rhododendron and azalea specialists have an extensive range of all classes, including some tender species and their own *Rhododendron yakushimanum* hybrids. They have a particularly comprehensive stock of evergreen azaleas, and also sell companion trees and shrubs, especially camellias (another speciality). The nursery extends over 25 acres: among the many fine trees are good, mature specimens of *Nothofagus dombeyi* and *N. antarctica*, as well as the two record-breakers. It is open over several weekends at Easter and during May.

Knap Hill Nursery Ltd

BARRS LANE, KNAPHILL, WOKING GU21 2JW

Tel 01483 481214   Fax 01483 797261
Website www.knaphillrhododendrons.co.uk
Location 2½ miles west of Woking, off A322
Opening hours 9 am – 5 pm; Monday – Friday. Closed on bank holidays

This large and famous rhododendron nursery is also one of England's oldest, founded in 1795: members of the Slocock family have been hybridising rhododendrons for several generations and their nursery covers more than 200 acres. Their extensive list includes hybrids, dwarf, semi-dwarf and *R. yakushimanum* hybrids, as well as deciduous and evergreen azaleas. The display area has about 600 different cultivars: not all are listed at any one time, but they will propagate to request. Over the years, the nursery has won 28 gold medals at the Chelsea Flower Show.

Loseley Park

GUILDFORD GU3 1HS

Tel 01483 304440   **Fax** 01483 302036
Website www.loseley-park.com
Location Off B3000 at Compton, south of Guildford
Opening hours 11 am – 5 pm; Wednesday – Sunday; May to September
Admission fee Adults £3; OAPs £2.50; Children £1.50. RHS members free from May to July

The walled garden attached to this fine Elizabethan house has recently been re-made and re-planted with over 1,000 old-fashioned roses framed by long, low, box hedges. The new herb garden is divided into six sections, respectively devoted to culinary, medicinal, ornamental, dye plants, cosmetic plants and an area of native wild flowers to attract wildlife. The fiery herbaceous borders come into their own in July and August, while the moat walk makes for a quiet amble at any season. The peaceful fountain garden is filled with plants of a cream, white and silver theme. The newest addition is the vegetable garden.

Owned by Michael More-Molyneux
Number of gardeners 3
Size 2½ acres

Millais Nurseries

CROSSWATER FARM, CHURT, FARNHAM GU10 2JN

Tel 01252 792698
Website www.rhododendrons.co.uk
Location In Crosswater Lane, signed from Churt village
Opening hours 10 am – 1 pm & 2 pm – 5 pm; Monday – Friday. Also Saturdays in spring and autumn. And daily in May

This important and dynamic rhododendron and azalea nursery has an extensive range of species and hybrids, including some new Himalayan species, late-flowering cultivars chosen to avoid the frost, large-leaved species for sheltered gardens, scented deciduous azaleas, *R. yakushimanum* hybrids for the smaller garden, dwarf cultivars for the rock garden and *Maddenia* series rhododendrons for the conservatory. In addition to the garden (six acres, ponds, stream and companion plantings, open daily for most of May and June) there is a trials garden where hundreds of new cultivars are labelled and tested.

Munstead Wood

HEATH LANE, BUSBRIDGE, GODALMING GU7 1UN

Tel 01483 417867   **Fax** 01483 425041
Location 1 mile south of Godalming on B2130: turn along Heath Lane. Parking in field 300 yards along on left
Opening hours 2 pm – 6 pm; 8 April, 20 May & 15 July
Admission fee Adults £3; OAPs £1.50; Children free

Munstead Wood is important for being Gertrude Jekyll's own garden. Here she worked out the principles she expounded in her best-known books *Wood and Garden* (1899) and *Colour in the Flower Garden* (1908). Her garden has now been split into several smaller holdings each in separate ownership, but the main parts are still attached to the house which Lutyens designed in 1896. The wood garden is fairly intact: the views up and down its main path to and from the lawn in front of the house seem just as they were 100 years ago: birches underplanted mainly with rhododendrons and azaleas. Closer to the house is a block of borders full of good plantings – roses and herbaceous plants, in particular. The Clarks have spent many years restoring the garden: the results are admirable.

Owned by Sir Robert & Lady Clark
English Heritage grade I

Painshill Park

PORTSMOUTH ROAD, COBHAM
KT11 1JE

Tel 01932 868113   **Fax** 01932 868001
Website www.brainsys.com/cobham/painshill
Location Signed from M25 Jct10 & A3
Opening hours 10.30 am – 6 pm (last tickets 4.30 pm); Tuesday – Sunday & Bank Holiday Mondays; April to October. 11 am – 4 pm (last tickets 3 pm) Tuesday – Thursday, Saturdays & Sundays; November to March. Closed 25 & 26 December
Admission fee Adults £4.20; Concessions £3.70; Children (under 16) £1.70

Charles Hamilton was the plantsman, painter and designer who created Painshill between 1738 and 1773, when he finally went bankrupt. His lasting achievement was to transform a barren heathland into ornamental pleasure grounds and parkland of dramatic beauty. A 14-acre lake is at the centre of the design: it offers a focus for the garden's most famous features, the white gothic temple and the grotto, which is approached across a 'Chinese' bridge. Hamilton sought to provoke the greatest variety of moods: other features included a ruined abbey and a Turkish tent. Hamilton was a pioneer of the naturalistic landscape style, and very influential, but never a rich man: he leased Painshill from the Crown and had little to spend, which makes his achievement all the more remarkable. He was also a great plantsman, importing many new species from North America for his shrubberies. After 1948 the garden fell into dereliction. Over the past 20 years it has been meticulously restored and the Painshill Trust has made enormous progress in raising the substantial funds needed. The Heritage Lottery Fund is a major supporter and has grant-aided the new Visitor and Education Centre which will be completed this spring.

Plant Highlights 'American' garden; tallest *Juniperus virginiana* (26m) in the British Isles.

Owned by Painshill Park Trust
Size 158 acres
English Heritage grade I

The Palm Centre

HAM NURSERY, HAM STREET, HAM, RICHMOND TW10 7HA

Tel 020 8255 6191   **Fax** 020 8255 6192
Website www.palmcentre.co.uk
Location Near Ham House
Opening hours 9 am – 6 pm; daily; all year

The Palm Centre is a five-acre nursery with one acre of glasshouses. It specialises in hardy exotic plants, especially palms, bamboos, tree ferns, cordylines, cycads, yuccas and citrus. It lists over 400 palm species. There are two planted-out gardens, one with a good number of mature palms of several different species, which customers are encouraged to wander through.

Pantiles Plant & Garden Centre

ALMNERS ROAD, LYNE, CHERTSEY KT16 0BJ

Tel 01932 872195   **Fax** 01923 874030
Website www.pantiles-nurseries.co.uk
Location 5 mins from M25 Jct11
Opening hours 8.30 am – 5.30 pm; Monday – Saturday. 11 am – 5 pm (summer) and 10 am – 4 pm (winter) on Sundays

The nursery specialises in outsize container-grown specimens up to eight metres high. It is popular with professionals and impatient amateurs alike – anyone, in fact, in search of that instant air of maturity which a large and well-grown tree can bring. The range of specimen trees is very impressive, and includes tree ferns like *Dicksonia antarctica* as well as large specimens of yew and box, cloud-pruned in the Japanese style.

Pinewood House

HEATH HOUSE ROAD, WORPLESDON HILL, WOKING GU22 0QU

Tel 01483 473241
Location Turning off A322, opposite Brookwood cemetery wall
Opening hours Parties by appointment, April to October

Admission fee Adults £3

This is an old and well-established woodland garden of great beauty – lakes, Scots pines, rhododendrons, Bagshot sand and a great sense of peace. The house is modern – built in the late 1980s as a copy of an ancient Roman villa.

Owned by Mrs R Van Zwanenberg
Number of gardeners 1
Size 4 acres

Planta Vera

LYNE HILL NURSERY, LYNE CROSSING ROAD, CHERTSEY KT16 0AT

Tel & Fax 01932 563011
Location Map in catalogue
Opening hours 9 am – 5 pm, last weekend of month and Bank Holidays, April to October; other times by appointment

Morris May rescued Lyne Hill Nursery from a derelict state six years ago and took over Richard Cawthorne's *Viola* collection in 1995. He continues Cawthorne's work by maintaining the world's largest collection of violas (*Melanium* section): some of the collection is in display beds at the nursery. Plants are propagated from autumn cuttings ready for sale in spring. Planta Vera's business is mainly wholesale, though there is a range of herbaceous perennials available as well as the violas.

Polesden Lacey

GREAT BOOKHAM, DORKING
RH5 6BD

Tel 01372 458203 **Fax** 01372 452023
Website www.nationaltrust.org.uk
Location Off A246 between Leatherhead & Guildford
Opening hours 11 am – 6 pm (or dusk, if earlier);
daily; all year
Admission fee Adults £4

Polesden Lacy is best for the long terraced walk, laid out by Sheridan, and the return through an Edwardian-style rose garden whose pergolas drip with ramblers. But the park is good and there are fine views.

Owned by The National Trust
English Heritage grade II*

Ramster

CHIDDINGFOLD GU8 4SN

Tel 01428 654167 **Fax** 01428 658345
Location 1½ miles south of Chiddingfold on A283
Opening hours 11 am – 5 pm; daily; 14 April to 1 July.
Parties by appointment at other times
Admission fee Adults £3; Children free

Ramster was first laid out in 1890, with help from a local nursery, Gauntletts of Chiddingfold, who were well known for their interest in flowering shrubs and especially for Japanese plants and planting. From this original influence date the ornamental stone lanterns, the large plantings of bamboos, and the avenue of *Acer palmatum* var. *dissectum* seedlings, now over 100 years old. In 1922 the property was bought by Miranda Gunn's grandparents Sir Henry and Lady Norman. Lady Norman was a keen gardener, the sister of the second

Lord Aberconway, who was President of the RHS. She had been brought up at Bodnant, where she imbibed the family's great love of rhododendrons: many of the plants at Ramster came from Bodnant, and some of the rhododendrons and azaleas are her own hybrids. Ramster is an important garden for rhododendrons and, in the part known as Ant Wood, the Gunns have been building up a comprehensive collection of the old Hardy Hybrids – over 200 plants. But the garden is full of other projects and developments: the bog garden has come together very quickly since it was planted in 1998, and there is a new Millennium Garden. The garden is maintained in such a way as to allow meadow grasses, wild flowers and orchids to flourish and flower later in the year, but Ramster is essentially a garden for spring and early summer.

 Plant Highlights Mature woodland garden with magnolias, camellias, azaleas, rhododendrons; bluebells; largest *Euonymus europaeus* (6m) in the British Isles.

Owned by Mr & Mrs Paul Gunn

Rupert Bowlby

GATTON, REIGATE RH2 0TA

Tel & Fax 01737 642221
Location Near M25, Jct8
Opening hours Saturdays & Sunday afternoons;
March & September. By appointment at other times

Rupert Bowlby is a bulb specialist: his displays of narcissi, tulips, fritillaries and *Allium* species have won him many prizes at the Chelsea Flower Show. He is now concentrating upon South African bulbs – babianas, cyanellas, dieramas, freesias, *Gladiolus*, ixias, lachenalias, moraeas and tritonias.

Savill Garden

C/O CROWN ESTATE OFFICE, THE GREAT PARK, WINDSOR SL4 2HT

Tel 01753 847518   **Fax** 01753 847536
Website www.savillgarden.co.uk
Location In Wick Lane at Englefield Green, 3 miles west of Egham off the A30 & 5 miles from Windsor
Opening hours 10 am – 6 pm (4 pm from November to February); daily except 25 & 26 December
Admission fee Adults £5; OAPs £4.50; Children £2 in April & May. Less in other months

This is quite simply the finest woodland garden in England, developed since 1932 on an undulating site framed by magnificent deciduous trees. There are, in fact, several gardens here, some formal and some informal, but all are seamlessly linked together. The woodlands contain unrivalled spring plantings with masses of camellias, rhododendrons, azaleas, maples and flowering dogwoods underplanted with subtle drifts of bulbs, ferns and herbaceous plants. Recent refurbishment of the bog garden has allowed the development of stunning associations of meconopsis, primulas, astilbes, hostas and wild narcissi. The primulas have just been replanted, and come in monospecific masses, from the earliest *P. rosea* and *denticulata* through to *P. florindae* in July and August. In high summer, the rose garden and tremendous set-piece double herbaceous borders are worth a long trip to see. The nearby gravel garden is one of England's oldest and largest: parts of it have recently been replanted with a fine display of drought-tolerant plants – many of them rare – and plants which benefit from the mulching effect of the gravel. Extensive and intelligent use is made of a wide range of summer perennials in the borders and in containers. By late summer the woods are filled with hydrangeas, whose cool blues and whites are stunningly effective. Then the deciduous broad-leaved trees begin their autumn spectacle. From November to March the newly created winter beds display flowers, stems and berries in effective colour groupings. But there are many reasons to visit the Savill Garden at other times of the years – the drifts of *Narcissus bulbocodium* (second only in their splendour to the alpine meadow at Wisley) in March, for example, and the floods of lysichitons in April. The collections of maples, camellias, rhododendrons and azaleas are also exemplary. The rock garden, the cool greenhouse and the monocot border are each full of interest in due season. The guide book, the plant centre and the website are all alike excellent.

Plant Highlights Woodland garden; roses (mainly modern); plantsman's collection of plants; camellias; fine collection of trees; Kurume azaleas; mahonias; magnolias; magnificent late summer borders; tallest silver birch *Betula pendula* (30m) in the British Isles (& 13 other record trees).

Owned by Crown Property
Number of gardeners 12
Size 35 acres
NCCPG National Collections *Ilex*; *Magnolia*; *Mahonia*; *Pernettya*; *Pieris*; *Rhododendron* (species & Glen Dale azaleas); Ferns; Dwarf Conifers
English Heritage grade I

Titsey Place

OXTED RH8 0SD

Tel 01273 407056 **Fax** 01273 478995
Location Off the B269 north of Limpsfield
Opening hours 1 pm – 5 pm; Easter Monday, then on
Wednesdays, Sundays & Bank Holiday Mondays from
15 May to 30 September
Admission fee Adults £2; Children £1

The historic garden at Titsey has been well
restored with advice from Elizabeth Banks
since it first opened to the public in 1993.
The lay-out is gardenesque and most of the
plantings date from the middle of the
nineteenth century. The large triple-trunked
horse chestnut (*Aesculus hippocastanum*) on
the upper terrace dates from that time. A
stream which rises in the grounds has been
dammed to make two lakes. The formal
gardens are planted with roses and
herbaceous plants, while the old walled
kitchen garden has been completely planted
as an example of how fruit, vegetables and
flowers were grown in Victorian times.

Owned by The Trustees of the Titsey Place Foundation
Number of gardeners 5
Size 12 acres

Toobees Exotics

BLACKHORSE ROAD, WOKING
GU22 0QT

Tel 01483 797534 **Fax** 01483 751995
Location On A324 between Woking & Brookwood
Opening hours 10 am – 5 pm; Thursday – Sunday & Bank
Holiday Mondays; 12 April to 30 September. And by
appointment

Toobees are well known to visitors to RHS
London shows: they have a constant flow of
new and rare succulents from Africa and
Madagascar. These include species of
euphorbia, pachypodium, carnivorous
plants, air-plants, palms and cycads. Visitors
are always welcome to inspect the
propagation areas and the amazing display
of large stock plants. The address for
correspondence is 20 Inglewood, Woking,
Surrey GU21 3HX.

Vale End

ALBURY, GUILDFORD GU5 9BE

Tel & Fax 01483 202296
Location 500 yards west of Albury on A248
Opening hours 10 am – 5 pm; 24 June & 29 July. Plus
6 pm – 9 pm on 21 June. Groups by arrangement
Admission fee Adults £2.50; Children free. £3 on 21 June

Vale End is a modern plantsman's garden,
the best we know on Bagshot sand, where a
love of plants has not been allowed to
obscure either the design or the landscape
beyond. It is walled around, and made on
many levels, on a site that faces south-west:
the owners have taken the opportunity to
grow sun-loving and Mediterranean plants.
Daphne Foulsham is chairman of the
National Gardens Scheme and can take
much of the credit for the scheme's
exponential success in recent years.

Owned by Mr & Mrs John Foulsham
Size 1 acre

Vann

HAMBLEDON, GODALMING GU8 4EF

Tel 01428 68 3413 **Fax** 017267 9344
Location 2 miles from Chiddingfold. Signs from A283 at
Hambledon on NGS days

Valley Gardens

C/O CROWN ESTATE OFFICE, GREAT PARK, WINDSOR SL4 2HT

Tel 01753 847518   **Fax** 01753 847536
Location At Englefield Green, 5 miles from Windsor, off A30: follow signs for Savill Garden
Opening hours 8 am – 7 pm (3.30 pm in winter); daily; all year
Admission fee Car & occupants £3.50 (£5 in April & May)

This is a woodland garden on a royal scale. The Valley Garden has over 200 acres of plantings across a site of great natural beauty which falls in vast sweeps to the open expanse of Virginia Water. As in the Savill Garden, huge trees of oak, beech, sweet chestnut and Scots pine provide a magnificent framework and have been used with great sensitivity. The whole composition conveys the feeling of a flowering forest from some far-off corner of Asia. From March and April until the end of June, a succession of camellias, azaleas and rhododendrons provide an unbelievable kaleidoscope of colour, most notably in the Punch Bowl where a natural combe is filled with terrace upon terrace of brightly coloured Japanese Kurume azaleas. Giant magnolias garland themselves overhead with thousands of chalice-shaped blooms. A huge array of supporting trees, shrubs and perennials jostles for attention. Enormous groups of hydrangeas provide late summer colour, from the white foaming flowers of *H. paniculata* to the blues and pale pinks of the lacecaps and mopheads. In autumn the hillsides light up in a spectacle unrivalled this side of the Appalachian Mountains. In the nearby heather garden an old gravel pit has been transformed into a horticultural wonder to rival the Punch Bowl: ostensibly

dominated by heathers and dwarf conifers (there is a National Collection here), the garden contains unrivalled collections of exotic and native birches, whitebeams and rowans, wild roses, cotoneasters and cistus. Recent plantings have made extensive use of ornamental grasses to provide relief amongst the stolid conifers. On the next hillside is to be found the National Collection of *Rhododendron* species, brought here in the 1950s from the famous garden of Tower Court near Ascot. A sweeping valley also contains a pinetum of some note, carpeted by countless thousands of dwarf narcissi in March and April. All in all a garden of the blue stocking variety.

Owned by Crown Property
Number of gardeners 16
Size 220 acres
NCCPG National Collections *Ilex*; *Magnolia*; *Mahonia*; *Pernettya*; *Pieris*; *Rhododendron* (species & Glenn Dale azaleas); Dwarf conifers

Opening hours 10 am – 6 pm; daily; 1 to 8 & 17 to 22 April; 1 – 6 May. Also 2 pm – 6 pm on 7 May for the National Gardens Scheme

Admission fee Adults £3; Children 50p. Pre-booked groups welcome

This high-profile Jekyll garden has been well restored and meticulously maintained by the present Caroes, the third generation to live here. Start at the back of the house and move along the Arts & Crafts pergola which leads straight to the lake. This is the heart of the garden, from which five or six distinct gardens lead from one to the next and melt into the Surrey woods: among them, a yew walk, a water garden, a woodland cherry walk, a hazel coppice and a woodland garden under vast oaks. The plantings are dense and thoughtful.

Owned by Mrs Martin Caroe
English Heritage grade II

The Vernon Geranium Nursery

CUDDINGTON WAY, CHEAM, SUTTON SM2 7JB

Tel 020 8393 7616   **Fax** 020 8786 7437
Website www.geraniumuk.com
Location South-west of Cheam
Opening hours 9.30 am – 5.30 pm; Monday – Saturday. 10 am – 4 pm; Sundays. March to July

As it names indicates, this is a specialist pelargonium nursery. The number of pelargonium cultivars here speaks for itself – over 1,100 doubles and semi- doubles, Deacons, stellars, rosebuds, finger-flowered, fancy-leaved, speckled, uniques, dwarfs, miniatures, angels and regals – the list seems

endless. Guided tours are given daily at 11 am and 2.30 pm between 14 and 29 July.

Winkworth Arboretum

HASCOMBE ROAD, GODALMING GU8 4AD

Tel 01483 208477
Website www.nationaltrust.org.uk
Location 2 miles south-east of Godalming, off B2130
Opening hours All year; dawn – dusk. Groups *must* pre-book in writing
Admission fee Adults £3.50

Winkworth is a true arboretum in the sense that it has a large collection of full-sized trees – as many taxa as possible – planted liberally over a large area. Many of the plantings are now in their prime. The acres of red oak (*Quercus coccinea*), *Nyssa sylvestris* and *Liquidamber styraciflua* are quite spectacular in autumn.

Plant Highlights Woodland garden; fine collection of trees; bluebells; wood anemones; autumn colour; tallest *Acer davidii* (19m) in the British Isles, and 5 further record trees.

Owned by The National Trust

NCCPG National Collections *Sorbus* (Aria & Micromeles groups)

RHS Garden Wisley

WOKING GU23 6QB

Tel 01483 224234 **Fax** 01483 211750
Location Near M25 Jct10
Opening hours 10 am (but 9 am at weekends) – 6 pm;
daily; all year except Christmas Day. Sundays from March
to October reserved for RHS members and their guests
only. Closes at 4.30 pm from November to February. Last
admissions 30 mins before closing
Admission fee Adults £5; Children £2. Discounts for
groups (pre-booked 21 days) – ring 01483 212307

Wisley is the most important horticultural demonstration garden in Europe – perhaps the world. It has many incidents of great intrinsic value – the vast Pulhamite rock garden which fills an entire hillside, for example – but its true worth lies in its comprehensiveness: everything that a gardener could possibly want to see and learn from is here within its 200 acres. The only problem is its very size: Wisley is not a garden you could ever hope to get round properly in just a day, let alone a few hours. It is somewhere to explore over many visits at different times of the year, until the layout and the principal features become familiar and you learn where you should go to see what is good and instructive at the time of your visit.

The Royal Horticultural Society moved its experimental garden from Chiswick in 1903 when Sir Thomas Hanbury bought the Wisley estate and gave it to the Society for 'the encouragement and improvement of the science and practice of horticulture in all its branches.' Wisley was then in a remote part of Surrey with no public transport to serve it. The move would not have been possible without the invention of the motor car: 6,000 Fellows (as members were then called) visited it during its first twelve months. Now

more than 700,000 visitors come to the garden every year. Wisley was unashamedly a trials garden where the Society practised the perfect cultivation of every type of plant that could be grown in the British Isles from alpines to hothouse orchids, whether in the open ground or in artificial conditions. This was backed up – then, as now – by an important system of trials which grew, tested, examined and made awards to flowers, fruit and vegetables. Those trials remain one of the garden's most important activities. Wisley was, above all, conceived as a scientific garden: to this day, the main building which dominates the formal garden near the entrance is known as the laboratory and contains scientific and administrative offices.

Sir Simon Hornby describes Wisley as 'a garden to delight, instruct and inspire.' His assertion is true at every time of the year. For many visitors the pulling power of Wisley is greatest in the short, dark days of winter. That is the time when such plants as cyclamen and narcissi fill the alpine pan house: there is always colour and flower-power here because suitable pots are brought from the growing-frames and plunged into its sandy benches specifically to maintain the display through every week of the year. In the landscaped alpine house, too, there is much of interest even in deep mid-winter. The main glasshouses certainly come into their own in winter. The display range has three sections – cool, warm and hot. Each is landscaped and supports a large number of plants growing in the soil that are suitable for greenhouses and conservatories at home. Sometimes the seasonal display is augmented by pots brought from the growing areas behind and placed on the benches: 'Charm' and 'Cascade' chrysanthemums in November, for example. There are many other houses open to visitors: the orchid collections and the cacti house are among the most popular.

Wisley really begins to come into its own in spring. The alpine meadow is the best of its kind anywhere in Britain: from about the middle of March onwards, for at least four weeks, it is completely carpeted with hoop-petticoat narcissi (forms of *N. bulbocodium*). Clearly the conditions and the regime of cultivation suit them, because the narcissi continue to spread and increase every year. In September, the same meadows are thick with autumn-flowering crocus. Beyond them is the Pulhamite rock garden, constructed in 1911–12 which is probably the finest in Britain. It does not provide the variety of habitats which more modern rock gardens offer, but it is a majestic and beautiful construction. It covers the whole hillside from the 'monocot border' (full of such plants as agapanthus, daylilies, amaryllis, nerines and kniphofias – best in late summer) at the top to the stream at the bottom of the valley, whose margins are thick with such plants as *Lobelia cardinalis* and lysichitons. Beyond is an area of light woodland where magnolias and tall rhododendrons give shelter to such woodlanders as meconopsis, hellebores and snowdrops and huge patches of candelabra primulas.

By late spring, one of the best areas is Battleston Hill, the highest point in the gardens, where winding paths take you through a beautifully laid out woodland garden underplanted with rhododendrons, azaleas, magnolias and camellias. Crocus in late winter, lilies in high summer and colchicums in autumn extend the season so that this is always an area of colour and interest. Here, and throughout the garden, are many unusual rare and interesting plants which add so much to the horticultural quality of Wisley. Also on Battleston Hill is a 'Mediterranean' garden where an extensive collection of plants with a reputation for tenderness shows what can be grown successfully on light, well-drained soil where trees provide shelter and frost rolls away downhill.

Wisley has a fine collection of roses, from such rare and tender species as the plant of *R. gigantea* on the wall of the laboratory to the massed ranks of modern roses which fill the beds around the Bowes-Lyon pavilion and in behind the mixed borders. Wisley is, in short, one of the best places in Britain to see roses of every sort, including some which are not seen elsewhere in English gardens open to the public. The mixed borders also come into their own from midsummer onwards: there are two of them, and they face each other on either side of the broad, grass ride which leads up to Battleston Hill. These borders are 140 yards long, backed by beech hedges and have a light framework of shrubs as a background for deep plantings of all the traditional perennials of the English herbaceous border.

Wisley has many other areas dedicated to the cultivation and display of particular plants. The pinetum is one example – an under-visited area of stately conifers, some of them record-breakers and all of them interesting at every season. The heather garden in Howard's Field is another dedicated garden with probably the best collection of heathers in England. The fruit fields too are a part of the garden that far too few venture into: over 1,400 cultivars of top, bush and soft fruit are grown here. The Society has been associated with the cultivation of fruit ever since its foundation in 1804, and displays of Wisley fruit have long been a feature of RHS London shows.

Wisley has its formal gardens too. These centre upon the long rectangular canal in front of the laboratory and the walled gardens beyond. Designed by Geoffrey Jellicoe and Lanning Roper, the canal is a formal setting for water lilies while the walled enclosures have spectacular summer and winter bedding displays. Rare and tender climbers cover their walls. Formal in a different sense are the model gardens which seem to grow and develop every year. The first were model fruit gardens, which showed people how to grow a great variety of fruit (and grow it *well*) in a small area. Nearby are model vegetable and herb gardens, now supplemented by many ornamental model gardens, which serve the same function – to show visitors what may be achieved in their own gardens. There have been several new developments in this area recently – part of the gardens' rolling programme of development. New last year was a country garden by Penelope Hobhouse, and the loan of some fine garden sculpture on Battleston Hill.

For many people, one of the most fascinating areas is the main Trials area in Portsmouth Field – over the brow of Battleston Hill and down towards the furthest boundary with the old Portsmouth road. This is where the Royal Horticultural Society runs most of its trials (some temporary and some permanent) of a very wide selection of annuals, perennials, shrubs, bulbs, fruit and vegetables. Trials of woody plants take place nearby at Deers Farm. The permanent trials are conducted (among others) with border carnations, chrysanthemums, daffodils, dahlias, daylilies, delphiniums, garden pinks, irises and sweet peas. These trials continue from year to year with periodic replanting, at which time additions and removals are made. They are of exceptional interest to visitors, and often of remarkable beauty too. There can be few horticultural experiences more exciting than to walk through the massed ranks of thickly planted delphiniums

or sweet peas that tower in over you in July or August.

The trials grounds are perhaps one of the main reasons why Wisley is so highly regarded by visitors, gardeners and professionals alike. The greatest testimonial to the importance of Wisley comes from the many specialist plant societies we have consulted in the course of writing *The RHS Garden Finder*. Time and again, when we asked them where the best collections of their special flowers could be seen – heathers, gladioli, delphiniums and dianthus among them – the list of gardens ended with the note 'and Wisley, of course'. It really is a garden to return to regularly to refresh one's appreciation, to see how plants can be grown and to learn something new. The plant centre at Wisley is also exceptionally good, especially as a source of rare and new plants.

Plant Highlights Woodland garden; snowdrops; roses (ancient & modern); rock garden; plantsman's collection of plants; plants under glass; fruit; mature conifers; good herbaceous borders; fine collection of trees; heather garden; herb garden; horticultural trials; vegetable gardens; tallest *Oystrya virginiana* (15.5m) in the British Isles, and 19 further record trees.

Owned by The Royal Horticultural Society
Number of gardeners 79
Size 240 acres
NCCPG National Collections *Calluna vulgaris; Crocus; Daboecia; Epimedium; Erica; Galanthus; Rheum*
English Heritage grade II*

SUSSEX, EAST

The two historic gardens in East Sussex which English Heritage has rated Grade I could not be more different – Great Dixter and Sheffield Park. Yet they have one thing in common which is typical of East Sussex gardens generally – they are gardens whose historic features have been overlaid with plants. Few of the other historic gardens in the county are open to the public, but garden-visitors are almost spoiled for choice. Every corner of East Sussex seems to brim with good modern gardens – those like Pashley Manor and Merriments have been widely recognised for their beauty and invention – and good collections of trees like those at Sheffield Park and Stanmer Park, near Brighton. The National Gardens Scheme does well in East Sussex, especially in the area around Crowborough where there are many medium-sized gardens to see. Nurseries, too, are good and fairly plentiful: some of the best are attached to gardens, like Great Dixter, or have a fine display garden attached to them, like Merriments. There are comparatively few National Collections: one of the most interesting is the collection of lilacs (*Syringa* cvs.) kept by the City of Brighton & Hove parks department. Members of the Royal Horticultural Society have free access to Sheffield Park throughout the year.

Bateman's

BURWASH, ETCHINGHAM TN19 7DS

Tel 01435 882302   **Fax** 01435 882811
Website www.nationaltrust.org.uk
Location Signed at west end of village
Opening hours 11 am – 5.30 pm; Saturday – Wednesday; 3 March to 4 November
Admission fee Adults £5; Children £2.50

These ten acres on the banks of the River Dudwell were Rudyard Kipling's home from 1902 until his death in 1936. The garden is fun for children, because there is a working flour mill, but not spectacular for the knowledgeable gardener, except for the *Campis grandiflora* on the house.

Owned by The National Trust
English Heritage grade II

Bates Green Farm

ARLINGTON, POLEGATE BN26 6SH

Tel & Fax 01323 482039
Location 3 miles south-west of Hailsham
Opening hours 10.30 am – 6 pm; 2, 9 & 16 April for National Gardens Scheme. And by appointment
Admission fee Adults £2; Children free

Made by the present owners since the mid-1970s, the garden at Bates Green Farm has several different areas: a large rock garden, a shady garden, and wonderful mixed borders planted for year-round colour associations. The owners seek perfection, but wonder if they will ever achieve it.

Owned by Mr & Mrs J R McCutchan
Size 2 acres

Brickwall House & Gardens

FREWEN COLLEGE, NORTHIAM TN31 6NL

Tel 01797 252001
Location Off B2088
Opening hours 2 pm – 4.30 pm; Bank Holidays. Plus Wednesdays in school holidays. And by appointment for groups (01797 253388)
Admission fee £3.50

This important historic garden, with seventeenth-century features which were re-worked in the nineteenth, has recently been re-designed as a Stuart garden, to match the house. Brickwall now has borders planted exclusively with old fashioned plants and a chess garden where green and yellow yew shapes are grown in squares of black or white chips. The bluebells in the arboretum are magnificent.

Plant Highlights Topiary; herbs; good herbaceous borders; fine collection of trees; bluebells; extensively redesigned since 1980.

Owned by Frewen Educational Trust
English Heritage grade II*

Cabbages & Kings Garden

WILDERNESS FARM, WILDERNESS LANE, HADLOW DOWN TN22 4HU

Tel 01825 830552   **Fax** 01825 830736
Location ½ mile south of A272
Opening hours 10.30 am – 5.30 pm; Thursday – Monday; Easter – October
Admission fee Adults £4; Concessions £3.50. RHS members free in September & October

Subtitled 'The Centre for Garden Design', this is the show garden of a leading modern garden designer. It is conceived as a series of interlinking garden-rooms, terraces and incidents, lushly and vividly planted. The idea is to give visitors lots of ideas for their own gardens – how to transform them, how to create garden rooms, and how to design sitting areas, features and focal points.

Owned by Andrew & Ryl Nowell

Clinton Lodge

FLETCHING, UCKFIELD TN22 3ST

Tel 01825 722952   **Fax** 01825 723967
Location In main village street
Opening hours 2 pm – 5.30 pm; 10, 11 & 20 June, 4 July & 1 August
Admission fee Adults £3; Children £2

Clinton Lodge is a rising star among new gardens, designed round a handsome seventeenth-century house. There are formal gardens of different periods, starting with a 'mediaeval' *potager* and an Elizabethan-style herb garden. The most successful parts are the pre-Raphaelite walk of lilies and pale roses, and the Victorian-

Great Dixter

DIXTER ROAD, NORTHIAM TN31 6PH

Tel 01797 252878   **Fax** 01797 252879
Location Off A28 at Northiam Post Office
Opening hours 2 pm – 5 pm; Tuesday – Sunday; April to October, plus Bank Holiday Mondays. Open at 11 am on Sundays & Mondays of Bank Holiday weekends
Admission fee Adults £4.50; Children £1

Christopher Lloyd's father Nathaniel bought Great Dixter in 1910: Lutyens did a conversion job on the house and laid out part of the gardens. Most of the brickwork, yew hedges, steps, walls, doorways and arts-and-crafts details date back to the original design – contemporary with Hidcote and earlier than Sissinghurst. The topiary was Nathaniel Lloyd's contribution – he wrote a book about it. But the main reason for the garden's pre-eminent reputation is the decades of horticultural skill which 'Christo' Lloyd himself has put into its planting. He is a knowledgeable plantsman who once taught horticulture at Wye College and has a remarkable eye for combining plants in harmonious groupings throughout the year. His books – especially the compilation of articles from *Country Life* published *as The Well-Tempered Garden* – have been popular and influential, so that the Lloyd style of planting and maintaining a garden is probably more widely copied now than any other. The heart of the garden is the Long Border, about seventy yards long and five yards deep, which has become a showcase and trial ground for his experiments. It is a series of compositions loosely strung together with a wide variety of weaving colours, heights and textures but kept together as much by good foliage as by flowers. Every section of it teaches you something new that could be made to work

in your own garden. One of Lloyd's strengths is his fondness for change – his desire to refine and improve his garden all the time. He was one of the first garden-owners to use lots of annuals and tender perennials to extend the summer season right through into autumn. He shocked the country's rosarians by replacing his parents' collection of old-fashioned roses with a late-summer explosion of dahlias, cannas and exotic foliage. And no-one has practised the gentle, patient art of long-term meadow-gardening so successfully as Christopher Lloyd: indeed, he has written so eloquently and prolifically about the principles and practices of meadow gardening that, even if he had never penned a word on any other aspect of ornamental horticulture, he would be established as a great apostle of this charming and relaxed art form which he sometimes refers to as 'tapestry gardening'. Visiting Great Dixter should be a compulsory part of every gardener's ongoing education.

Owned by Christopher Lloyd & Olivia Eller
Number of gardeners 5
Size 5 acres
English Heritage grade I

style herbaceous borders in soft pastel shades. New for 2001 are a canal garden and an *allée* of fastigiate hornbeams.

Owned by Mr & Mrs M R Collum
Number of gardeners 1½
Size 6 acres

Cobblers

MOUNT PLEASANT, JARVIS BROOK, CROWBOROUGH TN6 2ND

Tel 01892 655969
Location Turn off B2100 into Tollwood Road: ¼ mile on right
Opening hours For National Gardens Scheme

Tightly planned and beautifully planted, this garden down a narrow leafy lane has been made in an old apple-orchard by a retired architect who is also a plantsman. There is a great variety of habitats and plants (bog, alpine, hot-coloured, shade-loving etc.) within a design which opens out its perspectives slowly.

Owned by Mr & Mrs Martin Furniss
Size 2 acres

Merriments Gardens

HAWKHURST ROAD, HURST GREEN TN19 7RA

Tel 01580 860666 **Fax** 01580 860324
Website www.merriments.co.uk
Location On A229
Opening hours 9.30 am – 5.30 pm; daily; 1 April to mid-October
Admission fee Adults £3.50; Children £2

The gardens at this nursery are young – started in 1991 on a bare clay field – but the tail is already wagging the dog. Four remarkable acres of imaginative design and striking planting are kept meticulously tidy. The planting has been chosen so that each area blends seamlessly into the next and creates a satisfying and harmonious whole. The deep sweeping borders are designed and planted to combine colour, form and texture in endlessly imaginative planting schemes. The features include a Monet garden, foliage borders, two ponds, a border for spring, several borders designed to peak in summer and autumn, a blue garden – and dozens more. Recent developments include a dry area which has been transformed into a Mediterranean-inspired scree garden and a waterlogged area which has been turned into a bog garden and planted with moisture-loving plants. The nursery is good, too.

Owned by The Weeks & Buchele families
Size 4 acres

Michelham Priory

UPPER DICKER, HAILSHAM BN27 3QS

Tel 01323 844224 **Fax** 01323 844030
Website www.sussexpast.co.uk
Location Signed from A22 & A27
Opening hours 10.30 am – 4 pm; Wednesday – Sunday; 14 to 31 March & 1 to 28 October. 10.30 am – 5 pm; Wednesday – Sunday; April – July & September; 10.30 am – 5.30 pm; daily; August
Admission fee Adults £4.70; OAPs £4; Children £2.30

The old Augustinian priory has an Elizabethan barn, a blacksmith shop, a rope museum and a moat. Within the garden are several distinct areas, including a physic garden and cloister garden, with mediaeval plantings (faithful, if a little dull), some very good borders, a bog garden, a kitchen garden and several wildflower areas. It all makes for an enjoyable visit, highly educational for children and interesting for parents too.

Owned by The Sussex Archaeological Society
Size 7 acres

Moorlands

FRIARS GATE, CROWBOROUGH TN6 1XF

Tel 01892 652474
Location 2 miles north of Crowborough, off B2188
Opening hours 11 am – 5 m; Wednesdays; 1 April to 1 October. Plus 20 May & 15 July, and by appointment
Admission fee Adults £2.50; Children free

The garden at Moorlands was begun by Dr Smith's parents in 1929: Dr Smith took over in 1974, made a lake and a pond, and planted a lot of woodland and bog-loving plants. The garden now combines mature trees with modern herbaceous plantings. By the house, on a sloping site, is a long herbaceous border. This leads to the stream, red with iron ore but clean enough for trout and protected enough for kingfishers. Moorlands is a plantsman's garden of fine trees, rhododendrons and collectors' shrubs, underplanted with bog plants as well as wild flowers such as native daffodils (*Narcissus pseudonarcissus*) and orchids.

Owned by Dr & Mrs Steven Smith
Number of gardeners 4 part-time
Size 4 acres

Paradise Park

AVIS ROAD, NEWHAVEN BN9 0DH

Tel 01273 512123   **Fax** 01273 616005
Website www.paradisepark.co.uk
Location Signed from A26 & A259
Opening hours 10 am – 6 pm (but 5.30 pm in winter); daily; all year except 1 January & 25 December
Admission fee Adults £4.25; OAPs & Children £3.99

Part of a leisure complex attached to a garden centre, the most interesting features are a tropical house and a cactus house, each landscaped with handsome plant collections chosen for display. There are some imaginative garden designs – Caribbean, seaside, desert, oriental and rainforest gardens, for example. It is a haven in winter, and the outside gardens are a pleasure to explore in summer. They contain a Sussex history trail – beautiful models of important historic buildings in the county, each in a different setting.

Owned by Jonathan Tate

Pashley Manor Garden

TICEHURST, WADHURST TN5 7NE

Tel 01580 200888   **Fax** 01580 200102
Location On B2099 between A21 & Ticehurst
Opening hours 11 am – 5 pm; Tuesday – Thursday, Saturday & Bank Holiday Mondays; 7 April to 29 September
Admission fee Adults £5; OAPs & Children £4.50

A new/old garden, made or remade in the Victorian style over the last ten years with advice from Tony Pasley. The results are gentle shapes, spacious expanses, harmonious colours and solid plantings. It gets better every year.

Plant Highlights Roses (mainly old-fashioned & climbers); mature conifers; Victorian shrubberies; hydrangeas; irises; new late-summer herbaceous borders (1998); new plantings in water & bog gardens (1999); HHA/Christie's Garden of the Year in 2000.

Owned by James A Sellick
Number of gardeners 5
Size 12 acres

Rotherview Nursery with Coghurst Camellias

IVY HOUSE LANE, THREE OAKS, HASTINGS TN35 4NP

Tel 01424 756228   **Fax** 01424 428944
Location Follow brown tourist signs to Coghurst Hall Holiday Village (next door)
Opening hours 9 am – 5 pm; daily; March to October. 10 am – 4 pm; daily; November to February

Rotherview Nursery with Coghurst Camellias is an inter-nursery hybrid – two specialist nurseries recently combined on one site. Rotherview produces a wide range of alpines and perennials (especially hardy ferns) whilst Coghurst has a list of over 200 camellias, including the autumn-flowering *C. sasanqua* cultivars. Both nurseries have been regular exhibitors at RHS Flower Shows. The list of camellias is being expanded and the garden is already much improved, with raised beds for Rotherview's alpines and an area of trough gardens, as well as a camellia walk.

Sheffield Park

UCKFIELD TN22 3QX

Tel 01825 790231   **Fax** 01825 791264
Website www.nationaltrust.org.uk
Location Between East Grinstead & Lewes on A275
Opening hours 10.30 am – 4 pm; Saturdays & Sundays; January & February. 10.30 am – 6 pm; Tuesday – Sunday plus Bank Holidays; March to October. 10.30 am – 4 pm; Tuesday – Sunday; November & December
Admission fee Adults £4.60; Children £2.30. RHS members free

Sheffield Park (managed by the National Trust) is a beautiful 120-acre garden with four lakes linked by cascades and waterfalls. These were laid out in the eighteenth century by Capability Brown and Humphry Repton. The result is landscaping on the grandest of scales, though the lakes now reflect the twentieth-century plantings of exotics. Carpeted with daffodils and bluebells in spring, its rhododendrons, azaleas and stream garden are spectacular in early summer. In autumn, the garden is ablaze with wonderful leaf colours, and long beds of gentians. But the collection of rare trees and shrubs makes it a fascinating visit at any time of year.

 Plant Highlights Mature conifers; fine collection of trees; bluebells; daffodils; kalmias; autumn crocuses; rhododendrons; tallest *Nyssa sylvatica* (21m) in the British Isles, plus two other record tees.

Owned by The National Trust
Size 120 acres
NCCPG National Collections *Rhododendron* (Ghent azaleas)
English Heritage grade I

Standen

EAST GRINSTEAD RH19 4NE

Tel 01342 323029 **Fax** 01342 316424
Website www.nationaltrust.org.uk
Location 2 miles south of East Grinstead, signed from B2110
Opening hours 11 am – 6 pm;
Wednesday – Sunday & Bank Holiday Mondays;
28 March to 4 November. 11 am – 3 pm; Friday
– Sunday; 9 November to 16 December

Admission fee Adults £3

(P) (WC) (❀) (🏠) (☕)

This Edwardian garden has magnificent views across the valley. A series of enclosed gardens around and below the house gives way to woodland slopes and an old quarry furnished with ferns. Parts are rather overgrown, but there is much to trigger the imagination here.

Owned by The National Trust

SUSSEX, WEST

West Sussex is even better endowed with fine gardens and interesting nurseries than East Sussex. All five Grade I gardens are open to the public – Goodwood, Leonardslee, Parham, Petworth House and Stansted Park – though only Leonardslee and Parham are of great horticultural interest. However there is also a glut of Grade II* gardens open to the public, and all of them chiefly of importance for their plant collections – Borde Hill, Cowdray, Gravetye, Highdown, Nymans, High Beeches, Wakehurst and West Dean. These are matched by a great number of good medium-sized gardens which open for the National Gardens Scheme and a large number of good nurseries and garden centres. Apuldram Roses, Architectural Plants, Coghurst Camellias (now part of Rotherview Nursery), Croftway and Ingwersens are all nurseries of national or international status and often seen at RHS Flower Shows. The NCCPG has a good number of National Collections in the county. Borde Hill and Nymans offer free access to RHS members, though Borde Hill extends this privilege only in September and October. The old county horticultural society at Brinsbury is a RHS Partner College with a series of public lectures, demonstrations and workshops throughout the year: details from 020 7821 3408.

Apuldram Roses

APULDRAM LANE, DELL QUAY,
CHICHESTER PO20 7EF

Tel 01243 785769 **Fax** 01243 536973
Location 1 mile south-west of Chichester
Opening hours 9 am – 5 pm; Monday – Saturday;
daily, except for Christmas & New Year period.
10.30 am – 4.30 pm on Sundays and Bank Holidays

Apuldram sells a mixed range of mainly modern roses – about 300 cultivars. Most can be seen in the pretty display garden. The nursery has an annual pruning week in March.

Architectural Plants

COOKS FARM, NUTHURST, HORSHAM
RH13 6LH

Tel 01403 891772 **Fax** 01403 891056
Website www.architecturalplants.com
Location 3 miles south of Horsham, behind the Black
Horse pub in Nuthurst
Opening hours 9 am – 5 pm; Monday – Saturday

Somewhat out of the ordinary: Architectural Plants specialises in exotic-looking, evergreen foliage plants, often with architectural or sculptural shapes. 'Architectural' means that the plants themselves have their own architecture – strong, sometimes spectacular, shapes which bring a distinctive year-round presence to a garden. Examples include eucalyptus, bamboos, hardy palms, hardy bananas and evergreen magnolias. Larger specimens are available for immediate impact, and they deliver anywhere. The display area around the nursery is stylishly laid out and a pleasure to visit in its own right. The nursery also has a branch at Lidsey Road, Woodgate, near Chichester: it has phillyreas, arbutus and seaside exotics, but no display garden.

Borde Hill Garden

HAYWARDS HEATH RH16 1XP

Tel 01444 450326   **Fax** 01444 440427
Website www.bordehill.co.uk
Location 1½ miles north of Haywards Heath
Opening hours 10 am – 6 pm (or dusk); daily; all year
Admission fee Adults £5; OAPs £4.5; Children £2.50. RHS members free in September & October

This important woodland garden has been significantly developed and improved in recent years. It was originally planted in the early 1900s with exotic trees and a large collection of rhododendron species grown from such introducers as Forrest and Kingdon Ward. Some of those trees are now record-breakers, including a rare Chinese tulip tree (*Liriodendron chinense*) now 19m tall, a Greek beech (*Fagus orientalis*) of the same height, and a splendid *Pinus muricata* now 31m high. The garden has recently been substantially re-developed for the recreation market and is all the better for the new capital. The gardens surrounding the house are divided into 'rooms'. These include the Garden of Allah with a new (1999) wildlife pool; a ring of Knap Hill azaleas backed by rhododendrons from Farrer and Cox's

expedition to Burma and China in 1919; the newly-restored Victorian greenhouses, one of which is a peach house and another devoted to South African plants; a new Mediterranean garden designed by Robin Williams; a new rose garden planted mainly with David Austin roses; the Italian garden and two dells with *Trachycarpus* palms. The garden also has all sorts of family-friendly facilities like an adventure playground and a smart restaurant.

Plant Highlights Woodland garden; plantsman's collection of plants; fine collection of trees; rhododendrons; azaleas; magnolias; plants from original seed; new Italian Garden made with Lottery money (1999); Victorian greenhouses restored (1999); 48 different record trees, one of the largest collections in the British Isles.

Owned by Borde Hill Garden Ltd
Number of gardeners 5
Size 11 acres, plus 200 acres of parkland
English Heritage grade II*

Champs Hill

COLDWALTHAM, PULBOROUGH RH20 1LY

Tel 01789 831868   **Fax** 01789 831536
Location West of Coldwatham, on road to Fittleworth
Opening hours 11 am – 4 pm on Wednesdays & 2 pm – 6 pm on Sundays. 11,14,18, 21 & 25 March; 2, 9, 13 & 16 May; 5, 8, 12, 15 &19 August
Admission fee Adults £2.50; Children free

This garden has been developed around three disused sand-quarries since 1960. The woodlands are full of beautiful rhododendrons and azaleas, but the most striking feature is the collection of heathers – over 300 cultivars – interplanted with dwarf conifers. The garden also has some interesting sculptures, and stupendous views.

Owned by Mr & Mrs David Bowerman
Size 27 acres, including woodland

Coates Manor

FITTLEWORTH, PULBOROUGH
RH20 1ES

Tel 01798 865356
Location ½ mile off B2138, signed Coates
Opening hours 11 am – 5 pm; 14 October for autumn colour, and by appointment at other times
Admission fee Adults £1.50; Children 20p

Coates Manor has a small, neatly designed and intensely planted garden which crams a lifetime's learning into its plantings. Long-term colour effects are its outstanding quality: leaves, berries, trunks, stems, form, shadow and texture are all individually exploited to the maximum. This garden is a model of its kind, and beautifully maintained.

Owned by Mrs S M Thorp
Number of gardeners 1
Size 1 acre

Cooke's House

WEST BURTON, PULBOROUGH
RH20 1HD

Tel 01798 831353
Location Turn off A29 by White Horse at foot of Bury Hill
Opening hours 1 pm – 5 pm; 13 to 20 May. And by appointment
Admission fee Adults £1.50; Children free

This neat and well-maintained garden has a series of small enclosed gardens first planted

about 100 years ago by Leonard Borwick, a friend of Gertrude Jekyll. It is very pretty in spring, when the primulas and bulbs are out, and even better at midsummer when the roses and herbaceous plants crammed into the garden rooms create a sense of great richness and harmony.

Owned by Miss J B Courtauld
Number of gardeners 2
English Heritage grade II

Cowdray Park

MIDHURST GU29 0AQ

Tel 01730 812461   **Fax** 01730 812122
Location South of A272, 1 mile east of Midhurst
Opening hours 11 am – 5 pm on 20 May; 2 pm – 5 pm on 9 September
Admission fee Adults £2.50; Children free

Cowdray is seldom open, but worth a long journey to see the ornate house and its contemporary (100-year-old) collection of trees, particularly conifers – don't miss the avenue of wellingtonias up at the top. Some are now record-breakers, and the sweeps of rhododendrons and azaleas, especially the hardy hybrids down 'the dell', are on the grand scale too. There are also two lakes, waterfalls, wild flower areas and a lot of new planting.

Plant Highlights 300-year-old Lebanon cedar; wellingtonia avenue; rhododendrons; new lake (1998); new themes herbaceous border (1999); new collection of trees; grapes & fruit in the glasshouses; valley garden; tallest *Abies concolor* f. *violacea* (28m) and *Chamaecyparis pisifera* (29m) in the UK.

Owned by Viscount & Viscountess Cowdray
English Heritage grade II*

Croftway Nursery

YAPTON ROAD, BARNHAM, BOGNOR
REGIS PO22 0BQ

Tel 01243 552121   **Fax** 01243 552125
Website www.croftway.co.uk
Location Between Yapton & Barnham, on B2233
Opening hours 9 am – 5 pm; daily. Closed December to
February

There has been a nursery on the site of
Croftway for many years: *Monarda* 'Croftway
Pink' was raised here in the 1930s. The
present owners have been in business – it is
a *family* business – since 1988. Their most
important specialities are irises and hardy
geraniums – they think very highly of the
geraniums which Alan Bremner breeds in
Orkney – but they are also good for other
herbaceous perennials. They have a wide
choice of achilleas, astrantias, crocosmias,
daylilies, hostas, nepetas, penstemons,
phlox, salvias, and other labiates. The show
garden is excellent – there are many new
plants on trial there.

Denmans

FONTWELL, ARUNDEL BN18 0SU

Tel 01243 542808   **Fax** 01243 544064
Website www.denmans-garden.co.uk
Location Off A29 or A27, near Fontwell racecourse
Opening hours 9 am – 5 pm; daily; March to October.
Or by appointment
Admission fee Adults £2.95; OAPs £2.65;
Children (over 5) £1.75

This modern garden is a showpiece for John
Brookes's ideas and commitment to easy
care. He uses foliage, gravel mulches,
contrasts of form, coloured stems, winter
bark and plants as elements of design. The
garden's design is so fluid that you feel
carried along by its momentum and, of
course, it is a brilliant source of ideas for
your own garden.

Size 4 acres

Floraldene

FINDON ROAD, WORTHING
BN14 0BW

Tel 01903 261231
Location West side on Findon Road, next to Durrington
Cemetery
Opening hours For local charities in March, August
& September
Admission fee free

This garden is particularly good for heathers
– hundreds of different cultivars grown in a
small garden by a true devotee.

Owned by John Tucker
Number of gardeners owner
Size ½ acre

Gravetye Manor Hotel

EAST GRINSTEAD RH19 4LJ

Tel 01342 810567   **Fax** 01342 810080
Location 4 miles south-west of East Grinstead
Opening hours Hotel & restaurant guests only; all year.
The perimeter path is open to the public free of charge
from 10 am to 5 pm on Tuesdays & Fridays

Gravetye is William Robinson's own garden,
very influential about 100 years ago, and
scrupulously maintained by Peter Herbert as
it was in its prime. It was here that Robinson
put into practice the natural style of

gardening which he promoted so vigorously in his magazines and books. Robinson's own original woodland garden has many of the trees he planted – fine davidias and nyssas, for example. And the meadows below the house are planted with naturalised bulbs in the style that Robinson made popular through his writings. Gravetye is still a garden to learn from: there is much to admire and copy.

Owned by Peter Herbert
Number of gardeners 4
Size 30 acres
English Heritage grade II*

High Beeches

HANDCROSS RH17 6HQ

Tel 01444 400589   **Fax** 01444 401543
Website www.highbeeches.com
Location South of B2110, 1 mile east of M23 at Handcross
Opening hours 1 pm – 5 pm; daily, except Wednesdays; 24 March to 30 June, September & October. Plus Sunday to Tuesday in July & August
Admission fee Adults £4. Reductions for groups of 30+. Coaches by appointment

One of the best of the famous Sussex woodland gardens, High Beeches was originally part of a Loder garden, since sold and split up. It was acquired by the Boscawens in 1966 who have devoted many years to its maintenance and improvement. The original woodland was thinned and underplanted with exotics. Some are trees like nyssas, magnolias, davidias and *Tetracentron sinense*; others are shrubs – there is a 'Loderi Walk' planted with *Rhododendron × loderi* cultivars. A valley of ponds and woodland glades is beautifully planted with splendid rhododendrons, azaleas, and camellias for spring, but the garden has wonderful autumn

colours too, and a policy of letting good plants naturalise – wild orchids, willow gentians and *Primula helodoxa*.

 Plant Highlights Woodland garden; plantsman's collection of plants; mature conifers; fine collection of trees; rhododendrons; five-acre natural wildflower meadow; tallest *Stuartia monodelpha* (11m) in the British Isles.

Owned by High Beeches Gardens Conservation Trust
Number of gardeners 2
Size 25 acres
NCCPG National Collections Stewartia
English Heritage grade II*

Highdown

LITTLEHAMPTON ROAD,
GORING-BY-SEA BN12 6NY

Tel 01903 239999 ext 2539   **Fax** 01903 821384
Location Signed from A259
Opening hours 10 am – 6 pm (4.30 pm in February, March, October & November, and 4 pm in January & December); daily (but not weekends from October to March); all year
Admission fee free – donations welcome

This is the most famous garden to be made on chalk, and one of the best. It was actually laid out in a disused chalk quarry and on the surrounding, south-facing downland. Its maker, Sir Frederick Stern, was determined to try anything that might grow in these unusual conditions. Eighty years on, the results are some handsome trees, vigorous roses, and long-forgotten peony hybrids. The gardens are designed on a large grid and planted mainly as mixed borders. Mediterranean plants do especially well: hellebores, tulips, daffodils and anemones have naturalised over large areas. Stern was a fine plantsman and scholar, and wrote the classic

Leonardslee Gardens

LOWER BEEDING, HORSHAM RH13 6PP

Tel 01403 891212 **Fax** 01403 891305
Location 4 miles south-west of Handcross at Jct of B2110 & A281
Opening hours 9.30 am – 6 pm; daily; April to October
Admission fee Adults £5, but £6 on week-days & £7 at weekends in May; Children £3 at all times

Leonardslee is a plantsman's garden on an enormous scale: it was begun in 1889 by Sir Edmund Loder and still belongs to his descendants. It is important historically as one of the earliest examples of a collection of rare plants in a designed setting – a series of woodland valleys with panoramic views on the edge of the Wealden Forest. The gardens are beautiful when they first open in April with magnificent magnolias and camellias. Autumn colour is another feature: from the middle of September onwards maples, azaleas, liquidambars, carryas and nyssas produce one of the finest arrays of autumn colour in England. But Leonardslee is famous above all for its rhododendrons which line the many miles of paths up and down the hillsides and around the seven lakes. Sheets of bluebells accompany their main flowering in May, while the banks of the lakes and streams are densely planted with candelabra primulas, lysichitons and gunneras. There are many other fascinating features: magnificent conifers (but never in sufficient quantities to spoil the impression that this is a deciduous woodland garden); large plantings of modern *Rhododendron yakushimanum* hybrids; several original plants of *Rhododendron × loderi* hybrids; a large area naturalised by *Scilla liliohyacinthus*; rare shrubs like *Ilex dipyrena*; a European cork oak (*Quercus suber*) and the Amur cork oak (*Phellodendron amurense*); a

tree fern (*Dicksonia antarctica*) growing outside but protected in winter; a Pulhamite rock garden about 100 years old, which has a very striking clump of the hardy Chusan palm (*Trachycarpus fortunei*) and a bright mixture of evergreen azaleas; and a truly beautiful valley on the other side of the main lake which is filled from top to bottom with a flood of sweet-scented yellow azaleas (*Rhododendron luteum*).

Plant Highlights Woodland garden; rock garden; rhododendrons & azaleas; plantsman's collection of plants; plants under glass; mature conifers; bluebells; new alpine house; summer wildflower walk; new Millennium plantings (100 oak species; 100 maple species; many flowering *Cornus*); tallest fossil tree *Metasequoia glyptostroboides* (28m) and *Magnolia campbellii* (27m) in the British Isles, and 5 further champion trees.

Owned by R R Loder
Size 250 acres
English Heritage grade I

book *A Chalk Garden* as a memoir of his gardening experiences. He was also a distinguished plant breeder: Highdown has given us two very fine roses in *Rosa* × *highdownensis* and 'Wedding Day'. The garden is now well maintained by Worthing Borough Council and a pleasure to visit at any season, but perhaps especially in spring.

 Plant Highlights Woodland garden; roses (mainly old-fashioned); rock garden; plantsman's collection of plants; mature conifers; good herbaceous borders; fine collection of trees; tallest specimen of *Carpinus turczaninowii* in the UK, a handsome tree.

Owned by Worthing Borough Council
Number of gardeners 4
Size 10 acres
NCCPG National Collections plants introduced by Sir Frederick Stern
English Heritage grade II*

Holly Gate Cactus Nursery

BILLINGSHURST ROAD, ASHINGTON RH20 3BA

Tel 01903 892930
Location ½ mile from Ashington, on B2133 to Billingshurst
Opening hours 9 am – 5 pm; daily. Closed 25 – 26 December

Holly Gate specialises in cacti and succulents. It carries over 50,000 plants of all types in stock and sells them both retail and wholesale. Many are also planted in the cactus garden, which has some fine specimens and a wide range of taxa – fascinating for cognoscenti and an eye-opener for the uninitiated.

W E Th Ingwersen Ltd

BIRCH FARM NURSERY, GRAVETYE, EAST GRINSTEAD RH19 4LE

Tel 01342 810236
Location 4 miles south-west of East Grinstead
Opening hours 9 am – 1 pm & 1.30 pm – 4 pm; Monday – Saturday; all year. Closed on Saturdays from October to February

This was the first alpine nursery in the south of England: when it started in the 1920s, Mr Ingwersen was a tenant of William Robinson at nearby Gravetye Manor. Its exhibits at RHS Flower Shows have been a source of much praise. It still has one of the best collections in the country of traditional alpines, especially European primulas, sempervivums and autumn-flowering gentians, but it is also a good place to find less common rock plants, the smaller perennials, dwarf shrubs and conifers. There are many raised beds and troughs to see at the nursery (which is in a most beautiful setting): one can spend a long and very happy time here looking at alpines and browsing through possible purchases.

Parham

PARHAM HOUSE, PULBOROUGH RH20 4HS

Tel 01903 742021   **Fax** 01903 746557
Website www.parhaminsussex.co.uk
Location On A283 midway between Pulborough & Storrington
Opening hours 12 noon – 6 pm; Wednesdays, Thursdays, Sundays & Bank Holiday Mondays; April to October
Admission fee Gardens only: Adults £3.50; Children 50p

Nymans

HANDCROSS, HAYWARDS HEATH RH17 6EB

Tel 01444 400321   **Fax** 01444 400253
Website www.nationaltrust.org.uk
Location Handcross, off the main road
Opening hours 11 am – 6 pm; Wednesday – Sunday, plus Bank Holiday Mondays; 1 March to 4 November. 11 am – 4 pm; Saturdays & Sundays; November to March 2002. Closed 25 & 26 December & 1 January 2002
Admission fee Adults £6; Children £3. Reductions in winter. RHS members free

Ⓟ ⓌⒸ ⓖ ⓥ ⒢ ⒲

The garden at Nymans was made in the early years of the twentieth century by Leonard Messel, and his head gardener James Comber. Although it is now owned by the National Trust, there is still a substantial input from latter-day members of the Messel family, including Lord Snowdon and Alistair Buchanan of Hillbarn House (*q.v.*). Nymans is a stupendous plantsman's garden with a wonderful collection of plants of every type which have been marshalled with a fair degree of artistry and made to fit within a strong overall design. It is one of the best gardens of the Sussex hills, and one which retains much of the distinctive style dictated by its historic collection of shrubs and trees. The house is no more – burned to an empty shell long ago – yet almost the most abiding impression of a visit to Nymans is the sight of the house alive both inside and out with plants which enjoy the protection of its walls. In the walled garden are opulent yellow-and-blue herbaceous borders, a pioneering collection of old roses, a stupendous wisteria pergola and vast collections of magnolias and camellias. Further afield, the woodland and wild garden have a great collection of rare trees and shrubs. Nymans suffered very severely from the Great Storm of 1987, but has since made a brilliant recovery and many would say now that the garden looks better than ever.

Plant Highlights Woodland garden; topiary; roses (mainly old-fashioned); plantsman's collection of plants; good herbaceous borders; fine collection of trees; eight different record-breaking trees.

Owned by The National Trust
English Heritage grade II*

Parham is an ethereal English garden for the loveliest of Elizabethan manor houses. In the park are a landscaped lake and a cricket ground. The fun for garden-lovers is in the old walled garden: lush borders, colour plantings in yellow, blue and mauve, old and new fruit trees, and all maintained to the highest standard. The aim is to achieve 'Edwardian opulence ... without being too purist'.

 **Plant Highlights** Roses (mainly old-fashioned); plantsman's collection of plants; fruit; good herbaceous borders; new children's garden behind the Wendy House (1999); HHA/Christie's Garden of the Year in 1990.

Owned by Parham Park Trust
Number of gardeners 4½, plus volunteers
Size 11 acres
English Heritage grade I

Petworth House

PETWORTH GU28 0AE

Tel 01798 342207
Website www.nationaltrust.org.uk
Location At Petworth, well signed
Opening hours Garden: 12 noon – 6 pm; Saturday – Wednesday; 31 March to 4 November. Plus 17, 18, 24 & 25 March (12 noon – 4 pm) for spring bulbs. Plus Good Friday & Fridays in July & August. Park: 8 am – dusk if sooner; daily; all year (but closes at noon 29 June – 1 July)
Admission fee Garden ('Pleasure grounds'): £1. Park free

Ⓟ ⓨ ⓦⓒ ⓖ ⓨ ⓗ ⓢ

One of the best Capability Brown landscapes in England sweeps up to the windows of the house itself. The National Trust has decided to add modern attractions: herbaceous borders and acres of azaleas in a new woodland garden. Both park and garden

have enjoyed a renaissance since the Great Storm of 1987.

Owned by The National Trust
English Heritage grade I

Stonehurst

ARDINGLY RH17 6TN

Tel 01444 892052
Location 1 mile north of Ardingly on B2028
Opening hours 11 am – 5 pm; 16 April & 7 May
Admission fee Adults £2.50; Children £1

Ⓟ ⓨ ⓦⓒ ⓨ ⓗ ⓢ

The garden at Stonehurst was designed by Thomas Mawson in about 1910. In front of the house is a croquet lawn, which leads through a brick-and-tile pergola to a rose garden containing a swimming pool. Elsewhere is a tennis court surrounded by low brick walls and a viewing bastion at the corner. All of this makes the garden very interesting for the social and garden historian. But the horticultural joys are below the house, in a thick woodland garden: Stonehurst is in a rock-lined secret valley, where springs issue to form a series of small lakes, and rare liverworts have special scientific interest. The Strausses have made it known as a garden for rhododendrons, camellias and rare trees and shrubs which regularly win prizes at RHS shows in London. It is very well maintained.

Owned by D R Strauss
Number of gardeners 2½
Size 30 acres
English Heritage grade II

Wakehurst Place

ARDINGLY, HAYWARDS HEATH
RH17 6TN

Tel 01444 894066   **Fax** 01444 894069
Location On B2028 between Turner's Hill & Ardingly
Opening hours 10 am – 7 pm (6 pm in March, 5 pm in February & October, & 4 pm from November to January); daily except Christmas Day & New Year's Day; all year
Admission fee Adults £5; OAPs £3.50; Children £2.50. Subject to review. Free to National Trust members

Wakehurst Place, now managed and owned by the Royal Botanic Gardens at Kew as a country outlier, has a long horticultural history. Most of the planting, however, began after Gerald Loder bought the estate in 1903 and began to introduce exotic trees and shrubs – a development which continued throughout the mid-twentieth century under the next owner Sir Henry Price. The planting suffered badly in the Great Storm of 1987 but the survivors include many rare trees including the King William pine (*Athrotaxis selaginoides*). Among the record-breaking trees which survived the gales are *Cornus nuttallii* and *Torreya nucifera*, both 17m high, *Carya tomentosa* at 27 metres, and two cultivars of *Chamaecyparis lawsoniana* – 'President Roosevelt' at 15 metres and 'Winston Churchill' slightly shorter at 13 metres. A recent addition has been the 'iris dell', planted with authentic Japanese cultivars of water iris (*Iris ensata*), against a brilliant background of Kurume azaleas – Wakehurst has significant connections with Japan. The water garden is surrounded by sheets of blue meconopsis and the giant Himalayan *Cardiocrinum giganteum*. Wakehurst also has its botanic collections, including a Monocot border – wonderful ginger plants (*Hedychium*) in autumn – and specimen beds with especially comprehensive

collections of hypericums, hydrangeas and agapanthus. Many parts of the woodland garden are underplanted with rhododendrons, which are at their best in April and May. Wakehurst has also benefited from major funding by the Millennium Commission, which has enabled it to develop the world's largest seed bank: it aims to collect and conserve some ten per cent of the world's flora – 24,000 species – by the year 2010.

Plant Highlights Woodland garden; roses (mainly old-fashioned & climbers); rhododendrons & azaleas; plantsman's collection of plants; daffodils; camellias; fine collection of trees; alpine plants; bluebells; Asian heath garden; pinetum; cardiocrinums; good autumn colour; new *Iris ensata* dell (1998); tallest *Ostrya japonica* (15m) in the British Isles, plus 25 further tree records.

Owned by National Trust, but leased to Royal Botanic Gardens, Kew
Number of gardeners 40
Size 170 acres
NCCPG National Collections *Betula*; *Hypericum*; *Nothofagus*; *Skimmia*
English Heritage grade II*

West Dean Gardens

WEST DEAN, CHICHESTER PO18 0QZ

Tel 01243 811301   **Fax** 01243 811342
Website www.westdean.org.uk
Location 6 miles north of Chichester on A286
Opening hours 11 am – 5 pm; daily; March to October. Opens at 10.30 pm from May to September
Admission fee Adults £4.50; OAPs £4; Children £2

Laid out in the 1890s and 1900s, West Dean has now been extensively restored. Harold Peto's 100-metre pergola has been replanted with roses. Much of the damage to the

50-acre St Roche's arboretum caused by the 1987 storm has been made good. The great range of glasshouses in the walled garden has been repaired and the garden itself planted as a working kitchen garden which is now the crowning glory of West Dean. A huge variety of plants – from peaches to peppers, cucumbers to coleus, aubergines to orchids – grow in the 16 glasshouses and frames. Out of doors are orderly rows of cabbage, carrots, lettuce and beetroot, alongside herbaceous borders in rich red, oranges and yellows. No space is wasted: the kitchen garden has over one mile of walls covered in trained fruit trees – over 200 different apples, pears and plums. We know of no private garden with so many beautifully grown fruit and vegetables. Beyond the walled garden (two-and-a-half acres in size) are 35 acres of ornamental gardens and 240 acres of landscaped park. Herbaceous borders and annual bedding schemes have been reinstated, rustic summer houses rebuilt and the arboretum taken in hand. 2001 will see the redevelopment of the spring garden, including the 1820s rustic thatched summerhouse with its moss- and heather-lined interior and its floor of knapped flints and horses' molars.

Plant Highlights Roses (mainly old-fashioned & climbers); plants under glass; museum of old lawn mowers; 100-metre pergola with roses & clematis; tallest *Cupressus goveniana* (22m) and *Ailanthus vilmoriniana* (26m) in UK; amazing kitchen garden.

Owned by The Edward James Foundation
Number of gardeners 9
Size 90 acres in all
NCCPG National Collections *Aesculus*; *Liriodendron*
English Heritage grade II*

Yew Tree Cottage

CRAWLEY DOWN, TURNERS HILL RH10 4EY

Tel 01342 714633
Location Opposite Grange Farm on B2028
Opening hours By appointment from May to September
Admission fee Adults £1.50; OAPs £1

This miraculous small garden (about one third of an acre) has been designed, planted and maintained by the nonagenarian owner over many years. There is no better example of the cottage-garden style. It has won infinite plaudits for its display of plants, including a recent *BBC Gardener's World* interview with Gay Search. For years Mrs Hudson practised Jekyll-style planting. Then, in 1999, she decided to replace it with a gravel-and-grasses garden inspired by Piet Oudolf. The result is fascinating.

Owned by Mrs K Hudson

WARWICKSHIRE

Warwickshire has for centuries been a prosperous county: it has the rich clay soils, the country estates and the gardens to prove it. Many of its historic gardens are open to the public throughout the season, including such top attractions as Arbury Hall, Charlecote Park, Farnborough Hall, Packwood House, Upton House and Warwick Castle. The National Gardens Scheme is very successful in persuading the owners of modern gardens to open them to the public, especially by grouping several together within a village. Last year, for example, no less than eleven gardens in the village of Dorsington opened simultaneously for the Scheme, and the same number (on a different Sunday in June) in the up-market Earlsdon area of Coventry. Warwickshire has many first-rate garden centres and a few top-class specialist nurseries too – notably Fibrex Nurseries, who specialise in pelargoniums, ivies, hardy ferns and hellebores. Fibrex also has two of the county's National Collections. The Henry Doubleday Research Association, the organic gardening organisation, has its headquarters at Ryton near Coventry: it offers free access to RHS members throughout the year.

Arbury Hall

NUNEATON CV10 7PT

Tel 024 7638 2804   **Fax** 024 7664 1147
Location 3 miles south-east of Nuneaton off the B4102
Opening hours 2 pm – 6 pm; Sundays & Bank Holiday Mondays; Easter Sunday to September
Admission fee Adults £5; Children £3

Arbury is more important historically than horticulturally: Sanderson Miller was involved in some eighteenth-century improvements and there is a wonderfully landscaped sequence of canals and lakes. During the nineteenth century, many good trees were planted, now in the full-grown beauty of their maturity: purple beeches and a golden sycamore for example. Then there are bluebell woods, pollarded limes, a large rose garden, a walled garden and a huge wisteria. Nothing is outstanding in itself, but the ensemble is an oasis of peace on the edge of industrial Daventry and worth the journey from far away.

Owned by Viscount Daventry
English Heritage grade II*

Charlecote Park

WELLESBOURNE, WARWICK
CV35 9ER

Tel 01789 470277   **Fax** 01789 470544
Website www.nationaltrust.org.uk
Location Signed from A429

Opening hours 11 am – 6 pm; daily except Monday & Tuesday (open Bank Holiday Mondays); 3 February to 4 November. Plus Wednesdays in July & August

Admission fee £3 (garden only)

Fine cedars and a Capability Brown park are the main claims to Charlecote's fame, but the young William Shakespeare is reputed to have poached deer from the park, so the National Trust has planted a border with plants mentioned in his works.

Owned by The National Trust

English Heritage grade II*

Coughton Court

ALCESTER B49 5JA

Tel 01789 400777   **Fax** 01789 765544

Location 2 miles north of Alcester on A435

Opening hours 11 am – 5.30 pm; Saturdays & Sundays; 17 to 30 March and 1 to 28 October. Wednesday – Sunday; April to September. Plus Bank Holiday Mondays & Tuesdays, and Tuesdays in August. Closed 23 June

Admission fee Adults £5.10; Children £2.55

The garden at Coughton has all been made since 1992, designed by Christina Williams, the owner's daughter. An Elizabethan-style knot garden fills the courtyard, and extensive new plantings beyond lead the eye out to the distant landscape. There is a new rose labyrinth in the walled garden and a herb garden, as well as an orchard planted with local varieties of fruit. The bog garden, planted in 1997, has come together well.

Owned by Mrs Clare Throckmorton

Number of gardeners 4

Size 25 acres

Farnborough Hall

BANBURY OX17 1DU

Tel 01295 690002

Website www.nationaltrust.org.uk

Location Off A423, 6 miles north of Banbury

Opening hours 2 pm – 6 pm; Wednesdays & Saturdays; April to September. Also 6 & 7 May. Terrace Walk also open on Thursdays & Fridays

Admission fee Grounds £1.70; Terrace Walk £1 (Thursdays & Fridays only)

Farnborough Hall is Sanderson Millar's masterpiece – grand vistas, classical temples and a dominating obelisk, together with a long curving terraced walk to the adjoining estate of Mollington. No flowers, but space and peace.

Owned by The National Trust

English Heritage grade I

Fibrex Nurseries Ltd

HONEYBOURNE ROAD, PEBWORTH, STRATFORD-UPON-AVON CV37 8XT

Tel 01789 720788   **Fax** 01789 721162

Website www.fibrex.co.uk

Opening hours 10.30 am – 5 pm; Monday – Friday; all year. Plus weekends (12 noon – 5 pm) from March to July. Closed for last two weeks of December and first week of July

Fibrex is a family nursery, built up over more than 40 years and a regular prize-winner at RHS Flower Shows. It has four specialities: pelargoniums, ivies, hardy ferns and hellebores and holds National Collections at the nursery in two of them. The National Collection of pelargoniums has over 2,000 different species and cultivars and claims to be the largest in the world. The National Collection of ivies (*Hedera*)

has over 300 different species and cultivars. The ferns are planted out in the show garden in a natural manner using mature plants: the hellebores too are planted out for viewing when they are in flower.

NCCPG National Collections *Hedera; Pelargonium*

The Mill Garden

55 MILL STREET, WARWICK CV34 4HB

Location Off A425, beside castle gate

No garden has such an idyllic setting, on the banks of the Avon at the foot of Warwick castle: the views in all directions are superb. The garden is planted in the cottage style and seems much larger than its one acre: it burgeons with plants, and the use of annuals to supplement the varied permanent planting enables it to have colour and form, contrasts and harmonies, at every season. This garden was made by Arthur Measures over a long period. His family sold it last year, on condition that the new owner kept it open to the public. We have not yet been able to discover what plans the new owners have for 2001.

Packwood House

PACKWOOD LANE, LAPWORTH, SOLIHULL B94 6AT

Tel 01564 782024 Fax 01564 782014
Website www.nationaltrust.org.uk
Location 2 miles east of Hockley Heath: signed from A3400
Opening hours 11 am – 4.30; Saturdays & Sundays in March. Then 11 am – 5.30 pm; Wednesday – Sunday, plus Bank Holiday Mondays; 28 March to 28 October. Closes at 4.30 pm in April & October
Admission fee Garden only: Adults £2.50

(P) (WC) (&) (⌂) (☕)

Long famous for its topiary, Packwood also has magnificent herbaceous borders which make a visit in July or August particularly rewarding. We carry a photograph of these outstanding borders on the cover of this book.

Owned by The National Trust
English Heritage grade I

Ryton Organic Gardens

HENRY DOUBLEDAY RESEARCH ASSOCIATION, RYTON-ON-DUNSMORE, COVENTRY CV8 3LG

Tel 024 7630 3517 Fax 024 7663 9229
Website www.hdra.org.uk
Location 5 miles south-east of Coventry off A45
Opening hours 9 am – 5 pm; daily; all year except Christmas week
Admission fee Adults £3; Children free. RHS members free

(P) (WC) (&) (⌂) (⌂) (☕) (🍴)

Ryton is the UK centre for organic gardening where experiments are made in using only natural fertilisers and trying to operate without pesticides. It is very well laid out, with 35 different small gardens, all highly instructive. The staff's commitment is also impressive. The gardens include herb gardens, rose gardens, fruit and vegetable displays plus wildlife and conservation areas. A children's trail and guided tours are available. Gardening courses are held throughout the year. The excellent restaurant and substantial shop will add considerably to your enjoyment. The website is full of interest.

Owned by The Henry Doubleday Research Association (HDRA)
Number of gardeners 7
Size 10 acres

Upton House

BANBURY OX15 6HT

Tel 01295 670266
Website www.nationaltrust.org.uk
Location A422, 7 miles north-west of Banbury
Opening hours 1 pm – 5 pm; Saturday – Wednesday, plus Good Friday; 31 March to 31 October
Admission fee Adults £2.70

High on a ridge near the site of the battle of Edgehill, Upton is terraced right down to the pool at the bottom. The centrepiece is a kitchen garden, reached by flights of Italianate stairs. There are also modern formal gardens, one with standard *Hibiscus* 'Bluebird' underplanted with eryngiums, another a rose garden. Further down are a bog garden, a cherry garden and grand herbaceous borders to lead you back to the house. The garden is fascinating, and not at all what you expect when you first see the house.

Owned by The National Trust
NCCPG National Collections *Aster*
English Heritage grade II*

Warwick Castle

WARWICK CV34 4QU

Tel 01926 495421   **Fax** 01926 401692
Website www.warwick-castle.co.uk
Location In town centre
Opening hours 10 am – 6 pm (5 pm in winter); daily; all year except 25 December
Admission fee Adults £11.50; OAPs £8.20; Children £6.75. Less before May & after August

This classic eighteenth-century landscape looks good after some recent restoration, as do the late nineteenth-century formal garden, the Backhouse rock garden, and a rather 1980s Victorian-style rose garden.

Owned by Tussauds Group
Size 62 acres
English Heritage grade I

WEST MIDLANDS

As an administrative entity, West Midlands was a short-lived county: created in 1974 from parts of Warwickshire and Staffordshire: it is now entirely split up into unitary authorities. Its historic gardens are few, but they include what is left of the poet Shenstone's The Leasowes, together with the Birmingham Botanical Gardens and Castle Bromwich Hall. The latter are both highly visitable and highly visited – excellent gardens, deservedly popular still. Being such an urban county, West Midlands is short on old estates, landscaped parks and arboreta, but full of large villa-gardens like the one in Edgbaston which became the University of Birmingham Botanic Garden. This is the area too where the National Gardens Scheme does best. The county also has some good nurseries: Ashwood is one of the most innovative in the British Isles. It is also a designated RHS Partner Nursery, with four special RHS events due to take place there in 2001: further details from 020 7821 3408. The biggest RHS event in the Midlands takes place at the NEC from 13 to 17 June: *BBC Gardener's World Live* is very different from such shows as Chelsea and Hampton Court, though the great draw is the enormously long floral marquee which the Royal Horticultural Society runs with great aplomb. The ticket hotline is 0870 264 5555. The county, though small, also has a surprisingly large number of National Collections, including three (*Ceanothus*, *Gladiolus* and *Rudbeckia*) held by Dudley Borough Council.

Ashwood Nurseries Ltd

ASHWOOD LOWER LANE,
KINGSWINFORD DY6 0AE

Tel 01384 401996 **Fax** 01308 401108
Website www.ashwood-nurseries.co.uk
Location 2 miles west of Kingswinford, near A449
Opening hours 9 am – 6 pm; Monday – Saturday.
9.30 am – 6 pm; Sundays. All year, except
25 & 26 December

Ashwood is a rising star among nurseries. The owners have the happy knack of anticipating trends in fashion: they then put a lot of thought into developing new plants and, thus, new markets. They began in the 1970s with lewisias, crossing and selecting them until they could offer a remarkable range of colours. In 1996 they were awarded a gold medal for their lewisias at the Chelsea Flower Show, their first ever exhibit at the Royal Horticultural Society's most prestigious show. Next they began to breed hellebores – strains of *H. orientalis* in particular. The Ashwood hybrids are remarkable for their purity of colour, vigour and form – but, above all, for the new developments that they have brought to the genus: doubles, anemone-centred and upright forms. Now they are turning their attention to hybrids of *H. niger*. More recent, but no less promising, has been their involvement with hardy cyclamen, auriculas, and hepaticas. Hepaticas are extremely fashionable in Japan, where rare cultivars may cost the equivalent of several hundred pounds, and there is clearly money to be made from developing this genus yet further. Above all, Ashwood means quality: the exhibits the nursery brings to RHS Flower Shows are beautifully grown. A visit to their nursery is strongly recommended.

Birmingham Botanical Gardens & Glasshouses

WESTBOURNE ROAD, EDGBASTON, BIRMINGHAM B15 3TR

Tel 0121 454 1860 **Fax** 0121 454 7835
Website www.bham-bot-gdns.demon.co.uk
Location Follow brown tourist signs in Edgbaston
Opening hours 9 am (10 am on Sundays) – 7 pm, or dusk if earlier; daily; all year except Christmas Day
Admission fee Adults £4.80; Concessions £2.60. Rates will be reviewed in April

Part botanic garden, part public park, wholly delightful, the Birmingham Botanical Gardens can boast an historic lay-out (John Loudon), rare trees and shrubs, gardens for rhododendrons, roses, herbs and alpines, and four glasshouses (tropical, palm house, orangery and cacti house) as well as a good restaurant, brilliant standards of maintenance and a brass band playing on Sunday afternoons in summer. The plant highlights are innumerable, but include water hyacinths (the weed that is choking the Nile), rice plants, papyrus plants, coffee and sugar, bananas and pineapples, many

cycads, insectivorous plants, 'living stones', *Paulownia tomentosa,* good herbaceous plants (phlox, euphorbias, geraniums, delphiniums) and the National Collection of bonsai housed in a secure courtyard.

Plant Highlights Roses (ancient & modern); rock garden; plantsman's collection of plants; plants under glass; fruit; mature conifers; good herbaceous borders; alpine yard; bonsai; three 'historic' gardens – Roman, Mediaeval & Tudor.

Owned by Birmingham Botanical & Horticultural Society
Number of gardeners 10, plus students
Size 15 acres
English Heritage grade II*

Castle Bromwich Hall

CHESTER ROAD, CASTLE BROMWICH B36 9BT

Tel & Fax 0121 749 4100
Website www.cbhgt.swinternet.co.uk
Location 5 miles from city centre just off B4114
Opening hours 1.30 pm – 4 30 pm; Tuesday – Thursday. 2 pm – 6 pm; Saturdays, Sundays & Bank Holiday Mondays. April to October
Admission fee Adults £3; OAPs £2; Children £1

Castle Bromwich Hall is garden archaeology at work. The gardens at Castle Bromwich are being restored as they were in 1700 by a privately funded trust. For many years they were neglected, lost beneath a tangled mass of vegetation. Work began in 1985 and has been very successful: the result is both beautiful, inspiring and educational. The gardens contain a large collection of unusual period plants, and a nineteenth-century holly maze. There is also a holly walk – a broad path lined with variegated hollies. At its end, an elegant summerhouse looks across to an early greenhouse. Nearby is the formal vegetable garden, made to the design of Batty Langley's *New Principles of Gardening* (1728). Many historic vegetables and herbs are grown, along with unusual varieties like the black 'Congo' potato and white carrot. Fruit trees are formally trained – apples, pears, apricots, figs and cherries. The Upper and Lower Wildernesses have grown to maturity, but they have been underplanted well. The north garden has just been restored to the design shown in Henry Beighton's Prospect of 1726, its parterre outlined with yew, mown grass and gravel.

Owned by Castle Bromwich Hall Gardens Trust
Number of gardeners 3, plus volunteers
Size 10 acres
English Heritage grade II*

University of Birmingham Botanic Garden

58 EDGBASTON PARK ROAD, EDGBASTON B15 2RT

Tel 0121 414 4944   **Fax** 0121 414 5619
Website www.birmingham.ac.uk
Location Off A38 Bristol Road, ½ mile
Opening hours 11 am – 4 pm; Monday – Friday. Closed Bank Holidays, Easter & Christmas holidays
Admission fee Adults £2

This was originally a private garden, belonging to one of Birmingham's great-and-good families: it was given to the university in 1943 but still has the 'feel' of a private garden – one with an exceptional collection of plants. The rhododendrons and naturalised bulbs are very pretty: even the roses, chosen to illustrate their history in cultivation, fit well into an ornamental garden. Perhaps the most interesting plants

are the collection of alpines in troughs, in the sandstone rockery and in the scree beds. There are some geographic beds which put together plants that combine naturally in the wild, but everything else about the garden is horticultural, rather than botanic. It is a charming place to spend a couple of hours at almost any time of the year.

Owned by University of Birmingham
Number of gardeners 3
Size 6 acres
NCCPG National Collections *Rosa* (History of European roses)

Wightwick Manor

WIGHTWICK, WOLVERHAMPTON WV6 8EE

Tel 01902 761108   **Fax** 01902 764663
Website www.nationaltrust.org.uk
Location 3 miles west of Wolverhampton on A454
Opening hours 11 am – 6 pm on Wednesdays, Thursdays, Saturdays & Bank Holidays; March to December
Admission fee Adults £2.40

Wightwick is a substantial Victorian garden, designed by Thomas Mawson and planted by Alfred Parsons. It has topiary, a rose arbour, avenues of Irish yews and a Poets' Corner where all the plants were taken as cuttings from the gardens of literary men – Keats, Tennyson and Dickens among them.

Plant Highlights Topiary; roses (mainly old-fashioned & climbers); rock garden; good herbaceous borders.

Owned by The National Trust

WILTSHIRE

Wiltshire is the county that people travel through on their way to somewhere else. For gardeners, this is a mistake. Unlike so many counties whose great Grade I historic gardens are often rather dull, Wiltshire's are all supremely beautiful – Bowood, Iford, Longleat, Stourhead and Wilton. All are open to the public, as are many of the other graded gardens. Wiltshire also has a number of very good plantsman's gardens – notably Broadleas and Home Covert near Devizes, and the Old Vicarage at nearby Edington. It has some fine arboreta: tree-enthusiasts should also try to see the record-breaking multi-stemmed specimen of *Zelkova carpinifolia* at Wardour Castle – 35m high when last officially measured in 1977. The National Gardens Scheme does well in the county, particularly among the owners of medium-sized and large gardens. The Wiltshire Gardens Trust is active in conservation and also represents the NCCPG in the county: there is a sprinkling of National Collections among its members. Wiltshire does not, however, do so well for nurseries: perhaps only the Botanic Nursery at Atworth can be said to have a national profile. Geoffrey Jellicoe's masterpiece at Shute House, Donhead St Mary, has recently been open to groups by prior appointment. It is worth noting that, contrary to widespread belief, both Shute House and Larmer Tree Gardens are actually in Wiltshire, not in Dorset.

The Abbey House

MARKET CROSS, MALMESBURY
SN16 9AS

Tel 01666 822212 **Fax** 01666 822782
Location Town centre, behind abbey. Public carparks nearby
Opening hours 11 am – 6 pm; daily; March to October
Admission fee Adults £4.50; Concessions £4; Children £2. Free to RHS members in March & October

This remarkable 5-acre garden has all been made by the Pollards since 1995. They have planted 2,000 different roses to celebrate the millennium, and 2,000 different herb cultivars. Other features include an arcaded fruit walk, a knot garden, huge herbaceous borders, a striking laburnum tunnel and a formal garden. But it is the design and planting which are so distinctive: bold, varied and inspirational. Now a new woodland garden running down to the river below is under construction.

Owned by Ian Pollard

Avebury Manor

AVEBURY, MARLBOROUGH SN8 1RE

Tel 01672 539203
Website www.nationaltrust.org.uk
Location In the village, well signed
Opening hours 11 am – 5.30 pm; daily except Mondays
& Thursdays; April to October. Open Bank Holiday Mondays
Admission fee Adults £2.50; Children £1.25

A recent owner did much to revive this great
Edwardian garden. The National Trust is
continuing the work of restoration: the
results are well worth another visit.

Owned by The National Trust

Bolehyde Manor

ALLINGTON, CHIPPENHAM
SN14 6LW

Tel 01249 652105   **Fax** 01249 659296
Location 2 miles west of Chippenham
Opening hours 2.30 pm – 6 pm; 24 June. And by
appointment
Admission fee Adults £2.50; Children 50p

This charming house is surrounded by
outbuildings and walls of old Cotswold
stone, which form the background to a
series of enclosed gardens. Each is very
prettily designed and planted in the modern
style – using plants for their contrasts and
combinations of flower, shape, colour and
form. The gardens seem to brim over with
flowers and an abundance of beauty. If only
it were open more open.

Owned by Earl & Countess Cairns
Number of gardeners 2 part-time
Size 3 acres

The Botanic Nursery

COTTLES LANE, ATWORTH,
MELKSHAM SN12 8NU

Tel 01225 706597   **Fax** 01225 700953
Website www.botanicnursery.com
Location Just south of the A365 at the western end of
Atworth
Opening hours 10 am – 5 pm; Fridays & Saturdays; all
year except January. And by appointment

The Botanic Nursery built its reputation on
growing lime-tolerant plants, but has
become better known as a plantsman's
nursery, where a long browse will winkle out
all sorts of rare plants. It is best known at
RHS Flower Shows for its spectacular
displays of foxgloves (*Digitalis*) from its
National Collection, though it also has very
good collections of eryngiums and dieramas.

Bowood House

CALNE SN11 0LZ

Tel 01249 812102   **Fax** 01249 821757
Website www.bowood-estate.co.uk
Location Off A4 in Derry Hill village between Calne
& Chippenham
Opening hours 11 am – 6 pm; daily; 1 April to 28 October.
Separate rhododendron walks from mid April to early June
(telephone for exact dates, which depend upon the
flowering season)
Admission fee Adults £5.90; OAPs £4.90; Children £3.70

Beautifully maintained and welcoming,
Bowood has something from every period
of English garden history. Capability Brown
made the lake and planted many of the trees
and lawns which give such a beautiful setting
to the house. Charles Hamilton added the
famous cascade below the lake in the

picturesque style. There is an important nineteenth-century pinetum laid out on pre-Linnaean principles – geographically – with oceans of grass to separate the continents. It is not just a collection of magnificent conifers, but contains many rare and beautiful deciduous trees too, including the tallest specimen of the cut-leaved horse-chestnut (*Aesculus hippocastanum* 'Laciniata') in the British Isles. By the house are handsome Italianate formal gardens designed by Smirke and Kennedy in the nineteenth century and recently replanted by Lady Mary Keen. Up in the woods, and entered directly from the A342, is a magnificent display of modern rhododendrons around the Robert Adam mausoleum. The oceans of bluebells which surround these rhododendron drives is one of the finest in the south of England. Be sure to miss the reclining nude above the formal gardens.

 **Plant Highlights** Woodland garden; lake; Capability Brown landscape; famous old arboretum; topiary; azaleas & rhododendrons; mature conifers; bluebells; modern borders; tallest *Thuya occidentalis* 'Wareana' in the UK.

Owned by The Marquis of Lansdowne
Number of gardeners 4
English Heritage grade I

Broadleas

DEVIZES SN10 5JQ

Tel 01380 722035
Location 1 mile south of Devizes
Opening hours 2 pm – 6 pm; Wednesdays, Thursdays & Sundays; April to October
Admission fee Adults £3; Children £1

Lady Anne Cowdray started to make this garden – now owned by a charitable trust – in 1947. Since then it has grown into a very fine plantsman's garden, with lots of different kinds of plant but an especially good collection of ornamental trees and shrubs. Broadleas has a rose garden, a grey border, a rock garden and a 'secret' garden, all near the Regency house. But the main attraction is the Dell, a greensand combe that stretches down to the valley below, its sides just stuffed with good things. At the top are two tall magnolias, thought to be *M. sprengeri* var. *diva* and *M. sargentiana* var. *robusta*. Pass between them, and past a very tall paulownia, and you come into a world of rare trees, vast magnolias, sheets of *Primula whitei* and cyclamen. And Broadleas has two characteristics common to all good plantsman's gardens: it is worth visiting at any time of the year and it gets better all the time. The nursery sells surplus plants, many grown from wild-collected seed by members of the International Dendrology Society.

Owned by Broadleas Gardens Charitable Trust
Number of gardeners 2
Size 9 acres
English Heritage grade II

Conock Manor

DEVIZES SN10 3QQ

Tel 01380 840227
Location 5 miles south-east of Devizes off A342
Opening hours 2 pm – 6 pm; 20 May
Admission fee Adults £2; Children free

Beautiful parkland surrounds this covetable Georgian house. Behind the copper-domed stables an elegant shrub walk meanders past *Sorbus*, maples and magnolias. Some of the trees which have been planted in recent years are already making a good show.

Owned by Mrs Bonar Sykes
Size 2 acres, plus parkland
English Heritage grade II

Corsham Court

CORSHAM SN13 0BZ

Tel & Fax 01249 701610
Location Signed from A4 Bath to Chippenham
Opening hours 2 pm – 5.30 pm; Tuesday – Sunday
& Bank Holiday Mondays; 20 March to 30 September. Plus
2 pm – 4.30 pm; Saturdays & Sundays; 1 January
to 19 March and October to December
Admission fee Adults £2; OAPs £1.50; Children £1

Corsham is a major eighteenth-century
landscape garden, one of the few where both
Capability Brown and Humphry Repton
worked. Then the flower garden was
developed in the middle of the nineteenth
century: box-edged borders and a pretty
fountain, all kept up with some good
modern planting. An 18-acre arboretum was
planted in the 1980s which is growing up
well and is well worth exploring.

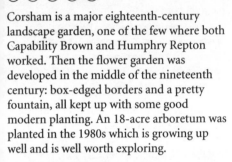 **Plant Highlights** Fine trees; designed
by Capability Brown and Humphry
Repton; young arboretum; amazing oriental
plane *Platanus orientalis* whose sweeping
limbs have rooted over a huge area.

Owned by James Methuen-Campbell
Number of gardeners 4
English Heritage grade II*

The Courts

HOLT, TROWBRIDGE BA14 6RR

Tel 01225 782340
Website www.nationaltrust.org.uk
Location In the middle of Holt village
Opening hours 1 pm – 5.30 pm; Sunday – Friday; 1 April
to 14 October
Admission fee Adults £3.50; Children £1.50

Holt Court (as it used to be called) is a 1920s
masterpiece in the Hidcote style. It has rich
colour plantings in a series of garden rooms
and excellent plants, beautifully used. It is
also well maintained by the Head Gardener
who came from Sissinghurst.

Owned by The National Trust
English Heritage grade II

Heale House Garden

MIDDLE WOODFORD, SALISBURY
SP4 6NT

Tel 01722 782504
Location Signed off the western Woodford valley road,
and from A345 & A360
Opening hours 10 am – 5 pm; daily; all year
Admission fee Adults £3.35; Children £1.50

Many would say that Heale is the prettiest
garden in southern England. It sits at the
bottom of a broad, chalk valley, with the
River Avon flowing through its midst. The
house is Jacobean, with substantial additions
so sympathetically designed by Detmar Blow
that it is difficult to know which parts
belong to the original house. Harold Peto
laid out the garden: you see his handiwork
in the formal gardens which run up towards
the south along an avenue of laburnums.
There are formal pools, terraces, balustrades
and Italianate garden architecture on the
way. Alongside the river are more
balustrading, old rambling roses and a lawn
which is richly planted with hybrid musk
roses and herbaceous plants. On an island in
the river is a Japanese garden, laid out in
1901 and much altered as a result of the
sheer growth of the original Japanese maples:
however, the scarlet lacquered bridge and
the neat tea-house seem quite as new.
Perhaps the best part of the garden is the old
kitchen garden, surrounded by cob walls

and hung around its topiary and pergolas. Here over 30 years from the mid-1960s onwards Lady Anne Rasch developed a wonderful series of mixed borders, exuberantly planted with roses, clematis and herbaceous plants which is one of the best examples of the genre in England. But the garden is open every day of the year, and there is always something to see, including swarms of cyclamen in autumn, and woodlands full of snowdrops and aconites in winter.

 Plant Highlights Snowdrops; roses (mainly old-fashioned); fruit; good herbaceous borders; Japanese gardens; good plant associations; first Christie's/HHA Garden of the Year in 1984.

Owned by Guy Rasch
Number of gardeners 2, plus owners
Size 8 acres
English Heritage grade II*

Hillbarn House

GREAT BEDWYN, MARLBOROUGH SN8 3NU

Tel 01672 870207   **Fax** 01672 871015
Location In High Street, opposite garage
Opening hours 2 pm – 6 pm; 15 July & 30 September. Plus parties by arrangement. There will also be a plant sale on 12 May 2001, starting at 10.30 am
Admission fee £2 Adults; 50p Children

Many consider Hillbarn to be Lanning Roper's masterpiece. It was a difficult site – small and steep – in which he created an illusion of size by dividing it up into small compartments. One is a French-style *potager*: among the first to be made in England, it has helped to create a fashion. Another compartment is a chequer-board with herbs and bulbs. The hornbeam hedges and arbours are exceptionally stylish. and

there are handsome plantings throughout the garden, which is very well maintained with a lot of family input.

Owned by Alistair J Buchanan
Number of gardeners 1
Size 2 acres

Home Covert

ROUNDWAY, DEVIZES SN10 2JA

Tel 01380 723407
Location 1 mile north of Devizes in Roundway Village
Opening hours 2 pm – 6 pm; 12 August for National Gardens Scheme; parties by appointment
Admission fee Adults £2.50; Children free

Home Covert is one of the most influential and largest plantsman's gardens in England. The knowledge and taste of the owners – together with their generosity towards visitors – have made it a cult garden among *cognoscenti* and learner-gardeners alike. The Phillips describe it as 'a botanical madhouse': it would be truer to call it a horticultural treasure-house. Every type of plant is grown but, above all, rare trees: *Cercis racemosa*, for example, and hundreds of plants – perhaps thousands – grown from seeds collected by such friends as Roy Lancaster, Martyn Rix and Maurice Foster. An older generation of plantsman is also commemorated here – Maurice Mason, Norman Haddon and Margery Fish, for example. Home Covert is a large garden, informally laid out within natural oak woodland, and it needs a long time to see round. Down in the bog garden are collections of willows and alders, naturalised *Lathraea clandestina* and swathes of candelabra primulas. Near the house is an enormous lawn, completely free of weeds, with a view for miles down the Avon valley. Raised beds, a rock garden, shade borders, protected beds for tender plants, swarms of erythroniums, fat clumps of lilies, old-fashioned roses and wild species – there seems no end to the number and variety of what is grown here.

 Plant Highlights Woodland garden; plantsman's plants of every kind; extensive new plantings (2001).

Owned by Mr & Mrs John Phillips
Number of gardeners owners only
Size 33 acres

Iford Manor

BRADFORD-ON-AVON BA15 2BA

Tel 01225 863146   **Fax** 01225 852364
Website www.ifordmanor.co.uk
Location 7 miles south-east of Bath, signed from A36 & Bradford-on-Avon
Opening hours 2 pm – 5 pm; Sundays & Easter Monday; April & October. Plus Tuesday – Thursday, Saturdays, Sundays & Bank Holiday Mondays from May to September
Admission fee Adults £3; OAPs & Children (over 10) £2.50

Ⓟ ⍟ ⓦⓒ ⍟

Harold Peto's own Italianate garden on a steep wooded hillside is meticulously maintained and imaginatively planted. Peto was a fashionable architect with a passion for classical Italian architecture and landscaping in an English setting. When he returned from working in France and Italy, he bought Iford to house his collections of statues and architectural marbles. He planted phillyreas, Italian cypresses and other Mediterranean species and laid out the garden as formal terraces. The architectural highlights include a Romanesque cloister, an octagonal cloister, and a gloriously colonnaded terrace. Every detail is wonderfully photogenic, especially when contrasted with wisterias, roses or the well-chosen National Collection of acanthus. The

woodland garden is worth exploring and there is much of horticultural interest too, notably a meadow of naturalised martagon lilies.

Owned by Mrs E Cartwright-Hignett
Number of gardeners 3
Size 1½ acres plus 12 acres of woodland
NCCPG National Collections Acanthus
English Heritage grade I

Larmer Tree Gardens

TOLLARD ROYAL, SALISBURY SP5 5PT

Tel 01725 516228   **Fax** 01725 516449
Location Follow brown signs from A354 or B3081
Opening hours 11 am – 6 pm; daily except Saturdays; Easter Sunday to 31 October
Admission fee Adults £3.50; OAPs £3; Children £1.50

Ⓟ ⓦⓒ ⓖ ⍟

The Larmer Tree Gardens were laid out by General Augustus Pitt Rivers as a public amenity. He put up a series of eccentric garden buildings around a spacious lawn, perhaps two acres across: they include the Singing Theatre, the Indian Room, the Roman Temple and the Lower Indian Building in the Nepalese style, brought here in 1880 after the Colonial Exhibition in London. In the 1880s and 1890s, trainloads of East-Enders were brought there by the philanthropic owner for a jolly cultural day in the country. His descendants have entirely restored the gardens since about 1990 and added some modern horticultural features. The best of these is a series of artificial pools in an artificial dell, surrounded by multi-coloured hydrangeas. All is set in light oak woodland with splendid thickets of cherry laurel. It is not a garden of the highest horticultural interest, though there are some venerable eucryphias, crinodendrons and stewartias. It is however spaciously laid out and very enjoyable to visit.

Owned by W Gronow-Davies & Trustees
Number of gardeners 3
Size 11 acres
English Heritage grade II

Longleat House

WARMINSTER BA12 7NW

Tel 01985 844400   **Fax** 01985 844885
Website www.longleat.co.uk
Location Off A362 Warminster to Frome road
Opening hours Daylight hours; daily; all year except
25 December. Maze and other attractions open from
24 March to 4 November. Please telephone for opening
times
Admission fee Grounds & gardens: Adults £2;
OAPs & Children £1

Forget the lions and the loins, Longleat has a classic eighteenth-century landscape by Capability Brown, a home park of 600 acres best seen from Heaven's Gate and a grand Victorian garden reworked by Russell Page in the 1930s. Capability Brown's landscape has been carefully managed and replanted over many years, so that it keeps its intended form. The Victorian garden between the house and the elegant conservatory built by Wyatville in the 1820s is now a very beautiful rose garden. The plantings of ornamental trees and rhododendrons woodlands have been thickened and updated with many new introductions. In short, Lord Bath (like his father before him) has conserved the best and is invigorating the rest of Longleat. Worth another visit.

Plant Highlights Woodland garden; topiary; rhododendrons & azaleas; good herbaceous borders; fine collection of trees; orangery; the world's longest maze;

'love labyrinth' with saucily-named roses; newly planted sun maze & lunar labyrinth.

Owned by The 7th Marquess of Bath
Number of gardeners 12
English Heritage grade I

The Mead Nursery

BROKERSWOOD, WESTBURY
BA13 4EG

Tel 01373 859990
Location Near Rudge, off A36 or A361
Opening hours 9 am – 5 pm, Wednesday – Saturday,
and Bank Holiday Mondays; 12 noon – 5 pm, Sundays,
1 February to 10 October

The Mead Nursery specialises in alpine plants, pot-grown bulbs and (mainly short-growing) herbaceous perennials, including varieties suitable for trough plantings. It is run organically and everything is propagated from the stock plants in the attractive display garden. There are areas of rock-garden and scree, and lots of attractive sinks and containers.

Oare House

OARE, MARLBOROUGH SN8 4JQ

Tel 01672 562428
Location In village, west side of A345
Opening hours 2 pm – 6 pm; 22 April & 29 July
Admission fee Adults £2; Children free

Oare has an approach along lime avenues and tall hedges whose grandeur is echoed by the main garden behind: a huge apron of walled lawn, with majestic mixed borders at the sides, lead the eye over a half-hidden swimming pool to a grand ride and on to the Marlborough Downs beyond. Intimacy exists only in some small enclosed gardens to the side and in the kitchen garden. Here are a magnificent herbaceous border in reds and yellows, a tunnel of fruit trees and vegetables in neat rows. Half a mile or so away, alongside the minor road to West Stowell, is the arboretum, with clumps of *Sassafras albidum* at the entrance and about 20 different record-breaking trees – quite a surprise in this rustic backwater.

Owned by Henry Keswick
Number of gardeners 3
Size 5½ acres garden & 40 acres arboretum
English Heritage grade II

Old Vicarage

EDINGTON, WESTBURY BA13 4QF

Tel & Fax 01380 830512
Location On B3098 in Edington village
Opening hours 2 pm – 6 pm; 10 June
Admission fee Adults £3.50; Children free

John d'Arcy bought the Old Vicarage in 1982: it is now one of the best examples of a plantsman's garden in southern England. The site offers a surprising range of mini-habitats, and d'Arcy took advantage of their potential to grow the widest possible number of plants. The features now include a sunken garden, a shady pergola, an avenue of fastigiate hornbeams *Carpinus betulus* 'Fastigiata', a gravel garden where *Morina afghanica* and *Ptilostemon afer* seed around, hot walls, raised beds, peat beds and shady beds – all blended with the rest of the garden so that no feature dominates any part of it. d'Arcy's great skill is as a cultivator: the fact that there is so much colour and interest at every time of the year proves that good plantsmanship can produce effects to challenge the most carefully designed and

planted of gardens. Trees are underplanted with shrubs, which are underscored in turn by herbaceous plants and bulbs, several different plants being placed together to give a succession of interest throughout the year. d'Arcy's special interests include Mexican mahonias, Oncocyclus irises, nerines and hollies. He is also well known as a plant collector. *Corydalis flexuosa* came from Sichuan in 1989; several new species of *Dierama* came from South Africa, together with such new species of *Geranium* as *G. harveyi* and *G. pulchrum*. All are still here, together with the living holotype of *Salvia darcyi*.

Owned by John d'Arcy
Number of gardeners 1
Size 2½ acres
NCCPG National Collections Oenothera

Pound Hill House

WEST KINGTON, CHIPPENHAM SN14 7JG

Tel 01249 782822   **Fax** 01249 782953
Location Signed in village
Opening hours 2 pm – 5 pm; daily; April to October
Admission fee Adults £2.50; Children free. RHS members free from July to October

The garden has been laid out and planted since about 1980 by Barbara and Philip Stockitt, with advice from their daughter, garden-designer Bunny Guinness, a Chelsea gold medal-winner. They supplemented the Cotswold dry-stone walls with hedges of yew and box to make a series of neat rooms, in scale with the substantial Cotswold farmhouse. Barbara is a nurserywoman, the owner of the highly successful wholesalers West Kington Nurseries and, incidentally, a sister of David Austin the rose-breeder. You approach the garden through an excellent small retail nursery which is beautifully laid out with a most inviting selection of plants, especially topiary and architectural plants, and well-integrated into the overall design. Inside the garden proper you encounter first a neat, formal kitchen garden, full of interesting vegetables, and a small rose garden of polyanthas 'The Fairy' and 'Little White Pet' grown as standards. The main part of the garden lies behind the house, most instructively laid out with structure given by box edging, yew cones and architectural plants at key points in the design. The plantings offer a stylish selection of plants, including many of the best modern cultivars, thickly planted and very well grown. Two particularly good features are a short avenue of Spanish chestnuts clipped to keep the trees small and the leaves large, and another of *Betula jacquemontii* entirely underplanted on both sides by pulmonarias – very striking in spring. But this excellent two-acre showcase-garden is interesting throughout the year. We carry a photograph of this outstanding modern garden on the cover of this book.

Owned by Mr & Mrs Philip Stockitt

Sharcott Manor

PEWSEY SN9 5PA

Tel 01672 563485
Location Off A345, one mile south-west of Pewsey
Opening hours 11 am – 5 pm; first Wednesday of every month; April to October. Plus 2 pm – 6 pm; 8 April & 8 July
Admission fee Adults £2; Children free

This extensive modern garden has been quite transformed over the last 20 years into a densely planted plantsman's paradise. There is much to see as you move gently between the garden rooms near the house and out into the spacious lawns and

woodland garden. There are harmonies and contrasts to please the most colour-conscious, while the dark shady lake at the bottom is a haven of romantic broodiness. Sharcott is an excellent garden which deserves to be better known.

Owned by Captain & Mrs David Armytage
Number of gardeners 2 part-time
Size 6 acres

Sherston Parva Nursery Ltd

MALMESBURY ROAD, SHERSTON SN16 0NX

Tel 01666 841066   **Fax** 01666 841132
Website www.sherstonparva.com
Location On B4040, 3 miles south of Westonbirt
Opening hours 10 am – 5 pm; daily; all year. Closed in January

Sherston Parva is an established nursery specialising in clematis and other climbing plants and wall shrubs. It also sells herbaceous plants. They have a stock of about 300 different clematis, though not all are propagated and available at one time so it is always worth asking if you want a particular cultivar. The nursery in any event makes it fairly clear that 'we feel it is more beneficial to our customers to remove from our list those varieties which have been so obviously superseded'. But there is always an excellent selection and their other climbers and wall-shrubs are well-chosen. They look wonderful against the nursery's own Cotswold stone walls.

Stourhead

STOURTON, WARMINSTER BA12 6QD

Tel & Fax 01747 841152
Website www.nationaltrust.org.uk
Location 3 miles north of Mere, signed off the
A303/B3092
Opening hours 9 am – 7 pm, or dusk if earlier; daily;
all year
Admission fee Adults £4.80; Children £2.90. Reductions
in winter

Whatever the weather or season, Stourhead
conveys a sense of majesty and harmony.
Try it early on a May morning, before it
opens officially, when the air is sweet with
azaleas. Or scuff the fallen leaves in late
November. Think of it 200 years ago,
without the rhododendrons, when all the
beech trees were interplanted with spruces.
Ponder the eighteenth century aesthetic,
which esteemed tones and shades more
highly than colours. Spot the change from
classical to gothic, from Pope to Walpole.
And wonder at the National Trust's ability
to maintain it so well with only six
gardeners.

Plant Highlights Snowdrops;
rhododendrons & azaleas; mature
conifers; fine collection of trees; bluebells;
good autumn colour; tallest tulip tree
Liriodendron tulipifera (37m) in the British
Isles, and twelve other record tree species.

Owned by The National Trust
English Heritage grade I

Stourton House Flower Garden

STOURTON, WARMINSTER BA12 6QF

Tel 01747 840417
Location Next to Stourhead, 2 miles north of A303 at
Mere
Opening hours 11 am – 6 pm; Wednesdays, Thursdays,
Sundays & Bank Holiday Mondays; April to November.
Groups at other times by appointment
Admission fee Adults £2.50; Children 50p

This five-acre garden next to Stourhead is
famous for its dried flowers, thanks to the
energy and personality of Elizabeth
Bullivant. It also has a strong design and
some beautiful plant combinations. The
baroque curves to the hedges are completely
original. Stourton is also a garden with a
tremendous number of different plants and
some particular favourites – hence the
enormous collection of hydrangeas, the
split-corona daffodils and the plantings of
rhododendrons, azaleas and camellias.
Mrs Bullivant has also been successful in
plant competitions at RHS shows, bringing
up a wide variety of plants to show a wider
audience. But Stourton is not a garden for
show – rather, it is a well-loved private
garden with a sideline in dried flowers. It is
also very good at all seasons – and especially
in early autumn when it is frankly stunning:
strongly recommended.

Plant Highlights Good herbaceous
borders; Victorian greenhouse;
elegantly curving hedges of Leylandii; 270
different hydrangeas; delphiniums; hosts of
daffodils, in innumerable shapes, sizes and
colours.

Owned by Mrs Anthony Bullivant
Size 4½ acres

Westdale Nurseries

HOLT ROAD, BRADFORD ON AVON
BA15 1TS

Tel & Fax 01225 863258
Location 1 mile east of Bradford town centre; left-hand side
Opening hours 9 am – 6 pm; daily except Christmas

Westdale has made quite an impact at RHS Flower Shows in recent years with its wonderful displays of bougainvilleas. It lists over 100 different cultivars, which are available in different sizes. All can be seen growing in their extensive glasshouses outside Bradford on Avon. But their range of other conservatory plants is very wide, and they are enthusiastic plantsmen, willing to try any plant which may have value as an ornament to the conservatory or greenhouse. Well worth a visit.

Wilton House

WILTON, SALISBURY SP2 0BJ

Tel 01722 746720   **Fax** 01722 744447
Location In village, 3 miles west of Salisbury on A30
Opening hours 10.30 am – 5.30 pm; daily; 4 April to 28 October but closed on 28 & 29 April
Admission fee Adults £3.75; Children £2.75

Wilton has a sublime eighteenth-century park around its classical Inigo Jones house, which is famous for its paintings. It is this stupendous parkland setting above the river Nadder which is the chief delight of visiting the gardens at Wilton. There are comparatively few horticultural excitements, though the house has pleasant mixed borders along one of its sides and a stylish modern garden, rather formal, in the entrance court designed by Lady Tollemache. On the edge of the park are a pretty new rose garden and an oriental water garden. A new fountain is planned for 2001.

Plant Highlights Roses; handsome cedars; famous Palladian bridge; magnificent golden-leaved oak.

Owned by Earl of Pembroke/Wilton House Trust
Number of gardeners 4
Size 21 acres
English Heritage grade I

Wiltshire College Lackham

LACOCK, CHIPPENHAM SN15 2NY

Tel 01249 466800   **Fax** 01249 444474
Website www.lackham.co.uk
Location 3 miles south of Chippenham on A350
Opening hours 10 am – 4 pm; Sundays & Bank Holiday Mondays; Easter to August
Admission fee Adults £2; Concessions £1.50; Children free

Lackham is among the best of the old county college gardens. A major extension was opened in 1996 – an Italian-style garden, an historic rose garden, a sensory garden, herbaceous borders and illustrations of English gardens over each of the last four centuries. The heart of Lackham is its walled garden of flowers, ornamentals, herbs, fruit and vegetables, beautifully laid out to educate and delight. In one of the glasshouses is the champion plant of *Citrus medica* which grew the largest citron ever seen in Britain (according to the Guinness Book of Records). The grounds are good for an exploration too, especially in bluebell time.

Number of gardeners 4, plus students
Size 20 acres
NCCPG National Collections *Populus*

WORCESTERSHIRE

Worcestershire has been reconstituted not as a county (which it was until 1974) but as a District Council. But such is the feeling of distinct identity that we have treated it in this book as a legal county again: the same applies to Herefordshire, to which it was yoked for 25 years. In fact, from a horticultural standpoint, Worcestershire has rather more going for it than its ex-partner: a flourishing National Gardens Scheme, the site of the only dedicated horticultural college in England at Pershore, the headquarters of the Alpine Garden Society, ten National Collection holders, and two of the most popular gardening shows in the country – the Spring Gardening Show (11–13 May) and the Autumn Garden & Country Show (29–30 September), both at the Three Counties Showground at Malvern. Worcestershire also has some excellent specialist nurseries, including Cotswold Garden Flowers, Old Court Nurseries and Stone House Cottage Garden. Though few of its historic parks and gardens are open to the public, they include that great plantsman's garden Spetchley Park (substantially re-made by a great-nephew of Miss Ellen Willmott) and Witley Court (made by an ancestor of Sir Simon Hornby, President of the Royal Horticultural Society).

Cotswold Garden Flowers

SANDS LANE, BADSEY, EVESHAM WR11 5EZ

Tel 01386 47337
Website www.cgf.net
Location On south-east edge of village
Opening hours 9 am – 5.30 pm; Monday – Friday. 10 am – 5.30 pm; Saturday – Sunday. March to mid-October. Other times by appointment
Admission fee free

Though it was founded as recently as 1991, Cotswold Garden Flowers is already the market leader for rare perennials and small

shrubs: over 8,000 different cultivars are grown here. The catalogue is both amusing and informative, but it is nothing compared to the joy of visiting the nursery and having the opportunity to see so many new and interesting plants. The owner has a knack for seeking out and introducing plants which are highly 'garden-worthy'.

NCCPG National Collections Lysimachia

Eastgrove Cottage Garden

SANKYNS GREEN, SHRAWLEY, LITTLE
WITLEY, WORCESTER WR6 6LQ

Tel 01299 896389
Website www.eastgrove.co.uk
Location On road between Great Witley (on
A443) & Shrawley (on B4196)
Opening hours 2 pm – 5 pm; Thursday – Monday; April
to July. Also Thursday – Saturday; 1 September to
13 October
Admission fee Adults £2

Eastgrove is a very pretty black-and-white
cottage, with an equally pretty cottage
garden that has been entirely made by the
Skinners since they bought the near-derelict
property in 1975. The scale is small, but the
quality and variety of the plantings are
stunning. There are herbs, dwarf conifers, a
developing collection of trees which they call
an arboretum, a bog garden and, above all,
thickly planted herbaceous plants. The
design and planting of the borders is
carefully thought through: the 'secret
garden' concentrates on mauves, pinks,
silvers and crimsons. Although perhaps best
in high summer, the garden is good enough
to visit at any time of the year. The nursery
propagates only plants from the garden and
has a list of over 1,100 different varieties.
Specialities include aquilegias, hardy
chrysanthemums, dianthus, heleniums,
irises, peonies, penstemons, rosemary,
salvias, violas, pelargoniums, and other
tender perennials.

Owned by Malcolm & Carol Skinner
Number of gardeners 2
Size 1½ acres

Gorsehill Abbey Farm

COLLIN LANE, BROADWAY
WR12 7PB

Tel 01386 852208 **Fax** 01386 858570
Location Off A44 at Collin House Hotel; ½ mile north-west
then left
Opening hours 2.30 pm – 6 pm; Thursday; July & August
Admission fee Adults £2; Children free

Gorsehill Abbey Farm is an organic garden
made in open countryside since 1992 and
still developing. The owners are keen
plantsmen, so they grow a wide variety of
interesting and unusual plants with the aim
of providing year-round interest. Features
include a large mixed border, pergolas,
ponds and water features, wildlife areas, a
fruit and vegetable garden, and the
permaculture forest garden.

Owned by Mike & Diane Stacey
Number of gardeners owners
Size 2 acres

The Manor House

BIRLINGHAM, PERSHORE WR10 3AF

Tel 01386 750005 **Fax** 01386 751288
Location In village
Opening hours 11 am – 5 pm; Thursdays; May & June.
Plus 17 June (Plant Fair)
Admission fee Adults £2; Children free

The garden was first set out in the late 1780s:
relics of these original plantings include
giant box hedges and a very fine *Phillyrea*, as
well as the ha-ha which allows the eye an
unhindered sweep to the River Avon and the
magnificent views of Bredon Hill. Jane
Williams-Thomas has replanted the garden
with a designer's eye, making terraces and

using hedges to create enclosed intimate areas. One important element of the design has been the use of many benches to encourage repose and create a peaceful atmosphere. Roses are a particular love – the garden has over 100 different cultivars – and they are interplanted with silver plants and perennials that will respond to the dry, warm site. The white garden is particularly successful: it has brick paths surrounded by yew hedges and the lush, romantic planting which characterises the whole garden. Rare plants are used in unusual combinations to bring out contrasts and harmonies of form and colour. The garden is a member of the Quiet Garden Trust.

Owned by Mr & Mrs David Williams-Thomas
Number of gardeners owners, plus part-time help
Size 1¾ acres

The Priory

KEMERTON, TEWKESBURY GL20 7JN

Tel 01386 725258
Location In Kemerton village
Opening hours 2 pm – 6 pm; Thursdays; 5 July to 27 September. Plus 1 & 15 July, 5 & 26 August, & 9 & 23 September. And parties by appointment between 20 June and 30 September
Admission fee Adults £2.50; Children free

The Priory is a late-summer comet, brilliant in August & September when annuals and tender plants supplement the perennial colour planting. Mrs Healing has spent many years studying plants and perfecting her colour gradings. The results are worth a long journey to see and to study: the crimson border is the best there has ever been.

Owned by The Hon Mrs Healing
Number of gardeners 1
Size 4 acres

Rickard's Hardy Ferns Ltd

KYRE PARK, TENBURY WELLS WR15 8RP

Tel 01885 410282   **Fax** 01885 410729
Location Off B4214 Bromyard road, 4 miles south of Tenbury Wells
Opening hours 11 am – 5 pm; Wednesday – Monday; April to October. And by appointment

Rickard is probably the best-known nursery specialising in ferns in the British Isles. It has won a succession of gold medals at the Chelsea Flower Show in recent years. A great number are for sale, including some of the fashionable half-hardy tree ferns. Nearly 1,000 different species and cultivars grow in the collection at the nursery. Kyre Park is an historic landscape – mainly a classical eighteenth-century landscape with lakes, but some of its elements date back to the seventeenth.

NCCPG National Collections Cystopteris; Polypodium; Thelypteridaceae
English Heritage grade II

Spetchley Park

WORCESTER WR5 1RS

Tel 01905 345224
Location 2 miles east of Worcester on A422
Opening hours 11 am – 5 pm; Tuesday – Friday & Bank Holiday Mondays, (plus 2 pm – 5 pm on Sundays); April to September
Admission fee Adults £3.40; Children £1.70

In a classic English landscaped park, three generations of Berkeleys have created one of the best plantsman's gardens in the Midlands.

Ellen Willmott was the owner's great aunt and many of the most exciting trees and shrubs date from her time – a gnarled specimen of the laciniate walnut (*Juglans nigra* 'Laciniata'), for example. In the walled garden, *Tulipa sprengeri* has seeded and naturalised over a large area. Other spring flowers include peonies, columbines and masses of bulbs. In summer, there are hundreds of different roses – old-fashioned roses, tea roses, David Austin roses, floribunda roses – every type of rose is here. Martagon lilies have naturalised in large quantities. The glasshouses are crammed with unusual plants. The planting continues: everywhere in the garden are new designs, new plants and new combinations. A whole new garden has been planted to commemorate the millennium, with tunnels of *Cercis canadensis* 'Forest Pansy' and *Robinia hispida* 'Macrophylla'. Because of its scale and variety, this garden offers something to everyone, but most especially to the plantsman.

Owned by R J Berkeley Esq
Number of gardeners 4
Size 30 acres
English Heritage grade II*

Stone House Cottage Garden

STONE, KIDDERMINSTER DY10 4BG

Tel 01562 69902   **Fax** 01562 69960
Location In village, 2 miles from Kidderminster on A448
Opening hours 10 am – 5.30 pm; Wednesday – Saturday; March to September. Plus Bank Holidays. And by appointment between October & March
Admission fee Adults £2.50; Children free

This is the garden of a famous nursery, which it matches for the range of beautiful

and unusual plants it offers. The owners are compulsive plantsmen and, as the garden is small, they have to move plants around or replace them altogether to make room for new arrivals. This means that the garden is constantly developing and improving – especially since much thought is given to the way each plant will associate with its neighbours. Around the walls is an eccentric collection of follies built as towers in the garden walls, which makes this garden quite unique.

Owned by Mr James & The Hon Mrs Arbuthnott
Number of gardeners 1
Size ¾ acre

The Walled Garden

6 ROSE TERRACE, WORCESTER WR5 1BU

Tel & Fax 01905 354629
Location Off Fort Royal Hill (which is off A44); ½ mile from Cathedral
Opening hours 12 noon – 5 pm; 16 June, 4 August. And for National Gardens Scheme
Admission fee Adults £1.50; Children 50p

This all-organic garden is a centre for the study of herbs: the owners sell herb plants and other herbal products. All takes place within a walled garden, dating from Victorian times, which they are in the process of restoring.

Owned by William & Julia Scott
Number of gardeners owners
Size ¾ acre

Webbs of Wychbold

WYCHBOLD, DROITWICH WR9 0DG

Tel 01527 861777   **Fax** 01527 861284
Website www.webbsofwychbold.co.uk
Location 1 mile from M5, Jct5: follow brown tourist signs
Opening hours 9 am – 6 pm; Monday – Friday (8 pm April – September). 9 am – 6 pm; Saturdays and Bank Holidays. 10.30 am – 4.30 pm; Sundays

Webbs are a major garden centre, a regional heavyweight with several trade awards for excellence. They have an extremely large stock of plants of every kind, as well as a wide range of in-house retail opportunities of interest to gardeners and non-gardeners alike. They have a reputation as plant-introducers too: a form of *Nemesia denticulata* which they call 'Confetti' and *Coryopsis* 'Calypso' are two of their plant introductions. Their display gardens include a herb garden, a series of patio gardens and a sequence of other model lay-outs which they call the Riverside Gardens. Tours of the nurseries and their National Collection of shrubby potentillas are also available. Good website.

Size 50 acres
NCCPG National Collections *Potentilla fruticosa* cvs.

Witley Court

GREAT WITLEY WR6 7JT

Tel 01299 896636
Location 10 miles north of Worcester on A443
Opening hours 10 am – 6 pm (5 pm in October); daily; April to October. 9 am – 4 pm; Wednesday – Sunday; November to March. Closed 24 to 26 December
Admission fee Adults £3.50; Concessions £2.60; Children £1.80

The gardens at Witley Court are undergoing extensive restoration and are increasingly in good condition, thanks to English Heritage. You enter through the rhododendron woods, planted mainly with hardy hybrids under a canopy of American conifers. At the bottom of the valley, below the cascade which runs from the lake, is an Elizabeth Frink statue – part of a planned sculpture park. More interesting, though, is the spectacular ruined mansion and the immense formal gardens behind. They are one of Nesfield's masterpieces, built on a monumental scale by the first Earl of Dudley: English Heritage has plans to restore them. The sheer size of the roofless conservatory and the fountains is remarkable: a place to fantasise about life among the plutocrats 100 years ago.

Owned by English Heritage
Number of gardeners 2
Size 40 acres
English Heritage grade II*

YORKSHIRE, EAST RIDING OF

Since the demise of the much-disliked Humberside, the East Riding has been reconstituted as an administrative area. Many of the Yorkshire's gardening institutions are organised on an all-Yorkshire basis: thus, for example, the Yorkshire Gardens Trust and the Yorkshire Group of the NCCPG are county-wide societies. Sledmere House is the outstanding historic garden in East Yorkshire, though Burton Constable is also well-known for its Capability Brown landscape garden. There are comparatively few good modern gardens in East Yorkshire, apart from the charming water-gardens at Burnby, where a National Collection of waterlilies (*Nymphaea*) is displayed in a beautifully landscaped site. There are four further National Collections in East Yorkshire, including a collection of *Crataegus laevigata* and *C. monogyna* cultivars at the University of Hull's garden at Cottingham – a botanic garden which has lost the botany department that was once the reason for its existence. There is a sprinkling of gardens that open for the National Gardens Scheme in East Yorkshire, which has its own county organiser. There are few nurseries of national repute: one which is not listed below is Swanland Nurseries, which has a good collection of *Pelargonium* cultivars – over 800 of them. Burnby Hall is the only garden which offers free entry to RHS members – and a very enjoyable garden it is.

Bishop Burton Botanic Garden

BISHOP BURTON COLLEGE, BEVERLEY HU17 8QG

Tel 01964 553000
Location In village
Opening hours 9 am – 5 pm; Monday to Friday; all year
Admission fee free

This is not a true botanic garden: Bishop Burton is a college where horticulture is taught, so this is closer to a demonstration garden to teach students about plants. The walled garden has areas where fruit, vegetables and herbs are grown, together with a display of good herbaceous plants and shrubs. There are also several glasshouses. Outside, in the park, is a nineteenth-century landscape with good wellingtonias, cedars and a cucumber tree (*Magnolia acuminata*).

Owned by Bishop Burton College
Number of gardeners 4, plus students
Size 2 acres walled garden, plus park

Burnby Hall Gardens

POCKLINGTON YO42 2QF

Tel 01759 302068   **Fax** 01759 388272
Location Off A1079 13 miles east of York
Opening hours 10 am – 6 pm; daily; 31 March to 30 September
Admission fee Adults £2.50; OAPs £2; Children £1. RHS members free

Burnby Hall is famed for its water lilies, planted by Frances Perry in the 1930 and now totalling over 80 different cultivars. They are grown in two long, landscaped lakes. But there is much more to Burnby: a rock garden, heather beds, a 'secret garden', seasonal bedding and a good collection of conifers all contribute to its visitor-friendly air. A woodland walk is due to open this spring, and the walled garden is being restored with a view to opening as soon as possible. Follow the tarmacadam path around the lakes: Burnby is a grand place for a promenade, especially when a brass band is playing on Sunday afternoons in summer.

Owned by Stewarts Trust
Number of gardeners 3½
Size 8 acres
NCCPG National Collections Nymphaea

Burton Agnes Hall Gardens

BURTON AGNES, DRIFFIELD YO25 0ND

Tel 01262 490324   **Fax** 01262 490513
Location On A166 Driffield-Bridlington road
Opening hours 11 am – 5 pm; daily; April to October
Admission fee Adults £4; OAPs £2; Children £1

The old walled garden has been redesigned in a neo-Elizabethan style to complement the house. As well as a *potager* and herb garden it has such unconventional features as a life-size games board for snakes & ladders, a jungle garden and a maze with a riddle. Rather more conventional are the plantings of shrub roses (lots of them), clematis and herbaceous plants. It is most enjoyable to visit.

Owned by Burton Agnes Hall Preservation Trust Ltd
NCCPG National Collections Campanula

Burton Constable

SKIRLAUGH, HULL HU11 4LN

Tel 01964 562400   **Fax** 01964 563229
Website www.burtonconstable.com
Location Via Hull B1238 to Sproatley follow HH signs
Opening hours 12 noon – 5 pm (last admission 4.15); Saturday – Thursday; Easter Sunday to 31 October
Admission fee Adults £1; Children 50p

The main feature around the massive house is a Capability Brown landscape: his original plans are still shown. However, the foundation has recently received lottery funding for a major restoration of the gardens, including the four acres of nineteenth-century pleasure grounds. So this is a garden to watch in future.

Owned by Burton Constable Foundation
Number of gardeners 3
English Heritage grade II

Sledmere House

SLEDMERE, DRIFFIELD YO25 3XG

Tel 01377 236637   **Fax** 01377 236500
Location Off A166 between York & Bridlington
Opening hours 11.30 am – 4.30 pm; daily except
Mondays & Saturdays; 13 April to 30 September.
Sundays only in April

Admission fee Adults £2; Children £1

Sledmere has a classical Capability Brown landscape: his originals plans can be seen in the museum. An Italianate formal garden was added in 1911, with Greek and Roman busts swathed in climbing roses. Over the last two years, Sledmere has seen extensive replanting in the eighteenth-century walled garden and around the house. A new knot garden is growing up quickly.

Owned by Sir Tatton Sykes
Number of gardeners 3
English Heritage grade I

YORKSHIRE, NORTH

North Yorkshire corresponds with the old North Riding of Yorkshire: it is a county of large estates and small market towns. Among its historic gardens are some of the grandest landscapes in England: Castle Howard, Duncombe Park and Studley Royal are all Grade I gardens. North Yorkshire also has three very important modern gardens – Harlow Carr, Newby Hall and Thorpe Perrow – each quite different in character but all horticultural heavyweights. Harlow Carr is the seat of the Northern Horticultural Society, which is modelled on the Royal Horticultural Society and enjoys a considerable following. The National Gardens Scheme does well in North Yorkshire and so does the NCCPG, which has over 20 National Collections in the county. The best nurseries are also in North Yorkshire, including R V Roger Ltd, which has a good line in exotic 'architectural' plants, and the *Pulmonaria* and rare plant specialist Stillingfleet Lodge Nurseries: Stillingfleet also has a good garden which Royal Horticultural Society members can visit free in May and June. Newby Hall, Millgate House and Harlow Carr are also free-access gardens for RHS members. The Royal Horticultural Society has a Partner College at Askham Bryan, the old county horticultural college: it has about a dozen public lectures and workshops throughout the year – details from the School Secretary on 01904 772230.

Beningbrough Hall

SHIPTON-BY-BENINGBROUGH, YORK
YO30 1DD

Tel 01904 470666   **Fax** 01904 470002
Website www.nationaltrust.org.uk
Location 8 miles north-west of York off the A19
Opening hours 11 am – 5.30 pm; Saturday – Wednesday, plus Good Friday & Fridays in July & August; 31 March to 31 October
Admission fee Adults £3.60; Children £1.80

Beningbrough is approached by an avenue of limes through stately parkland. Apart from a gloomy Victorian shrubbery, the gardens are modern and pretty. Two small formal gardens, one with reds and oranges and the other with pastel shades, lie on either side of the early Georgian house. A sumptuous mixed border, graded from hot colours to cool, runs right to the gate of the walled kitchen garden. Restoration has begun here in earnest: there are exciting plans for further developments.

Plant Highlights Fruit; good herbaceous borders; American garden; good conservatory on house; traditional Victorian kitchen garden undergoing restoration; 'Lady Downe's Seedling' grape,

Castle Howard

YORK YO6 7DA

Tel 01653 648444   **Fax** 01653 648501
Website www.castlehoward.co.uk
Location 15 miles north-east of York, off A64
Opening hours 10 am – 4.30 pm (last entry); daily;
16 March to 4 November. Ray Wood on Wednesdays
and at weekends
Admission fee Adults £4.50; Children £2.50

Be prepared to spend all day at Castle Howard: it is essential visiting both for plantsmen and for anyone with a sense of history. At every time of the year, there are really good walks through woodlands and formal gardens, along the terraces and beside the water, and views of the buildings and sculptures in the landscape. The heroic megapark (originally about 300 acres, but now closer to 3,000) was first laid out by the 3rd Earl of Carlisle in 1700. Vanburgh filled the five axes with landscapings and important buildings: the south lake, the terraces, the statues and the waterfalls down to the new river are all his. Vanburgh's masterpiece, built in 1724–6, is the Temple of the Four Winds. The Mausoleum was designed by Hawksmoor in 1728. In front of the house are the remains of a vast nineteenth-century parterre, whose centre point is the Atlas fountain built by Nesfield in the 1850s. Within a walled garden is a series of grand 1980s rose gardens (slightly Surrey) designed by Jim Russell, with every type of rose from ancient to modern. Of more interest to gardeners and plantsmen is Ray Wood, where a fine and historic collection of rhododendrons and other ericaceous plants (all meticulously labelled) is destined to develop as one of the greatest woodland gardens in Europe. The rhododendrons and other plants of

twentieth-century plant hunters are well represented – collections by Forrest, Rock, Kingdon Ward, Ludlow and Sheriff are all well represented, as are more recent collections from Nepal, Bhutan, Japan, and China. Since 1999 it has been managed jointly by Castle Howard and the Royal Botanic Gardens at Kew: there is a small additional charge to visit it.

Plant Highlights Impressive landscape; woodland garden; roses (ancient & modern); good herbaceous borders; tallest elm *Ulmus glabra* (37m) in British Isles.

Owned by Castle Howard Estates Ltd
Size 1,000 acres
English Heritage grade I

raised at Beningbrough in 1835; vast Portuguese laurel *Prunus lusitanica*.

Owned by The National Trust
English Heritage grade II

Daleside Nurseries

RIPON ROAD, KILLINGHALL, HARROGATE HG3 2AY

Tel 01423 506450   **Fax** 01423 527872
Website www.dalesidenurseries.co.uk
Location 4 miles north of Harrogate (A61)
Opening hours 9 am – 5 pm, Monday – Saturday;
10 am – 12 noon, 1.30 pm – 4.30 pm, Sundays

Daleside is a well-established (founded 1958) general nursery with a wide range of plants available including clematis, conifers, rhododendrons and azaleas, roses, trees and shrubs. It also has a speciality, which is soft fruit and fruit trees.

Duncombe Park

HELMSLEY YO62 5EB

Tel 01439 770213   **Fax** 01439 771114
Website www.duncombepark.com
Location Off A170; signed from Helmsley
Opening hours 10.30 am – 6 pm or dusk if earlier;
Sunday – Thursday; 13 April to 28 October
Admission fee Adults £4; Children £2

Duncombe is a major eighteenth-century landscape garden: the views from Thomas Duncombe's Rievaulx Terrace are constantly changing – 'a moving variation' Arthur Young called it in 1770. The long, spacious terrace near the top of the steep hillside curves for more than half a mile between a domed Ionic cupola and a pedimented

Tuscan temple. Sometimes the gothic ruins of Rievaulx Abbey far below are framed by woodland rides and sometimes they disappear altogether. Crucial to Duncombe's effect is the contrast between the smooth classical landscape and the sublime decay of the ancient abbey. It foreshadows the rise of the picturesque as a significant development of the landscape movement.

Owned by Lord Feversham
Number of gardeners 1
Size 30 acres, plus parkland
English Heritage grade I

Harlow Carr Botanical Gardens

BECKWITHSHAW, HARROGATE HG3 1QB

Tel 01423 565418   **Fax** 01423 530663
Website www.harlowcarr.fsnet.co.uk
Location Crag Lane off Otley Road (B6162), 1½ miles from Harrogate centre
Opening hours 9.30 am – 6 pm, or dusk if earlier; daily; all year
Admission fee Adults £4.50; OAPs £3.50; Students £2; Children (under 11) free. RHS members free

Not for nothing is Harlow Carr known as 'the Wisley of the North': for more than 50 years, it has set itself the challenge of educating, inspiring and delighting northern gardeners. The gardens are comprehensive and spectacular. The features include rock gardens, heathers, alpine houses, streamside and water gardens, woodland gardens, a rhododendron collection, peat terraces, a winter garden, a shrub rose border, vegetable and fruit plots, and an extensive arboretum. New features appear every year: look out for the new kitchen garden and fruit garden, the redesigned and replanted herb garden, and the new border which mixes herbaceous plants with ornamental grasses. The Northern Horticultural Society also ensures that Harlow Carr is an important centre for horticultural learning, with a splendid list of events and courses all through the year for amateurs and professionals alike. Its website is comprehensive, accessible and informative.

Owned by Northern Horticultural Society
Number of gardeners 7
Size 68 acres
NCCPG National Collections Calluna (provisional); Dryopteris; Fuchsia magellanica (provisional); Polypodium; Rheum

Millgate House

RICHMOND DL10 4JN

Tel 01748 823571 **Fax** 01748 850701
Location Bottom of Market Place; first house in Millgate
Opening hours 10 am – 6 pm; daily; April to October
Admission fee Adults £1.50; Children free. RHS members free in June & July

This is a walled garden in the middle of the town, and thus remarkably sheltered. Since starting work in the garden in 1980, the owners' aim has been to create structure, bulk, year-round interest and a sense of profusion. They have achieved this by re-designing the garden to suggest that it is much larger than it really is, and by planting only the best plants of every type. The most prominent are roses, clematis, hostas, snowdrops, hellebores, ferns and foliage shrubs. By 1995 they had won the National Garden Competition, against 3,200 other entries. The garden continues to improve. It is immensely stylish, a model for all town gardens.

Owned by Tim Culkin & Austin Lynch
Number of gardeners owners
Size one-third of an acre

Mount Grace Priory

STADDLEBRIDGE, NORTHALLERTON DL6 3JG

Tel 01609 883494 **Fax** 01609 883361
Website www.nationaltrust.org.uk
Location 12 miles north of Thirsk on A19
Opening hours 10 am – 6 pm; daily; April to September. 10 am – 5 pm; daily; October. 10 am – 1 pm and 2 pm – 4 pm; Wednesday – Sunday; November to March
Admission fee Adults £2.90; Concessions £2.20; Children £1.60

The herb garden, designed by Stephen Anderton in 1994, is of most interest to gardeners. It is a recreation of a fifteenth-century monastic garden. Around the house, the 1920s flower borders are being restored: there are terraces, acers, rhododendrons and azaleas. It is not a garden in which to dally, but an interesting add-on to the whole experience of a visit.

Owned by The National Trust (managed by English Heritage)
Number of gardeners 2

Newby Hall

RIPON HG4 5AE

Tel 01423 322583 **Fax** 01423 324452
Website www.newbyhall.co.uk
Location Off B6265, 2 miles from A1 between Boroughbridge & Ripon
Opening hours 11 am – 5.30 pm; Tuesday – Sunday & Bank Holiday Mondays; April to September
Admission fee Adults £5; OAPs £4; Children £3.50. RHS members free in April, May & September

Newby is the garden with everything: firm design, an endless variety of features, great plantsmanship and immaculate maintenance. Its axis is a bold, wide, double border stretching endlessly down to the River Ure. The National Collection of *Cornus* now extends to 35 species and 65 cultivars, planted to give colour, beauty and interest. Newby also has a large number of other rare trees and shrubs and a comprehensive collection of shrubby salvias, many of them collected in central and southern America by the owner's brother Dr Jamie Compton. Newby is second only to Hidcote as an example of twentieth-century gardening, but very much grander: visit it at any season and expect to spend all day there.

 Plant Highlights Woodland garden; roses (mainly old-fashioned & climbers); rock garden; plantsman's collection of plants; daffodils; good herbaceous borders; HHA/Christie's Garden of the Year in 1986; tallest *Acer griseum* (15m) in UK.

Owned by Richard Compton
Number of gardeners 7
Size 25 acres
NCCPG National Collections *Cornus*
English Heritage grade II*

Parcevall Hall Gardens

SKYREHOLME, SKIPTON BD23 6DE

Tel 01756 720311 **Fax** 01756 720441
Website www.parcevallhallgardens.co.uk
Location Off B6160 from Burnsall
Opening hours 10 am – 6 pm; daily; April to October; winter visits by appointment
Admission fee Adults £3; Children 50p

Ⓟ 🅗 🆆 ⊕

The gardens at Parcevall Hall have a breathtaking architectural layout and views of the Yorkshire dales. They were largely designed and planted by Sir William Milner in 1927 and benefit from a great variety of soils (limestone and gritstone) which means

that rhododendrons and camellias grow alongside limestone outcrops. It is something of a plantsman's garden too: the naturalised daffodils in the orchard include 'W F Milner' while the *Primula florindae* given by Kingdon Ward has now naturalised around the lily pond. Within the grounds are 14 Stations of the Cross.

Owned by Walsingham College (Yorkshire Properties) Ltd
Number of gardeners 3
Size 16 acres

Ripley Castle

RIPLEY, HARROGATE HG3 3AY

Tel 01423 770152 **Fax** 01423 771745
Website www.ripleycastle.co.uk
Location 3½ miles north of Harrogate, off A61
Opening hours 9 am – 5 pm (or dusk if earlier); daily; all year
Admission fee Adults £3; OAPs £2.50; Children £1.50

Ⓟ 🆆 🅖 ⊕ 🏠 ⊕

Ripley has a garden with something for everyone: a fourteenth-century castle (restored); temples; a landscape designed by Capability Brown; a fine Regency conservatory; a Victorian formal garden; evergreen shrubberies (handsome yews); rare vegetables from HDRA in the traditional Victorian walled garden; colour at every season; over 2,000 hyacinths in 40 varieties; woodland walks; herbaceous borders; and hundreds of thousands of bulbs – daffodils in hosts.

Owned by Sir Thomas Ingilby Bt
Number of gardeners 4
NCCPG National Collections *Hyacinthus orientalis*
English Heritage grade II

R V Roger Ltd

THE NURSERIES, PICKERING
YO18 7HG

Tel 01751 472226
Location 1 mile south of Pickering, on A169
Opening hours 9 am – 5 pm; Monday – Saturday.
1 pm – 5 pm; Sundays

There has been a change of emphasis at
Roger's over the years. It used to be known
most for its all-round range of alpines,
bulbs, conifers, perennials, roses, trees and
shrubs. Then it started to develop a
speciality for trained fruit trees – everything
from espaliered apples to gooseberries
grown as standards. Now it is also one of the
top places for architectural plants like
bamboos from China and tree ferns from
Australia. The list of Australian natives is
also expanding – clematis, kennedyas and
hardenbergias among the climbers, and
xanthorrhoeas and macrazamias among the
woody plants.

Sleightholmedale Lodge

FADMOOR, KIRKBYMOORSIDE
YO6 6JG

Tel 01751 431942
Location Signed from Fadmoor
Opening hours 2 pm – 6 pm; 21 May, 15 & 16 July. And
by written appointment
Admission fee Adults £2; Children 50p

This family garden – Mrs James is the third
generation to garden here – is a plantsman's
paradise right on the edge of the moors. The
walled garden was built on a south-facing
slope, which makes it possible to grow a
wide range of plants that might not

otherwise survive. As well as magnificent
meconopsis and hardy herbaceous plants it
has Mexican and Mediterranean rarities (a
cistus walk, for example) which are a
triumph for good cultivation and
manipulation of the microclimate. The
herbaceous borders are held together by
repeating certain plants throughout:
foxgloves, campanulas, martagon lilies, for
example. Outside the walled garden is an
orchard underplanted with snowdrops and
narcissi. Up at the top is a hollyhock walk.
And there are roses of every sort – hundreds
of them, perhaps thousands.

Owned by Mrs R James

Stillingfleet Lodge Nurseries

STILLINGFLEET, YORK YO4 6HW

Tel & Fax 01904 728506
Location 6 miles south of York: turn opposite the church
Opening hours 1 pm – 4 pm; Wednesdays; May to
September. Plus Fridays in May & June
Admission fee Adults £2; Children 50p. RHS members
free in May & June

Stillingfleet is a series of small gardens
surrounding a late eighteenth-century
farmhouse. The emphasis is on a cottage
garden style of planting, for ease of
maintenance. Foliage is used to add interest
and texture: the result is a sequence of
sumptuous herbaceous borders – a living
lesson in how to plant a garden. The
collection of pulmonarias is fascinating: 13
species and over 150 cultivars flower over a
long period. A wildflower walk leads to a
pond planted for natural effect. The nursery
has an excellent herbaceous list with a high
proportion of unusual plants: the catalogue

changes each year but is always good for geraniums and pulmonarias.

Number of gardeners owner plus a little part-time help
Size 1½ acres
NCCPG National Collections *Pulmonaria*

Studley Royal

FOUNTAINS, RIPON HG4 3DZ

Tel 01765 608888   **Fax** 01765 608889
Website www.nationaltrust.org.uk
Location 3 miles west of Ripon off B6265, via the Visitor Centre
Opening hours 10 am – 5 pm (7 pm in summer) or dusk if sooner; daily; all year, except Fridays from November to January & 24 & 25 December. Closes at 4 pm on 6 & 7 July
Admission fee Adults £4.50; Children £2.20

Studley Royal is inextricably linked to Fountains Abbey: nothing can beat the surprise view of the ruined Cistercian abbey from Anne Boleyn's Seat. The most spectacular water garden in England was laid out in between 1716 and 1781 in the sheltered flat bottom of the River Skell. The abbey is at one end, the 400-acre deer park at the other. The combination of the formal canal, moon pools, grotto springs, rustic bridge, sculptures and the Temple of Filial Piety against a dark background of trees is a supreme example of eighteenth-century landscaping at its most individual.

Plant Highlights Topiary; snowdrops; World Heritage site; newly restored water garden; biggest *Prunus avium* (bird cherry) in British Isles.

Owned by The National Trust
English Heritage grade I

Sutton Park

SUTTON-ON-THE-FOREST, YORK
YO6 1DP

Tel 01347 810249   **Fax** 01347 811251
Website www.statelyhome.co.uk
Location 8 miles north of York on B1363
Opening hours 11 am – 5 pm; daily; 1 April to 30 September
Admission fee Adults £2.50; OAPs £1.50; Children 50p

Capability Brown was here in the eighteenth century, but the joy of Sutton is the formal garden laid out on terraces below the house by Percy Cane in the 1960s and planted by the late Nancie Sheffield with exquisite taste. It was one of the first to throw off the austerity of the post-war years and insist upon floral profusion and segregated colour schemes. It is still quite the prettiest garden in Yorkshire. In the grounds are a Georgian ice-house and a woodland walk which takes you round some of the best trees on the estate – oaks, wellingtonias, and some fine Victorian conifers.

Plant Highlights Fine formal gardens; woodland garden; roses (mainly old-fashioned); plantsman's collection of plants; good herbaceous borders; walled pond garden; new fern garden & herb garden (1998).

Owned by Sir Reginald & Lady Sheffield
Number of gardeners 2½
Size 8 acres, plus parkland

Thorp Perrow Arboretum

BEDALE DL8 2PR

Tel & Fax 01677 425323
Location On the Bedale-Ripon road, 2 miles south of Bedale
Opening hours Dawn to dusk; daily; all year
Admission fee Adults £5; OAPs & Students £3.75; Children £2.75

Thorp Perrow is the most important arboretum in the north of England, with more than 20 record-breaking trees among the thousands planted since Sir Leonard Ropner started work in 1931. There was already a pinetum on the estate, planted by Lady Augusta Milbank in the 1840s and 1850s. Ropner surrounded it with his new plantings – over 1,000 different taxa still survive, to which his son Sir John has added at least another 300. There are handsome avenues to walk along, often lined with a single genus or species – red oaks, rowans, cherries or cypresses, for example. Many are thickly lined with daffodils in spring, as are the glades and bays where you can study a particular collection like acers or hollies. The only downside to Thorp Perrow is that all the trees are identified only with a number, which you then have to look up in the catalogue of plantings. The reason for this is that labels with names on them tend to get lost more easily. This minor irritation apart, Thorp Perrow is in every way an inspiring and enjoyable place to visit.

Owned by Sir John Ropner Bt
Size 85 acres
NCCPG National Collections Fraxinus; Juglans; Tilia
English Heritage grade II

Valley Gardens

HARROGATE BOROUGH COUNCIL, HARROGATE

Tel 01423 500600   **Fax** 01423 556720
Website www.harrogate.gov.uk
Location Harrogate
Opening hours Dawn – dusk; daily; all year
Admission fee free

The Valley Gardens at Harrogate are one of the best examples of plantsmanship in a public garden in England. They were first laid out 1880–1900 and have recently been substantially refurbished with a grant from the Lottery. The gardens have alpine rarities in spring, a romantic rhododendron dell, good roses, a magnificent dahlia display in late summer and the best colour bedding in Yorkshire.

Owned by Harrogate Borough Council
Size 17 acres
English Heritage grade II

YORKSHIRE, SOUTH

The county of South Yorkshire was invented in 1974 and is, in effect, a Greater Sheffield. Nevertheless it has a couple of good historic gardens which are open to the public – Wentworth Castle and Brodsworth Hall. The Sheffield Botanical Gardens too are of great horticultural interest, having been planted and maintained over many years as a garden of ornamental plants of every kind. Both the Sheffield Botanical Gardens and the gardens at Wentworth Castle have benefited from lottery funding in recent years and are much more visitor-friendly as a result, though it is still possible to visit Wentworth only as part of a guided tour. The National Gardens Scheme has very few gardens opening for it in the county and, though it is well provided with garden centres, South Yorkshire has no specialist nurseries of national importance. There are eight NCCPG National Collections – including two at Sheffield Botanical Gardens and three at Wentworth Castle.

Brodsworth Hall

ENGLISH HERITAGE, BRODSWORTH, DONCASTER DN5 7XJ

Tel 01302 722598   **Fax** 01302 337165
Location 6 miles north-west of Doncaster
Opening hours 12 noon – 6 pm; Tuesday – Sunday & Bank Holiday Mondays; 1 April to 4 November. Then 11 am – 4 pm; weekends only; until Christmas
Admission fee Garden only: Adults £2.60; OAPs £2; Children £1.30. Cheap rates in winter

Brodsworth was unkempt for fifty years, acquired by English Heritage in 1990, and is now being restored as first laid out in the 1860s. It offers Italianate terraces, statues and classical follies, a rose garden where ramblers are trained on ironwork arcades, magnificent trees including monkey puzzles and 30-ft *Arbutus* trees, and bright Victorian bedding. Newly planted for 2001 is a fine fern collection in the restored rock garden.

Owned by English Heritage
Number of gardeners 4
Size 13 acres
English Heritage grade II

The Earth Centre

KILNER'S BRIDGE, DONCASTER ROAD, DENABY MAIN DN12 4EA

Tel 01709 512000   **Fax** 01709 512010
Location Signed off to A6023 about one mile east of Denaby Main
Opening hours Not yet known: probably opening in May.
Admission fee Not yet known

The gardens at the Earth Centre include forest gardens, twenty-first-century gardens, bog gardens and dry gardens. All are part of a larger project created to promote and demonstrate the idea of sustainability. It has had a few teething problems, but the owners hope to be fully open by late spring.

Number of gardeners 4

Size 25 acres

Sheffield Botanical Gardens

CLARKEHOUSE ROAD, SHEFFIELD S10 2LN

Tel 0114 250 0500   **Fax** 0114 255 2375

Location Jct33 of M1, follow A57 signs to Glossop, left at Royal Hallamshire Hospital, 500yds on left

Opening hours 7.30 am (10 am at weekends) – 7.45 pm (4 pm in winter); daily; all year

Admission fee free

The Sheffield Botanical Gardens were founded in 1833 by public subscription and still burgeon with civic pride. The garden has been awarded a £5.1m lottery grant and has a phased programme of work leading up to March 2004. This summer, the 'Paxton' pavilions (actually built by Robert Marnock) are being repaired. The layout of the garden is a good example of the 'gardenesque' style made popular by John Loudon but there is much to interest the plantsman, too. The features include good camellias and magnolias; heathers; a peat garden; a rock garden; demonstration vegetable gardens; a lilac collection; good trees. The garden has splendid summer bedding too, and lots of seats and waste bins: an exemplary combination of botany and amenity.

Owned by Sheffield Town Trust

Number of gardeners 5, plus 2 part-time

Size 19 acres

NCCPG National Collections Diervilla; Weigela

Wentworth Castle Gardens

LOWE LANE, STAINBOROUGH, BARNSLEY S75 3ET

Tel 01226 731269

Location Signed 'Northern College'. 3 miles south of Barnsley; 2 miles from M1

Opening hours Principally open in spring by guided tours on Tuesdays at 10 am and Wednesdays & Thursdays at 2 pm from 18 April to 28 June. Also 2 pm – 5 pm on 13 & 20 May & 3 June; and 10 am – 5 pm on 27 & 28 May

Admission fee Adults £2.50; Concessions £1.50

Wentworth has a major landscape garden, one of the earliest in England, which accounts for the amazing series of buildings in the grounds – among them are an Ionic rotunda, a gothic folly and an obelisk to Queen Anne. It was then overlaid with a seriously important collection of hardy hybrid rhododendrons at the end of the nineteenth century. This has been the basis of its current development as an educational and cultural resource, backed by lottery funding. It is twinned with the Kunming Academy of Sciences, China. There is only problem about visiting it – you have to go with a guided tour.

Plant Highlights Historic landscape; woodland garden; newly excavated nineteenth-century rock garden; educational collection of rhododendrons.

Owned by Barnsley Metropolitan Borough Council

Number of gardeners 5

Size 40 acres

NCCPG National Collections Rhododendron (Falconeri series); Magnolia species; Camellia × williamsii

English Heritage grade I

YORKSHIRE, WEST

West Yorkshire corresponds to the old West Riding. It is a county of great contrasts, from the industrial and commercial cities of Bradford and Leeds to the wool towns of Huddersfield and Halifax, with a chunk of the Peak District in the south-west and some large agricultural estates in the north. The most important historic gardens are Bramham Park – a remarkable pre-landscape garden on a big scale – and the opulent Harewood House. But they are matched for sheer horticultural value by four gardens which all have an historic past but are now owned and managed by Leeds City Council as gardens for public recreation– Lotherton Hall, Temple Newsam, The Hollies, and the Canal Gardens & Tropical World in Roundhay Park. The NCCPG has no less than eleven National Collections in the care of the Leeds City Parks Department. It therefore comes as a surprise to discover that the Royal Horticultural Society has as yet no partnership arrangements with any garden, nursery or college in West Yorkshire. There are, in fact, rather few specialist nurseries of national standing in the county, though it is well served by garden centres. The standards of horticultural displays in both private and public gardens are greatly aided by the activities of the Yorkshire in Bloom competition.

8 Dunstarn Lane

ADEL, LEEDS LS16 8EL

Tel 0113 267 3938
Location Off Long causeway, Adel
Opening hours 2 pm – 7 pm; 24 June, 1 & 11 July, 5 August
Admission fee Adults £1.50; Children free

The house at 8 Dunstarn Lane is modern, built as a retirement house in the grounds of his old family home by Richard Wainwright, the distinguished lawyer and retired member of parliament. The part of the garden which he retained includes the area

where he (and his father before him) have grown delphiniums for more than half a century. It is probably the finest and most extensive collection of delphiniums in private hands, with nearly 70 cultivars. They are interplanted with their traditional border companions – roses (mainly modern), phlox, dahlias, Michaelmas daisies and annuals.

Owned by Mr & Mrs Richard Wainwright
Number of gardeners 1
Size 3 acres

Bramham Park

WETHERBY LS23 6ND

Tel 01937 846002 **Fax** 01937 845923
Location 5 miles south of Wetherby on A1
Opening hours 10.30 am – 5.30 pm; daily; April to September. Closed for horse trials from 4 to 10 June and occasionally for other events. Ring before visiting
Admission fee Gardens only: Adults £4; OAPs £2; Children £2

Bramham has very important pre-landscape formal gardens, laid out in the grand manner in the style of Le Nôtre in the early eighteenth century. Long straight rides cut through dense woodland, with ornamental ponds, cascades, loggias, temples and an obelisk. The standard of maintenance is exemplary: all credit to the Lane Foxes for the care they have lavished upon Bramham over such a long period.

Owned by George Lane Fox
Number of gardeners 3
Size 66 acres
English Heritage grade I

Canal Gardens & Tropical World

ROUNDHAY PARK, STREET LANE, LEEDS LS8 2ER

Tel 0113 266 1850 **Fax** 0113 237 0077
Location 3 miles north-west of city centre, off A6120 ring road
Opening hours Open 10 am all year. Close at 4 pm in January & December; 5 pm in February & November; 6 pm in March & October; 7 pm in April & September; 8 pm from May to August

Admission fee Tropical World: Adults £1.50; Children 75p. Gardens free

Tropical World's glasshouses contain South American rain forest plants, bromeliads, hoyas, cacti and a butterfly house. It is said to have the largest collection of tropical plants outside Kew. It is in any event a wonderful retreat from a Yorkshire winter and a triumph of municipal horticultural excellence. Roundhay Park has a £6.1m project to preserve and enhance the gardens which has received support from the Heritage Lottery Fund. This means that Tropical World will be shut until about March 2001.

Plant Highlights Sub-tropical plants; roses (mainly modern); plants under glass; good carpet bedding; orchids; new floral clock (1998); new French & Spanish gardens (May 1999); new desert house.

Owned by Leeds City Council
English Heritage grade II

Golden Acre Park

OTLEY ROAD, BRAMHOPE, LEEDS LS16 5NZ

Tel 0113 267 3729
Website www.leeds.gov.uk
Location 4 miles north on A660 Otley Road
Opening hours Dawn – dusk; daily; all year
Admission fee free

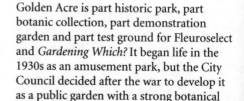

Golden Acre is part historic park, part botanic collection, part demonstration garden and part test ground for Fleuroselect and *Gardening Which?* It began life in the 1930s as an amusement park, but the City Council decided after the war to develop it as a public garden with a strong botanical interest. Perhaps the best of the five impressive public gardens in Leeds, it is certainly the most popular.

Owned by Leeds City Council
Size 137 acres
NCCPG National Collections *Primula auricula*; *Syringa*

Harewood House

THE ESTATE OFFICE, HAREWOOD, LEEDS LS17 9LQ

Tel 0113 288 6331 **Fax** 0113 288 6467
Website www.harewood.org
Location Between Leeds & Harrogate on A61
Opening hours 10 am – 6 pm; daily; 1 March to 29 October
Admission fee Grounds: Adults £6; OAPs £5; Children £3.50

Capability Brown was the first famous landscaper to work at Harewood for the super-rich Lascelles family: he was followed by Repton, Loudon and Barry. The latter came in the 1840s, to build the stupendous Italianate terrace which has recently been restored with a European grant. Its grand parterre and ornate fountains are the perfect link between the house and the landscaped park. Around the lake are hundreds of rhododendrons, unusual shrubs and bulbs, particularly daffodils. The waterfall at the end feeds a rocky garden where primulas, astilbes, hostas and gunneras grow rampantly in the damp. The modern rose garden at the end of the lakeside walk is an extra delight.

 Plant Highlights Woodland garden; Japanese garden; rhododendrons.

Owned by The Earl of Harewood
English Heritage grade I

The Hollies Park

WEETWOOD LANE, LEEDS LS16 5NZ

Tel 0113 278 2030 **Fax** 0113 247 8277
Website www.leeds.gov.uk
Location 3 miles north of city off A660
Opening hours Dawn – dusk; daily; all year
Admission fee free

This public park is made in a plantsman's garden, and is well run by a hard-pressed and enthusiastic team. Visitors wishing to see the National Collections are advised to make a prior appointment.

Owned by Leeds City Council
Size 93 acres
NCCPG National Collections *Deutzia*; *Hemerocallis* (Coe hybrids); *Hosta* (large-leaved); *Philadelphus*; *Syringa*

Land Farm Gardens

COLDEN, HEBDEN BRIDGE, HALIFAX HX7 7PJ

Tel 01422 842260
Location On right, 2 miles from Hebden Bridge on Colden road
Opening hours 10 am – 5 pm; Saturdays, Sundays & Bank Holiday Mondays; May to August
Admission fee Adults £2.50. Guided tours for parties (in evening) £3.50 per person, including refreshments

This is a pioneering plantsman's garden, high in the Pennines and facing north. The range of plants that can successfully be grown in such an unpromising situation is an eye-opener – lots of hardy rhododendrons, shrubs, trees and alpines. There is also a good collection of sculpture, with more pieces arriving all the time.

Owned by John Williams
Size 4 acres

Lotherton Hall

ABERFORD, LEEDS LS25 3EB

Tel 0113 281 3259 **Fax** 0113 281 3068
Website www.leeds.gov.uk
Location Off A1, ¾ mile east on B1217
Opening hours 8 am – 8 pm or dusk, if earlier; daily; all year
Admission fee £2 per car (£5 all year)

This showpiece garden was laid out about 1885–1915 by a friend of Ellen Willmott. It was given to the Council in 1968 and has been well restored in recent years. It offers gazebos, walks, yew hedging, rose gardens, and a lily pond recently replanted with period varieties. The rock garden known as the Dell is especially good. The formal garden is laid out with gravel paths and lots of bedding. Lotherton is a garden that is on the move again, with a woodland trail recently added for disabled users. There will be a series of Japanese exhibitions and events throughout the year.

Owned by Leeds City Council
Number of gardeners 2
Size 10 acres
English Heritage grade II

Temple Newsam Park

LEEDS LS15 0AE

Tel 0113 264 5535
Website www.leeds.gov.uk
Location 3 miles south-east of city, off A63 Selby Road
Opening hours Dawn – dusk; daily; all year
Admission fee free. Admission charge to house

This prodigious house on a windy bluff, surrounded by 1,200 acres of parkland, has been a 'green lung' for Leeds since 1923.

Somewhat dilapidated in the past, the garden is now improved by some recent plantings. These include a traditional herb garden; a spring garden full of bulbs; and the Italian garden with formal flower beds, box, yew and beech hedges, pleached laburnum walks and a clipped hornbeam stilt hedge. A fine rhododendron and azalea walk runs down to the lakes. Nearby is an arboretum and a bog garden. Further on still, the old walled kitchen garden is planted with roses and wide herbaceous borders. The long conservatory has a fine display of flowering plants, ivies and cacti: its back wall (1788) still has the flues which were used to keep it warm with hot air.

Owned by Leeds City Council
NCCPG National Collections Aster; Delphinium; Phlox paniculata
English Heritage grade II

York Gate

BACK CHURCH LANE, ADEL, LEEDS LS16 8DW

Tel 0113 267 8240
Website www.gardeners-grbs.org.uk
Location Behind Adel Church, off A660
Opening hours 2 pm – 5 pm; Thursdays; May to August. Plus 11 February, 11 March, 8 April, 13 & 28 May, 10 June, 8 July, 12 & 27 August. 6 pm – 9 pm, 3 May, 27 June, 26 July
Admission fee Adults £2.50 (£3 for evening visits); Children free

In 1977, Robin Spencer summed up his garden at York Gate for the Yellow Book *Gardens Open to the Public in England and Wales* as 'an owner-made and maintained garden of particular interest to the plantsman, containing orchard with pool, an arbour, miniature pinetum, dell with stream, a folly, a nut walk, peony bed, iris borders, fern border, herb garden, summerhouse, alley, white and silver garden, two vegetable gardens, and pavement maze all within one acre.' All of which is absolutely true. And he could have mentioned the Japanese garden, bog garden, collection of bonsai, Italianate loggia and several arbours too. It is now safely in the care of the Gardeners' Royal Benevolent Society – a masterpiece of tight design, invention, colour sense and sheer creative opportunism.

Owned by The Gardeners' Royal Benevolent Society
Number of gardeners 1
Size 1 acre

SCOTLAND

Scottish gardens are very variable – this is a factor of their soil and climate. All along the west coast, from Dumfries & Galloway up to Ullapool and beyond, are fine, subtropical woodland gardens, where one can enjoy acres of large-leaved rhododendrons and eucalyptus trees and all manner of curiosities like *Myosotidium hortensia* which would not be hardy in any but the most favoured parts of England. There is no better place to go visiting gardens in May or June – provided the weather is kind. There are comparatively few good gardens in inland Scotland. Historically, the big estates were (and still are) in remote places where the land is unsuitable for agriculture and, in consequence, their gardens tend to be few and disappointing. In the Borders, for example, there are several estates along the valleys of Tweed and the Teviot whose gardens are open to the public: all have collections of nineteenth-century conifers underplanted with hardy hybrid rhododendrons or common *R. ponticum*, but little else in the way of horticultural interest. On the East Coast, however, there are once again many worthy gardens, above all the superb botanic garden at Edinburgh, which (like all botanic gardens nowadays) is laid out to please visitors, and other good botanic gardens at Dundee, St Andrews and Aberdeen. There are interesting gardens too near Edinburgh (especially Malleny at Balerno) and on Deeside (Crathes, Kildrummy and Drum).

Trees flourish in much of Scotland – especially those North American conifers for which the cool, damp west coast provides perfect growing conditions: many of the tallest pines, firs and spruces in Britain are in

Scotland. The largest collection of record-breaking trees is at the Royal Botanic Garden in Edinburgh, which has 45.

We have listed the gardens to visit in Scotland under the old 1974 regions, rather than the historic counties or the plethora of more recent local councils. The regions divide the country into areas of acceptable size for the purpose of this book, though there is a preponderance of gardens in the old region of Strathclyde – as indeed there still is in Argyll & Bute. If readers can suggest a better way than the old regions to list gardens, we would be pleased to hear from them. Scotland's Garden Scheme divides the country into areas which are even more confusing – 'Etterick & Lauderdale', for example, and 'Lochaber, Badenoch & Strathspey'. The 1974 regions do at least have the advantage of having been administrative areas until very recently.

Scotland has many great historic gardens. The basis of the protection they enjoy is the *Inventory of Gardens & Designed Landscapes in Scotland* which was published in 1987. The Inventory lists 275 sites, which are graded in a more specific way than the gardens on the English register, for example according to the value of their horticultural content or historic importance. Historic Scotland has employed Krystyna Campbell to extend the Inventory: she expects to be able to add some further 155 sites. The additions which she has already completed identify and describe the new gardens with exemplary thoroughness. The supplement for Lothian region will be published this spring, and the one for Highland and Western Isles will follow later in 2001.

No-one has done more to acquire, save, restore and redevelop Scotland's great gardens than The National Trust for Scotland. Its portfolio of properties includes many of the best historic and horticultural gardens in the country: Branklyn, Brodick, Crathes, Culzean and Inverewe are gardens of international renown. The Royal Botanic Garden at Edinburgh too has developed four of the finest gardens anywhere in the world – Dawyck, Logan, Benmore (Younger Botanic Garden) and its own incomparable garden in north Edinburgh.

Members of the Royal Horticultural Society have free access for at least some months of the year to a dozen Scottish gardens: Abriachan, Cawdor Castle, Dundee Botanic Garden, Dunrobin Castle, Geilston Garden, Glenwhan, Harmony Garden, Hill of Tarvit, Kellie Castle, Leith Hall, St Andrews Botanic Garden, and the great teaching garden at Threave. More may be added during the course of the year: see the Society's website (www.rhs.org.uk) for the latest news. Scotland also has its own Yellow Book called *The Gardens of Scotland*, available from Scotland's Gardens Scheme, 31 Castle Terrace, Edinburgh EH1 2EL. It lists over 350 gardens throughout Scotland and, like its English equivalent, is the essential starting point for choosing more gardens to visit than this book recommends. The only other guide to Scottish gardens we can recommend is *Good Scottish Gardens* by Joyce & Maurice Lindsay (Chambers, 1995), which is thoroughly researched, accurate and informative: although it is now out of print – and ought to be republished in a new edition – it is widely available in public libraries.

Scotland is well served by garden centres, especially by such chains as Dobbie's in the Lowlands. It has some excellent specialist nurseries too: Jack Drake is Britain's premier alpine nursery; no-one has bred more or better new rhododendrons than Peter Cox at Glendoick; and Cally in Dumfries & Galloway has a great reputation for rare plants. However, it is fair to say that there are fewer nurseries *per capita* in Scotland as a whole than in England.

Scotland also has its own rather basic horticultural structure: these include, for example, such societies as the Scottish Rock Garden Club, the Scottish Rhododendron Society, the Royal Caledonian Horticultural Society and the Scottish Orchid Society. All are excellent organisations and some, like the Scottish Rock Garden Club and the Scottish Rhododendron Society, are substantial societies with good programmes of events and publications of record. Scotland also has a number of horticultural training colleges, notably Threave, Oatridge and the Scottish Agricultural College at Auchincruive – the latter is a RHS Partner College.

Nevertheless, the Royal Horticultural Society has not found it easy to make progress in Scotland. The Scotland's National Gardening Show, which ran from 1997, was cancelled in 2000 because the Society felt 'no longer able to sustain the considerable subsidy that the show required due to lower-than-expected visitor numbers'. The figures tell their tale. It needed 50,000 visitors to break even: there were only 35,000 at the last show in 1999. There is still a need for a national show in Scotland, and both the Royal Horticultural Society and the Royal Caledonian Horticultural Society are considering how to satisfy that unmet need. However, there are those who believe that, as with other aspects of cultural life in Scotland, gardening may still be too widely regarded north of the border as an English import.

BORDERS

Abbotsford

MELROSE TD6 9BQ

Tel 01896 752043   **Fax** 01896 752916
Location Off A7, two miles from Melrose
Opening hours 9.30 am – 5 pm (but 2 pm – 5 pm on Sundays in April, May & October); daily; 20 March to 31 October. And on 5 August for Scotland's Garden Scheme
Admission fee Adults £4; Children £2

Sir Walter Scott laid out the gardens at Abbotsford in the 1820s: he designed the formal Court garden by the house and planted the surrounding woodlands. The walled garden centres on a handsome orangery, with roses, fruit trees and herbaceous borders planted for late summer effect.

Owned by Dame Jean Maxwell-Scott DCVO
Number of gardeners 2
Size 1 acre

high in the hills where the climate is more continental than temperate. The trees for which the garden is famous were first planted in the 1830s: the owners subscribed to the great plant-hunting expeditions of the day, including those of David Douglas. This explains the many fine North American conifers in the garden. In the early twentieth century, the owners received plants from the early Chinese collections of E H Wilson. The gardens are also famous for their berberis, rhododendrons and cotoneasters and – of course – the Dawyck beech, an upright, fastigiate form of the common beech, first found in the policies in the mid-nineteenth century.

Plant Highlights Good herbaceous borders; meconopsis; Chinese conifers; Dawyck beech; Douglas fir from original seed; tallest *Fagus crenata* (21m) in the British Isles, and 18 further record trees.

Owned by Royal Botanic Garden, Edinburgh
Size 60 acres

Dawyck Botanic Garden

STOBO EH45 9JV

Tel 01721 760254   **Fax** 01721 760214
Website www.rbge.org.uk
Location 8 miles south-west of Peebles on B712
Opening hours 9.30 am – 6 pm; daily; March to October
Admission fee Adults £3; Concessions £2.50; Children £1

Dawyck is a woodland garden, run as an annexe of the Royal Botanic Garden in Edinburgh. It is very different from Edinburgh's other outliers: its 60 acres are

Edrom Nurseries

COLDINGHAM, EYEMOUTH TD14 5TZ

Tel & Fax 01890 771386
Location A1107, 5 minutes from A1
Opening hours 9 am – 5.30 pm; Monday – Friday; March to October

This nursery specialises in alpine primulas, gentians and meconopsis. The list of these three genera is particularly comprehensive, and includes many forms that are not available elsewhere. As with the other

alpines it lists, many are new to commerce or grown under collectors' numbers.

Floors Castle

ROXBURGHE ESTATES OFFICE, KELSO TD5 7SF

Tel 01573 223333 **Fax** 01573 226056
Location Signed in Kelso
Opening hours 10 am – 4.30 pm (4 pm in October); daily; 13 April to 28 October
Admission fee £3

Floors has handsome traditional herbaceous borders in the walled garden and the castle is impressively sited in its parkland. But change and restoration continue too: a new two-acre parterre in front of the castle is surmounted by a ducal coronet, while the 'star plantation' was entirely replanted with azaleas and rhododendrons in 1998. There are some good trees in the park, including a holm oak (*Quercus ilex*) and a Dawyck beech (*Fagus sylvatica* 'Fastigiata'), and a venerable holly on the spot where King James II of Scotland was blown up while besieging Roxburgh Castle in 1460.

Owned by The Duke of Roxburghe
Number of gardeners 5

Harmony Garden

ST MARY'S ROAD, MELROSE TD6 9LJ

Tel 01721 722502
Location In Melrose, opposite the abbey
Opening hours 10 am – 5.50 pm; daily; April to September. Opens at 1.30 pm on Sundays
Admission fee £2. RHS members free

'Harmony' takes its name from the Jamaican pimento plantation where its original builder James Waugh made his fortune. It is a modest, quiet walled garden with lawns, herbaceous and mixed borders, vegetable and fruit areas, and a rich display of spring bulbs. The views of Melrose Abbey and the Fildon Hills are a bonus.

Owned by The National Trust for Scotland
Number of gardeners 1
Size 2 acres

Kailzie Gardens

KAILZIE, PEEBLES EH45 9HT

Tel & Fax 01721 720007
Location On B7062 2 miles east of Peebles
Opening hours 11 am – 5.30 pm; daily; all year
Admission fee Adults £2.50; Children 75p (but £2 & 50p respectively from mid-October to 20 April)

Kailzie has been revived over the last 20 years. The large walled garden has a mixture of flowers and produce: a laburnum alley, a rose garden and double herbaceous borders are some of the attractions. There are meconopsis and primulas in the rhododendrons woodland walks outside. There will be a special week in June 2001 for the sale of geraniums and fuchsias.

Owned by Lady Angela Buchan-Hepburn
Number of gardeners 3
Size 20 acres

Lilliesleaf Nursery

GARDEN COTTAGE, LINTHILL,
LILLIESLEAF TD6 9HU

Tel & Fax 01835 870415
Location On B6359 between Midlem & Lilliesleaf
Opening hours 9 am – 5 pm, Monday – Saturday;
10 am – 4 pm, Sundays. December to March, phone first

This nursery has a general plant range, with an emphasis on perennials and hard-to-find plants of every kind. It is particularly good for epimediums, and offers a number of hybrids listed by no other nursery. It is worth seeing the demonstration garden, too: attractive mixed borders in a walled garden.

NCCPG National Collections *Epimedium*

Manderston

DUNS TD11 3PP

Tel 01361 883450   **Fax** 01361 882010
Website www.manderston.co.uk
Location On A6105 2 miles east of Duns
Opening hours 2 pm – dusk; Sundays & Thursdays;
10 May to 30 September, plus 28 May & 27 August.
Parties at any time by appointment
Admission fee Gardens only: Adults £3.50; Children £1.50

The house is Edwardian, built in classical neo-Georgian style. Below it are four expansive terraces with rich planting around clipped yews and hollies and fountains on the upper terrace. Below is a small lake with an ornamental boathouse and an eighteenth-century Chinese-style bridge. On the other side of the lake are the woodland gardens with a large collection of unusual species of trees and shrubs: the extensive collection of rhododendrons and azaleas dates back 100 years. This woodland garden is criss-crossed with numerous paths so that visitors can see all parts of it. On the north side of the house, after crossing wide lawns set about with mature trees, visitors reach the formal garden and herbaceous borders, both at their best in summer.

Owned by Lord Palmer
Number of gardeners 2
Size 52 acres

Mellerstain

GORDON TD3 6LG

Tel 01573 410225   **Fax** 01573 410636
Website http://muses.calligrafix.co.uk/mellerstain
Location 1 mile west of A6089 Kelso – Edinburgh road
Opening hours 11.30 pm – 6 pm; daily, except Saturdays;
21 April to 30 September
Admission fee £2

The house has extensive views south to the Cheviots: it was built by the Adams (father and son) between 1725 and 1778. It is set off by Sir Reginald Blomfield's formal garden, balustraded and terraced, but now rather covered by lichen. It is planted with floribunda roses and lavender. Beneath it runs the landscaped park, also laid out by William and Robert Adam, sauntering down to a lake. The whole picture is uncompromisingly grand.

Plant Highlights Topiary; roses (mainly modern); Italian terraced garden by Sir Reginald Blomfield; lake restored (1997/98).

Owned by Mellerstain Trust
Number of gardeners 1
Size 4½ acres

Mertoun Gardens

St Boswells, Melrose TD6 0EA

Tel 01835 823236 **Fax** 01835 822474
Location B6404, 2 miles north-east of St Boswells
Opening hours 2 pm – 6 pm; Saturdays, Sundays
& Public Holiday Mondays; April to September
Admission fee Adults £2; OAPs £1.50; Children 50p

Originally part of the Duke of Sutherland's
estates, Mertoun is best known for its
traditional kitchen garden. A long
herbaceous border within it has recently
been replanted. For many years now, the
Dukes have grown a strain of pea which is
said to have come from one found by Lord
Carnarvon in the tomb of Tutenkhamen.

Owned by Mertoun Gardens Trust
Number of gardeners 3
Size 26 acres

Monteviot House Gardens

Jedburgh TD8 6UQ

Tel 01835 830380 **Fax** 01835 830288
Location Off A68 north of Jedburgh & B6400 to Nisbet
Opening hours 12 noon – 5 pm; daily; April to October
Admission fee Adults £2; Children free

The gardens at Monteviot lie along a
dramatic slope of the Teviot valley. The
box-hedged herb garden and terrace along
the front of the house have a breathtaking
view of the river below. The sheltered
terraced rose garden is Victorian: the river
garden at the bottom was originally
designed in the 1930s by Percy Cane.
Italianate in inspiration, this sheltered
garden slopes down between curved borders
of herbaceous plants, shrubs, bulbs and
roses, to a broad stone landing stage above
the waters of the Teviot itself. In the nearby
water garden, fed by a natural spring, three
islands are linked by elegant curved wooden
bridges. Here are bog plants and bamboos.
The dramatic impact of the garden as a
whole is heightened by the contrast between
formal and the informal and by the way that
the planting leads seamlessly through the
different parts. The trees in the arboretum
are exceptional: recent clearing has
displayed them in their glory. *Fagus sylvatica*
'Riversii' is 30m high.

Number of gardeners 3

Priorwood Garden

Melrose TD6 9PX

Tel 01896 822493
Website www.nts.org.uk
Location Next to Melrose Abbey
Opening hours 10 am (1.30 pm on Sundays) – 5.30 pm;
daily; April to September. 10 am (1.30 pm on Sundays)
– 4 pm; daily; October to 24 December
Admission fee Adults £2; Concessions £1. Honesty box

Priorwood is best known for its shop, which
was recently extended and improved.
Everything in the garden is geared towards
dried flowers. Most of the plants are chosen
because they are suitable for drying, but they
are also very colourful. Courses on drying
flowers are also held here. In the orchard is a
collection of historic apple cultivars, all
organically grown.

Owned by The National Trust for Scotland
Number of gardeners 1

Traquair House

INNERLEITHEN EH44 6PW

Tel 01896 830323   **Fax** 01896 830639
Website www.traquair.co.uk
Location Signed from Innerleithen
Opening hours 10.30 am – 5.30 pm; daily; 22 April to 31 October
Admission fee Grounds only: Adults £2; Children £1

The main attraction is a large maze, planted in 1980 of beech and Leyland cypress. The house is a Catholic time-warp, said to be the oldest inhabited and most romantic house in Scotland. The Bear Gates in the park, once the main entrance to the estate, have been closed ever since Bonnie Prince Charlie passed through them for the last time in 1746.

Owned by Mrs Maxwell Stuart
Number of gardeners 3
Size 30 acres

DUMFRIES & GALLOWAY

Broughton House Gardens

12 HIGH STREET, KIRKCUDBRIGHT DG6 4JX

Tel & Fax 01557 330437
Location Signed in centre of Kirkcudbright
Opening hours 1 pm – 5.30 pm; daily; April to October. Open at 11 am, 13 to 16 April and throughout July & August. Open 11 am – 4 pm on 24 & 25 February, and from Monday to Friday in November
Admission fee Adults £3.50; Concessions £2.50

E A Hornel the artist laid out the Japanese-style garden in the 1900s: it is the best known part of the garden and featured in many of his portraits. Most of the rest is a 'Scottish' garden with a fine position above the Dee. The house contains many of Hornel's works and an extensive collection of Scottish books.

Owned by Hornel Trust (managed by National Trust for Scotland)
Number of gardeners 1
Size 2 acres

Cally Gardens

GATEHOUSE OF FLEET, CASTLE DOUGLAS DG7 2DJ

Tel none
Location 12 miles west of Castle Douglas, on Gatehouse road off A75

Opening hours 10 am – 5.30 pm; Saturdays & Sundays; plus 2 pm – 5.30 pm from Tuesday to Friday. Easter to early October.

Cally is a nursery for the horticultural *avant-garde*. It specialises in new and rare perennials, including some from wild-collected and botanic garden seed. Many are culled from a collection of over 3,500 plants, which makes it one of the most interesting in Scotland – the owner, Michael Wickenden, has an excellent eye for quality. The walled garden has 30 large borders where all these novelties and rarities can be seen growing. The list of what is for sale changes by as much as half each year.

Craigieburn Classic Plants

BY MOFFAT DG10 9LF

Tel & Fax 01683 221250
Location 2½ miles east of Moffat, on A74. On the left, beyond Craiglochan signs
Opening hours 12 noon – 6 pm; Saturdays & Sundays; Easter to September
Admission fee For charity

The nursery at Craigieburn is now playing second fiddle to the garden, which is under-going substantial development and imp-rovement as a collection of Himalayan plants. It is particularly good for *Meconopsis*, of which the Wheatcrofts used to have a National Collection. The mild climate means that

Castle Kennedy Garden

STAIR ESTATES, REPHAD, STRANRAER DG9 8BX

Tel 01776 702024   **Fax** 01776 706248
Location 5 miles east of Stranraer on A75
Opening hours 10 am – 5 pm; daily; April to September
Admission fee Adults £3; OAPs £2; Children £1

Castle Kennedy is a ruined keep, destroyed in the first half of the eighteenth century when the bedding which was being aired for the return of the master, the 2nd Earl of Stair, caught fire. Its imposing bulk overlooks the walled garden, which is a riot of herbaceous colour in the summer, with gnarled old apple trees heavy with lichen in its midst, and some interesting tender shrubs, including bottle-brushes (*Callistemon* species) against its walls. The main horticultural interest lies outside, although the romantic planting continues. The 2nd Earl was a military man, and bequeathed to the garden its highly original structure of dashing rides, ridges and earthworks which represent battle encampments. They were made by the Royal Scots Greys and the Inniskilling Fusiliers when they should have been occupied suppressing religious dissent in the area. The extensive gardens now occupy an isthmus bounded by two lochs, with the ruined castle at one end, and its nineteenth-century replacement Lochinch Castle at the other – the place where *Buddleja* 'Lochinch' originated. There is a two-acre round pond, from which an ancient, slightly decrepit avenue of monkey puzzle trees leads off. These trees, *Araucaria araucana*, were grown from original seed sent from Chile: elsewhere are plants garnered by Stair forbears who subscribed to the collecting expeditions of Sir Joseph Hooker (*Rhododendron arboreum* for example). The

gardens generally are well stocked with rhododendrons, at their best in April and May. Later in the season, in an area known as the dancing green, a semi-circle of crimson *Embothrium coccineum* (June) is interplanted with flower-decked *Eucryphia* × *nymansensis* (August). There are more conventional flower borders in the area beside Lochinch Castle. In gardens as old as these, time has started to take its toll, but restoration and replanting is underway. The gardens recommend visitors to follow one of four graded walks to get the most out of their visit. For the energetic, this is a marvellous place just to wander at will.

Plant Highlights Woodland garden; good herbaceous borders; rhododendrons; embothriums; eucryphias; monkey puzzle avenue; tallest *Pittosporum tenuifolium* (17m) in the British Isles, tallest *Rhododendron arboreum* (16m) and three other record-breaking trees.

Owned by Lochinch Heritage Estate

Glenwhan Garden

DUNRAGIT, BY STRANRAER DG9 8PH

Tel & Fax 01581 400222
Website www.glenluce.org.uk/glenwhan.htm
Location 1 mile off A75 at Dunragit Village. Follow brown tourist signs
Opening hours 10 am – 5 pm; daily; mid-March to mid-October
Admission fee Adults £3; OAPs £2.50; Children £1. RHS members free from August to October

Glenwhan is a plantsman's garden which has been created since 1979 by its present owners, starting from wild fields and scrub. Ambitious in scale, the heart of the garden is a pair of lochans or bog lakes. Above them rises a series of roped terraces, planted with heathers, azaleas, small conifers, golden elders, hardy fuchsias and massed Rugosa roses. A small folly stands at the peak. In prospect, the whole design is beautifully composed and tranquil. From the folly there are extensive views across the garden to Luce Bay and the Mull of Galloway beyond. Tessa Knott's first plantings were a sturdy shelter belt of small trees, including native Scots pines, English oaks and mountain ashes. Now 20 years old, there are occasional glimpses through these lichen-stained ancients to the gorse scrub and bog which surround the garden. The shelter belt is a transitional feature: it is a refinement of the more primitive vegetation beyond the perimeter fence, and it introduces planting themes which are then developed within the garden, in the form, for example, of collections of choicer *Sorbus* and *Quercus* species (including *Q. × bushii* and *Q. dentata*). Pools have been cut out of the blackest peat to make an attractive sequence of grassy water gardens, planted with primula and meconopsis cultivars.

Glenwhan is very much a plantsman's garden, but Tessa Knott also uses plants to create effects, and she has capitalised upon the lie of the land to produce different habitats. The new plantings include large-leaved rhododendrons (*R. fictolacteum* for example), and some interesting southern hemisphere plants, including eucalyptus and olearias around the summerhouse. Another highlight is the dappled woodland walk with yet more new planting. Indeed many parts of this garden are 'work in progress' which will be worth returning to see again as they mature.

Owned by Mr & Mrs William Knott
Number of gardeners 3
Size 12 acres

Logan Botanic Gardens

PORT LOGAN, STRANRAER DG9 9ND

Tel 01776 860231 **Fax** 01776 860333
Website www.rbge.org.uk/intro/logan.htm
Location 14 miles south of Stranraer on B7065
Opening hours 9.30 am – 6 pm; daily; March to October
Admission fee Adults £3; Concessions £2.50; Children £1;
Family £7

Ⓟ ⓦⓒ 🌱 🎁 🍵 🍴

These extraordinarily exotic gardens, started by the McDouall family in the nineteenth century, are now part of the Royal Botanic Garden at Edinburgh. Logan's sheltered aspect and proximity to the warming waters of the Atlantic, enable a wide range of tender and southern hemisphere plants to be grown out of doors. The bedding out of thousands of half-hardy perennials makes the garden a blaze of colour on bright sunny days. In the walled garden, overlooked by the slender remains of Castle Balzieland, there is a fine collection of established tree ferns (*Dicksonia antarctica*). They are underplanted with the smaller fern, *Blechnum chilense*, which creates an impression of lush fertility, as if the dicksonias have seeded themselves everywhere. The formal lily pond is partly framed by a diagonal avenue of 30-ft cabbage palms (*Cordyline australis*). Around the pond are waving wands of *Dierama pulcherrimum* and *Kniphofia*, and the air glints with dragonflies in summer. Among the trees which flower in the sheltered walls are a tall *Metrosideros umbellatus* and the flame tree, *Embothrium coccineum*. Also flowering freely here, as it does in other gardens in south-west Scotland, is *Eucryphia* × *nymansensis* 'Nymansay'. Beyond the brilliance of the walled garden, and past an avenue of Chusan palms (*Trachycarpus fortunei*), lies Logan's woodland garden.

Some of its pleasures are more hidden than others, but a spectacular specimen of *Magnolia campbellii* 'Charles Raffill' stands on the edge, in flower in April, and decked with swollen red pods by August. Look out in particular for plants from the southern hemisphere, including *Leptospermum lanigerum*, *Crinodendron hookerianum*, and the Chatham Island daisy bush, *Olearia semidentata* (syn. *O.* 'Henry Travers'). Do not miss the gunnera bog either, where this giant rhubarb-like plant grows so tall and thick that you can lose yourself under its prickly, slightly sinister canopy. In the Discovery Centre there are reference books, computers and microscopes which the visitor can use – perhaps to learn more about the *Maddenia* section of the genus *Rhododendron*, in which the garden specialises. Visitors can borrow innovative free audio guides, which are keyed to numbers marked on labels throughout the gardens. It is slightly surreal to see your fellow visitors wandering around clasping these futuristic wands, but the guide is informative and chatty.

Owned by Royal Botanic Garden, Edinburgh
Size 30 acres

Lobelia tupa grows to 8 ft. The nursery now sells mainly surplus plants from the garden.

Owned by Andrew & Janet Wheatcroft
Size 8 acres

Elizabeth MacGregor

ELLENBANK, TONGLAND ROAD, KIRKCUDBRIGHT DG6 4UU

Tel 01557 330620
Location On A711, 1 mile north of Kirkcudbright
Opening hours 10 am – 5 pm; Mondays, Fridays & Saturdays; May to mid-October

Violas – over 100 of them – are the speciality at this excellent nursery: some are not available from any other source. They are complemented by a lively selection of perennials and shrubs for cottage gardens and mixed-border planting. The walled garden is worth a visit in its own right.

Galloway House Gardens

GARLIESTON, NEWTON STEWART DG8 8HF

Tel 01988 600680
Location Off B7004 at Garlieston
Opening hours 9 am – 5.30 pm; daily; March to October
Admission fee £1

Galloway House is where Neil McEacharn learnt to garden, before moving to Lake Maggiore to create the great gardens of Villa Taranto. A vast *Davidia involucrata* dates from his ownership, as do many of the tender trees and shrubs which he planted to take advantage of the mild maritime climate – eucryphias, for example. The fine conifers date back to the Earls of Galloway in the nineteenth century, while most of the

Rhododendron species were planted after the war. The garden is still undergoing restoration, but is already a great pleasure to visit, especially in late spring.

Owned by Galloway House Gardens Trust
Number of gardeners 1
Size 65 acres

Threave Garden

CASTLE DOUGLAS DG7 1RX

Tel 01556 502575 **Fax** 01556 502683
Website www.nts.org.uk
Location Off A75, 1 mile west of Castle Douglas
Opening hours 9.30 am – sunset; daily; all year. Walled garden and glasshouses close at 5 pm
Admission fee Adults £4.50; Concessions £3.50; Children £1. RHS members free in April, May, September & October

Threave is a teaching garden with a very wide range of attractions – something to interest every gardener, in fact. It has been developed over the last 35 years with the needs of students at the School of Horticulture, garden-owners and tourists all in mind. Threave has quickly acquired the reputation of a Scottish Wisley. There are over 200 daffodil cultivars to admire in spring; a fine collection of old roses in the summer; colourful herbaceous borders; and good autumn colour. The modern designs are inspirational and a new Victorian-style conservatory has recently been built in the walled garden.

Plant Highlights Woodland garden; roses (ancient & modern); rock garden; plantsman's collection of plants; plants under glass; fruit; good herbaceous borders; fine collection of trees; peat garden; heath garden; tallest *Alnus rubra* (23m) in the British Isles, and two other record trees.

Owned by The National Trust for Scotland
Number of gardeners 2, plus 3 instructors
Size 64 acres

FIFE

Cambo Gardens

KINGSBARNS, ST ANDREWS
KY16 8QD

Tel 01333 450054   **Fax** 01333 450987
Location On A917 between Kingsbarns & Crail
Opening hours 10 am – dusk; daily; all year
Admission fee Adults £2.50; Children free

Cambo's large Victorian walled garden is
built around the Cambo Burn and has a very
fine display of annuals and perennials as
well as fruit and vegetables. A waterfall and
elegant oriental bridge give the garden its
unique character. It is spectacular when the
snowdrops and snowflakes flower, and
dedicates one Sunday at the end of the
February to Scotland's Garden Scheme.

Owned by Mr & Mrs T P N Erskine

Falkland Palace

FALKLAND, CUPAR KY15 7BU

Tel 01337 857397   **Fax** 01337 857980
Website www.nts.org.uk
Location On A912, 11 miles north of Kirkcaldy. 10 miles
from M90, Jct t8
Opening hours 11 am (1.30 pm on Sundays) – 5.30 pm;
daily; April to October. Opens at 10 am on weekdays from
June to August
Admission fee Adults £2.50; Concessions £1.70

The palace at Falkland is old: it dates from
the first half of the sixteenth century.
Today's garden was built in about 1950 by
Percy Cane: his reconstruction of a Scottish
renaissance garden has a herb garden in the
Jacobean style, an astrolabe walk and formal
parterres prettily planted in pastel colours.

Owned by The National Trust for Scotland
Number of gardeners 2
Size 11 acres

Hill of Tarvit

CUPAR KY15 5PB

Tel & Fax 01334 653127
Website www.nts.org.uk
Location Off A916, 2½ miles south of Cupar
Opening hours 9.30 am – sunset; daily; all year
Admission fee Adults £2; Concessions £1 in honesty box.
RHS members free

Hill of Tarvit is an established plantsman's
garden, formally designed but opulently
planted and maintained, in keeping with the
Lorimer house. The Edwardian plantings,
now splendidly mature, have been
complemented by modern additions. The
Trust has begun to restore and replant the
borders on the top terrace in the Edwardian
style.

Owned by The National Trust for Scotland
Number of gardeners 2
Size 20 acres

Kellie Castle

PITTENWEEN KY10 2RF

Tel 01333 720271 **Fax** 01333 720736
Website www.nts.org.uk
Location On B9171, 3 miles north-west of Pittenween
Opening hours 9.30 am – sunset; daily; all year
Admission fee Adults £2; Concessions £1 in honesty box.
RHS members free

Kellie Castle is Sir Robert Lorimer's own
family house: it was he who remade the
garden in its present form and designed
both the 'secret garden' and 'Robin's
corner'. It is no more than one acre in
extent, but strong lines and thick planting
create a sense of both space and enclosure.
Much of the planting is modern. The
organic walled garden contains a fine
collection of old-fashioned roses, fruit trees
and herbaceous plants: there are displays in
the summerhouse about the history of the
walled garden. The yew hedges are threaded
with scarlet *Tropaeolum speciosum*.

Plant Highlights Roses (mainly
old-fashioned); fruit; good herbaceous
borders; strong design; extended collection
of historic vegetables.

Owned by The National Trust for Scotland
Number of gardeners 2
Size 16 acres

St Andrews Botanic Garden

THE CANONGATE, ST ANDREWS
KY16 8RT

Tel 01334 477178 **Fax** 01334 476452
Website www.st-and.ac.uk/standrews/botanic
Location A915, Largo Road, then entrance in
The Canongate
Opening hours 10 am – 7 pm (4 pm October – April);
daily; all year. Greenhouses closed at weekends
October – April
Admission fee Adults £2; OAPs & Children £1. RHS
members free

The University botanic garden at
St Andrews is currently undergoing much
change and improvement. The garden's
main asset, the peat, rock and water
complex (crag, scree, moraine, alpine
meadow and bog) is being repaired and
replanted. Work on the cactus house has
been completed, a new alpine house is now
open, and the orchid house re-opened
recently. There is also a tropical house and a
house for *Maddenia* rhododendrons. The
garden caters particularly well for children
and is interesting to visit at every season. In
2001, the gardens will be hosting two special
RHS events: details from 020 7821 3408.

Owned by Fife Council
Size 18 acres

GRAMPIAN

Blackhills

BY ELGIN, MORAY IV30 3QU

Tel 01343 842223 **Fax** 01343 843136
Website www.blackhills.co.uk
Location 1 mile south of Lhanbryde, near Elgin on the B9103
Opening hours Last two Sundays in May, and by appointment
Admission fee Donation

Blackhills is a magnificent collection of rhododendrons in two steep-sided glacial valleys: these possess a microclimate which allows many plants to grow which are normally considered too tender for the north-east coast of Scotland. The rhododendrons were planted throughout the twentieth century by successive generations of the Christie family, along with many other Himalayan and Chinese plants, in a woodland garden which is now fully mature. There are about 360 different rhododendron species growing at Blackhills, all of wild origin: most were collected in the Himalayas, some came from North America, Central Asia and Northern Europe. The garden now contains one of the finest and most extensive private collections of species rhododendrons in the world. Some of the species self-seed.

Owned by T S Christie
Number of gardeners 1
Size 50 acres

Brodie Castle

BRODIE, FORRES, MORAY IV36 2TE

Tel 01309 641371 **Fax** 01309 641600
Website www.nts.org.uk
Location Signed from A96
Opening hours Grounds: 9.30 am – sunset; daily; all year
Admission fee £1 in honesty box

Brodie Castle came to the National Trust for Scotland in 1980. It sits in a landscaped park and there are rhododendrons in the woodland policies, but Brodie is famous, above all, for its daffodils. Many were bred here at the turn of the nineteenth century and the Trust has tried assiduously to identify them, propagate them and distribute them more widely. They are a glorious sight when they bloom in the lawns around the baronial battlements.

Owned by The National Trust for Scotland
Number of gardeners 6, plus 2 part-time
Size 80 acres
NCCPG National Collections *Narcissus*

Crathes Castle

BANCHORY AB31 5QJ

Tel 01330 844525 **Fax** 01330 844797
Website www.nts.org.uk
Location On A93, 15 miles west of Aberdeen
Opening hours 9 am – sunset; daily; all year
Admission fee Adults £3.50; Concessions £2.50

Crathes is famous for its walled garden, which started as a kitchen garden and was developed as a flower garden in the 1920s and 1930s. It is divided into eight distinct gardens, each with its own character. These include a white border, a yellow enclosure known as the Golden Garden, a misty blue garden, and a dreamy high summer border with pastel shades for long Highland evenings. Less than four acres, the garden is intensively planted to give colour all the year round. Some of the topiary yew hedges date back to 1702.

 Plant Highlights Woodland garden; roses (ancient & modern); plantsman's collection of plants; mature conifers; specimen trees; colour borders; tallest *Zelkova × verschaffeltii* in the British Isles, and four further tree records.

Owned by The National Trust for Scotland
Number of gardeners 5
Size 3¾ acres
NCCPG National Collections *Viburnum*; *Dianthus* (Malmaison carnations)

Cruickshank Botanic Garden

UNIVERSITY OF ABERDEEN, DEPT OF PLANT AND SOIL SCIENCE, ST MACHAR DRIVE, ABERDEEN AB24 3UU

Tel 01224 272704   **Fax** 01224 272703
Location Follow signs for Aberdeen University and/or Old Aberdeen
Opening hours 9 am – 4.30 pm; Monday – Friday; all year. Plus 2 pm – 5 pm; Saturdays & Sundays; May to September
Admission fee free

Ⓟ ⓦⓒ ⓖ ⓧ

Cruickshank Botanic Garden was founded in 1898 for the teaching and study of botany at the university of Aberdeen. Its twelve acres still have an educational element but

also serve as an amenity for the wider public. Its leading features include: a rock garden for alpine plants and bulbs, where wild orchids seeds around; an arboretum, planted quite recently – in about 1970 – with natives, exotics and garden cultivars, many of them now semi-mature; collections of native plants, including all the endemic *Sorbus* species of the British Isles; and a rose garden which has been laid out to illustrate the history of the rose in cultivation. They garden is well-maintained and – like all botanic gardens – worth visiting at any time of the year. It is also supported by an enthusiastic Friends organisation. The latest development is a wildflower meadow.

Owned by Aberdeen University
Number of gardeners 3

Drum Castle

DRUMOAK, BANCHORY AB31 3EY

Tel 01330 811204   **Fax** 01330 811962
Website www.nts.org.uk
Location Off A93, 10 miles west of Aberdeen
Opening hours Grounds: 9.30 – sunset; daily; all year. Garden: 10 am – 6 pm; daily; 13 April to 30 September, plus weekends in October
Admission fee Adults £1; honesty box or ticket machine

Ⓟ ⓦⓒ ⓖ

The gardens at Drum are modern – begun in 1991 with the intention of providing an appropriate historic setting for the castle and a place where old Scottish roses could be grown. There is a knot garden planted with herbs in the style of the early seventeenth century and a formal garden with *allées* and topiary to represent the early eighteenth century. Most of the borders are designed and planted in the twentieth-century style as mixtures of roses, other shrubs and perennials. Scattered all around the gardens is the best collection of Scottish roses (hybrids of *Rosa pimpinellifolia*) in Britain.

Owned by The National Trust for Scotland
Number of gardeners 2
Size 20 acres

Kildrummy Castle

KILDRUMMY, ALFORD AB33 8RA

Tel 01975 571203/571277
Location On A97, off A944
Opening hours 10 am – 5 pm; daily; April to October
Admission fee Adults £2; Children free

Kildrummy has a glen-garden, laid out about 100 years ago. The richly planted pools and ponds are complemented by a plantsman's collection on the hillside, and a large mature rock garden made from the natural sandstone. It is one of the most romantic gardens in Scotland.

Owned by Kildrummy Castle Garden Trust

Leith Hall

KENNETHMONT, HUNTLY AB54 4NQ

Tel 01464 831216   **Fax** 01464 831594
Website www.nts.org.uk
Location On B9002 west of Kennethmont
Opening hours 9.30 am – sunset; daily; all year
Admission fee Adults £2; Concessions £1.30.
RHS members free

From this garden's historic past come two ponds and an ice house, but richly planted borders are the pride of Leith Hall today: they are full of colour all through the summer. Also impressive is the rock garden, restored and replanted by that most

successful of societies, the Scottish Rock Garden Club. Leith gets better and better.

Plant Highlights Roses (mainly modern); rock garden; good herbaceous borders; bluebells; recent restorations & improvements; new sculptures in woodland walk.

Owned by The National Trust for Scotland
Number of gardeners 2
Size 6 acres

Pitmedden

ELLON, ABERDEEN AB4 7PD

Tel 01651 842352   **Fax** 01651 843188
Website www.nts.org.uk
Location 1 mile west of Pitmedden on A920
Opening hours 10 am – 5 pm; daily; May to September.
Last entry 5.30 pm
Admission fee Adults £5; Concessions £4

The spectacular formal garden at Pitmedden was meticulously created in the 1950s by the National Trust for Scotland, using seventeenth-century Scottish designs. Three of the four parterres came from patterns associated with Holyroodhouse: the fourth is an heraldic design based on the coat-of-arms of Sir Alexander Seton, who first laid out a garden here in 1675. The result has three miles of box hedging and uses 40,000 bedding plants every summer. It may not be completely authentic, but it certainly looks genuine enough, as well as being both impressive, satisfying and peaceful.

Owned by The National Trust for Scotland
Number of gardeners 5
Size 15 acres

HIGHLAND

Abriachan Gardens

LOCH NESS SIDE, BY INVERNESS
IV3 8LA

Tel & Fax 01463 861232
Location Just off the A82
Opening hours 9 am – 7 pm (5 pm from October to March); daily; all year
Admission fee Adults £2; OAPs £1; Children 20p. RHS members free from April to September

These unique gardens on the shores of Loch Ness wind their way through the native hazel and oak woodland and offer spectacular views down the Great Glen. Many choice plants are grown here: their specialities are hardy perennials and shrubs. There are extensive garden walks among dry stone dykes and raised beds.

Owned by Mr & Mrs D Davidson
Number of gardeners 2
Size 4 acres

Allangrange

MUNLOCHY, BLACK ISLE IV8 8NZ

Tel 01463 811249 **Fax** 01463 811407
Location Signed off A9, 5 miles north of Inverness
Opening hours 2 pm – 5.30 pm; 6 May & 10 June; or by appointment
Admission fee £1.50

Colour gardening by Mrs Cameron, a botanical artist, has made this one of the loveliest summer gardens in the British Isles. The spring flowers are good, too.

Owned by Major Allan Cameron
Number of gardeners 1
Size 3 acres

Ardfearn Nursery

BUNCHREW, INVERNESS IV3 6RH

Tel 01463 243250
Location Off A862 west of Inverness
Opening hours 9 am – 5.30 pm; daily

Alpines and small ericaceous shrubs in quantity are produced at this nursery in a lovely Highland setting. It is particularly good for celmisias, gentians and above all, primulas. But the stock is always changing, which is what draws back the nursery's discriminating clientèle year after year.

Attadale Gardens

STRATHCARRON, WESTER ROSS
IV54 8YX

Tel 01520 722217 **Fax** 01520 722546
Location ON A890 between Strathcarron & South Strome
Opening hours 10 am – 5.30 pm; Monday – Saturday; April to October. Coaches by prior arrangement only
Admission fee Adults £2; Children £1

The gardens at Attadale were started in the 1890s: many rhododendrons, azaleas and specimen trees date from that time. The recent expansion of planting began in the 1980s, with over 2,000 trees and shrubs, which are now underplanted with irises, candelabra primulas, gunneras and bamboos. There is also a vegetable garden and herb garden.

Owned by Mr & Mrs Ewen Macpherson
Number of gardeners 3½
Size 20 acres

Cawdor Castle

CAWDOR, NAIRN IV12 5RD

Tel 01667 404615 **Fax** 01667 404674
Website www.cawdorcastle.com
Location Between Inverness & Nairn on B9090.
Opening hours 10 am – 5 pm; daily; 1 May to 14 October
Admission fee £3. RHS members free in May, June, September & October

Cawdor Castle could claim to be the most romantic castle in the Highlands – the fourteenth-century home of the Thanes of Cawdor. It has several gardens: the earliest dates from the sixteenth century and has the maze. There is also an eighteenth-century flower garden with large herbaceous borders and roses and a nineteenth-century wild garden with a good collection of rhododendrons and spring bulbs as well as splendid trees. Recent additions include a holly maze, a laburnum walk and coloured planting schemes. Earth, Purgatory and Paradise are somehow represented in the new plantings, but they are best enjoyed as colours and shapes. The effect is neither cranky nor grand, just extremely charming.

Owned by The Dowager Countess Cawdor
Number of gardeners 4
Size 3½ acres

Coiltie Garden

DIVACH, DRUMNADROCHIT IV63 6XW

Tel 01456 450219
Location Take the small uphill road out of Drumnadrochit to Divach
Opening hours 12 noon – 7 pm; daily; 16 June to 31 July
Admission fee Adults £1.50; Children free

There was little except a few old trees when the Nelsons came to Coiltie in 1980. Now the four acres of sandy, rocky soil on a cold upland wooded site have been turned into a beautiful summer garden. Roses are one of their successes, and the garden is also getting quite a name for its herbaceous borders.

Owned by Mr & Mrs David Nelson
Number of gardeners 1
Size 4 acres

Dochfour Gardens

INVERNESS IV3 6JY

Tel 01463 861218 **Fax** 01463 861336
Location 5 miles south-west of Inverness on the A82
Opening hours 10 am – 5 pm; Monday – Friday; April to September
Admission fee Adults £1.50; Concessions £1

Dochfour is a substantial garden, landscaped and terraced down to the River Ness. Though best when the daffodils and rhododendrons colour the hillside, it is most famous for the size and number of its nineteenth-century conifers.

 Plant Highlights Conifers; rhododendrons & azaleas; naturalised daffodils; parterres; water gardens; tallest

Thuja occidentalis 'Lutea' in the British Isles, plus two further tree records.

Owned by The Hon Alexander Baillie
Number of gardeners 1½
Size 19 acres

Dunrobin Castle Gardens

GOLSPIE, SUTHERLAND KW10 6SF

Tel 01408 633177   **Fax** 01408 634081
Website www.great-houses-scotland.co.uk
Location 1 mile north of Golspie on A9
Opening hours Dawn to dusk; daily; all year round. Castle gardens: 10.30 am (12 noon on Sundays except in July & August) – 5.30 pm (4.30 pm in April, May & October); 1 April to 15 October. Last entry 30 minutes before closing
Admission fee Castle & garden: Adults £6; OAPs £4. RHS members free. Reductions for groups. Gardens open free when castle closed.

The grand terraced gardens at Dunrobin were laid out in 1850 by Sir Charles Barry, architect of the Houses of Parliament. Their formal French style, striding down to the Dornoch Forth, is appropriate to the French-style *château*. Three parterres surround the fountains, two bedded out traditionally and one planted with hardy geraniums and underplanted with tulips and lilies. Recent restoration and replanting have produced a line of whitebeams, gunneras, new rhododendrons and three herbaceous borders. Another addition has been some 20 wooden pyramids planted with clematis and climbing roses – very pretty.

Owned by The Sutherland Trust
Number of gardeners 3
Size 5 acres

The Hydroponicum

ACHILTIBUIE, ULLAPOOL IV26 2YG

Tel 01854 622202   **Fax** 01854 622201
Location Signed off A835, 25 miles north of Ullapool
Opening hours 10 am – 6 pm; daily; 2 April to 30 September. Guided tours on the hour (last one at 5 pm). Plus tours at 12 noon and 2 pm from Monday to Friday in October
Admission fee Adults £4.75; Concessions £3.50; Children £2.75

The Hydroponicum has three glasshouses, each individually heated and featuring plants from different climatic zones. Salads, herbs and tree fruits grow in the 'cottage garden' house. Tomatoes, citrus fruit and olives fill the 'South of France' house. And the 'Canary Island zone' is planted with vines, figs, tamarillos and bananas. 'Planted' is not quite the right word: hydroponics are all about soilless cultivation – essential in places like Saudi Arabia but a small miracle here in the north-west of Scotland.

Owned by Viscount Gough
Number of gardeners 2
Size ¼ acres glasshouses & 2 acres grounds

Inverewe

POOLEWE, ROSS AND CROMARTY IV22 2LQ

Tel 01445 781200   **Fax** 01445 781497
Website www.nts.org.uk
Location On A832, 6 miles north of Gairloch
Opening hours 9.30 am – 9 pm (5 pm from 1 November to 14 March); daily; all year
Admission fee Adults £5; Concessions £4

Inverewe is one of the wonders of the horticultural world, a subtropical garden in the north west Highlands. Its position on a sheltered peninsular, warmed by the Gulf Stream, explains the luxuriance of its plantings. It is also the reason why, even so far north, it has much to interest the plantsman at every time of the year. The garden owes its origins to Osgood Mackenzie, who from 1862 to 1922 planted windbreaks to protect more delicate exotics within. Fabulous large-leaved Himalayan rhododendrons, magnolias, eucalyptus, tree ferns, palms and tender rarities are underplanted with drifts of blue poppies and candelabra primulas. Among Inverewe's record trees are specimens of *Eucalyptus cordata* and *Salix magnifica*, neither of which would be fully hardy in the home counties of England. Inverewe is exceptionally well maintained, though perhaps best on a sunny dry day in May, before the midges breed.

Plant Highlights Woodland garden; sub-tropical plants; rock garden; plantsman's collection of plants; mature conifers; good herbaceous borders; fine collection of trees; autumn colour; meconopsis; candelabra primulas; lilies; tallest *Eucalyptus cordata* (30m) in the British Isles, and three further record trees.

Owned by The National Trust for Scotland
Number of gardeners 8
Size 50 acres
NCCPG National Collections *Olearia*; *Brachyglottis*; *Rhododendron* (*Barbatum*, *Glischra* & *Maculifera* sections)

Jack Drake

INSHRIACH ALPINE NURSERY, AVIEMORE, INVERNESS-SHIRE PH22 1QS

Tel 01540 651287 Fax 01540 651656
Website www.kincraig.com/
Location Take B970 to Inverdruie. Turn right, ¾ mile after the Spey Bridge

Opening hours 10 am – 5 pm; Monday – Friday. 10 am – 4 pm; Saturdays. Most of the year

This famous Highland nursery is a Mecca for devotees of alpine and rock garden plants. It offers a large number of selected or collected forms. True alpines rub shoulders with species for wild and bog gardens. The nursery is laid out with demonstration gardens – screes, peat walls, wild gardens and bog gardens.

Leckmelm Arboretum

BY ULLAPOOL IV23 2RN

Location 3 miles south of Ullapool on the A835
Opening hours 10 am – 6 pm; daily; April to September
Admission fee Adults £1.50; Children free

The Leckmelm arboretum was laid out in the 1870s, and it is from those days that many of the finest trees date – wellingtonias, cedars, monkey puzzles and a huge weeping beech (*Fagus sylvatica* 'Pendula'). Some of the trees are record-breakers, including an *Abies amabilis* 40m high, a good *Chamaecyparis lawsoniana* 'Wisselii' and a *Kalopanax pictus*, whose presence at such a northerly point may be explained by the mild climate. The Troughtons have taken advantage of the arboretum's position on the shores of Loch Broom by making new plantings in recent years: they have put in such rhododendrons as *R. sinogrande* and *R. macabeanum*, and even a selection of dicksonias, palms, olive-trees and bananas.

Owned by Mr & Mrs Peter Troughton
Number of gardeners 1
Size 12 acres

Lochalsh Woodland Garden

BALMACARA, BY KYLE OF LOCHALSH, ROSS IV40 8DN

Tel 01599 566325 **Fax** 01599 566359
Website www.nts.org.uk
Location On A87, 3 miles from Kyle
Opening hours 9 am – sunset; daily; all year
Admission fee Adults £2; Concessions £1. Honesty box

This woodland garden is becoming much better known, and deservedly. The structure is about 100 years old – tall pines, oaks and larches with ornamental underplantings started in the late 1960s. Rhododendrons from Euan Cox at Glendoick came first: newer plantings include collections of hardy ferns, bamboos, fuchsias, hydrangeas and *Maddenia* rhododendrons, as well as plants from Tasmania and New Zealand. The season of interest extends from early spring well into autumn.

Owned by The National Trust for Scotland
Number of gardeners 1
Size 13 acres

LOTHIAN

Binny Plants

BINNY ESTATE (SUE RYDER),
ECCLESMACHAN ROAD, BROXBURN
EH52 6NL

Tel & Fax 01506 858931
Location 2 miles north of Uphall
Opening hours 10 am – 5 pm; Thursday – Monday;
mid-march to 31 October

This excellent nursery has an expanding
range. Its original specialities were
euphorbias, geraniums, hostas and small
shrubs, but it has now added a good range
of grasses and ferns. The catalogue has good,
helpful plant descriptions, with some shrewd
observations that give the reader confidence.

Dalmeny House

ROSEBERY ESTATES, SOUTH
QUEENSFERRY EH30 9TQ

Tel 0131 331 1888   **Fax** 0131 331 1788
Location B924 off A90
Opening hours 2 pm – 5.30 pm; Sunday – Tuesday;
July & August. And for Scotland's Garden Scheme in
snowdrop time
Admission fee Grounds only: free

The grounds at Dalmeny are extensive, and
visitors are encouraged to see the valley walk
with rhododendrons, wellingtonias and
other conifers. But the estate concentrates

upon the house and its remarkable
collections rather than promoting the
gardens and grounds.

Owned by The Earl of Rosebery

Inveresk Lodge

24 INVERESK VILLAGE, MUSSELBURGH
EH21 7TE

Tel 01721 722502
Website www.nts.org.uk
Location A6124 south of Musselburgh, 6 miles east of
Edinburgh
Opening hours 10 am – 6 pm, Monday – Friday;
12 noon – 6 pm, Saturdays & Sundays; April to October.
10 am – 4.30 pm, Monday – Friday; 2 pm – 5 pm, Sundays;
November to March
Admission fee Adults £2; Concessions £1. Honesty box

This modern, terraced garden has been
tailor-made for a modest estate and is
maintained to a high standard. In its fine
Edwardian conservatory are an aviary and
some tree ferns. Elsewhere are good
herbaceous borders and interesting climbing
plants. Graham Thomas designed the rose
borders.

Owned by The National Trust for Scotland
Number of gardeners 1
Size 13 acres

Royal Botanic Garden, Edinburgh

INVERLEITH ROW, EDINBURGH EH3 5LR

Tel 0131 552 7171 **Fax** 0131 248 2901
Website www.rbge.org.uk
Location 1 mile north of Princes Street
Opening hours 9.30 am – 7 pm; daily; April to August.
Closes at 6 pm in March & September, 5 pm in
February & October, 4 pm from November to January
Closed 1 January & 25 December
Admission fee free. Guided tours at 11 am & 2 pm, daily
from April to September

The gardens at the Royal Botanic Garden in Edinburgh have an important amenity function for both tourists and local people, but they are principally a collection of plants of scientific and educational importance. They are internationally renowned for their collection of plants from the Himalaya, west China and Japan; their rhododendron collection – the best in the world; their collection of orchids from south-east Asia; their alpines; and their flora of Arabia. So far as possible, these have been displayed within the gardens in a naturalistic setting which hints at their native habitats. The landscaping in the glasshouses in particularly good and recreates a whole series of different environments from arid deserts to humid tropics. It goes without saying that everything is extremely well labelled and the standard of maintenance is among the highest in any garden anywhere in the world. The members of staff are also invariably courteous and helpful. The rock garden is nearly a hectare and composed of many different micro-habitats, most of them helped by the naturally light sandy soil and low rainfall. More than 5,000 species (from areas as different as high mountains, the arctic regions and the Mediterranean) flourish in the mounds and

gullies of sandstone and conglomerate alongside the stream and in the screes. The heath garden is in the process of renovation and will open later this year as a Scottish moorland habitat garden. The arboretum has nearly 2,000 different trees, many of them seldom seen in cultivation – the sort that visitors find attractive and are then disappointed find unavailable commercially. There are also extensive areas dedicated to azaleas and to systematic demonstration gardens. A must for any keen gardener in Scotland.

Plant Highlights Woodland garden; sub-tropical plants; roses (ancient & modern); rock garden; rhododendrons & azaleas; herbs; plants under glass; mature conifers; good herbaceous borders; fine collection of trees; alpine plants; peat beds; 45 UK record-breaking trees, more than any other Scottish garden.

Owned by Board of Trustees
Size 77 acres

Malleny House Garden

BALERNO EH14 7AF

Tel 0131 449 2283
Website www.nts.org.uk
Location In Balerno, south-west of Edinburgh, off A71
Opening hours 9.30 am – 7 pm (4 pm from November to March); daily; all year
Admission fee Adults £2; Concessions £1. Honesty box

Malleny is one of the National Trust for Scotland's best gardens, much praised for its 'personal' quality. The nineteenth-century shrub roses are richly underplanted with herbaceous plants which carry the display through into the autumn: there is a sense of opulence about the garden throughout the summer and autumn. The bonsai collection creates quite another dimension, as do the magnificent conservatory and the huge cones of yew topiary, relics of a seventeenth-century formal garden. It is, above all, a very peaceful garden – and far too little visited.

Owned by The National Trust for Scotland
Number of gardeners 1
Size 3 acres
NCCPG National Collections *Rosa* (nineteenth-century shrubs)

Suntrap Garden

43 GOGARBANK, EDINBURGH EH12 9BY

Tel 0131 339 7283
Location 1 mile west of Edinburgh bypass, between A8 & A71
Opening hours 10 am – 4.30 pm; daily; all year, but weekdays only from October to March, and closed for Christmas fortnight
Admission fee Adults £1; Children free

Suntrap has three acres of demonstration gardens attached to Oatridge Agricultural College: it is one of the best places in Lothian to learn how to be a better gardener. The features include island beds, a rock garden, a peat garden, sculptures, vegetable plots, a rose garden, annual borders – and much more.

Owned by Oatridge Agricultural College
Size 3 acres

STRATHCLYDE

Achamore Gardens

ISLE OF GIGHA PA41 7AD

Tel 01583 505254   **Fax** 01583 505244
Website www.isle-of-gigha.co.uk
Location Take Gigha ferry from Tainloan (20 mins) then
easy walking for 1½ miles
Opening hours Dawn – dusk; daily; all year
Admission fee Adults £2; Children £1

Achamore is one of the best rhododendron gardens in the British Isles, and started as recently as 1944. Despite such a short existence (many rhododendrons gardens date well back into the nineteenth century) Achamore has also had its fair share of ups and downs. It was largely planted by Sir James Horlick, with advice from Jim Russell. It has about 20 distinct areas cut out of the woodland (overgrown with *R. ponticum*) but they all have rhododendrons in common: their names include the Loderi garden, Thomson Garden and Macabeanum Wood. Camellias, eucalyptus and nothofagus also grow well here, as do many of the Surrey-type trees recommended by Russell – flowering cherries, sorbus and birches. And there are good herbaceous plantings too, from daffodils through to pulmonarias and primulas.

 Plant Highlights Woodland garden; sub-tropical plants; rhododendrons; azaleas; biggest *Larix gmelinii* in the British Isles.

Owned by Holt Leisure Parks Ltd (Mr D N Holt)
Number of gardeners 2
Size 40+ acres

Achnacloich

CONNEL, OBAN PA37 1PR

Tel 01631 710221   **Fax** 01631 710796
Location On A85, 3 miles east of Connel
Opening hours 10 am – 6 pm; daily; 7 April
to 31 October
Admission fee Adults £1.50; OAPs £1; Children free

A substantial woodland garden made in three stages. First there were the Scots pine and European larch, which have grown to great heights. Then came the large-scale plantings of rhododendrons, particularly the *Triflora* species which have begun to naturalise. The latest stage has been the creation of a plantsman's garden using the tender shrubs and trees which flourish on the west coast on Argyll. Some of the embothriums are taller than the native oaks.

Owned by Mrs J Nelson
Number of gardeners 1
Size 35 acres

An Cala

ISLE OF SEIL PA34 4RF

Tel & Fax 01852 300237
Location In village of Easdale
Opening hours 10 am – 6 pm; daily; April to September
Admission fee Adults £1.50; Children free

This sheltered garden on the wild west coast has a natural rock garden and several streams which have been dammed and planted with moisture-loving species. The result is a garden of great lushness.

Owned by Mrs T Downie
Number of gardeners 1
Size 5 acres

Angus Garden

BARGUILLEAN, TAYNUILT PA35 1HY

Tel 01866 822254   **Fax** 01866 822048
Location Turn south off A85 at Taynuilt: 3 miles on right
Opening hours dawn – dusk; daily; March to October
Admission fee Adults £2; Children free

This young garden in a beautiful setting on the shores of Loch Etive has a particularly fine collection of modern rhododendrons in light oak woodland. It doubles up as a test ground for new hybrids introduced from USA by the adjacent Barguillean Nurseries. There are plans for a substantial expansion of the gardens to create more summer and autumn interest. Rather short on labels, but a garden to watch.

Owned by Sam Macdonald
Number of gardeners 1
Size 11 acres

Ardanaiseig Hotel Garden

ARDANAISEIG, KILCHRENAN, BY TAYNUILT PA35 1HE

Tel 01866 833333   **Fax** 01866 833222
Website www.ardanaiseig-hotel.com
Location On Loch Awe, 4 miles up from Kilchrenan
Opening hours 9 am – 5 pm; daily; all year
Admission fee Adults £2; Children free

Ardanaiseig has a fine woodland garden with an important collection of rhododendrons and azaleas. Most were planted about 100 years ago. The hotel is in a stunning position on a promontory.

Owned by Bennie Gray

Ardchattan Priory

CONNEL, OBAN PA37 1RQ

Tel 01631 750274
Location 5 miles east of Connel Bridge, on the north shore of Loch Etive
Opening hours 9 am – 6 pm; daily; April to October
Admission fee Adults £2; Children free

Best in spring, when daffodils flower in light ornamental woodland, but Ardchattan is also planted for high summer, with an emphasis on roses and herbaceous borders. The autumn colour, too, is surprisingly good for a west coast garden.

Owned by Mrs Sarah Troughton
Number of gardeners 1½
Size 4 acres

Ardkinglas Woodland Garden

CAIRNDOW PA26 8BH

Tel & Fax 01499 600263
Website www.ardkinglass.com
Location On A83 at Cairndow
Opening hours Daylight hours; daily; all year
Admission fee £2

Formerly known as Strone Gardens, Ardkinglas is famous for its magnificent conifers but has been substantially improved by recent restoration and new plantings. Among the rhododendrons are many hybrids bred by the late Lord Ardkinglas, when he was Secretary of State for Scotland. The nearby

Tree Shop, run by the Ardkinglas Estate, is a nursery specialising in trees and shrubs – especially rhododendrons. It is open seven days a wekk and has a handsome list of unusual plants.

 Plant Highlights Woodland garden; rhododendrons & azaleas; mature conifers; new gazebo looking over Loch Fyne; tallest tree in all Europe *Abies grandis* (63m), and 4 further UK record trees.

Owned by S J Noble Esq
Number of gardeners 1
Size 25 acres
NCCPG National Collections *Abies; Picea*

Ardtornish Garden

LOCHALINE, MORVERN, BY OBAN
PA34 5VZ

Tel 01967 421288   **Fax** 01967 421211
Location 2 miles north of Lochaline
Opening hours Not known as we went to press. In 2000 the garden was open 10 am – 5 pm; daily; May to October
Admission fee £2 (in 2000)

(P) (ﾂ) (WC) (ﾂ)

This is Faith Raven's other garden – see Docwra's Manor in Cambridgeshire – and a complete contrast: 28 acres of rocky hillside full of Edwardian hybrid rhododendrons like 'Pink Pearl' and 'Cynthia'. Mrs Raven has actively improved it with a great range of interesting plants. Remote, but worth every inch of the journey.

Owned by Mrs John Raven

Arduaine Garden

ARDUAINE, BY OBAN PA34 4XQ

Tel & Fax 01852 200366
Website www.nts.org.uk
Location On A816 between Oban & Lochgilphead

Opening hours 9.30 am – sunset; daily; all year
Admission fee Adults £3; Concessions £2

(P) (WC)

Arduaine is a luxuriant woodland garden in a sheltered, south-facing valley at the edge of the sea. Stout conifers and 40-ft thickets of *Griselinia* protect the spectacular rhododendrons which two nurserymen planted in the 1970s. *Primula denticulata* and *Narcissus cyclamineus* have naturalised in grassy glades. *Cardiocrinum giganteum* and *Myosotidium hortensia* grow vigorously. There are several outsize and champion trees, including *Eucryphia glutinosa, Gevuina avellana, Nothofagus antarctica, Trochodendron aralioides* and the upright form of the tulip tree known as *Liriodendron tulipifera* 'Fastigiatum'. But the sheer variety of all the plantings is an education, while the whole garden is handsomely maintained.

 Plant Highlights Sub-tropical plants; rhododendrons; tallest *Nothofagus antarctica* (26m) in the British Isles and 6 further records.

Owned by The National Trust for Scotland
Number of gardeners 3
Size 20 acres

Barwinnock Herbs

BARRHILL, GIRVAN KA26 0RB

Tel & Fax 01465 821338
Opening hours 10 am – 6 pm; daily; April to October

(P) (ﾂ)

Although not far from such tourist destinations as Galloway Forest Park, Barwinnock Herbs is set among wonderfully wild scenery, which forms a spectacular backdrop to this beautifully laid out nursery. Primarily a nursery which specialises in organically grown culinary, medicinal and aromatic herbs, there is a small garden too, in which these plants are prettily displayed. The plant yard itself is most attractive, with the pots arranged on rustic tables amidst a collection of agricultural bygones. There is a small rural museum attached, with some local produce and seed on sale and, for those who want to venture further afield, there are some enticing walks mapped out from the nursery. If you do not want to take your purchases with you, they are happy to post them for you.

Biggar Park

BIGGAR ML12 6JS

Tel 01899 221085
Location ¼ mile south-west of Biggar on A702: white gates & lodge
Opening hours By appointment for groups, May to August; and for Scotland's Garden Scheme
Admission fee Adults £2; Children 50p

Biggar is a mixture of woodland, spacious lawns (with an ornamental pond), unusual plants and shrubberies. It is 700ft up, so somewhat susceptible to late spring frosts. In the formal walled garden are traditional herbaceous borders – the poppies are especially fine in June – plus fruit and vegetables, and a greenhouse. Roses are a special interest: there are good collections of both old and modern cultivars. The most recent development is the start of a Japanese garden.

Owned by Captain & Mrs David Barnes
Number of gardeners 1
Size 10 acres

Brodick Castle

ISLE OF ARRAN KA27 8HY

Tel 01770 302202   **Fax** 01770 302312
Website www.nts.org.uk
Location Ferry from Ardrossan to Brodick, follows signs
Opening hours 9.30 am – sunset; daily; all year. Walled garden closes at 5 pm
Admission fee Adults £2.50; Concessions £1.70

This lush rhododendron garden was begun by Molly, Duchess of Montrose, in 1923. The climate at Brodick is mild and wet: the sloping hillside is almost frost-free. Some of the Duchess's plantings are now record-breakers, including *Embothrium coccineum* at more than 20m, the seldom-seen *Euonymus tingens*, the wild form of *Leptospermum scoparium* more than 10m high, and the rare *Nothofagus nervosa* which is over 30m high. In the woodland are fine magnolias, camellias, crinodendrons and olearias too, but none of these plantings is a match for the rhododendrons, many of which were grown from collectors' seed. The work of collectors Forrest, Ludlow and Kingdon Ward are all represented here. The walled garden has been restored as it might have been in Victorian times. For those with longer to dally, Brodick also has a fine park with further features including a restored ice-house.

Plant Highlights Sub-tropical plants; good herbaceous borders; fine trees; candelabra primulas; meconopsis; lilies; good bedding; tallest *Drimys winteri* (21m) and *Embothrium coccineum* (20m) in the British Isles (& three further records).

Owned by The National Trust for Scotland
Number of gardeners 6, plus 2 part-time
Size 80 acres
NCCPG National Collections *Rhododendron* (subsections *Falconera, Grandia* and *Maddenia*)

Colzium Walled Garden

LENNOX ESTATE, OFF STIRLING
ROAD, KILSYTH, GLASGOW G65 0PY

Tel 01236 828150 **Fax** 01236 826322
Location Signed from Kilsyth on B803
Opening hours Noon – 7 pm; daily; Easter to mid-September.
Noon – 4 pm; Saturdays & Sundays; rest of year
Admission fee free

Colzium Walled Garden is an up-and-
coming young garden, which the Council has
developed on an ancient site since 1978. A
wide range of plants is grown within the
protection of high walls, particularly ornamental trees and shrubs, and the standards
of maintenance and labelling are excellent.

Owned by North Lanarkshire Council
Size ½ acre

Crarae Gardens

CRARAE, BY INVERARY PA32 8YA

Tel 01546 886614 **Fax** 01546 886388
Website www.crarae-gardens.org
Location South of Inverary on A83

The future of Crarae was rather uncertain as
we went to press. The trustees were finding
maintenance costs too much for them, and
were in discussion with the National Trust
for Scotland about a possible arrangement
that would enable the gardens to be preserved.
In 2000, it was open daily from 9 am – 6 pm
from Easter to October and thereafter
during daylight hours. It is a garden of major
importance for its collection of plants.

Plant Highlights Woodland garden;
camellias; rhododendrons; autumn
colour; tallest *Acer pensylvanicum* in the
British Isles (and 12 further tree records).

Owned by The Crarae Garden Charitable Trust
Size 50 acres
NCCPG National Collections *Nothofagus*

Culzean Castle & Country Park

MAYBOLE, AYRSHIRE KA19 8LE

Tel 01655 884455 **Fax** 01655 884503
Website www.nts.org.uk
Location Off A719, west of Maybole & South of Ayr
Opening hours 9.30 am – sunset; daily; all year
Admission fee Park & garden only: Adults £4;
Concessions £3

Culzean is the flagship of the National Trust
for Scotland, thoroughly restored and
seriously open to the public (more than
400,000 visitors a year). The gardens are
important and include a deer park, a ruined
arch, a viaduct, an ice house, a beautiful
gothic camellia house, gazebos, a pagoda
and a vinery. The three areas of horticultural
interest are the walled garden, the fountain
court and 'Happy Valley', which is a
woodland garden with fine specimen trees.
Record-breakers include an upright Irish
yew (*Taxus baccata* 'Fastigiata') at 20m, and
the rare southern Japanese hemlock *Tsuga
sieboldii* at 25m.

Plant Highlights Woodland garden;
herbs; plants under glass; good
herbaceous borders; deer park; formal
garden; tallest Irish yew *Taxus baccata*
'Fastigiata' (19m) in the British Isles (plus
two further tree records).

Owned by The National Trust for Scotland
Number of gardeners 7, plus 4 groundsmen
Size 120 acres

Finlaystone

LANGBANK PA14 6TJ

Tel 01475 540 285
Location On A8, 10 mins west of Glasgow
Opening hours 10.30 am – 5 pm; daily; all year
Admission fee Adults £2.50; OAPs & Children £1.50

Much of the garden at Finlaystone was laid out in about 1900. The formal garden dates from this period: it is enclosed within a yew hedge which was castellated by 'an enthusiastic family governess and a French aunt' in about 1920. But most of today's imaginative and beautiful garden is more recent. The New Garden dates from 1959: the banks of a burn are lined with hostas, *Peltiphyllum peltatum* – spectacular in autumn – and azaleas which blend into the woodland beyond. In fact, throughout Finlaystone, the woodland areas are thick with azaleas, as well as rhododendrons, bluebells and snowdrops. Celtic themes have inspired the MacMillans to construct several new gardens on the hillside above the house. The Celtic Garden has an intricate pattern of paving set into grass: the design is based on one from the Book of Kells. In the walled garden is a 'garden oasis' in the form of a Celtic cross with a pool at the centre but all enclosed by a circular brick rose pergola. There is also a garden of scented plants for blind visitors which is sometimes known as the 'Fragrant Garden' and on other occasions as the 'Smelly Garden'.

Owned by George MacMillan

Geilston Garden

CARDROSS, DUMBARTON G82 5EZ

Tel 01389 841867
Location On A814, at western end of Cardross

Opening hours 9.30 am – 5 pm; daily; April to October
Admission fee £2. RHS members free

Geilston is a nice example of the many small country houses, villas and estates which were put together by successful Glasgow industrialists along the banks of the Clyde. The garden retains a sense of being a private space in which the visitor is an invited guest. The many attractive features include a fruit and vegetable garden with a central 'dipping pond', a walled garden with traditional glasshouses and a burn which winds through the wooded glen.

Owned by The National Trust for Scotland
Number of gardeners 1
Size 7 acres

Glasgow Botanic Garden

730 GREAT WESTERN ROAD, GLASGOW G12 0UE

Tel 0141 334 2422   **Fax** 0141 339 6964
Location On A82 2 miles from city centre
Opening hours Grounds: 7 am – dusk; daily; all year. Glasshouses & Kibble Palace: 10 am – 4.45 pm (4.15 pm in winter); daily; all year. Special opening for Scotland's Garden Scheme on 8 & 9 September
Admission fee free

Most of the elements of the traditional botanic garden are here, including chronological beds, but the glory of Glasgow is its two glasshouses – the Kibble Palace and the Main Range. The Kibble Palace is a fine nineteenth-century cast-iron and steel structure, now in need of the restoration which will start later this year. It houses collections from South Africa, China, South America and the Canaries: a walk around its outer circle takes the visitor round the horticultural globe. There is no better place to enjoy a winter's day in Glasgow. The Main Range is a more conventional construction – though also showing signs of disrepair – with good glasshouse collections of plants arranged by family and use, from tree ferns to palms and from cacti to orchids. In 2001, the gardens will be hosting four special RHS events: details from 020 7821 3408.

Owned by Glasgow City Council
NCCPG National Collections Begonia; Dendrobium; Dicksoniaceae

Glenarn

RHU, HELENSBURGH G84 8LL

Tel 01436 820493 **Fax** 0141 21 8450
Location Turn up Pier Road at Rhu Marina, first right is Glenarn Road
Opening hours Dawn to dusk; daily; mid-March to mid-September
Admission fee Adults £2; OAPs & Children £1

Glenarn's ten acres of woodland garden has rhododendrons dating from Sir Joseph Hooker's Himalayan expedition and others from the 1930s trips of Kingdon Ward and Ludlow and Sheriff. The many good hybrids include the original Gibson plants. But there are plenty of magnolias, camellias, pieris, and other good plants too.

Owned by Mr & Mrs Michael Thornley

Greenbank Garden

FLENDERS ROAD, CLARKSTON, GLASGOW G76 8RB

Tel 0141 639 3281
Website www.nts.org.uk

Location One mile along Mearns Road from Clarkston Toll, take 1st left
Opening hours Garden: 9.30 am – sunset; daily; all year. Walled garden closes at 5 pm. Closed 1 & 2 January, 25 & 26 December
Admission fee Adults £3.50; Concessions £2.50

Greenbank is a demonstration garden: it was left to the Trust in 1976 on condition that it was developed as a teaching resource for people with small gardens. The walled garden has therefore been divided into a great number of sections which represent different interests and skills: a rock garden, fruit garden, dried flower plot, raised beds, winter garden, and so on.

Owned by The National Trust for Scotland
Number of gardeners 3
Size 2½-acre walled garden; 15 acres of policies

Mount Stuart

ISLE OF BUTE PA20 9LR

Tel 01700 503877 **Fax** 01700 505313
Website www.mountstuart.com
Location 5 miles south of Rothesay
Opening hours 10 am – 5 pm; daily except Tuesdays & Thursdays; May to September
Admission fee Adults £3.50; Children £2

Mount Stuart has a vast and fascinating garden to accompany the sumptuous house. Its 300 acres include: a Victorian pinetum, recently expanded by a further 100 acres dedicated to the Royal Botanic Garden at Edinburgh's Conifer Conservation Programme; a two-acre rock garden designed by Thomas Mawson and thickly planted with rare collected plants; a 'wee' garden of five acres, planted with tender exotics from Australia and New Zealand; and a kitchen garden recently redesigned by Rosemary Verey. Add in the relics of an eighteenth-century landscape, a tropical greenhouse, acres of bluebells and established rhododendrons, and you have the measure of a long and fascinating visit.

Owned by The Mount Stuart Trust
Number of gardeners 8
Size 300 acres

Torosay Castle & Gardens

CRAIGNURE, ISLE OF MULL PA65 6AY

Tel 01680 812421   **Fax** 01680 812470
Website www.holidaymull.org
Location 1½ miles from Craignure on A849 to Iona
Opening hours House: 10.30 am – 5.30 pm; daily; April to mid-October. Gardens: 9 am – dusk; daily; all year
Admission fee Adults £4.50; Concessions £3.50; Children £1.50. RHS members free

The best feature of the gardens at Torosay is the Italian Statue Walk, lined with 19 figures by Antonio Bonazza. The formal terraces (attributed to Lorimer) are covered with rambling roses, other climbers and perennials. The Japanese garden, bog garden, greenhouses and rock garden add to the sheer variety. The woodland garden is stuffed with interesting specimens: *Eucryphia*, *Embothrium* and *Crinodendron* among many, underplanted with meconopsis and primulas.

Owned by Mr C James
Number of gardeners 2½ plus seasonal extras
Size 12 acres

Younger Botanic Garden

DUNOON PA23 8QU

Tel 01369 706261   **Fax** 01369 706369
Website www.rbge.org.uk

Location 7 miles north of Dunoon on A815
Opening hours 9.30 am – 6 pm; daily; March to October
Admission fee Adults £3; OAPs £2.50; Children £1; Family £7

The Younger Botanic Garden at Benmore has been an annexe of the Royal Botanic Garden at Edinburgh since 1929, having been given to the nation a few years earlier by the brewer Harry Younger. The stupendous redwood avenue which greets the visitor at the entrance dates from 1863 and was the start of a systematic programme of planting conifers on the estate, into which the Youngers introduced ornamental trees and shrubs. The mild, wet climate makes possible the cultivation of tender plants from lower altitudes of the Sino-Himalaya, Bhutan, Japan and the New World. Benmore is a living textbook of the genus *Rhododendron*: over 350 species and sub-species grow at Benmore, and a further 300 hybrids and cultivars. Their background is of conifers planted early in the nineteenth century, perhaps the best collection in Scotland. The conifers are at the heart of RBGE's conservation programme and have been supplemented by new ecological plantings including a Bhutanese glade and a Chilean glade. But the whole garden is spacious, educational and beautifully maintained.

Plant Highlights Woodland garden; mature conifers; fine collection of trees; giant redwood avenue planted in 1863; rhododendrons; ferns; new Chilean plant collection; ten record-breaking trees, including *Nothofagus betuloides* at over 20m.

Owned by Board of Trustees/RBG, Edinburgh
Size 125 acres

TAYSIDE

Bell's Cherrybank Gardens

CHERRYBANK, PERTH PH2 0NG

Tel 01738 627330   **Fax** 01738 472823
Location Take Perth road from M90 Jct11 & first right onto B9112
Opening hours 10 am – 5 pm; daily; May to September. Plus 12 noon – 4 pm on Sundays. By appointment at other times
Admission fee Adults £3

These immaculately maintained show gardens make good use of water and incorporate some striking modern sculptures. They are best known for the collection of heaths and heathers, the most comprehensive in the British Isles with over 900 cultivars. There are plans to expand the gardens substantially which may be put into effect shortly.

Owned by United Distillers UK plc
Number of gardeners 2
Size 6½ acres
NCCPG National Collections Erica

Bolfracks Garden

ABERFELDY PH15 2EX

Tel 01887 820207
Location 2 miles west of Aberfeldy on A827
Opening hours 10 am – 6 pm; daily; 14 March to 31 October
Admission fee Adults £2.50; Children free

Bolfracks is a plantsman's garden, made mainly by Mr Hutchison over many years. It is unusual among Scottish gardens for having a good display of flowers throughout the year. There are rhododendrons and azaleas, of course, but they are principally dwarf species and hybrids, and are joined by a large number of daphnes, phyllodoces, pieris, quinces and berberis. Midsummer sees the shrub roses, of which there is a good collection, with everything from gallicas through to modern shrub roses. But Bolfracks is particularly good for its herbaceous borders: the perennials make a good display by June and continue through until autumn, when gentians, cyclamen and colchicums take over.

Owned by J D Hutchinson CBE
Number of gardeners 1
Size 3 acres

Branklyn Garden

116 DUNDEE ROAD, PERTH PH2 7BB

Tel 01738 625535
Website www.nts.org.uk
Location Off Dundee Road, on eastern edge of Perth, ½ mile from Queen's Bridge
Opening hours 9.30 am – sunset; daily; March to October
Admission fee Adults £3; OAPs £2

The apotheosis of Scottish rock gardening, Branklyn is a suburban garden absolutely crammed with rare plants growing in a series of artificial microhabitats. This is a garden to go round slowly, looking at all the plants – small rhododendrons, alpines, herbaceous plants and peat-lovers. It was built up between 1922 and 1967 by John Renton, who bequeathed it to the National Trust for Scotland on his death. This sort of garden depends for its success upon the understanding and plantsmanship of the gardeners who work in it, and the Trust has been fortunate with their employees at Branklyn since they took it on.

Owned by The National Trust for Scotland
Number of gardeners 2
Size 2 acres
NCCPG National Collections Cassiope

Christie's Nursery

DOWNFIELD, WESTMUIR, KIRRIEMUIR
DD5 8LP

Tel & Fax 01575 572977
Website www.christiealpines.co.uk
Location On A926 1 mile west of Kirriemuir
Opening hours 10 am – 5 pm; daily except Sundays & Tuesdays; March to October

This alpine nursery has an impressive list, particularly strong on gentians, hardy orchids, corydalis and lewisias. The owners reckon to have about 1,000 different items in stock at any time, and about 2,000 growing in their pretty display garden. In 2001, the nursery will be hosting four special RHS events: details from 020 7821 3408.

NCCPG National Collections Gentiana

Cluny House

BY ABERFELDY, PERTHSHIRE
PH15 2JT

Tel 01887 820795
Location 3½ miles from Aberfeldy, on the Weem to Strathtay Road
Opening hours 10 am – 6 pm; daily; March to October

Admission fee Adults £2.50; Children under 16 free.

Cluny is a plantsman's garden, largely made in the 1950s by Mrs Mattingley's father, who subscribed to the Ludlow and Sherriff expeditions. Some older trees date from the nineteenth century – notably two vast wellingtonias – and the Mattingleys have continued to develop the garden since they took over in 1987. It is very much a woodland garden, with a natural appearance, except that the canopy is now of rhododendrons, acers, sorbus, euonymus, and birches. It has superb rhododendrons and many other ornamental trees and shrubs from the Himalayas and North America, as well as an underplanting of meconopsis, trilliums, gentians, nomocharis, cardiocrinums, erythroniums, lilies, arisaema and hellebores. But it is memorable, above all, for primulas – starting with the early-flowering petiolarid species – *P. whitei, P. tanneri, P. sonchifolia* and *P. edgeworthii*, for example. Then come sheets of candelabra species: the first is yellow *P. chungensis*, followed by purple *P. pulverulenta*, the dark pink and white forms of *P. japonica*, purple *P. beesiana*, orange *P. bulleyana*, yellow *P. sikkimensis* and yellow *P. florindae* – as well as naturally occurring hybrids between them. Many exotic species – and not just primulas – seed and regenerate freely in the acid, humus-rich soil. The whole garden is hand-weeded and chemical-free: interesting seedlings are thereby spotted and protected.

Plant Highlights Plantsman's collection of plants; fine collection of trees; meconopsis; primulas; cardiocrinums; wellingtonia (*Sequoiadendron giganteum*) with the widest girth in the British Isles.

Owned by Mr J & Mrs W Mattingley
Size 6 acres
NCCPG National Collections Primula (Asiatic species)

Drummond Castle Gardens

MUTHILL, CRIEFF PH7 4HZ

Tel 01764 681257 **Fax** 01764 681550
Location South of Crieff on A822
Opening hours 2 pm – 6 pm; daily; Easter weekend, then from May to October
Admission fee Adults £3.50; OAPs £2.50; Children £1.50

Drummond has probably the most important formal garden in Scotland, laid out in about 1830 as a St Andrew's cross, with complex parterres filled since the 1950s with roses, statues, clipped cones, herbaceous plants, gravel and lots more beside. The result is order, shape, structure, mass, profusion and colour. There is also a copper beech planted by Queen Victoria to commemorate her visit in 1842. Parts of the film *Rob Roy* were shot in the gardens.

Owned by Grimsthorpe & Drummond Castle Trust Ltd
Number of gardeners 5
Size 12 acres

Dundee Botanic Garden

RIVERSIDE DRIVE, DUNDEE DD2 1QH

Tel 01382 566939 **Fax** 01382 640574
Location Signed from Riverside Drive (A85), near its junction with Perth Road
Opening hours 10 am – 4.30 pm (3.30 pm from November to February); daily; all year
Admission fee Adults £1.50; OAPs & Children 75p. RHS members free

Dundee has a fine modern botanic garden which caters well for visitors: its gentle south-facing slopes are just above the banks of the River Tay. Founded in 1971, it can now boast fine collections of conifers and broad-leaved trees, good shrubs, tropical and temperate glasshouses, a water garden and a herb garden. There are also systematic and chronological borders and a whole series of native plant communities from montane to coastal habitats. These include a collection of *Sorbus* species native to Britain. There are also plant groupings which demonstrate adaptations for survival, such as drought resistance (the Mediterranean garden) and specialised pollination. Among the more surprising collections are *Nothofagus* species from South America and a large collection of *Eucalyptus* trees from Australia. In 2001, the gardens will be hosting two special RHS events: details from 020 7821 3408.

Owned by University of Dundee
Number of gardeners 3
Size 23 acres

Edzell Castle

EDZELL, ANGUS DD9 7VE

Tel 01356 648631
Website www.historic-scotland.gov.uk
Location On B966 to Edzell Village, then signed for 1 mile
Opening hours 9.30 am – 6.30 pm; daily; April to November. But not open until 2 pm on Sundays in October & November
Admission fee Adults £2.50; OAPs £1.90; Children £1. May go up in April

Edzell has a 1930s formal garden in the seventeenth-century style, designed to be seen from the ruined keep. It is shaped like a quincunx of sorts, with yew bobbles, box edging and roses in the beds. The four main segments have the motto of the Lindsey family *DUM SPIRO SPERO* cut round their edges in box. But, once you have seen the parterre, Edzell is not a garden to linger in.

Owned by Historic Scotland

Glendoick Gardens

GLENDOICK, PERTH PH2 7NS

Tel 01738 860205   **Fax** 01738 860630
Website www.glendoick.com
Location A90 between Perth & Dundee
Opening hours 2 pm – 5 pm; 6 & 20 May. And pre-booked parties of 20+ during May
Admission fee £2

Everyone knows of the Glendoick nursery, but the garden is even more important. Started by Farrer's friend Euan Cox in the 1920s, it has one of the best collections of plants, especially rhododendron species, forms and hybrids, in the British Isles. More's the pity that it is so seldom open. The nursery started in 1953, and all its stock is propagated on site. Peter Cox has specialised in breeding low-growing rhododendrons for small gardens: his successes include such well-known cultivars as 'Curlew', 'Razorbill' and 'Egret'. He has also continued to hunt for plants in China, as his father did before him. There is a good demonstration garden in the nursery.

Owned by Mr & Mrs Peter A Cox

House of Dun

MONTROSE, ANGUS DD10 9LQ

Tel 01674 810264   **Fax** 01674 810722
Website www.nts.org.uk
Location On A395, halfway between Montrose & Brechin
Opening hours 9.30 am – sunset; daily; all year

Admission fee £1 in honesty box

The first thing you notice at House of Dun, particularly in winter, is the magnificent line of mature wellingtonias, but there are sheets of spring bulbs, a Victorian rose garden for summer, a border of *Nerine bowdenii* over 100 metres long, and a collection of old fruit trees of interest in autumn. The walled garden (rather small) has been restored as it might have been in the late nineteenth century and planted with cultivars that date back to the 1880s.

Owned by The National Trust for Scotland
Number of gardeners 1
Size 45 acres

House of Pitmuies

BY FORFAR, ANGUS DD8 2SN

Tel 01241 828245
Location Off A932 Forfar to Arbroath Road
Opening hours 10 am – 5 pm; daily; April to October
Admission fee Adults £2.50; Children free

House of Pitmuies is one of the most beautiful modern gardens in Scotland, and still expanding. Laid out and planted in the Hidcote style, Pitmuies has wonderful shrub roses in mixed plantings, clever colour schemes, and innumerable different gardens within the garden: a delphinium border, cherry walk, an alpine meadow for wild flowers, rhododendrons glades, vast hollies and splendid monkey puzzles inherited from Victorian times. Enchanted and enchanting.

Plant Highlights Roses (ancient & modern); plants under glass; fruit; good herbaceous borders; alpine meadow; ferns; colour schemes; new woodland garden (2000); tallest *Ilex aquifolium* 'Argenteomarginata' in the British Isles.

Owned by Mrs Farquhar Ogilvie

Kinross House

KINROSS KY13 7ET

Tel 01577 863467
Location In Kinross
Opening hours 10 am – 7 pm; daily; April to September
Admission fee Adults £2; Children 50p

Kinross is the most beautiful house in Scotland, with extensive views across Loch Leven. It is approached along a magnificent avenue of lime trees. The elegant walled garden has herbaceous borders and roses and, above all, a seventeenth-century sense of proportion. It is one of the few Scottish gardens which is genuinely at its best in July and August.

Owned by Sir David Montgomery Bt

Scone Palace

PERTH PH2 6BD

Tel 01738 552300   **Fax** 01738 552588
Website www.scone-palace.co.uk
Location Signed from A93
Opening hours 9.30 am – 5.45; daily; April to October.
10 am – 4 pm in winter
Admission fee Gardens only: Adults £2.90; OAPs £2.50;
Children £1.70. RHS members free

Scone is best known for its pinetum and for the Douglas firs (*Pseudotsuga menziesii*) grown from original seed sent back by their discoverer David Douglas, who was born on the estate here. Lord Mansfield has the

largest private collection of orchids in the country.

Plant Highlights Established pinetum; woodland walks; rhododendrons & azaleas; daffodils; new 'Murray' maze; tallest *Tilia platyphyllos* (37m) in the British Isles, and 4 further record trees; largest private collection of orchid hybrids in Britain.

Owned by The Earl of Mansfield
Number of gardeners 7
Size 100 acres

WALES

Most of the best-known gardens of Wales are close to the sea – as, indeed, are most of its larger centres of population. This gives the principality a reputation for being able to grow tender plants that would not be hardy – say – in Surrey. There is some truth in this, though no Welsh garden is truly described as sub-tropical in the way that Tresco and Inverewe are. The National Gardens Scheme offers gardens to visit in every part of Wales, and in respectable numbers. The Royal Horticultural Society has negotiated free access for its members, for some or all of the year, to Bodnant, the National Botanic Garden of Wales and Picton Castle.

This book lists gardens in Wales under the old 1974 counties, rather than the historic counties or the present administrative units. The 1974 counties are a useful size for the purpose of this book, and their names are readily recognised.

Wales has many historic gardens, made mainly in the eighteenth and nineteenth centuries and usually in the styles that were fashionable in England at the time. The National Trust has played an important part in preserving and restoring some of the finest. Bodnant, Plas Newydd and Powis Castle are gardens of the utmost international importance. By and large, however, they share with other Welsh gardens the characteristic of having acquired their horticultural importance during the twentieth century: the same is true of other classic Welsh gardens like Portmeirion and Dyffryn. Though it cannot rival such major botanic gardens as Kew and Edinburgh, the new National Botanic Garden of Wales does give a new focus to Welsh horticulture.

Wales's historic gardens are well supported by the Welsh Historic Gardens Trust which has taken action to identify, evaluate and conserve the principality's heritage. Comparatively few historic gardens in Wales are open to the public.

CADW, the Welsh Historic Monuments Commission in Cardiff, has nearly finished a Register of Parks and Gardens of Special Historic Interest in Wales. All the county registers have now been published except for Dyfed's, which is due later this year. The prices of the registers for the other five counties are Gwent £15, Clwyd £20, Powys and Glamorgan £21 each, and Gwynedd £30.

The best collection of trees in Wales is at Bodnant, which has a large number of rarities and some 20 champions among them. There are good tree collections also at Dyffryn and Margam in Glamorgan. The NCCPG has 20 National Collections in Wales, of which seven are in National Trust gardens and four in the care of the gardens belonging to the City of Swansea.

Wales has comparatively few top-class nurseries, and practically none in South Wales near Cardiff or Swansea. However, the outstanding examples elsewhere in the principality are among Britain's best. Celyn Vale has a unique list of Australasian trees; Dibleys Nurseries are the leading nursery for *Streptocarpus* and other house plants; and Crûg Farm Plants is a true plantsman's nursery which introduces more new collected plants into cultivation than any other in Britain.

CLWYD

Aberconwy Nursery

GRAIG, GLAN CONWY, COLWYN BAY
LL28 5TL

Tel 01492 580875
Location South of Glan Conwy, 2nd right off A470. Turn right at top of hill: nursery is on the right
Opening hours 10 am – 5 pm; Tuesday – Sunday; February to October

This RHS Partnership Nursery is best known as one of our leading nurseries for alpine plants and a steady introducer of new cultivars, especially autumn-flowering gentians. But it also offers unusual shrubs, herbaceous and woodland plants, including many dwarf rhododendrons and small ericaceous plants. Other specialities are dieramas, epimediums and its hybrids of *Helleborus niger*.

Celyn Vale Nurseries

ALLT-Y-CELYN, CARROG, CORWEN
LL21 9LD

Tel & Fax 01490 430671
Website www.eucalyptus.co.uk
Location 3 miles east of Corwen & 1 mile from Carrog, near A5
Opening hours 9 am – 4 pm; Monday – Friday; January to November

Specialist growers of eucalyptus and acacias: they use seed from high altitude specimens to maximise hardiness and will advise also on suitable species for coppicing, poor drainage, alkaline soils, hedging, salt tolerance and so on. They say that the hardiest gum trees are *E. archeri*, *E. coccifera*, *E. pauciflora* subsp. *debeuzevillei*, *E. kybeanensis*, *E. niphophila*, *E. parvifolia* and *E. subcrenulata*.

Chirk Castle

CHIRK LL14 5AF

Tel 01691 777701   **Fax** 01691 774706
Website www.nationaltrust.org.uk
Location 1½ miles west of Chirk off A5
Opening hours 11 am – 6 pm (last admission 4.30 pm); Wednesday – Sunday, plus Bank Holiday Mondays; 28 March to 28 October. Closes at 5 pm in October
Admission fee Adults £2.80; Children £1.40

Chirk has handsome nineteenth-century formal gardens, one planted with roses and another with billowing yew topiary. There is also a good 1930s collection of trees and shrubs, the relics of a garden by Norah Lindsay. The National Trust has done much to provide shelter from the wind, so that more tender plants may be grown.

Plant Highlights Woodland garden; topiary; snowdrops; roses (ancient & modern); rock garden; rhododendrons & azaleas; good herbaceous borders; eucryphias; hydrangeas; lime avenue.

Owned by The National Trust

Bodnant Gardens

TAL-Y-CAFN, COLWYN BAY LL28 5RE

Tel 01492 650460 **Fax** 01492 650448
Website www.oxalis.co.uk/bodnant.htm
Location 8 miles south of Llandudno & Colwyn Bay on
A470. Entrance ½ mile along Eglwysbach Road
Opening hours 10 am – 5 pm; daily; 17 March to
31 October
Admission fee Adults £5; Children £2.50. RHS members
free

(P) (WC) (&) (🌳) (🏛) (🍴) (¶)

Two Lords Aberconway, both past-Presidents of the Royal Horticultural Society, and three generations of the Puddle family, as Head Gardeners, have made Bodnant compulsory visiting. Set in the valley of the River Conwy, Bodnant combines dramatic formal terraces with extensive woodland plantings on the grandest of scales. A deep herbaceous border, backing onto a high wall, is instantly striking, with mature, often tender climbers rampant above bold, warm plantings. Although this is North Wales, and the views from the lawns are across the valley to the Carneddau mountains and Snowdonia National Park, parts of the garden feel distinctly Italianate. Beside the house, two enormous cedars overshadow a formal lily pond, on the first of a succession of terraces, where hydrangeas abound. A crisply shaved yew hedge curves above a mezzanine rose pergola, and there are specimens of *Magnolia grandiflora* everywhere. Below is a stately gazebo from the early eighteenth century, the Pin Mill, which looks across a flat pool to a grassy stage at the opposite end of its terrace, edged with cut cubes of topiary. Plantings of pencil-thin cypresses, and *Cistus* and *Potentilla* cultivars, help to create an intensely Mediterranean feel on clear summer days. Behind the Pin Mill, the

mood changes, as the grassy valley fills with tall specimen trees, marching beside a fast flowing mill stream and a stern old mill. Along the stream there are hostas, bergenias and meconopsis. Some of the massive *Sequoiadendron* specimens bear planting plaques which show them to be in their second century. Winding back in an extended arc towards the house, there are gentler woodland plantings, with shrubbery borders, and smaller trees growing in grass. There is a magnificent collection of magnolias, rhododendrons and camellias. Other good plants include *Viburnum × bodnantense*, hybrid camellias, huge rhododendrons, white wisterias, a vast *Arbutus × andrachnoides*, and flaming embothriums. The garden is admirably maintained, and is popular with visitors, too. The walled plant-yard is strong on many of the tender climbers from the garden, and reasonably priced.

Plant Highlights An important collection of plants; rhododendrons & azaleas; camellias; good herbaceous borders; fine collection of trees; magnolias; good autumn colour; tallest Californian redwood *Sequoia sempervirens* (47m) in the British Isles and 18 further record-breaking tree species – more than any other garden in Wales.

Owned by The National Trust
Size 80 acres
NCCPG National Collections *Embothrium*; *Eucryphia*; *Magnolia*; *Rhododendron forrestii*

Dibleys Nurseries

LLANELIDAN, RUTHIN LL15 2LG

Tel 01978 790677 **Fax** 01978 790668
Website www.dibleys.com
Location 6 miles south of Ruthin, off the B5429
Opening hours 10 am – 5 pm; daily; April to September.
Plus weekdays in March & October

Dibleys are the leading British nursery for gesneriads – especially streptocarpus, of which they have a comprehensive collection of cultivars, from 'Constant Nymph' to the latest modern hybrids like the ever-blooming 'Crystal Ice'. They have made a great impact on RHS Flower Shows in recent years, and won gold medals at Chelsea in 1998, 1999 and 2000. They will be introducing three new cultivars in 2001. Dibleys also have a long list of other gesneriads like *Kohleria* and *Columnea*, and a good line in foliage begonias. An excellent nursery, in top form.

NCCPG National Collections *Streptocarpus*

Erddig

WREXHAM LL13 0YT

Tel 01978 355314 **Fax** 01978 315151
Website www.nationaltrust.org.uk
Location Signed from A483 &A525
Opening hours 11 am – 6 pm; Saturday – Wednesday;
31 March to 4 November. Opens at 10 am in
July & August; closes at 5 pm in October
Admission fee Gardens only: Adults £4; Children £2

More of a re-creation than a restoration, Erddig today majors on domestic life in the early eighteenth century. There are old-fashioned fruit trees (an excellent collection of cultivars of apples, plums, pears and cherries, beautifully trained), an avenue of pleached limes, and a long canal to frame the house, but all are slightly awed by the Victorian overlay – avenues of monkey puzzles and wellingtonias.

Plant Highlights Woodland garden; roses (mainly old-fashioned); fruit; spring bulbs.

Owned by The National Trust
Size 13 acres
NCCPG National Collections *Hedera*

DYFED

Aberglasney Gardens

LLANGATHEN SA32 8QH

Tel & Fax 01558 668998
Location 4 miles west of Landeilo, signed from A40
Opening hours 10 am – 6 pm; daily; April to October.
Then 10.30 am – 3 pm; Monday – Friday & first Sunday of
month; November to March
Admission fee Adults £3.95; OAPs £3.45; Children £1.95

Aberglasney has a garden that lay dormant
for about 400 years, until plans were made to
restore it in the style of the sixteenth and
seventeenth centuries. The structure remains
fairly intact from that time – including a
covered walk – and reproduction gardens
have been put within that structure. Hal
Moggridge and Penelope Hobhouse have
both been involved with the project: the
dense yew tunnel dates from about 1700.

Owned by Aberglasney Restoration Trust
Number of gardeners 4
Size 9 acres

Cae Hir

CRIBYN, LAMPETER SA48 7NG

Tel & Fax 01570 470839
Location In village
Opening hours 1 pm – 6 pm; daily except Mondays (but
open on Bank Holiday Mondays). Closed in winter
Admission fee Adults £2.50; OAPs £2; Children 50p

This vigorous and expanding garden was
begun in 1985 and has already been featured
many times on television. Mr Akkermans'
energy and achievement are an inspiration.

He has taken six acres from the surrounding
meadows and made them into a series of
beautiful colour-conscious gardens. All
different types of plants are here: trees,
shrubs and herbaceous plants, often used in
original ways. Mr Akkermans is now
experimenting with half-hardy trees and
shrubs, allowing wild flowers to mix with
cultivated ones in some parts of his
immaculately tidy garden.

Owned by Wil Akkermans
Number of gardeners owner
Size 6½ acres

Colby Woodland Garden

AMROTH, NARBERTH SA67 8PP

Tel 01834 811885
Website www.nationaltrust.org.uk
Location Signed from A477
Opening hours 10 am – 5 pm; daily; 1 April to
4 November. Walled garden opens at 11 am
Admission fee Adults £2.80; Children £1.40

Colby is an attractive woodland garden, best
in May when the rhododendrons and
azaleas are in full flower. Among the
nineteenth-century plantings are vast
cryptomerias, clumps of *Embothrium
coccineum* and a huge plant of
Rhododendron falconeri subsp. *eximium*
planted in 1883. In the walled garden, a rill
runs down from the *trompe l'oeil* gazebo to a
pool. There have been many new plantings
recently throughout the garden.

Owned by The National Trust

The National Botanic Garden of Wales

MIDDLETON HALL, LLANARTHNE, CARMARTHEN SA32 8HG

Tel 01558 668768   **Fax** 01558 668933
Website www.gardenofwales.org.uk
Location 7 miles east of Carmarthen
Opening hours From 10 am, daily, except Christmas Day. Closing times vary from 4.30 pm to 6 pm according to the time of year
Admission fee Adults £6.50; Concessions £5; Children £3. RHS members free

The landscaped park and gardens of the original eighteenth-century Middleton Hall Estate are the setting for this new national botanic garden which opened to the public last year amid great public acclamation. The Gardd Fotaneg Genedlaethol Cymru near Llanarthne in the Vale of Towy sees itself as the Welsh Kew, and will carry out research into conservation and biology. Near the entrance to the garden is a 'Welsh landscape' with native meadows and woodlands. Then comes the Broadwalk, 220m long, with a rill which runs down through a geological display of Welsh rocks. The garden's collection of herbaceous plants is planted along its edges, with narrow paths leading into the plantings to facilitate access. There is also a herb garden, named after the Physicians of Myddfai, with an ethnobotanical collection of native pharmacological Welsh plants. However, it is the Great Glasshouse which has received most of the adulation, and rightly so, because it is a stunning piece of architecture – the largest single span glasshouse in the world. It concentrates upon the Mediterranean floras of the world – cheaper to maintain than tropical floras – including Chile, California, south-west Australia, South Africa, the Mediterranean basin and the Canary Isles.

Owned by Trustees of the National Botanic Garden, Wales
Number of gardeners 12
Size 180 acres

Picton Castle

PICTON, HAVERFORDWEST, PEMBROKESHIRE SA62 4AS

Tel & Fax 01437 751326
Location 4 miles east of Haverfordwest off A40
Opening hours 10.30 am – 5 pm; Tuesday – Sunday & Bank Holiday Mondays; April to October
Admission fee Adults £3.95; OAPs £3.75; Children £1.95. RHS members free from April to September

This thirteenth-century castle has been the home of the Philipps family for some 400 years, and the 40 acres of grounds include fine collections of rhododendrons, azaleas, magnolias, camellias, myrtles, embothriums and eucryphias, some of which have been bred by the castle gardeners. Older specimens like a vast multi-trunked *Abies alba* have been joined by new plantings of recent introductions – *Taiwania cryptomerioides* and *Calocedrus formosana* among them. The climate is mild, and supports normally tender plants like *Pittosporum tobira* 'Variegatum' and *Vestia lycoides*. The display is at its best in May to June: summer and autumn bring woodland walks among the massive oaks and giant redwoods. The walled garden has a fish pond, a fernery, rose beds, herbaceous borders and a fountain in the centre.

Owned by Picton Castle Trust
Number of gardeners 4, plus 2 part-time
Size 40 acres

GLAMORGAN

Clyne Gardens

MILL LANE, BLACK PILL, SWANSEA
SA3 5BD

Tel 01792 401737 **Fax** 01792 635408
Website www.swansea.gov.uk/leisure/allparks.html
Location 3 miles west of Swansea on coast road
Opening hours Dawn to dusk; daily; all year
Admission fee free

Clyne is a stupendous woodland garden, the best in South Wales, well cared for by enthusiastic and knowledgeable staff. It is best as a magic rhododendron valley in May, but the range of rare and tender plants provides interest all year. Bluebells, lysichitons and gunneras are among its other features. It was planted between 1921 and 1952 by a local landowner called Algernon Walker-Heneage-Vivian, who subscribed to many of the Himalayan and Chinese plant-hunting expeditions of the day. The forms and hybrids of *Rhododendron niveum* which the head gardener brought to the RHS flower shows in 1996 and 1997 are still remembered by the London rhododendron fraternity. The mild climate means that *R. fragrantissimum* grows happily outside, and there is a group of *R. 'Loderi King George'* 50ft high. The car park is small, and tends to fill up early in the day. There are band concerts on Sunday afternoons in summer.

Owned by City & County of Swansea
NCCPG National Collections *Pieris; Enkianthus; Rhododendron (Triflora & Falconera subsections)*

Dyffryn Botanic Garden

ST NICHOLAS, CARDIFF CF5 6SU

Tel 029 2059 3328 **Fax** 029 2059 1966
Location Jct33 M4 on A48 then follow signs
Opening hours 10 am – 5.30 pm; daily; mid-April to October
Admission fee Adults £3; OAPs & Children £2.50. Subject to review

Dyffryn has 55 acres of sumptuous gardens designed by Thomas Mawson around an Edwardian prodigy house. They are now being restored with a chunky £3.23m millennium grant. Intended partly for display – there is even a Roman garden with a temple and fountain – and partly for the owners' own pleasure, Dyffryn has a huge collection of good plants built up by Reginald Cory in the early years of the twentieth century. Watch it revive over the next year or so: the garden as a status symbol.

Plant Highlights Woodland garden; roses (mainly modern); azaleas and rhododendrons; good herbaceous borders; spring bulbs; summer bedding; tallest purple birch *Betula pendula* 'Purpurea' in the British Isles (and ten other record trees).

Owned by Vale of Glamorgan Council

Margam Park

PORT TALBOT SA13 2TJ

Tel 01639 881635 **Fax** 01639 895897
Location Follow directions from M4 Jct38
Opening hours 10 am – 7 pm (5 pm in winter); daily; all year
Admission fee Adults £3.85; OAPs & Children £2.85. Subject to review

Margam is a popular country park with lots to interest the garden historian and plantsman: a wonderful range of conservatories and glasshouses, including the orangery for which Margam is famous, big trees and rhododendrons (some grown from Kingdon Ward's seed), and cheerful bedding out. Recent additions include a collection of dwarf conifers, a permanent exhibition of modern sculptures, a maze (one of the largest in Europe) and a new pergola 450 yards long: further work is promised. Margam is also the seat of Fuchsia Research International, where almost all the *Fuchsia* species are grown under glass in a naturalistic landscape.

 **Plant Highlights** Roses (mainly modern); fine collection of trees; bedding out; daffodils; rhododendrons; maze; orangery; tallest bay tree *Laurus nobilis* (21m) in the British Isles.

Owned by Neath Port Talbot County Borough Council

Plantasia

PARC TAWE, SWANSEA SA1 2AL

Tel 01792 474555/298637 **Fax** 01792 652588
Website www.swansea.gov.uk/leisure/
Location Off main Eastern approach to Swansea
Opening hours 10 am – 5 pm; Tuesdays – Sundays & Bank Holidays; all year. Closed 1 January, 25 & 26 December
Admission fee Adults £2.20; Concessions £1.50. Subject to review

Plantasia is a large glasshouse (1600 sq m) with three climatic zones – arid, tropical, and rain forest. Each is full with exotic plants – palms, strelitzias, tree ferns, nepenthes, cacti and such economic plants as coconuts and pineapple. The authorities say that some of the 5,000 plants represent species which are actually extinct in the wild. It is the perfect goal for a winter expedition, and not expensive, but you may not enjoy the insects, birds, monkeys and reptiles as much as the flowers.

Owned by Swansea City Council

GWENT

Penpergwm Lodge

ABERGAVENNY NP7 9AS

Tel & Fax 01873 840208
Website www.penplants.com
Location 3 miles from Abergavenny on B4598, opposite King of Prussia pub
Opening hours 2 pm – 6 pm; Thursday – Sunday; end of March to end of September
Admission fee Adults £2; Children free

Catriona Boyle has developed the garden at Penpergwm over the last 20 years, using some of the structure created when the house was built in Edwardian times – mature trees, open lawns, formal areas and old hedges. She has added two exuberant terraces, each planted to a colour theme and linked by a parterre and vine walk. The original vegetable garden has been redesigned and renamed a *potager*, with flowers, standard roses and vegetables. The result is both clever and satisfying – Mrs Boyle runs a well-regarded garden school. The nursery has lots of home- propagated plants, mostly unusual herbaceous plants, bulbs, climbers and shrubs, but also half-hardy perennials which extend the garden season. Specialities include *Aconitum*, euphorbias, cistus, philadelphus, clematis, loniceras, camassias, erythroniums, *Melianthus major* and salvias.

Owned by Mrs C Boyle
Number of gardeners 1
Size 4 acres

The Veddw

DEVAUDEN NP6 6PH

Tel & Fax 01291 650836
Location Signed from the green at Devauden
Opening hours 2 pm – 5 pm; Sundays & Bank Holiday Mondays; April to September
Admission fee Adults £2.50; Children £1

This is a young and expanding garden – enjoyable to see now, and to watch as the owners' ideas for its expansion develop. It is also interesting because it is a low-budget garden and the owners are happy to tell you about their mistakes as well as their successes. For example, the front garden was at first planted as a careless, random 'cottage garden': then they decided that it just 'looked a mess' and have started to add structural elements like clipped box. The main garden is the other side of the house, and includes a magnolia walk, a 'Buff Beauty' garden and a crescent-shaped border which is planted with pastel colours to provide flowers from spring to autumn. Much attention is given to colour planting throughout the garden: pinks, mauves, whites and purples are definitely preferred to the stronger colours. But there is much variety within its two acres, and good design and many good plants too. The two-acre woodland is also destined to become part of the garden proper, but the owners say they are finding it difficult to get the ornamental underplantings established. All in all, a garden of great charm – and promise.

Owned by Anne Wareham & Charles Hawes
Number of gardeners owners
Size 4 acres

GWYNEDD

Bodysgallen Hall

LLANDUDNO LL30 1RS

Tel 01492 584466   **Fax** 01492 582519
Location On right, off A470 to Llandudno
Opening hours Daily; all year
Admission fee Open only to Hotel Guests. Children over 8 welcome

These are good gardens and good grounds for a good hotel. Partly 1920s and partly modern, the gardens include a knot garden divided into eight segments, an extremely busy kitchen garden, woodland walks, a little sunken garden with a lily pond and a modern parterre with white floribundas in the old walled garden. And it is handy for Bodnant, too.

Owned by Historic House Hotels Ltd

Cefn Bere

CAE DEINTUR, DOLGELLAU LL40 2YS

Tel 01341 422768
Location At Cae Deintur, behind primary school, up short steep hill, left half way up, 4th house
Opening hours By appointment from early spring to late autumn
Admission fee Contribution to National Gardens Scheme

Cefn Bere is a plantsman's garden within a disciplined design: the owners say that it encapsulates their own development as gardeners over the last 40 years. It has a great variety of rare plants within a small compass, especially alpines, perennials, grasses, ferns and evergreens. And wonderful views.

Owned by Mr & Mrs G M Thomas
Number of gardeners owners
Size one-fifth of an acre

Crûg Farm Plants

GRIFFITH'S CROSSING, CAERNARFON LL55 1TU

Tel & Fax 01248 670232
Website www.crug-farm.co.uk
Location 2 miles north-east of Caernarfon, off A487, follow signs to Bethel
Opening hours 10 am – 6 pm; Thursday – Sunday & Bank Holidays; 24 February to 30 September

This RHS Partnership Nursery is unusual in specialising in plants for shade: perennials, shrubs and climbers. The range is extensive and interesting. Their selection of hardy geraniums equals many specialists in the genera. Their collecting expeditions to Korea, Sikkim, Japan, China, Vietnam, Laos, the Philippines and Taiwan are making an impact on the gardens of many discerning plantsmen: new-to-science names a-plenty. The display garden and private garden are worth seeing when they are open for the National Gardens Scheme.

NCCPG National Collections Coriaria; Paris

Penrhyn Castle

BANGOR LL57 4HN

Tel 01248 353084 **Fax** 01248 371281
Website www.nationaltrust.org.uk
Location 3 miles east of Bangor on A5122, signed from A55 – A5 junction
Opening hours 12 noon – 5 pm; daily except Tuesday; 28 March to 2 November. Open at 10 am – 5.30 pm in July & August. Last admission 4.30 pm
Admission fee Adults £4; Children £2

A Norman castle (actually a Victorian fake) with a distant walled garden of parterres and terraces merging into the slopes of rhododendrons and camellias. There is much of dendrological interest (ancient conifers, holm oaks, champion eucryphias and naturalised arbutus trees) and a 'dinosaur landscape' of tree ferns, gunneras and aralias.

Owned by The National Trust
Size 47 acres

Plas Brondanw Gardens

LLANFROTHEN, PANRHYNDEUDRAETH LL48 6SW

Tel 01766 770484
Location On Croesor road off A4085
Opening hours Details not available as we went to press
Admission fee Adults £1.50; Children 25p (in 2000)

Plas Brondanw is the highly original and architectural Edwardian garden laid out by Clough Williams-Ellis 17 years before he began Portmeirion, and now assiduously restored by his granddaughter Menna. It is one of the best-kept secrets in North Wales, full of slate stonework and such original design ideas as the arbour of four red-twigged limes. The garden rooms are inward looking and almost cottagey in their planting, but the mountain peaks are ever present.

Owned by Trustees of the Second Portmeirion Foundation

Plas Newydd

LLANFAIRPWLL, ANGLESEY LL61 6EQ

Tel 01248 714795 **Fax** 01248 713673
Website www.nationaltrust.org.uk
Location 2 miles south-west of Llanfairpwll on A4080
Opening hours 11 am – 5.30 pm; Saturday – Wednesday; 31 March to 31 October
Admission fee Adults £2.50; Children £1.25

Plas Newydd has a grand collection of rhododendrons (plus azaleas, magnolias and acers) within a Repton landscape on a spectacular site above the Menai Straits. Its many other horticultural attractions include an avenue of *Chamaecyparis pisifera* 'Squarrosa' running down to the sea. Some of the rhododendrons came as a wedding present to Lord & Lady Anglesey from Lord Aberconway at Bodnant: many others followed. There are examples of the more tender species of considerable size, including a *R. montroseanum* which is probably the largest in Britain. Late-flowering hybrids like 'Polar Bear' extend the season well into July. The fine Italianate garden below the house is 1930s, most surprising.

Owned by The National Trust
Size 31 acres

Plas-yn-Rhiw

RHIW, PWLLHELI LL53 8AB

Tel & Fax 01758 780219
Website www.nationaltrust.org.uk
Location 12 miles from Pwllheli on south coast road to Aberdarow
Opening hours 12 noon – 5 pm; daily except Tuesday; 31 March to 29 September. Also on Saturdays & Sundays in October. Closed on Wednesdays until 16 May
Admission fee Adults £2; Children £1. £2.50 for snowdrops in February (telephone for exact times & dates)

(P) (WC)

This pretty garden is small and fairly formal: it is divided into a series of rooms which are hedged with cherry laurel and bay to protect them from the sea-gales. Box-edged parterres are filled with rambling roses and billowing cottage garden flowers. Tender trees and shrubs flourish in the mild coastal climate: embothriums, desfontaineas, crinodendrons and lapagerias.

Owned by The National Trust
Size 10 acres

Portmeirion

PENRHYNDEUDRAETH LL48 6ET

Tel 01766 770000   **Fax** 01766 771331
Website www.portmeirion.com
Location Between Penrhyndeudraeth & Porthmadog
Opening hours 9.30 – 5.30; daily; all year
Admission fee Adults £5; OAPs £4; Children £2.50

(P) (WC) (✿) (⊞) (☕)

Portmeirion is where the architect Clough Williams-Ellis worked out his Italianate fantasies. The television series *The Prisoner* was filmed here. The gardens are carved out of a rhododendron woodland but formal, with a mixture of Mediterranean plants and exotic palms, and full of architectural bric-a-brac of every period. Other attractions include tree ferns, gunneras, phormiums, ginkgos and holm oaks. Williams-Ellis began to lay out the garden at Portmeirion as soon as he made his first purchase of land along the coastline of north-west Wales in 1926. He bought up further estates in later years, by which he acquired one of the chief attractions of the gardens at Portmeirion today – the collection of rhododendrons and azaleas which is known as the Gwyllt gardens. *Rhododendron arboreum* has grown to enormous size and in parts of the garden is still impenetrable. The peak display comes in May: the mainstay of late summer and autumn is thousands of hydrangeas throughout the Portmeirion estate. Much of the development of the garden has taken place in the last 20 years, taking advantage of the mild climate. One garden – almost at the furthest end of the estate and planted with a background of eucalyptus trees – is known as the 'ghost garden' because of the way the wind whistles in the leaves.

 Plant Highlights Woodland garden; sub-tropical plants; rhododendrons & azaleas; giant yuccas; exuberant summer bedding; tallest *Maytenus boaria* (18m) in the British Isles.

Owned by Portmeirion Ltd
Number of gardeners 11
Size 70 acres

POWYS

Ashford House

TALYBONT-ON-USK, BRECON
LD3 7YR

Tel 01874 676271
Location 1 mile east of Talbont along B4588
Opening hours 2 pm – 6 pm; Tuesdays; April to September
Admission fee Adults £2; Children free

There are two parts to the garden at Ashford: both have been made by the Andersons. First there is the walled garden, about an acre in extent, with raised beds (lots of alpines), and a plantsman's collection of plants of every kind. Then there is the woodland garden, which the Andersons have underplanted with suitable shrubs, especially rhododendrons, and other plants.

Owned by Mr & Mrs D A Anderson
Number of gardeners 1 part-time
Size 3½ acres

The Dingle

WELSHPOOL SY21 9JD

Tel 01938 555145 **Fax** 01938 555778
Location Left turn to Nurseries off A490 to Llanfyllin
Opening hours 9 am – 5 pm; daily except Tuesdays; all year except Christmas week
Admission fee Adults £1.50; Children free

This steep garden attached to a successful nursery is essentially a plantsman's private garden still. It is mainly made up of unusual trees and shrubs, mulched with bark, but it has some herbaceous plantings too. The beds are put together with a carefully co-ordinated colour mixtures and designed to look good all through the year.

Owned by Mr & Mrs Roy Joseph
Number of gardeners 1
Size 4 acres

Dolwen

CEFN COCH,
LLANRHAEADR-YM-MOCHNANT
SY10 0BU

Tel & Fax 01691 780411
Location Right at Three Tuns Inn, ¾ mile up lane
Opening hours 2 pm – 4.30 pm; Fridays, plus last Sunday of month; April to August. And by appointment
Admission fee Adults £2; Children free

Old garden: new owners. This plantsman's garden on a steep 2½-acre site was energetically made by Mrs Denby in the 1980s: it continues to be open under the enthusiastic guidance of the new owners who have started replanting some of the beds and adding features of their own. There are stupendous views and beautiful plantings around three large ponds, fed by natural springs and connected by waterfalls. It remains one of the best modern gardens in Wales, of ever-growing interest.

Owned by Bob Yarwood & Jeny Marriott
Number of gardeners 4 part-time
Size 2½ acres

Glansevern Gardens

GLANSEVERN, BERRIEW, WELSHPOOL
SY21 8AH

Tel 01686 640200   **Fax** 01686 640829
Location On A483, 4 miles south-west of Welshpool
Opening hours 12 noon – 6 pm; Fridays, Saturdays
& Bank Holiday Mondays; May to September. And
parties by appointment
Admission fee Adults £3; OAPs £2; Children free

The handsome Greek-revival house at
Glansevern sits in a landscaped park (1802),
complete with its lake, rhododendrons and
splendid Victorian specimen trees. The
1840s rock garden incorporates a spooky
grotto. But it is the modern planting which
really distinguishes Glansevern: luxuriant
primulas in the water-garden, island beds
around the house and roses in the walled
garden.

Owned by Neville Thomas
Number of gardeners 2
Size 18 acres

plants on the walls – they include Banksian
roses, pomegranates and a hefty *Feijoa
sellowiana*. At other times it is the structure
which impresses: the terraces, lead statues
and yews. The views are always a big draw,
but especially when the rhododendrons and
azaleas are in flower on the ridge opposite
the castle. There is much wonderfully rich
colour planting by Graham Thomas and in
early autumn the maples colour the lower
slopes. The aspect is south-east, so Powis is
best seen in the morning light:
photographers please note.

Plant Highlights Famous terraces
gardens; woodland garden; topiary;
good herbaceous borders; tender plants;
colour plantings; good autumn colour;
largest (i.e. thickest trunk) sessile oak
Quercus petraea in the British Isles, and four
other record trees.

Owned by The National Trust
Size 24 acres
NCCPG National Collections *Aralia*; *Laburnum*

Powis Castle

WELSHPOOL SY21 8RF

Tel 01938 554338   **Fax** 01938 554336
Website www.nationaltrust.org.uk
Location 1 mile south of Welshpool off the A483
Opening hours 11 am – 6 pm; Wednesday – Sunday plus
Bank Holiday Mondays; 31 March to 4 November. Plus
Tuesdays in July & August
Admission fee Adults £5; Children £2.50

The hanging terraces swamped by bulky
overgrown yews and exuberant summer
bedding are famous. If you visit Powis in
late summer or early autumn, you will be
completely distracted by the rare and tender

NORTHERN IRELAND

Northern Ireland has some fine historic landscapes dating back to the eighteenth century: Florence Court is one of them, and another – which we do not list – is Castle Ward in Co Down. However, there is no doubt that the two best gardens in Northern Ireland are the twentieth-century masterpieces – Mount Stewart and Rowallane. Both are in the care of the National Trust, which has maintained them as major tourist attractions. It is a pity that so few people from Britain know them at first hand. Given good weather, they are among the most enchanting and extensive gardens anywhere in the British Isles – and especially lovely in late spring.

Many trees and shrubs flourish in the mild, damp climate of Co Down and Co Antrim. The National Arboretum at Castlewellan has a very fine collection of mature trees: 38 of them are record-breakers. Nevertheless, it is fair to say that gardening and garden visiting are not such popular activities in Northern Ireland as on the mainland of the United Kingdom. Prices reflect this: the cost of admission to National Trust properties in Northern Ireland is substantially less than one would pay to visit a garden of equivalent quality in England.

Northern Ireland has a few gardening clubs and societies of its own: there is, for example, a Northern Ireland Daffodil Group

and a Rose Society of Northern Ireland. Daffodils have for long been a Northern Irish speciality: Brian Duncan and Carncairn Daffodils are two of the world's leading breeders, and their owners follow in the footsteps of other great Ulster daffodil men like Sir Frank Harrison and Guy Wilson. Roses are very popular: the roses in the Sir Thomas & Lady Dixon Park in south Belfast are a great draw in summer and the Dickson roses nursery – now only wholesale – has been at Newtonards for over 100 years. Since the closure of the Slieve Donard nursery, there has been no outstanding plantsman's nursery in Northern Ireland, though Gary Dunlop at Ballyrogan comes close to it, and Patrick Ford at Seaforde is a particularly good source of rare trees and shrubs. There are eight National Collections in Northern Ireland, most of them held by corporate owners like the National Trust.

Northern Ireland's only horticultural college is Greenmount College of Agriculture & Horticulture in Antrim, which is a RHS Partner College and is running about a dozen public lectures and demonstrations in 2001: details are available from the college on 028 9442 6661. RHS members also have free access to a number of gardens in Northern Ireland during the summer, most notably Benvarden Garden and Carnfunnock Country Park in Co Antrim.

Ballyrogan Nurseries

THE GRANGE, BALLYROGAN,
NEWTOWNARDS, CO DOWN
BT23 4SD

Tel 01247 810451 (evenings)

This is a small part-time nursery with a
remarkable stock of rare plants derived from
the owners' large collections. The plants are
mostly herbaceous. The nursery used to
have National Collections of celmisias,
crocosmias and euphorbias, so these three
genera are especially well-represented.
Recent enthusiasms include agapanthus,
dieramas and rodgersias.

Benvarden
Garden & Grounds

BENVARDEN, DERVOCK, BALLYMONEY,
CO ANTRIM BT53 6NN

Tel 028 2074 1331   Fax 028 2074 1955
Location Follow the brown signs on B67
Opening hours 1.30 pm – 5.30 pm; Tuesday – Sunday,
plus Bank Holiday Mondays; June to September
Admission fee Adults £2.50; Children free. RHS members
free

The main feature of the two-acre walled
garden is a spectacular curved red brick wall,
12ft high, dating from approximately 1780.
Around the walls are espalier-trained apples
and pear trees. Other features include a
splendid rose garden, several herbaceous
borders, a new box parterre, and a fully
working kitchen garden. There are also
walks around a small lake planted with
rhododendrons, azaleas, magnolias and fine
trees.

Owned by Mr & Mrs Hugh Montgomery
Number of gardeners 2
Size 5 acres

Carnfunnock
Country Park

COAST ROAD, DRAINS BAY, LARNE,
CO ANTRIM BT40 2QG

Tel 028 2827 0451   Fax 028 2827 0852
Location On A2, 3½ miles north of Larne
Opening hours 10 am – dusk; daily; all year. Closed
1 January & 25 December
Admission fee Parking fees; no fee for RHS members in
July & August

The walled garden is set within
Carnfunnock Country Park, 181 hectares of
varied parkland within the Antrim Coast
Area of Outstanding Natural Beauty. The
walled garden was originally the cottage
garden of the Cairndhu Estate owned and
run by Sir Thomas and Lady Dixon. The
gardens contain a wide collection of plants
from all over the world and enjoy a
microclimate which allows plants such as
the bottle brush (*Callistemon*) and
eucalyptus to flourish. The gardens also
boast an amphitheatre, while one of the
central features to the walled garden is a
unique collection of sundials tracing the
history of time.

Owned by Larne Borough Council
Number of gardeners 3
Size 500 acres

Castlewellan National Arboretum

CASTLEWELLAN FOREST PARK,
CASTLEWELLAN, CO DOWN
BT31 9BU

Tel 028 4377 8664   **Fax** 028 4377 1762
Location 30 miles south of Belfast, 4 miles west of Newcastle
Opening hours dawn – dusk; daily; all year
Admission fee £3.80 per car

Castlewellan means trees: 40 record-breakers and many rarities. The heart of the collection is in a huge walled garden, interplanted with rhododendrons and other shrubs. The central path has mixed borders at the top: dwarf rhododendrons are prominent even here. Much has been restored in recent years: labelling is good, and the standard of maintenance high. There are plans to make the collections of *Taxus* and *Eucryphia* comprehensive.

 Plant Highlights Woodland garden; mature conifers; fine collection of trees; autumn colours; embothriums; eucryphias; tallest *Chamaecyparis nootkatensis* 'Lutea' (22m) in the British Isles, plus 39 other tree records; new 'fragrant garden' around a Lutyensesque tea house.

Owned by Department of Agriculture, Forest Services
Number of gardeners 3
Size 15 acres

Florence Court

THE NATIONAL TRUST, FLORENCE
COURT, ENNISKILLEN,
CO FERMANAGH BT92 1DB

Tel 028 6634 8249   **Fax** 028 6634 8873
Website www.nationaltrust.org.uk
Location 8 miles south-west of Enniskillen
Opening hours Grounds: 10 am – 7 pm (4 pm October to March); daily. Closed Christmas Day
Admission fee Adults £3; Children £1.50

Florence Court has an eighteenth-century parkland, with stupendous views of Lough Erne and some magnificent trees. These include the original 'Irish Yew' (*Taxus baccata* 'Fastigiata') and many specimens of a beautiful form of weeping beech with a broad curving crown. The rhododendrons are, for the most part, huge ancient hybrids of *R. arboreum*, but there has been much new planting in recent years and the horticultural interest is now considerable.

Plant Highlights Woodland garden; fine collection of trees; rhododendrons.

Owned by The National Trust
Size 9 acres

Guy Wilson Daffodil Garden

UNIVERSITY OF ULSTER, COLERAINE,
CO DERRY BT52 1SA

Tel 028 7044 4141
Location Signed from sports centre, or entry via Portstewart Road
Opening hours Dawn – dusk; daily; all year
Admission fee free

Mount Stewart

THE NATIONAL TRUST, MOUNT STEWART ESTATE, GREY ABBEY, NEWTOWNARDS, CO DOWN BT22 2AD

Tel 028 4778 8387 **Fax** 028 4278 8569
Website www.nationaltrust.org.uk
Location East of Belfast on A20
Opening hours 11 am – 6 pm; daily; April – October.
2 pm – 5 pm on Sundays in March, and 11 am – 6 pm
on St Patrick's Day
Admission fee Adults £3; Children £1.50

Mount Stewart is the greatest garden in Northern Ireland, arguably in all Ireland. There are two factors which have made this possible: the exceptionally mild climate which allows plants to thrive that would not survive in all but the mildest parts of the British Isles; and the willingness of the gardens' principal maker, Edith, Marchioness of Londonderry, to spend money on a large scale on design, plants and staff. The formal garden in front of the house is grandly laid out with all manner of inventive details: best known are the stone carvings of animals known as the dodo terrace. Beyond the formal garden is a sunken Spanish garden and off to one side is the shamrock garden where a bed designed by Lady Londonderry to represent the Red Hand of Ulster has been surrounded in these more politically correct times by a green shamrock. The rare plants begin on the walls of the house itself: *Rosa gigantea* covers a large area and there are huge plants of *Ceanothus* 'Trewithen Blue'. Here too are the wonderfully flowing beds of the lily wood where exotic myrtles, pittosporums and phormiums are underplanted with primulas, cyclamen, narcissi and lilies, but here – as in every part of the garden – one is never far from amazing large-leaved rhododendrons, cordylines and tree ferns. Better still is the walk around the lake, where rhododendrons flood the woodlands: for many visitors in spring it is the highlight of a tour of Mount Stewart. The views across the lake are dominated by the mausoleum and the exceptional collection of rhododendrons is interplanted with collections of rare shrubs like mimosas, clianthus, prostantheras, pittosporums and grevilleas. They are underplanted in places with meconopsis and candelabra primulas and, at one point, you catch a glimpse of a white stag in a glade. The outstanding area is the Jubilee Glade where plants in shades of red, white and blue provide colour all through the year. For design, variety, plants and plantings, Mount Stewart is a place of miracles. Allow lots of time for your visit.

Owned by The National Trust
Size 78 acres
NCCPG National Collections *Phormium; Dianella; Libertia*

Rowallane Garden

SAINTFIELD, BALLYNAHINCH, CO DOWN BT24 7LH

Tel 028 9751 0131 **Fax** 028 9751 1242
Website www.nationaltrust.org.uk
Location One mile south of Saintfield on A7
Opening hours 10.30 pm – 6 pm, Monday – Friday;
12 noon – 6 pm, Saturday & Sunday; 17 March to
31 October. Then 10.30 am – 5 pm; Monday – Friday;
November to March 2002. Closed 1 January,
25 & 26 December
Admission fee Adults £3. Reductions in winter

Ⓟ 🐕 ⓦⓒ ⓑ 🌳 🏫 ☕

The extensive gardens at Rowallane can be
dated back to 1903, when Hugh
Armytage Moore inherited the estate from
his uncle John Moore. Uncle John had
planted some of the larger trees – beeches,
wellingtonias and rhododendrons – but
everything else you see today dates from the
twentieth century. Hugh Armytage Moore
was a great plantsman – not just a collector
of horticultural curiosities, but a selector of
good forms. As his appetite for plants grew,
so the garden expanded into the little fields
which pattern the estate. The seedlings grew
and needed to be planted. The hedges and
walls which surround these enclosures
remain as the boundary features of each
compartment, so that you still have the
impression of walking from field to field
although each is thickly planted with
ornamental trees and shrubs. Moore
subscribed to the plant collecting expeditions
of E H Wilson and Frank Kingdon Ward. It
is to those expeditions that the vast collection
of rhododendrons owes its origins. No garden
can match it on a sunny day in April or May,
as you amble from a glade of R. augustinii
forms to a line of R. macabeanum or back
through R. yakushimanum hybrids: the
large-leaved species are particularly
prominent. Because of the mild climate,
many other good plants flourish here which
are rare elsewhere – Lomatia ferruginea,
Grevillea rosmarinifolia and Nothofagus
cunninghamii, for example. Other rarities
include Helwingia japonica and Cupressus
duclouxiana, the latter a record-breaking
specimen. Rowallane has also given us
some good garden hybrids (e.g.
Hypericum × 'Rowallane') and selected
forms (e.g. Viburnum plicatum 'Rowallane').
Another notable feature is the rock garden
– an outcrop of natural whinstone rock
which actually has few plants growing in it,
but many around the base of the boulders,
including the striking candelabra primula
'Rowallane Rose'. And the walled garden too
is a treasure-house of rare plants, including
Feijoa sellowiana and the National
Collection of Penstemon species, which gives
colour long after the rhododendrons have
faded. But it is still the rhododendrons and
azaleas for which the garden is best
remembered.

Plant Highlights Rhododendrons &
azaleas; a great plantsman's collection
of plants; fine collection of trees; good
autumn colour; snowdrops; rock garden;
tallest Cupressus duclouxiana (14m) in the
British Isles and three other record trees.

Owned by The National Trust
Size 50 acres
NCCPG National Collections Penstemon

The name says it all – this is both a celebration of Guy Wilson as a daffodil breeder and a museum of his hybrids. Drifts of his hybrids, and others of Irish raising, sweep through the university gardens.

 Plant Highlights An exceptional collection of daffodils, best in second half of April.

Owned by University of Ulster at Coleraine

NCCPG National Collections *Narcissus*

Seaforde Gardens

SEAFORDE, DOWNPATRICK, CO DOWN BT30 8PG

Tel 028 44 81 1225   **Fax** 028 44 81 1370

Location Between Belfast & Newcastle

Opening hours 10 am – 5 pm; Monday – Saturday. 1 pm – 6 pm; Sundays. Closed at weekends from November to February

Seaforde is an important nursery for trees and shrubs, including Irish specialities (*Eucryphia* × *intermedia* 'Rostrevor') and tender taxa. The list now includes a growing number of rhododendrons grown from Patrick Forde's own collecting expeditions to Bhutan, Yunnan, Tibet and Vietnam. The gardens – open all year – are extensive and important: they have drifts of primulas, camassias and bluebells, as well as both pink forms of *Eucryphia lucida*.

NCCPG National Collections *Eucryphia*

REPUBLIC OF IRELAND

Until quite recently, gardens were widely thought of in Ireland as part of the culture of the Anglo-Irish: real Irishmen possessed neither the resources nor the cultural points of reference to occupy themselves with horticulture. There was a grain of truth in this: one of the consequences of the troubles and the land reforms has been the loss of many of the historic gardens, parks and demesnes which accompanied the houses of the landed gentry. It is a problem of which the Irish are acutely aware and where such groups as the Irish Georgian Society have done much to change people's perceptions. The new wealth and confidence which Ireland has found within the European Union have helped to dispel the notion that gardens are yet another manifestation of British superiority: now they are seen as something which the Irish can seize upon and adapt to their own cultural styles, traditions, needs and conditions.

The old order is still there, of course. Most of the big gardens attached to big houses and open to the public date back to the nineteenth century – examples are Lismore, Derreen, Tullynally and Powerscourt. But a number were also made in the middle of the twentieth century, often with English pounds (Birr and Malahide) or American dollars (Glenveagh and Mount Congreve). And the best modern gardens in Ireland have most certainly been made by Irishmen – one has only to think of Jim Reynolds's amazing combination of plantsmanship, artistry and style at Butterstream.

Irish gardens tend to be tagged on at the end of guidebooks to UK gardens. The truth is that they are one of the best reasons for visiting Ireland in the first place. This has been made clear from time to time by books that do not always receive the currency they deserve. Two recent titles with a heavy photographic input are *Glorious Gardens of Ireland* with pictures by Melanie Eclare (Kyle Cathie, 1999) and *Irish Gardens* by Olda Fitzgerald (Conran Octopus, 1999).

Ireland is well supplied with garden centres, but has few specialist nurseries. Good garden plants are difficult to come by. Irish gardeners often say that their best herbaceous plants tend to come from Britain and are then more widely distributed through an informal system of gifting. The NCCPG is represented by the Irish Garden Plant Society: there are only three National Collections in the country – *Garrya* and *Potentilla fruticosa* (cvs.) at National Botanic Gardens, Glasnevin, and *Olearia* in the care of Fingal County Council at Malahide Castle. It is also to be hoped that the new Irish interest in gardening will benefit the Royal Horticultural Society of Ireland, whose 'Royal' title hints at its ties to the United Kingdom but which has less than 2,000 members.

Altamont Garden

ALTAMONT GARDEN TRUST,
ALTAMONT, TULLOW, CO CARLOW

Tel 00 353 503 59444
Location Signed from N80 & N81
Opening hours 11 am – 7 pm (or dusk, if sooner);
Wednesday – Sunday; all year
Admission fee Adults £3; Children (under 10) £1

Altamont is a charming and romantic woodland garden, stretching to nearly 100 acres, and full of huge specimens of rare plants, together with lakes, islands, a bog garden and a shady glen. Altamont is a place of contemplation and wonder, and very old-world Irish: it will be interesting to see how Dúchas, the Irish Heritage Service, manages it.

Owned by Dúchas, The Heritage Service

Annes Grove Gardens

CASTLETOWNROCHE, MALLOW,
CO CORK

Tel 00 353 22 26145
Location 1 mile north of Castletownroche on N72
Opening hours 10 am – 5 pm, Monday – Saturday;
1 pm – 6 pm, Sundays; mid-March to 30 September
Admission fee Adults £3; OAPs & Students £2; Children £1

Annes Grove has long been famous for its 30-acre garden, begun in 1907: 'Robinsonian' is the word most often used to describe it. The walled garden is a flower garden, with a seventeenth-century mount and a Victorian gothic summer house on top. The river garden is lushly wild with lysichiton, gunnera and candelabra primulas around the pools. In the glen garden lies a wonderfully dense collection of azaleas and rhododendrons many from Kingdon Ward's seed.

Plant Highlights Woodland garden; plantsman's collection of plants; good herbaceous borders; rhododendrons from wild seeds; rare trees; tallest *Azara microphylla* (11m) in the British Isles.

Owned by Patrick Annesley

Ardgillan Park

BALBRIGGAN, CO DUBLIN

Tel 00 353 1 8727777 **Fax** 00 353 1 8727530
Location Coast road between Skerries & Balbriggan
Opening hours 10 am – 5 pm; daily; all year
Admission fee free

Ardgillan was all but lost in the troubles, but restored by the Council as a public amenity in the late 1980s. A new rose garden and herbaceous borders have been added. The four-acre walled garden is being developed too – it has a herb garden now and fruit trees grown against the walls.

Plant Highlights Roses (ancient & modern); rock garden; herbs; fruit; good herbaceous borders; 200-year-old yew walk; restored Victorian glasshouse in rose garden.

Owned by Fingal County Council
Size 4 acres
NCCPG National Collections *Potentilla*

Ardnamona

LOUGH ESKE, CO DONEGAL

Tel 00 353 73 22650 **Fax** 00 353 73 22819
Website www.tempoweb.com/ardnamona
Location On Lough Eske, 5 miles north-east of Donegal

Opening hours 10 am – 6 pm; daily; all year
Admission fee Adults £2; Children free

Ardnamona is wilderness of huge rhododendrons, some as much as 60ft high, like a Himalayan forest. Reclamation and replanting are under way: the owners have already made a big impact on the 40 acres of *Rhododendron ponticum.*

Owned by Mr & Mrs Kieran Clarke

Ballymaloe Cookery School Garden

BALLYMALOE, SHANAGARRY, CO CORK

Tel 00 353 21 646785 **Fax** 00 353 21 646909
Location Ballymaloe, signed from Castlemartyr & Shanagarry
Opening hours 9 am – 6 pm; daily; 1 April to 1 October
Admission fee Adults £4; OAPs £2; Children £1.50

The garden attached to the famous Ballymaloe cookery school is full of unusual fruit, vegetables and herbs. Seldom is a functional garden so stylishly designed and planted, or so extensive.

Owned by Tim & Darina Allen
Number of gardeners 3
Size 3 acres

Ballynacourty

BALLYSTEEN, CO LIMERICK

Tel 00 353 61 396409 **Fax** 00 353 61 396733
Location 3 miles from Askeaton, on River Shannon
Opening hours By appointment
Admission fee £3

Ballynacourty is a fine modern family garden: four densely planted acres won from open farmland. It is interesting, too, for its selection of lime-tolerant trees and shrubs.

Owned by George & Michelina Stacpoole

Birr Castle Demesne

BIRR, CO OFFALY

Tel 00 353 509 22154 **Fax** 00 353 509 21583
Website www.ireland.iol.ie/birr-castle
Location Rosse Row in Birr, Co Offaly
Opening hours 9 am – 6 pm or dusk; daily; all year
Admission fee Adults £5; OAPs £4; Children £2.50

The best garden in the Irish Midlands, Birr has 125 acres of grounds, a huge collection of trees and shrubs, and a wonderful walled garden with a tunnel down the middle. Many of the plants are grown from original collectors' material: some were collected in the wild by the owner's parents, Michael and Anne Rosse. Birr also has the tallest box hedges in the world. In the grounds is the famous telescope, once the largest in the world, now fully restored and witness to the polymath abilities of the owner's family over the generations. Three new features have been added for the millennium: a *teatro verde*, a winter garden and a new river garden.

Plant Highlights Topiary; roses (mainly old-fashioned); plantsman's collection of plants; herbs; good herbaceous borders; fine collection of trees; *Paeonia* 'Anne Rosse'; *Magnolia* 'Anne Rosse'; tallest *Acer monspessulanum* (15m) and boxwood *Buxus sempervirens* (12m) in the British Isles, plus 49 other record species.

Owned by Earl of Rosse
Number of gardeners 7
Size 125 acres

Butterstream

KILDALKEY ROAD, TRIM, CO MEATH

Tel 00 353 46 36017 Fax 00 353 46 31702
Location Outskirts of Trim on Kildalkey Road
Opening hours 11 am – 6 pm; daily; April to September
Admission fee Adults £4; Students £2; Children £1

Ireland's Sissinghurst is just over 20 years old, and still expanding. Jim Reynolds has made a series of garden rooms (13 at the last count) in the modern style around an old farmhouse. Each is different but connected to the next. They include a green garden, a white garden, a hot-coloured garden, a Roman garden, a pool garden (with Tuscan portico reflected in it), an obelisk garden, and many others. The plants are determined by the soil – heavy, cold, limey clay.

Owned by Jim Reynolds
Number of gardeners 2
Size 8 acres, plus semi-parkland

Coolcarrigan Gardens

COOLCARRIGAN, NAAS, CO KILDARE

Tel 00 353 45 863512 Fax 00 353 45 8641400
Location 12 miles north of Naas
Opening hours By appointment only, from April to August
Admission fee £3

This garden owes everything to a gale which knocked the heart out of the established plantings in 1974. Harold Hillier advised on the replanting and the result is one of the best modern collections of trees and shrubs in Ireland – over 1,100 different species and cultivars. The owners, keen plantsmen, have added late summer borders and a rock garden.

Owned by Mr & Mrs John Wilson-Wright
Number of gardeners 1
Size 10 acres

Creagh Gardens

SKIBBEREEN, CO CORK

Tel & Fax 00 353 28 22121
Location 4 miles from Skibbereen on the Baltimore road
Opening hours 10 am – 6 pm; daily; March to September
Admission fee Adults £3; Children £2

Creagh (pronounced Cree) has 20 acres of exotic woodland glades on the edge of a sea estuary and lushly planted by the late Peter & Gwendoline Harold-Barry in the style of a Douanier Rousseau painting. The one-acre, traditional, organically cultivated kitchen garden has long runs of glasshouses and a pretty rustic summerhouse. Recent restorations confirm it as one of the great gardens of southern Ireland. But there is a cloud on the horizon: the house and gardens are up for sale as we go to press.

Owned by Gwendoline Harold-Barry Trust
Number of gardeners 2 plus part-timers
Size 20 acres

Curraghmore

PORTLAW, CO WATERFORD

Tel 00 353 51 387102 Fax 00 353 51 387481
Location 14 miles west of Waterford: enter by Portlaw gate
Opening hours 2 pm – 5 pm; Thursdays & Bank Holidays; Easter to mid October. Groups by appointment may visit the handsome Palladian house too
Admission fee £2

Lord Waterford's family has lived at Curraghmore since 1170, which is a long time even by Irish standards. It has fine terraced gardens with balustrades and an excellent collection of trees and shrubs, dating mainly from the nineteenth and early twentieth centuries. The outstanding feature is the Shell Grotto which was built in 1754 by the heiress to the property, Catherine, Countess of Tyrone. She personally decorated the interior walls with shells which were collected from all round the world. Curraghmore is a magnificent estate which deserves to be better known.

Owned by The Marquess of Waterford

Derreen

LAURAGH, KILLARNEY, CO KERRY

Tel 00 353 64 83588
Location 15 miles from Kenmare on the Castletown Road
Opening hours 11 am – 6 pm; daily; April to September
Admission fee Adults £3; Children £1.50

Derreen is quite extraordinary. The rocky outcrops come right to the front door, but the fast lush growth of its trees and shrubs is boundless. Tree ferns *Dicksonia antarctica* and myrtles *Myrtus communis* have gone native, and seed themselves everywhere. Moss, lichen and ferns abound. Large-leaved rhododendrons grow to great heights. It is a place of wonder on a sunny day in late April.

Owned by The Hon David Bigham
Number of gardeners 2

The Dillon Garden

RANELAGH, DUBLIN 6, CO DUBLIN

Tel 00 353 1 4971308   **Fax** 00 353 1 4971308
Website www.dillongarden.com
Location 45 Sandford Road

Opening hours 2 pm – 6 pm; daily; March, July & August. Plus Sundays, April to June, & September. Groups by appointment
Admission fee Adults £3; OAPs £2

This much acclaimed plantsman's garden offers a fantastic range of rarities, from snowdrops and hellebores in spring, to tropaeolums in autumn. Unlike some collectors' gardens, Helen Dillon's is immaculately maintained, strictly planted according to colour and beautifully designed as a series of garden rooms. Last year (2000), she replaced the lawn with a series of formal beds and small cascades set in limestone paving. The website is excellent.

Owned by Helen & Val Dillon
Number of gardeners 1
Size ½ acre

Fairfield Lodge

MONKSTOWN AVENUE, MONKSTOWN, CO DUBLIN

Tel & Fax 00 353 1 2803912
Location In Monkstown village
Opening hours By appointment
Admission fee Adults: £2.50

Fairfield is a small town garden, made to appear much larger by division into a series of outdoor rooms. Its formal design, informal planting and clever colour combinations have made it a modern classic.

Owned by John Bourke

Fernhill

SANDYFORD, CO DUBLIN

Tel 00 353 1 295 6000
Location 7 miles south of central Dublin on the Enniskerry Road
Opening hours 11 am – 5 pm (2 pm – 6 pm on Sundays & Bank Holidays); Tuesday – Sunday (& Bank Holidays); March to September
Admission fee Adults £3; OAPs £2; Children £1

This popular garden on the outskirts of Dublin has a good collection of rhododendrons and other woodland plants and some magnificent trees 150 years old. There are steep woodland walks and an excellent nursery which sells plants on Saturday afternoons in April and September.

Owned by Mrs Sally Walker
Number of gardeners 2
Size 30 acres

Fota

FOTA ISLAND, CARRIGTWOHILL, CO CORK

Tel 00 353 214 812728   **Fax** 00 353 214 270244
Location 9 miles from Cork city, off Cobh road
Opening hours 10 am (11 am on Sundays) – 6 pm (5 pm in winter); daily; all year. Closed for Christmas holidays and at weekends in winter
Admission fee Cars £1; Pedestrians free of charge

Fota has a handsome formal garden and walled garden, now undergoing restoration, but is famous above all for its trees, most of them planted by the Smith-Barrys towards the end of the nineteenth century. As well as a fine collection of Victorian conifers (huge redwoods and wellingtonias), there are flowering mimosas, a wonderful *Cornus*

capitata and such tender trees as the Canary Islands palm (*Phoenix canariensis*). Many are record-breakers, including two *Cryptomeria japonica* each over 100ft high and three very rare trees indeed – *Juniperus bermudiana*, *Nothofagus moorei* and *Phyllocladus trichomanoides*. In 1975 the estate was acquired by University College, Cork, but in 1996 it was transferred to the Gaeltacht and the collection is now growing again – with additions from central America in particular.

Plant Highlights Woodland garden; mature conifers; fine collection of trees; 165 Irish-bred daffodil cultivars; wildlife park; tallest Italian cypress *Cupressus sempervirens* (25m) in the British Isles, plus 18 other record trees.

Owned by Dept of Arts, Heritage & the Gaeltacht

Gash Gardens

GASH, CASTLETOWN, PORTLAOISE, CO LAOIS

Tel 00 353 502 32247   **Fax** 00 353 502 32857
Location ½ mile from N7 at Castletown
Opening hours 10 am – 5 pm; daily; May to October. Opens at 2 pm on Sundays
Admission fee £2.50. Group rates by appointment. Not suitable for children

Gash is a young, award-winning plantsman's garden, started in 1984, full of unusual plants and maintained to very high standard. It has four acres, on either side of the River Nore, with streams and other water features. There is a large rock and alpine garden, colourful herbaceous borders and an extensive collection of trees and shrubs. The garden bursts into life with a display of alpine plants and rhododendrons in spring and early summer. In June comes the laburnum arch, followed by the herbaceous borders which carry through to autumn – autumn colour is particularly good. The garden was initially laid out and developed by Noël Kennan as a complement to his nursery business: his daughter is continuing to develop and maintain it.

Owned by Mary Kennan
Number of gardeners owner plus part-time
Size 4 acres

Glenveagh Castle

CHURCHILL, LETTERKENNY, CO DONEGAL

Tel 00 353 74 37090   **Fax** 00 353 74 37072
Location 14 miles north-west of Letterkenny on R251
Opening hours daily; dawn to dusk; all year
Admission fee Adults £2; OAPs £1.50; Students £1. Subject to review

Glenveagh was built for its view down the rocky slopes of Lough Veagh, and part of the gardens is known as the View Garden. Lanning Roper laid out a formal Italianate courtyard garden. Jim Russell advised on planting. There are wonderful borders and conservatories as well as rhododendrons and camellias. The unusual shrubs are magnificent: tree-like griselinias and *Michelia doltsopa*, for instance. There are new plantings from Royal Botanic Garden in Edinburgh and a trip to Yunnan in 1996.

Owned by Dúchas, The Heritage Service

Glin Castle

GLIN, CO LIMERICK

Tel 00 353 68 34173   **Fax** 00 353 68 34364
Website www.glincastle.com
Location On N69, 32 miles west of Limerick
Opening hours By appointment
Admission fee Adults £3

Simple formal gardens run down towards the park and merge with the surrounding woodland. The walled kitchen garden has recently received a make-over: cutting borders, herbs, herbaceous borders and such vegetables as sea-kale and asparagus. In the pleasure gardens are some fine ornamental trees – dogwoods, magnolias, cherries and parrotias, as well as rhododendrons and camellias. Taken with the gothicised castle and its magnificent position on the Shannon estuary, Glin is a place of rare enchantment.

Owned by Desmond Fitzgerald, Knight of Glin
Number of gardeners 2
Size 5 acres

Heywood Gardens

BALLINAKILL, CO LAOIS

Tel 00 353 502 33563
Location In grounds of Ballinakill College
Opening hours Dawn – dusk; daily; all year
Admission fee free

This interesting garden was originally designed by Lutyens, then was taken into State care and is in the middle of careful restoration and replanting by Graham Thomas. Go now, to see what an Edwardian garden looked like when newly made.

Owned by Office of Public Works

Hillside

ANNMOUNT, GLOUNTHANE,
CO CORK

Tel 00 353 21 4353119
Location From Cork, turn left at Glounthane Church, up hill, under bridge, 100 yards on right
Opening hours 9 am – 6 pm; daily; May to September. And by appointment
Admission fee £3

This is an intensely cultivated plantsman's garden in a setting of mature trees and rhododendrons. It burgeons with alpine plants in every part – stone troughs, a scree bed and gravel areas. But it also won the 'Top Garden in Ireland' award last year (2000) for its all-season attractions.

Owned by Mrs Mary Byrne

Japanese Gardens & St Fiacra's Garden

TULLY, KILDARE TOWN, CO KILDARE

Tel 00 353 45 521617   **Fax** 00 353 45 522964
Website www.irish-national-stud.ie
Location Signed in Kildare
Opening hours 9.30 am – 6 pm; daily; 12 February to 12 November
Admission fee £6 Adults; £4.50 OAPs; £3 Children

The Japanese garden is a sequence which symbolises Man's journey through life. It was made for Lord Wavertree by Japanese gardeners in the early years of the twentieth century. A very substantial new garden, dedicated to St Fiacre the patron saint of gardeners, was opened in 1999, and provides a grand contrast.

Owned by Irish National Stud
Number of gardeners 3
Size 4 acres

John F Kennedy Arboretum

NEW ROSS, CO WEXFORD

Tel 00 353 51 388171   **Fax** 00 353 51 388172
Location 8 miles south of New Ross off R733
Opening hours 10 am – 8 pm, May to August; 10 am – 6.30 pm, April and September; 10 am – 5 pm, October to March. Closed 13 April & 25 December
Admission fee Adults £2; OAPs £1.50; Children & Students £1

This is a memorial arboretum founded in 1968 with financial help from Irish/American citizens on 623 acres near the Kennedy homestead. 30 years on, the statistics are impressive: 4,500 types of trees and shrubs arranged taxonomically, and 200 plots by geographical distribution. All are meticulously labelled, and planted with artistry. There is one circuit for broadleaves and another for conifers, interwoven at times to improve the overall appearance of the collection. Special features include an 'ericaceous garden' with 500 different rhododendrons, and many varieties of azaleas and heathers. There is also a slow-growing conifer collection, a hedge collection, a display of ground covers and a selection of climbing plants on a series of stone and timber shelters. In summer a miniature railway runs through plantings that represent each continent.

Plant Highlights Mature conifers; fine collection of trees; eight different tree records for the British Isles.

Owned by Dúchas, The Heritage Service
Number of gardeners 14
Size 623 acres

Johnstown Castle Gardens

WEXFORD, CO WEXFORD

Tel 00 353 53 42888 **Fax** 00 353 53 42004
Location 4 miles south-west of Wexford
Opening hours 9 am – 5.30 pm; daily; all year except Christmas Day
Admission fee £3 per car & passengers

Johnstone Castle has 50 acres of ornamental grounds with good trees, tall cordylines, three lakes and the Irish Agricultural Museum.

 **Plant Highlights** Woodland garden; mature conifers; walled gardens; tallest *Cupressus macrocarpa* (40m) in the British Isles.

Owned by TEAGASC (Food & Agriculture Development Authority)

Kilfane Glen & Waterfall

THOMASTOWN, CO KILKENNY

Tel 00 353 56 24558 **Fax** 00 353 56 27491
Website www.NicholasMosse.com
Location Off N9, 2 miles north of Thomastown
Opening hours 2 pm – 6 pm; Sundays; April to June & September. 11 am – 6 pm; daily; July & August
Admission fee Adults £4; Children £3

A romantic landscape garden laid out in the 1790s and vigorously restored by the present owners. Sit in the tiny *cottage ornée*, admire

the exquisite form of the waterfall across the ravine, and dream of Rousseau.

Owned by Nicholas & Susan Mosse
Number of gardeners 2
Size 20 acres

Lismore Castle

LISMORE, CO WATERFORD

Tel 00 353 58 54424 **Fax** 00 353 58 54896
Location Centre of Lismore
Opening hours 1.45 pm – 4.45 pm; daily; 14 April to 14 October. Opens at 11 am in high season
Admission fee Adults £3; Children £1.50

Lismore is best for the castellated house: the gardens are interesting rather than exceptional, but there is a pretty grove of camellias and a double yew walk planted in 1707. The upper enclosure is even older, a Jacobean survivor. Visit the walled garden for some fine traditional kitchen gardening: the vinery was designed by Paxton – this is the Irish Chatsworth.

Owned by Lismore Estates
Number of gardeners 4
Size 7 acres

Lodge Park Walled Garden

STRAFFAN, CO KILDARE

Tel 00 353 1 628 8412 **Fax** 00 353 1 627 3477
Location Follow sign to Steam Museum Straffan from Maynooth & Kill
Opening hours 2.30 pm – 5.30 pm; Tuesday – Friday (plus Sunday in June/July only); June to August
Admission fee £2

As it did in the eighteenth century, the walled garden at Lodge Park continues to produce fruit and vegetables with much more besides. The edible crops grow alongside an ever-increasing collection of lesser-known ornamental plants. Coloured borders of white, blue and yellow greet the visitor and a pink border begins the main walk of the garden, near a collection of peonies. Behind a new classical entrance, the original cold greenhouse allows semi-tender plants to be displayed. A more modern heated greenhouse gives protection for plants such as cymbidiums and daturas. The main walk of the garden is lined with box hedges, interrupted by topiary yews: behind the box lies a south-facing border of shrubs and perennials. In the centre is an ornamental salad garden, a fruit garden and a more conventional vegetable garden. The main herbaceous border has a backdrop of roses and is spectacular in July. The rose garden includes a circular iron structure clad in climbing roses topped by a copper rosebud. The north-facing border allows for a collection of shade-loving plants, especially hellebores and pulmonarias.

Owned by Mr & Mrs Robert Guinness
Number of gardeners 1
Size 2 acres

Mount Usher Gardens

ASHFORD, CO WICKLOW

Tel 00 353 404 40205   **Fax** 00 353 404 40116
Location Ashford, 30 miles south of Dublin on the N11
Opening hours 10.30 am – 6 pm; daily; 14 March to 31 October
Admission fee Adults £4; OAPs & Children £3. Guided tours for groups available.

These 20 acres of garden have the River Vartry through the middle: both sides of the river are crowded with unusual trees and shrubs – 5,000 different species and cultivars, some of them *very* rare. The self-sown *Pinus montezumae* are justly famous. There are good herbaceous plants too, and lilies in July. It is a truly remarkable plantsman's garden made by four generations of Walpoles from 1868 to 1980 and extensively restored by the present owner.

Plant Highlights Woodland garden; sub-tropical plants; plantsman's collection of plants; mature conifers; fine trees; spring bulbs; new millennium arboretum (2000); tallest *Cornus capitata* (18m) in the British Isles, plus 28 other record tree species.

Owned by Mrs Madelaine Jay
Number of gardeners 4
Size 20 acres

Muckross House & Gardens

MUCKROSS, KILLARNEY, CO KERRY

Tel 00 353 64 31440   **Fax** 00 353 64 33926
Location 4 miles south of Killarney on N71
Opening hours Dawn – dusk; daily; all year except one week at Christmas
Admission fee free

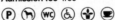

Killarney National Park provides a most beautiful setting for the gardens of Muckross House. There are a young arboretum (25 acres and now fully open to visitors) and some enormous old rhododendrons, but the woodland is of Scots pines and arbutus trees and, even more exciting for a garden-visitor, the rock garden is a natural one, of carboniferous limestone. Well maintained.

National Botanic Gardens

GLASNEVIN, DUBLIN 9, CO DUBLIN

Tel 00 353 1 837 4388   **Fax** 00 353 1 836 0080
Location 3 miles north of City Centre between N1 & N2: exit from M50 to City Centre at Jct X or Y
Opening hours 9 am – 6 pm (10 am – 4.30 pm in winter); daily except 25 December. Open at 11 am on Sundays
Admission fee free. Cars £1

Glasnevin was founded in 1795 to promote a scientific approach to the practice of agriculture: education remains a priority at the gardens which have a flourishing school of horticulture. The design of the botanic garden is classically Victorian, laid out as a beautiful public park in undulating ground on the south bank of the River Tolka: plants are comprehensively documented, labelled and classified. Notable trees include a magnificent Caucasian ironwood (*Zelkova carpinifolia*) near the new Herbarium building, good specimens of *Tetradium daniellii, Gymnocladus dioica* and *Davidia involucrata* and notable plants of a prostrate form of maidenhair tree (*Ginkgo biloba*) and weeping Atlantic cedar (*Cedrus atlantica* 'Pendula'). Recent years have seen a dramatic programme of restoration and renewal. The elegant curvilinear range of glasshouses built by Richard Turner 1843–1868 has been magnificently restored. It has – among many tropical plants – a good collection of cycads. The cactus and fern houses – the borders around them are planted with arum lilies and white watsonias – each have extensive collections, including a 400-year-old tree fern presented by the Melbourne Botanic Garden in the 1890s. Now the restoration of the great palm house is under way. The gardens are a focal point for horticulture in Ireland and still fulfil the function of distributing new introductions

among the gardens of Ireland. New education and visitor facilities have recently been added and it remains the finest collection of plants in Ireland. Allow a full day to do justice to the garden and its attractions.

Plant Highlights Large collection of trees including conifers; plant families collection; rock garden and alpine yard; rose garden; vegetable garden; native plants; arboretum; herbaceous borders; seasonal bedding and displays; serpentine pond and heather garden; four ranges of public glasshouses; ferns; tropical water lilies; succulents; tender conifers and cycads; Vireya rhododendrons; house plants; palms; orchids; tallest variegated Plane tree *Platanus × hispanica* 'Suttneri' (21m) in the British Isles, plus 25 further tree records.

Owned by Office of Public Works
Number of gardeners 18
Size 50 acres
NCCPG National Collections Garrya; Potentilla fruticosa

Plant Highlights Woodland garden; rock garden; mature conifers; fine collection of trees; rhododendrons; azaleas; greenhouse collection; extensive young conifer plantings in arboretum.

Owned by Dúchas, The Heritage Service
Size 15 acres, plus 25-acre arboretum

National Garden Exhibition Centre

KILQUADE, KILPEDDER, CO WICKLOW

Tel 00 353 1 2819890   **Fax** 00 353 1 2810359
Website www.clubi.ie/calumet
Location Signed from the N11
Opening hours 10 am (1 pm on Sundays) – 6 pm (dusk in winter); daily; all year
Admission fee Adults £2.50; OAPs £2; Groups (10+) £2

This is a permanent exhibition of contemporary style attached to a garden centre. It has some 19 linked but distinct gardens: the Herb Garden; the Geometric Garden; the Contemplative Garden; the Seaside Garden; the 'Pythagoras at Play' Garden; and so on. Each was made by a different designer and construction team. It adds up to the best of modern Irish design for small gardens: a shop window for ideas on style, plants and materials.

Owned by Tim & Suzanne Wallis

Powerscourt Gardens

POWERSCOURT ESTATE, ENNISKERRY, CO WICKLOW

Tel 00 353 1 204 6000   **Fax** 00 353 1 204 6900
Website www.powerscourt.ie
Location 12 miles south of Dublin off N11

Opening hours 9.30 am – 5.30 pm (dusk in winter); daily except 25 & 26 December; all year
Admission fee Adults £4; Students £3.50; Children £2

Powerscourt is a wonderful mixture of awesome grandeur and sheer fun. It is also extremely well organised for visitors. The main Italianate garden, a stately 1860s staircase down to a lake, has Great Sugarloaf Mountain as an off-centre backdrop. It is lined with bedding plants, statues and urns (look out for the sulky cherubs). To one side is the Japanese garden – not strongly Japanese – but full of twists and hummocks and scarlet paintwork. In the arboretum, Alan Mitchell designed a tree trail. Powerscourt is busy in summer, but you can escape into solitude along the avenue of monkey puzzles. The magnificent house has been restored and is now open to visitors again.

Plant Highlights Woodland garden; mature conifers; fine collection of trees; much recent restoration, including the Bamberg gates, and a remodelling of the Japanese garden; tallest *Abies spectabilis* (32m) in the British Isles, plus 10 other record tree specimens.

Owned by Powerscourt Estate
Number of gardeners 6
Size 47 acres

Primrose Hill

PRIMROSE LANE, LUCAN, CO DUBLIN

Tel 00 353 1 6280373
Location Lucan village, at top of Primrose Lane, through black iron gates
Opening hours 2 pm – 6 pm; daily; February, then June to the beginning of August. And by appointment
Admission fee Adults £3; Children £1

Primrose Hill is a plantsman's garden, particularly interesting for its rare forms of herbaceous plants and its snowdrops. The planting continues, and includes a small arboretum.

Owned by Robin & Cicely Hall
Size 4 acres

Ram House Garden

COOLGREANY, GOREY, CO WEXFORD

Tel 00 353 402 37238   **Fax** 00 353 402 37238
Location N11 to Inch and turn inland 1½ miles to Coolgreany
Opening hours 2.30 pm – 6 pm; Fridays to Sundays & Bank Holidays; 27 April to 9 September. And by appointment
Admission fee Adults £3; Children £2

Ram's two acres are laid out in the modern style, as a series of garden rooms, full of good plants and clever plantings. The owners are keen plantsmen, so that the garden and its collections are forever expanding and improving.

Owned by Godfrey & Lolo Stevens
Number of gardeners owners
Size 2 acres

Talbot Botanic Gardens

MALAHIDE CASTLE, MALAHIDE, CO DUBLIN

Tel 00 353 1 8727777   **Fax** 00 353 1 8727530
Location 10 miles north of Dublin on Malahide Road
Opening hours 2 pm – 5 pm (or by appointment); daily; May to September
Admission fee £2.50

The Talbot Botanic Garden at Malahide Demesne was the work of Milo Talbot, a passionate amateur botanist with a particular interest in southern hemisphere plants, notably the flora of Tasmania and Chile. He built up a collection of 5,000 different taxa and, since the soil is limey, they are in the main calcicole plants. The gardens include a four-acre walled garden, divided into seven distinct areas which give the impression of a series of secret gardens each with its own particular range of plants. It is in this walled garden that the rarer and tender species will be found. There are seven small glasshouses including a Victorian Conservatory at the end of the central path – a prominent focal point. Each house is very different in style and plantings The smallest has a collection of *Primula auricula* cultivars, while the Victorian house has a collection of Australasian plants. There are extensive collections of escallonias, *Syringa*, philadelphus, nothofagus and pittosporum as well as the National Collection of *Olearia*. Malahide is best visited at 2 pm on Wednesday afternoons when guided tours are offered of the walled garden (not otherwise open).

Owned by Fingal County Council
Size 22 acres
NCCPG National Collections *Olearia*

Tullynally Castle

CASTLEPOLLARD, CO WESTMEATH

Tel 00 353 44 61159   **Fax** 00 353 44 61856
Location Signed from Castlepollard
Opening hours 2 pm – 6 pm; daily; May to October
Admission fee Adults £3; Children £1

Tullynally has a grand garden for a grandly turreted house. Formal terraces lead down to the park and into the woodland gardens.

A fine avenue of centennial Irish yews is the centrepiece of the walled garden. Tom Pakenham wrote the acclaimed *Meetings with Remarkable Trees* (Weidenfeld, 1996. £25), some of whose photographs were taken at Tullynally. And he is starting to introduce exotics from his travels abroad: some are available for purchase.

Plant Highlights Woodland garden; daffodils; bluebells; grotto; new Tibetan garden (1999); biggest beech tree *Fagus sylvatica* in the British Isles and tallest *Griselinia littoralis* (20m).

Owned by The Hon Mr & Mrs Thomas Pakenham

Valclusa Gardens & Nursery

WATERFALL ROAD, ENNISKERRY, CO WICKLOW

Tel 00 353 1 286 9485   **Fax** 00 353 1 286 1877

Location Signed from Enniskerry to waterfall

Opening hours 10 am – 7 pm; Saturdays, Sundays & Bank Holiday Mondays; Easter to October. Plus Wednesdays & Fridays in May & June

Admission fee Adults £2.50; Children free

The garden has a fine position by the famous waterfall. Among its established trees (huge specimens of redwood, embothriums, *Cornus capitata* and a weeping form of *Liriodendron tulipifera*) is a modern plantsman's garden of rhododendrons, grasses, hostas and over 100 geraniums.

Owned by Duncan & Susan Forsythe

RHS GARDENS OVERSEAS

During the last ten years or so there has been an explosion of good English-style gardens in northern France and Belgium: gardening *à l'anglais* has become very fashionable. The Royal Horticultural Society has been an important influence in this development and enjoys very cordial relations with such moving spirits as Patrice Fustier, who runs the 'French Chelsea' at Courson. Many English visitors have discovered the delights of the Paris gardens at Haÿ-les-Roses and Bagatelle, as well as Monet's garden near Vernon. It is beyond the remit of this book to describe such gardens: the best guides are *Gardens of The Netherlands and Belgium* by Barbara Abbs (Mitchell Beazley, 1999) and *Gardens of France* by Patrick Taylor (Mitchell Beazley, 1996).

This small section lists the gardens to which the Royal Horticultural Society has been able to secure free entry for its members. Pride of place must go to the remarkable Arboretum Kalmthout in Belgium, which is very much an English-style plantsman's garden with many plants not yet known and grown in UK. The French gardens to which RHS members have free access for some or all of the year

are of mixed interest and quality: Arboretum National des Barres, Château d'Ainay-le-Vieil, Château de Beauregard, Château de Bouges, Château de la Bourdaisière, Château de la Bussière, Château de Valmer, Château de Villiers, Ferme Médiévale de Bois-Richeux, Les Jardins de Château Rivau, Château de Bosmelet, Manoir du Grand Courtoiseau, Parc Botanique du Prieuré d' Orchaise, Notre Dame d' Orsan, Parc Floral de la Source, Saint Laurent de Manzay, Jardins de Sasnières, Villandry Château Gardens, and Villeprévost. Of these, Villandry and Parc Floral de la Source are of exceptional interest – one for its huge formal gardens and the other for its floral displays.

There is an ever-increasing number of gardens in France which are open to the public and have historical connections with England – Bagatelle for a start, and Villa Noailles near Grasse and Serre de la Madone on the Riviera. It is to be hoped that the Royal Horticultural Society will establish closer links with some of these gardens, so that more of its members have the opportunity to discover a part of the English gardening tradition which is not actually in England itself.

Château d'Ainay-le-Vieil

18200 AINAY-LE-VIEIL, FRANCE

Tel & Fax 00 33 2 48 63 36 14
Location 55 km south of Bourges, signed from the N144
Opening hours 10 am – noon and 2 pm – 7 pm; daily; 15 May to 1 November
Admission fee Adults FF40; Children FF20. RHS members free in June

This is a proper fortified castle from the fourteenth and fifteenth centuries, adjoining a seventeenth-century charterhouse. Within the walls are five themed gardens: a cut-flower garden, a formal orchard, a garden of meditation, an enclosed herb-garden, and a white garden. Elsewhere are the rose gardens, with a large collection of old roses, all properly labelled.

Arboretum Kalmthout

HEUVEL 2, KALMTHOUT, B-2920, BELGIUM

Tel 00 32 36 666741 **Fax** 00 32 36 663396
Location 20 km north of Antwerp
Opening hours 10 am – 5 pm; daily; 15 March to 15 November
Admission fee Adults BEF 150; Children BEF 50. RHS members free all year

The beautiful continental garden at Kalmthout comprises a network of wide, mown paths winding between islands and banks of trees and shrubs, opening out into large spaces or narrowing into shadowy, enclosed alleys. It is home to one of Europe's finest woody plant collections. Highlights include witch hazels, an impressive array of ericaceous plants and the wonderful flowering cherry trees.

Arboretum National des Barres

45290 NOGENT-SUR-VERNISSON, FRANCE

Tel 00 33 2 38 97 62 21 **Fax** 00 33 2 38 97 65 15
Location Signed from N7 at Nogent, 18 km south of Montargis
Opening hours 10 am – 6 pm; daily; 15 March to 15 November
Admission fee Adults FF30; Children FF15. RHS members free in June & July

The National Arboretum at Barres is a seriously important botanical collection. It was founded by the Vilmorin family (France's leading nurserymen and seedsmen) in 1866 and its 35 hectares (86 acres) include over 8,000 different taxa. Most are species, arranged both geographically and systematically: round the château are ornamentals and cultivars. Worth a long visit: think of it as a nineteenth-century Hillier Arboretum and you will not be disappointed. Excellent plants for sale.

Château de Beauregard

41120 CELLETTES, FRANCE

Tel & Fax 00 33 2 54 70 40 05
Location 6 km south of Blois, on the D956
Opening hours 9.30 am – 12 noon & 2 pm – 6.30 pm (5 pm in winter); daily except Wednesdays; all year. Open Wednesdays from April to September, and between 12 noon & 2pm in July & August
Admission fee Adults FF40; Children free. RHS members free in June & July

Highlights include a fountain which marks the path into colour-themed gardens gathered within the clematis and rose-covered walls of a former kitchen garden.

Ferme Médiévale de Bois-Richeux

28130 PIERRES MAINTENON, FRANCE

Tel 00 33 2 11 88 20 20   **Fax** 00 33 2 46 24 56 00

Location 3 km west of Maintenon, 25 km north-north-west of Chartres

Opening hours 10 am – 12 noon & 2 pm – 6 pm; Saturday & Sundays; 1 May to 1 October. Daily in July & August

Admission fee Adults FF25; Children FF20. RHS members free in June

The manor house is set within a frame of aromatic and culinary plants and herbs with medicinal plants laid out in a chessboard pattern. A secluded courtyard and kitchen garden are protected from the winds by a fine trellis of climbing vines and osier.

Château de Bouges

36110 BOUGES-LE-CHÂTEAU, FRANCE

Tel 00 33 2 54 35 88 26   **Fax** 00 33 2 54 35 16 96

Location Take exit 10 or 11 from the A20: 13 km by D2 or D37

Opening hours 10 am – noon and 2 pm – 5 pm; Saturdays & Sundays; March & November. 10 am – noon and 2 pm – 6 pm; daily except Tuesday; April, May, September & October. 10 am – noon and 2 pm – 7 pm; daily except Tuesday; June. 10 am – 1 pm and 2 pm – 7 pm; daily; July & August

Admission fee Adults FF25; Children free. RHS members free from June to September

Several different periods and styles of gardening are represented at Bouges: the formal French garden, a nineteenth-century English park (fine trees and a lake), a flower garden (especially good for dahlias), a kitchen garden laid out with cones of yew, and a large tropical greenhouse.

Château de la Bourdaisière

25 RUE DE LA BOURDAISIÈRE, 37270 MONT-LOUIS-SUR-LOIRE, FRANCE

Tel 00 33 2 47 45 26 31   **Fax** 00 33 2 47 45 09 11

Location 14 km east of Tours, signed from D140

Opening hours 10 am – 7 pm; daily; June to September

Admission fee Adults FF35; Children FF28. RHS members free

This English style park contains a kitchen garden with over 400 types of tomato and a herb collection to satisfy the greatest of gastronomes. The formal gardens have recently been restored in a striking modern design.

Owned by Prince de Broglie

Château de la Bussière

45230 LA BUSSIÈRE, FRANCE

Tel 00 33 2 38 35 93 35   **Fax** 00 33 2 38 35 94 13

Location 1 hour from Paris on the N7 (12 km north-east of Gien)

Opening hours 10 am – 12 noon & 2 pm – 6 pm; daily; 1 April to 15 November. But 10 am – 7 pm in July & August

Admission fee Adults FF35; Children FF25. RHS members free in June & July

This eighteenth-century garden is abundant in fresh fruit and vegetables decoratively arranged in little squares and rows edged in boxwood.

Château de Bosmelet

76720 AUFFAY, FRANCE

Tel 00 33 2 35 52 81 07 **Fax** 00 33 2 35 32 84 62
Opening hours 1 June – 30 September
Admission fee Adults FF30; Children free. RHS members free in September

In the walled garden is a display of more than 800 varieties of fruit, vegetables and flowers, arranged in a rainbow colour-scheme.

Owned by Baronne Laurence de Bosmelet

Manoir du Grand Courtoiseau

45220 TRIGUÈRES, FRANCE

Tel 00 33 2 80 24 10 83 **Fax** 00 33 2 38 94 10 64
Location Take the D943 between Château-Renard & Triguères
Opening hours Saturdays, Sundays & Bank Holidays; end of April to end of October. Daily except Tuesdays, Wednesdays & Bank Holidays from end of July to end of August.
Admission fee Adults FF40; Children FF30. RHS members free in June & July

Le Grand Coutoiseau is an eighteenth-century manor house, surrounded by a contemporary garden which reflects that period. Beautiful planted borders contain old roses, perennials, bulbs, shrubs and topiaries of yews and box, which thrive around the planted moats.

Parc Botanique du Prieuré d'Orchaise

PLACE DE L'EGLISE, 41190 ORCHAISE, FRANCE

Tel & Fax 00 33 2 45 03 36 11
Location 11 km west of Blois by the D766 towards Angers
Opening hours 3 pm – 7 pm; first & third Sunday afternoons from March to October
Admission fee Adults FF35. RHS members free

Not so much a botanic garden, more the collection of an enthusiastic plantsman, Orchaise boasts over 2,000 plant cultivars from around the world. Flowering cherries, water lilies, azaleas and rhododendrons are among the garden's specialities, but it is especially well known for its beautiful plantings of peonies and roses.

Notre Dame d'Orsan

18170 MAISONNAIS, FRANCE

Tel 00 33 2 48 56 27 50 **Fax** 00 33 2 48 56 39 64
Location A71 Motorway, exit St Amand Montrond; 10 km south-south-east of Lignières by D65
Opening hours 10 am – 7 pm; daily; 1 April – 1 November
Admission fee Adults FF50; Children FF25. RHS members free in September

The priory has disappeared (the house is seventeenth-century) and the garden is entirely modern, laid out by two enthusiasts since 1991 and yet already seemingly mature. It is a mediaeval theme-garden whose vineyards, rose arbours, maze, herb garden and secret garden are planted in a loose evocation of the spirit of the middle ages. Unhistorical it may be, but it is also inspirational and very pretty.

Owned by Sonia Lesot & Patrice Taravella

Parc Floral de la Source

45072 ORLÉANS, CEDEX 2, FRANCE

Tel 00 33 2 38 49 30 00 **Fax** 00 33 2 38 49 30 19
Location 7 km south-south-east from Orléans by the N20
Opening hours 9 am – 6 pm; daily; 1 April to
15 November. 2 pm – 5 pm; daily; 16 November to
31 March
Admission fee Adults FF40; Children free. RHS members
free in May & June

La Source was started as an exhibition
garden for the Orléans nursery trade in
1963, though nowadays nurseries from all
over France compete to be allowed a
permanent site there. The château at the
centre is eighteenth-century, and takes its
name from the source of the River Loiret
which surges out of a hole in the ground.
The trade displays are mainly of trees and
shrubs, each individually designed (often
very strikingly) but include international iris
trials, thousands of modern roses (a
spectacular sight), millions of bulbs in
spring and a good display of dahlias and
chrysanthemums in autumn. There are
some inspirational designs and good
colour-plantings too. Worth at least half a
day: and there is even a narrow-gauge
railway to chuff you round.

Les Jardins de Château Rivau

37120 LÉMERÉ, FRANCE

Tel 00 33 2 47 95 77 47 **Fax** 00 33 2 47 95 78 46
Location 9 km south of L'Ile Bouchard
Opening hours 1 pm – 7 pm; Saturdays, Sundays & Bank
Holidays; May to September. Daily except Tuesday from
1 June to 16 September

Admission fee Adults FF35; Children FF20. RHS members
free at weekends in May & June

The gardens at Le Rivau surround a fairy-
tale moated fifteenth-century castle. On
about 12 acres the sensitively recreated
gardens are inspired by fifteenth- and
sixteenth-century illuminated manuscripts,
supplying something of interest to all
gardeners. The chessboard of the secret
garden is resplendent in May and June with
a collection of apothecary roses.

Saint Laurent de Manzay

CONSERVATOIRE DES PLANTES
TINCTORIALES ET AROMATIQUES,
PRIEURÉ DE MANZAY, 18120 LIMEUX,
FRANCE

Tel & Fax 00 33 2 48 57 13 08
Opening hours 3 pm – 7 pm; Saturdays, Sundays & Bank
Holidays; May, June, September & October. Daily except
Tuesdays in July & August
Admission fee Adults FF30; Children free. RHS members
free in June & July

The garden has 400 varieties of plants with
now forgotten virtues. These neolithic plants
from the sixteenth century were used for
painting or textiles and medicinal and
culinary purposes.

Jardins de Sasnières

LE CHÂTEAU, 41310 SASNIÈRES,
FRANCE

Tel 00 33 2 54 82 92 34 **Fax** 00 33 2 54 82 93 30
Location 17 km south west of Vendôme by the N10
& D108

Opening hours 10 am – 6 pm; Thursday – Monday; Easter to 1 November
Admission fee Adults FF40; Children free. RHS members free in May & June

The gardens are situated in the hollow of a small valley and as visitors walk along the grassy paths and by the wild pond, filled with rainbow trout and prettily fringed with candelabra primulas, they will discover rare plants carefully chosen for their unusual stems, flowers and foliage.

Château de Valmer

CHANÇAY, 37210 VOUVRAY, FRANCE

Tel 00 33 2 47 52 93 12 **Fax** 00 33 2 47 52 26 92
Location 11 km north-east of Vouvray by the D46
Opening hours 2 pm – 7 pm; Saturdays & Sundays; May to September. Daily except Monday in July & August
Admission fee Adults FF35; Children free. RHS members free in August

Valmer is an elegant example of the Italian influence on French gardens of the seventeenth century in the Loire Valley. Steps lead down from flower-covered terraces to kitchen gardens arranged in the style popularised by Marie-Antoinette. All are surrounded by an English-style park, and vines: the estate is famous for its Vouvray wine.

Villandry
Château Gardens

37510 VILLANDRY, FRANCE

Tel 00 33 2 47 50 02 09 **Fax** 00 33 2 47 50 12 85

Location 15 km west of Tours on the D7
Opening hours Open every day, all year from 9 am (8.30 am in July & August), closing between 5.30 pm & 8 pm according to season
Admission fee Adults FF33; Children FF22. RHS members free in September

One of the greatest gardens in the world, and certainly the most complete reconstructed example of a sixteenth-century garden. Villandry was laid out on a massive scale in the early years of the twentieth century, based upon designs from 1540 by the royal gardener Androuet de Cerceau. The formal *potager* alone, a three-acre square, has over 50,000 vegetables formally planted in nine eye-catching patterns. And it is renewed with different patterns every six months. Above it are formal flower gardens and the 'garden of love', full of colour-symbolism. The whole contains over 50 kilometres of box edging and trained yew-trees which give structure to the garden throughout the year.

Owned by Henri Carvallo

Villeprévost
Château Park

28140 TILLAY-LE-PÉNEUX, FRANCE

Tel 00 33 2 37 99 45 17
Location 1 hour from Paris, on the A10; 10 km south-west of exit 12
Opening hours 2 pm – 6.30 pm; Saturdays & Sundays; Easter to 15 November
Admission fee Adults FF25; Children FF20. RHS members free in July & August

Enjoy walks along paths lined with hornbeam hedges, wild flora, hyacinths and herbaceous peonies.

Château de Villiers

18800 CHASSY, FRANCE

Tel 00 33 2 48 77 53 20   **Fax** 00 33 2 47 77 53 29
Location 38 km east of Bourges by the D976 to Nérondes and then by the D6 to Villiers
Opening hours 10 am – 7 pm; daily except Tuesdays; 1 May to 23 September. Closed throughout July

Admission fee Adults FF35; Children FF25. RHS members free in June

This is the very personal garden of a good plantswoman, formally designed and lavishly planted. Roses, perennials and clematis abound, but there are also rare plants, gazebos, a quincunx of medlars and a collection of lilac species.

PLANT-LOVER'S GUIDES

NCCPG NATIONAL COLLECTIONS

ABELIA
Pleasant View Nursery & Garden,
Devon, England

ABIES
Ardkinglas Woodland Garden,
Strathclyde, Scotland

ACACIA
Tresco Abbey, Cornwall, England

ACANTHUS
Iford Manor, Wiltshire, England

ACER
Hergest Croft Gardens,
Herefordshire, England

ACER (Japanese cvs.)
Westonbirt Arboretum,
Gloucestershire, England

ACHILLEA
Capel Manor, London, England

ADENOPHORA
Padlock Croft, Cambridgeshire,
England

ADIANTUM
Tatton Park, Cheshire, England

AESCULUS
West Dean Gardens, Sussex, West,
England

ALCHEMILLA
Cambridge University Botanic
Garden, Cambridgeshire, England

ANEMONE NEMOROSA
Kingston Lacy, Dorset, England

ANEMONE (Japanese)
Broadview Gardens, Kent, England
Heath Lands, Hampshire, England

AQUILEGIA
Hardwicke House, Cambridgeshire,
England

ARALIA
Powis Castle, Powys, Wales

ARBUTUS
Dunster Castle, Somerset, England

ARGYRANTHEMUM
Lower Icknield Farm,
Buckinghamshire, England

ARISTOLOCHIA
The Plantsman Nursery, Devon,
England

ARTEMISIA
Elsworth Herbs, Cambridgeshire,
England

ASPLENIUM
SCOLOPENDRIUM
Sizergh Castle, Cumbria, England

ASTER
Temple Newsam Park, Yorkshire,
West, England
Upton House, Warwickshire,
England

ASTER (autumn-flowering)
Old Court Nurseries, Herefordshire,
England

ASTILBE
Holehird, Cumbria, England
Marwood Hill Gardens, Devon,
England

AUBRIETA
University of Leicester Botanic
Garden, Leicestershire, England

AZARA
Exeter University Gardens, Devon,
England
Trelissick Garden, Cornwall,
England

BEGONIA
Glasgow Botanic Garden,
Strathclyde, Scotland
Rhodes & Rockliffe, Essex, England

BERBERIS
Mill Hill Plants, Nottinghamshire,
England

BERGENIA (species
& primary hybrids)
Cambridge University Botanic
Garden, Cambridgeshire, England

BETULA
Hergest Croft Gardens,
Herefordshire, England
Wakehurst Place, Sussex, West,
England

BRACHYGLOTTIS
Inverewe, Highland, Scotland

BUDDLEJA
Longstock Water Gardens,
Hampshire, England

BUXUS
Ickworth, Suffolk, England
Langley Boxwood Nursery,
Hampshire, England

CALAMINTHA
Marle Place Gardens, Kent, England

CALLUNA VULGARIS
RHS Garden Wisley, Surrey, England

CALLUNA (provisional)
Harlow Carr Botanical Gardens,
Yorkshire, North, England

CAMELLIA
Mount Edgcumbe Gardens,
Cornwall, England

CAMELLIA JAPONICA
Antony Woodland Garden,
Cornwall, England

CAMELLIA × WILLIAMSII
Wentworth Castle Gardens,
Yorkshire, South, England

CAMPANULA
Burton Agnes Hall Gardens,
Yorkshire, East Riding of, England
Lingen Nursery and Gardens,
Shropshire, England
Padlock Croft, Cambridgeshire,
England

CARPINUS
Beale Arboretum, Hertfordshire,
England
The Sir Harold Hillier Gardens &
Arboretum, Hampshire, England

CASSIOPE
Branklyn Garden, Tayside, Scotland

CATALPA
Cliveden, Buckinghamshire, England

CEANOTHUS (deciduous)
Knoll Gardens, Dorset, England

CELMISIA (species)
St Luke's Cottage, Northumberland
and Tyne & Wear, England

CHAMAECYPARIS
LAWSONIANA
University of Leicester Botanic
Garden, Leicestershire, England

CHAMAECYPARIS
LAWSONIANA (cvs).
Bedgebury National Pinetum, Kent,
England

CIMICIFUGA
Bridgemere Garden World,
Cheshire, England

CISTUS
Chelsea Physic Garden, London,
England

CITRUS
Reads Nursery, Norfolk, England

CLEMATIS ORIENTALIS
Bridgemere Garden World,
Cheshire, England

CLEMATIS VITICELLA
Longstock Water Gardens,
Hampshire, England

CLEMATIS
Burford House Gardens, Shropshire,
England

COLCHICUM
Felbrigg Hall, Norfolk, England

CONOPHYTUM
Abbey Brook Cactus Nursery,
Derbyshire, England

CONVALLARIA
Kingston Lacy, Dorset, England

COPROSMA
County Park Nursery, Essex,
England

CORIARIA
Crûg Farm Plants, Gwynedd, Wales

CORNUS
Newby Hall, Yorkshire, North,
England
RHS Garden Rosemoor, Devon,
England
The Sir Harold Hillier Gardens &
Arboretum, Hampshire, England

CORYLUS
The Sir Harold Hillier Gardens &
Arboretum, Hampshire, England

CORYLUS (cobnuts & filberts)
Brogdale, Kent, England

COTONEASTER
The Sir Harold Hillier Gardens &
Arboretum, Hampshire, England

CROCOSMIA
Lanhydrock, Cornwall, England

CROCUS
RHS Garden Wisley, Surrey, England

× CUPRESSOCYPARIS
Bedgebury National Pinetum, Kent,
England

CYCLAMEN
Tile Barn Nursery, Kent, England

CYDONIA OBLONGA
Norton Priory Museum & Gardens,
Cheshire, England

CYSTOPTERIS
Rickard's Hardy Ferns Ltd,
Worcestershire, England
Sizergh Castle, Cumbria, England

DABOECIA
RHS Garden Wisley, Surrey, England

DAPHNE
Brandy Mount House, Hampshire,
England

DELPHINIUM
Rougham Hall Nurseries, Suffolk,
England
Temple Newsam Park, Yorkshire,
West, England

DENDROBIUM
Glasgow Botanic Garden,
Strathclyde, Scotland

DEUTZIA
The Hollies Park, Yorkshire, West,
England

DIANELLA
Mount Stewart, Co Down, Northern
Ireland

DIANTHUS
Kingstone Cottage Plants,
Herefordshire, England

DIANTHUS (Malmaison
carnations)
Crathes Castle, Grampian, Scotland

DICKSONIACEAE
Glasgow Botanic Garden,
Strathclyde, Scotland

DIERVILLA
Sheffield Botanical Gardens,
Yorkshire, South, England

DRYOPTERIS
Harlow Carr Botanical Gardens,
Yorkshire, North, England
Sizergh Castle, Cumbria, England

DWARF CONIFERS
Savill Garden, Surrey, England
Valley Gardens, Surrey, England

ECHINACEA
Elton Hall, Herefordshire, England

ECHINOPSIS (hybrids)
Abbey Brook Cactus Nursery,
Derbyshire, England

ELEAGNUS
Beale Arboretum, Hertfordshire,
England

EMBOTHRIUM
Bodnant Gardens, Clwyd, Wales

ENKIANTHUS
Clyne Gardens, Glamorgan, Wales

EPIMEDIUM
Lilliesleaf Nursery, Borders, Scotland
RHS Garden Wisley, Surrey, England

ERICA
Bell's Cherrybank Gardens, Tayside,
Scotland
RHS Garden Wisley, Surrey, England

ERYTHRONIUM
Greencombe Gardens, Somerset,
England

EUCALYPTUS
Meon Orchard, Hampshire, England

EUCRYPHIA
Bodnant Gardens, Clwyd, Wales
Seaforde Gardens, Co Down,
Northern Ireland

EUPHORBIA
Oxford Botanic Garden,
Oxfordshire, England

FAGUS
Kirkley Hall Gardens,
Northumberland and Tyne & Wear,
England

FALLOPIA
Rowden Gardens, Devon, England

FERNS
Savill Garden, Surrey, England

FICUS
Reads Nursery, Norfolk, England

FRAGARIA × *ANANASSA*
Brogdale, Kent, England

FRAXINUS
The Quinta, Cheshire, England
Thorp Perrow Arboretum,
Yorkshire, North, England

FRITILLARIA (European species)
**Cambridge University Botanic
Garden,** Cambridgeshire, England

FUCHSIA MAGELLANICA
(provisional)
Harlow Carr Botanical Gardens,
Yorkshire, North, England

FUCHSIA
Croxteth Hall & Country Park,
Lancashire, Greater Manchester
& Merseyside, England
**University of Leicester Botanic
Garden,** Leicestershire, England

FUCHSIA (hardy)
Kathleen Muncaster Fuchsias,
Lincolnshire, England

GALANTHUS
Brandy Mount House, Hampshire,
England
RHS Garden Wisley, Surrey, England

GARRYA
National Botanic Gardens,
Co Dublin, Republic of Ireland

GAULTHERIA
Greencombe Gardens, Somerset,
England

GENTIANA
Christie's Nursery, Tayside, Scotland

GERANIUM
Catforth Gardens, Lancashire,
Greater Manchester & Merseyside,
England
East Lambrook Manor, Somerset,
England

GERANIUM (species
& primary hybrids)
**Cambridge University Botanic
Garden,** Cambridgeshire, England

GREVILLEA
Pine Lodge, Cornwall, England

GYMNOCALYCIUM
Abbey Brook Cactus Nursery,
Derbyshire, England

HAMAMELIS
**The Sir Harold Hillier Gardens &
Arboretum,** Hampshire, England
Swallow Hayes, Shropshire, England

HAWORTHIA
Abbey Brook Cactus Nursery,
Derbyshire, England

HEBE (dwarf)
Siskin Plants, Suffolk, England

HEDERA
Erddig, Clwyd, Wales
Fibrex Nurseries Ltd, Warwickshire,
England

HELIOTROPIUM
Hampton Court Palace, London,
England

HELLEBORUS
Broadview Gardens, Kent, England

HELLEBORUS (part)
Longthatch, Hampshire, England
White Windows, Hampshire,
England

HEMEROCALLIS
Antony House, Cornwall, England

HEMEROCALLIS (Coe hybrids)
The Hollies Park, Yorkshire, West,
England

HESPERIS
**University of Leicester Botanic
Garden,** Leicestershire, England

HIBISCUS SYIACUS (cvs.)
Notcutts Nurseries, Suffolk, England

'HILLIER' PLANTS
**The Sir Harold Hillier Gardens &
Arboretum,** Hampshire, England

HOHERIA
Abbotsbury Sub-Tropical Gardens, Dorset, England

HOSTA (large-leaved)
The Hollies Park, Yorkshire, West, England

HOSTA (small leaved)
Apple Court, Hampshire, England

HYACINTHUS ORIENTALIS
Ripley Castle, Yorkshire, North, England

HYDRANGEA
Holehird, Cumbria, England

HYPERICUM
Wakehurst Place, Sussex, West, England

ILEX
RHS Garden Rosemoor, Devon, England
Savill Garden, Surrey, England
Valley Gardens, Surrey, England

IRIS
Belsay Hall, Northumberland and Tyne & Wear, England
Myddelton House, London, England

IRIS (species)
The Harris Garden, Berkshire, England

IRIS ENSATA
Marwood Hill Gardens, Devon, England

IRIS SIBIRICA
Lingen Nursery and Gardens, Shropshire, England

IRIS UNGUICULARIS
Great Barfield, Buckinghamshire, England

JUGLANS
Thorp Perrow Arboretum, Yorkshire, North, England
Wimpole Hall, Cambridgeshire, England

JUNIPERUS
Bedgebury National Pinetum, Kent, England

KNIPHOFIA
Barton Manor, Isle of Wight, England

LABURNUM
Powis Castle, Powys, Wales

LAVANDULA
Downderry Nursery, Kent, England

LAVANDULA (sect. Lavandula, Dentata, Pterostoechas & Stoechas)
Norfolk Lavender, Norfolk, England

LEUCOJUM
Great Barfield, Buckinghamshire, England

LIBERTIA
Mount Stewart, Co Down, Northern Ireland

LIGUSTRUM
The Sir Harold Hillier Gardens & Arboretum, Hampshire, England

LIRIODENDRON
West Dean Gardens, Sussex, West, England

LITHOCARPUS
The Sir Harold Hillier Gardens & Arboretum, Hampshire, England

LITHOPS
Abbey Brook Cactus Nursery, Derbyshire, England

LONICERA (species & primary hybrids)
Cambridge University Botanic Garden, Cambridgeshire, England

LUPINUS (Russell strains)
Swallow Hayes, Shropshire, England

LYSIMACHIA
Cotswold Garden Flowers, Worcestershire, England

MAGNOLIA
Bodnant Gardens, Clwyd, Wales
Savill Garden, Surrey, England
Valley Gardens, Surrey, England

MAGNOLIA (species)
Wentworth Castle Gardens, Yorkshire, South, England

MAHONIA
Savill Garden, Surrey, England
Valley Gardens, Surrey, England

MALUS
Granada Arboretum, Cheshire, England

MALUS (apples, ornamental cvs. & cider apples)
Brogdale, Kent, England

MECONOPSIS
Houghall, Co Durham, England

MENTHA
Iden Croft Herbs, Kent, England

MONARDA
Leeds Castle, Kent, England

NARCISSUS
Brodie Castle, Grampian, Scotland
Guy Wilson Daffodil Garden, Co Derry, Northern Ireland

NARCISSUS (miniature)
Broadleigh Gardens, Somerset, England

NERIUM OLEANDER
Elsworth Herbs, Cambridgeshire, England

NOTHOFAGUS
Crarae Gardens, Strathclyde, Scotland
Wakehurst Place, Sussex, West, England

NYMPHAEA
Bennetts Water Lily Farm, Dorset, England
Burnby Hall Gardens, Yorkshire, East Riding of, England
Kenchester Water Gardens, Herefordshire, England
Stapeley Water Gardens, Cheshire, England

OENOTHERA
Old Vicarage, Wiltshire, England

OLEARIA
Inverewe, Highland, Scotland
Talbot Botanic Gardens, Co Dublin, Republic of Ireland

ORIGANUM
Hexham Herbs & Hardy Plants, Northumberland and Tyne & Wear, England
Iden Croft Herbs, Kent, England

OSMUNDA
Sizergh Castle, Cumbria, England

PAEONIA
Hidcote Manor, Gloucestershire, England

PAEONIA LACTIFLORA
Kelways Ltd, Somerset, England

PAPAVER ORIENTALE
Water Meadow Nursery and Herb Farm, Hampshire, England

PARAHEBE
County Park Nursery, Essex, England

PARIS
Crûg Farm Plants, Gwynedd, Wales

PASSIFLORA
National Collection of Passiflora, Somerset, England

PELARGONIUM
Fibrex Nurseries Ltd, Warwickshire, England

PENSTEMON
Kingston Maurward Gardens, Dorset, England
Rowallane Garden, Co Down, Northern Ireland

PERNETTYA
Savill Garden, Surrey, England
Valley Gardens, Surrey, England

PERSICARIA
Rowden Gardens, Devon, England

PHILADELPHUS
The Hollies Park, Yorkshire, West, England

PHLOMIS
Just Phlomis, Gloucestershire, England

PHLOX PANICULATA
Temple Newsam Park, Yorkshire, West, England

PHORMIUM
Charney Well, Cumbria, England
Mount Stewart, Co Down, Northern Ireland

PHOTINIA
The Sir Harold Hillier Gardens & Arboretum, Hampshire, England
Trelissick Garden, Cornwall, England

PHYGELIUS
Knoll Gardens, Dorset, England

PICEA
Ardkinglas Woodland Garden, Strathclyde, Scotland

PIERIS
Clyne Gardens, Glamorgan, Wales
Savill Garden, Surrey, England
Valley Gardens, Surrey, England

PINUS
The Quinta, Cheshire, England

PINUS (excl. dwarf cvs.)
The Sir Harold Hillier Gardens & Arboretum, Hampshire, England

PLATANUS
Mottisfont Abbey, Hampshire, England

PLATYCODON
Padlock Croft, Cambridgeshire, England

POLYPODIUM
Harlow Carr Botanical Gardens, Yorkshire, North, England
Rickard's Hardy Ferns Ltd, Worcestershire, England

POLYSTICHUM
Greencombe Gardens, Somerset, England
Holehird, Cumbria, England

POPULUS
Wiltshire College Lackham, Wiltshire, England

POTENTILLA
Ardgillan Park, Co Dublin, Republic of Ireland

POTENTILLA FRUTICOSA
National Botanic Gardens, Co Dublin, Republic of Ireland

POTENTILLA FRUTICOSA (cvs.)
Webbs of Wychbold, Worcestershire, England

PRIMULA (Asiatic species)
Cluny House, Tayside, Scotland

PRIMULA (Cortusoides section}
Plant World Botanic Gardens, Devon, England

PRIMULA AURICULA
Golden Acre Park, Yorkshire, West, England
Martin Nest Nurseries, Lincolnshire, England

PRUNUS (cherry)
Brogdale, Kent, England

PRUNUS (plums)
Brogdale, Kent, England

PSEUDOPANAX
Ventnor Botanic Garden, Isle of Wight, England

PULMONARIA
Stillingfleet Lodge Nurseries, Yorkshire, North, England

PYRUS
Brogdale, Kent, England

QUERCUS
The Sir Harold Hillier Gardens & Arboretum, Hampshire, England

RANUNCULUS FICARIA
Rowden Gardens, Devon, England

RHEUM
Harlow Carr Botanical Gardens, Yorkshire, North, England
RHS Garden Wisley, Surrey, England

RHODODENDRON
Highclere Castle, Hampshire, England

RHODODENDRON (Barbatum}, Glischra & Maculifera sections}
Inverewe, Highland, Scotland

RHODODENDRON (Falconeri series)
Wentworth Castle Gardens, Yorkshire, South, England

RHODODENDRON (subsections Falconera, Grandia and Maddenia)
Brodick Castle, Strathclyde, Scotland

RHODODENDRON (Ghent azaleas)
Sheffield Park, Sussex, East, England

RHODODENDRON (Knap Hill azaleas)
Sherwood, Devon, England

RHODODENDRON (Kurume azaleas, the Wilson 50)
Isabella Plantation, London, England

RHODODENDRON (species & Glen Dale azaleas)
Savill Garden, Surrey, England
Valley Gardens, Surrey, England

RHODODENDRON (Triflora & Falconera subsections)
Clyne Gardens, Glamorgan, Wales

RHODODENDRON FORRESTII
Bodnant Gardens, Clwyd, Wales

RIBES (gooseberries)
Rougham Hall Nurseries, Suffolk, England

RIBES (species & primary hybrids)
Cambridge University Botanic Garden, Cambridgeshire, England

RIBES GROSSULARIA (gooseberries)
Brogdale, Kent, England

RIBES NIGRUM (blackcurrants)
Brogdale, Kent, England

RIBES SATIVUM (currants other than blackcurrants)
Brogdale, Kent, England

RODGERSIA
Hadspen Garden, Somerset, England

ROHDEA JAPONICA
Apple Court, Hampshire, England

ROSA
Mottisfont Abbey, Hampshire, England

ROSA (History of European roses)
University of Birmingham Botanic Garden, West Midlands, England

ROSA (nineteenth-century shrubs)
Malleny House Garden, Lothian, Scotland

ROSA (species)
Peter Beales Roses, Norfolk, England

ROSA (species & cultivars)
The Gardens of the Rose, Hertfordshire, England

ROSMARINUS
Downderry Nursery, Kent, England

RUDBECKIA
Elton Hall, Herefordshire, England

RUSCUS
Cambridge University Botanic Garden, Cambridgeshire, England

SALIX
Westonbirt Arboretum, Gloucestershire, England

SALVIA
Kingston Maurward Gardens, Dorset, England
Pleasant View Nursery & Garden, Devon, England

SAMBUCUS
Wallington, Northumberland and Tyne & Wear, England

SANTOLINA
Marle Place Gardens, Kent, England

SARCOCOCCA
Capel Manor, London, England

SAXIFRAGA
Waterperry Gardens, Oxfordshire, England

SAXIFRAGA (European species)
Cambridge University Botanic Garden, Cambridgeshire, England

SCABIOSA CAUCASICA
Hardwick Hall, Derbyshire, England

SKIMMIA
University of Leicester Botanic Garden, Leicestershire, England
Wakehurst Place, Sussex, West, England

SORBUS
Granada Arboretum, Cheshire, England
Houghall, Co Durham, England

SORBUS (Aria & Micromeles groups)
Winkworth Arboretum, Surrey, England

SIR FREDERICK STERN, PLANTS INTRODUCED BY
Highdown, Sussex, West, England

STEWARTIA
High Beeches, Sussex, West, England

STREPTOCARPUS
Dibleys Nurseries, Clwyd, Wales

STYRACACEAE (incl. Halesia, Pterostyrax, Styrax, Sinojackia)
Holker Hall, Cumbria, England

SYMPHYANDRA
Padlock Croft, Cambridgeshire, England

SYRINGA
Golden Acre Park, Yorkshire, West, England
The Hollies Park, Yorkshire, West, England

TAXUS
Bedgebury National Pinetum, Kent, England

THALICTRUM
Bridgemere Garden World,
Cheshire, England

THELYPTERIDACEAE
Rickard's Hardy Ferns Ltd,
Worcestershire, England

THUJA
Bedgebury National Pinetum, Kent,
England

THYMUS
Hexham Herbs & Hardy Plants,
Northumberland and Tyne & Wear,
England

TILIA
Thorp Perrow Arboretum,
Yorkshire, North, England

TRILLIUM
Spinners, Hampshire, England

TULBAGHIA
Marwood Hill Gardens, Devon,
England

TULIPA (species & primary
hybrids)
**Cambridge University Botanic
Garden,** Cambridgeshire, England

VACCINIUM
Greencombe Gardens, Somerset,
England

VIBURNUM
Crathes Castle, Grampian, Scotland
RHS Garden Hyde Hall, Essex,
England

VICARY GIBBS PLANTS
Lyme Park, Cheshire, England

VINCA
Monksilver Nursery,
Cambridgeshire, England

VITIS VINIFERA
Brogdale, Kent, England

VITIS VINIFERA (grapes)
Reads Nursery, Norfolk, England

WEIGELA
Sheffield Botanical Gardens,
Yorkshire, South, England

WOODWARDIA
Apple Court, Hampshire, England

YUCCA
Renishaw Hall, Derbyshire, England

ZELKOVA
Hergest Croft Gardens,
Herefordshire, England

WHERE TO SEE PARTICULAR PLANTS

ALPINES

Cambridge University Botanic Garden
Cambridgeshire, England
Hillside
Co. Cork, Republic of Ireland
W E Th Ingwersen Ltd
Sussex, West, England
Jack Drake
Highland, Scotland
National Botanic Gardens
Co. Dublin, Republic of Ireland
RHS Garden, Wisley
Surrey, England
Royal Botanic Garden, Edinburgh
Lothian, Scotland
Royal Botanic Gardens, Kew
London, England
St Luke's Cottage
Northumberland and Tyne & Wear, England
University of Durham Botanic Garden
Co. Durham, England
University of Leicester Botanic Garden
Leicestershire, England

ARBORETA

Bath Botanic Gardens
Somerset, England
Batsford Arboretum
Gloucestershire, England
Bicton Park Gardens
Devon, England
Cambridge University Botanic Garden
Cambridgeshire, England
Cruickshank Botanic Garden
Grampian, Scotland
Dawyck Botanic Garden
Borders, Scotland

Exeter University Gardens
Devon, England
Fota
Co. Cork, Republic of Ireland
Lynford Arboretum
Norfolk, England
Marwood Hill Gardens
Devon, England
National Botanic Gardens
Co. Dublin, Republic of Ireland
Ness Botanic Gardens
Cheshire, England
Nymans
Sussex, West, England
RHS Garden, Hyde Hall
Essex, England
RHS Garden, Rosemoor
Devon, England
RHS Garden, Wisley
Surrey, England
Rowallane Garden
Co. Down, Northern Ireland
Royal Botanic Garden, Edinburgh
Lothian, Scotland
Royal Botanic Gardens, Kew
London, England
Sheffield Park
Sussex, East, England
Stourhead
Wiltshire, England
Talbot Botanic Gardens
Co. Dublin, Republic of Ireland
Torosay Castle & Gardens
Strathclyde, Scotland
Winkworth Arboretum
Surrey, England

BEGONIA

Blackmore & Langdon
Somerset, England

BLUEBELLS

Emmetts Garden
Kent, England
Haughley Park
Suffolk, England
Royal Botanic Gardens, Kew
London, England
Sheffield Park
Sussex, East, England
Stourhead
Wiltshire, England
Winkworth Arboretum
Surrey, England

CACTI

Abbey Brook Cactus Nursery
Derbyshire, England
Birmingham Botanical Gardens & Glasshouses
West Midlands, England
Cambridge University Botanic Garden
Cambridgeshire, England
Holly Gate Cactus Nursery
Sussex, West, England
National Botanic Gardens
Co. Dublin, Republic of Ireland
RHS Garden, Wisley
Surrey, England
Royal Botanic Garden, Edinburgh
Lothian, Scotland
Royal Botanic Gardens, Kew
London, England
Toobees Exotics
Surrey, England
University of Durham Botanic Garden
Co. Durham, England

CAMELLIAS

Burncoose Nurseries & Gardens
Cornwall, England

Marwood Hill Gardens
Devon, England
RHS Garden, Wisley
Surrey, England
Rotherview Nursery with Coghurst Camellias
Sussex, East, England
Trehane
Cornwall, England

CARNATIONS
RHS Garden, Wisley
Surrey, England

CHRYSANTHEMUMS
Halls of Heddon
Northumberland and Tyne & Wear, England
RHS Garden, Wisley
Surrey, England
Philip Tivey & Son
Leicestershire, England

CLEMATIS
J Bradshaw & Son
Kent, England
Burford House Gardens
Shropshire, England
Sherston Parva Nursery Ltd
Wiltshire, England
Thorncroft Clematis Nursery
Norfolk, England

CONIFERS
Batsford Arboretum
Gloucestershire, England
Clumber Park
Nottinghamshire, England
Cragside
Northumberland and Tyne & Wear, England
Dawyck Botanic Garden
Borders, Scotland
Dochfour Gardens
Highland, Scotland
Foggy Bottom
Norfolk, England
Fota
Co. Cork, Republic of Ireland

Mount Stuart
Strathclyde, Scotland
National Botanic Gardens
Co. Dublin, Republic of Ireland
Nymans
Sussex, West, England
RHS Garden, Wisley
Surrey, England
Royal Botanic Gardens, Kew
London, England
Scone Palace
Tayside, Scotland
Sheffield Park
Sussex, East, England
Trelissick Garden
Cornwall, England
Winkworth Arboretum
Surrey, England
Younger Botanic Garden
Strathclyde, Scotland

CYCLAMEN
Ashwood Nurseries Ltd
West Midlands, England
Cadenza
Surrey, England
RHS Garden, Wisley
Surrey, England
Tile Barn Nursery
Kent, England

DAFFODILS
Acorn Bank Garden
Cumbria, England
Broadleigh Gardens
Somerset, England
Brodie Castle
Grampian, Scotland
Clandon Park
Surrey, England
Erddig
Clwyd, Wales
Fota
Co. Cork, Republic of Ireland
Guy Wilson Daffodil Garden
Co. Derry, Northern Ireland
Petworth House
Sussex, West, England
RHS Garden, Wisley
Surrey, England

Stourhead
Wiltshire, England
Threave Garden
Dumfries & Galloway, Scotland

DAHLIAS
Biddulph Grange
Staffordshire, England
Butterfields Nursery
Buckinghamshire, England
Halls of Heddon
Northumberland and Tyne & Wear, England
Sam Oldham
Somerset, England
Philip Tivey & Son
Leicestershire, England
Valley Gardens
Yorkshire, North, England

DELPHINIUMS
8 Dunstarn Lane
Yorkshire, West, England
Blackmore & Langdon
Somerset, England
Falkland Palace
Fife, Scotland
Godington Park
Kent, England
Haddon Hall
Derbyshire, England
RHS Garden, Wisley
Surrey, England
Rougham Hall Nurseries
Suffolk, England

FERNS
Brodsworth Hall
Yorkshire, South, England
National Botanic Gardens
Co. Dublin, Republic of Ireland
Rickard's Hardy Ferns Ltd
Worcestershire, England
Royal Botanic Garden, Edinburgh
Lothian, Scotland
Royal Botanic Gardens, Kew
London, England
Sherborne Garden
Somerset, England

Sizergh Castle
Cumbria, England

FUCHSIAS
Margam Park
Glamorgan, Wales

GLADIOLI
RHS Garden, Wisley
Surrey, England

GLASSHOUSES
Birmingham Botanical Gardens & Glasshouses
West Midlands, England
Cambridge University Botanic Garden
Cambridgeshire, England
Canal Gardens & Tropical World
Yorkshire, West, England
The Eden Project
Cornwall, England
The Living Rainforest
Berkshire, England
The National Botanic Garden of Wales
Dyfed, Wales
National Botanic Gardens
Co. Dublin, Republic of Ireland
Ness Botanic Gardens
Cheshire, England
Plantasia
Glamorgan, Wales
RHS Garden, Wisley
Surrey, England
Royal Botanic Garden, Edinburgh
Lothian, Scotland
Royal Botanic Gardens, Kew
London, England
Sir George Staunton Country Park
Hampshire, England
University of Durham Botanic Garden
Co. Durham, England
University of Leicester Botanic Garden
Leicestershire, England

HEATHERS
The Bannut
Herefordshire, England
Bell's Cherrybank Gardens
Tayside, Scotland
Bicton Park Gardens
Devon, England
Blencathra
Berkshire, England
Champs Hill
Sussex, West, England
Exeter University Gardens
Devon, England
Floraldene
Sussex, West, England
Jack Drake
Highland, Scotland
National Botanic Gardens
Co. Dublin, Republic of Ireland
Ness Botanic Gardens
Cheshire, England
RHS Garden, Wisley
Surrey, England
Royal Botanic Garden, Edinburgh
Lothian, Scotland
Threave Garden
Dumfries & Galloway, Scotland
Valley Gardens
Surrey, England

HEBES
Siskin Plants
Suffolk, England
University of Bristol Botanic Garden
Gloucestershire, England

HEMEROCALLIS
Antony House
Cornwall, England
Apple Court
Hampshire, England
Ann & Roger Bowden
Devon, England
Goldbrook Plants
Suffolk, England
Rosewood Daylilies
Kent, England

HERBACEOUS PLANTS
Barrington Court
Somerset, England
Beningbrough Hall
Yorkshire, North, England
Beth Chatto Gardens
Essex, England
Buscot Park
Oxfordshire, England
The Courts
Wiltshire, England
The National Botanic Garden of Wales
Dyfed, Wales
National Botanic Gardens
Co. Dublin, Republic of Ireland
Nymans
Sussex, West, England
Packwood House
Warwickshire, England
RHS Garden, Hyde Hall
Essex, England
RHS Garden, Wisley
Surrey, England
Royal Botanic Gardens, Kew
London, England
Savill Garden
Surrey, England
Tintinhull House
Somerset, England
Upton House
Warwickshire, England
Wallington
Northumberland and Tyne & Wear, England

HERBS
Acorn Bank Garden
Cumbria, England
The National Botanic Garden of Wales
Dyfed, Wales
RHS Garden, Rosemoor
Devon, England
RHS Garden, Wisley
Surrey, England
Royal Botanic Gardens, Kew
London, England
Salley Gardens
Nottinghamshire, England

University of Leicester Botanic Garden
Leicestershire, England

The Walled Garden
Worcestershire, England

HOSTAS

Apple Court
Hampshire, England

Ann & Roger Bowden
Devon, England

Goldbrook Plants
Suffolk, England

Park Green Nurseries
Suffolk, England

IRISES

Broadleigh Gardens
Somerset, England

Croftway Nursery
Sussex, West, England

Kelways Ltd
Somerset, England

Marwood Hill Gardens
Devon, England

Mill Hill Plants
Nottinghamshire, England

LILIES

Ness Botanic Gardens
Cheshire, England

Old Rectory Cottage
Berkshire, England

MAGNOLIAS

Batsford Arboretum
Gloucestershire, England

Caerhays Castle Gardens
Cornwall, England

Lanhydrock
Cornwall, England

Marwood Hill Gardens
Devon, England

RHS Garden, Wisley
Surrey, England

Savill Garden
Surrey, England

Spinners
Hampshire, England

Valley Gardens
Surrey, England

ORCHIDS

Butterfields Nursery
Buckinghamshire, England

Glasgow Botanic Garden
Strathclyde, Scotland

Kelways Ltd
Somerset, England

RHS Garden, Wisley
Surrey, England

Royal Botanic Garden, Edinburgh
Lothian, Scotland

Royal Botanic Gardens, Kew
London, England

Scone Palace
Tayside, Scotland

PLANTSMAN'S GARDENS

Beth Chatto Gardens
Essex, England

Biddulph Grange
Staffordshire, England

Birkheads Cottage Garden Nursery
Northumberland and Tyne & Wear, England

Cally Gardens
Dumfries & Galloway, Scotland

Cambridge University Botanic Garden
Cambridgeshire, England

Cannington College Heritage Garden
Somerset, England

Copton Ash Gardens
Kent, England

Cotswold Garden Flowers
Worcestershire, England

The Courts
Wiltshire, England

Crûg Farm Plants
Gwynedd, Wales

Cruickshank Botanic Garden
Grampian, Scotland

Dell Garden
Norfolk, England

The Dillon Garden
Co. Dublin, Republic of Ireland

Dundee Botanic Garden
Tayside, Scotland

The Garden House
Devon, England

Great Dixter
Sussex, East, England

Greencombe Gardens
Somerset, England

Harlow Carr Botanical Gardens
Yorkshire, North, England

The Harris Garden
Berkshire, England

Hinton Ampner House
Hampshire, England

Home Covert
Wiltshire, England

Longthatch
Hampshire, England

The Manor House
Somerset, England

Marwood Hill Gardens
Devon, England

National Botanic Gardens
Co. Dublin, Republic of Ireland

Nymans
Sussex, West, England

Old Rectory Cottage
Berkshire, England

Oxford Botanic Garden
Oxfordshire, England

RHS Garden, Hyde Hall
Essex, England

Rowallane Garden
Co. Down, Northern Ireland

Royal Botanic Garden, Edinburgh
Lothian, Scotland

Royal Botanic Gardens, Kew
London, England

Savill Garden
Surrey, England

Scotney Castle
Kent, England

Sheffield Park
Sussex, East, England

Sherborne Garden
Somerset, England

Spetchley Park
Worcestershire, England

St Andrews Botanic Garden
Fife, Scotland

Talbot Botanic Gardens
Co. Dublin, Republic of Ireland
University of Birmingham Botanic
Garden
West Midlands, England
University of Durham Botanic
Garden
Co. Durham, England
Valley Gardens
Surrey, England

PRIMROSES
Edrom Nurseries
Borders, Scotland

RHODODENDRONS & AZALEAS
Achamore Gardens
Strathclyde, Scotland
Angus Garden
Strathclyde, Scotland
Blackhills
Grampian, Scotland
Borde Hill Garden
Sussex, West, England
Cannizaro Park
London, England
Clyne Gardens
Glamorgan, Wales
Crarae Gardens
Strathclyde, Scotland
Dawyck Botanic Garden
Borders, Scotland
Dorothy Clive Garden
Staffordshire, England
Glenarn
Strathclyde, Scotland
Glendoick Gardens
Tayside, Scotland
Highclere Castle
Hampshire, England
Hodnet Hall Gardens
Shropshire, England
Hydon Nurseries
Surrey, England
Isabella Plantation
London, England
Knap Hill Nursery Ltd
Surrey, England

Lanhydrock
Cornwall, England
Lydney Park Gardens
Gloucestershire, England
Marwood Hill Gardens
Devon, England
Millais Nurseries
Surrey, England
Mount Stewart
Co. Down, Northern Ireland
Muncaster Castle
Cumbria, England
National Botanic Gardens
Co. Dublin, Republic of Ireland
Ness Botanic Gardens
Cheshire, England
Nymans
Sussex, West, England
The Old Glebe
Devon, England
Petworth House
Sussex, West, England
Plas Newydd
Gwynedd, Wales
Ramster
Surrey, England
RHS Garden, Wisley
Surrey, England
Rowallane Garden
Co. Down, Northern Ireland
Royal Botanic Gardens, Kew
London, England
Savill Garden
Surrey, England
Scotney Castle
Kent, England
Sheffield Park
Sussex, East, England
Sherwood
Devon, England
Stourhead
Wiltshire, England
Trengwainton Gardens
Cornwall, England
Valley Gardens
Surrey, England
Wentworth Castle Gardens
Yorkshire, South, England
Younger Botanic Garden
Strathclyde, Scotland

ROCK GARDENS
Cambridge University Botanic
Garden
Cambridgeshire, England
Cruickshank Botanic Garden
Grampian, Scotland
Dorothy Clive Garden
Staffordshire, England
Mount Stuart
Strathclyde, Scotland
National Botanic Gardens
Co. Dublin, Republic of Ireland
Ness Botanic Gardens
Cheshire, England
RHS Garden, Wisley
Surrey, England
Royal Botanic Garden, Edinburgh
Lothian, Scotland
Royal Botanic Gardens, Kew
London, England

ROSES, MODERN
Benvarden Garden & Grounds
Co. Antrim, Northern Ireland
Chartwell
Kent, England
David Austin Roses
Shropshire, England
The Gardens of the Rose
Hertfordshire, England
Mannington Gardens
Norfolk, England
Mattocks Roses
Oxfordshire, England
RHS Garden, Hyde Hall
Essex, England
RHS Garden, Rosemoor
Devon, England
RHS Garden, Wisley
Surrey, England
Royal Botanic Gardens, Kew
London, England
University of Birmingham Botanic
Garden
West Midlands, England

ROSES, OLD
Cruickshank Botanic Garden
Grampian, Scotland

David Austin Roses
Shropshire, England
Drum Castle
Grampian, Scotland
The Gardens of the Rose
Hertfordshire, England
Hardwick Hall
Derbyshire, England
Hunts Court
Gloucestershire, England
Kiftsgate Court
Gloucestershire, England
Mottisfont Abbey
Hampshire, England
Ness Botanic Gardens
Cheshire, England
Nymans
Sussex, West, England
Peter Beales Roses
Norfolk, England
RHS Garden, Hyde Hall
Essex, England
RHS Garden, Rosemoor
Devon, England
Royal Botanic Gardens, Kew
London, England
University of Birmingham Botanic Garden
West Midlands, England
Westbury Court
Gloucestershire, England
Wiltshire College Lackham
Wiltshire, England

SNOWDROPS
Benington Lordship
Hertfordshire, England
East Lambrook Manor
Somerset, England
Hodsock Priory
Nottinghamshire, England
Plas-yn-Rhiw
Gwynedd, Wales
Snape Cottage
Dorset, England

SUBTROPICAL PLANTS
Abbotsbury Sub-Tropical Gardens
Dorset, England

Achamore Gardens
Strathclyde, Scotland
Derreen
Co. Kerry, Republic of Ireland
Dunster Castle
Somerset, England
The Eden Project
Cornwall, England
Exeter University Gardens
Devon, England
Fota
Co. Cork, Republic of Ireland
Knoll Gardens
Dorset, England
Logan Botanic Gardens
Dumfries & Galloway, Scotland
Meon Orchard
Hampshire, England
Mount Stewart
Co. Down, Northern Ireland
Mount Stuart
Strathclyde, Scotland
The Palm Centre
Surrey, England
Penrhyn Castle
Gwynedd, Wales
Rowallane Garden
Co. Down, Northern Ireland
Royal Botanic Gardens, Kew
London, England
Talbot Botanic Gardens
Co. Dublin, Republic of Ireland
Torosay Castle & Gardens
Strathclyde, Scotland
Trelissick Garden
Cornwall, England
Trengwainton Gardens
Cornwall, England
University of Bristol Botanic Garden
Gloucestershire, England
Ventnor Botanic Garden
Isle of Wight, England
Westdale Nurseries
Wiltshire, England

TOPIARY
Abbotsford
Borders, Scotland

Athelhampton
Dorset, England
Chirk Castle
Clwyd, Wales
Drummond Castle Gardens
Tayside, Scotland
Graythwaite Hall
Cumbria, England
Herterton House Gardens
Northumberland and Tyne & Wear, England
Langley Boxwood Nursery
Hampshire, England
Levens Hall
Cumbria, England
Packwood House
Warwickshire, England
Pitmedden
Grampian, Scotland
The Romantic Garden Nursery
Norfolk, England

VIOLAS
Elizabeth MacGregor
Dumfries & Galloway, Scotland
C W Groves & Son
Dorset, England

WILD FLOWERS
The Garden House
Devon, England
Naturescape
Nottinghamshire, England

WOODLAND GARDENS
Hodnet Hall Gardens
Shropshire, England
Mount Stewart
Co. Down, Northern Ireland
RHS Garden, Wisley
Surrey, England
Rowallane Garden
Co. Down, Northern Ireland
Savill Garden
Surrey, England
Spinners
Hampshire, England
Valley Gardens
Surrey, England

UNITED KINGDOM &
REPUBLIC OF IRELAND

ATLANTIC OCEAN

NORTH SEA

MAP 20

SCOTLAND

MAP 19

NORTHERN
IRELAND

MAP 18

MAP 17

ENGLAND

MAP 22

MAP 16

Irish Sea

REPUBLIC
OF
IRELAND

MAP 15

MAP 14

MAP 12 MAP 13

MAP 21 MAP 11

WALES

MAP 10

MAP 8

MAP 9

MAP 7

MAP 5

Celtic Sea

MAP 6

MAP 4

MAP 2 MAP 3

MAP 1

English Channel

0   40   80 Km
0   20   40 Miles

Key To Garden Location Maps

———— Coastline	M1 Motorway	Urban Area
———— International Border	A5 Dual Carriageway	○ Settlement
———— Regional Border	A15 Main Road	❋ Garden Location
———— County Border	———— Minor Road	

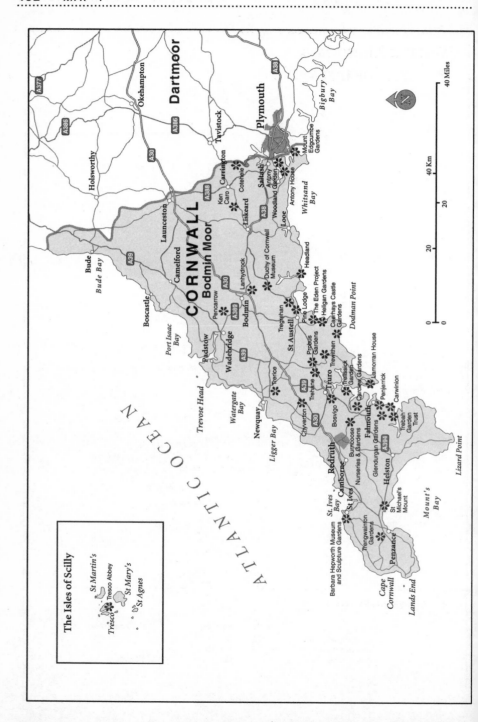

MAP 2 • **433**

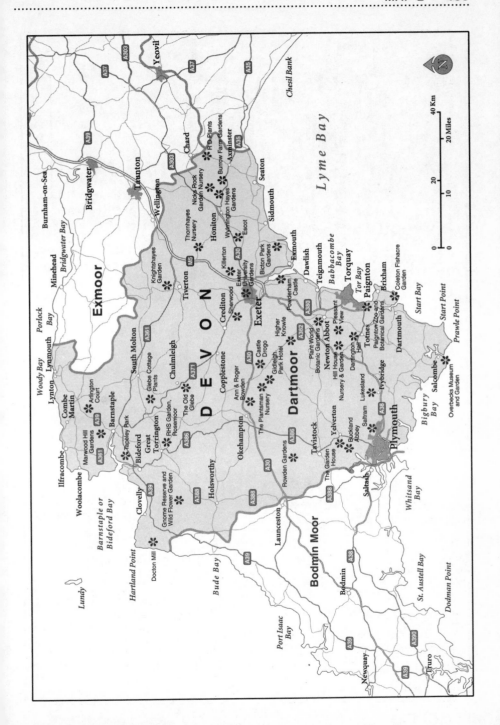

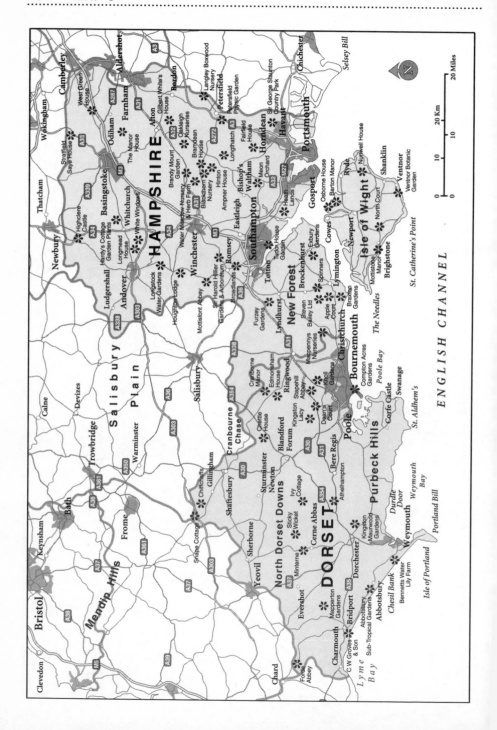

MAP 4 • **435**

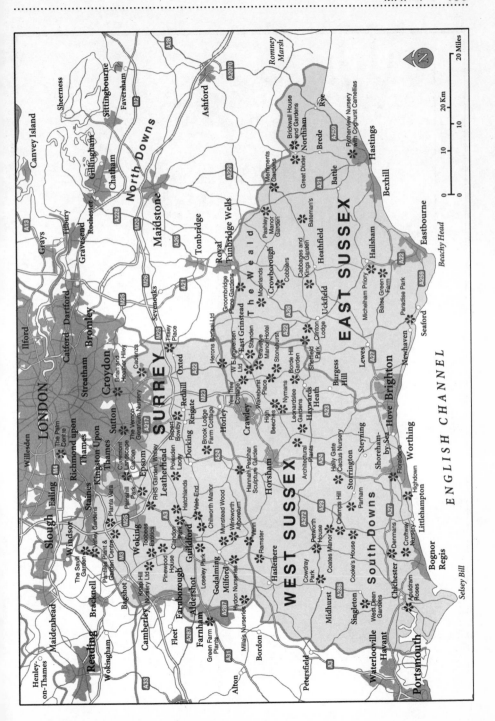

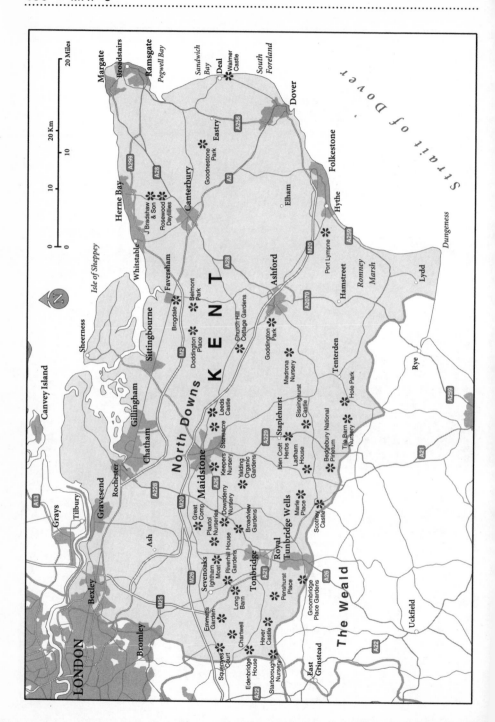

MAP 6 • **437**

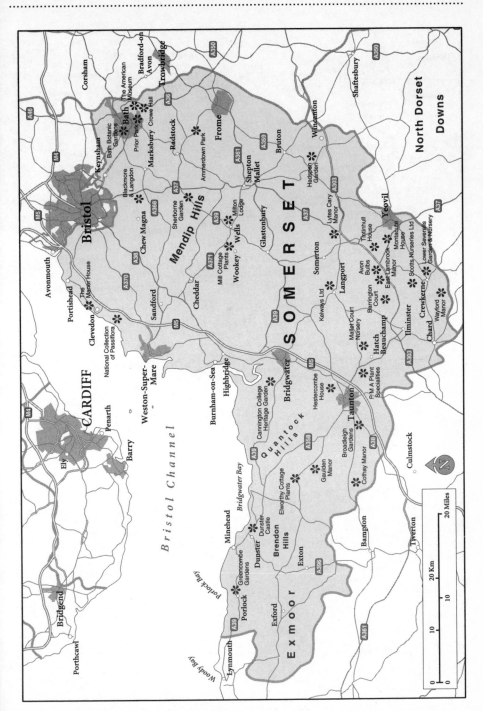

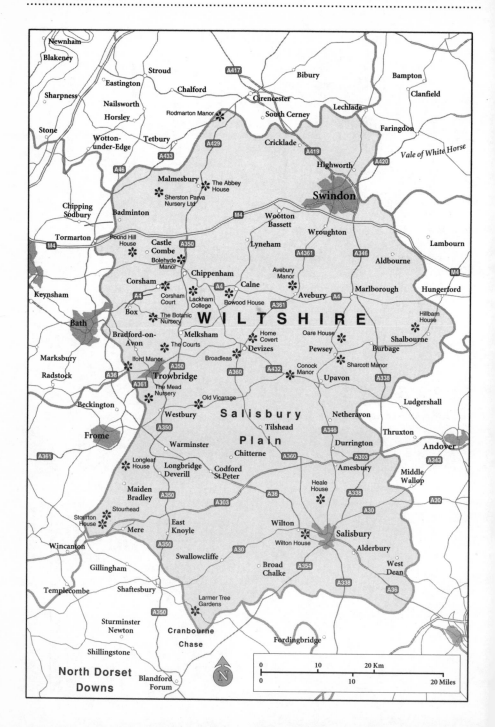

MAP 8 • **439**

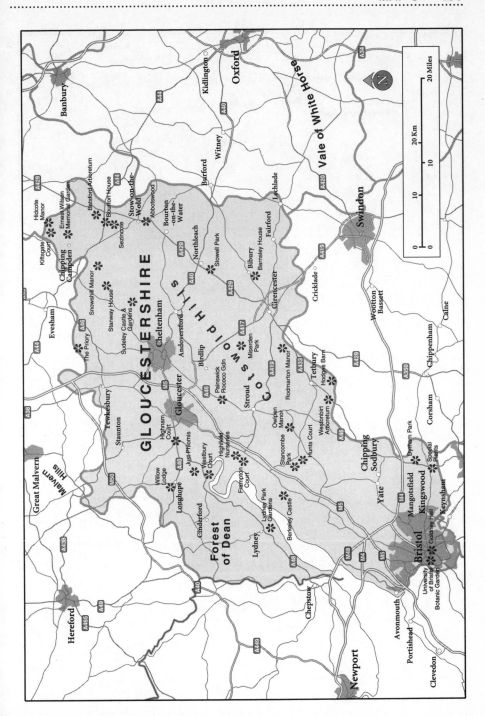

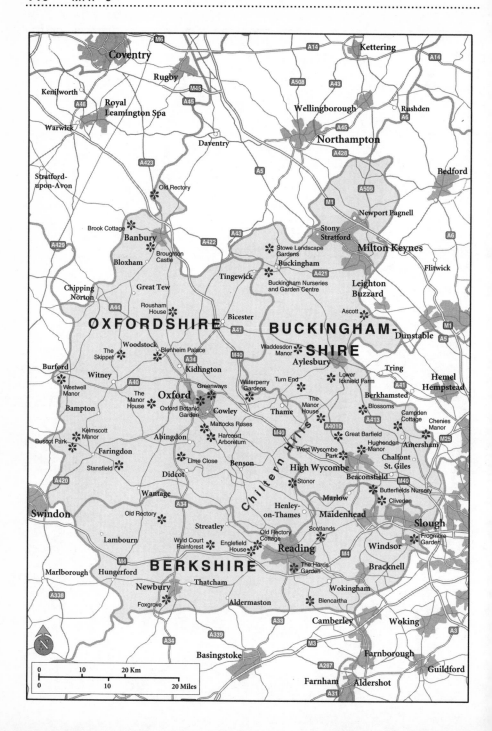

MAP 10 • 441

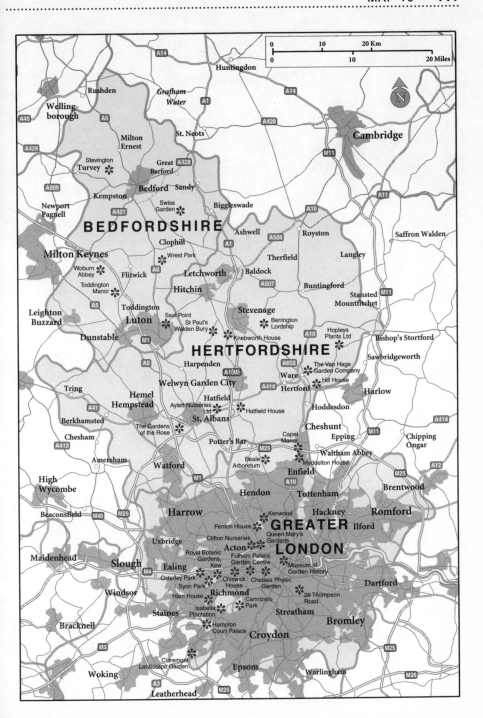

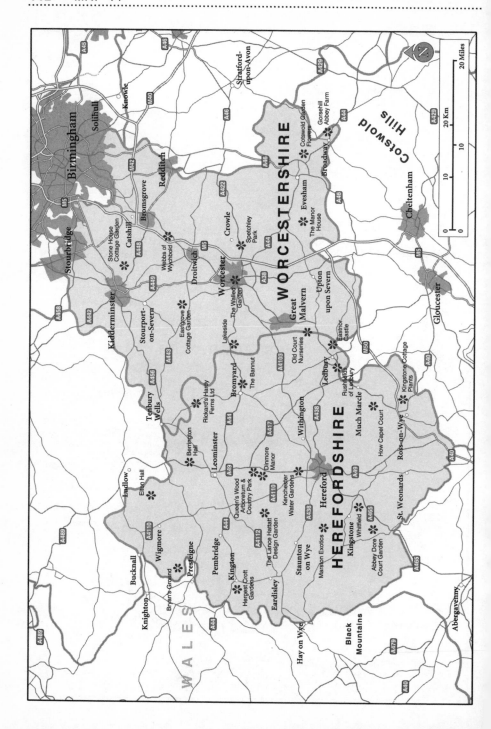

MAP 12 • **443**

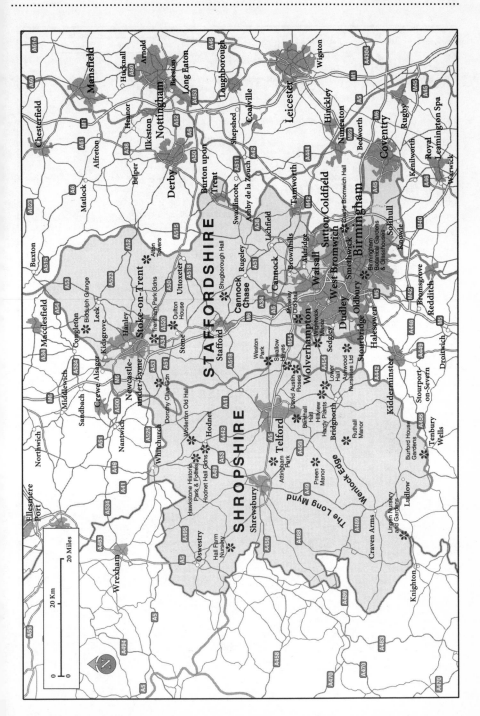

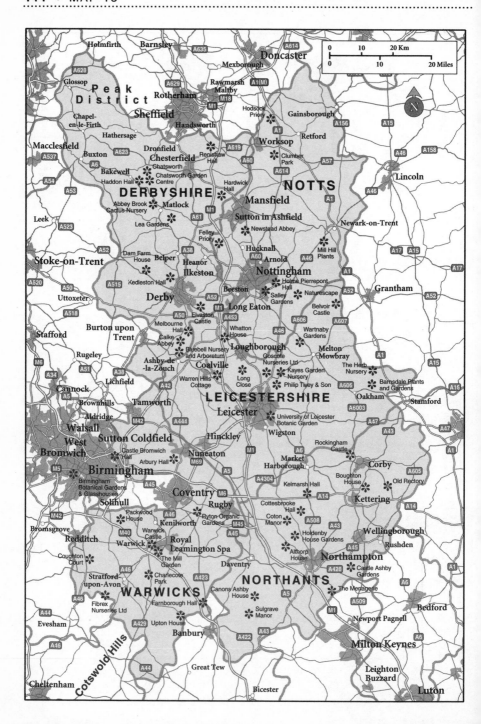

MAP 14 • **445**

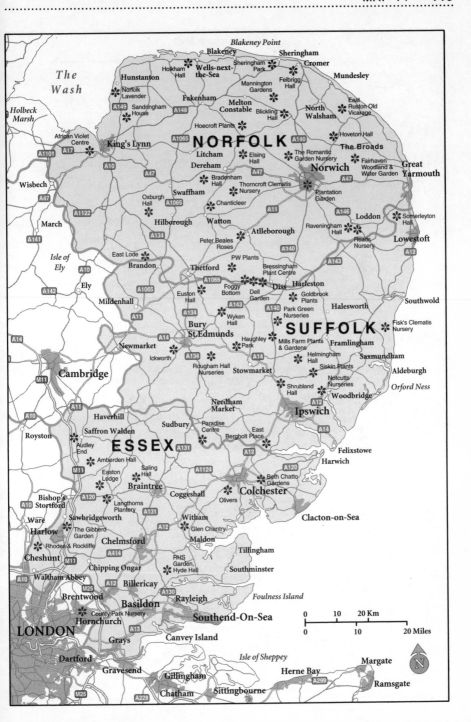

The Wash

Holbeck Marsh

NORFOLK

Blakeney Point
Blakeney
Sheringham
Sheringham Park
Cromer
Hunstanton
Holkham Hall
Wells-next-the-Sea
Mundesley
Norfolk Lavender
Mannington Gardens
Felbrigg Hall
Sandringham House
Fakenham
Melton Constable
Blickling Hall
North Walsham
East Ruston Old Vicarage
Hoecroft Plants
Hoveton Hall
African Violet Centre
King's Lynn
Litcham
Dereham
Elsing Hall
The Romantic Garden Nursery
The Broads
Norwich
Fairhaven Woodland & Water Garden
Great Yarmouth
Wisbech
Bradenham Hall
Thorncroft Clematis Nursery
Oxburgh Hall
Swaffham
Chanticleer
Plantation Garden
March
Hilborough
Watton
A146
Loddon
Somerleyton Hall
Peter Beales Roses
Atlleborough
Raveningham Hall
Lowestoft
Isle of Ely
East Lode
Brandon
PW Plants
Reade Nursery
Ely
Thetford
Bressingham Plant Centre
Mildenhall
Foggy Bottom
Dell Garden
Diss
Harleston
Euston Hall
Goldbrook Plants
Southwold
Wyken Hall
Park Green Nurseries
Halesworth
Fisk's Clematis Nursery
SUFFOLK
Bury St Edmunds
Haughley Park
Mills Farm Plants & Gardens
Framlingham
Newmarket
Ickworth
Helmingham Hall
Saxmundham
Cambridge
Rougham Hall Nurseries
Stowmarket
Siskin Plants
Aldeburgh
Shrubland Hall
Notcutts Nurseries
Orford Ness
Woodbridge
Needham Market
Ipswich
Haverhill
Saffron Walden
Sudbury
Paradise Centre
East Bergholt Place
ESSEX
Royston
Audley End
Amberden Hall
Felixstowe
Harwich
Easton Lodge
Saling Hall
Braintree
Coggeshall
Olivers
Beth Chatto Gardens
Colchester
Bishop's Stortford
Langthorns Plantery
Clacton-on-Sea
Ware
Sawbridgeworth
Witham
Glen Chantry
Harlow
The Gibberd Garden
Chelmsford
Maldon
Tillingham
Rhodes & Rockliffe
Cheshunt
RHS Garden, Hyde Hall
Southminster
Chipping Ongar
Waltham Abbey
Billericay
LONDON
Brentwood
Basildon
Rayleigh
Foulness Island
County Park Nursery
Hornchurch
Southend-On-Sea
Grays
Canvey Island
Dartford
Isle of Sheppey
Margate
Gravesend
Gillingham
Herne Bay
Ramsgate
Chatham
Sittingbourne

0   10   20 Km
0   10   20 Miles

N

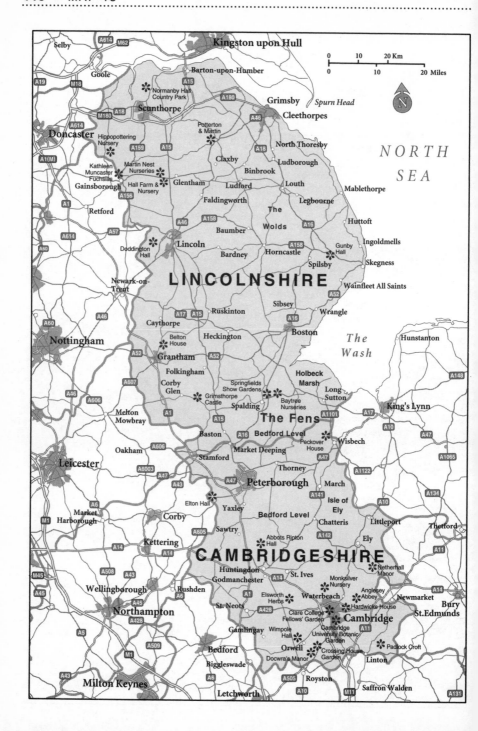

MAP 16 • **447**

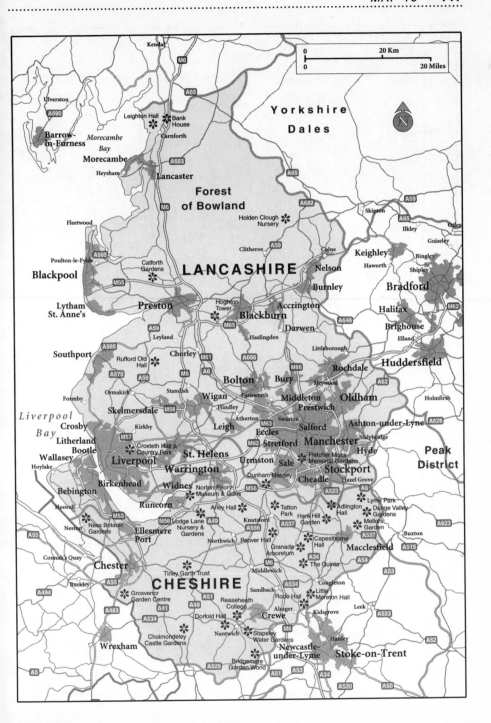

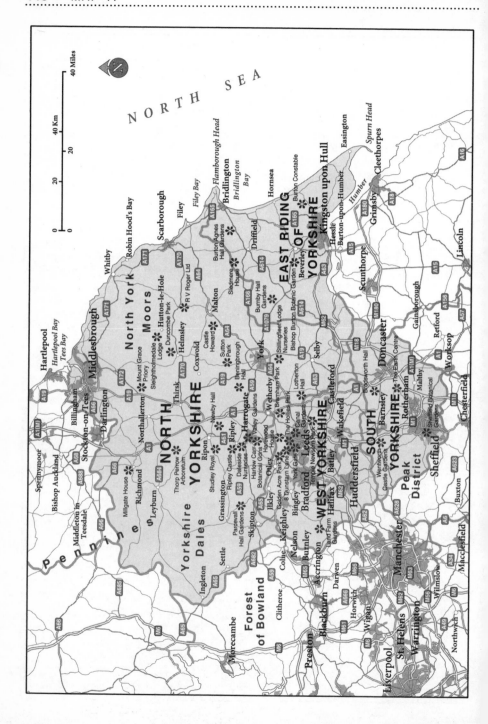

MAP 18 • 449

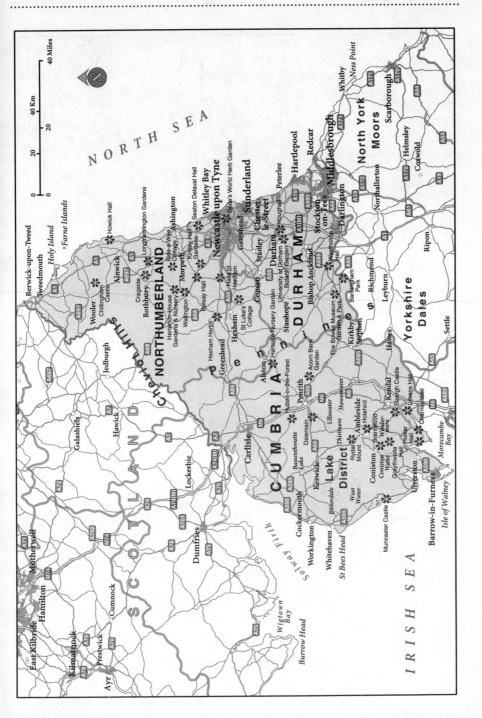

MAP 20 • 451

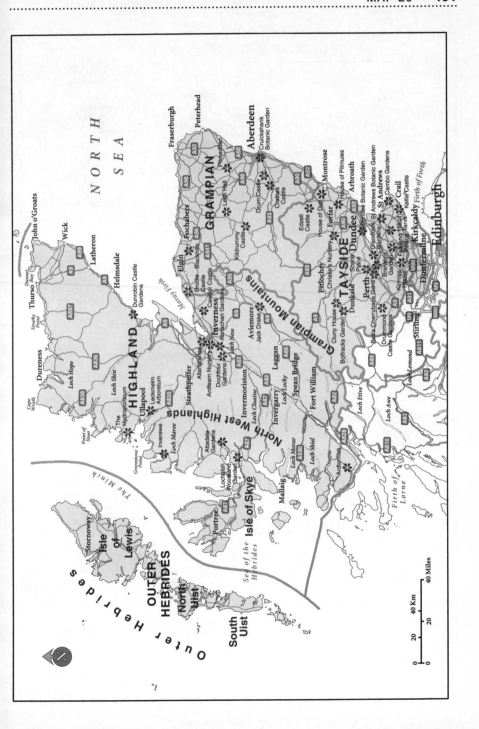

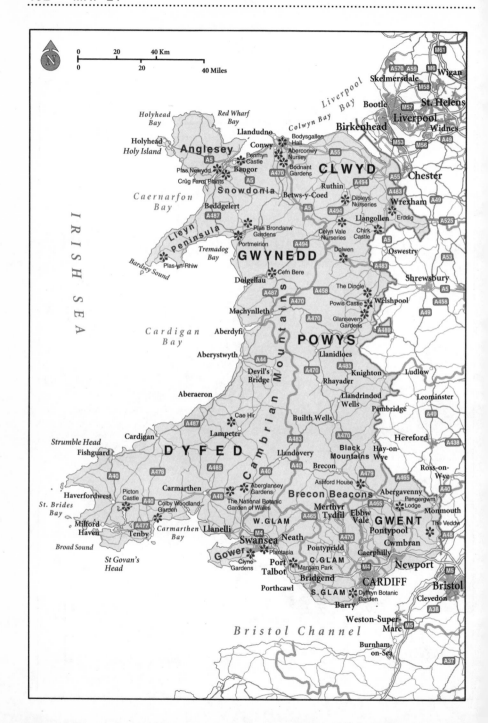

N

0   20   40 Km
0   20   40 Miles

Holyhead Bay
Red Wharf Bay
Holyhead
Holy Island
Llandudno
Anglesey
Conwy
Penrhyn Castle
Bangor
Bodysgallen Hall
Colwyn Bay
Birkenhead
Aberconwy Nursey
Bodnant Gardens
A5
A470
CLWYD
A55
Chester
A55
A483
Plas Newydd
Crûg Farm Plants
Snowdonia
Ruthin
Betws-y-Coed
Dibleys Nurseries
Wrexham
A49
Erddig
A525
Caernarfon Bay
Beddgelert
A487
Plas Brondanw Gardens
Portmeirion
Llangollen
Celyn Vale Nurseries
Chirk Castle
A5
Oswestry
A53
Lleyn Peninsula
Tremadog Bay
GWYNEDD
A494
Dolwen
A483
Bardsey Sound
Plas-yn-Rhiw
Cefn Bere
The Dingle
Shrewsbury
A5
Dolgellau
A487
A470
Powis Castle
Welshpool
A458
Cardigan Bay
Machynlleth
A470
Glansevern Gardens
A489
A49
Aberdyfi
POWYS
Aberystwyth
Llanidloes
Ludlow
Devil's Bridge
A44
A470
A483
Knighton
Rhayader
Leominster
Aberaeron
Llandrindod Wells
Pembridge
A49
Cae Hir
Builth Wells
Hereford
A438
Cardigan
Lampeter
A487
Strumble Head
Fishguard
A483
A470
DYFED
Llandovery
Black Mountains
Hay-on-Wye
Picton Castle
A40
A478
A485
Carmarthen
Aberglansey Gardens
Brecon
Ross-on-Wye
A465
A40
Haverfordwest
St. Brides Bay
Colby Woodland Garden
A40
The National Botanic Garden of Wales
A48
Ashford House
Brecon Beacons
Abergavenny
Pengerrwm Lodge
Monmouth
A465
A48
Milford Haven
A477
Tenby
Carmarthen Bay
Llanelli
W. GLAM
Merthyr Tydfil
Ebbw Vale
GWENT
The Veddw
Broad Sound
Swansea
Neath
A470
Pontypool
Cwmbran
St Govan's Head
Gower
Plantasia
Clyne Gardens
Port Talbot
Pontypridd
Margam Park
C. GLAM
Caerphilly
M4
Newport
M5
Bridgend
CARDIFF
Bristol
Porthcawl
S. GLAM
Dyffryn Botanic Garden
Clevedon
A38
Barry
Weston-Super-Mare
M5
Bristol Channel
Burnham-on-Sea
A37

I R I S H   S E A

Liverpool Bay
Skelmersdale
Wigan
A570 A59 M6
M58
Bootle
St. Helens
M57
Liverpool
Widnes
M53
M56
A49

Cambrian Mountains

MAP 22 • **453**

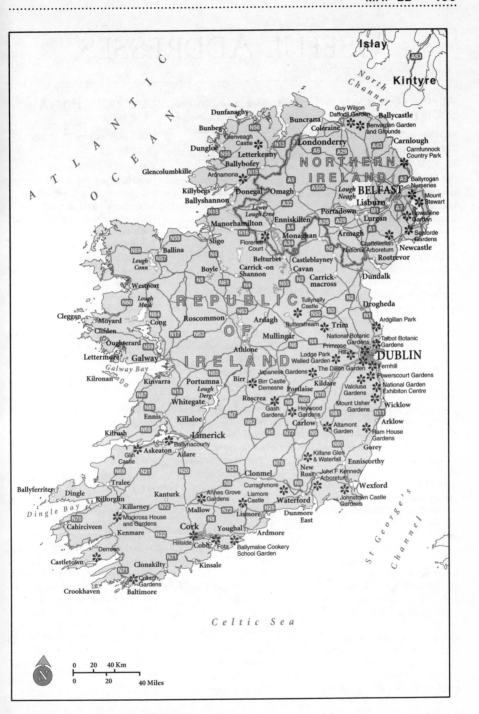

Islay

Kintyre

North Channel

A83

A T L A N T I C   O C E A N

Dunfanaghy
N56
Bunbeg
Glenveagh Castle
Dunglo
N56
N13
Letterkenny
Ballybofey
Glencolumbkille
Ardnamona
N15
Killybegs
Donegal
Omagh
Ballyshannon
Lower Lough Erne
N15
Manorhamilton
N59
Sligo
N4
Florence Court
Belturbet
Carrick-on Shannon
Ballina
Lough Conn
N57
Boyle
N5
N61
N4
N55
Westport
Lough Mask
N60
Cleggan
Moyard
N84
Cong
Roscommon
N63
Ardagh
Clifden
N17
N63
Oughterard
N59
Mullingar
Lettermore
Galway
Galway Bay
Athlone
N6
N4
Kilronan
Kinvarra
N67
Portumna
Lough Derg
N18
Birr
Whitegate
N65
Japanese Gardens
Ennis
Killaloe
N7
Roscrea
N8
Kilrush
N68
Limerick
N62
N8
Ballynacourty
Askeaton
Adare
Glin Castle
N69
N21
N20
N24
Clonmel
Tralee
N8
Curraghmore
Ballyferriter
Dingle
Kanturk
Annes Grove Gardens
Killorglin
Killarney
Mallow
N72
Lismore Castle
Cahirciveen
N70
Muckross House and Gardens
N22
Youghal
Kenmare
Hillside
Cobh
Fota
Ardmore
Castletown
Derreen
N71
Clonakilty
Kinsale
Crookhaven
Creagh Gardens
Baltimore

Guy Wilson Daffodil Garden
Buncrana
Coleraine
Ballycastle
Benvarden Garden and Grounds
N13
Londonderry
A6
A29
A43
Carnlough
Carnfunnock Country Park
N56
NORTHERN
A5
IRELAND
A505
Lough Neagh
BELFAST
A2
Ballyrogan Nurseries
A32
Lisburn
Mount Stewart
Portadown
M1
A7
Rowallane Garden
Enniskillen
A28
A29
Lurgan
A1
Monaghan
A4
A34
Armagh
Castlewellan National Arboretum
Seaforde Gardens
N2
Newcastle
Cavan
Carrick-macross
N3
Rostrevor
N55
Dundalk
N2
Tullynally Castle
Drogheda
N3
N1
Ardgillan Park
N52
Trim
National Botanic Gardens
Talbot Botanic Gardens
Butterstream
Primrose Hill
DUBLIN
Lodge Park Walled Garden
The Dillon Garden
Fernhill
Birr Castle Demesne
Kildare
Valclusa Gardens
Powerscourt Gardens
National Garden Exhibiton Centre
Portlaoise
N80
N78
N8
Heywood Gardens
Mount Usher Gardens
Wicklow
Gash Gardens
N81
N11
Carlow
Altamont Garden
Arklow
N77
N9
Ram House Gardens
N80
Gorey
Kilfane Glen & Waterfall
N76
Enniscorthy
New Ross
John F Kennedy Arboretum
N9
Wexford
Lismore
Waterford
N25
Johnstown Castle Gardens
Lismore
Dunmore East
Ballymaloe Cookery School Garden

Cork
N71

St George's Channel

Celtic Sea

N

0   20   40 Km
0   20   40 Miles

USEFUL ADDRESSES

ALPINE GARDEN SOCIETY

AGS Centre, Avon Bank, Pershore, Worcester WR10 3JP
Tel 01386 554790
Fax 01386 554801
www.alpinegardensoc.org

Founded in 1929. The AGS caters for anyone interested in rock gardening or alpine plants. You join the national organisation which entitles you to numerous benefits including free entry to the 20 or so shows, the bulletin, the seed exchange scheme, and the advisory service. If you wish you can also join one of some 60 local groups: there is a small additional subscription which varies from group to group. You have to be a member of the national AGS in order to join. Local groups organise their own busy programmes of events, including lectures, shows and visits. The *Quarterly Bulletin of the Alpine Garden Society* is an authoritative illustrated magazine which covers alpines in cultivation and in the wild. The AGS organises guided expeditions to many countries for its members, and these are both popular and respected. It also publishes monographs and alpine title: members can also use the slide and postal book libraries. At local level, AGS groups are an excellent and informal way to learn and develop an interest in alpines. Some groups are more active than others: it depends on local demand. Many of the lecturers are acknowledged experts, as will be some of the group members. The dates for the national shows, and a number of group events, appear in the Event Finder on the RHS

website (www.rhs.org.uk). Most local groups allow members to bring guests and will usually admit visitors for a small charge, though if you expect to attend regularly then you should really sign up properly. AGS headquarters can put you in touch with your nearest group. The Society's newly-made rock garden at the AGS Centre, Pershore, is well worth a visit.

AMERICAN CONIFER SOCIETY

P O Box 3422, Crofton, MD 211–0422, USA
Tel 00 1 410 721 6611
www.conifersociety.org

A thriving international society – the best in its field – with a excellent Bulletin and a long calendar of events and tours. Members may attend regional meetings throughout USA and Canada. The emphasis is upon conifers that are dwarf or unusual. It also issues an annual US$500 grant to conserve and propagate dwarf or unusual cultivars.

AMERICAN HEMEROCALLIS SOCIETY

Department WWW, P O Box 10, Dexter, GA 31019, USA
www.daylilies.org

The Society's quarterly publication *The Daylily Journal* is both colourful and informative: it has articles on cultivation, hybridisation, new cultivars and forthcoming events. There are dozens of advertisements by nurseries in the States, where *Hemerocallis* are a major horticultural interest.

AMERICAN HOSTA SOCIETY

338 East Forestwood Street, Morton, IL 61550, USA
Tel 001 309 266 6013
www.hosta.org

The society brings together the activities of *Hosta* enthusiasts throughout North America. Some 50 local and state *Hosta* societies are amalgamated into half-a-dozen US regions, with a seventh for Canada. *The Hosta Yearbook* has details of all the societies' activities and a complete membership list. The quarterly *Hosta Journal* carries good articles on botany, classification, cultivation and new varieties from correspondents in US and abroad. The society also publishes a source list of some 30 US nurseries offering quality *Hosta* plants and acts as the international registrar for new varieties: sometimes over 100 a year.

AMERICAN IRIS SOCIETY

8426 Vine Valley Drive, Sun Valley, CA 9135–3656, USA
Tel 00 1 408 722 1810
www.irises.org

The society's main event is the National Convention, which will be held in York, Pennsylvania, on 21–24 May 2001. There are several dedicated specialist iris societies in USA, including the Spuria Iris Society, the Society for Japanese Iris and the Aril Society International: details on the website.

AMERICAN ORCHID SOCIETY

16700 AOS Lane, Delray Beach, FL 33446–4351, USA
Tel 00 1 561 404 2000
Fax 00 1 561 404 2100
www.orchidweb.org
A well-established, large (and growing) society with members all over the world and more than 500 affiliated societies. Members receive the monthly *AOS Bulletin*, a substantial publication with over 100 pages, many in full colour: the advertisements alone are an education. The *Awards Quarterly* and the society's scientific review *Lindleyana* are published separately. The society's website is very comprehensive and includes hundreds of images of orchids and a long list of international orchid shows and conferences.

AMERICAN PENSTEMON SOCIETY

P O Box 33, Plymouth, VT 05056, USA
Tel 001 412 238 4208
Members have access to the excellent Seed Exchange (15 free packets a year) as well as receiving the quarterly *Bulletin of the American Penstemon Society* which has articles on collecting, cultivation and hybridisation.

AMERICAN RHODODENDRON SOCIETY

11 Pinecrest Drive, Fortuna, CA 95540, USA
Tel 00 1 707 725 3043
Fax 00 1 707 725 1217
www.rhododendron.org
This is the leading, world-wide *Rhododendron* society, represented in UK by the Scottish Rhododendron Society. The American Rhododendron Society exists to encourage interest in and disseminate knowledge about rhododendrons and azaleas.

AMERICAN ROSE SOCIETY

P O Box 30,000, 8877 Jefferson Paige Road, Shreveport, LA 71130–0030, USA
Tel 00 1 318 938 5402
Fax 00 1 318 938 5405
www.ars.org
The world's largest rose society, founded in 1892 and based in the 118-acre Gardens of the American Rose Center. It has nearly 400 affiliated societies and a steady membership. Traditionally concerned with modern roses, it is increasingly involved in the heritage rose movement. The monthly *American Rose Magazine* and the yearly *American Rose Annual* are quality publications.

ARBORICULTURAL ASSOCIATION

Ampfield House, Romsey, Hampshire SO51 9PA
Tel 01794 368717
Fax 01794 368978
www.trees.org.uk
A registered charity and the professional body for over 2,000 arboriculturists. The AA publishes a useful directory of consultants and contractors who have met the organisation's stringent standards for training, work and insurance: contact the Secretariat for details. A range of other publications is also available. There is a local group structure, and keen amateurs can join as part of the Tree Club.

ASSOCIATION OF GARDEN TRUSTS

70 Cowcross Street, London EC1M 6EJ
Tel 020 7251 2610
www.gardenstrusts.Couk
The association is a national organisation representing county gardens trusts. It provides support for the trusts and encourages the sharing of information, resources, training and experience. It aims to promote a proper understanding of the importance of parks and gardens at local and national level. The is a list of all the individual county gardens trusts on the AGT's website, plus links to those which have websites of their own.

THE ASSOCIATION OF SOCIETIES FOR GROWING AUSTRALIAN PLANTS

P O Box 744 Place, Blacktown, NSW 2148, Australia
Tel 0061 2 9621 3437
Fax 0061 2 9621 7603
http://farrer.riv.csu.edu.au/ASGAP/
There are societies for growing native plants in every Australian state – this is the address of the New South Wales society – and many local societies within each state. The main benefits to members overseas are the excellent publications (a quarterly newsletter and an annual) and the comprehensive seed lists.

ASSOCIATION POUR LA SAUVEGARDE DU PATRIMOINE FRUITIER

4, avenue de la Résistance, F-30270 Saint Jean-du-Gard, France
Tel 00 33 4 66 85 33 37
Fax 00 33 4 66 86 19 66
A conservation group devoted to fruit – everything from apples and pears to olives and figs. The

excellent quarterly bulletin *Fruits Oubliés* is subtitled *Revue de Pomologie Vivante* and *Sauve qui Pomme.*

BIO-DYNAMIC AGRICULTURE ASSOCIATION

Woodman Lane, Clent, Stourbridge, West Midlands DY9 9PX
Tel 01562 884933
Offers help to bio-dynamic growers: bio-dynamics are based on the anthroposophical theories of Rudolph Steiner and combine organic principles with celestial ones. The phase of the moon is believed to influence planting times.

BONSAI CLUBS INTERNATIONAL

P O Box 1176, Brookfield, WI 53008–1176, USA
Tel 00 1 414 860 8807
Fax 00 1 414 641 0757
The top American organisation for Bonsai clubs publishes the excellent bi-monthly magazine *Bonsai.*

BOTANIC GARDENS CONSERVATION INTERNATIONAL

Descanso House, 199 Kew Road, Richmond, Surrey TW9 3BW
Tel 020 8332 5953
Fax 020 8332 5956
www.bgci.org.uk
Based at Kew, this organisation supports botanic gardens all over the world to use their resources for wild plant research, conservation, education and the promotion of environmental awareness.

BOTANICAL SOCIETY OF SCOTLAND

c/o Royal Botanic Garden, Edinburgh, Lothian EH3 5LR
Tel 0131 552 7171
www.rbge.org.uk/bss
This society was founded in 1836 – it was formerly the Botanical Society of Edinburgh. Based in Edinburgh, with regional branches in Scotland, the society includes amateur and professional botanists. It holds regular lectures, conferences and field meetings. Its publications include a newsletter and a scientific journal.

BOTANICAL SOCIETY OF SOUTH AFRICA

Kirstenbosch, Claremont, Cape Town 7735, South Africa
Tel 00 27 21 797 2090
www.botanicalsociety.org.za
Based at Kirstenbosch in Cape Province, the society has for many years been very successful in spreading information about the rich native flora of South Africa. Members have free entry to all the many regional gardens which it runs throughout the republic, as well as Kirstenbosch itself. The chief benefit to overseas members is the generous annual allocation of seed of native Cape species. The Society's exhibits have for many years been one of the sensations of the Chelsea Flower Show and, more recently, the Hampton Court Palace Flower show.

BOTANICAL SOCIETY OF THE BRITISH ISLES

c/o 41 Marlborough Road, Roath, Cardiff CF23 5BU
Tel 029 2049 6042
This association of amateur and professional botanists traces its history back to 1836. Three regular publications (*Watsonia, BSBI Abstracts* and *BSBI News*) cover the society's activities, articles on the taxonomy and distribution of plants in the British Isles, and an annual bibliography. The society also arranges conferences, exhibitions and study trips, and undertakes research projects and surveys. Members have access to a panel of experts on the British flora and can buy works on British botany at reduced prices.

BRITAIN IN BLOOM

Tidy Britain Group, The Pier, Wigan, Lancashire WN3 4EX
Tel 01942 824620
Fax 01942 8247778
www.tidybritain.org.uk
This popular organisation is dedicated to beautifying our cities, towns, villages and countryside. For administrative purposes it is split into about a dozen regions throughout the UK. Entry forms and advice are available from the regional organisers.

BRITISH & EUROPEAN GERANIUM SOCIETY

8 Roses Close, Wollaston, Wellingborough, Northamptonshire NN29 7ST
www.fitzjohn.linkuk.Couk/main.htm
The British & European Geranium Society is dedicated to growing, hybridising and exhibiting *Pelargonium*. The society is divided into regional groups which organise programmes of events including lectures and shows. There is an annual national show; every other year a conference is also staged. Members receive three *Gazettes* and a Year Book. The society has other publications too. A new service is a computerised plant finder which has details of sources for any pelargonium which is available in Europe.

BRITISH BEE-KEEPERS' ASSOCIATION

National Agricultural Association, Stoneleigh, Warwickshire CV8 2LZ
Tel 01203 696679
Fax 01203 690682
www.bbka.demon.Couk/index.htm
The BBA represents about 13,000 bee-keepers, mainly in England. It produces leaflets, runs seminars and conventions, supports local groups of bee-keepers and supervises examinations. It also represents the industry at UK and European government levels. There are membership associations throughout the country.

BRITISH CACTUS & SUCCULENT SOCIETY

15 Brentwood Crescent, York, North Yorkshire YO10 5HU
Tel 01904 410512
www.cactus-mall.com/bcss
Founded in 1983 by the amalgamation of two earlier cactus and succulent societies, the BCSS is the premier national society with associated branches in more than 100 towns throughout the British Isles. Members receive the quarterly *Journal*, a quality magazine with a wide range of good articles. The yearbook *Bradleya* is available for an extra payment. There is a good choice of activities to cater for all interests. The website is first-rate.

BRITISH CLEMATIS SOCIETY

4 Springfield, Lightwater, Surrey GU18 5XP
Tel 01276 476387
www.britishclematis.org.uk
A fast-growing society which organises meetings throughout the country and publishes a substantial illustrated journal, *The Clematis*, each year as well as supplements and newsletters. The society organises visits to gardens and nurseries. Members can obtain advice on clematis cultivation and join in the seed exchange programme. The society also produces a list of good clematis gardens and a list of clematis nurseries. It has established its trial grounds at the Gardens of the Rose.

BRITISH FUCHSIA SOCIETY

15 Summerfield Lane, Summerfield, Kidderminster, Hereford & Worcester DY11 7SA
Tel 01562 66688
The British Fuchsia Society organises a number of regional shows and a London show. Members receive the *Fuchsia Annual* and a twice-yearly bulletin, as well as three rooted cuttings. They can also obtain advice from the society's experts, either by post or telephone. Special interest groups are devoted to old cultivars and hybridising. Some 300 societies are affiliated to the national society, many of which organise programmes of events and festivals.

BRITISH GLADIOLUS SOCIETY

10 Greenway, Ashbourne, Derbyshire DE6 1EF
Tel 01335 346446
Founded in 1926 the British Gladiolus Society stages four major shows each year: the National, the Southern, the Midland and the Northern. There are regional groups in Sussex and Buckinghamshire. Members keep in touch with society news through three bulletins and the yearbook, *The Gladiolus Annual*, which is published each spring. The society runs trials at three sites, and also has a book, slide and video library available for members and affiliated societies. Council members can advise on gladiolus cultivation, and the society raises money by distributing cormlets. A small range of booklets on showing and growing gladiolus is also available.

BRITISH HOSTA & HEMEROCALLIS SOCIETY

Toft Monks, The Hithe, Rodborough Common, Stroud, Gloucestershire GL5 5BN
Founded in 1981, the British Hosta & Hemerocallis Society has members spread throughout the world. It publishes an annual bulletin, and regular newsletters to keep members informed of news and events. Garden visits and lectures are arranged, and members can borrow by post from the society's specialist and comprehensive library. An annual award is presented to a hosta and a hemerocallis. Expert advice is provided via the secretary. There are some eleven relevant NCCPG national collections.

THE BRITISH IRIS SOCIETY

1 Sole Farm Close, Great Bookham, Surrey KT23 3ED
Tel 01372 454581
The British Iris Society was founded in 1922 and caters for all levels of interest in this varied genus. The illustrated and authoritative *Iris Year Book* is supplemented by three newsletters. The society's programme includes three annual shows and occasional lectures. There are regional groups in Mercia and Kent, and special interest groups for species, Japanese, Siberian and Pacific Coast irises. Members can borrow from the reference library, and the

society has an extensive slide collection. As well as a plant sales scheme there is also a seed distribution scheme, and expert advice is available on request. New hybrids are trialled at Wisley, and the Dykes Medal is awarded to the best British-bred hybrid in the trial.

BRITISH MYCOLOGICAL SOCIETY

Dr Stephen Moss, School of Biological Sciences, Universioty of Portsmouth, Hampshire PO1 2DY
Tel 023 9252 5902
www.ulst.ac/faculty/science/bms/
This learned society was founded in 1896 and promotes the study of all types of fungi, from mushrooms to moulds. It has about 30 local groups.

THE BRITISH NATIONAL CARNATION SOCIETY

Linfield, Duncote, Towcester, Northamptonshire NN12 8AH
Tel 01327 351594
The British National Carnation Society was founded in 1949 and organises several shows annually: the principal ones are at RHS Westminster shows in June and October. Members receive the illustrated *Carnation Year Book* each year as well as two newsletters. New members can also choose one of the society's cultural booklets when they join. Medals and show cards are available for affiliated societies, and together the society and its affiliates hold area shows throughout the country. A coupon in the autumn newsletter gives a discount on plants from selected nurseries. A panel of experts can be called on to answer questions. Other societies can hire lectures: a fee is charged to non-affiliated societies.

THE BRITISH PELARGONIUM & GERANIUM SOCIETY

75 Pelham Road, Bexleyheath, Kent DA7 4LY
Tel 01322 525947
www.bpgs.org.uk
The British Pelargonium & Geranium Society was founded in 1951. It publishes a Year Book and three issues of *Pelargonium News* annually. The society's annual show, held in June, moves around the country, and includes classes for beginners and flower arrangers. Every other year a conference is held. Members can take advantage of a postal advisory service, and free seeds. They stage publicity and information stands at Chelsea, Malvern and the RHS London shows, and encourage other societies to join as affiliated members.

BRITISH PTERIDOLOGICAL SOCIETY

42 Crown Woods Way, Eltham, London SE9 2NN
www.nhm.ac.uk/hosted_sites/bps/
Now over 100 years old, this international society includes amateur and professional members. An annual *Bulletin* contains society news, whilst the *Pteridologist* prints articles and book reviews for the amateur enthusiast. The twice-yearly *Fern Gazette* includes more scientific papers: members who do not wish to receive this journal pay the lower optional subscription rate. According to season, activities include indoor meetings and field trips and garden visits. A spore exchange distributes fern spores from all over the world, whilst a postal plant exchange scheme helps members obtain rarely available or surplus plants. The society takes a

stand at the Malvern Spring Show and the Southport Show. Members can obtain advice on fern cultivation through the Hon. General Secretary.

BRITISH SOCIETY OF PLANT BREEDERS

Woolpack Chambers, Market Street, Ely, Cambridgeshire CB7 4ND
Tel 01353 664211
Fax 01353 661156
Represents the interests of commercial and state sector plan breeders covering farm crops, vegetables and ornamentals. The Society issues sub-licences and collects royalties from sub-licensees on behalf of plant breeders. It is an officially recognised body for conducting trials that are a legal requisite for National Listing of new varieties.

BRITISH TOURIST AUTHORITY

Thames Tower, Black's Road, Hammersmith, London W6 9EL
Tel 020 8846 9000
www.visitbritain.com
The BTA has an excellent website, full of information on gardens in England, Scotland and Wales. A list of British tourist information centres is available. Local centres can often provide information on gardens and events in their area.

BRITISH TRUST FOR CONSERVATION VOLUNTEERS (BTCV)

36 St Mary's Street, Wallingford, Oxfordshire OX10 0EU
Tel 01491 839766
Fax 01491 839646
www.btcv.org.uk/
Carries out practical conservation projects, including tree-planting. They run training courses and offer working conservation

holidays, including some involving garden restoration.

BUTTERFLY CONSERVATION

Manor Yard, East Lulworth, Wareham, Dorset BH20 5QP
Tel 01929 400209
Fax 01929 400210
www.butterfly-conservation.org
This thriving society works to safeguard the future of butterflies and moths. One way of doing so is to promote butterfly-friendly gardening.

CACTUS & SUCCULENT SOCIETY OF AMERICA

P O Box 2615, Pahrump,
NV 89041–2615, USA
Fax 001 702 751 1357
www.cssainc.org
The leading society in its field, with a good number of members from Europe and about 100 affiliated societies all over North America. All members receive the impressive bi-monthly *Cactus and Succulent Journal*. The society also publishes a scientific journal *Haseltonia*. The 2001 convention will be in Woodland Hills, California, from 1 to 6 July.

CADW: WELSH HISTORIC MONUMENTS

National Assembly for Wales, Cathays Park, Cardiff CF10 3NQ
Tel 029 2050 0200
Fax 029 2082 6375
www.wales.gov.uk
Cadw has nearly finished publishing its register of Parks & Gardens of Special Historic Interest in Wales. The standard modern work on the subject is *The Historic Gardens of Wales* by Elizabeth Whittle [HMSO, 1992].

CARNIVOROUS PLANT SOCIETY

100 Lambley Lane, Burton Joyce, Nottingham, Nottinghamshire NG14 5BL
The Carnivorous Plant Society publishes an annual colour journal and four newsletters. It organises a number of events including visits to nurseries, field trips and open days. A plant search scheme is run, and members have free access to the seed bank. The information officer can provide advice on all topics.

CENTRE FOR ALTERNATIVE TECHNOLOGY

Machynlleth, Powys SY20 9AZ
Tel 01654 702400
www.cat.org.uk
The centre demonstrates a range of sustainable technologies, including organic food production. It also runs courses, sells books and publishes information leaflets on environmental approaches to gardening.

COMMON GROUND

P O Box 25307, London NW5 1ZA
Tel 020 7267 2144
www.commonground.org.uk
Common Ground is rather an unusual environmental group. They publicise National Apple Day (21 October) and promote local distinctiveness. They initiated the idea of community orchards and have a very interesting publications list. Their main concern is to preserve and promote links between the environment and social culture.

CORNWALL GARDENS SOCIETY

Poltisko, Silver Hill, Parranwell Station, Truro, Cornwall TR3 7LP
Tel 01872 863300
A scaled-down model of the RHS, with an excellent magazine, good bulletins and a famous show. It also organises a garden scheme and publish a splendid Gardens Open guide.

THE COTTAGE GARDEN SOCIETY

Hurstfield House, 244 Edleston Road, Crewe, Cheshire CW2 7EJ
Tel 01270 250776
Fax 01270 250118
www.alfresCodemon.Couk/cgs/
The Cottage Garden Society promotes and conserves worthwhile old-fashioned garden plants, and encourages owners of small gardens to garden in the informal cottage style. Members receive a quarterly bulletin and can take part in the annual seed distribution. The society has a growing number of active regional groups: each organises lectures, meeting, visits and other events. The society hires out slides to members.

THE COUNTRYSIDE AGENCY

John Dower House, Crescent Place, Cheltenham, Gloucestershire GL50 3RA
Tel 01242 521381
www.countryside.gov.uk
The Countryside Commission is the agency charged with advising the government on matters relating to the countryside and landscape of England. It aims to ensure that the English countryside is protected and that it can be used and enjoyed now and for the future.

COUNTRYSIDE COUNCIL FOR WALES

Plas Penrhos, Ffordd Penrhos, Bangor, Gwynedd LL57 2LQ
Tel 01248 370444
Fax 01248 385506
www.ccw.gov.uk
The Council is the statutory advisor on wildlife and conservation in Wales and the executive authority for the preservation of its landscape.

THE CYCLAMEN SOCIETY

Tile Barn House, Standen Street, Iden Green, Benenden, Kent TN17 4LB
cyclamen.org.uk
The Cyclamen Society has an international membership but is based in Britain. Its work includes research and conservation, whilst members benefit from the twice-yearly journal, a seed distribution scheme and access to expert advice through the society's advisory panel. It exhibits and stages shows, organises meetings and lectures, and maintains a specialist library of literature and slides on cyclamen.

DAFFODIL SOCIETY

The Meadows, Puxton, Weston-super-Mare, Somerset BS24 6TF
Tel 01934 833641
www.daffsoc.freeserve.Couk
Established in 1898, the Society caters for breeders, exhibitors and lovers of daffodils. It also has over 200 affiliated societies as members. It is closely involved in the competitions at RHS London Flower shows, the Harrogate Spring show as well its own shows. Members receive the annual *Journal* in February and the *Newsletter* in July. In addition to the Seed Scheme, there are good

opportunities to acquire new cultivars in the annual Bulb Lottery.

THE DELPHINIUM SOCIETY

Takakkaw, Ice House Wood, Oxted, Surrey RH8 9DW
Tel 01883 715049
www.delphinium.demon.Couk
The Delphinium Society dates back to 1928. New members receive a mixed packet of seed when they join, and all members can buy the society's hand-pollinated seeds of garden hybrids and species. The illustrated Year Book is a unique source of information about the genus. Two shows, at which cups are awarded, are held each year. Members gain free entry to the shows, and can also take advantage of advice on cultivation and a number of social events.

DEUTSCHE KAKTEEN-GESELLSCHAFT E V

Oos-Strasse 18, D-75179 Pforzheim, Germany
Tel 00 49 7231 281550
www.deutschekakteengesellschaft.de
Founded in 1892, and one of the most distinguished horticultural associations in Europe. The Society has about 7,000 members and 125 affiliated local groups, and specialist working groups for *Astrophytum, Echinopsis, Gymnocalycium, Rebutia* and *Tephrocactus*. There is a large lending library of specialist books for members' use. The society also publishes a list of about 40 specialist cactus nurseries in Germany. The illustrated monthly journal *Kakteen und andere Sukkulenten* is of high quality, with informative articles of botanical and horticultural interest.

DEUTSCHE RHODODENDRON GESELLSCHAFT

Botanischer Garten und Rhododendronpark, Marcusallee 60, D-28359 Bremen, Germany
Tel 00 49 421 361 3025
Fax 00 49 421 361 3610
This Bremen-based society is a fair match for the RHS Rhododendron Group. Its publications illustrate its botanical and horticultural qualities: the *Jahrbuch* is an authoritative scientific publication while the handsomely illustrated quarterly magazine *Immergrüner Blätte* is of more horticultural interest but of equally high standard. In addition to the seed exchange, members are entitled to take a number of cuttings and pollen from the Rhododendron-park in Bremen: the Rhododend-ronpark is Germany's answer to the Savill Gardens and Valley Gardens in Windsor Great Park. The society gives awards to new *Rhododendron* cultivars and mounts a big exhibition every four years (next in 2002). Its annual study tours are an important feature of its events programme.

ENGLISH HERITAGE

Fortress House, 23 Savile Row, London W1X 1AB
Tel 020 7973 3000
Fax 020 7973 3146
www.english-heritage.org.uk
English Heritage is responsible for the national register of parks and gardens of special historic interest. Dr Harriet Jordan is currently overseeing a comprehensive upgrade of the register, with the aim of publishing a fully revised edition in 2001. Excellent website.

THE EUROPEAN BOXWOOD & TOPIARY SOCIETY

The Dower House, Crimp Hill, Old Windsor, Berkshire SL14 2HL
Tel 01753 854982
This young society has got off to a flying start with visits to famous topiary gardens in several European countries. The magazine *Topiarius* is a quality publication.

FAUNA & FLORA INTERNATIONAL

Great Eastern House, Tenison Road, Cambridge, Cambridgeshire CB1 2DT
Tel 01223 571000
Fax 01223 461481
www.fauna-flora.org.uk
The society was founded in 1903, which makes it the world's oldest conservation society: it now has over 4,000 individual members. Much of its energy is currently directed at the trade in wild-collected bulbs and creating indigenous plant areas in such countries as Turkey.

FORESTRY COMMISSION

231 Corstorphine Road, Edinburgh, Lothian EH12 7AT
Tel 0131 334 0303
Fax 0131 334 4473
www.forestry.gov.uk
The Commission's objectives are to protect Britain's forests and woodlands, expand Britain's forest area, enhance the economic value of our forest resources, conserve and improve the biodiversity or woodlands, develop recreational opportunities and increase public participation and understanding. It publishes an extremely useful telephone and address directory which outlines the work of every British organisation concerned with forestry. It has three divisions:

Forestry Authority and Forest Enterprise, and Forest Research.

FRIENDS OF BROGDALE

The Brogdale Horticultural Trust, Brogdale Farm, Faversham, Kent ME13 8XZ
Tel 01795 535286
Fax 01795 531710
The Brogdale Experimental Horticultural Station was bought from the government by the Brogdale Trust in 1991 to safeguard its work. It carries out commercial research and trialling, and maintains exceptional reference collections of fruit varieties, including over 2,300 different apples. Friends receive free entry to the site, priority booking for events, and access to a Friday afternoon information line. There is also a quarterly newsletter.

FRIENDS OF THE EARTH

26–28 Underwood Street, London N1 7JQ
Tel 020 7490 1555
Fax 020 7490 0881
www.foe.Couk
Friends of the Earth claims to campaign on more issues than any other environmental group in the country. Its website is extremely active.

FRIENDS OF THE ROYAL BOTANIC GARDEN EDINBURGH

The Royal Botanic Garden, Inverleith Row, Edinburgh EH3 5LR
Tel 0131 552 5339
http://rbge-sun1.rbge.org.uk/friends
The Friends raise funds for and promote the work of the Royal Botanic Garden Edinburgh. There is no admission charge to this great garden, but friends have free entry to the three regional gardens (Logan, Dawyck and Younger).

There is a regular newsletter, and an excellent series of lectures and other social events.

FRIENDS OF THE ROYAL BOTANIC GARDENS KEW

Cambridge Cottage, Kew Green, Kew, Richmond, Surrey TW9 3AB
Tel 020 8332 5922
Fax 020 8332 5901
The Friends of the Royal Botanic Gardens, Kew, raises funds for Kew's scientific work, hence the relatively high subscription (£34 for a single membership). That said, free entry to Kew, Wakehurst and 15 further gardens in Britain is a valuable benefit. The Friends' journal *Kew*, published three times a year, is colourful and outstandingly good. Lectures are given monthly throughout the year, and there is an annual plant auction in the autumn. Friends receive discounts on shop purchases, and complimentary day passes to the gardens for their guests.

FRUIT GROUP OF THE ROYAL HORTICULTURAL SOCIETY

80 Vincent Square, London SW1P 2PE
Tel 020 7630 7422
Fax 020 7233 9525
Membership of the Fruit Group is open to all members of the RHS. The Group exhibits at the Chelsea Flower Show, the RHS Great Autumn Show, the Harrogate Autumn Show and the Malvern Autumn Show. Members have the opportunity to exhibit at RHS shows and join Group outings, but perhaps the best meetings are those at RHS Garden Wisley, where they can study the RHS's fruit collection at close quarters, in the company of knowledgeable members of staff and other experts. These meetings

often have a practical aspect: the occasional 'gooseberry tastings' are not to be missed. The Group balances its activities between top fruit and soft fruit, so that all members' interests are accommodated within the annual programme. It has also begun to set up sub-groups e.g. in the West Midlands (based at Pershore) and the south west (run from Rosemoor).

THE GARDEN HISTORY SOCIETY

70 Cowcross Street, London EC1M 6EJ
Tel 020 7608 2409
Fax 020 7490 2974
www.gardenhistorysociety.org
Founded in 1965. This learned society is concerned with the study of garden and landscape history. It is also actively involved in conservation and regularly advise local authorities on such issues. The twice-yearly journal *Garden History* publishes new research, whilst regular newsletters carry details of conservation matters and society events. These events include lectures and garden visits, at home and abroad. There is a regional group in Scotland. Events are limited to society members only but the public are admitted to the excellent winter lectures in London.

GESELLSCHAFT DER STAUDENFREUNDE

Meisenweg 1, D-65975 Hattersheim, Germany
Tel & Fax 00 49 6190 3642
The German Perennial Society developed from the Iris and Lily Society but now encompasses all hardy perennials. There are over 30 regional and five special interest groups (alpines, *Hemerocallis*, lilies, peonies and wildflowers) which all

organise their own lectures and outings. Members receive the excellent quarterly journal *Der Staudengarten*, which is comparable to *The Hardy Plant*. The society's seed scheme centres on an annual list, not confined to perennials, which offers about 4,000 items. We strongly recommend all Hardy Planters to consider membership.

THE HARDY ORCHID SOCIETY

83 Ladysmith, East Gomeldon, Salisbury, Wiltshire SP4 6LE
Tel 01980 610151
www.drover.demon.Couk.HOS/
The society is interested in all terrestrial orchids, British and foreign. There are two meetings a year, at Pershore, as well as fields meetings in Europe. The website is excellent.

THE HARDY PLANT SOCIETY

Little Orchard, Great Comberton, Pershore, Hereford & Worcester WR10 3DP
Tel 01386 710317
www.hardy-plant.org.uk
The Hardy Plant Society has its own garden at the Pershore College of Horticulture. Members join the national society and can then choose to join one of over 40 regional groups. In addition there are four special interest groups (Hardy Geraniums; Pulmonarias; Peonies; and Variegated Plants) and a Correspondents Group for those who cannot come to meetings. Two journals are sent to members each year, along with regular newsletters. The national society attends Chelsea, whilst area groups patronise local shows and arrange their own programmes of events. An annual seed distribution list is circulated to all members.

The society is also involved in conserving old cultivars and introducing new ones, and has produced a number of useful publications. It has grown fast in recent years and is going through a period of change. The local groups organise their own busy programmes of meetings, trips and garden visits: the additional cost of joining such a group is usually very small. Full details of the local and specialist groups are available from the national society: only HPS members can join a local or specialist group.

THE HEATHER SOCIETY

Denbeigh, All Saints Road, Creeting St Mary, Ipswich, Suffolk IP6 8PJ
Tel & Fax 01449 711220
www.users.zetnet.Couk/heather
The Heather Society was founded in 1963. Members receive the society's authoritative *Year Book*, which is edited by Dr Charles Nelson, and a twice-yearly bulletin of news and events. Competitions are held through the RHS at Westminster. A slide library is maintained, and expert advice on cultivation and other technical queries is available. Regional groups arrange a series of local events, and an annual weekend conference, linked to the AGM, is held at a different location each year (Hereford, 7–10 September in 2001).

THE HEBE SOCIETY

Rosemergy, Hain Walk, St Ives, Cornwall TR26 2AF
Tel 01736 795225
www.gwynfryn.demon.Couk/hebesoc/
An international society, based in Britain. It was established in 1985, and has since expanded its brief to include other New Zealand plants. Quarterly issues of *Hebe News* keep members in touch with activities,

and include botanical and horticultural articles. Local groups have been formed in the north-west of England, Cornwall and the Cotswolds. The society maintains a slide library, operates a cutting exchange service and produces booklets about hebes and parahebes. Society members can also obtain written advice on request.

HEMEROCALLIS EUROPA

Homburg 14, D-79761 Waldshut-Tiengen, Germany
Tel & Fax 00 49 7741 63068
Germany-based but bilingual (German and English) society that seeks to study, evaluate and popularise the best daylilies for Europe. It has members all over the continent. The society encourages the breeding of new varieties, and runs trials for their garden-worthiness in Germany and at Ventnor Botanic Gardens in the Isle of Wight. Members receive three newsletters and a substantial Yearbook.

HENRY DOUBLEDAY RESEARCH ASSOCIATION (HDRA)

Ryton Organic Gardens, Ryton-on-Dunsmore, Coventry CV8 3LG
Tel 01203 303517
Fax 01203 639229
www.hdra.org.uk
Europe's largest organic organisation, founded in 1958. At the Ryton headquarters there is a ten-acre garden, and a reference library which members can use. Members are kept up to date with HDRA events through a quarterly magazine. In addition there are over fifty local groups around the country. The society provides free advice on organic gardening to its members, and they receive discounts on HDRA products and books. They can also join the Heritage Seed programme for a small extra charge: this scheme propagates and preserves vegetable varieties which have been squeezed out of commerce by current legislation. Since they are not allowed to be sold, the HDRA gives them away to subscribers. The HDRA also carries out scientific research, consultancy work for industry and public bodies, and worldwide research and agricultural aid projects. The association publishes a directory of organic gardens belonging to members and open to fellow-members.

THE HERB SOCIETY

Deddington Hill Farm, Warmington, Banbury, Oxfordshire OX17 1XB
Tel 01295 692000
www.herbsociety.Couk
Founded in 1927 as the Society of Herbalists, the Society aims to bring together all with an interest in herbs. Members receive three copies of the Society's magazine *Herbs*, and four copies of the newsletter *Herbarium* each year. Seminars and workshops are arranged nationwide in appropriate settings. Information on suppliers, literature and all aspects of growing herbs is available to members. The Society's garden is part of the Henry Doubleday Research Association's garden at Yalding in Kent.

THE HISTORIC GARDENS FOUNDATION

34 River Court, London SE1 9PE
Tel 020 7633 9165
Fax 020 7401 7072
This conservation charity was set up in 1995 to create links between everyone concerned with the preservation, restoration and management of historic parks and gardens. It is particularly strong in France and UK.

HISTORIC SCOTLAND

Longmore House, Salisbury Place, Edinburgh, Lothian EH9 1SH
Tel 0131 668 8600
www.historic-scotland.gov.uk
Responsible for the maintenance of historic houses and gardens in the care of the Secretary of State for Scotland: Edzell Castle is one of the leading examples. Krystyna Campbell is working on an extension to the *Inventory of Gardens & Designed Landscapes in Scotland*.

HORTICULTURAL TRADES ASSOCIATION (HTA)

Horticulture House, 19 High Street, Theale, Reading, Berkshire RG7 5AH
Tel 0118 930 3132
Fax 0118 932 3453
www.martex.Couk/hta
The trade association for amenity and leisure horticulture, with around 2,000 members. It publishes a magazine, *Nurseryman and Garden Centre* and a useful reference *Yearbook*: both are also available to non-members. Business advice and negotiated discounts are provided to members. The HTA also promotes the HTA National Garden Gift Tokens.

THE INSTITUTE OF HORTICULTURE (IOH)

14–15 Belgrave Square, London SW1X 8PS
Tel 020 7245 6943
www.horticulture.demon.Couk
The professional body for horticulturists of all descriptions. The strict membership

requirements demand a combination of education and experience, so membership confers recognised professional status. Student membership is also available. The IoH acts as a forum for the collection and dissemination of horticultural information to its members and the public. It also promotes and represents the horticultural industry. Its website is one of the best we know, and especially helpful for those contemplating horticulture as a career.

INTERNATIONAL CAMELLIA SOCIETY

329 London Road, St Albans, Hertfordshire AL1 1DZZ
www.camellia-ics.org
Founded in 1962, the ICS now has some 1,600 members worldwide. Members receive the *International Camellia Journal* annually, and a UK newsletter twice a year. The society takes a stand at the main spring shows, and holds weekend meetings in spring and autumn. Informal advice on camellias is available to members, as is a worldwide network of fellow enthusiasts.

INTERNATIONAL CLEMATIS SOCIETY

3 Cuthberts Close, Cheshunt, Waltham Cross EN7 5RB
Tel 01992 636524
The society is international in its membership and aspirations: it aims to provide a channel of communication for clematis growers across the world. Its main event is the annual tour, attended by international members, during which there are shows and meetings. Members receive an annual *Journal.* The excellent seed list contains up to 100 items.

INTERNATIONAL DENDROLOGY SOCIETY

Hergest Estate Office, Kington, Hereford & Worcester HR5 3EGF
This prestigious international society has a worldwide membership. It encourages and helps fund conservation and research projects by registered charities, and has established a bursary to allow a dendrological student from Eastern Europe to study in the UK every year. The IDS holds a dendrological symposium every two years. Members also receive the *Year Book* and newsletters, and can take part in the seed exchange scheme and the excellent botanical tours. Membership is restricted, i.e. at the invitation of existing members only and subject to the approval of the council.

INTERNATIONAL LILAC SOCIETY

Norman's Farm, Wyverstone, Stowmarket, Suffolk IP14 4SF
This is the address of the English contact, Sheelagh Chapman, of this society, many of whose members live in North America. In addition to receiving the informative *Quarterly Journal of the International Lilac Society,* members can purchase rare *Syringa* taxa and take part in the annual convention.

INTERNATIONAL OAK SOCIETY

23 Crescent Road, Alverstoke, Gosport, Hampshire PO12 2DH
Tel 01705 585972
www.saintmarys.edu/~rjensen/ios/html
Although the Secretary is English, the society has a particularly strong American membership. The society gives members all over the world an opportunity to acquire rare species on its annual acorn day.

INTERNATIONAL OLEANDER SOCIETY INC

P O Box 3431, Galveston, TX 77552-0431, USA
Tel 00 1 409 762 9334
www.oleander.org
Galveston is the Oleander City and the society has its reference collection of varieties at the Moody gardens there. The main publication is the quarterly *Nerium News*, but the society has also issued videos on oleanders and their cultivation.

INTERNATIONAL TREE FOUNDATION

Sandy Lane, Crawley Down, Crawley, West Sussex RH10 4HS
Tel 01342 712536
Fax 01342 718282
Formerly Men of the Trees, this is an international tree planting and conservation organisation, founded in the 1920s.

INTERNATIONAL VIOLET ASSOCIATION

Devon Violet Nursery, Rattery, South Brent, Devon TQ10 9LG
Tel 01364 643033
This is a relatively young and growing international society which originated in the USA, though the president is British. Its aims include bringing the violet back into gardens, assisting in the preservation of its natural habitats, and recording and introducing new cultivars. Membership is not limited to growers and collectors. A newsletter is produced four times a year, and the president offers an advisory service to European members.

INTERNATIONAL WATER LILY SOCIETY

92 London Road, Stapeley, Nantwich, Cheshire CW5 7LH
Tel 01270 628628
Fax 01270 624188

The International Water Lily Society is based in the USA but has members throughout the world and this is the UK contact address. The membership spans amateurs and professionals, and the society carries out a range of research and educational work, including hybrid registration. Members receive the quarterly journal.

IRISH GARDEN PLANT SOCIETY

c/o National Botanic Gardens, Glasnevin, Dublin 9, Republic of Ireland

Formed in 1981 as the Irish equivalent to the NCCPG, the Society has a particular mission to locate and propagate plants raised in Ireland, whether by amateurs or nurserymen. The Society is the only group within Ireland that is registered with the NCCPG. There are branches in Munster and Northern Ireland, each with their own programme. Members receive a quarterly newsletter as well as the society's journal *Moorea*, which has articles of a historical nature about Irish plants, gardens and gardeners.

JAPANESE GARDEN SOCIETY

Groves Mill, Shakers Lane, Long Itchington, Warwickshire CV23 8QB
Tel 01926 632746

This society is devoted to gardens influenced by the Japanese tradition of design. It is compiling a register of Japanese gardens in the UK and works for the conservation of existing gardens and the creation of new ones. The Society organises tours to Japan and publishes a list of Japanese gardens open for the NGS. It has several regional groups: members receive the quarterly journal *Shakkei*.

LILY GROUP OF THE ROYAL HORTICULTURAL SOCIETY

Wilton Cottage, Drakes Bridge Road, Eckington, Pershore, Hereford & Worcester WR10 3BN
Tel 01386 750794
Fax 01386 750524

Membership of the Lily Group is open to all members of the RHS. It is the largest lily society in Europe and the only one in Britain. Members receive three newsletters a year. Lectures are associated with RHS shows at Westminster (at least two a year), and the Group also exhibits at Hampton Court. There is an annual bulb auction at the late-autumn show and the Group issues a Seed List early in the year: it offers a remarkable choice of lily and *Liliaceae* seed sent by donors at home and abroad. Advice on all aspects of growing these plants is available from the General Secretary, via the RHS.

THE MAGNOLIA SOCIETY INC

6616 81st Street, Cabin John, MD 20818, USA
Tel & Fax 00 1 301 320 4296
www.supernet.net/~magnolia

Founded in 1963 to promote the exchange of knowledge about magnolias, the Society is the major association devoted to this genus. Members receive the twice-yearly journal *Magnolia* as well as a newsletter. The journal has articles on cultivation, propagation, breeding, and gardens. The society offers a seed exchange, library and registration service for new cultivars.

MARCHER APPLE NETWORK

Orchard Barn, Ocle Pychard, Hereford, Hereford & Worcester HR1 3RB
Tel 01432 820304

This society was formed by a group of people living in the Welsh Marches with the aim of rescueing old apple cultivars from extinction. They identify old trees, propagate them and establish new orchards to preserve them. They also organise events to celebrate and encourage the revival of interest in traditional fruit varieties.

THE MEDITERRANEAN GARDEN SOCIETY

P O Box 14, Peania 190 02, Greece
Tel 00 30 1 664 3089
www.support.net/Medit-Plants

This excellent young society is principally for people who live in the Mediterranean region and want to garden in the English manner i.e. with plants! It has members all over the world.

THE MERLIN TRUST

The Dower House, Boughton House, Kettering, Northamptonshire NN14 1BJ
Tel 01536 482279
Fax 01536 482294

The leading UK charity dedicated to helping young horticulturists to extend their knowledge. Applicants must be aged between 18 and 30 and show how their project would help their present work. All ideas are considered: travel, work experience, photography, seed collection, conservation work, travel to study plants. The trustees say that personal enthusiasm counts for more than qualifications.

MINISTRY OF AGRICULTURE, FISHERIES AND FOOD

3 Whitehall Place, London SW1A 2HH
Tel 020 7270 8080
Fax 020 7270 8443
www.maff.gov.uk
General enquiries on the above number. See your local telephone directory (under 'Agriculture') for the addresses of MAFF's regional centres.

MUSEUM OF GARDEN HISTORY

Lambeth Palace Road, London SE1 7LB
Tel 020 7261 1891
www.compulink.Couk/~museumgh/
The only museum of its kind, housed in the (now disused) church where the two John Tradescants, father and son, were buried. Further details are available in our Gardens of England section.

THE NATIONAL ASSOCIATION OF FLOWER ARRANGEMENT SOCIETIES

21 Denbigh Street, London SW1V 2HF
Tel 020 7828 5145
Fax 020 7821 0587
Founded in 1959. NAFAS is the umbrella organisation for nearly 1,500 flower-arrangement clubs. The Association is very active in training and teaching arrangers of all skill levels. Local clubs organise demonstrations and competitions, and area groups stage exhibits at NAFAS and local shows. Regular flower festivals are organised to raise money for charitable causes, and arrangements in hospitals are another important part of the NAFAS activity. Members co-ordinate the flowers at Westminster Abbey, and do the arrangements for major occasions including royal weddings. *The Flower Arranger* is circulated quarterly; members can use the book service, and there is a book and slide library at the London headquarters. Prospective members should write to headquarters in the first instance: they will put you in touch with a local club. Subscriptions to these clubs vary and are usually modest. All clubs are represented at area level: there are over 20 areas throughout Britain. The 7th International Show of the World Association of Flower will take place in Glasgow on 13–16 June 2002.

NATIONAL AURICULA AND PRIMULA SOCIETY (MIDLAND & WEST SECTION)

6 Lawson Close, Saltford, Somerset BS18 3LB
Tel 01225 872893
Founded in 1900. Members receive the year book *Argus* and two newsletters every year. The society also publishes information sheets on cultivation, guides to varieties and a history of auriculas. Plant sales are held at the society's three annual shows: some varieties are not available commercially.

NATIONAL AURICULA AND PRIMULA SOCIETY (SOUTHERN SECTION)

67 Warnham Court Road, Carshalton Beeches, Surrey SM5 3ND
Founded in 1876. Members receive a year book and an annual newsletter. Three shows will be held this year. Plants are for sale at the shows. Members can seek advice on all aspects of primula cultivation and exhibition. The society has a third section serving the North (146 Queens Road, Cheadle Hulme, Cheshire SK8 5HY).

NATIONAL BEGONIA SOCIETY

33 Findern Lane, Willington, Derbyshire DE65 6DW
Tel 01283 702681
This society was established in 1948. New members receive a cultural handbook, and the journal appears three times a year. Meetings are arranged through the regional groups, five of which also organise an annual area show. In addition there is a national show with many classes. New cultivars can be submitted for awards to the floral committee. An advisory service is available through the secretary. The Society is producing a register of all cultivars in cultivation.

NATIONAL CHRYSANTHEMUM SOCIETY

George Gray House, 8 Amber Business Village, Amber Close, Tamworth, Staffordshire B77 4RD
Tel & Fax 01827 310331
The National Chrysanthemum Society holds two national shows each year in Bingley Hall, Stafford (September and November). The advisory bureau helps with queries about chrysanthemums and handles membership enquiries.

NATIONAL COUNCIL FORTHE CONSERVATION OF PLANTS AND GARDENS

The Pines, RHS Garden, Wisley, Woking, Surrey GU23 6QP
Tel 01483 211465
Fax 01483 212404
www.nccpg.org.uk
Founded in 1978. The NCCPG is divided into about forty local and

county groups who organise their own programmes of events. The national body works to preserve individual plants and endangered gardens. The society's most successful innovation has been the establishment of more than 600 National Collections of genera (and part genera). These gather together as many representatives of the genus as possible and form a unique resource. Many can be visited: full details appear in the *2001 National Plant Collections Directory*. The NCCPG has close relations with similar movements throughout the world.

NATIONAL DAHLIA SOCIETY

19 Sunnybank, Marlow, Buckinghamshire SL7 3BL
Tel 01628 473500
The National Dahlia Society holds two main shows, runs trials at Leeds and Wisley, and gives an annual award for the best new British and new overseas seedlings. Members receive the society journal twice a year, and can take part in its annual conference and lecture programme. There are about 900 affiliated societies: they can use the society's medals and certificates for their own shows. A range of books and pamphlets is available for members at reduced prices.

NATIONAL GARDENS SCHEME

Hatchlands Park, East Clandon, Guildford, Surrey GU4 7RT
Tel 01483 211535
www.ngs.org.uk
The National Gardens Scheme was founded in 1927. Ninety percent of its income comes from the 3,500 or so gardens which are open to the public and from sales of the Yellow Book. In 2000 it donated nearly £1.5m to gardening and nursing

charities. The website has an excellent searchable database of all gardens which open for the Scheme, plus those in Scotland's Garden Scheme.

NATIONAL POT LEEK SOCIETY

147 Sea Road, Fulwell, Sunderland SR6 9EB
Tel 0191 549 4274
The society produces a yearbook and two newsletters for its members. Advice can be provided by letter or phone, and the society produces a growing guide, *Sound All Round*, and a video, *Growing Leeks with the Experts*. Among the items on sale are measuring equipment and charts and a video. Most of the members live in the north-east of England.

THE NATIONAL SWEET PEA SOCIETY

3 Chalk Farm Road, Stokenchurch, High Wycombe, Buckinghamshire HP14 3TB
Tel 01494 482153
The National Sweet Pea Society was founded in 1900. Its *Annual* appears every June, and further Bulletins in February and September. The *Annual* is a substantial publication. There are three major shows every. Each county has an area representative who arranges programmes for local members. The society actively promotes new varieties, and members can send their own seedlings to the trials at RHS Garden Wisley each year.

NATIONAL TRUST

36 Queen Anne's Gate, London SW1H 9AS
Tel 020 7222 9251
www.nationaltrust.org.uk
The UK's leading conservation body has many outstanding

gardens and landscapes under its care. Membership gives admission to all the Trust's properties and is strongly recommended to anyone who is interested in gardens. Numerous events are organised throughout the year. The Trust has an excellent website, full of information about the trust, including all its gardens.

NATIONAL TRUST FOR SCOTLAND

5 Charlotte Square, Edinburgh EH2 4DU
Tel 0131 226 5922
Fax 0131 243 9501
www.nts.org.uk
This Scottish conservation body has a number of excellent gardens in its care; members also receive free entry to National Trust properties under a reciprocal arrangement. The website gives good descriptions of the gardens in its care.

NATIONAL VEGETABLE SOCIETY

56 Waun-y-Groes Avenue, Rhiwbini, Cardiff, South Glamorgan CF4 4SZ
Tel 01222 627994
www.nvsuk.org.uk
The National Vegetable Society was founded in 1960 and caters for individual members and societies. The latter can use the NVS medals and award cards. Membership spans the expert and the novice vegetable grower. The new quarterly National Bulletin and the regional Bulletins that members receive contain advice on all aspects of growing and showing vegetables. A National Newsletter gives details of all Society activities. The National Vegetable Championships are held at a different location each year and major awards are presented at it.

NATIONAL VIOLA AND PANSY SOCIETY

Cleeway, Eardington, Bridgnorth, Shropshire WV16 5JT
Tel 01746 766909
Founded in 1911. The Midlands-based society encourages and popularises the growing of exhibition varieties, and helps its members with advice on propagation and cultivation. A newsletter is circulated irregularly, and there is an annual show. Surplus cuttings and plants form the basis for occasional exchanges.

NORTH AMERICAN ROCK GARDEN SOCIETY

P O Box 67, Millwood, NY 10546, USA
Tel 00 1 914 762 2948
www.nargs.org
The society (NARGS for short) offers an excellent quarterly journal and the longest society seed list we know of (5000+ items): as a result, it has many members in UK.

THE NORTH OF ENGLAND ROSE, CARNATION AND SWEET PEA SOCIETY

10 Glendale Avenue, Whitley Bay, Tyne & Wear NE26 1RX
Tel 0191 252 7052
The society – Rosecarpe, for short – was founded in 1938. Its interests extend beyond its three main flowers. Members can attend the regular meetings, usually on the first Monday of most months in the Civic Centre, Gateshead, for lectures or demonstrations. The four shows play an important part in the society's life, notably the Gateshead Spring and Summer Flower Shows organised in association with the Metropolitan Borough Council, and two

Rosecarpe Flower Shows. Trophies are presented at all shows. An annual year book is produced, and members can also borrow the society's books and videos, and draw on the advice of the society's experts. Rosecarpe attends other shows and horticultural college events, and is affiliated to the national Rose, Carnation, Sweet Pea and Daffodil societies.

NORTHERN HORTICULTURAL SOCIETY

Harlow Carr Botanical Gardens, Crag Lane, Harrogate, North Yorkshire HG3 1QB
Tel 01423 565418
Fax 01423 530663
www.harlowcarr.fsnet.Couk
Founded in 1946, the Northern Horticultural Society is a focus for gardeners in the north of England. Members receive free entrance to the Harlow Carr Botanical Gardens which are the society's headquarters. The annual programme includes a series of day and longer courses throughout the year at the garden. The garden also trials vegetable and flower varieties specifically for their suitability to northerly climates, and visitors can assess the new and unreleased varieties which are undergoing trial. An illustrated journal, *The Northern Gardener*, appears four times a year. Members can also take advantage of the seed scheme, the reference and lending library, and an advisory service (in writing only). There are special interest sections for alpines, bonsai, bulbs, delphiniums, ferns, rhododendrons and roses. A reciprocal arrangement with the Royal Horticultural Society allows free access to the three RHS gardens and members also have free entry to another eleven throughout England.

NORTHERN IRELAND DAFFODIL GROUP

77 Ballygowan Road, Hillsborough, Co Down, Northern Ireland BT26 6EQ
Daffodils are a major interest in Northern Ireland. The NIDG has many affiliated societies, who exhibit at the City of Belfast Spring Show. It also issues two newsletters a year to all members.

NORTHERN IRELAND TOURIST BOARD

St Anne's Court, 59 North Street, Belfast BT1 1NB
Tel 028 9024 6609
Fax 028 9024 0960
This very helpful organisation publishes *The Gardens of Northern Ireland*, available from its tourist information offices.

ORCHID SOCIETY OF GREAT BRITAIN

Athelney, 145 Binscombe Village, Godalming, Surrey GU7 3QL
Tel 01483 421423
The nationwide orchid society. It produces an informative journal four times a year and stages two major shows annually. In addition there is a monthly meeting in London which may include a lecture and a show. The library lends books and slides, and members can obtain cultural advice in person or in writing from the Cultural Adviser. There is a plant exchange forum, and a sales table at most meetings. The society publishes a small booklet on orchid cultivation which is a useful introduction to the subject.

RHODODENDRON, CAMELLIA & MAGNOLIA GROUP OF THE ROYAL HORTICULTURAL SOCIETY

Netherton, Buckland Monachorum, Yelverton, Devon PL20 7NL

Tel & Fax 01822 854022

Membership is open to all members of the RHS. New members are assigned to the nearest regional branch and advised of the garden visits and lectures programme. The Group organises a Spring Tour and an Autumn Weekend, and mounts a display at the main Rhododendron Show at Vincent Square. The *Bulletin* is published three times a year. The year book (*Rhododendrons with Camellias and Magnolias*) is issued every January.

THE ROYAL CALEDONIAN HORTICULTURAL SOCIETY

28 Silverknowes Southway, Edinburgh EH4 5PX

Tel 0131 336 5488

Fax 0131 336 1847

The Royal Caledonian Horticultural Society was founded in 1809. It publishes an annual *Journal*, and a newsletter *Preview* three times a year. There is a regular lecture programme from October to April, whilst in the summer months a series of garden visits takes place. The society's president is the custodian of their library. There is an annual spring show and an AGM, at which the society presents three prestigious awards: the Queen Elizabeth the Queen Mother Medal, the biennial Neill Prize to a botanist, and the Scottish Horticultural Medal, the number of whose recipients is limited to 50. The 'Caley' has

begun to establish a co-ordinating function among Scottish horticultural societies.

THE ROYAL GARDENERS' ORPHAN FUND

48 St Alban's Road, Codicote, Hertfordshire ST4 8UT

Tel 01438 8207783

Founded in 1887 to help the orphans of gardeners 'by giving them regular allowances and grants for special purposes'. The fund also offers assistance to needy children whose parents are employed full-time in horticulture.

THE ROYAL HORTICULTURAL SOCIETY (RHS)

P O Box 313, 80 Vincent Square, London SW1P 2PE

Tel 020 7834 4333

www.rhs.org.uk

The Royal Horticultural Society is the premier horticultural society in the country and probably the world. Membership has grown steadily in recent years and the society's activities have expanded correspondingly. As well as the extensive RHS gardens at Wisley in Surrey, there are now also regional gardens at Rosemoor, Devon, and Hyde Hall, Essex. On production of a valid Individual Membership card, members are entitled to free entry to nearly 80 gardens throughout the UK and in northern France and Belgium. Some are free throughout their opening period: others for a month or so. There is also a full range of courses, lectures, specialist events and demonstrations right across the country. Members are admitted to these events at concessionary rates, and free of charge to most lectures: you should apply for tickets in writing. The

show programme is formed around the London shows at the RHS Halls in Westminster (see the RHS website for details and dates). The RHS and specialist societies hold plant competitions at these shows, and members can bring along plants for exhibition or cultural awards. Schedules are available from the RHS. Members no longer receive free entrance to Chelsea Flower Show, but they can buy tickets at reduced prices and the Tuesday and Wednesday of Chelsea week are reserved for members. Members are entitled to reduced price admission to the increasing number of shows which the RHS now runs, among them the Hampton Court Palace Flower Show, the Tatton Park Flower Show and the established shows at Malvern. The illustrated RHS journal *The Garden* is sent free to members every month. Long a journal of record, the magazine is in top form with a mixture of society news, horticultural and botanical articles: every edition offers much of interest to all gardeners. Its sister title is *The New Plantsman*: aimed at the specialist, there is a separate subscription. A number of other publications are produced, and the society promotes a collection of gardening titles in association with commercial publishers. RHS members are entitled to technical advice from the society's experts: this service is accessible by post, at the society's own shows and a number of other major events which it attends, and in person at Wisley. Members may use and borrow from the Lindley Library in Westminster: its holdings are of world standing. A distribution of seed from the Wisley garden is made each year for a nominal charge. Membership benefits apply to the named holder only but members can enrol up to three people who live at their address as associate members: they are entitled to all the normal benefits except free entry to those gardens which are not owned by the RHS. Only one copy of the journal is sent to each address. There are some specialist sections (an additional subscription is payable) for Fruit, Lilies, and Rhododendrons, Camellias & Magnolias. Behind the scenes the RHS is involved in scientific and technical horticulture, including its regular trial programme. The trials can be viewed at Wisley (Portsmouth field). The society liaises with national and trade organisations in the interests of horticulture, and is increasingly active in the international arena. Up-to-date information about events is published monthly in *The Garden*. The website, too, is a mine of useful information.

ROYAL HORTICULTURAL SOCIETY OF IRELAND

Swanbrook House, Bloomfield Avenue, Morehampton Road, Dublin 4
Tel 00 353 1 668 4358
Founded in 1830, the society encourages people to make gardens and grow a wide variety of plants. Lectures, demonstrations, courses, garden visits and plant sales are held throughout the year. The newsletter (three a year) keeps members up to date with activities.

THE ROYAL NATIONAL ROSE SOCIETY

The Gardens of the Rose, Chiswell Green, St Albans, Hertfordshire AL2 3NR
Tel 01727 850461
Fax 01727 850360
Founded in 1876, the society has its headquarters near St Albans: the Gardens of the Rose display over

1800 different roses. Members enter free. The society also maintains about a dozen regional rose gardens. An illustrated quarterly journal *The Rose* gives news of the society and the rose world, and there are regular shows including the British Rose Festival at the Hampton Court Palace Flower Show. The society always has hundreds of new roses on trial for awards at St Albans: the trial fields can be visited. There is a full advisory service for members and regular pruning demonstrations which anyone can attend. There are some regional groups, and special interest sections for exhibitors and rose breeders (The Amateur Rose Breeders Association). For an additional fee RNRS members can join the Historic Roses Group, which organises its own programme of events and visits. The Society is hoping to fund a major expansion of its gardens in the next few years.

ROYAL SOCIETY FOR THE PROTECTION OF BIRDS

The Lodge, Sandy, Bedfordshire SG19 2DL
Tel 01767 680551
Fax 01767 692365
www.rspb.org.uk
This charity takes action for wild birds and the environment. It is the largest wildlife conservation charity in Europe.

THE SAINTPAULIA & HOUSEPLANT SOCIETY

33 Church Road, Newbury Park, Ilford, Essex IG2 7ET
Tel 020 8590 3710
The society holds regular Tuesday evening meetings at the RHS, usually to coincide with the London shows. There are competitions at the meetings, and

an annual show in the Lawrence Hall (formerly known as the New Hall) at the June show. Members receive the bulletin four times a year. The society arranges visits and also has several local groups with their own programmes. Members can borrow from the society's specialist library, and take part in the annual leaf distribution.

SCOTLAND'S GARDEN SCHEME

31 Castle Terrace, Edinburgh EH1 2EL
Tel 0131 229 1870
Fax 0131 229 0443
www.ngs.org.uk
Over 300 gardens open for the SGS, which is closely modelled on the English National Gardens Scheme and shares its website. Owners are encouraged to open their gardens to the public and the proceeds are then distributed among various charities. The SGS is proud to be able to show a higher return per gardens than the NGS.

SCOTTISH RHODODENDRON SOCIETY

Stron Ailne, Colintraive, Argyll, Strathclyde PA22 3AS
Tel 01700 841285
The Scottish Rhododendron Society was founded as a forum where Scottish growers could meet and exhibit. Many of the best Scottish rhododendron gardens belong, but a fair proportion of the members live outside Scotland. An excellent newsletter is produced three times a year, and there are at least two meetings annually. Their national show, at a different venue each year, is probably the top show in Britain for rhododendrons. Members can purchase a range of books at reduced prices, seek specialist advice through the

ecretary, and gain free admission o Arduaine Gardens in Strathclyde. The society is also a chapter of the excellent American Rhododendron Society, which means that members automatically belong directly to the American society too. This gives them the scholarly quarterly journal, access o all the other ARS chapters (from Denmark and Holland to India), and the opportunity to raise seeds from the ARS seed bank.

SCOTTISH ROCK GARDEN CLUB

P O Box 14063, Edinburgh, Lothian EH10 4YE

www.srgc.org.uk

Founded in 1933 this is now the largest horticultural society in Scotland, with overseas members in nearly 40 countries. There are regional groups throughout Scotland, each responsible for organising a programme of events including lectures. Some members also open their gardens. The society journal, *The Rock Garden*, appears twice a year: it is a well-produced and authoritative magazine which covers rock garden plants both in cultivation and in the wild. The seed exchange scheme is among the best of its kind.

SOCIÉTÉ NATIONAL D'HORTICULTURE DE FRANCE

84, rue de Grenelle, Paris F-75007, France

Tel 00 33 1 44 39 78 78

Fax 00 33 1 45 44 96 57

The SNHF was founded in 1827 and operates through a dozen sub-societies for the promotion of particular plants, including orchids, cacti, fuchsias and roses. Members receive the excellent monthly magazine *Jardins de France*.

SOCIETY OF GARDEN DESIGNERS

14–15 Belgrave Square, London SW1X 8PS

Tel 020 7838 9311

www.society-of-garden-designers.Couk

The leading professional body for full-time garden designers. Only a fraction of its 1,000+ members are recognised as Full Members or Fellows. Membership depends upon a combination of training and experience, and work is inspected. The society distributes information about its members to enquirers free of charge: contact The Secretary. Full members use the initials FSGD and MSGD.

SOIL ASSOCIATION

Bristol House, 40–56 Victoria Street, Bristol, Gloucestershire BS1 6BY

Tel 0117 929 0661

Founded in 1949, the association exists to promote and develop alternatives to intensive agriculture. It calls its headquarters the Organic Food & Farming Centre. The British Organic Farmers and Organic Growers Association are also based here.

SPORTS TURF RESEARCH INSTITUTE

St Ives Estate, Bingley, West Yorkshire BD16 1AU

Tel 01274 565131

Fax 01274 561891

www.stri.org.uk

Founded in 1929 to carry out research into grasses and turf management. The institute advises the National Trust and private owners, at home and overseas, as well as sports associations and golf course managers.

STANLEY SMITH HORTICULTURAL TRUST

Cory Lodge, P O Box 365, Cambridge CB2 1HR

This trust makes grants every year totalling more than £50,000 and welcomes applications from individuals, organisations and institutions. The trustees try to maintain a balance across the whole spectrum ofamenity horticulture and between small (up to £1,500) and larger grants. Recent projects supported include plant collecting, books on horticultural subjects, garden restoration and the breeding of new hybrids. Grants are awarded twice a year, in April and October.

THRIVE

The Geoffrey Udall Building, Trunkwell Park, Beech Hill, Reading, Berkshire RG7 2AT

Tel 0118 988 5688

www.thrive.org.uk

This charity (formerly known as Horticultural Therapy) is dedicated to helping people with special needs gain independence, new skills and quality of life through gardening. It has set standards through its pioneering work in the community, helping projects and groups, and assisting individuals with information and educational opportunities.

TREE REGISTER OF THE BRITISH ISLES

77a Hall End, Wootton, Bedfordshire MK43 9HP

Tel 01234 768884

The Register aims to aims to identify and record full details of exceptional trees. We have used it widely as a source of information about record-breaking trees. Its Newsletter is a fascinating read for anyone who enjoys the sheer variety and size of old trees.

VEREIN DEUTSCHER ROSENFREUNDE

Waldseestrasse 14, D-76530 Baden-Baden, Germany
Tel 00 49 7221 31302
Fax 00 49 7221 38337
Lieben Sie Rosen? Dann sollten Sie VDR Mitglied werden. The German rose society is the best-run rose society in Europe and offers good value to members abroad through its informative quarterly *Rosenbogen* and its quality *Jahrbuch.* There are three great rose gardens: at Westfalenpark in Dortmund, at Sangerhausen and at Wilhelmshöhe in Kassel. Each has more than twice as many cultivars as any garden in UK.

WAKEFIELD & NORTH OF ENGLAND TULIP SOCIETY

70 Wrenthorpe Lane, Wrenthorpe, Wakefield, West Yorkshire WF2 0PT
This long-established society, devoted to florists' tulips, publishes an annual journal and holds two shows each year. Other events include formal and informal meetings and garden visits. Surplus bulbs are distributed in October. *The English Tulip and its History* is available from the society, as are slide lectures.

WELSH HISTORIC GARDENS TRUST

Ty Leri, Talybont, Ceredigion SY24 5ER
Tel & Fax 01970 832268
The Welsh Historic Gardens Trust assists and initiates the conservation of important gardens, parks and landscapes in Wales. Members can become involved in research, surveying and other conservation work: there are branches throughout the principality. The Newsletter is informed and informing, while the Trust itself has become a powerful force for conservation within the principality.

THE WILDLIFE TRUSTS

Harling House, 62 Copperfield Street, London SE1 0DJ
Tel 020 7921 5400
Fax 020 7921 5411
www.wildlifetrust.org.uk

The Wildlife Trusts are made up of the 46 local wildlife trusts and over 150 urban groups with a total of 325,000 members. They manage some 2,300 nature reserves, campaign on conservation issues, and encourage people to become involved in conservation.

WOMEN'S FARM & GARDEN ASSOCIATION

175 Gloucester Street, Cirencester, Gloucestershire GL7 2DP
Tel 01285 658339
A useful voluntary organisation for women whose livelihood is connected with the land. Among its activities is the Women's Returners to Amenity Gardening Scheme which arranges placements in private gardens for women wishing to return to work.

WORSHIPFUL COMPANY OF GARDENERS

25 Luke Street, London EC2A 4AR
Tel 020 7739 8200
Fax 020 7739 8470
A City Guild, incorporated in 1605. It has always played an active part in horticultural affairs. Its charity fund makes grants to deserving projects, including horticultural therapy schemes and garden designs for special schools.

INDEX

26 Thompson Road   187
8 Dunstarn Lane   333, 426

Abbey Brook Cactus Nursery   69,
   419, 420, 421, 425
Abbey Dore Court Garden   139
Abbey House, The   304
Abbots Ripton Hall   31
Abbotsbury Sub-Tropical
   Gardens   92, 421, 430
Abbotsford   340, 430
Abbotswood   110
Aberconwy Nursery   377
Aberglasney Gardens   380
Abriachan Gardens   355
Achamore Gardens   363, 429, 430
Achnacloich   363
Acorn Bank Garden   63, 426, 427
Adlington Hall   37
African Violet & Garden
   Centre   196
Allangrange   355
Alpine Garden Society   454
Altamont Garden   397
Althorp   208
Alton Towers   252
Amberden Hall   104
American Conifer Society   454
American Hemerocallis
   Society   454
American Hosta Society   454
American Iris Society   454
American Museum   240
American Orchid Society   455
American Penstemon Society   455
American Rhododendron
   Society   455
American Rose Society   455
Ammerdown Park   240
An Cala   363
Anglesey Abbey   32
Angus Garden   364, 429
Annes Grove Gardens   397
Antony House   48, 420, 427
Antony Woodland Garden   49,
   419
Apple Court   124, 421, 423, 424,
   427, 428
Apuldram Roses   286

Arboretum Kalmthout   411
Arboretum National des
   Barres   411
Arboricultural Association   455
Arbury Hall   297
Architectural Plants   286
Ardanaiseig Hotel Garden   364
Ardchattan Priory   364
Ardfearn Nursery   355
Ardgillan Park   397, 422
Ardkinglas Woodland
   Garden   364, 418, 422
Ardnamona   397
Ardtornish Garden   365
Arduaine Garden   365
Arley Hall   38
Arlington Court   77
Arrow Cottage see Lance Hattatt
   Design Garden
Ascott   24
Ashford House   388
Ashwood Nurseries Ltd   301, 426
Association of Garden Trusts   455
Association of Societies for
   Growing Australian Plants,
   The   455
Association pour la Sauvegarde du
   Patrimoine Fruitier   455
Athelhampton   93, 430
Attadale Gardens   355
Attingham Park   233
Audley End   104
Avebury Manor   305
Avon   7
Avon Bulbs   240
Aylett Nurseries Ltd   146

Ballymaloe Cookery School
   Garden   398
Ballynacourty   398
Ballyrogan Nurseries   391
Bank House   172
Bannut, The   140, 427
Barbara Hepworth Museum &
   Sculpture Garden   49
Barningham Park   102
Barnsdale Plants and
   Gardens   176
Barnsley House Garden   111

Barrington Court   241, 427
Barton Manor   152, 421
Barwinnock Herbs   365
Bateman's   279
Bates Green Farm   279
Bath Botanic Gardens   241, 425
Batsford Arboretum   111, 425,
   426, 428
Baytree Nurseries   181
Beale Arboretum   148, 419, 420
Bede's World Herb Garden   214
Bedgebury National
   Pinetum   157, 419, 421, 424
Bell's Cherrybank Gardens   371,
   420, 427
Belmont Park   157
Belsay Hall   216, 421
Belton House   181
Belvoir Castle   177
Beningbrough Hall   323, 427
Benington Lordship   148, 430
Bennetts Water Lily Farm   93, 422
Benthall Hall   233
Benvarden Garden &
   Grounds   391, 429
Berkeley Castle   112
Berrington Hall   140
Beth Chatto Gardens   105, 427,
   428
Bicton Park Gardens   77, 425, 427
Biddulph Grange   253, 426, 428
Bide-a-Wee Cottage   215
Biggar Park   366
Binny Plants   360
Bio-Dynamic Agriculture
   Association   456
Birkheads Cottage Garden
   Nursery   216, 428
Birmingham Botanical Gardens &
   Glasshouses   302, 425, 427
Birr Castle Demesne   398
Bishop Burton Botanic
   Garden   320
Blackhills   352, 429
Blackmore & Langdon   241, 425,
   426
Blackthorn Nursery   124
Blencathra   19, 427
Blenheim Palace   225

Blickling Hall   196
Blossoms   25
Bluebell Nursery &
   Arboretum   70
Bodnant Gardens   378, 420, 421,
   423
Bodysgallen Hall   385
Bolehyde Manor   305
Bolfracks Garden   371
Bonsai Clubs International   456
Borde Hill Garden   287, 429
Bosvigo   49
Botanic Gardens Conservation
   International   456
Botanic Nursery   305
Botanical Society of Scotland   456
Botanical Society of South
   Africa   456
Botanical Society of the British
   Isles   456
Boughton House   208
Bourton House   112
Bowden, Ann & Roger   77, 427,
   428
Bowes Museum Garden & Park,
   The   102
Bowood House   305
Bradenham Hall   197
Bradshaw, J & Son   157, 426
Bramdean House   124
Bramham Park   334
Brandy Mount House   126, 419,
   420
Branklyn Garden   371, 419
Brantwood   64
Braxton Gardens   125
Bressingham Plant Centre   197
Brickwall House & Gardens   280
Bridgemere Garden World   38,
   419, 424
Britain in Bloom   456
British & European Geranium
   Society   456
British Bee-Keepers'
   Association   457
British Cactus & Succulent
   Society   457
British Clematis Society   457
British Fuchsia Society   457
British Gladiolus Society   457
British Hosta & Hemerocallis
   Society   457
British Iris Society   457
British Mycological Society   458

British National Carnation
   Society   458
British Pelargonium & Geranium
   Society   458
British Pteridological Society   458
British Society of Plant
   Breeders   458
British Tourist Authority   458
British Trust for Conservation
   Volunteers (BTCV)   458
Broadlands   127
Broadleas   306
Broadleigh Gardens   242, 421,
   426, 428
Broadview Gardens   158, 418, 420
Brodick Castle   366, 423
Brodie Castle   352, 421, 426
Brodsworth Hall   331, 426
Brogdale   158, 419, 420, 421, 422,
   423, 424
Brook Cottage   226
Brook Lodge Farm Cottage   265
Broughton Castle   226
Broughton House Gardens   345
Bryan's Ground   140
Buckingham Nurseries and Garden
   Centre   25
Buckland Abbey   78
Burford House Gardens   234, 419,
   426
Burnby Hall Gardens   321, 422
Burncoose Nurseries &
   Gardens   50, 425
Burrow Farm Gardens   78
Burton Agnes Hall Gardens   321,
   419
Burton Constable   321
Buscot Park   227, 427
Butterfields Nursery   26, 426, 428
Butterfly Conservation   459
Butterstream   399

Cabbages & Kings Garden   280
Cactus & Succulent Society of
   America   459
Cadenza   265, 426
Cadw: Welsh Historic
   Monuments   376, 459
Cae Hir   380
Caerhays Castle Gardens   51, 428
Calke Abbey   70
Cally Gardens   345, 428
Cambo Gardens   350

Cambridge University Botanic
   Garden   33, 418, 420, 421, 423,
   424, 425, 427, 428, 429
Campden Cottage   26
Canal Gardens & Tropical
   World   334, 427
Cannington College Heritage
   Garden   242, 428
Cannizaro Park   187, 429
Canons Ashby House   209
Capel Manor   187, 418, 423
Capesthorne Hall   38
Carclew Gardens   50
Carnfunnock Country Park   391
Carnivorous Plant Society   459
Carwinion   50
Castle Ashby Gardens   209
Castle Bromwich Hall   302
Castle Drogo   78
Castle Howard   324
Castle Kennedy Garden   346
Castlewellan National
   Arboretum   392
Catforth Gardens   173, 420
Cawdor Castle   356
Cefn Bere   385
Celyn Vale Nurseries   377
Centre for Alternative
   Technology   459
Champs Hill   287, 427
Chanticleer   198
Charlecote Park   297
Charney Well   64, 422
Chartwell   158, 429
Château d'Ainay-le-Vieil   411
Château de Beauregard   411
Château de Bosmelet   413
Château de Bouges   412
Château de la Bourdaisière   412
Château de la Bussière   412
Château de Valmer   415
Château de Villiers   416
Chatsworth   71
Chatsworth Garden Centre   71
Chelsea Physic Garden   188, 419
Chenies Manor   26
Chettle House   93
Chiffchaffs   94
Chillingham Castle   216
Chilworth Manor   265
Chirk Castle   377, 430
Chiswick House   188
Cholmondeley Castle Gardens   39
Christie's Nursery   372, 420
Church Hill Cottage Gardens   159

Chyverton 52
Clandon Park 265, 426
Clare College Fellows' Garden 32
Claremont Landscape
  Garden 266
Cleveland 7
Clifton Nurseries 188
Clinton Lodge 280
Cliveden 27, 419
Clumber Park 221, 426
Cluny House 372, 422
Clyne Gardens 382, 420, 422,
  423, 429
Coates Manor 288
Cobblers 282
Coiltie Garden 356
Colby Woodland Garden 380
Coleton Fishacre Garden 79
Colzium Walled Garden 367
Common Ground 459
Compton Acres Gardens 94
Conock Manor 306
Cooke's House 288
Coolcarrigan Gardens 399
Copton Ash Gardens 159, 428
Cornwall Gardens Society 459
Corsham Court 307
Cotehele 52
Cothay Manor 243
Coton Manor 209
Cotswold Garden Flowers 315,
  421, 428
Cottage Garden Society 459
Cottesbrooke Hall 210
Coughton Court 298
Countryside Agency, The 459
Countryside Council for
  Wales 460
County Park Nursery 106, 419,
  422
Courts, The 307, 427, 428
Cowdray Park 288
Cragside 217, 426
Craigieburn Classic Plants 345
Cranborne Manor 95
Crarae Gardens 367, 421, 429
Crathes Castle 352, 419, 424
Creagh Gardens 399
Croftway Nursery 289, 428
Crossing House Garden 32
Crowe Hall 243
Croxteth Hall & Country
  Park 173, 420
Crûg Farm Plants 385, 419, 422,
  428

Cruickshank Botanic
  Garden 353, 425, 428, 429
Culzean Castle & Country
  Park 367
Curraghmore 399
Cyclamen Society 460

Daffodil Society 460
Dalemain 64
Daleside Nurseries 325
Dalmeny House 360
Dam Farm House 70
Dartington Hall 79
David Austin Roses 234, 429, 430
Dawyck Botanic Garden 340,
  425, 426, 429
Deacon's Nursery 152
Dean's Court 95
Dell Garden 198, 428
Delphinium Society 460
Denmans 289
Derreen 400, 430
Deutsche
  Kakteen-Gesellschaft 460
Deutsche Rhododendron
  Gesellschaft 460
Dibleys Nurseries 379, 423
Dillon Garden, The 400, 428
Dingle, The 388
Dinmore Manor 141
Dochfour Gardens 356, 426
Docton Mill 79
Docwra's Manor 34
Doddington Hall 182
Doddington Place Gardens 159
Dolwen 388
Dorfold Hall 39
Dorothy Clive Garden 254, 429
Downderry Nursery 160, 421,
  423
Drum Castle 353, 430
Drummond Castle Gardens 373,
  430
Duchy of Cornwall Nursery 52
Duncombe Park 325
Dundee Botanic Garden 373, 428
Dunge Valley Gardens 39
Dunham Massey 173
Dunrobin Castle Gardens 357
Dunster Castle 243, 418, 430
Dyffryn Botanic Garden 382
Dyrham Park 112

Earth Centre, The 331

East Bergholt Place 257
Eastgrove Cottage Garden 316
East Lambrook Manor 244, 420,
  430
East Lode 198
Eastnor Castle 141
Easton Lodge 106
East Ruston Old Vicarage 199
Eden Project, The 53, 427, 430
Edenbridge House 160
Edmonsham House 96
Edrom Nurseries 340, 429
Edzell Castle 373
Elizabeth MacGregor 349, 430
Elsing Hall 200
Elsworth Herbs 34, 418, 421
Elton Hall, Cambridgeshire 34
Elton Hall, Herefordshire 141,
  420, 423
Elvaston Castle 72
Elworthy Cottage Plants 244
Emmetts Garden 160, 425
Englefield House 19
English Heritage, 14, 460
Erddig 379, 420, 426
Ernest Wilson Memorial
  Garden 112
Escot 80
European Boxwood & Topiary
  Society 461
Euston Hall 256
Exbury Gardens 127
Exeter University Gardens 80,
  418, 425, 427, 430

Fairfield House 128
Fairfield Lodge 400
Fairhaven Woodland & Water
  Garden 201
Falkland Palace 350, 426
Farnborough Hall 298
Fauna & Flora International 461
Felbrigg Hall 201, 419
Felley Priory 222
Fenton House 189
Ferme Médiévale de
  Bois-Richeux 412
Fernhill 401
Fibrex Nurseries Ltd 298, 420,
  422
Finlaystone 368
Fisk's Clematis Nursery 258
Fletcher Moss Botanical
  Gardens 174
Floors Castle 341

Floraldene 289, 427
Florence Court 392
Foggy Bottom 201, 426
Forde Abbey 96
Forestry Commission 461
Fota 401, 425, 426, 430
Foxgrove 20
Frampton Court 113
Friends of Brogdale 461
Friends of the Earth 461
Friends of the Royal Botanic
  Garden Edinburgh 461
Friends of the Royal Botanic
  Gardens Kew 461
Frogmore Gardens 20
Fruit Group of the Royal
  Horticultural Society 461
Fulham Palace Garden
  Centre 189
Furzey Gardens 128

Galloway House Gardens 349
Garden History Society 462
Garden House, The 83, 428, 430
Gardens of the Rose, The 147,
  423, 429, 430
Gash Gardens 401
Gaulden Manor 244
Geilston Garden 368
Gesellschaft der
  Staudenfreunde 462
Gibberd Garden, The 106
Gidleigh Park Hotel 81
Gilbert White's House 128
Glansevern Gardens 389
Glasgow Botanic Garden 368,
  418, 419, 428
Glebe Cottage Plants 81
Glen Chantry 107
Glenarn 369, 429
Glendoick Gardens 374, 429
Glendurgan Gardens 53
Glenveagh Castle 402
Glenwhan Garden 347
Glin Castle 402
Gnome Reserve & Wild Flower
  Garden 81
Godington Park 161, 426
Goldbrook Plants 258, 427, 428
Golden Acre Park 334, 422, 424
Goldney Hall 113
Goodnestone Park 161
Gorsehill Abbey Farm 316
Goscote Nurseries Ltd 177
Granada Arboretum 40, 421, 423

Gravetye Manor Hotel 289
Graythwaite Hall 65, 430
Great Barfield 27, 421
Great Comp 162
Great Dixter 281, 428
Greenbank Garden 369
Greencombe Gardens 245, 420,
  422, 424, 428
Green Farm Plants 128
Greenways 228
Grimsthorpe Castle 182
Groombridge Place Gardens 162
Grosvenor Garden Centre 40
Groves, C.W. & Son 96, 430
Gunby Hall 182
Guy Wilson Daffodil
  Garden 392, 421, 426

Haddon Hall 72, 426
Hadspen Garden 245, 423
Hall Farm & Nursery 183
Hall Farm Nursery 234
Halls of Heddon 217, 426
Ham House 189
Hampton Court Palace 190, 420
Hannah Peschar Sculpture
  Garden 266
Harcourt Arboretum 228
Hardwick Hall 73, 423, 430
Hardwicke House 35, 418
Hardy Orchid Society 462
Hardy Plant Society 462
Hardy's Cottage Garden
  Plants 129
Hare Hill Garden 40
Harewood House 335
Harlow Carr Botanical
  Gardens 325, 419, 420, 422,
  423, 428
Harmony Garden 341
Harris Garden, The 21, 421, 428
Hartside Nursery Garden 65
Hatchlands 266
Hatfield House 149
Haughley Park 258, 425
Hawkstone Historic Park &
  Follies 235
Headland 53
Heale House Garden 307
Heath Lands 129, 418
Heather Society 462
Hebe Society 462
Heligan Gardens 54
Helmingham Hall 259
Hemerocallis Europa 463

Henry Doubleday Research
  Association (HDRA) 463
Herb Nursery, The 177
Herb Society 463
Hergest Croft Gardens 142, 418,
  424
Herons Bonsai Ltd 267
Herterton House Gardens &
  Nursery 217, 430
Hestercombe Gardens 246
Hever Castle 162
Hexham Herbs & Hardy
  Plants 218, 422, 424
Heywood Gardens 402
Hidcote Manor 114, 422
High Beeches 290, 423
Highclere Castle 130, 423, 429
Highdown 290, 424
Higher Knowle 82
Highfield Nurseries 113
Highnam Court 113
Hiley, Brian & Heather 267
Hill House 148
Hill House Nursery & Garden 82
Hill of Tarvit 350
Hillbarn House 308
Hillside 403, 425
Hillview Hardy Plants 235
Hinton Ampner House 130, 428
Hippopottering Nursery 183
Historic Gardens
  Foundation 463
Historic Scotland 463
Hodges Barn 115
Hodnet Hall Gardens 235, 429,
  430
Hodsock Priory 223, 430
Hoecroft Plants 202
Hoghton Tower 174
Holden Clough Nursery 174
Holdenby House Gardens 210
Hole Park 163
Holehird 65, 418, 421, 422
Holker Hall 66, 424
Holkham Hall 202
Hollies Park, The 335, 419, 420,
  421, 422, 424
Holly Gate Cactus Nursery 292,
  425
Holme Pierrepont Hall 223
Home Covert 308, 428
Hopleys 150
Horticultural Trades Association
  (HTA) 463
Houghall, Durham 103, 421, 423

Houghton Lodge 130
House of Dun 374
House of Pitmuies 374
Hoveton Hall 203
How Caple Court 142
Howick Hall 218
Hughenden Manor 27
Humberside 7
Hunts Court 115, 430
Hutton-in-the-Forest 66
Hyde Hall see RHS Garden Hyde Hall
Hydon Nurseries 267, 429
Hydroponicum, The 357

Ickworth 260, 418
Iden Croft Herbs 163, 421, 422
Iford Manor 309, 418
Ightham Moat 163
Ingwersen, W E Th Ltd 292, 425
Institute of Horticulture (IoH) 463
International Camellia Society 464
International Clematis Society 464
International Dendrology Society 464
International Lilac Society 464
International Oak Society 464
International Oleander Society Inc 464
International Tree Foundation 464
International Violet Association 464
International Water Lily Society 465
Inveresk Lodge 360
Inverewe 357, 418, 422, 423
Irish Garden Plant Society 465
Isabella Plantation 191, 423, 429
Ivy Cottage 97

Jack Drake 358, 425, 427
Japanese Garden Society 465
Japanese Gardens & St Fiacra's Garden 403
Jardins de Château Rivau 414
Jardins de Sasnières 414
John F Kennedy Arboretum 403
Johnstown Castle Gardens 404
Just Phlomis 116, 422

Kailzie Gardens 341
Kathleen Muncaster Fuchsias 183, 420
Kayes Garden Nursery 178
Kedleston Hall 73
Keepers Nursery 164
Kellie Castle 351
Kelmarsh Hall 211
Kelmscott Manor 228
Kelways Ltd 246, 422, 428
Ken Caro 54
Kenchester Water Gardens 143, 422
Kenwood 191
Kiftsgate Court 116, 430
Kildrummy Castle 354
Kilfane Glen & Waterfall 404
Killerton 82
Kingston Lacy 97, 418, 419
Kingston Maurward Gardens 97, 422, 423
Kingstone Cottage Plants 143, 419
Kinross House 375
Kirkley Hall Gardens 218, 420
Knap Hill Nursery Ltd 267, 429
Knebworth House 150
Knightshayes Garden 84
Knoll Gardens 98, 419, 422, 430

Ladham House 164
Lakeside 143
Lamorran House 54
Lance Hattatt Design Garden 142
Land Farm Gardens 335
Langley Boxwood Nursery 131, 418, 430
Langthorns Plantery 108
Lanhydrock 55, 419, 428, 429
Larmer Tree Gardens 309
Lea Gardens 73
Leckmelm Arboretum 358
Leeds Castle 164, 421
Leighton Hall 175
Leith Hall 354
Leonardslee Gardens 291
Levens Hall 66, 430
Lilliesleaf Nursery 342, 420
Lily Group of the Royal Horticultural Society 465
Lime Close 229
Lingen Nursery and Gardens 236, 419, 421
Lismore Castle 404
Little Moreton Hall 40

Living Rainforest, The 22, 427
Lochalsh Woodland Garden 359
Lodge Lane Nursery & Bluebell Cottage Gardens 41
Lodge Park Walled Garden 404
Logan Botanic Gardens 348, 430
Long Barn 165
Long Close 178
Longframlington Gardens 219
Longleat House 310
Longmead House 131
Longstock Water Gardens 132, 418, 419
Longthatch 131, 420, 428
Loseley Park 268
Lotherton Hall 336
Lower Hall 236
Lower Icknield Farm 28, 418
Lower Severalls Gardens & Nursery 246
Lukesland 84
Lydney Park Gardens 117, 429
Lyme Park 41, 424
Lynford Arboretum 203, 425
Lytes Cary Manor 246

Macpennys Nurseries 98
Madrona Nursery 165
Magnolia Society Inc 465
Malleny House Garden 362, 423
Mallet Court Nursery 247
Manderston 342
Mannington Gardens 203, 429
Manoir du Grand Courtoiseau 413
Manor House, The, Bedfordshire 16
Manor House, The, Buckinghamshire 28
Manor House, The, Hampshire 133
Manor House, The, Oxfordshire 229
Manor House, The, Somerset 247, 428
Manor House, The, Worcestershire 316
Mapperton Gardens 99
Marcher Apple Network 465
Margam Park 383, 427
Marle Place Gardens 165, 418, 423
Marston Exotics 144
Martin Nest Nurseries 184, 422

Marwood Hill Gardens 85, 418, 421, 424, 425, 426, 428, 429
Mattocks Roses 229, 429
Mead Nursery, The 310
Mediterranean Garden Society 465
Melbourne Hall 74
Mellerstain 342
Mellors Garden 42
Menagerie, The 211
Meon Orchard 133, 420, 430
Merlin Trust 465
Merriments Gardens 282
Mertoun Gardens 343
Michelham Priory 282
Mill Cottage Plants 247
Mills Farm Plants and Gardens 260
Mill Garden, The 299
Mill Hill Plants 223, 418, 428
Millais Nurseries 268, 429
Millgate House 326
Milton Lodge 248
Ministry of Agriculture, Fisheries and Food 466
Minterne 99
Miserden Park 117
Monksilver Nursery 35, 424
Montacute House 248
Monteviot House Gardens 343
Moorlands 283
Moseley Old Hall 254
Mottisfont Abbey 134, 422, 423, 430
Mottistone Manor 153
Mount Edgcumbe Gardens 55, 419
Mount Grace Priory 326
Mount Stewart 393, 419, 421, 422, 429, 430
Mount Stuart 369, 426, 429, 430
Mount Usher Gardens 405
Muckross House & Gardens 405
Muncaster Castle 67, 429
Munstead Wood 268
Museum of Garden History 191, 466
Myddelton House 194, 421

National Association of Flower Arrangement Societies 466
National Auricula and Primula Society (Midland & West Section) 466

National Auricula and Primula Society (Southern Section) 466
National Begonia Society 466
National Botanic Garden of Wales 381, 427
National Botanic Gardens 406, 420, 422, 425, 426, 427, 428, 429
National Chrysanthemum Society 466
National Collection of Passiflora 248, 422
National Council for the Conservation of Plants and Gardens 466
National Dahlia Society 467
National Garden Exhibition Centre 407
National Gardens Scheme 467
National Pot Leek Society 467
National Sweet Pea Society 467
National Trust 467
National Trust for Scotland 467
National Vegetable Society 467
National Viola and Pansy Society 468
Naturescape 224, 430
Ness Botanic Gardens 43, 425, 427, 428, 429, 430
Netherhall Manor 35
Newby Hall 326, 419
Newstead Abbey 224
Nicky's Rock Garden Nursery 86
Norfolk Lavender 204, 421
Normanby Hall Country Park 184
North American Rock Garden Society 468
North Court 153
North of England Rose, Carnation and Sweet Pea Society 468
Northern Horticultural Society 468
Northern Ireland Daffodil Group 468
Northern Ireland Tourist Board 468
Norton Priory Museum & Gardens 42, 419
Notcutts Nurseries 260, 421
Notre Dame d'Orsan 413
Nunwell House 153
Nymans 293, 425, 426, 427, 428, 429, 430

Oakleigh Nurseries 134

Oare House 310
Old Court Nurseries 144, 418
Old Glebe, The 86, 429
Old Rectory Cottage 22, 428
Old Rectory, Berkshire 23
Old Rectory, Oxfordshire 229
Old Rectory, Northamptonshire 212
Old Vicarage 311, 422
Olivers 108
Orchid Society of Great Britain 468
Osborne House 155
Osterley Park 194
Oulton House 254
Overbecks Museum & Garden 86
Owlpen Manor 117
Oxburgh Hall 204
Oxford Botanic Garden 230, 420, 428

Packwood House 299, 427, 430
Padlock Croft 36, 418, 419, 422, 424
Paignton Zoo & Botanical Gardens 86
Painshill Park 269
Painswick Rococo Garden 118
Palm Centre, The 269, 430
Pantiles Plant & Garden Centre 270
Paradise Centre 261
Paradise Park 283
Parc Botanique du Prieuré d'Orchaise 413
Parc Floral de la Source 414
Parcevall Hall Gardens 327
Parham 292
Park Green Nurseries 261, 428
Pashley Manor Garden 283
Peckover House 36
Pencarrow 56
Penjerrick 56
Pengergwm Lodge 384
Penrhyn Castle 386, 430
Penshurst Place 166
Peover Hall 42
Peter Beales Roses 204, 423, 430
Petersfield Physic Garden 135
Petworth House 294, 426, 429
Picton Castle 381
Pine Lodge 58, 420
Pinewood House 270
Pitmedden 354, 430

Plant World Botanic Gardens 87, 422
Planta Vera 270
Plantasia 383, 427
Plantation Garden 205
Plantsman Nursery, The 87, 418
Plas Brondanw Gardens 386
Plas Newydd 386, 429
Plas-yn-Rhiw 387, 430
Plaxtol Nurseries 166
Pleasant View Nursery & Garden 87, 418, 423
P M A Plant Specialities 249
Polesden Lacey 271
Port Lympne 166
Portmeirion 387
Potterton and Martin 184
Pound Hill House 311
Powderham Castle 88
Powerscourt Gardens 407
Powis Castle 389, 418, 421
Preen Manor 237
Primrose Hill 407
Prior Park 249
Priorwood Garden 343
Priory, The 317
Probus Gardens 57
P W Plants 204

Queen Mary's Gardens 194
Queen's Wood Arboretum & Country Park 144
Quinta, The 44, 420, 422

Ram House Garden 408
Ramster 271, 429
Raveningham Hall Gardens 205
R D Plants 88
Reads Nursery 205, 419, 420, 424
Reaseheath College 44
Renishaw Hall 74, 424
Rhodes & Rockliffe 108, 418
Rhododendron, Camellia & Magnolia Group of the Royal Horticultural Society 469
RHS Garden Hyde Hall 109, 424, 425, 427, 428, 429, 430
RHS Garden Rosemoor 88, 419, 421, 425, 427, 429, 430
RHS Garden Wisley 276, 418, 419, 420, 423, 425, 426, 427, 428, 429, 430
Rickard's Hardy Ferns Ltd 317, 419, 422, 424, 426

Ripley Castle 327, 421
Riverhill House Gardens 167
Rockingham Castle 212
Rode Hall 44
Rodmarton Manor 118
Romantic Garden Nursery, The 206, 430
Rosemoor see RHS Garden Rosemoor
Rosewood Daylilies 167, 427
Rotherview Nursery with Coghurst Camellias 284, 426
Rougham Hall Nurseries 261, 419, 423, 426
Rousham House 230
Rowallane Garden 394, 422, 425, 428, 429, 430
Rowden Gardens 89, 420, 422, 423
Royal Botanic Garden, Edinburgh 361, 425, 426, 427, 428, 429
Royal Botanic Gardens, Kew 192, 425, 426, 427, 428, 429, 430
Royal Caledonian Horticultural Society 469
Royal Gardeners' Orphan Fund 469
Royal Horticultural Society 469
Royal Horticultural Society of Ireland 470
Royal National Rose Society 470
Royal Society for the Protection of Birds 470
Rufford Old Hall 175
Rupert Bowlby 271
Rushfields of Ledbury 145
Ruthall Manor 237
R V Roger Ltd 328
Rydal Mount 67
Ryton Organic Gardens 299

Saint Laurent de Manzay 414
Saintpaulia & Houseplant Society 470
Saling Hall 109
Salley Gardens 224, 427
Saltram 89
Sam Oldham 250, 426
Sandringham House 206
Savill Garden 272, 420, 421, 422, 423, 427, 428, 429, 430
Scone Palace 375, 426, 428
Scotland's Garden Scheme 470
Scotlands 23

Scotney Castle 168, 428, 429
Scottish Rhododendron Society 470
Scottish Rock Garden Club 471
Scotts Nurseries Ltd 250
Seaforde Gardens 395, 420
Seal Point 17
Seaton Delaval Hall 219
Sezincote 118
Sharcott Manor 312
Sheffield Botanical Gardens 332, 420, 424
Sheffield Park 284, 423, 425, 426, 428, 429
Sherborne Garden 250, 426, 428
Sheringham Park 207
Sherston Parva Nursery Ltd 312, 426
Sherwood 90, 423, 429
Shrubland Park Gardens 262
Shugborough Hall 255
Sir George Staunton Country Park 135, 427
Sir Harold Hillier Gardens & Arboretum, The 136, 421, 419, 420, 421, 422, 423
Siskin Plants 262, 420, 427
Sissinghurst Castle 168
Sizergh Castle 68, 418, 419, 420, 422, 427
Skippet, The 230
Sledmere House 322
Sleightholmedale Lodge 328
Snape Cottage 99, 430
Snowshill Manor 119
Société National d'Horticulture de France 471
Society of Garden Designers 471
Soil Association 471
Somerleyton Hall 262
Special Plants 119
Spetchley Park 317, 428
Spinners 135, 424, 428, 430
Sports Turf Research Institute 471
Springfields Show Gardens 185
Squerryes Court 169
St Andrews Botanic Garden 351, 428
St Luke's Cottage 219, 419, 425
St Michael's Mount 58
St Paul's Walden Bury 150
Stancombe Park 119
Standen 285

Stanley Smith Horticultural Trust 471
Stansfield 231
Stanway House 120
Stapehill Abbey 101
Stapeley Water Gardens 45, 422
Starborough Nursery 169
Steven Bailey Ltd 137
Sticky Wicket 100
Stillingfleet Lodge Nurseries 328, 423
Stone House Cottage Garden 318
Stoneacre 169
Stonehurst 294
Stonor 231
Stourhead 313, 425, 426, 429
Stourton House Flower Garden 313
Stowe Landscape Gardens 29
Stowell Park 120
Stratfield Saye House 137
Studley Royal 329
Sudeley Castle & Gardens 120
Sulgrave Manor 212
Suntrap Garden 362
Sutton Park 329
Swallow Hayes 237, 420, 421
Swiss Garden 17
Syon Park 192

Talbot Botanic Gardens 408, 422, 425, 429, 430
Tapeley Park 90
Tatton Park 45, 418
Temple Newsam Park 336, 418, 419, 422
Thorncroft Clematis Nursery 207, 426
Thornhayes Nursery 90
Thorp Perrow Arboretum 330, 420, 421, 424
Threave Garden 349, 426, 427
Thrive 471
Tile Barn Nursery 170, 419, 426
Tintinhull House 250, 427
Tirley Garth Trust 46
Titsey Place 273
Tivey, Philip & Son 178, 426
Toddington Manor 17
Toobees Exotics 273, 425
Torosay Castle & Gardens 370, 425, 430
Traquair House 344

Trebah Garden Trust 58
Tree Register of the British Isles 471
Tregrehan 59
Trehane 59, 426
Trehane Camellia Nursery 101
Trelissick Garden 59, 418, 422, 426, 430
Trengwainton Gardens 60, 429, 430
Trentham Gardens 255
Trerice 60
Tresco Abbey 61, 418
Trewithen 60
Tudor House Garden 137
Tullynally Castle 408
Turn End 29

University of Birmingham Botanic Garden 303, 423, 429, 430
University of Bristol Botanic Garden 121, 427, 430
University of Durham Botanic Garden 103, 425, 427, 429
University of Leicester Botanic Garden 178, 418, 419, 420, 421, 423, 425, 427, 428
Upton House 300, 418, 427

Valclusa Gardens & Nursery 409
Vale End 273
Valley Gardens, Yorkshire, North 330, 426
Valley Gardens, Surrey 274, 420, 421, 422, 423, 427, 428, 429, 430
Van Hage Garden Company 151
Vann 273
Veddw, The 384
Ventnor Botanic Garden 154, 422, 430
Verein Deutscher Rosenfreunde 472
Vernon Geranium Nursery, The 275
Villandry Château Gardens 415
Villeprévost Château Park 415

Waddesdon Manor 30
Wakefield & North of England Tulip Society 472
Wakehurst Place 295, 418, 421, 423
Walled Garden, The 318, 428

Wallington 220, 423, 427
Walmer Castle 170
Warren Hills Cottage 179
Wartnaby Gardens 179
Warwick Castle 300
Water Meadow Nursery and Herb Farm 138, 422
Waterperry Gardens 231, 423
Wayford Manor 251
Webbs of Wychbold 319, 422
Welsh Historic Gardens Trust 472
Wentworth Castle Gardens 332, 419, 421, 423, 429
West Dean Gardens 295, 418, 421
West Green House 138
West Wycombe Park 30
Westbury Court 121, 430
Westdale Nurseries 314, 430
Westholme Hall 103
Weston Park 255
Westonbirt Arboretum 122, 418, 423
Westwell Manor 232
Whatton House 180
White Windows 138, 420
Wightwick Manor 303
Wildlife Trusts, The 472
Willow Lodge 123
Wilton House 314
Wiltshire College Lackham 314, 422, 430
Wimpole Hall 36, 421
Winkworth Arboretum 275, 423, 425, 426
Wisley see RHS Garden Wisley
Witley Court 319
Woburn Abbey 18
Wollerton Old Hall 238
Women's Farm & Garden Association 472
Worshipful Company of Gardeners 472
Wrest Park 18
Wyken Hall 263
Wylmington Hayes Gardens 91

Yalding Organic Gardens 171
Yew Tree Cottage 296
York Gate 336
Younger Botanic Garden 370, 426, 429